HILLEL AND JESUS

CONTRIBUTORS

P. S. Alexander
Oxford Centre for Postgraduate
    Hebrew Studies
Oxford, England

J. P. Arnold
Reunion Institute
Houston, Texas

D. E. Aune
Saint Xavier College
Chicago, Illinois

J. H. Charlesworth
Princeton Theological Seminary
Princeton, New Jersey

J. D. G. Dunn
University of Durham
Durham, England

C. A. Evans
Trinity Western University
Langley, British Columbia

D. Fiensy
Grape Grove Church of Christ
Jamestown, Ohio

D. Flusser
Hebrew University
Jerusalem, Israel

A. Goshen-Gottstein
Tel Aviv University
Tel Aviv, Israel

L. L. Johns
Bluffton College
Bluffton, Ohio

L. Levine
Hebrew University
Jerusalem, Israel

H. Lichtenberger
Eberhard-Karls-Universität
Tübingen, Germany

S. E. Robinson
Brigham Young University
Provo, Utah

C. Safrai
Amstelveen, The Netherlands

S. Safrai
Hebrew University
Jerusalem, Israel

D. Schwartz
Hebrew University
Jerusalem, Israel

J. Sievers
Pontifical Biblical Institute
Rome, Italy

J. F. Strange
University of South Florida
Tampa, Florida

B. T. Viviano
École Biblique et Archéologique
    Française
Jerusalem, Israel

M. Weinfeld
Hebrew University
Jerusalem, Israel

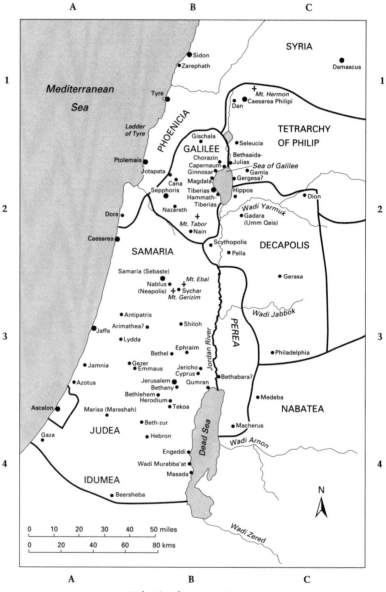

Palestine from 6 to 44 C.E.

HILLEL AND JESUS

COMPARATIVE STUDIES OF
TWO MAJOR RELIGIOUS LEADERS

Edited by
James H. Charlesworth
and Loren L. Johns

FORTRESS PRESS
MINNEAPOLIS

BM
535
.H54
1997

HILLEL AND JESUS
Comparative Studies of Two Major Religious Leaders

Acknowledgements
Photographs in chapter 5 are used by permission of Meir Ben-Dov, Jerusalem; Yad Izhak Ben-Zvi, Jerusalem; and The Israel Exploration Society, Jerusalem. The map on p. iv and the illustrations in chapter 13 are from *Jesus and His World,* ed. John J. Rousseau and Rami Arav (Fortress Press, 1995).

ISBN 0-8006-2564-1

The paper used in this publication meets the minimum requirements of American National Standard for Information Sciences—Permanence of Paper for Printed Library Materials, ANSI Z329.48–1984.

Manufactured in the U.S.A.

01   00   99   98   97   1   2   3   4   5   6   7   8   9   10

In Memory of Joan Hart

CONTENTS

Contributors .... *ii*
Foreword (J. H. CHARLESWORTH) .... *xiii*
Preface (L. L. JOHNS) .... *xvii*
Abbreviations .... *xxv*

PART ONE
INTRODUCTION

1. J. H. CHARLESWORTH   3
   Hillel and Jesus: Why Comparisons Are Important

2. A. GOSHEN-GOTTSTEIN   31
   Hillel and Jesus: Are Comparisons Possible?

3. M. WEINFELD   56
   Hillel and the Misunderstanding of Judaism in Modern
      Scholarship

4. D. FLUSSER   71
   Hillel and Jesus: Two Ways of Self-Awareness

PART TWO
SOCIAL AND HISTORICAL STUDIES

5. L. I. LEVINE   110
   Archaeology and the Religious Ethos of Pre–70 Palestine

6. S. E. ROBINSON   121
   Apocalypticism in the Time of Hillel and Jesus

7. J. SIEVERS   137
Who Were the Pharisees?

8. J. D. G. DUNN   156
Jesus and Factionalism in Early Judaism

9. D. E. AUNE   176
Jesus and Cynics in First-Century Palestine: Some Critical
    Considerations

10. B. PIXNER   193
Jesus and His Community: Between Essenes and Pharisees

11. D. A. FIENSY   225
Jesus' Socioeconomic Background

12. J. P. ARNOLD   256
The Relationship of Paul to Jesus

PART THREE
THE SAYINGS OF HILLEL AND JESUS

13. J. F. STRANGE   291
The Sayings of Jesus and Archaeology

14. C. SAFRAI   306
Sayings and Legends in the Hillel Tradition

15. S. SAFRAI   321
The Sayings of Hillel: Their Transmission and
    Reinterpretation

16. D. R. SCHWARTZ   335
Hillel and Scripture: From Authority to Exegesis

17. P. S. ALEXANDER   363
Jesus and the Golden Rule

18. H. LICHTENBERGER 389
Jesus and the Dead Sea Scrolls

19. C. A. EVANS 397
Reconstructing Jesus' Teaching: Problems and Possibilities

20. B. T. VIVIANO 427
Hillel and Jesus on Prayer

EPILOGUE

21. J. H. CHARLESWORTH 460
Retrospective and Prospective Reflections

Indexes *463*

J. H. CHARLESWORTH

FOREWORD

THE CENTRAL QUESTION that unites these chapters is the following: How and in what ways, if at all, can we learn more about Hillel by comparing him with Jesus, and how can we learn more about Jesus by comparing him with Hillel? A presupposition shared by the contributors is that both are clearly real men who lived in Palestine before the destruction of the nation Israel and the burning of the Temple in 70 C.E. In contrast to some publications of approximately 100 years ago, no one assumes or seeks to demonstrate that an objective biography of Hillel can be created out of Rabbinics or of Jesus from the New Testament. The sources that historians use to suggest what is probably historical about Hillel or Jesus are clearly posterior to each of them and composed by those who celebrated them, often in mythical terms.

The contributors vary among themselves regarding the degree to which a reliable portrait of Hillel or Jesus is possible; generally the younger scholars tend to be more skeptical about a solid historical depiction, especially of Hillel. The main reason is that we have written traditions about Jesus that not only derive from the century in which he lived, but in some cases only a decade or two from the time of his ministry. With Hillel we are forced to evaluate traditions that in some cases were not written down until the sixth century C.E., or approximately 500 years after Hillel.

Using historical critical methodology, scholars have clarified that neither Hillel nor Jesus are fictitious characters created respectively by the Hillelites or by Christians. Both Hillel and Jesus were Palestinian teachers who taught before the destruction of Jerusalem in 70 C.E. While the purpose of the present reference work is to clarify how we can know more about Hillel by comparing him with Jesus—and conversely, how we may know more about Jesus by comparing him with Hillel—the inquiries are not focused only on the historical persons, but also include a perception of the legends and mythology that developed around each. All contributors demonstrate why an objective historical account of these men is simply not possible. A secondary reason, beside the often late date of compositions celebrating Hillel, is that those who recorded traditions about them were primarily interested in presenting the abiding importance of each for a meaningful life. Virtually all records of Hillel and Jesus are presented with concerns and perspectives that are not strictly historical. In the following pages experts on Hillel or Jesus demonstrate how they seek to discern historical data within Rabbinics or the New Testament, and why it is simply not possible sometimes to move backward in time before the needs and concerns of post-70 or even, with Hillel, before post-fifth-century communities. At the same time, the specialists recognize and appreciate the celebrations of Hillel by the Rabbis and Jesus by Christians.

The edited chapters of this book originally were papers delivered and discussed in Jerusalem in 1992. While I was Lady Davis Professor in the History Department in the Hebrew University in Jerusalem, I observed the retirement of the older generation of Israelis and the emergence of those who had been trained in Israel, many of whom had been born in Israel. While both generations were highly trained and gifted, only the older generation represented especially by David Flusser, Moshe Weinfeld, and Shmuel Safrai had been trained in European cultures, learning the classics and Hebrew while children and often speaking German, French, and other languages fluently. The two generations tended not only to reflect different environments, but also sometimes considerably different perspectives on ancient sources, especially Rabbinics. I thought it wise to focus on a subject that would capture this major period not only in the history of Israel, but also in scholarship, and to bring both together with others, especially Christian experts on Judaism and Christian Origins. The best place is obviously Jerusalem and in the Hebrew University on Mount Scopus. The topic seemed evident by the emergence, since 1980, of Jesus Research, which is different from the earlier attempts to portray the historical Jesus by the importance given to the topography and archaeology of ancient Israel, the new insights and perspectives obtained from the Jewish Pseudepigrapha and the Dead Sea Scrolls, as well as the freedom from questions shaped by theological agendas.

A question addressed to me by G. Ernest Wright in Jerusalem during the spring of 1969 helped focus my thoughts for the symposium:

"What do we really know about Hillel?" I thus thought it wise to focus on Hillel and Jesus and to call an international symposium in Jerusalem for June 8–11, 1992.

In organizing the symposium and in preparing the papers for publication, I am indebted to many, notably to Eve Marie Charlesworth, Joel Fleishman, Petra Heldt, Teddy Kollek, Henry Luce III, Tru Madsen, and Doron Mendels. I wish to express my appreciation also to Loren Johns, who worked closely with me in editing these chapters, and to Michael Davis for preparing the indexes. The symposium succeeded thanks to the assistance of Princeton Theological Seminary, the Jerusalem Hyatt, the Hebrew University, and the Jerusalem Center for Near Eastern Studies, support from the Foundation on Christian Origins, and a major grant from the Henry Luce Foundation, Inc.

The symposium would not have come into existence without the initiative and generosity of Mr. and Mrs. Stanley Hart. They could not attend the conference because of the fading health of Joan Hart. This volume is thus dedicated to the memory of Joan Hart, who passed away while I was editing the contributions. Joan was a cornucopia overflowing with joy and compassionate love. I never heard her say anything unkind or thoughtless. I will be buoyed up in sinking moments ahead by the encouraging warmth she left behind on this side of that vast unknown sea. My mind mirrors many marvelous memories; notably two: her excited face looking up from an archaeological balk near an early fountain in Magdala (she had discovered and held in her right hand a first-century potsherd that she dated accurately), and her youthful gait as she ascended Hippus and then contemplated life as the sun set across the Sea of Galilee. When I hand this tome to Stanley, I feel she too will be reaching out to receive it.

PREFACE

WHO WAS HILLEL? Who was Jesus? Although many scholars are pursuing these questions today, another significant question has received less attention: How does what we know of Jesus help to clarify Hillel, and vice versa? Can what we might know about the comparison of these different traditions bring further light to each set of traditions? Ultimately, are we not thereby better informed about the historical persons behind those traditions?

The task of answering the above questions is fraught with both promise and challenge. Such a comparison of traditions requires all the work of tradition criticism. And tradition criticism itself stands on the shoulders of the array of historical-critical methodologies that have properly come to characterize attempts to recover the "historical Hillel" and the "historical Jesus." But even further considerations complicate the project. Historically, such projects have been charged with hidden theological agenda; namely, to demonstrate the superiority of one of these historical figures (and derivatively, one of the religious traditions) over the other. Thus, some of the authors understandably express some caution in these essays about such possible hidden agendas on the part of the other writers even as they take tentative steps toward a common historical understanding.

Past attempts to compare these figures have foundered on one or more of these problems. Furthermore, as J. H. Charlesworth notes in the foreword, there are differences between generations of scholars regarding the relative reliability of the Hillel traditions, to say nothing about the Jesus traditions. How reliable are those traditions? Written Jesus traditions can confidently be dated within 50 years of his death; written Hillel traditions postdate his death by 200 or even 500 years.

Nevertheless, while acknowledging the above challenges, the essays in this book demonstrate the value of comparing and contrasting these two remarkable Jewish figures. They lived and worked at the turn of the era and gave rise to two distinct bodies of traditions that live on through the centuries.

PART ONE

Because of the methodological complexity of the task undertaken in this book, the essays included here reflect an array of methodological approaches. The book has three parts. The first part contains an introduction to the central questions of the book and to the methodological challenges facing such a project. In the first chapter, J. H. Charlesworth introduces the project. After touching on some of the missteps and false starts in comparing Hillel and Jesus in the past, he examines some of the basic methodological considerations requisite for such a project. Finally, he offers some general similarities and differences between Hillel and Jesus as a starting point in the discussion.

In chapter 2, A. Goshen Gottstein characterizes past comparisons of Jesus with other religious figures as a "Jesus and X topos." This sort of project is especially problematic, he argues, since a nontheological, history-only, pursuit is not even possible. To place these figures in the same category (e.g., as early Palestinian teachers) is to misuse the very sources containing the traditions of these respective figures. Rabbinical figures were unique individuals who resisted "type-casting." As a result, Goshen Gottstein suggests that the contrasts between Hillel and Jesus may be more significant.

In chapter 3, M. Weinfeld offers a stinging (yet appropriate) exposé of attempts by Christian scholars of 50 to 100 years ago to characterize both Hillel and the presumedly monolithic Judaism of the first century of the Common Era. The gross reductionism of Judaism which resulted led in turn to tendentious caricatures which served primarily as a foil for the presumed superior teachings of Jesus. Unfortunately, these scholars did not recognize that the rabbinic literature itself revels that criticisms of "Pharisaic hypocrisy" represented a debate *within* the Judaisms of the first and second centuries C.E. Jesus' denunciations must therefore be read as an intramural debate within Judaism, rather than as a symbolic rejection of Judaism as such.

In chapter 4, D. Flusser compares Hillel and Jesus with regard to their "self-awareness." Building on earlier studies on this subject, Flusser concludes that the "I" of Jesus and of Hillel differed significantly, due to their differing self-awareness. Both had a "high" self-awareness, stemming from their own respective convictions about the importance of their mission. But Flusser argues that the move from the Jesus of history to the Christ of faith is not as difficult as has been imagined, since a majority of the New Testament christological motifs are attested already in the high self-awareness of the "historical" Jesus himself. In fact, he probably understood himself to be the Messiah and the "Son of Man." In contrast, Hillel understood himself to be a representative of humanity and thus an exemplar.

PART TWO

After this introduction to the problem, Part Two of the book consists of a collection of specific social and historical studies aimed at clarifying the contexts in which Hillel and Jesus functioned. In chapter 5, L. I. Levine investigates the significance of archaeology for clarifying the religious ethos of pre–70 Palestine. For instance, recent archaeology has clarified the imposing significance and centrality of the Temple as well as those of the priestly class for life in pre–70 Palestine. Similarly, archaeological evidence suggests that we be cautious about identifying the function of the emerging post–70 synagogue with that of the pre–70 synagogue. Archaeology is also shedding further light on the intra-Jewish debate about ritual purity and the crisis of purity faced by turn-of-the-era Jews in the Hellenistic environment of first-century Palestine-an environment archaeology is increasingly revealing as pervasive.

In chapter 6, S. E. Robinson evaluates the "jaundiced eye" with which much of modern scholarship has looked on the apocalypticism of Second Temple Judaism. Robinson traces this modernist skepticism toward nonrational modes of thought and the negative emotional valuation of apocalypticism that accompanied it. After tracing the profound influence of apocalyptic thought on Jesus, Robinson asks how it is that apocalypticism failed to influence Hillel as heavily. Robinson concludes that whereas apocalypticism represented various ways of *resisting* Hellenism and its influences, the sages sought in various ways to *accommodate* Hellenism. By helping Judaism to accommodate some forms of Hellenism, Hillel ultimately empowered Judaism to survive Hellenism.

In chapter 7, J. Sievers examines once again that critical question, "Who were the Pharisees?" Sievers' own approach is to tighten the controls for who qualifies as a Pharisee by admitting only individuals who have explicitly been identified as Pharisees and who can reliably be confirmed as such. This greatly diminishes the number of known Pharisees before the fourth century C.E. to only around twelve. Was Hillel a Pharisee? Ironically, the greatest gain and the one "assured result" of recent study in this area is the conclusion that we know less about the Pharisees than we thought we knew.

In chapter 8, J. D. G. Dunn recalls two points of emerging consensus among students of Second Temple Judaism and Christian origins. These are: (1) that Judaism was a diverse phenomenon at the beginning of the first century C.E.; and (2) that Jesus must be understood within that diverse Judaism. Dunn wishes to push beyond that consensus to ask how first-century Jews would have interpreted that diversity. That is, would various groups within the Judaisms of Jesus' day have maintained the normativity of their own theological perspectives? If so, how did Jesus fit into all of this? To answer these questions, Dunn analyzes the function of the designation "sinner" within the literatures of that period. Dunn argues, contra E. P. Sanders, that the designation "sinner" is no minor matter in comparison with the designation "Jew" but that Jesus himself protested against using *sinner* in a factional way.

In chapter 9, D. E. Aune examines the recent consensus among *some* scholars engaged in Jesus research that the historical Jesus is best understood against the background of Jewish or Hellenistic wisdom traditions (e.g. as a Cynic philosopher) rather than against the background of Jewish apocalypticism. In order to address this consensus, Aune first assesses what we can know of Cynicism as such in the first century C.E. Was there a Cynic "school" in the first century C.E.? Aune then tackles the more methodologically challenging issue of how to assess parallels in the sayings, systems, and thought structures of the first-century world. He concludes that although the formal similarities between the *chreiai* attributed to Jesus and the Cynics are striking and deserve detailed study, the Jewish-Cynic Jesus hypothesis as articulated so far has fallen short in its potential to clarify the historical Jesus.

In chapter 10, B. Pixner suggests that the earliest Christian community in Jerusalem lived in close proximity to the Essene community there. Pixner reviews his discovery of the Essene Gate in the southwestern corner of Jerusalem. He then reviews connections between the Essenes and the Christian Jews of the first century. He suggests, for instance, that the Last Supper was probably held in an Essene guesthouse. A crucial link for such connections is James, the brother of Jesus. Pixner explores the various possible connections between the family of Jesus and the Jerusalem Essenes and then lays out a three-stage understanding of the tenuous relationship between the early Christians and the Jerusalem Essenes, a connection which could no longer be maintained after James's death.

In chapter 11, D. Q. Fiensy examines the socioeconomic conditions of Herodian Palestine in an attempt to recover an understanding of the ancient agrarian society in which Jesus lived. Two specific questions form the heart of Fiensy's investigation: "What was the socioeconomic environment structure of Galilee during the tetrarchy of Antipas?" and, "From which socioeconomic rung did Jesus come?" Fiensy concludes that only about 1% of the population of Palestine belonged to the elite class in Jesus' day. As a skilled carpenter, Jesus would have come from Palestine's artisan class. Thus, while the socioeconomic distance between Jesus and the elite classes would have been enormous, Jesus was probably not economically destitute before his ministry.

In chapter 12, J. P. Arnold addresses the assumed "paradigm of discontinuity" between Paul and Jesus. Arnold challenges past characterizations of a Pauline school that was antithetical to Jesus' own thought and teachings. This antithesis was most visible in the Tübingen school and has been rearticulated most recently (in revised form) by G. Lüdemann. In contrast, Arnold emphasizes the continuity between Paul and Jesus, primarily with regard to Paul's knowledge and use of traditional material about Jesus. More specifically, he points to evidence of Paul's appreciation of the historical Jesus in Paul's "*transmission* of traditional material about Jesus, his *application* of these traditions to the needs of Gentile converts, and his *defense* of these traditions against opposing Jesus traditions which represented 'another Jesus' and a 'different gospel.'"

PART THREE

With these social and historical studies as background, Part Three looks more specifically at the sayings of Hillel and Jesus and the ways in which those sayings have been used in subsequent scholarship. In chapter 13, J. F. Strange argues for greater appreciation for the role and importance of archaeology in developing the social and historical context for the New Testament writings. Strange laments simple and unnecessary mistakes made by some New Testament scholars due to their inadequate knowledge of the geography and archaeology of Palestine. The undervaluing of archaeology as a discipline stems in part from a too-narrow understanding of its task. It is not primarily the unearthing of artifacts, though this represents one elementary level of the discipline. The deeper, more significant layer of archaeology as a discipline is the reconstruction of past social systems and relations. With these comments as backdrop, Strange goes on to demonstrate some of the pay-offs of the archaeology of Galilee—Sepphoris in particular—for understanding Jesus and Galilean Judaism of the first century C.E.

In chapter 14, C. Safrai examines the nature and function of sayings and legends in the Hillel tradition. Safrai begins with a four-part typology of Hillel sayings: (1) sayings attributed to Hillel himself in m.AB 1 and 2 and in Abot de Rabbi Nathan (ARN); (2) sayings by others that were incorporated into a story or legend *about* Hillel; (3) sayings attributed to Hillel found in other rabbinic literature; and (4) otherwise unknown or hidden sayings of Hillel that can be extracted from existing stories and legends. Safrai then does a form-critical analysis of sayings from each of these categories in order to trace their distinctive literary dynamics.

In chapter 15, S. Safrai follows up on C. Safrai's work with an investigation of the manner in which some of Hillel's sayings were transmitted and how they were understood and interpreted by later generations. S. Safrai is specifically interested in whether and how the sayings were reinterpreted and adapted to changing situations by later sages. In pursuit of this task, Safrai considers several sayings, following their use and reinterpretation by later generations of sages within the rabbinic tradition.

In chapter 16, D. R. Schwartz analyzed Hillel's use of Scripture. Schwartz suggests that Hillel was above all a sage of oral tradition, not an interpreter of texts. Hillel's ethical and legal teachings are grounded most clearly on his own authority and that of his teachers in the Pharisaic tradition, *not* on that of Scripture. Thus, for Hillel, the Oral Law has primacy despite evidence that later sages were more interested in Hillel as an interpreter of Scripture. For Hillel, opinion usually preceded exegesis, not vice versa. Instead of assuming that biblical warrant does and must exist for legal rulings, "the same type of common sense approach which limited his reading of Scripture also allowed for rulings based on tradition or on his own authority." By the time of Yavneh, the need was for greater stability and controls over such readings and thus Hillel's hermeneutical/theological approach lost sway.

In chapter 17, P. S. Alexander focuses on the Golden Rule. After clarifying that the Golden Rule is more a general proposition than a fixed form of words, Alexander investigates the reliability of Golden Rule traditions and their meaning. Alexander concludes that the historical reliability of the traditions connecting Hillel to the Golden Rule is not as strong as those connecting Jesus to it. In fact, the link is weak enough to invalidate any attempt to compare how the historical Hillel and the historical Jesus used the Rule. Although the Rule clearly originated long before Hillel or Jesus lived, one cannot trace confidently the trail or direction by which the Rule passed between Chinese, Graeco-Roman, and Jewish traditions. Alexander does suggest, however, that although the traditions tell us nothing reliable about Hillel and Jesus as historical figures, the appeal to the Rule as *summum ius* in both traditions does illuminate the traditions themselves in helpful ways.

In chapter 18, H. Lichtenberger revisits the fateful 1865-66 essay by Franz Delitzsch in which he compared Jesus and Hillel. Lichtenberger points out that "unlike other Christian scholars who depicted Jews or representatives of Judaism ... in a derogatory way, Delitzsch portrayed Hillel favorably—but only in order to show how much superior Jesus is in comparison to him." Echoing the cautions of others in this volume about the theological motivations of such comparisons, Lichtenberger does suggest, however, several promising ways in which the Dead Sea Scrolls illuminate Jesus traditions once thought original to him.

In chapter 19, C. A. Evans focuses on the problems and prospects or reconstructing Jesus' teaching. In contrast to some tradition critics, Evans argues that the biggest challenge is not determining what saying or tradition is original to Jesus—a big enough challenge!—but in determining what the saying or tradition originally meant. At the heart of Evans' essay is his appeal for a reexamination of Jesus' teaching "in a manner that is more sensitive to the first-century Palestinian context." Careless or misinformed assumptions about a saying's original meaning have often led to inaccurate historical assessments of its originality. Misunderstandings of the original *Sitz im Leben* of many sayings have also contributed to such inaccurate assessments. Evans illustrates his thesis by reexamining the Parable of the Prodigal Son and the Parable of the Pounds. He shows how these parables may plausibly have been spoken by Jesus by demonstrating how Jesus' own understanding of their meaning may have differed from Luke's later interpretation of them.

In chapter 20, B. T. Viviano concludes this section with a comparative analysis of Hillel and Jesus on prayer. After briefly rehearsing some of the high points in twentieth-century studies on prayer, Viviano compares Hillel and Jesus traditions with regard to prayer, concluding that the evidence—sparse as it is with regard to Hillel and prayer—suggests that both had mystical and prophetic moments and both were simultaneously lovers of and wrestlers with God. Viviano then analyzes the "Lord's Prayer" and revisits Joachim Jeremias's comments on the significance of Jesus' address of God as "Abba." He concludes by suggesting that while Hillel represents a more "creation-centered, sapiential outlook on prayer," Jesus' prayers reflect his sense of apocalyptic urgency regarding the coming redemption.

Finally, J. H. Charlesworth concludes this collection with an epilogue of retrospective and prospective reflections on the exercise. He suggests nine positive points of consensus that have emerged from this project and argues that the results clearly demonstrate the value in and need for interdisciplinary and interconfessional projects such as this.

ABBREVIATIONS

RABBINIC WRITINGS

Mishnah

m.Ab	Pirqé 'Abot
m.'Arak	'Arakhim
m.AZ	'Abodah Zarah
m.BB	Baba Batra
m.Bek	Bekorot
m.Ber	Berakot
m.Bik	Bikkurim
m.BMeṣ	Baba Meṣiah
m.BQam	Baba Qamma
m.'Eduy	'Eduyot
m.Giṭṭ	Giṭṭin
m.Hag	Ḥagigah
m.Kel	Kelim
m.Keṭ	Keṭubbot
m.Kid	Ḳiddushin
m.Mak	Makkot
m.Meg	Megillah
m.Men	Menaḥot?
m.MK	Mo'ed Ḳatan
m.Ned	Nedarim
m.Nid	Niddah
m.Pe'a	Pe'ah
m.Pes	Pesaḥim
m.RH	Rosh Ha-Shanah
m.Sanh	Sanhedrin
m.Shab	Shabbat
m.Shevi	Shevi'it
m.Soṭ	Soṭah
m.Suk	Sukkah
m.Taan	Ta'anit
m.Yad	Yadayim

m.Yeb   Yebamot
m.Yoma   Yoma
m.Zeb   Zebaḥim

Tosefta
t.BB   Baba Batra
t.Beṣ   Beṣah
t.Ber   Berakot
t.BMeṣ   Baba Meṣiah
t.ʿEduy   ʿEduyot
t.Hag   Ḥagigah
t.Keṭ   Keṭubbot
t.Kid   Ḳiddushin
t.Maas   Maʾaserot
t.Meg   Megillah
t.Neg   Negaim
t.Nez   Nezirot
t.Peʾa   Peʾah
t.Pes   Pesaḥim
t.RH   Rosh Ha-Shanah
t.Sanh   Sanhedrin
t.Shab   Shabbat
t.Soṭ   Soṭah
t.Suk   Sukkah
t.Taan   Taʿanit

Palestinian Talmud
y.AZ   ʿAbodah Zarah
y.Ber   Berakot
y.Hag   Ḥagigah
y.Keṭ   Keṭubbot
y.Ned   Nedarim
y.Peʾa   Peʾah
y.Pes   Pesaḥim
y.Sanh   Sanhedrin
y.Shab   Shabbat
y.Shevi   Sheviʾit
y.Soṭ   Soṭah

y.Suk	Sukkah
y.Taan	Taʿanit
y.Ter	Terumot
y.Yoma	Yoma

Babylonian Talmud

b.AZ	ʿAbodah Zarah
b.BB	Baba Batra
b.BQam	Baba Qamma
b.Ber	Berakot
b.Beṣ	Beṣah
b.BMeṣ	Baba Meṣiah
b.ʿErub	ʿErubin
b.Hag	Ḥagigah
b.Hull	Ḥullin
b.Keṭ	Keṭubbot
b.Kid	Ḳiddushin
b.Mak	Makkot
b.Meʿ	Meʿilah
b.Ned	Nedarim
b.Pes	Pesaḥim
b.Sanh	Sanhedrin
b.Shab	Shabbat
b.Soṭ	Soṭah
b.Sukk	Sukkah
b.Taan	Taʿanit
b.Yeb	Yebamot
b.Yoma	Yoma

Sifra

SifQed	Qedoshim
SifBehar	Behar

Sifre

SifDeut	Deuteronomy
SifLev	Leviticus
SifNum	Numbers

Rabbah
GenRab   Genesis Rabbah
ExRab   Exodus Rabbah
LevRab   Leviticus Rabbah
EcclRab   Ecclesiastes Rabbah
SongRab   Song of Songs Rabbah

Other Rabbinic Writings
ARN   Abot de-Rabbi Nathan
Hillel   Midrash Hillel (Beit Hamidrash; בית המדרש)
KalRab   Kallah Rabbati
PesRab   Pesiqta Rabbati
Neof   Targum Neofiti, Pseudo-Jonathan
SefMa'as   Sefer Ha-Ma'asiyyot
TanYash   Tanḥuma Yashan

OTHER ANCIENT WRITINGS

Agr   Cato's *De Agri Cultura*
Ant   Josephus's *Antiquities*
Dial Meret   Lucian's Dialogue with Meret.
GEgyp   Gospel of the Egyptians
Horace, *Sat* *Satires*
Life   Josephus's Life
Or   Dio Chrysostom's *Orations*
POxy   Oxyrhynchus Papyri
ProtJames   Protevangelium of James
War   Josephus's *Jewish War*

MODERN WORKS

AB   Anchor Bible (commentaries)
ABD   Anchor Bible Dictionary
AGAJU   Arbeiten zur Geschichte des Antiken Judentums
              und des Urchristentums
AnBib   Analecta Biblica
ANRW   Aufstieg und Niedergang der Römischen Welt
BAR   Biblical Archaeology Review
BBB   Bonner biblische Beiträge

BETL	Bibliotheca ephemeridum theologicarum lovaniensium
BibOr	Biblica et orientalia
BJRL	*Bulletin of the John Rylands University Library of Manchester*
BJS	Brown Judaic Studies
CII	Corpus inscriptionum iudaicarum
CSEL	Corpus scriptorum ecclesiasticorum latinorum
DE	Eusebius's *Demonstratio Evangelica*
EAEHL	*Encyclopaedia of Archaeological Excavations in the Holy Land*
ELS	*Enchiridion Locorum Sanctorum*
ET	English translation
FRLANT	Forschungen zur Religion und Literatur des Alten und Neuen Testaments
GCS	Griechische christliche Schriftsteller
HE	Eusebius's *Ecclesiastical History*
HeyJ	Heythrop Journal
HTKNT	Herders Theologische Kommentar zum Neuen Testament?
HTR	Harvard Theological Review
HUCA	Hebrew Union College Annual
ICC	International Critical Commentary
IDB	Interpreter's Dictionary of the Bible
IEJ	Israel Exploration Journal
JBL	Journal of Biblical Literature
JE	Jewish Encyclopedia
JQR	Jewish Quarterly Review
JR	Journal of Religion
JSNT	Journal for the Study of the New Testament
JSNTSup	Journal for the Study of the New Testament Supplement Series
KJV	King James Version
LAB	Librorum Antiquitatum Biblicarum
LD	Lectio divina
LEP	Diogenes Laertius's Lives of Eminent Philosophers
LSJM	Liddell, H. G., and R. Scott. *A Greek-English*

	Lexicon, rev. by H. S. Jones and R. MacKenzie, Oxford, 1940.
MGWJ	Monatsschrift für Geschichte und Wissenschaft des Judentums
NCB	New Century Bible
NIBC	New International Bible Commentary
NJBC	The New Jerome Bible Commentary
NJPS	New Jewish Publication Society translation of the Tanakh
NovT	Novum Testamentum
NTD	Das Neue Testament Deutsch
NTS	New Testament Studies
OBO	Orbis biblicus et orientalis
OCD	Oxford Classical Dictionary
OTP	Charlesworth, J. H., ed. *The Old Testament Pseudepigrapha*. 2 vols. Garden City, N.Y., 1983, 1985.
PE	Eusebius's *Praeparatio Evangelica*
PEFQS	Palestine Exploration Fund, Quarterly Statement
PG	J. Migne, *Patrologia graeca*
PJ	Palästina-Jahrbuch
PL	J. Migne, *Patrologia latina*
PW	Pauly-Wissowa, *Real-Encyclopädie der classischen Altertumswissenschaft*
RevScRel	Revue des sciences religieuses
S-B	H. L. Strack and P. Billerbeck, *Kommentar zum Neuen Testament aus Talmud und Midrasch*, 6 vols. (Munich, 1926).
SBF	Studii biblici franciscani
SBFLA	Studii biblici franciscani liber annuus
SBLDS	Society of Biblical Literature Dissertation Series
SBLMS	Society of Biblical Literature Monograph Series
SJ	Studia Judaica
SJLA	Studies in Judaism in Late Antiquity
SNTSMS	Society for New Testament Studies Monograph Series
StTh	Studia Theologica
TB	Tyndale Bulletin

TDNT	Theological Dictionary of the New Testament
TS	Theological Studies
TSAJ	Texte und Studien zum Antiken Judentum
TU	Texte und Untersuchungen
WUNT	Wissenschaftliche Untersuchungen zum Neuen Testament
ZDPV	Zeitschrift des deutschen Palästina-Vereins
ZNW	Zeitschrift für die neutestamentliche Wissenschaft
ZTK	Zeitschrift für Theologie und Kirche

PART ONE

INTRODUCTION

HILLEL AND JESUS:
WHY COMPARISONS ARE IMPORTANT

FOR NEARLY 2,000 years, Hillel has been studied by Jewish historians with few references to Jesus; and he was often seen unhistorically in light of Christian orthodox worship. During the same centuries, Jesus was studied by Christian scholars with virtually no references to Hillel.

When Hillel was mentioned, it was often as one who was a precursor of Jesus.[1] In 1922 the Jewish expert Adolph Büchler could discuss Jewish-Palestinian piety before 70 C.E. without including Jesus of Nazareth.[2] The classic books by the Christian scholars Albert Schweitzer and Rudolph Bultmann on Jesus could assess what can be known about him historically without asking how and in what ways he was influenced by the greatest teacher in Judaism of his day, namely Hillel.[3] Even today, major volumes on pre–70 Judaism hardly mention the two most influential teachers in Palestinian Judaism.[4] For example, the multi-volumed Compendia Rerum Iudaicarum ad Novum Testamentum discusses at length Philo, Josephus, and Gnosticism; it contains numerous sections on the Dead Sea Scrolls and the Pseudepigrapha; but it has not one chapter on Hillel or on Jesus.

---

[1] See A. Danziger, *Jewish Forerunners of Christianity* (New York, 1903) and especially chap. 1: "Hillel, the Forerunner of Christ."

[2] A. Büchler, *Types of Jewish-Palestinian Piety from 70 B.C.E. to 70 C.E.: The Ancient Pious Men* (London, 1922).

[3] A. Schweitzer, *The Quest of the Historical Jesus: A Critical Study of Its Progress from Reimarus to Wrede*, with a preface by F. C. Burkitt, trans., W. Montgomery (New York, 1910, 1911 [second edition], reprinted many times). R. Bultmann, *Jesus and the Word*, trans. L. P. Smith and E. H. Lantero (London, 1958).

[4] The important "New Schürer," which claims to be about the history of Judaism during the time of Jesus Christ, contains no section on Jesus; but it does present a major section on Hillel; see E. Schürer, *The History of the Jewish People in the Age of Jesus Christ*, ed. G. Vermes, et al. (Edinburgh, 1979) vol. 2, pp. 363–67.

Perhaps this failure to deal with these two great teachers is because of the opinion that modern Judaism and Christianity must no longer dictate the descriptions of the past. An ideal has become a misconception; that is, the desire to avoid the claims of modern religions has caused historians to be blind to the significance of Hillel and Jesus. Obviously after 70 C.E. rabbinic schools and Christian scholars respectively elevated Hillel and Jesus far above their own importance within the society of pre-70 Judaism, but that fact does not allow the historian to ignore them or to proceed as if behind the historic person is no historical man.[5]

The discipline has now moved far beyond these misleading assessments. How and in what ways, if at all, can we learn more about the historical Hillel by comparing him to Jesus, and how can we learn more about the historical Jesus by comparing him to Hillel?

At the close of the twentieth century it is timely and wise to focus on these two geniuses in the history of Early Judaism.[6] Both Hillel (c. 60 B.C.E. to c. 20 C.E.) and Jesus (c. 7 B.C.E. to 30 C.E.)[7] were devout Jews who lived during a pivotal time in Jewish history, specifically between the kingship of Herod the Great (37–4 B.C.E.) and the destruction of Jerusalem and the Temple in 70 C.E. Both began with humble beginnings and both apparently engaged in common labor. Both were great and influential scholars. From the view of the two Jewish groups that survived the conflagration of 70—namely Rabbinic Judaism and Christianity[8]—they are the most influential Jewish teachers in the period from Ezra to the destruction of 70.[9]

---

[5] As C. A. Evans perceives, "much of the current discussion pays insufficient attention to history, parallel traditions, and relevant figures and events." Evans, *Jesus and His Contemporaries* (AGAJU 25; Leiden, 1995) p. vii.

[6] For sources on Hillel, see the following: J. Neusner, "Hillel," *The Rabbinic Traditions About the Pharisees Before 70*, 2 parts (Leiden, 1971) part 1, pp. 212–302; A. Hyman, *Toldoth Tannaim Ve'Amoraim* [Hebrew], 3 vols. (Jerusalem, 1987) vol. 1, pp. 362–73; M. Margalioth, ed., *Encyclopedia of Talmudic and Geonic Literature Being a Biographical Dictionary of the Tanaim, Amoraim and Geonim*, 2 vols. (Tel Aviv, 1987) vol. 1, pp. 246–51 [Hebrew].

[7] The dates for Hillel are debated; the ones for Jesus are widely accepted (but not certain). For a discussion of the latter, see esp. J. P. Meier, *A Marginal Jew: Rethinking the Historical Jesus*, 2 vols. (AB; New York, 1991, 1994) vol. 1, pp. 212–14, 229 and note.

[8] Note how Hillel is remembered in the Talmud: "In ancient days when the Torah was forgotten from Israel, Ezra came up from Babylon and reestablished it. Then it was again forgotten until Hillel the Babylonian came up and reestablished it."

At the outset many will be suspicious that a Christian, especially one who is ordained by an established institution,[10] cannot with balanced judgment compare Hillel and Jesus. Will not many wonder whether the conclusion will celebrate Jesus to the detriment of Hillel? Frankly, I am willing to admit that in some ways the historical Hillel is more appealing than the historical Jesus. Hillel's ingenious interpretation of Torah, leniency, and openness to prospective converts to Judaism is far more appealing than some of the episodes in Jesus' life that cannot be explained away by Redaction Criticism or other forms of higher criticism. Jesus most likely told a young man who wanted to follow him but needed to return home to bury his father, "Let the dead bury the dead."[11] He also probably rejected as unworthy of him the wise and searching request of a woman from the northern coast of Palestine, specifically Syrophonecia. No sayings so cutting, so harsh—indeed so tasteless—were attributed to Hillel.

Hillel apparently had room for Gentiles within Judaism. Jesus rejected Gentile converts, at least during most of his ministry, and it has not been possible to deny that he did instruct his disciples to go only to Israelites.[12] Is it not ironic that Christians today, virtually all of whom are Gentiles, follow Jesus and not Hillel? Why should Gentiles follow Jesus; deliberations will be wisely guided by the words of Krister Stendahl:

---

b.Sukkah 20a.

[9] Obviously Sirach was an important Jewish teacher in Jerusalem during the second century B.C.E.; but he never obtained the prominence of Hillel or Jesus. It is odd that his teachings were considered more "canonical" within early Christianity than within post-135 Judaism. The Righteous Teacher, the founder of the community that produced the Dead Sea Scrolls, cannot be portrayed as in any way as important as Hillel or Jesus. They same applies to the Galilean miracle workers, like Honi, who were also attributed wise and important teachings.

[10] I am an ordained Methodist minister, but have never during my professional career felt constrained or limited in pursuing questions.

[11] See M. Hengel, *The Charismatic Leader and His Followers*, trans. J. C. G. Greig (Studies of the New Testament and Its World; Edinburgh, 1981).

[12] Most experts involved in Jesus Research today tend to reject many of the Gentile mission pericopes as redactional. Matthew, who concludes with the great comission, which obviously includes Gentiles (28:19), is pro-Gentile (10:18; 3:9; 8:11; 21:43; 22:1-14; 23:38-39); he cannot have created Jesus' words in 10:5. They most likely derive from earlier, probably authentic, Jesus traditions.

It is the resurrection of Jesus which gives enough of an anticipation to warrant the church to move beyond the limitations of the very words of its Master who as the Messiah *designatus* had said: "Do not go to the Gentiles."[13]

Hillel's view of the Endtime also is more palatable to modern tastes than was Jesus' stress on an imminent apocalyptic cataclysm. Hillel was not caught up in the eschatological and apocalyptic fervor that had been building up within Palestinian Judaism for at least a century. In contrast Jesus probably said, at least on one occasion, something like what is recorded in Mark, "Behold there are some standing here who will not taste death until they see God's Kingdom come in power" (Mark 9:1). It is conceivable, at least to many scholars from Albert Schweitzer to Richard H. Hiers (and many others), that Jesus was carried away by eschatology and the view that the world would end in his own lifetime.[14] Followers of Hillel do not have the embarrassment of trying to work with Jesus' misunderstandings of eschatology, although followers of Jesus surely can refer to such passages as Mark 13:32, which indicates that he refused to specify the time of the End; only God knew that hour.[15]

It is clear from these preliminary observations, even though they are rather sweeping generalizations, that it is fruitful to compare and contrast Hillel and Jesus.[16] The fruits of such work will depend upon our ability to attempt to overcome our own biases, commitments, and to write, as Polybius[17] would urge, to aim for a reliable historical assess-

---

[13] K. Stendahl, *The Scrolls and the New Testament*, ed. by K. Stendahl with J. H. Charlesworth (New York, 1992) p. 17.

[14] See esp. R. H. Hiers, *The Historical Jesus and the Kingdom of God: Present and Future in the Message and Ministry of Jesus* (Gainesville, Florida, 1973).

[15] The historian should consider the probability that "distasteful" elements in Hillel's teachings were suppressed or removed as the rabbinic tradition evolved. If so, perhaps we may now raise the following question without fear of suggesting that Jesus was superior to Hillel: "Why is it that Christian transmitters of tradition allowed more problematic or 'distasteful' traditions to survive than did the House of Hillel?"

[16] This statement would hold true even if it is not clear that we can have "certain" knowledge about the historical Hillel and Jesus. For further reflections, see the cautious methodological comments by A. Goshen Gottstein in chapter two.

[17] See esp. Polybius's comment that the historian should "inquire from as many people as possible, to believe those worthy of belief and to be an adequate critic of the reports that reach him." *Histories* 12.4.5.

ment. The pertinence of this research leads many of us to wonder why no scholar has recently attempted to write a book on Hillel and Jesus, although many have appeared on other related topics, like the Qumran Essenes' Teacher and Jesus, the Cynic Philosophers and Jesus, the Zealots and Jesus, and especially the Pharisees and Jesus. No symposium or colloquium has been organized to confront the issues raised by these two great thinkers, even though archaeological discoveries in Israel, especially in Jerusalem and Galilee, that date from their time have been outstanding, and at times incredible. Since the forties we have obtained archaeological evidence of crucifixion near the time of Jesus' death, have found a stone with Pilate's name on it, and discovered the putative tomb of Caiphas's family.[18] Even more significant have been the ever increasing documentary evidence that dates, without editing or alteration through copying, directly from the time of Hillel and Jesus, including the numerous inscriptions, and especially the hundreds of documents preserved in the Qumran Caves and popularly called the Dead Sea Scrolls. It is therefore imperative to see how and in what ways we learn more about Hillel and Jesus, and their time, by comparing them.

Probably most historians today will disagree with those who think that Hillel and Jesus were normal people, as P. Winter advocated for the latter;[19] and many will be impressed by the evidence marshalled by David Flusser that Hillel, and not only Jesus, had a rather well developed ego and elevated self-perception.[20]

Few will conclude that Jesus attached himself to Hillel, who was his "real teacher," as Ernst Renan wrote when he penned a romantic portrait of Jesus.[21] I also doubt that anyone will follow the lead of Paul Rieger, who in *Hillel und Jesus* concluded, "so it is to be accepted with the highest probability that Jesus was a pupil of Hillel."[22] I also doubt

[18] See the discussions in Charlesworth, *Jesus Within Judaism: New Light from Exciting Archaeological Discoveries* (AB; New York, 1988) and in Charlesworth, ed., *Jesus and the Dead Sea Scrolls* (AB; New York, 1992).

[19] P. Winter, *On the Trial of Jesus* (Berlin, 1961) p. 148.

[20] See Flusser's paper in this collection and also his "Hillel's Self-Awareness and Jesus," *Immanuel* 4 (1974) 31–36.

[21] E. Renan, *The Life of Jesus* (New York, 1863).

[22] "Hat also Hillel noch mindestens 20 Jahre nach Beginn der üblichen Zeitrechnung gelebt, so ist mit höchster Wahrscheinlichkeit anzunehmen, dass Jesus ein Schüler Hillels gewesen ist" (P. Rieger, *Hillel und Jesus* [Hamburg, 1904] p. 7).

that a scholar abreast of research on the Dead Sea Scrolls and Pseudepigrapha will conclude, as the distinguished Abraham Geiger did in 1864
and as Harvey Falk claimed in 1985, that Jesus was a Pharisee who
belonged to the Hillelites.[23] The reasons for these opinions are not
primarily because Hillel had died before Jesus was born, even though
there is evidence that Hillel antedates Jesus,[24] or because Jesus was so
different from Hillel; it is because for all the similarities between Jesus
and Hillel, they were also often appreciably different. Unlike Hillel,
Jesus was significantly influenced by apocalypticism and eschatology;
and he shared these perspectives with other Jews, notably the Righteous
Teacher of the Dead Sea Scrolls. It is fascinating to ponder this question: Was Jesus closer to the Righteous Teacher or to Hillel? Perhaps
this symposium will take up this question. In my judgment, Jesus was
closer to the Righteous Teacher on apocalypticism and disenchantment
with the ruling priestly family, but closer to Hillel on purity issues and
the appreciation of the Temple and its services. Unlike the Righteous
Teacher—but like Hillel—Jesus was more liberal and had a place for all
Jews in the house of Israel.

No one today would simply take up the method or advocate the
conclusions of Franz Delitzsch who wrote a book on Hillel and Jesus
over 100 years ago.[25] Reacting clearly to Renan's romanticism and
Geiger's popular portrait and elevation of Hillel, and attempting to
prove the superiority of Christianity over Judaism, Delitzsch strove to
praise Jesus at the expense of Hillel.[26] He claimed that Jesus was a
reformer, but Hillel never was, leaving "everything as he found it" (p.
141). Jesus was free from "any existing" rabbinical system, drinking
"of the fullness of the Divine Spirit," but Hillel "simply propagated the

---

[23] A. Geiger, *Vorlesungen über das Judentum and seine Geschichte* (1864):
"dass Jesus ein Pharisäer war, der in den Wegen Hillels ging ..." H. Falk, *Jesus the
Pharisee: A New Look at the Jewishness of Jesus* (New York, 1984): "It shall be the
goal of this book to demonstrate that Jesus' debates with the Pharisees were actually disputes recorded in the Talmud between Bet Shammai and Bet Hillel, with Jesus adopting
the views of Bet Hillel" (p. 8). This method is not that of inductive historiography. See
the erudite prosopographical study in this volume by J. Sievers.

[24] D. Flusser stated that Hillel "died before Jesus was born." See his "Hillel's
Self-Awareness and Jesus," *Immanuel* 4 (1974) 31.

[25] Note in particular the English translation: F. Delitzsch, *Jesus and Hillel*,
trans. P. Monkhouse (London, 1877).

[26] See especially the critical insights in this volume by H. Lichtenberger.

scholastic lore of Shemaiah and Abtalion" (pp. 148–49). Jesus' teaching is judged to be "universally religious, moral, and humane," but Hillel's is "juristic, casuistic, and narrow-mindedly national" (p. 161). Such comments are of no help in our attempt to compare Hillel and Jesus; they simply disclose that until the present century such comparisons violated the canons of historiography, which we should not think are our own creations. They surely antedate Hillel and Jesus, and were fashioned by Herodotus, Thucydides, and especially Polybius.

Most historical-critical scholars eschew portraits of Jesus as a deluded visionary or as Mary's illegitimate son, even though some scholars have attempted to defend such conclusions.[27] They probably will also not portray Hillel as Jesus' precursor. Such contentions are now marked as the relics of Christian or Jewish apologetics and polemics or the result of a distorted methodology.

One of the great benefits of the latter half of this century is that promising discoveries have enticed us scholars out of the ivory-palaced halls of modern academia, especially the German institutions in which historical pessimism was born and bred, into a focused perception of ancient Palestine and the creative world of pre–70 Palestinian Judaism. The unexpected and indeed phenomenal archaeological discoveries from Hillel and Jesus' time help us become more empathetic with that ancient world, in which we strive to understand the lives and teachings of Hillel and Jesus.[28]

With so many helmsmen helping it will be possible to sail more accurately and carefully past the scholarly extremes of the Scylla and Charybdis. We need to avoid claims like those of Rieger and Falk which force Jesus into the school of Hillel and the biased conclusions like those of Delitzsch which cast Jesus out of the Bet Hillel. Our research should proceed so that Hillel and Jesus will be more realistically and accurately portrayed, and allow for Jesus to be in many ways similar to (and also different from) Hillel without applying the adjective "Hillelite" to him. We must surely avoid the pitfalls of positivistic historicism; in no way should we seek only on an attempt to recapture the

---

[27] See the helpful insights by Meier, "Birth and Lineage," in *A Marginal Jew*, vol. 1, pp. 208–52.

[28] See Charlesworth, "The Jesus of History and the Archaeology of Palestine," in *Jesus Within Judaism*, pp. 103–30, and N. Avigad, *Discovering Jerusalem* (Nashville, New York, 1983).

ipsissima verba of these giants. All we can hope to do is to approximate the purpose or intentionality of the putative utterances.

In our research we need to comprehend the diversity of the many groups within Early Judaism, the factionalism often among them,[29] the probability that Hillel was already dead before Jesus was mature, the geographical (and perhaps cultural) difference between them,[30] and the lack of data indicating that they engaged in dialogue. Cumulatively, these insights or "facts" lead me to conclude that Jesus was not directly influenced by Hillel.

Before proceeding further it is imperative to ponder to what degree the traditions associated with Hillel and Jesus are reliable. In the mid-nineteenth century the erudite Rabbi Abraham Geiger, who lived in Frankfort-on-Main, in his *Judentum und seine Geschichte*, argued that "Hillel is a strictly historical personage."[31] He went on to claim that Hillel, unlike other figures such as Jesus, was not hidden behind legends.[32] In 1922 A. Büchler felt he could discuss Hillel and his teachings without having to assess to what degree what was attributed to him in the Mishnah and Tosephta, as well as the Targumim, could be traced reliably back to him.[33] These are dated and untenable views which were forged in the crucible of a minority religion trying to survive within a hostile ostensibly Christian culture. As I. Elbogen,[34] A. Kaminka,[35] J.

---

[29] See the contribution in this volume by J. G. D. Dunn.

[30] Hillel probably represented Judea, Jesus Galilee. Jesus did not have good relations with those from Judea.

[31] "Hillel ist eine vollkommen geschichtliche Persönlichkeit; ... ." A. Geiger, *Das Judenthum und seine Geschichte bis zur Verstörung des zweiten Temples* (Breslau, 1865 [second edition]) vol. 1, p. 100.

[32] Geiger, *Das Judenthum und seine Geschichte*, pp. 99–107. For his discussion of Jesus see L. Geiger, ed., *Abraham Geiger's Allgemeine Einleitung in die Wissenschaft des Judenthums* (Berlin, 1875) pp. 78–86.

[33] For example, Büchler described Hillel's humility, patience, and calmness without asking if the accounts about Hillel are trustworthy; *Types of Jewish-Palestinian Piety*, see esp. pp. 11, 16–17, 21. At times Büchler attributed anonymous sayings to Hillel (see p. 38, n. 3). Büchler also wanted to prove that Hillel was humble and that the great moral attributes of the *hasidim* were not represented only by the Essenes.

[34] I. Elbogen, "Hillel," *Encyclopaedia Judaica* vol. 8, cols. 42–51: "Von seinem Leben sind nur wenige Einzelheiten bezeugt, hingegen hat sich ein Legendenkranz um seine Person gebildet" (col. 42).

[35] A. Kaminka, "Hillel's Life and Work," *JQR* 30 (1939–40) 107–22: "The sources, from which we may derive facts about the lives of the Tannaim of the century before the destruction of the Temple, are very meager. We must rely on legends as most of the historians do; but unfortunately these legends, although numerous, are

Goldin,[36] and many, including notably J. Neusner,[37] have demonstrated Hillel's life and teachings were altered during the transmission from his death, around 20 C.E. to the writing down of his teachings around 200 C.E. and even much later. Moreover, his life was celebrated through redaction and through legendary expansions.[38] We cannot assume that because the later Pharisees adopted him he must have been a pre-70 Pharisee; here we benefit from the research conducted by Neusner and J. Sievers.[39]

Ever since the time of Reimarus at the close of the 18th century, and surely since David Strauss in 1835, as A. Schweitzer clarified, it is common coin in universities and seminaries throughout the world, to recognize that the Gospels are celebrations of Jesus' life in light of the Easter faith. Although M. Kähle and R. Bultmann exaggerated the creative abilities of the post-Easter communities and missed the vast amount of reliable traditions about Jesus, especially his actions,[40] it is a consensus today that the Gospels are not biographies which describe the life of a Galilean Jew. They preach him in light of the Easter faith.

It is unlikely that Hillel was a descendant of David.[41] The assertion that Jesus was a descendant of David is so clearly enveloped in the Christian kerygma that it is difficult to be certain that he was a Davidad. These claims that either Hillel or Jesus is a Davidad appear in the chain of traditions attributed to them. While in both instances the

---

mostly figments of the imagination" (p. 107).

[36] J. Goldin rightly stated that Hillel "is flanked by legends" (p. 263). Goldin, "Hillel the Elder," *The Journal of Religion* 26 (1946) 263–77.

[37] J. Neusner, "The Figure of Hillel," *Judaism in the Beginning of Christianity* (Philadelphia, 1984) pp. 63–88.

[38] See the helpful insights by P. Schäfer in *Studien zur Geschichte und Theologie des Rabbinischen Judentums* (AGAJU 15; Leiden, 1978) esp. pp. 1–44.

[39] Neusner concluded, "My only firm conclusion is that Hillel was likely to have lived sometime before the destruction of the Temple and to have played an important part in the politics of the Pharisaic party" (*Rabbinic Traditions*, part 1, p. 301). Also see the paper by J. Sievers in this collection.

[40] See M. Kähler, *The So-Called Historical Jesus and the Historic Biblical Christ*, trans. C. E. Braaten, with a foreword by P. J. Tillich (Philadelphia, 1964 [originally published in 1896] and R. Bultmann, *History of the Synoptic Tradition*, trans. J. Marsh, rev. ed. (New York, 1963).

[41] *Pace Encyclopedia of Talmudic and Geonic Literature*, vol. 1, p. 246. Neusner, *History*, vol. 1, pp. 190–91; Neusner, *Rabbinic Traditions*, part 1, p. 268.

historical figure has been embellished with legends, it is far more likely that Jesus was a Davidad than Hillel. Such traditions appear within a decade of Jesus' death; Hillel's traditions are centuries later.[42]

Likewise expansionistic to a historical kernel are the anecdotes which laud Hillel at the expense of Shammai and Jesus at the expense of the "Pharisees."[43] In both instances we are confronted with the legendary Hillel or Jesus and not the historical Hillel or Jesus. In both instances the expansion is due to Jewish schools, in one case with the Johannine ben Zakkai School and the Rabbinic School at Usha and on the other the Jewish-Christian school behind the Gospel of Matthew.

We must, therefore, be aware of the possibility that when discussing Hillel or Jesus we might be building hypotheses or theses on data that are vastly separated from the historical figures by time and space.[44] A picture of Hillel uncritically built upon second-century and later traditions and a portrait of Jesus constructed from post-70 traditions will seriously undermine our attempt to reconstruct the lives and teachings of these two Jews who lived in ancient Palestine before the destruction. We must *weigh every passage* that contains either Hillel or Jesus traditions to ascertain if it derives ultimately from Hillel or Jesus.

THE TIME OF TRANSITION AND THE AGE OF STANDARDIZATION

Before assessing the major similarities and differences that ostensibly derive from comparing the historical Hillel with the historical Jesus, we should emphasize the importance of the time in which they lived. It was a chaotic period. During the time of Herod the Great no less than seven different priests served as high priests. After Herod the Great the stability he achieved through brutality and demagoguery vanished.[45] It

---

[42] For further on the unreliability of Hillel traditions, see H. L. Strack and G. Stemberger, *Introduction to the Talmud and Midrash*, trans. Markus Bockmuehl (Minneapolis, 1992), pp. 66–68, 71–72.

[43] It is true that m.Eduyot includes "40 cases in which the Shammaites interpret more leniently and the Hillelites more severely," as Strack and Stemberger reported (*Introduction to the Talmud and Midrash*, p. 129).

[44] I have tried to omit from our considerations in the present discussion the episodes in which the historical Hillel is replaced by the Hillel celebrated in Rabbinics. My attempt is to see how we can catch a glimpse of the historical Hillel and the historical Jesus—perhaps only from shadows of these real Palestinian men. See the judicious methodological comments by Goshen Gottstein in the following chapter.

[45] See the suggestive study by R. Fenn in *The Death of Herod: An Essay in the Sociology of Religion* (Cambridge, New York, 1992).

was a crucial time; in fact it is difficult to think of a period more important in Jewish history. It was the time of transition and the age of standardization. Four pillars in the ediface of Judaism were being chiseled into the shape they still have today.

The Hebrew and Aramaic script developed from the ancient Hasmonean uneven writing to the elegant and square bookhand of the Herodian period. Thus the script moved from a form that is incomprehensible to one who has studied the Talmudim for decades to a form in which a young Israeli can read it, and do so easily. From the time of Hillel and Jesus the Hebrew script continued to preserve the shape it obtained then; there was no further significant evolution.

The text of the Hebrew Bible essentially also moved to a standard form during the time of Hillel and Jesus. The text had been divergent, and extremely so with the books of Jeremiah and Samuel. During the decades of the first century, when Hillel and Jesus taught, the text of the Hebrew Bible reached the form in which we know it today. There was no further alteration; the Masoretic text took shape long before the addition of the vowels in the early middle ages.

The books to be judged sacred were finally selected during this time of Hillel and Jesus. The intense rivalry to the so-called Mosaic books and Davidic Psalter by, for example, the Books of Enoch and the other psalters, like the Psalms of Solomon and the Qumran Psalm Scroll, came to an end. Most of the debate over the books to be included in the Torah and Prophets antedated the time of Hillel and Jesus by at least two centuries, and the final inclusion of Esther and exclusion of Sirach came a century later, at Usha. That means the shape of the canon was essentially set by the time of Hillel and Jesus. When Jesus refers to the Law and the Prophets,[46] he seems to reflect the *status quo*; that is to say that the Law (תורה) and the Prophets (נביאים) were closed collections, but the Writings (כתובים) remained open. The Hebrew canon of scriptures was standardized during this early period in Jewish history; it would not be opened again and other books added, even if the consensus among the Rabbis was that the Oral Law was also given at Sinai and now embodied in writing in Mishnah, Tosephta, and Talmudim.

---

[46] See esp. Mt 5:17; 7:12; Lk 16:16.

The liturgy also developed to a recognized form during the time of Hillel and Jesus. It was during this period that for the first time in the history of Judaism prayers appeared in set or statutory forms, even if spontaneous prayer was encouraged.[47] Some Rabbis offered the opinion that only spontaneous prayer was pleasing to God, but their words only demonstrate that statutory prayers had appeared as part of the synagogal liturgy. This new creation was foreshadowed by earlier liturgies, such as the Passover Haggadah, which is probably the earliest form of Jewish synagogal liturgy. Obviously, the Davidic Psalter, in its final form of text and collection, without the apocryphal compositions as are know in the Qumran Psalm Scroll, was the hymnbook of the Second Temple. Hence it was during the time of Hillel and Jesus that Jewish liturgy, which is known today and recited in synagogues throughout the world, took its first recognizable form—and of course there was additional development. The Temple and its liturgy also reached their pinnacle of development with the grandeur suggestive to us today by the spectacularly massive stones and installations in and near the Temple mount. These would loom of more significance if after the time of Hillel and Jesus the Temple had not been destroyed by the Roman troops who disobeyed the orders of Titus in the early autumn of 70. And it needs little emphasis to bring to the fore the realization that both Hillel and Jesus revered the Temple and worshipped there. Hillel and Jesus taught in Jerusalem and revered the Temple.

This time of transition—from approximately 63 B.C.E., when Pompey entered the Land, to 132 C.E., when Bar Cosiba was defeated—produced *a standard script, text, collection or canon, and the first statutory prayers in Jewish liturgy.* The cummulative process produced the data and perspectives from which and according to which Jews could, and would, articulate a clear normative self-definition. Thus the borders and boundaries of being a Jew were specified. In the process all early Jewish groups—which totaled more than a dozen—were reduced to only two: one group followed the teachings of Hillel and the other the teachings of Jesus. Eventually, sometime late in the century in which these two giants lived the boundaries became clearer and "Christians" could be distinguished from Jews. The boundary was

---

[47] See esp. J. Heinemann, *Prayer in the Talmud: Forms and Patterns*, trans. R. S. Sarason (SJ 9; Berlin, New York, 1977).

erected by the completion of the wording of the Birkath ha-Minim and the expulsion from the synagogues of those Jews who followed Jesus; a sociological phenomenon represented in the appearance of the word ἀποσυνάγωγος (aposynagōgos) in the Gospel of John, which ironically—yet understandably—is both the most Jewish of the Gospels and one in which Ἰουδαῖοι (Ioudaioi), usually translated incorrectly "Jews," are targeted as the enemies of truth and of Jesus.

Why is the time of transition also the age of standardization? Why is the time for the movement from Early Judaism to rabbinic Judaism and Christianity one of standardization? One of the reasons is the fact that beginning with 63 B.C.E. (at least, if not earlier), Jews were facing increasing pressure from Rome and the Romans were threatening the pride and self-understanding that had been inherited. The sacred books seemed too diverse and too "archaic," at least to many Jewish youths, to provide answers to the new questions. Beginning in 63 B.C.E., the kingdom established by the Hasmoneans—and eventually freedom itself—were lost to the Romans. Many Jews would have uttered words similar to those recorded in Fourth Ezra; they would have wondered what happened to God's promises.

Second, accelerating after the conquest by Alexander the contiguous cultures began in a far more intense way to threaten the efficaciousness and power of the traditions beloved by the Fathers. The creative insights and energies from Persia, Egypt, Greece, and Rome intoxicated the spirit of the Jews, especially in Palestine and among the young.[48] What was so wrong with being like the Greeks? Why should not one remove the signs of circumcision? Ultimately the question became, "What defines a Jew?" Many Jewish males were embarrassed by the traditions that had galvanized society and defined their fathers and grandfathers. Some, perhaps many, underwent epispasm and removed the marks of circumcision.[49] Obviously traditions were being challenged and the sacred threatened by the profane. Standards and norms were needed.

---

[48] See Charlesworth, "Greek, Persian, Roman, Syrian, and Egyptian influences in Early Jewish Theology: A Study of the History of the Rechabites," in *Hellenica et Judaica: Hommage à Valentin Nikiprowetzky*, ed. A. Caquot, et al. (Leuven-Paris, 1986) 219–43.

[49] See R. G. Hall, "Epispasm and the Dating of Ancient Jewish Writings," *Journal for the Study of the Pseudepigrapha* 2 (1988) 71–86.

Third, though most Palestinian Jews believed that Jerusalem was the center of the world and the link between heaven and earth (the *axis mundi*), there was a growing fear that God was no longer involved in history and at times too far removed from the laments of his chosen ones. Although prayers were acknowledged to be heard by God, even by the apocalyptists, there was a perception that God, unlike during the time of Abraham, was now far removed to the highest of highest heavens. Jewish thought became increasingly more preoccupied with the perception that the present was close to the Endtime and the dawning of a new day, the Age to Come, and with the presupposition that meaning and God's promises were possible to reaffirm because of an act from heaven or from the future. In many Jewish centers of learning reflection about history and learning Torah was replaced by speculations about the heavens above or the coming future age. These two forces, "eschatology" and apocalypsology,[50] shaped the *Zeitgeist* of Hillel's and Jesus' time. In the time of transition each of them, in similar ways, sought to establish standards by which God's will could be discerned and obeyed and life could be bearable in the present and on this earth.

Fourth, with experienced sense of the loss of some promises to Abraham, especially the Land, and with the failure of the promised coming one—the Messiah—to appear in time and space there appeared in many Jewish circles the assumption that this earth and time may not be the source of meaning. In some ways it was a time like ours; in many centers of learning there was a fear among some and a conviction among others that the traditions had lost their force or value. The Enoch groups that produced the most brilliant compositions just before the time of Hillel and Jesus were convinced that Wisdom, that wonderful hypostatic being who was with God, had come to the earth but could not find a home and so returned into the heavens (1En 42).[51] In this

---

[50] That is, the process of thinking apocalyptically, with its sociological ramifications.

[51]   "Wisdom could not find a place in which she could dwell;
         but a place was found (for her) in the heavens.
         Then Wisdom went out to dwell with the children of the
         people, but she found no dwelling place.
         (So) Wisdom returned to her place
         and she settled permanently among the angels."
                                    1 Enoch 42:1-2; E. Isaac in *OTP* 1.33

ideological setting the average folk sought to find meaning and sacredness in life and traditions, and some of the Am ha-aretz were devoutly
religious. In contrast to many of the Jewish groups, especially the
Essenes, the Sadducees, and the Shammaities, Hillel and Jesus
apparently directed their message so as to include the disenfranchised.

Just how Hillel and Jesus fit into their time, and how they helped
the Time of Transition become the Age of Standardization has not been
clearly perceived and articulated. In any case, they lived at a time of
major transition.[52] Obviously, neither Hillel nor Jesus helped standard-
ize the script or the text; neither ruled on which books to be included in
or excluded from the canon. Probably neither helped form the Jewish
liturgy. Surely, however, both Hillel and Jesus stood against the frag-
mentation being caused by sectarian movements such as the Essenes.
Both urged fellow Jews to remain loyal to community, and both resisted
the growing might of the Zealots, or zealous ones, advocating peace and
love. Both struggled against the rigidity and insensitivity of the priestly
aristocracy in Jerusalem.[53] Despite the difficulty of discerning which
sayings of Hillel and Jesus ultimately are authentic, the broad clusters
of traditions attributed to each tend to support such generalizations. In
any case, the followers of Hillel and Jesus certainly understood their
masters to have taught and inculcated such perspectives.

How did Hillel help the time of Transition become the age of
standardization? It is not yet clear; but some reflections seem to be in
order. He emphasized set ways to interpret Torah so that a standard
methodology for exegesis could be observed.[54] He probably did inherit,
not create as S. Lieberman and Neusner indicate,[55] something like the

[52] For example, see the title of N. N. Glatzer book: *Hillel the Elder: The
Emergence of Classical Judaism*, revised edition (New York, 1956, 1966).
[53] See A. Geiger, "Hillel's Kampf gegen das Priesterthum," in *Sadducäer*
(Breslau, 1863) pp. 36–48 and E. P. Sanders, *Jesus and Judaism* (Philadelphia, 1985).
[54] J. Jeremias argued that Paul utilized Hillel's middot; see Jeremias "Paulus als
Hillelit," in *Neotestamentica et Semitica* (Edinburgh, 1974) pp. 88–94. F. Manns suggests that the author of John utilized the middot; Manns, "Exégèse rabbinique et exégèse johannique," *Revue biblique* 92 (1985) 525–38. Manns is convinced that the middot are ancient and rightly linked with Hillel (pp. 527–28).
[55] S. Lieberman, *Hellenism in Jewish Palestine* (New York, 1950) pp. 53–54;
Neusner, *Rabbinic Traditions*, part 1, p. 241. For text, translation, and exegetical comments on the middot, see D. I. Brewer, *Techniques and Assumptions in Jewish Exegesis
Before 70 CE* (TSAJ 30; Tübingen, 1992) pp. 17–23.

seven middot attributed to him: *a fortiori* (קל וחומר), analogy (גזרה שוה), deduction from a verse (בנין אב מכתוב אחד), deduction from two verses (בנין אב משני כתובים), deduction from the general to the particular and from the particular to the general (כלל ופרט ופרט וכלל), coherence with another passage (כיוצא בו במקום אחר), and deduction from the context (דבר הלמד מעניינו).[56] Along with the establishment of the *Bet Kennesset* and the *Bet Midrash* the formalizing of normative hermeneutical praxis stabilized the meaning of Torah and protected the community from the centrifugal forces of sectarian hermeneutics, as found in the Dead Sea Scrolls.[57]

Hillel—according to the Hillelites—developed the *Prosbul*, which protected both the borrower and lender.[58] The *Prosbul* antedates 56 C.E. since a document found in a Murabba'at dated to the second year of Nero apparently alludes to it.[59] This legislation was necessary—and part of the standardization process—because Jews were losing their land, which they had received as a divine promise, to the Romans and the Herods. It is easy to imagine why pre-70 Palestinian Jews considered Romans and Herods sinful landlords and oppressive overlords.[60] Jesus' parables make clear the threat to Jews who were becoming tenant farmers.[61]The *Prosbul* was intended primarily to help the small land-

---

[56] t.San 7:11; ed. Suckermandel, p. 427, lines 4–8; also see ARN ch. 37, trans. Goldin, p. 154. See Neusner, *Rabbinic Tradition*, part 1, pp. 240–42, 174–75; also see G. Vermes, et al., *The History of the Jewish People in the Age of Jesus Christ (175 B.C.–A.D. 135)*, by Emil Schürer (Edinburgh, 1979) vol. 2, pp. 343–44.

[57] See the observations of S. Towner, "Hermeneutical Systems of Hillel and the Tannaim: A Fresh Look," *HUCA* 53 (1982) 101–35.

[58] m.Sheb 10.3; Sifré Deut 113, ed. Friedman, pp. 97b–98a. See the comments by E. E. Urbach in *The Sages: Their Concepts and Beliefs*, trans. I. Abrahams (Jerusalem, 1979) vol. 1, p. 580; and R. Goldenberg, "Hillel/Hillelschule (Schammaj/Schammajschule)," *Theologische Realkenzyklopädie* 15 (1986) 326–30; see esp. p. 327. Extremely important are the texts cited by and the critical comments by J. Neusner, "Hillel," part 1, pp. 212–302; see esp. 217–20, 262–62. Neusner shows that it is possible that two stories were brought together and that the historical circumstances in which Hillel ordained the *Prosbul* are impossible to reconstruct; but it remains probable that it was Hillel, and no other, who instituted the *Prosbul*. I am convinced that it was remembered, reliably, that Hillel instituted the *Prosbul* and that then later additions were added to this historical kernel.

[59] See DJD 2, pp. 100–104.

[60] See, for example, the comments against them found in 1En 1–37.

[61] See my discussion, and works consulted, in *Jesus Within Judaism*, pp. 131–64.

owner and business persons without substantial means.[62]

Most importantly, Hillel may well have developed a program in which the demands of Torah, which were becoming unbearable for some Jews, were interpreted liberally and leniently, and in which a wise attitude to non-Jews was fostered.[63] Hence, for those inside the boundaries—that is the religious Jews—it was possible to hear God's word and not be crushed by it, and for those outside—the Gentiles—it was possible to live with some respect and toleration that would make life less precarious and the future less treacherous.

At such points Jesus stands shoulder to shoulder with Hillel. Both most likely resisted the curse of increased rules for purification and acceptance by the Jewish aristocracy and the enslavement through conquest and over taxation by the occupying Roman forces. In a vein similar to Hillel, Jesus taught that Torah was not a burden but a joy, and that rules like the Sabbath were made for the human not the human for them.[64] Hillel and Jesus most likely warned against rebellion and war against Rome. Jesus allegedly taught that he who lives by the sword dies by the sword.[65] He noted the ways that Torah was being interpreted, how the people were becoming confused with excessive and idiosyncratic exegesis, and affirmed that it was a living text that revealed its meaning through pneumatic and eschatological exegesis.

MAJOR SIMILARITIES

It is obvious that Hillel and Jesus share enough similarity that an intensive comparison may prove fruitful. Let us then continue by focusing on the major similarities they apparently shared.

Their followers preserved traditions that each of them could summarize Torah succinctly. Hillel allegedly told a proselyte: "What is hateful to you, do not do to your neighbor; that is the whole Torah. The

---

[62] Sanders correctly states that the *Prosbul* "is aimed at helping the small landowner or businessman" (*Judaism: Practice & Belief 63 B.C.E.–66 C.E.* [London, Philadelphia, 1992], p. 427).

[63] Here I mean the contrast between the putative attitude of Shammai and Hillel to the question of what is the foundation of Torah.

[64] See esp. j.Pess. chap. 6. Mk 2:27.

[65] The saying that he who takes the sword will perish by the sword is found only in Mt 26:52; but it seems to convey the intention of Jesus as found in other passages (cf. Jn 18:11; also see Lk 1:79, Acts 10:36, Rom 14:17-19, 1Cor 7:15).

rest is commentary. Go, study."[66] Jesus ostensibly summarized Torah by quoting the first two commandments; and he also may well have taught the so-called Golden Rule in a positive form.[67] It is only conceivable, but barely probable, that Jesus inherited this maxim from Hillel. This famous piece of wisdom antedated them, is found also in non-Jewish cultures, may have made its way into Judaism through the Sayings of Ahikar[68] where the author of Tobit 4:15 most likely obtained it in its negative form. Philo and possibly Paul knew it in the negative form cited by Hillel.[69] It is recorded in the Jewish Pseudepigrapha, specifically it is mirrored in Pseudo-Philo 11:12, where it is incorrectly attributed to "the Lord," and in an odd form of the negative, as with Hillel, in Syriac Menander 250-51. Even the Roman Emperor Alexander Severus, according to his biographer Lampridius, was famous for saying *quod tibi non vis alteri ne feceris*, "that which you do not wish for yourself, do not do to another."[70] This maxim—the so-called Golden Rule—is a part of universal human learning; there is nothing peculiarly Jewish or Christian about it.[71]

Both Hillel and Jesus attracted disciples and lived in ancient Palestine during the harsh years of Roman occupation. Both taught in Jerusalem; and both are famous for speaking the language of the common folk.[72] With little qualification it seems probable that both Hillel and Jesus can be described as a *hasid* who feared God and preached love of others.

Neither supported the growing power of the Jews who wanted open revolt against Rome, even though the Romans were probably per-

---

[66] j.Shabb 31a. This epigrammatic saying does not appear in earlier sources (contrast m.Ab 2); hence, it is far from certain that it is historically accurate. E. P. Sanders rightly states that "we cannot attribute it to him with confidence." Sanders, *Judaism*, p. 258.

[67] Mt 7:12, Lk 6:31.

[68] Ahikar 8:88 [Arm.].

[69] See Philo, *Hypothetica* 7. Sanders thinks that Rom 13:10 indicates that "Paul knew the negative form of the saying and found it useful." *Judaism*, p. 258.

[70] I am indebted to the erudition and insights of T. Baarda, published in *OTP* 2.587-88.

[71] Similar thoughts are shared by P. Alexander in a following chapter.

[72] See j.Yev 15:3; j.Ket 4:8; Neusner, *Rabbinic Traditions*, esp. part 1, p. 251. Research on Mk 4 shows that allegorical embellishment is typical of redaction to the Jesus tradition. It is widely accepted that Jesus spoke in clear pictorial language, and I am convinced he did so to communicate because of his feeling for others.

ceived as enemies of God's rule here on earth. Both also probably had severe clashes with the sacerdotal aristocracy in Jerusalem and with those affluent Sadducees who thought no compromise was unthinkable.

In contrast to both Philo and Josephus, those two great bookends of the first century, Hillel and Jesus were far more dedicated to Jewish traditions and the purity of Jewish faith. The force of the traditions associated with both Hillel and Jesus indicate that both attempted to find Jewish ways to interpret Torah, God's will recorded in writing. Philo and Josephus sought to adapt Judaism to the realities of Hellenistic culture. Jesus and Hillel sought to reform Judaism and to rearticulate its inner genius in light of contemporary needs and crises. Philo and Josephus smoothed the boundaries between Judaism and the non-Jewish world. Hillel and Jesus were far more dedicated to the Land than either Philo or Josephus,[73] and each was primarily an interpreter of Torah and oral tradition.

The Dead Sea Scrolls have sprung again into the consciousness of the public throughout the world. Attention has been shifted, in many quarters, from space-age explorations of the future to a fascination with the past, and especially the time of Hillel and Jesus. It would be helpful, perhaps, to briefly comment on some ways the Dead Sea Scrolls have helped us understand Hillel and Jesus.[74]

By far the most important contribution has been to give us actual documents from their time. When we work with the Pseudepigrapha, Josephus, the New Testament, and all the rabbinic writings we are confronted with documents that postdate their time and are almost always heavily edited and shaped by the concerns of a different age. The Dead Sea Scrolls reveal clearly the strong eschatological and apocalyptic concerns of Jews during the time of Hillel and Jesus.

The More Precepts of the Torah (4QMMT) shows that interest in so-called halachot as in the Mishna antedates Hillel's time by about a century. Hillel certainly did not create this major dimension of Judaism.[75]

---

[73] I mean to ground this claim in the fact that Hillel and Jesus lived and remained in Palestine. Philo chose to stay in Alexandria, although he did make at least one pilgrimmage to Jerusalem. Josephus left the land and resided in Rome with those who destroyed the Temple.

[74] See further the chapter by Lichtenberger.

[75] T. Herford suggested that "possibly Hillel, but more probably R. Akiba, made the first attempt at a classified arrangement of them (halachoth)." Herford, *The*

An unpublished Qumran document, 4Q521, clearly contains the word מְשִׁיחוֹ, "his (or God's) Messiah." The line must be restored, but it seems to state that "[the hea]vens and the earth shall obey his Messiah." The Hebrew script is in a hand that dates from about the time of Hillel's birth. Understandably not only Christians but also Jews, and others also, have become interested in what can now be known about messianic speculations during the time of Hillel and Jesus.[76] According to rabbinic sources Hillel did not discuss or refer to Jewish speculations on the Messiah. No passage in the canonical New Testament portrays Jesus as referring to, discussing, or answering questions regarding the Messiah. While Hillel certainly did not think he was the Messiah, it is possible, perhaps probable that Jesus did possess some messianic self-understandings.[77] Nevertheless, it must be stressed that neither Hillel's nor Jesus' teachings are defined by messianology.[78] If rabbinic specialists are correct in concluding that Hillel shunned the preoccupation with messianism of some of his contemporaries,[79] and if scholars are right in concluding that Jesus admonished Peter for confessing that he was the Messiah,[80] then certainly Hillel and probably Jesus would have concurred that only God will clarify who the Messiah is.[81]

Pharisees (Boston, 1924, 1952, 1962) p. 84. For 4QMMT, see E. Qimron and J. Strugnell, eds., *Qumran Cave 4 V: Miqsat Maʻase HaTorah* (DJD 10; Oxford, 1994).

[76] See esp. J. J. Collins, *The Scepter and the Star: The Messiahs of the Dead Sea Scrolls and Other Ancient Literature* (AB; New York, 1995).

[77] See my comments in the concluding chapter of *Jesus Within Judaism*. Also, see Flusser's chapter in which he articulates his conclusion that Jesus claimed to be the Messiah.

[78] N. Glatzer suggested that in Hillel's teachings "the place of messianism is taken by the concept of the life in the world-to-come" (p. 244). See N. Glatzer, "Hillel the Elder in the Light of the Dead Sea Scrolls," in *The Scrolls and the New Testament*, pp. 232–44.

[79] See Megillah 3a. N. N. Glatzer, "Messianism," in *Hillel the Elder*, pp. 69–71.

[80] See the judicious insights of R. H. Fuller in *Foundations of New Testament Christology* (New York, 1965).

[81] Moving beyond the limits of historiography, I must add theologically that Christians claim that God's resurrection of Jesus by God proves his uniqueness and that he has now received God's anointing. It may not so logically follow that God's resurrection of Jesus discloses that he is (or was) his Messiah. This title is one of the most opaque in the history of Jewish teaching. According to the author of the Gospel of John, Thomas did not acknowledge that Jesus was the Messiah; he confessed that he was "my Lord and my God" (Jn 20:28). Yet the complexity is scarcely removed by such a passage, since the author of John certainly believed that Jesus had been the long-awaited

Surely there should be no longer doubt that the Dead Sea Scrolls belonged to a form of the Essenes. This was not a monolithic group, and Qumran Essenism was probably the most strict dimension of it. The Qumran Essenes probably deposited an ancient Jewish library in caves west of the Dead Sea in the year 68 C.E. as they fled before the Roman army that was approaching from the north. Near the beginning of this century Böcher strove to show that Hillel was not an Essene.[82] Soon after the discovery of the Dead Sea Scrolls the well-known scholar Nahum N. Glatzer claimed that Hillel probably adopted some of the teachings of the Qumran Essenes, directed some of his teachings against the Essene's sectarian exclusiveness and their separation of humanity into two absolute groups: the wicked and the righteous.[83] The magisterial Talmudists E. E. Urbach suggested that Hillel directed some harsh criticisms against the Qumran sect.[84]

Clearly neither Hillel nor Jesus were Essenes, nor were they strongly influenced by them.[85] I, however, think it is possible, even likely, that Hillel and Jesus confronted Essenes, since most of them lived throughout the Land and on the outskirts of most cities, if we can trust the reports of Philo and Josephus. Hillel and Jesus may well have accepted the concept of free will dominant in Early Judaism; they would then have disagreed with the Essene's concept of predestination, which—as M. Broshi points out—was a teaching unique to the Essenes.[86] In contrast to the Essenes they had great concern for and respect for the average Jew. They both would have abhorred the Essene sectarianism, superior attitude, and exhortation to hate all who are not Essenes, the Sons of Light. Both were attributed teachings on the Sabbath that contrasted with the Essene elevation of this holy day to the exclusion and detriment of other Torah teachings. Both would surely have rejected the claim that only the Moreh has-Sedeq had been given

---

Messiah (see esp. Jn 4:25-26).

[82] Böcher, *Types of Jewish-Palestinian Piety*, pp. 34, 39.

[83] Glazer in *The Scrolls and the New Testament* and in *Hillel the Elder*, esp. pp. 31–33.

[84] Urbach, *Sages*, vol. 1, p. 585.

[85] See the contributions in Charlesworth, ed., *Jesus and the Dead Sea Scrolls*.

[86] M. Broshi argues, and I agree, that "the most significant theological concept setting the sectarians apart" is "predestination." [M. Sekine], *The Dead Sea Scrolls* (Tokyo, 1979) p. 16.

by God the revelation that explains the meaning of Torah.[87] Both would most likely have argued against the Essene concept of the solar calendar, since both worshipped in the Temple during the prescribed feasts. I am also convinced that not only Jesus, but also Hillel would have resisted the crippling demands for purity stressed by the Essenes and also by the ruling sacerdotal aristocracy in Jerusalem.

MAJOR DIFFERENCES

These reflections disclose, of course, areas of difference between Hillel and Jesus. Hillel was probably from Babylon;[88] Jesus was certainly from Palestine. Hillel studied under Shemaiah and Abtalyon; no early tradition indicates that Jesus studied under a sage, but then such traditions may have been lost (perhaps intentionally). Hillel began in poverty and at one stage of his career Jesus may have endured humble conditions. Hillel was most likely revered, giving rise to the probably false report that he was elected Nasi (Head of the Sanhedrin) for 40 years[89] but Jesus was crucified by the occupying Roman forces. Hillel was married and his descendants were famous in the founding of Rabbinic Judaism, namely his grandson, Gamaliel I under whom Jesus' follower Paul studied according to the author of Acts 22:3, Gamaliel II, and especially Rabbi Judah the Prince, compiler of the Mishna.[90] Jesus was not married and had no descendants, although some of his relatives apparently were significant in and around Jerusalem after 70.[91] Hillel was clearly linked with the establishment and taught at least some of the legislation attributed to him; Jesus was in conflict with the establishment, and his death may well be related to his attack against some of the sacerdotal aristocracy centered in Jerusalem and living in the palatial mansions on the western hill.

While Hillel and Jesus apparently emphasized the commandment to love others as oneself, found in Leviticus 19, only Jesus extended it

---

[87] 1QpHab 7.

[88] This tradition is passed on in Rabbinics as a formula and lynch pin for other, usually much later, traditions. There is no reason to doubt that Hillel was from Babylon; and this conclusion is defended by most experts.

[89] See, e.g. Hyman, *Toldoth*, vol. 1, p. 362.

[90] See Neusner's caveats in *Rabbinic Traditions*, part 1, p. 294.

[91] See R. J. Bauckham, *Jude and the Relatives of Jesus in the Early Church* (Edinburgh, 1990).

to include everyone, including enemies (Mt 5:44). Only Jesus is reputed to have warned clearly against the dangers of military conflict with Rome. His warnings and predictions about the fall of Jerusalem probably lie behind the heavily edited verses of Mark 13.

Their approach to Torah was different. It appears that Hillel was most interested in halacha (legislation for daily life), but Jesus in haggadah (stories and parables). Hillel reputedly focused on formulating rules for conduct, Jesus on the prophets who were interpreted in light of apocalyptic and eschatological thought.

The form of their putative sayings is also distinct. Most experts on the New Testament conclude that Jesus chose to speak in parables, and that in his parables we find Jesus' peculiar (not unique) style and message. Hillel was not known for parabolic utterances; and this is significant when it is observed that early Tannaitic Rabbis are konwn for their parables. Noteworthy among them are R. Gamaliel the Elder, R. Yohanan ben Zakkai (eight parables), R. Pinhas, R. Hanina ben Gamaliel, R. Eleazar ben Azariah, R. Eleazar ben Arak, R. Yose the Priest, R. Gamaliel II (five parables), R. Eleazar ben Zadok, R. Samuel the Younger, and R. Aqiba (seven parables).

An extreme difference pertains to Hillel's and Jesus's views on divorce. Shammai had a rather open view on divorce. Hillel was even more liberal, if we can trust the traditions. Akiba was extremely liberal. According to Mark, one of our earliest source for Jesus' sayings, Jesus prohibited divorce. Matthew softened Jesus' rule, providing for divorce in case of a woman's unfaithfulness. Until the last few decades we have had no parallel to Jesus' strict ruling on divorce. Now, in the Temple Scroll, the largest of all the Dead Sea Scrolls, we find a prohibition on polygamy and a possible prohibition against divorce. The king, and therefore even more so all others, must not take another wife so long as his wife is alive. Hence, Hillel is in line with the Jewish majority opinion on divorce, even represented in the first century in one of the schools of Jesus, specifically the School of Matthew; Jesus is extremely strict and only paralleled to a certain extent by the teachings preserved in the Temple Scroll.

Hillel, according to a critical dating of the traditions and in contrast to the House of Hillel, apparently neither taught about the Holy Spirit nor received it,[92] although the Rabbis claimed if anyone in his

---

[92] Many Hillel scholars, perhaps most, assume that the sayings about the Holy

generation deserved to receive the Holy Spirit it was he. This latter rabbinic statement has apparently confused some experts who cannot explain the social setting that gave rise to the polemic.[93] It may well be a response by the House of Hillel to the claims by Jesus' followers in the late first century C.E. To state that Hillel was the only one of his generation who was worthy to receive the Holy Spirit may be intended, *inter alia*, to suggest that Jesus, who belonged to Hillel's generation, did not receive the Holy Spirit. Such observations lead us away from the beginning of the first century C.E. to the end of it, and to subsequent centuries—that is, from the historical Hillel and Jesus to the historic and mythical Hillel and Jesus.

What is the major difference between Hillel and Jesus? It is surely the end of the story for each. Neither Hillel nor Jesus were of Davidic or priestly descent, neither were chosen as the legitimate high priest. Hillel, however, was honored in his time, although I doubt that he was elevated to the highest position available to him, even though tradition claims he was Nasi—President of the Sanhedrin—for nearly 40 years.[94]

In stark contrast, Jesus ran into trouble with the priestly establishment; probably he intended for just reasons to confront the wealthy priestly aristocrats. He was executed as a common rebel against Rome; but his disciples and some women close to him claimed that he appeared to them again as their resurrected Lord with a message of salvation and hope. The historical Hillel exits from a bed surrounded by his disciples;[95] Jesus dies on a cross and his disciples later confront an empty tomb. These are major differences.

Spirit attributed to Hillel are not authentic to him. See, e.g. Urbach, *The Sages*, vol. 1, pp. 576-77. I am influenced by the study of the transmission of Hillel's sayings by Neusner; see esp. *Judaism in the Beginning of Christianity*, pp. 71-76; esp. p. 76: "It seems unlikely to me that any of this contains a shred of historically usable information." I consider this important; see esp. p.Pes 6:1.

[93] Neusner seems to be referring to it when he admits, "But I cannot suggest who would have wanted to allege in Hillel's name that the holy spirit is upon Israel, or what polemic was involved in so stating." *Judaism in the Beginning of Christianity*, p. 75.

[94] Vermes is also convinced that Hillel did not become Nasi; *History*, vol. 2, pp. 364, 68.

[95] The account by Glatzer is amazingly brief and a mixture of fact and fiction; see Glatzer, "Hillel's Death and the Rise of Johanan ben Zakkai," *Hillel the Elder*, pp. 83-84.

It is in this contrast that we find the main reasons for the chasm that develops between Hillel's followers and Jesus' followers. Hillel was remembered as a man and he was not hailed as divine.[96] Hillel may well have been memorialized in some early celebrations of the Passover haggadah, if J. Petuchowski's argument can be sustained[97]; Jesus was surely remembered during the first century in the celebrations of Passover and Eucharist, as 1 Corinthians 11 indicates.

Both Hillel's and Jesus' followers knew the claim that Jesus had been resurrected by God was rather absurd, especially when he had not won over the nation and accomplished none of the tasks allegedly to be performed by the One-who-was-to-come, and the Gentiles—especially in the form of despised and insensitive Roman occupying troops—had not been driven from Jerusalem, the center of the world.[98] Eventually some followers of Hillel will include in the Jewish statutory liturgy a curse on the Notzrim, the Christians; and subsequently the latter will be expelled from the synagogue. We know that this happened by the end of the century in which Hillel and Jesus lived because of the appearance of the word ἀποσυνάγωγος (aposynagōgos) in the Gospel of John. The much later Hillelites will claim that Jesus' virginal birth is to be explained by noting that Mary had a paramour; but then the Christians will proceed to contend that Jesus is identical with God in substance, and thence charge "Jews," not just some of the priestly aristocracy, with Deicide. From there matters only get worse, but this history is so well known that it does not merit repeating here.

What is important is to comprehend that the strife between the Hillelites and the Christians cannot be derived from animosities between Hillel and Jesus. In fact there are abundant reasons to conclude that in many ways Hillel and Jesus would have admired each other and would have enjoyed debating. Hillel would probably have been offended by Jesus' charisma and strong apocalyptic and eschatological preaching.

---

[96] A. Geiger wrote, "Auch an ihn mögen manche Sagen sich knüpfen, aber sie sind vollkommen seinem Wesen entsprechend, Wunderbares wird von ihm gar nicht berichtet; er bleibt ein Mensch, ein gesunder, voller Mensch, mehr soll er nicht sein, deshalb ist er grade um so grösser." *Judenthum und seine Geschichte*, p. 100.

[97] J. Petuchowski, "'Do this in Remembrance of Me' (I Cor 11 24)," *JBL* 76 (1957) 293–98.

[98] For the concept of the Messiah see PssSol 17 and 18; for the idea that Jerusalem is the center of the world see, among other texts, Jub.

One can speculate that Jesus would have scolded Hillel for not having a vision and realizing that the Endtime was rapidly approaching. In summation, perhaps eschatology and apocalypsology is what separates the putative teachings of Hillel from Jesus.

CONCLUSION

What should a historical and obvious sweeping overview of Hillel and Jesus contribute to the cultures represented by those writing in this volume? We all readily admit that the high values of western culture have been eroding for some time. No longer do our poets and great thinkers produce works on utopia; seldom do we hear about a better future—only the drugged homeless people and wild Hasidim seem to talk about dreams. Our pluralistic world needs to hear and heed—in the great sense of *shema‘*—the salubrious teachings of Hillel and Jesus. For example, at least some of the following:

> Hillel: "If I am not for myself, who is for me? But if I am only for myself, what am I? And if not now, when?"[99]

> Jesus: "The (first) commandment is, 'Hear, O Israel: The Lord our God, the Lord is one; and you shall love the Lord your God with all your heart, and with all your soul, and with all your mind, and with all your strength.' The second is, 'You shall love your neighbor as yourself.' There is no other commandment greater than these."[100]

> Hillel: "The more Torah, the more life;
> the more study, the more wisdom;
> the more counsel, the more discernment;
> the more righteousness, the more peace."[101]

> Jesus: "Think not that I have come to abolish the Torah and the Prophets; I have come not to abolish them but to fulfill them."[102]

[99] m.Ab 1.14.
[100] Mk 12:29-31.
[101] m.Ab 2.8.
[102] Mt 5:17.

Hillel: "Do not keep aloof from the congregation and do not trust in yourself until the day of your death, and do not judge your fellow until you have come to his place."[103]

Jesus: "Give to him who begs from you,
and do not refuse him who would borrow from you."[104]

Hillel: "Be of the disciples of Aaron: love peace and pursue peace, love fellow-creatures, and bring them near to the Torah."[105]

Jesus: "Blessed are the peacemakers, for they shall be called sons of God."[106]

Hillel: "If a man has gained a good name he has gained (something valuable) for himself; if he has gained for himself words of the Torah he has gained for himself life in the world to come."[107]

Jesus: "In my Father's house are many rooms."[108]

Having heard these words—cherished long ago by others like us—more may come to admire, even revere, Hillel and Jesus, two men who were not only extraordinary teachers but also holy men.

Hillel and Jesus saw and experienced what each of us today would sacrifice much to have seen and experienced; they entered into the majestic Herodian Temple. Jesus lauded the Temple, and quoting Isaiah 56:7,[109] he called it a "house of prayer for all nations." They both saw the gold glimmer in the noon day sun. They smelled the incense. They watched as the smoke of sacrifice wound its way heaven-

---

[103] m.Ab 2.5.

[104] Mt 5:42.

[105] m.Ab 1.:12. "Fellow-creatures" is from the feminine noun derived from *br'*.

[106] Mt 5:9.

[107] m.Ab 2.7.

[108] Jn 14:2.

[109] Mk 11:17. The tradition here seems reliable, although we must not hold on to the quotation from Isaiah or claim *ipsissima verba Jesu*. John 2:16 has Jesus call the Temple "my Father's house."

ward. They chanted from the same hymn book, the Davidic Psalter. They most likely joined the Levites in "singing" psalms dear to each of us. From 2,000 years away, they reveal to us that they knew how to pray; and they urge us to experience what they experienced, specifically that the Lord our God is near and does hear. They remind us that they lived among a people that knew how to pray.[110]

---

[110] Hillel and Jesus did not invent something new; they strove to recover the traditions that make God's people great. See Neusner, *Judaism in the Beginning of Christianity*, p. 66. Charlesworth, *Jesus Within Judaism*, passim. Flusser in *Jesus' Jewishness*, pp. 153-76.

HILLEL AND JESUS:
ARE COMPARISONS POSSIBLE?

THE "JESUS AND X" TOPOS AND THEOLOGICAL AGENDA

THE JESUS-HILLEL QUESTION ought to be viewed as a particular spec-
imen of a wider topos in the history of religion in general and the history of Christianity in particular. We can call this topos: Jesus and X.
The ultimate purpose of such a juxtaposition would be to gain a better
understanding, in some way, of the two parties being contrasted.
Ideally, such a comparison should be carried out using one of the methodologies available to the historians of religions. Theology should not
be one of the factors governing such an investigation. The purpose of
comparison is not to "prove" who is better or to demonstrate a lack of
singularity, but simply to understand.

Two types of "Jesus and X" comparisons are possible. It is possible to compare Jesus and religious figures of other traditions and periods. Indeed, this has been done. Thus, a comparative portrait of Jesus
and the Buddha is meaningful, as is the contrast between Jesus and the
Baal Shem Tov. An underlying assumption of such a comparison is that
the two parties being compared belong to the same class. This class may
be that of founders of religious movements, prophets, teachers, saviors,
etc. Clearly, any such comparison predetermines the perspective
through which it addresses the figure of Jesus.

Another way of employing the "Jesus and X" topos is historical.
What concerns us in this case are the historical background of Jesus, its
potential influences upon him, etc. Employing the historical form of the
topos need not, *a priori*, make the same assumptions regarding class. In
order to clarify the *historical* links between Jesus and any other figure,
one need not assume the two figures constitute the same type of person
or reflect similar types of work. One could therefore investigate the

work of Jesus in relation to that of any Palestinian Rabbi in order to gain a better understanding of both the background and the uniqueness of Jesus.

The way in which "Jesus and X" studies have been carried out historically has not always matched up to this ideal description. The primary cause for this seems to be the theological interests motivating the investigation. When conducted by a scholar who is theologically motivated, the "Jesus and X" topos does not serve exclusively the purpose of understanding. It is often informed by an attempt to establish spiritual superiority.[1] This theological goal could be achieved independent of historical connections. The theologian has no difficulty asserting the superiority of Jesus to Moses. Such a claim to superiority does not rest upon a historical relationship between the two figures, but upon some resemblance in type. Some point of similarity must be found between Moses and Jesus for such a comparison to make sense. Perhaps the similarity lies in their being great prophets, or religious figures. Nevertheless, once Jesus is seen as greater than Moses, he may well be perceived as belonging to a different class or category. Thus, for instance, if Jesus is not merely a prophet, but a Messiah, and therefore greater than Moses, both the point of similarity and the essential difference are employed in the service of this comparison. Neither the similarity nor the difference need rest upon historical relations. Theology need not, perforce, resort to history.

However, when an ostensibly *historical* contrast is theologically motivated, error may creep in. One ought to turn to history in order to gain a better understanding of individuals against the background of their time. Instead, however, we often see historical background used to demonstrate the understanding that the man was better than his time. Under such conditions, one will refer to whatever may be available in the background of Jesus, regardless of how similar or dissimilar it may be to Jesus.

Against this theoretical statement we should test the application and the applicability of the "Jesus and X" topos to the case of Hillel the Elder. "Jesus and Hillel" has been in circulation for over a century.[2]

---

[1] This is all the more so when the X is not just a particular person, but the totality of Judaism. See E. P. Sanders, *Jesus and Judaism* (London, 1985), pp. 1–2; in particular his implied differences with E. Käsemann, p. 356, note 19.

[2] See the papers in this volume by J. H. Charlesworth and H. Lichtenberger.

Not surprisingly, the application of the topos is heavily colored theologically. Franz Delitzch employed it to illustrate the superiority of Jesus over the finest of Rabbis. Somewhat earlier, Abraham Geiger used it, in the opposite direction, with clear theological gain in mind—Jesus is no news at all.

Charlesworth's attempt to draw a series of correspondences between Hillel and Jesus is not free from theological agenda, either. (The return from "Christ" to "Jesus" is a theological prerequisite for the exercise at hand.) Fundamental to the present argument is the placing of Jesus and Hillel in the same basic category. As Charlesworth would have it, Hillel is not merely part of the historical background of Jesus. He is essentially similar in kind. This is why the comparison ought to be meaningful.

Though he does not explicitly state this, Charlesworth implies that the various differences between the two persons do not undermine our ability to place them in the same category—that of early Palestinian teachers. I would claim that the decision to group Hillel and Jesus in the same category is not only a scholarly historical evaluation. It may reflect a theological understanding as well. Such an understanding may seek to reverse trends current in theological circles for centuries. However, precisely when seen against such a background, one realizes that any hermeneutical move through which the historical Jesus is seen has a corresponding theological correlative.

This does not mean that any particular historical view of Jesus ought to be disqualified because of its potential theological ramifications. It means only that when Christians and Jews come together to evaluate the question of "Hillel and Jesus" against a heavily colored theological background, we cannot totally disregard the theological factor when we assess why certain moves or choices are made. As an observant Jew, I cannot help but examine the theological motivation for the moves that follow and for the positions expressed.

Unfortunately, having raised the question, I am less able to give a clear-cut answer. The thesis I am about to present can serve opposing theological interests. Whether it indicates my own theological complexity or my freedom from theological agenda, I cannot tell. Even if I cannot provide an answer to the question I myself raise, I feel it is important that as Jews and Christians struggling together with the question at hand, we recognize the difficulty, if not the impossibility, of participating in a totally neutral and objective discourse.

I personally would argue *against* placing these two personalities within the same category. For phenomenological reasons—as well as for reasons that stem from my understanding of the nature of rabbinic society, literature, and culture—the very presentation of our theme as "Hillel and Jesus" not only prejudges the issue at hand, but misjudges it as well. If our interest lies in learning more about the background of the historical Jesus, then Hillel is significant, but not more so than any other Rabbi of his time—perhaps no more significant than the witness of the sum total of rabbinic literature, which we may choose to limit to a specific historic period. However, the very grouping of Hillel and Jesus together implies concerns beyond those of historical background. Such a discussion assumes a similarity *in type*, such that the phenomenologist of religion could discuss. This assumption is not borne out by the rabbinic material concerning Hillel.

QUALITATIVELY DIFFERENT SOURCES

We must be reminded of some basic differences between the nature of Talmudic literature and the nature of the Gospels. We have no Talmudic Gospel of any Rabbi.[3] No Rabbi in the Talmudic period—in contrast to

---

[3] This point has already been the subject of discussion. See P. Alexander, "Rabbinic Biography and the Biography of Jesus: A Survey of the Evidence," in *Synoptic Studies: The Ampleforth Conferences of 1982 and 1983*, ed. C. M. Tuckett (JSNTSS 7; Sheffield, 1984), pp. 19–50. According to Alexander, the reason nothing equivalent to Gospel writing appears in rabbinic literature is that no Rabbi has a status equivalent to the status of Jesus for the Gospel writers (p. 41). The rabbinic centerpoint is the Torah, whereas the Gospel's centerpoint is the person of Jesus. (See also M. Smith, *Tannaitic Parallels to the Gospels* [JBL Monograph Series 6; Philadelphia, 1951], p. 159).

Nevertheless, Alexander himself remains unsatisfied with this answer because early Christian hagiography is not limited to the life of Jesus. Why then are there no lives of Jewish Rabbis? As Alexander points out, the question is particularly pressing in view of the fact that writing the lives of religious figures is not dependent upon contemporary Roman practices, but ultimately follows biblical precedent.

A more extensive treatment of this question is found in J. Neusner, *Why No Gospels in Talmudic Judaism* (Brown Judaic Studies 135; Atlanta, 1988). At certain points in his discussion, Neusner offers the same answer as Alexander (see pp. 45–47, 52, 72). Although Neusner does not attempt to address directly the question at hand, his discussion seems to take a different turn. His discussion of rabbinic authorship, as a form of collective writing (as opposed to the individual authoring of the Gospels), touches upon the collective nature of rabbinic literature (see pp. 70–72). Neusner's discussion seems to relate the collective nature of the rabbinic enterprise to the centrality of Torah for the Rabbis. As a result, he does not use the latter point to explain the lack

later periods[4]—is deemed by Talmudic culture to be worthy of exclusive attention. This contrasts sharply to the very nature of the Gospels. This observation reflects not only on the nature of the respective literatures, but on the nature of their heroes, as well.

Why were the Gospels written?[5] The Gospels tell the story of one special man who is understood to be unique, to stand in his own right, and therefore merits the telling of a special story. Seen as biographies of one special holy man, the Gospels can be taken as hagiography. Like any biography, or perhaps even more so, the writing of hagiography requires an individual who is recognized and set apart from his immediate cultural context. Hagiography is founded upon a certain distance between the venerated person and his immediate context.

This distance is composed of two factors. The first factor is the recognition of the venerated subject as significantly different from his surrounding. He may possess special power, knowledge, virtue, or merit that set him apart from others. The other, and perhaps more basic factor that contributes to the distance between the venerated subject and his context, is the recognition of this subject as individuated, and therefore, as worthy of distinct and individual attention. Thus, a precondition

---

of hagiography in rabbinic literature. What Neusner seems to offer as a correlative to the centrality of Torah in rabbinic culture we will use as the main reason for the absence of hagiography from rabbinic literature.

[4] In later forms of Jewish writing, we do find hagiographical treatises that constitute a genre, known as praises (שבחים). Examples of this genre may be found in the praise of such figures as the *Ari*, or the *Baal Shem Tov*.

[5] This question obviously touches upon the question of the nature of Gospel as literary genre. For the most recent discussion of this question, see R. A. Burridge, *What Are the Gospels?* (Cambridge, 1992). Over the course of the last century, scholarship has alternatively viewed the Gospels as a kind of biography and as a unique literary creation resembling no other known literary genres. The theological *Tendenz* of the latter position, strongly upheld by R. Bultmann, is obvious (see R. Bultmann, "Evangelien," ET in J. Pelikan, ed., *Twentieth Century Theology in the Making* (New York, 1971), vol. 1, pp. 86–92).

According to this position, Gospel writing would be the product of the particular religious understanding of the messianic, and therefore—salvific, activity of Jesus. The lack of Gospels in rabbinic literature would then be a less significant issue, since no salvific claim is attached to any particular Rabbi. Following Burridge's discussion, the present discussion assumes Gospel writing to be a form of biography. One could therefore ask why we do not have any instances of rabbinic biography, and receive the same answer.

for the writing of hagiography is the ability to isolate a person from his environment and to treat him as distinct. When the religious personality is not isolated from his environment, no hagiography can result.

Talmudic stories concerning various Rabbis, including Hillel, lack both conditions necessary for the writing of a Gospel, or hagiography. Stories about Rabbis within Talmudic literature are not always stories of saints.[6] They are stories that include teaching and morals. They may extol specific virtues, convey struggles, or illustrate special powers attached to certain individuals.[7] And yet Talmudic stories do not present their heroes as saintly ideals, nor does the telling of stories about Rabbis necessarily constitute a call to emulate those Rabbis.

More important is the absence from Talmudic literature of the second condition necessary for the writing of hagiography. Rabbinic literature is a collective enterprise. Individual Rabbis are assimilated to

---

[6] Many rabbinic stories portray Rabbis amid power struggles and human temptations and do not attempt to uphold any image of saintliness. Furthermore, as Y. Fränkel has shown, stories about Rabbis in Talmudic and midrashic literature have particular characterization. They are not intended to be historical or true to reality. Rather, they are literary creations that attempt to convey a particular worldview by means of telling a story about a rabbinic hero (see Y. Fränkel, *Darchei Ha'agada ve'Hamidrash* [1991], chapter 9, pp. 235–85). This worldview is not the image of saintliness of any Rabbi, but the general religious truths of the culture, as perceived by the story teller. Stories about Rabbis can therefore not serve as raw material for a hagiography—not only because of the actual content of the stories, but because of the literary and ideological nature of rabbinic story telling.

[7] Neusner's discussion seems, at one point, to collapse Gospel writing into the record of miracle-making. This is how I understand his examination of rabbinic miracle legends in the context of his discussion of Gospel writing (see Neusner, *Why No Gospels?* chapter 2). I find this attempt to bridge the gap between Gospel writing and Talmudic legends unconvincing. As hagiographies, the Gospels are more than collections of miracle stories. Therefore, the examination of rabbinic miracle stories is irrelevant in this context.

A good illustration of the gap between miracle stories and Gospel writing can be found in the stories of the great miracle workers Ḥoni the Circle-drawer and Ḥanina ben Dosa. We may possess miracle stories concerning these two personalities. Yet we possess almost no teachings of theirs nor do we know enough about their religious virtue to enable the writing of a hagiography. These ancient Jewish figures serve as part of the Jewish background against which Jesus is to be appreciated, yet they do not occupy such a place of importance—nor is enough known about them—to warrant a literary work devoted exclusively to them. See G. Vermes, *Jesus the Jew* (London, 1976), pp. 69–78.

the larger collective of Rabbis. Stories about individual Rabbis must be assessed against the general background of the collective nature of rabbinic literature. The attempt to depict the character or teaching of any individual Rabbi is difficult not only because of the problems associated with the history of rabbinic texts. It is difficult because of the more fundamental question concerning the degree of individuation of a Rabbi within the total rabbinic framework.

INDIVIDUATION WITHIN THE RABBINIC COMMUNITY

Clearly the Rabbis are not so many clones of one prototype. Personality, virtue, understanding, power, and religious genius distinguish one Rabbi from another. Yet, when seen in the context of rabbinic literature as a whole, how fundamentally different is a Hillel from a Rabbi Yoḥanan, or a Rabbi Akiba from a Rabbi Abbahu. Even the most distinguished of Rabbis is not sufficiently set apart from the company of other Rabbis to deserve exclusive attention.

A brief glance at Pirqé ʾAbot will illustrate the point. Even though we can point to the religious genius of Rabbi Akiba in some of his formulations,[8] or notice the thick concentration of statements attributed to Hillel,[9] the reader is impressed more than anything by the fact that so many different teachers from different generations seem to be doing the same thing. The common concerns indicate an ongoing discussion of a collective culture in which the individual voice is merged. His individual voice is never lost. Yet we come to know it only in the context of a collective enterprise. This is why the success of any study that focuses upon the person or teaching of any individual Rabbi will always be limited.[10] It may uncover some of the features of the particu-

---

[8] See m.Ab 3:17-20 (numberings of statements in ʾAbot may vary from edition to edition).

[9] Hillel traditions are found in m.Ab 1:12-14; 2:5-8.

[10] Such a study is contingent upon the existence of a large corpus of statements that are attributed to a particular sage. It would naturally be more suited to figures with an active public life, where their teachings, actions, and policies help us to draw a profile of the particular person.

A more fruitful way of bringing to light the nuances that distinguish one sage from another is to analyze controversies. In a controversy, two positions—and therefore possibly also two personalities—are juxtaposed. Such a juxtaposition offers us points of demarcation within what would otherwise be a homogeneous whole. It is not surprising that some scholars have chosen this route in their attempt to get at the figures and schools within rabbinic literature. See A. Marmorstein, *The Old Rabbinic Doctrine of*

lar Rabbi. Yet the meaning of these features depends upon the features of the Rabbis in whose context he is seen. These are all too often similar, if not identical.

This basic trait of rabbinic literature accounts for some of the technical difficulties confronting the student of this literature. The anonymous nature of so much of rabbinic literature underscores the collective nature of the enterprise. Despite ostensibly meticulous care taken to record the names of individual tradents, the history of the transmission of the text includes creative manipulation of these traditions, as well as of the ascriptions to individual teachers.[11] This is not a betrayal of historic responsibility; it is a natural product of the understanding of tradition as a collective enterprise.

Let me illustrate what has been said up to now with regard to Hillel himself. The first two chapters of 'Abot are a tradition history. They record the stages of tradition history from the so-called generation of the men of the great assembly down to the generation of the disciples of Rabbi Yoḥanan ben Zakkai, two generations after Hillel. Within the history of tradition, the place occupied by Hillel is typically contextual and in no way outstanding. What is more striking, however, is that Hillel is not really viewed independently at all. Hillel is presented alongside another sage: Shammai. "Hillel and Shammai received [the Law] from them."[12] Another ancient tradition list also places the two sages alongside one another.

> Jose ben Joezer says: [On a Festival day a man] may not lay [his hands on the offering before it is slaughtered]; Joseph ben Johanan says: He may. Joshua b. Perahyah says: He may not; Nittai the Arbelite says: He may. Judah b. Tabbai says: He may not. Simeon b. Shetah says: He may. Shemaiah says: He may not; Abtalion says: He may. Hillel and Menahem did not differ, but Menahem went forth, and Shammai entered in. Shammai says: He may not lay his hands; Hillel says: He

---

God, Part 2: Essays in Anthropomorphism (London, 1937), pp. 29–42. See further, A. J. Heschel, *Theology of Ancient Judaism* (in Hebrew), vol. 1 (London and New York, 1962), pp. 3–5.

[11] See H. L. Strack, and G. Stemberger, *Introduction to the Talmud and Midrash* (Edinburgh, 1991), pp. 60, 64–66.

[12] m.Ab 1:12.

may. The former [of each of these pairs] were Presidents, and the others were Fathers of the Court.[13]

This tradition list, which is identical to that found in the first chapter of 'Abot, is the earliest record of a halakhic controversy. The controversy continues over the course of several generations. In this list, Hillel's place is typically contextual. He is assimilated to the chain of tradents and his position is identical to that of all Fathers of the Court. This position is not viewed in isolation, but in relation to the alternative position. Thus, the full significance of Hillel's position can only be appreciated when viewed alongside Shammai's position. The only point in the history of this disputation in which no controversy exists is when Menahem is paired to Hillel. Yet our source does not indicate that the lack of controversy in any way reflects Hillel's authority or exclusive power.

None of this means that Hillel is not important. That he is the most frequently quoted authority in 'Abot[14] is not insignificant. However, he is only significant within this context. When we isolate him from this context, we imply an understanding of Hillel that betrays this rabbinic self-understanding. What we then imply is that the religious genius of this man allows us to regard him in his own light—indeed, as a product of his culture, yet transcending it in some significant manner. This implied understanding is false. Nothing in the life or teachings of Hillel radically distinguishes him from Shammai, let alone from any of the other Rabbis.

A comparison of the statements of these two sages, as brought in 'Abot 1, will illustrate my point.

Hillel and Shammai received [the Law] from them. Hillel said: Be of the disciples of Aaron, loving peace and pursuing peace, loving mankind and bringing them nigh to the Law.[15]

---

[13] m.Hag 2:2.

[14] We find seven statements attributed to Hillel in the first two chapters of 'Abot. Furthermore, Hillel is the only rabbinic authority quoted by another Rabbi in 'Abot (4:5). The next most frequently quoted authority is Rabbi Akiba, with four statements, in chapter three. Most Rabbis are mentioned by one or two statements only.

[15] m.Ab 1:12.

Two values are emphasized in the words of Hillel: loving-kindness and the study of Torah. When we contrast Hillel's statement with that of Shammai, we realize that precisely the same values are emphasizes in Shammai's adjacent statement.[16]

> Shammai said: Make thy [study of the] Law a fixed habit; say little and do much, and receive all men with a cheerful countenance.[17]

Here too we encounter the same basic values: Torah and loving-kindness, only in different order and with different emphasis. Here is precisely the point: the individual teacher (in this case, Hillel) may offer us a different emphasis of the same collective values, but he does not offer us a new or different teaching.

This point is further adumbrated when we examine the context of the first chapter of 'Abot. Nearly all the traditions of the generations preceding Hillel and Shammai emphasize similar values and thrash out the implications and the priorities of two basic value concepts: Torah and loving-kindness.[18] Therefore, if we do not ask about political power

---

[16] Because of the particular interest in statements of Hillel, Shammai's counterstatement does not appear immediately after Hillel's statement. Two other statements of Hillel have been inserted in the middle of what was originally one more controversy in the list of pairs, as we find it in the first chapter of 'Abot. That Hillel and Shammai ought to be viewed as a pair and that the original statement of Hillel is the one quoted in our discussion are both obvious from the opening words of Mishna 12: "Hillel and Shammai received from them."

[17] m.Ab 1:15.

[18] These two values are first brought in m.Ab 1:2 in the teaching of Simeon the Just. "Simeon the Just was of the remnants of the Great Synagogue. He used to say: By three things is the world sustained: by the Law, by the [Temple] service, and by deeds of loving-kindness." Whereas in Simeon's words the Temple service figures alongside Torah and loving-kindness, the authorities immediately following him seem to emphasize either Torah or acts of loving-kindness. Despite the fact that we are dealing with pre-70 authorities, the pairs that follow Simeon seem to dispute precisely this point: which of the two is greater: Torah or deeds of loving-kindness. [The lack of mention of the Temple and the consistent thematic discussion of Torah vs. deeds of loving-kindness obviously expose our text to questions of tendency, editorial activity, and historical reliability. For the present discussion, these questions are less vital. If indeed we cannot learn about the actual statements of Hillel and Shammai because they have been stamped by a homologizing editor, this only strengthens the point we are making].

The first pair seem to be disputing over which of the two values is the greatest. "Jose b. Joezer of Zeredah and Jose b. Johanan of Jerusalem received [the Law] from them. Jose b. Joezer of Zeredah said: Let thy house be a meeting house for the Sages, and sit amid the dust of their feet and drink their words with thirst. Jose b. Johanan of

and authority, but about religious personality and teaching, I would suggest that Hillel was a man of his culture and context. He is a fine representative of a Rabbi. But he is in no way unique. Even those statements that indicate a high degree of self-awareness[19] do not place Hillel outside the scope of the collective enterprise.

The function of Hillel within tradition history illustrates my claims. Virtually all traditions prior to Hillel are anonymous. The anonymous nature of early halakha concords with the absence of any disputation in the earliest stages of received tradition.[20] Except for the above-mentioned controversy concerning the laying of hands on the sacrifice, the earliest point in tradition history in which a controversy exists regarding matters of the law is between Hillel and Shammai. We find three controversies between them.[21] A greater number is found

---

Jerusalem said: Let thy house be open wide and let the needy be members of thy household; and talk not much with woman-kind" (m.Ab 1:4-5). Both sages discuss the purpose of the home. Both share the assumption that the spiritual significance of the home is a function of the activity that takes place in it. For the former sage, it is the activity of Torah that endows the home with meaning. For the latter—doing acts of loving-kindness, such as receiving the poor.

In the next pair, we find differing emphases upon these two values. "Joshua b. Perahyah and Nittai the Arbelite received [the Law] from them. Joshua b. Perahyah said: Provide thyself with a teacher and get thee a fellow [disciple] and when thou judgeth any man incline the balance in his favour. Nittai the Arbelite said: Keep thee far from an evil neighbour and consort not with the wicked and lose not belief in retribution" (m.Ab 1:6-7). Though less obvious than the previous case, here too the differing emphases accent Torah and deeds of loving-kindness respectively. The former sage emphasizes Torah related issues—the teacher and the friend, with whom one can study Torah. The latter emphasizes aspects of social relations, warning what is to be avoided.

The next pair on the list changes the topic of discussion, even though their two statements are related to each other. One could also make the point we have been making concerning the pair immediately preceding Hillel and Shammai. The controversy of Hillel and Shammai themselves, as our discussion indicates, is typically contextual.

[19] See D. Flusser, "Hillel's Self-Awareness and Jesus," *Judaism and the Origins of Christianity* (Jerusalem, 1988), pp. 509-14. Flusser points out that unlike Jesus, Hillel's self-awareness is not exclusive of him, but that he partakes of an awareness that appertains to all humankind (p. 513).

[20] See E. E. Urbach, *The Halakhah* (1986), p. 93.

[21] See b.Shab 14b-15a, expounding the implications of the first three *mishnayot* of tractate ʿEduyot.

between their disciples.[22] The phenomenon is thereafter so widespread as to constitute a hallmark of Talmudic literature.

We should immediately notice here that the greatest rabbinic authorities do not stand on their own right, but are always viewed within the context of disputations and disagreements. This is not only an indication of their lack of singular authority. It is not only that Hillel is not great enough to impose his view upon all. It is an expression of the fact that when we look at the Rabbis only through the perspective of a Hillel, we are looking at only one side of a coin. For all the greatness of Rabbi Akiba, he comes to us embedded in a context of controversy with Rabbi Ishmael. No Rabbi is an island.

THE DEVELOPMENT OF CONTROVERSY IN RABBINIC TRADITION

The issue of controversy is of further importance for understanding Hillel's significance within tradition. We may view the development of controversy within tradition as concomitant to the growth and development of a certain form of learning,[23] and therefore as essentially positive. In this context, one may even reflect upon Hillel's contribution to the promulgation of this new way of learning.[24] Yet, Talmudic tradition itself struggles with the sudden entry of controversy into a tradition that claims its roots in the Sinaitic revelation. In his disputes with Shammai, Hillel becomes a problem, rather than an ideal.

---

[22] See y.Hag 2:2, p. 77d.

[23] Though this is not clearly stated, this fact is implied in Urbach's argument in the seventh chapter of his book, *The Halakha*. The origins of midrashic interpretation are related to attempts to deviate from an existing norm. The halakha itself undergoes transformation when midrash becomes a source of authority, rather than received tradition. When we note that controversy becomes prevalent at the same point in which halakha undergoes the above-mentioned transformation, we recognize the relationship between controversy and the new form of learning.

[24] The common position is that Hillel inherited, and did not create, the hermeneutic methods employed by him. See S. Lieberman, *Hellenism in Jewish Palestine* (New York, 1950), p. 54. However, Urbach notes that a new way of learning became prevalent from the times of Hillel and Shammai (*Halakha*, p. 94). Even if Hillel is not personally responsible for the creation of a new way of learning, it seems fair to assume that he cultivated this way of learning. The existence of halakhic controversy from Hillel's time onward supports this claim. It serves not only as testimony to the lack of clear authority (as Urbach, p. 93, implies), but to the rise in a new form of learning in which Hillel is active.

We have noted above that Hillel and Shammai are involved in the earliest known halakhic controversies. This fact is of concern to the integrity of tradition.

> Said R. Yossi: In the beginning there was no controversy in Israel. ... Now, once the disciples of Shammai and Hillel who did not adequately serve their master had become many, controversy multiplied in Israel, and they became two Torahs.[25]

R. Yossi clearly understands controversy as a negative phenomenon. Two conflicting opinions now compete for religious truth instead of the one certain word of God. R. Yossi pegs the blame for the spread of controversy on the disciples of Hillel and Shammai. This accords with the proliferation of halakhic controversy after Hillel and Shammai. Responsibility for the presence of controversy is thus shifted from Hillel and Shammai themselves to their disciples. Thus, Hillel and Shammai stand at the turning point from tradition in its integrity to tradition in crisis.

R. Yossi does not offer any positive solution to the problem he describes.[26] Other sources attempt to integrate controversy within tradition's self-understanding.

> R. Abba stated in the name of Samuel: For three years there was a dispute between Beth Shammai and Beth Hillel, the former asserting, 'The halacha is in agreement with our views,' and the latter contending, 'The halacha is in agreement with our views.' Then a heavenly voice issued announcing: [The utterances of] both are the words of the living God, but the halacha is in agreement with the rulings of Beth Hillel.[27]

The strategy employed by this text enables the inclusion of controversy within an ideal view of tradition. If for R. Yossi controversy impairs the single and unequivocal word of God, in this text both sides

---

[25] t.Hag 2:9.

[26] The elaboration of his tradition in y.Hag 2:2 (p. 77d) expresses the opinion that the messianic solution is the only possible solution to this problem of tradition.

[27] b.ʿErub 13b.

engaged in controversy are expressing the divine voice. The emphasis is not upon truth, but upon the religious value of the opposing positions expressed in controversy. The religious value is acquired by the relation established with God. Thus, both sides are not proclaimed to be correct, but to be expressing the words of the living God. Even though in practical terms a decision must be reached that favors the position of Beth Hillel, in the religious sense, both parties share in the fullness of one divine reality.

Serving as an *a posteriori* justification for the existence of controversy within tradition, our text does not explain in what way both parties express the words of the living God. Several possibilities emerge in attempting to understand how opposing opinions express one religious reality.

> Perhaps a man might imagine, 'Since the House of Shammai declare unclean and the House of Hillel clean, Mr. so and so prohibits, and Mr. such and such permits, why should I henceforward learn Torah?' Scripture says 'Words ... , The words ... , These are the words (Deut. 1:1), all these words have been given by a single Shepherd, one God made them, one provider gave them, the Lord of all deeds, blessed be He, has spoken it. So you, open many chambers in your heart and bring into it the words of the House of Shammai and the words of the House of Hillel, the words of those who declare unclean and the words of those who declare clean.[28]

Our text starts with the recognition that controversy poses a threat to the integrity of tradition. Why should one study Torah if there is no clear-cut position? The answer our text affords is that both sides of the controversy are divinely given. This answer is similar in kind to the answer found in the previous text. However, it seems that where the previous text brought God into the picture only after controversy had become rife, the present text sees God as the historical point of origin of both sides of the controversy. All the different words were given by God as part of the original giving of the Torah.[29] In similar fashion,

---

[28] t.Soṭ 7:12 (trans. J. Neusner [New York, 1979], p. 179).

[29] The choice of capitalization in Neusner's translation indicates where he thinks God, rather than Moses, is the subject of the statement. One may disagree with some of his choices—in particular with the reading of "shepherd" in relation to God. Variations in the manuscript tradition of the Tosephta also exhibit different understand-

one is called to open various chambers of the heart in order to place within them the different components of the Torah. This position obviously facilitates dealing with controversy, though it does not address the fundamental question of why God would choose to make equivocal statements as part of his revelation.

It should be noted that in this passage, too, Shammai and Hillel, or their schools, are exemplary of rabbinic controversy. What one places in the different chambers of the heart are the words of Beth Shammai and Beth Hillel.

Another way of endowing both sides of rabbinic controversy with religious significance is to address the intention of the disputing parties.

> Any controversy that is for God's sake shall in the end be of lasting worth, but any that is not for God's sake shall not in the end be of lasting worth. Which controversy was for God's sake? Such was the controversy of Hillel and Shammai.[30]

Hillel and Shammai, and not their houses, are here the archetype of the ideal controversy. What legitimates both sides of the controversy is the intention of the disputing parties. Both parties are arguing for the sake of God. Purity of motive is the guarantee of religious authenticity. Here it is not divine intervention or historical transmission that legitimates the conflicts of Shammai and Hillel, but the pure intentions of Shammai and Hillel.

What is common to the series of texts we have just analyzed is not only the attempt to justify the existence of controversy within Torah, but the view that Hillel and Shammai are representative, perhaps even symbolic, of this particular feature of rabbinic tradition. In this context,[31] Hillel comes to us not only embedded in the wider network of rabbinic relations, but as representative of a problem that threatens

---

ings of the same question (see Lieberman's edition of the Tosephta, pp. 194–95). In the Erfurt manuscript we read, "one shepherd received them." In any event, it is clear that both God and Moses are referred to in this passage. The theory of tradition is not merely that the different positions are all part of the original meaning or scope of the Torah, but that they are part of the historically transmitted body of knowledge.

[30] m.Ab 5:17.

[31] Unlike a context in which Hillel makes a *takanna*, such as the *prozbul*.

rabbinic authority. Hillel lacks unequivocal authority and his teaching threatens, at least temporarily, the very authority of Torah itself.

HILLEL AND RABBINIC AUTHORITY

Being a part of the collective rabbinic enterprise raises the question of Hillel's authority. What is the authority upon which his teaching rests? I believe we can single out three components that imbue Hillel's teaching with authority. The first component is his posturing within a tradition. Hillel is a link in an ongoing tradition. His teaching is accepted because he transmits the teachings of former generations.[32] Alongside this component we find Hillel's reliance on scriptural interpretation as a source of authority. The story of Hillel and Bnei Beteira exemplifies the relation and the tension that exists between these two components.

> Our Rabbis taught: This *halacha* was hidden from Bnei Beteira. On one occasion the fourteenth of Nisan fell on the Sabbath [and] they forgot and did not know whether the Passover overrides the Sabbath or not. They said: 'Is there any man who knows whether the Passover overrides the Sabbath or not?' They were told: 'There is a certain man who has come up from Babylonia, Hillel the Babylonian by name, who served the two greatest men of the time, and he knows whether the Passover overrides the Sabbath or not. [Thereupon] they summoned him [and] said to him: 'Do you know whether the Passover overrides the Sabbath or not? Have we then [only] one Passover during the year which overrides the Sabbath?' Replied he to them, 'Surely we have many more than two hundred Passovers during the year which override the Sabbath.' Said they to him: 'How do you know it?' He answered them: *'In its appointed time'* (Num 28:2) is stated in connection with the Passover, and *in its appointed time* is stated in connection with the *tamid*. Just as *its appointed time* which is said in connection with the *tamid* overrides the Sabbath, so *its appointed time* which is said in connection with the Passover overrides the Sabbath.' ... They immediately set him at their head and appointed him Patriarch. ... Said they to him: 'Master, what if a man forgot and did not bring a knife on the eve of the Sabbath?' 'I have heard this law,' he answered, 'but have

---

[32] See the tradition lists from m.Ab and m.Hag, discussed above.

forgotten it.' ... [Seeing the people act, he] recollected the *halacha* and said: 'Thus have I received the tradition from the mouth of Shemaiah and Abtalyon.'[33]

Hillel is commended in two different ways in this passage. The first thing we know about him is that he served the two greatest men of his generation—Shemaiah and Abtalyon. What commends him at the outset is a particular posturing within tradition. Hillel is a recipient of tradition, and therefore can solve a difficulty others are unable to solve. The next part of the story shows Hillel's exegetical skills. His exegesis does not seem to derive from a received tradition, but is portrayed as his own ingenuity. However, lest we think too much of Hillel personally, the last part of our story portrays him in the same light in which Bnei Beteira were portrayed in the previous section. He too forgets his received tradition. There his exegetical wits do not seem to count, and he relies upon common practice as a way of determining the rule. The final words of our passage close the circle of this story. The people's actions remind Hillel of the teaching of Shemaiah and Abtalyon.

This story plays out different forms of establishing authority against each other. Hillel's authority rests both upon his hermeneutical abilities and upon his received tradition.[34] The logic of the story seems to present received tradition as the ultimate source of authority, surpassing Hillel's interpretive abilities. Thus, a balance, which contains within

---

[33] b.Pes 66a-b.

[34] Without entering into the problem of this story's tradition history, I have preferred, for the sake of illustrating my argument, to present the Babylonian Talmud's version of the story rather than that of the Palestinian Talmud. According to the version of the story in y.Pes 6:1 (p. 33a), Bnei Beteira reject Hillel's hermeneutic exercises and accept his teaching only when he announces this is a tradition he received from Shemaiah and Abtalion. Thus, tradition is presented as the main source of authority, while exegesis is strongly underplayed.

We are not concerned here with the historicity of a particular incident, but with the methods of establishing authority in the particular culture to which Hillel belongs. Both texts discuss the relationship between scriptural interpretation and received tradition as sources of authority. Even if different versions of the same story offer different positions on the same question, what concerns us is the very existence of the question. It is sufficient indication for the existence of varying sources of authority within rabbinic culture. The Bavli is merely a clearer illustration of the dual source of authority in this culture.

it a tension, is found between these different modes of establishing authority.

As transmitter of tradition, Hillel is a mere vehicle who does not leave his stamp on tradition. His exegetical activity involves Hillel in the process in a personal way. Interpretation relies on the authority of Scripture, yet it is dependent upon the authority of the sage himself.

THE RABBI AS SAGE

We thus come to the third component of authority, that of the sage as sage. We find this factor most clearly in the nonlegal haggadic passages. There, the need for reliance upon Scripture or tradition is less acute. The sayings in ʾAbot do not, on the whole, rely upon scriptural proof texts; they are expressions of that very wisdom that constitutes the identity of the sage as sage. This wisdom may be legitimated in that the sages are links in a chain of tradition. However, because they are linked in this way, the sages come to possess a status and an authority that reflects not only tradition, but their very identity as sages.

The first chapters of ʾAbot demonstrate the intertwining of authority that is founded upon occupying a place in the history of a transmitted tradition and the autonomous authority of the sage as sage. However, ʾAbot records only nonlegal statements. The autonomous authority of the sage is largely restricted to the field of haggada. As concerns halakha, the story of Hillel and Bnei Beteira is a typical representation of the delicate balance that exists between scriptural interpretation and received tradition as sources of authority.

The explicit attention paid to these two sources of authority does not eliminate the role of the sage. We may claim that the sage is ultimately responsible for the interpretation of Scripture, since the hermeneutic process is founded upon a certain degree of autonomy of the interpreter vis-à-vis the interpreted text. Only thus can the meaning of the text be transformed through the process of interpretation, as is so often the case in rabbinic hermeneutics. Yet, no matter how ingenious the interpretation, how subversive the hermeneutic strategy, or how awkward the grounding of the sage's own understanding in the biblical text may be, the ultimate authority rests with the biblical text, rather than with the sage himself. Even if implicit in the midrashic *oeuvre* is the recognition of the power and authority of the interpreting sages, the ultimate source of authority is not the sage, but the word of Scripture.

As seen in the last quote, Hillel's halakhic authority does not rest upon himself, but upon those factors that are the sources of authority in rabbinic culture in general.

When we analyze Hillel against the background of rabbinic authority in general, we are again forced to conclude that Hillel may not be isolated from rabbinic culture and viewed in his own right. He may be clearly distinct within the wider context of Rabbis. He may even advance rabbinic culture significantly. Nevertheless, he is a part of that collective endeavor. His authority rests upon the conventional means of sanctioning authority. No matter how highly evolved his own sense of self-awareness may be,[35] it never filters directly into the halakhic process. At most, it colors his haggadic statements. When Hillel is engaged in halakhic controversy, tradition is threatened and a new theory of tradition history has to be formulated. We therefore conclude that Hillel is never isolated from the totality of the rabbinic enterprise.

All this is so different to the case of Jesus that it disables significant comparison between the two personalities. Jesus is totally his own distinct personality. We cannot confuse him with any other hero of the New Testament. No matter what he may have drawn from any of the available first-century Judaisms, he is not a part of any particular tradition. Never does he quote teachings of former generations, other than Scripture itself. In his hands, even Scripture serves less as prooftext (as it does for the Rabbis) and more as an illustration and example of his teachings.[36] Perhaps too much has been made of Jesus' teaching with authority.[37] Yet even after we discount the theological history of this theme and attempt to see Jesus against the background of his time, the reader has the clear impression that Jesus is not merely a first-century Rabbi. He is not a part of that collective creative effort, he

---

[35] See above, note 19.

[36] In *The Charismatic Leader and his Followers*, M. Hengel claims that Jesus uses prooftexts only in the context of debates, when his authority is challenged (ET [Edinburgh, 1981], p. 46; see also p. 47).

[37] See the extensive discussion of M. Hengel, *Charismatic Leader*, pp. 65–69; G. Friedrich, Προφήτης, TDNT, 6.841; M. Y. H. Lee, *Jesus und die Jüdische Autorität: Eine Exegetische Untersuchung zu Mk 11,27–12,12* (Wurzburg, 1986); see also the extensive bibliographic footnote in C. Marucci, S.J., "Die implizite Christologie in der sogenannten Vollmachtsfrage (Mk 11,27-33)," *Zeitschrift für katholische Theologie* 108 (1986) 292, note 1.

does not resort to their means of claiming authority, and he appeals to
another type of authority.

GOD

At this point we come to what may be the most striking difference
between Jesus and Hillel: God. The importance of God for the life and
teaching of Jesus can hardly be overemphasized. Jesus enjoys a special
relationship with God, is strongly aware of his presence, makes constant mention of him, and addresses him frequently. This close relationship of Jesus to God would seem to account both for the individuality of
Jesus and for the authority he exudes.[38] It is precisely here that the
greatest difference between Hillel and Jesus emerges. To make the point
as blunt as possible: we do not find Hillel referring to God even once in
all the traditions that refer to Hillel.[39]

Clearly Hillel was a God-fearing man. I have no doubt that he
enjoyed a personal relationship with God. It is likely that he taught his
disciples something concerning God. However, that is not what tradition chose to record in his name. We are limited by the fact that Hillel
comes to us through the mediation of a tradition that is distinguished by
particular emphases. We therefore do not know all we would like to
know about the personal religious life of Hillel. Yet this very limitation
illustrates our claim. Hillel comes to us as part of a collective enterprise, sharing the concerns of that collective. Pre–70 Rabbis hardly talk
of God.[40] Again, this does not mean that God is absent from their lives,

---

[38] See Hengel, *Charismatic Leader*, p. 69.

[39] In his discussion of Hillel's self-awareness, Flusser raises the possibility that
according to the Bavli's adaptation of Hillel's statements, God is the subject of some of
Hillel's sayings, and not Hillel himself (p. 513). However, as Flusser's discussion indicates, this possibility is somewhat forced.

[40] Of course, pre–70 Rabbis hardly talk of anything, because of the scarcity of
sources that have come to us from that period. Any claim based on the silence of pre–
70 sources is obviously hampered by this essential reservation. However, in dealing
with religious literature, it may not be too much to expect some understanding of God
and his works to find expression in a given body of statements, no matter how limited.
When Antigonos of Socho speaks in m.Ab 1:3 of servants serving their master, some
understanding of the human and the Divine is obviously expressed therein. However,
the focus of this statement is the proper religious intention of a human. Except for what
emerges from the parable itself, we learn little from it about God himself and his works.
On this point, one can draw a clear contrast with later rabbinic literature.

but it does mean that the collective cultural concerns deemed important to teach, record, and transmit are different. These concentrate upon Torah and the way of life that constitutes the service of God. God is not one of the actors upon the rabbinic stage.[41]

PRAYER

Closely related to the place God occupies in the lives of Jesus and Hillel respectively, as portrayed in the traditions that record their teachings, is the role of prayer in their respective teachings. As stated, the rabbinic stage, as early as we can find it, is a stage upon which a person acts in the service of God. One of the central means of service is the study of Torah.[42] It should be noted that only gradually does prayer come to play a central role in rabbinic religiosity.[43]

The pre-70 rabbinic authorities, living under the shadow of the Temple, did not practice regular prayer and therefore do not discuss it.[44] We therefore do not possess any statement of Hillel's concerning

---

[41] The clearest expression of this is to be found in the express rejection of God from the context of rabbinic discussion, in the famous controversy in b.BMeṣ 59b. Of course, two opinions are expressed in this passage, and in other passages in Talmudic literature a heavenly voice is used to settle disputes (see b.ʿErub 13b). However, a general rabbinic consensus is reflected in the position of the majority opinion, in b.BMeṣ. This consensus is highly typical of rabbinic religion, that accords humans a very active role in the constitution of reality and of Torah.

[42] See m.Ab 1:2, quoted above, note 18. Prayer is not listed as one of the cardinal values that uphold the world. This is obvious, since the Temple service is mentioned there. Prayer only emerges as a major form of religious expression with the destruction of the Temple. See also the following note.

[43] One indication of rabbinic preference of Torah to prayer is to be found in the fact that compared to the many statements encouraging the study of Torah in m.Ab, we find hardly any mention of prayer in this tractate. The only mention of prayer in a rabbinic dictum in ʾAbot is in 2:13, during the first generation after the destruction of the Temple, by R. Simeon ben Netanel. Following our discussion (above, note 18), one finds in the earlier traditions of ʾAbot that Torah and acts of loving-kindness are the natural substitutes for the destroyed Temple. Gradually, however, prayer comes to take the place of acts of loving-kindness and emerges as a substitute for the missing Temple service. See ARN A 4 (Schecter, p. 21). The new emphasis upon prayer agrees with the new halakhic obligation of fixed regular prayer. See E. Fleischer, "On the Beginnings of Obligatory Jewish Prayer" (in Hebrew), *Tarbiz*, 59 (1990) 397–441.

[44] Again, there is a general scarcity of sources and statements from pre-70 authorities: the bulk of rabbinic literature is of a later date. Therefore, the lack of statements on any particular topic, including that of prayer, does not indicate total absence of reflection on that topic. It only means the topic was not central enough—either to the

prayer. Even though we may safely assume that Hillel practiced some form of prayer, we have no testimony of his prayer activity, nor is any prayer particular to him recorded.[45] In this light, Jesus, as portrayed in the Gospels, stands out once again as different from Hillel or any other pre-70 Rabbi. His frequent prayer and his instruction in prayer seem to reflect the centrality of God in his life and teaching.

It would be wise to refrain from value judgment at this point regarding the respective concerns of two cultures, or schools of teaching. However, a certain clarification is necessary. Rabbinic culture constitutes a conscious choice to endow humanity with great responsibility in the service of God. It extols the sage over the prophet. "A sage is greater than a prophet."[46] In this culture of sages, Wisdom (or Torah, in its latter day form[47]) is the focus of a God-fearing culture. It ought to be viewed as an extension of biblical wisdom literature. This is particularly true for pre-70 rabbinic Judaism. Only a God-fearing culture propagates the wisdom of God. Wisdom and Torah are to a certain degree autonomous of God.[48] Therefore, personal relationship with God

---

teachers of that period or to the tradition that preserved their teaching—to be recorded or addressed by the literature.

[45] We have scarcely any texts of prayer that are ascribed to pre-70 authorities (see perhaps t.Ber 3:7, in the name of R. Zadok). An early mention of rabbinic prayer is to be found in t.RH 5:17. However, this is a record of a prayer event, and not the record of a particular text of prayer. The lack of prayer texts from this period may be less surprising when we consider the evolution of fixed prayer. Following Fleischer's position (above, note 43) that no fixed obligatory prayer existed prior to the destruction of the Temple, the lack of prayer attributed to any particular Rabbi need not surprise us. What this culture chose to record and make significant are teachings of Torah, and not formulas of prayer.

[46] b.BB 12a. See Shimon Ravidovitch, *Iyunim Bemachshevet Israel*, vol. 1 (Jerusalem, 1969), pp. 34–36.

[47] The identification of wisdom and Torah is found already in Ben Sira 24. It is commonplace in rabbinic sources. See, for example, GenRab 1:1.

[48] Interestingly, out of hundreds of rabbinic statements about the importance of Torah and its study, hardly any discuss the way in which Torah can serve as a means of approaching God, nor is Torah study, unlike most commandments, viewed from the angle of the relationship with God. The implication of such passages as SifDeut 49 is that the Torah is equivalent to God. Thus, Torah constitutes a representation of God. Where clinging to God is not possible, clinging to the Torah is religiously equivalent. However, no precise understanding of the nature of this equivalence is offered. Because of the supposed equivalence of God and Torah, Torah is rarely perceived as instrumental in leading one toward a higher aspect, such as a relationship with God. Torah is thus functionally autonomous, within the structure of rabbinic thinking, much as wisdom is, within certain sections of biblical thought.

is not at the fore of pre–70 Judaism. Religiosity and piety are indeed central to individual lives. However, the common concerns, as recorded in the transmitted sources, place a greater emphasis on Wisdom.

THE BIBLICAL PROPHETIC TRADITION

The sapiential aspect of the teaching of Jesus is a commonplace. However, alongside the continuation of wisdom tradition, Jesus also continues the biblical prophetic tradition.[49] One expression of this prophetic tradition is the apocalyptic and eschatological message of Jesus. This dimension of the prophetic is not unique to Jesus, in relation to the Rabbis. Various rabbinic apocalyptic utterances are similar in kind to those of Jesus.[50] However, one must take into account not only the existence of apocalyptic statements, but the relative importance of the eschatological and apocalyptic dimensions in the teachings of Jesus and the Rabbis. Despite similarities in respective sayings, the eschatological—and in this sense, the prophetic—dimension, is clearly far more central to the teaching of Jesus than it is to the world outlook of the rabbis. It thus sets him apart from the totality of rabbinic express-ion.[51]

When we speak of the prophetic, we refer not only to the content and message of the prophet, but to the quality of relationship with God that characterizes the prophet. The close personal relationship to God and the force of God's presence in the life of Jesus are as typical of the biblical prophetic type as the Rabbis are of the biblical wisdom type. Thus, when we view rabbinic culture as a whole, and pre–70 Rabbinism in particular, we may look not only to the tasks this group has set before itself and to its function in the widest context of Jewish history; we may also evaluate it against the background of biblical types of reli-giosity and their latter-day manifestations in late Second Temple period.[52]

---

[49] On the relationship of the sapiential and the prophetic dimensions in the per-son of Jesus, see M. Hengel, *Charismatic Leader*, pp. 47–49, 63.

[50] See b.Ṣot 48b; b.Sanh 68a, 98a–b; see also my "Testaments in Rabbinic Lit-erature: Transformations of a Genre," *JSJ* 25.2 (1994).

[51] See Hengel, *Charismatic Leader*, pp. 63–69.

[52] On the typological affinities between Ḥasidim and biblical prophets, see G. B. Sarfatti, "Pious Men, Men of Deeds, and the Early Prophets" (in Hebrew), *Tarbiz* 26 (1957) 126–53; see also G. Vermes, *Jesus the Jew* (London, 1976), pp. 76–77. It is noteworthy that Ḥanina ben Dosa, when asked if he is a prophet replies, "I am neither a

Another crucial aspect distinguishes the work of Jesus from that of Hillel. Jesus is indeed a teacher-prophet. Yet the Gospels record that one particular type of activity occupied a primary place in the life of Jesus—one that was not an essential part of the work of a Rabbi. I refer to the work of Jesus as a healer. The healing work of Jesus, as portrayed in the Gospels, encompasses not only physical healing, but spiritual healing as well. Great significance is placed on Jesus' powers of exorcism. In fact, exorcism serves to indicate the unique presence manifest in Jesus and the eschatological significance of his actions.[53] Healing is not incidental to Jesus the teacher. It represents a unique, distinct, and central aspect of his work.

When we compare this with what we know about Rabbis, the contrast is obvious. We do have records of Rabbis performing works of healing.[54] On rare occasions we also have mention of rabbinic exorcism.[55] However, Hillel is never regarded as a healer, nor is any other pre-70 Rabbi. Moreover, healing is never seen as part of the self-understanding of any Rabbi, or of rabbinic culture. Healing may be an incidental byproduct of the wisdom of certain Rabbis and may serve as testimony to God's power in them. It is not, however, constitutive of their self-understanding. The relation between the special role of prayer in the life of Jesus and the work of healing that is ascribed to him seems obvious. Both types of activity indicate a method of work and an emphasis that is different from that of Hillel, as seen against the background of rabbinic culture. This difference points once more to a major class distinction between Hillel and Jesus. It is not that they were two of

---

prophet nor the son of a prophet" (b.Ber 34b). This denial of prophetic status derives in fact from Amos 7:14. This quote captures the complexity of the relationship between the Ḥasidim and early prophets. One may further view the tension between classical rabbinic authority and the power manifest in the acts of the Ḥasidim as another expression of the tension between the types of sage and prophet in this period of Jewish religion. For this tension, see b.Ber 34b; m.Taan 3:8; see further, Vermes, *Jesus the Jew*, pp. 80–82.

[53] See M. Hengel, *Charismatic Leader*, pp. 65–67.

[54] See b.Ber 5a; see also J. Preuss, *Biblical and Talmudic Medicine*, ET (1978), pp. 21–23. However, much of this healing relies on herbs and medicaments, not on the power of the healer himself.

[55] See b.Me᾽ 17b; see also Meʿir Bar Ilan, "Exorcism by Rabbis," *Daʿat* (forthcoming).

a kind, with certain minor variances. They are two fundamentally different types.

CONCLUSION

Let us now return to the ramifications of the above discussion upon our theme: Jesus and Hillel. If such a juxtaposition presupposes an essential *identity in type*, there is little to commend it. However, if we see Hillel as a prime example of a pre–70 Rabbi, in part a contemporary of Jesus, then the historical *contrast* is of great significance. Through this contrast, both figures emerge more clearly, both in their distinctness and in their relation to the culture in which they were embedded. However, Hillel is only one expression of the wider historical background of Jesus. To understand Jesus, we need to refer to the Essenes, as well as to the Pharisees, the Ḥasidim, and the Rabbis.

The particular type of analogy implied by the grouping of Hillel and Jesus may be significant, yet its significance is limited. Hillel should be seen as a part of his collective culture. Jesus should be seen against the background of the various cultures with which he could have had contact. It may be that when all the historical parallels are drawn, we will not be able to assume an essential similarity between Jesus and any of the existing types of Palestinian spirituality. Jesus may emerge as more than just a mixture of various elements, derived from different historical sources. This degree of *historical* uniqueness calls into question how much sense there is in applying the "Jesus and X" topos to the historical background of Jesus.

In the future, we ought to separate the quest for parallels and sources for the historical Jesus from the "Jesus and X" topos. Framing a discussion under such a category ought to be specific to those instances in which a typological comparison is possible. If Jesus is unique when seen against his background, he may yet be seen in a comparative light when viewed typologically and phenomenologically. The application of this topos to figures in later Jewish history, as well as in other religious traditions, is both possible and beneficial.

HILLEL AND THE MISUNDERSTANDING OF JUDAISM IN MODERN SCHOLARSHIP

MY POINT OF departure for the discussed topic will be the view of J. Wellhausen on Judaism. Wellhausen was an outstanding scholar in Old Testament and New Testament whose life ambition was "historical interpretation based on philological examination."[1] Yet he readily admitted that he did not include rabbinic literature in his historical reconstruction of the Second Temple period. He read only Josephus. He admitted also that the theologians did not study even that.[2]

In his entry on "Israel" in *Encyclopedia Britannica*, Wellhausen defined Judaism as follows:

> Judaism is historically comprehensible, and yet it is a mass of antinomies. ... The Creator of heaven and earth becomes the manager of a petty scheme of salvation; the living God descends from His throne to make way for the law [the very law which was the basis of Jesus' education! —M.W.]. The law thrusts itself in everywhere; it commands and blocks up the access to heaven; it regulates and sets limits to the understanding of the divine working on earth. As far as it can, it takes the soul out of religion and spoils morality. It demands a service of God, which, though revealed, may yet with truth be called a self-chosen and unnatural one, the sense and use of which are apparent neither to the understanding nor to the heart. The labour is done for the sake of the exercise. It does no one any good, and rejoices neither God nor man. ... The ideal is a negative one, to keep one's self from sin, not a positive one, to do good upon earth. The occupation of the hands

---

[1] See note 12.
[2] See note 12.

and the desire of the heart fall asunder. ... There is no connection between the Good One and goodness.[3]

He goes on to claim that the gospel

developes hidden impulses of the Old Testament, but it is a protest against the ruling tendency of Judaism. Jesus understands monotheism in a different way from his contemporaries. ... He feels the reality of God dominating the whole of life, he breathes in the fear of the Judge who requires an account for every idle word. This monotheism is not to be satisfied with stipulated services, how many and great soever; it demands the whole man, it renders doubleness of heart and hypocrisy impossible. Jesus casts ridicule on the works of the law, the washing of hands and vessels, the tithing of mint and cumin, the abstinence even from doing good on the Sabbath. Against unfruitful self-sanctification He sets up another principle of morality, that of the service of one's neighbor.[4]

What follows is much in the same vein. Wellhausen continues extolling the church and denigrating Judaism.

The same bias appears in Wellhausen's *Israelitische und jüdische Geschichte*.[5] Here the New Testament is presented as the apex of the spiritual creativity of the "true Israel," while the vast Hebrew literature which flourished in the Middle Ages did not, Wellhausen argues, emerge from the true roots of Israel's tradition.[6] Unlike Christianity, Judaism sees salvation as a miraculous event, unrelated to the religious and ethical behavior of the individual. The idea of individual responsibility before God, he concludes, is far-removed from Judaism.[7]

Wellhausen presents here a completely distorted view of the situation.[8] While it is true that Jewish halakha is, and has always been, a

---

[3] *Encyclopedia Britannica*, 9th ed., 1881, Vol. XIII, pp. 369–431.

[4] Reprinted in J. Wellhausen, *Prolegomena to the History of Israel*, trans. J. Black and A. Menzies (Edinburgh, 1885), pp. 508–10. The German edition of this study appeared in J. Wellhausen, *Skizzen und Vorarbeiten: Erstes Heft* (Berlin, 1884).

[5] 7th ed. (Berlin, 1914; originally published in 1894).

[6] "Die ausgedehnte jüdische Literatur des spätern Mittelalters kann man nicht eigentlich als ein Gewächs aus der alten Wurzel betrachten" (p. 358).

[7] "Israel," pp. 364ff.

[8] His views correspond to those of his contemporaries in Germany, esp. E. Schürer and W. Bousset. Many of these never made an effort to study rabbinical

labor for its adherents,[9] its observance has never been a matter of "labour done for the sake of the exercise" but was rather an instructive discipline in the demanding multi-faceted service of God. A claim that halakha ignores the commandment of the heart and the "reality of God dominating the whole of life" is simply misrepresentation. Wellhausen was apparently unaware that the biblical words "I have set the Lord always before me" (Ps 16:8)[10] are displayed prominently upon the lectern of every synagogue, and he apparently knew nothing of that

---

sources or to read the literature of the Jewish school and synagogue. Nevertheless, they dared to define Judaism in a confident manner. Cf., e.g., the words of G. F. Moore: "What Bousset lacked in knowledge, he made up, however, in the positiveness and confidence of his opinions ... [by] unsupported assertion coming by force of sheer reiteration" ("Christian Writers on Judaism," *HTR* 14 [1921] 242).

On the prevailing anti-Jewish atmosphere of German theologians in the 19th century, cf. J. Blenkinsopp, *Prophecy and Canon* (Notre Dame, 1977), pp. 19–20. See also W. McKane and his reaction to Blenkinsopp in *JSOT* 17 (1979) 66–67, and Blenkinsopp's response to McKane in *JSOT* 18 (1980) 105–7. On the religious sentiments of Wellhausen's own time, see recently: L. H. Silberman, "Wellhausen and Judaism: Julius Wellhausen and his *Prolegomena to the History of Israel*," *Semeia* 25 (1982) 75–82.

R. Smend in his article, "Wellhausen und das Judentum" (*ZTK* 79 [1982] 249–82), has presented a thorough and valuable discussion of Wellhausen's attitude towards Jews and Judaism. Smend rightly concludes that in those days nobody would be blamed for thinking or talking like him. To be sure, this does not mean that he and his contemporaries were free of anti-Semitic feelings. Wellhausen was not happy at all about the survival of the Jews. On other occasions he did not hide his feelings of aversion to Jews. (See R. Smend, "Wellhausen und das Judentum," p. 269, note 95.)

According to W. R. Nicoll in the protocol of his meeting with Wellhausen in Eldena near Greifswald (March 8, 1881): "Wellhausen hates Jews" (see T. H. Darlow, *William Robertson Nicoll: His Life and Letters* (London, 1925), p. 42. See, however, the reservations of R. Smend in *ZTK* 78 (1981) 165. We should admit that Wellhausen's personal feelings do not count when it comes to scholarly matters. What we try to show is that whatever Wellhausen's personal feelings towards Jews may have been, his characterization of Judaism is false.

[9] Hence the various complaints about its rigidity, stiffness, etc. See references, esp. the ones concerning Buber, in R. Smend, *ZTK* 79 (1982) 278, notes 140–41. On Buber's attitude toward institutionalized religion, see Y. Amir, "Buber and the Synagogue," *Here and Now: Studies in the Social and Religious Thoughts of M. Buber* (Jerusalem, 1982), pp. 115–18 [Hebrew].

[10] In the translations of this and other biblical passages, I have made use of the recent translations of the Scriptures published by the Jewish Publication Society of America. I have, where the context required, deviated from the Society's rendering.

Judaism which struggles against "a commandment of men, learned by rote" (מצות אנשים מלומדה).[11]

Wellhausen himself testifies that besides some Mishnah and Mekhilta, he never studied any rabbinic literature,[12] which makes him ill-

---

[11] See, e.g., Baḥya ibn Paquda's *Duties of the Heart*, trans. M. Hyamson (Jerusalem, 1962), esp. Vol. II, pp. 144–51 ("Repentance," Chapter V) and 198–201 ("Spiritual Accounting," Chapter III). The medieval philosopher's idea and its formulation derive from Isa 29:13 (despite Wellhausen's idea of the inauthentic roots of medieval Jewish writings!).

[12] See *Die Pharisäer*, p. 123, note 1. In another note (p. 19, note 1), he says that the Mishnah from beginning to end is characteristic of the Pharisees, and that there is no point in going to detail *as it is all the same*. Clearly no one who had studied Mishnah properly would make such a statement.

As pointed out by H. Liebeschütz in his survey of Wellhausen (*Das Judentum im deutschen Geschichtsbild von Hegel bis Max Weber* (Tübingen, 1967), pp. 245–68), this conscious decision to forego the careful study of rabbinic literature is especially astonishing on the part of a scholar whose life's ambition was historical interpretation based on philological examination. Liebeschütz's study was brought to my attention by the late Professor I. L. Seeligman. As for Wellhausen's work on the Pharisees, his devoted friend Wilamowitz-Moelendorf testified that he wrote this work without any training in rabbinics. Wellhausen stated, "I read only Josephus, the theologians do not do even that," *Erinnerungen* (1848–1914[2]; [Leipzig, 1928], p. 188).

This ignorance of Jewish sources crippled Wellhausen not only in his study of the Pharisaic period (i.e., the time of Jesus), but also in his evaluation of topics treated in the Priestly Code of the Pentateuch. For instance, in his discussion of the "shoulder, the two cheeks, and the maw" given to the priests, he makes reference to Josephus (*Prolegomena*[6], p. 14, note 8 (ET, p. 154), but not to the Mishnah (Hulin 10:1; compare Sifra 17:6). Elsewhere, discussing P's outlawing of the high places since the time of the erection of the tabernacle, he cites (in Latin!) the Mishnah in Zebaḥim 14:4, but neglects to mention the Mishnayot which follow and speak of the subsequent legalization of the high places (*Prolegomena*[6], p. 37, note 1 [not found in ET]). Y. Kaufmann accuses Wellhausen of willful distortion (*History of the Israelite Religion*, vol. 1 [Tel Aviv, 1938], p. 132, note 34 [Hebrew]), but it is just as likely that the case is one of citation from faulty, incomplete secondary sources. Wellhausen's superficiality in dealing with rabbinic material is far more serious a shortcoming than his hatred of Talmudists, a hatred he certainly did not lack (cf. *Die Pharisäer*, p. 123).

Regarding the lack of training in Judaic sources among the New Testament scholars of Wellhausen's age, cf. G. F. Moore in "Christian Writers on Judaism" (Note 4): "It is not without significance that all these authors—Schürer, Baldensperger, Weiss, Bousset—were New Testament scholars, the oldest of them scarcely past thirty years old. Schürer was the only one who thought it necessary to know anything about the rabbinical sources, and he found in Surenhusius' Mishnah just the right material for the demonstration of 'legalism.' Beyond this he never went; the others did not go so far."

One of the biggest distortions of Judaism in Bousset's book about Jesus (*Jesus Predigt in ihrem Gegensatz zum Judentum*, 1892) is his statement that "later Judaism had neither in name nor in fact the faith of the Father-God; it could not possibly rise to

qualified to say what Pharisaic Judaism is and is not. One Mishnaic passage which he certainly did not learn is the dictum that "a man may offer much or little, *so long as he directs his mind toward heaven* (m.Men 13:11). Had he learned it, he could not have claimed that Judaism separates the legal act from the proper thought and the "understanding of the heart."

It is also evident that Wellhausen failed to see that the Jewish religious experience is one of joy in fulfilling a commandment. The law is observed not for the sake of the exercise, but to perform the will of the Creator. Wellhausen entirely missed the fact that Judaism sanctifies life by eradicating the separation of *jus* from *fas* (of law from religion) by rendering all aspects of life—the synagogue, the home, and the market— a continous act of divine service. Every step taken by the Jew is directed by awareness that he or she is fulfilling God's will.

The notion, which Wellhausen ascribed to Jesus as the antithesis of Judaism, that true monotheism is "not to be satisfied with stipulated services ...; it demands the whole man" is actually an authentically Jewish view. Rabbi Jose is quoted as saying "and let all your deeds be done for the sake of Heaven" (m.Ab 2:12). Elsewhere, this statement is attributed to Hillel the Elder, who is said to have performed such deeds as eating, drinking, and bathing for the sake of Heaven.[13] This same concept is expressed in the words of the amora Bar Kappara (b.Ber 63a): "Under which short passage are all the laws of the Torah subsumed? 'In all your ways know him' (Prov 3:6)."

Jesus was perpetuating a dispute current in the Judaism of his age: Hillel demanded, as we have seen, that one direct all his deeds to

---

it" (cf. G. F. Moore, "Christian Writers on Judaism," p. 242). Whoever opens a Jewish prayer book will hardly miss the phrases אבינו מלכנו ("our Father, our king") or אבינו שבשמים ("our Father in heaven").

[13] ARN B 30 (cf. Schechter edition, p. 66); see also E. E. Urbach, *The Sages: Their Concepts and Beliefs*, vol. 1 (Jerusalem, 1975), pp. 339–42. Urbach writes, "One cannot overlook the danger to the observance of the precepts from the standpoint of Hillel, for if every act can be done in the name of Heaven, then something is abstracted from the absolute value of the precept and a way is opened for nullification the worth of the ritual laws whose connection with the knowledge of the Lord is not clear or simple. In truth, Jesus reached such extreme conclusions in his polemic against the Halakha, as is reported in the Gospels" (p. 341).

At any rate, it was not Jesus who invented this sort of monotheism.

Heaven. Shammai held that such religious intent is necessary only for deeds which go into the performance of a divine command; it was not necessary for other actions.[14]

Although Wellhausen quoted Shammai and not Hillel, Judaism adopted Hillel's view.[15] Judaism understands the commandments as the concretization of a few ethico-religous principles:

> R. Simlai preached: Six hundred thirteen precepts were uttered to Moses: Three hundred sixty-five prohibitions, corresponding to the number of days in the solar year, and two hundred forty-eight injunctions corresponding to the number of organs of a man's body. ... David reduced the number to eleven as it is written: 'A Psalm of David: Lord, who may dwell in Your tent?' He who lives without blame, who does what is right ... who has never done harm to his fellow' (Ps 15:1-5). ... Isaiah proceeded to reduce the number to six, as it is written, 'He who walks in righteousness, speaks uprightly' (Isa 33:15). ... Micah further reduced the number to three, as it is written, 'He has told you, O man, what is good, and ... the Lord requires of you to do justice ... to love kindness ... and to walk humbly' (Micah 6:8). ... Again came Isaiah and reduced the number to two, as it is said, 'Thus said the Lord: Observe what is right and do what is just' (Isa 56:1). ... Amos finally reduced the number to one, as it is said, 'Thus said the Lord to the House of Israel: Seek me, and you will live' (Amos 5:4). (b.Mak 23b–24a)

The point of the homily is that the essence of the divine command and all the individual precepts it entails can be expressed in any number, however small, of the general religious-ethical demands, and that the classical prophets and psalmists had affirmed this fact. Another Talmudic view, that of R. Nahman bar Yiṣhak, is that the reduction of the number of commandments to one, expressed according to R. Simlai in the passage from Amos, is better expressed in the words of Habakuk, "The righteous shall live by his faith (באמונתו)" (Hab 2:4). This notion

---

[14] See Urbach, *Sages*, p. 450.

[15] To characterize the Pharisaic attitude, Wellhausen quoted Shammai's and not Hillel's view about the Sabbath, and thus distorted the picture (*Die Pharisäer*, p. 19; ET, p. 116). On the theological aspects of the controversy between Shammai and Hillel, see Urbach, *Sages*, p. 340.

that the "faith of the righteous" is equal to the whole of the Law is found in Gal 3:11-12. However, as opposed to the Talmudic passage, it appears there as part of the Pauline polemic against the observance of the precepts of the Torah.

Urbach realized that R. Simlai's homily was intended primarily to express the idea that humanity is to be wholly engaged in the fulfillment of God's will—both spacially and temporally.[16] The individual commandments are thus no more than a detailed elaboration and concretization of humanity's submission to and nearness to the Divine. Such a view is directly opposed to that voiced by Wellhausen in his book on the Pharisees:

> Die Summe des Abgeleiteten erstickte die Quelle, die 613 Gebote des geschriebenen und die tausend anderen des ungeschriebenen Gesetzes liessen für den Gewissen keinen Platz. Die Summe der Mittel wurde der Zweck, man vergass Gott über der Thora und der Zugang zu ihm über der Etikette, durch welche er ermöglicht werden sollte.[17]

The same R. Simlai preached that the Torah both begins and ends with acts of kindness. It opens with God's providing raiment for Adam and his wife, and ends with his attending to the burial of Moses (m.Soṭ 14a). The lesson is an obvious one: lovingkindness (חֶסֶד) as practised by God himself, is the alpha and omega of the Law.[18] Wellhausen's claim that Pharisaic Judaism was an outgrowth of the priestly religion

---

[16] Urbach, *Sages*, pp. 343-45.

[17] *Die Pharisäer*, p. 19. Most Christian scholars failed to acquire a true understanding of the nature of Judaism and thus held views like this. The English biblical scholar G. A. Smith writes on Deut 4:7, "For what great nation is there that has a God so close? ... Legal Judaism lost this sense of constant nearness of God [i.e., the one operative in Deut 4:7] and did not compensate for the loss by its apocalypses" (*Deuteronomy*, Cambridge Bible [Cambridge, 1918], p. 60). Only recently has the trend been reversed as Christian scholars have begun to get acquainted with Judaism; see C. Klein, *Theologie und Anti-Judaismus* (München, 1975).

[18] Cf. Pseudo-Jonathan to Deut 34:6 and compare Mt 25:31-39. Rabbi Simlai, a third-century sage, was a kind of 'apostle' (or emissary-sage). In his preaching he polemicized with Christians (cf. B. Z. Rosenfeld, "The Activity of Rabbi Simlai: A Chapter in the Relations Between Eretz-Israel and the Diaspora in the Third Century," *Zion* 48 [1983] 229-39). It is against this background that we should understand the affinities of his sermons to the New Testament.

and was therefore characterized by moral insensitivity is untenable.[19] Lev 19 (cf. esp. vv. 14, 18, 32-34) and 25 (cf. esp. vv. 1, 17, 36, 43) are replete with moral demands, such as not putting a stumbling block before the blind (19:14), loving the neighbor (19:18), standing up before an old man (19:32), loving the foreigner (19:39), not cheating (25:17), not charging interest (25:36), and not ruling over a slave ruthlessly (25:43). The idea that the Priestly Code is morally apathetic is as distorted as the notion that Pharisaic Judaism is. Wellhausen did not feel the true pulse of Judaism. Proper intent (*kavvanah*) while performing the commandments was always a crucial issue to the Rabbis.[20] There would have been no place for the many Talmudic discussions of this topic if, as Wellhausen contended, the commandments were merely exercise.

CHRISTIAN MORALITY

According to Wellhausen, religion reached its height in Christian morality. Yet this Christian morality itself is rooted in Pharisaic Judaism, as the Gospels themselves attest. Thus we read in Mt 22:35f,

And one of them [the Pharisees], a legal expert [νομικός][21] asked him, to test him: 'Master, which is the great commandment [ἐντολὴ μεγάλη] in the law?' And he said to him, '"You shall love the Lord your God with all your heart, and with all your soul, and with all your mind."[22] This is the first and great commandment, and the second is

[19] "For what holiness required was not to do good, but to avoid sin," "Israel," *Encyclopedia Britannica*, reprinted in ET of *Prolegomena*, p. 500.

[20] Cf. Urbach, *Sages*, pp. 390-95.

[21] Compare Lk 10:25. In 4Mac 5:4, Eleazar standing before Antiochus is called νομικός. In 2Mac 6:18 he is called "one of the first scribes" (πρωτευόντων γραμματέων), i.e., one engaged in the interpretation of the Torah (δευτέρωσις, מדרש התורה); compare *tōpeś Torah* (Sir 15:1) and *dōreś Torah* (35:15; see also Qumran passages). The latter are occasionally reckoned among the Pharisaic scribes, but are not identical to them; see, for example, Lk 11:45, where the νομικός does not see himself as one of the Pharisees. The Pharisees are the members of the sect; the *soferim* are the officials and assorted Temple scribes, and the νομικοί are the learned preachers and interpreters of the Law. On Moses as a νομικός, see S. Lieberman, *Hellenism in Jewish Palestine* (New York, 1950), pp. 81-82.

[22] ἀγαπήσεις κύριον τὸν θεόν σου ἐν ὅλῃ τῇ καρδίᾳ σου ... ψυχῇ σου ... διανοίᾳ σου. The word διανοία (cf. Mk 12:30; Lk 10:27) never appears in the LXX for Heb. דעת, and represents, I believe Heb. יצר, as in the LXX of Gen 6:5; 8:21; 1Chr 29:18;

like it: "You shall love your neighbor as yourself." On these two commandments hang all the law and the prophets.'   (Mt 22:36-39)[23]

The Pharisee's questions about the "great commandment" correspond in large measure to the dictum of Rabbi Akiba: "'Love your neighbor as yourself': that is a major principle [כלל גדול] in the Law" (SifLev 19:18).[24]

On the other hand, Jesus' statement that all the law and the prophets hang on these two commandments corresponds to Hillel's reaction to the heathen who wanted to be converted on the condition that Hillel teach him the entire Torah "while standing on one foot." Hillel replied, "What is hateful to you do not do to your neighbor. This is the entire Torah; all the rest go and study [i.e., all the rest is a commentary]" (b.Shab 31a).[25] This saying appears in the Palestinian Targum as a

---

in accord with the Midrashic comment on "with all thy heart" (i.e., with both your inclinations יצריך; Sifre Debarim 32, ed. Finkelstein, p. 55 and refs.). In contrast, σύνησις in Mk 12:35 is the equivalent of Heb. mada' of da'at, which replaced classical leb in rabbinic Hebrew (see A. Ben David, Leshon Miqra Uleshon Hakamim, Vol. 1 [Tel Aviv, 1967], p. 92; cf. also the commentary of Abraham Ibn Ezra to Deut 6:5. לבבך נפשך ומאדך appear in Qumran as "intelligence [דעת], strength [כח], and fortune [הון]" (1QS 1.12; cf. 3.2). The LXX rendered מאד in Deut 6:5 with Greek ἰσχύς or δύναμις (see note 25 below). The Aramaic translations render מאד nks (property) or mmwn (money; see below). Cf. also CD 13.11 and my article in Iyunim bemiqra: Sefer zikkaron le-Y. M. Grintz (Tel Aviv, 1982), pp. 41–47.

[23] See Sifra, Kedoshim 1:1: "Why was [this chapter] said to the entire people? Because the essentials of the Law are subsumed in it." See also D. Flusser, Yahadut umeqorot hanatsrut (Tel Aviv, 1979), p. 36.

[24] See Flusser, Yahadut. It is best to avoid interpreting ἐντολή as "principle" (כלל) as Flusser does, since כלל is not the same as מצוה at all (see M. Smith, Parallels Between the Gospels and Tannaitic Literature (Jerusalem, 1945).

The phrase ἐντολὴ μεγίστης appears in the letter of Aristeas in connection with the honoring of parents (§228). Second in importance is the love of neighbor, expressed in the language of the LXX, "your friend who is as yourself" (ὁ φίλος ὁ ἴσος τῆς ψυχῆς σου; Deut 13:7). For the view that honoring one's parents is the most important commandment, see y.Pe'a 1:1 (15d): "R. Simeon ben Yohai says, the respect of father and mother is so great that the Holy One, Blessed be He, preferred it above His own honor.... Said R. Abba bar Kahana: "Scripture equates the easiest of the commandments with the most stringent. The easiest is to let [the mother-bird] leave the nest, the most stringent is the honoring of father and mother." This same view may be present in Sif-Deut 13:7: "Your friend who is as yourself; this is your father" (ed. Finkelstein, p. 151).

[25] Cf. ARN B 26 (Schechter ed., p. 53).

translation of Lev 19:18: "Love your neighbor as yourself."[26] In the parallel of Mk 12:28-33 we read:

> And one of the [Pharisaic] scribes came, and ... asked him, 'Which is the first commandment of all?' And Jesus answered him, 'The first of all the commandments is, "Hear, O Israel; the Lord our God is one Lord: And you shall love the Lord you God with all your heart, and with all your soul, and with all your mind, and with all your strength."[27] This is the first commandment. And the second is like it, namely, "You shall love your neighbor as yourself." There is none other commandment greater than these.' And the scribe said unto him, 'Well, Master, thou hast said the truth, for there is but one God; and there is none other but he: And to love him with all the heart, and with all the understanding [σύνεσις] and with all the soul, and with all the strength, and to love his neighbor as himself, is more than all whole burnt offerings and sacrifices.'

Both Luke 10:25-28 and Matthew 22 state clearly that the legal expert approached Jesus to test him, and Jesus stood the trial. Jesus thus revealed his awareness that the two commandments mentioned are the basis of Pharisaic Judaism.

By expressing the view of the Pharisees, Jesus reveals his own opinion as well. Christian interpreters have always realized this, though they have consistently felt compelled to stress the difference between the position of the Pharisees and that of Jesus. Bousset, for example, writes as follows:

> Die Heraushebung und Zusammenstellung der zwei Gebote tritt also nicht eigentlich als eigener Gedanke Jesu auf, sondern auch ein ehrlicher und nach dem Heil verlangender Schriftgelehrter konnte wissen, dass dies die wichtigsten Gebote des alten Bundes waren. ...

---

[26] For this saying and its sources, see Urbach, *Sages*, p. 589, and p. 955, note 93.

[27] The word used here is ἰσχύς. In Deut 6:5, the word δύναμις appears (LXX). However, ἰσχύς is used in 2Kgs 23:25. In Hebrew and Aramaic sources of the Second Commonwealth and thereafter, *me'od* is interpreted as "money." See CD 9.1; 12.10; m.Ber 9:5; Onkelos and Yerushalmi to Deut 6:5. The scribes at Qumran apparently understood *me'od* as fortunes (see note 18 above).

Aber die einzelnen ernsten Rabbiner haben nicht vermocht, diese Erkenntnis für die Welt fruchtbar zu machen; erst dadurch, dass Jesus für diese Anschauung eintrat, hat er gewissermassen die Seele der alten Religion entdeckt, aus der Umklammerung einer tausendgliederigen Gesetzesüberlieferung befreit und ihren edelsten Gehalt in die neue Religion überfuhrt. Der ganze Wust des Zeremonial-Gesetzes aber mit seinen zahllosen Einzelheiten ist damit zurückgedrangt und zum Absterben gezwungen.[28]

The tendentious inaccuracy of such interpretation speaks for itself. Neither the Pharisees nor Jesus considered the traditional meticulous observance of the commandments in any way a contradiction to the precepts of love of God and neighbor, nor did the authors of the Gospels themselves (cf. Mt 5:17-20; Lk 16:17). As a matter of fact, as we have stressed, the Pharisees considered observance to be the very realization of these ideals. It was Hillel, one of the greatest of the Pharisees, who saw—as indicated—in Leviticus 19:18 the basis of the whole Torah. And it was this same Pharisee Hillel who taught that man must "love his fellow men and bring them near to the Law" (m.Ab 1:12), a lesson which recalls Jesus' befriending of the sinners in order to bring them to faith. Hillel's school indeed ruled that Torah is to be taught to all men, even sinners, since "many sinners in Israel, after having been brought to the study of the Torah, have become righteous, pious and proper men." This view was opposed by the school of Shammai, who taught that "one should teach only those who are wise, humble, of distinguished ancestry, and rich.[29]

The difference between the attitudes of Hillel and Shammai in matters of formalities and etiquette comes to clear expression in the manner of recitation of the Shema credo.[30] According to the school of Shammai, one should stand while reciting the Shema in the morning, as written in Deut 6:7: ובקומך ("at your rising"), whereas the recital of Shema in the evening should be performed while reclining (בשכבך). In

---

[28] W. Bousset and W. Heitmüller, *Die Schriften des Neuen Testaments*[4], Band 1 (Göttingen, 1929), p. 186.

[29] ARN A 3 (ed. Schechter, pp. 14–15).

[30] Cf. I. Knohl, "A Parasha Concerned with Accepting the Kingdom of Heaven," *Tarbiz* 53 (1983) 11–32.

contrast, the school of Hillel says, "Everyone recites in his own way: one may stand, recline, walk, and even work during the recital."

Shammai stresses the formal act: the ceremony during the recital. Hillel ignores altogether the ceremony and stresses instead the intention of the heart. R. Meir interprets Deut 6:6, "The words which I charge you will be on your heart" (והיו הדברים האלה על לבבך): the words will follow the intention of the heart.

Concerning the objection to formal attire and etiquette, most interesting is the critique of hypocrisy in rabbinic literature. Here we find the same accusations as in Matthew 23. As in the Gospels, so in the rabbinic literature, we read about חנפי תורה, "hypocrites in regard to the Torah," as I show elsewhere.[31]

I shall briefly refer to two accusations: the ostentatious display of formal attire and the arrogant demonstration of piety. First, ostentatious display of formal attire referred to parading in cloaks (ἐν στολαῖς; cf. Mk 12:38 and Lk 20:46). This accusation is quite common in rabbinic literature. In the passage from Sotah 22b, R. Nahman B. Isaac denounces the sin of those who wrap themselves with cloaks in order to show off. Thus ben Azzai said, "It is easier to rule the world than to teach in the presence of two men wrapped in cloaks (העטופים בסדינים)."[32] A somewhat different version is found in the Midrash on Psalm 18:44:

'You have rescued me from strife'—so that I will be saved from being judged before them. Ben-Azzai said: 'It is easier to rule the world than to rule [influence] two men wrapped in robes.'[33]

This refers to the judges who used to wrap themselves in their robes before taking up a case.[34] This kind of admonition is directed toward judges and official leaders who care about their prestigious position, but do not pay attention to the oppressed who need help.

---

[31] Cf. my article, "The Charge of Hypocrisy in Matthew 23 and in Jewish Sources," *Immanuel* 24/25 (1992).

[32] ARN A 25 (end, Schechter ed.). On the attire of rabbinic scholars, cf. S. Krauss, "The Cloak of Rabbinic Scholars" (Hebrew), Jubilee Volume for M. S. Bloch (Budapest, 1905), pp. 83–93.

[33] Midrash on Psalms, p. 81 (Buber ed.).

[34] Buber, Ibid, notes.

It is not the formal attire itself which is condemned here, but the abuse of it. Sometimes, therefore, praise is given to those who, though wrapped in robes, do not flaunt their importance. Commenting on the meaning of Isaiah 23:18, "Rather shall her profits be to those who abide before the Lord," the sage says to R. Ishmael b. R. Jose: "It refers to people like you and your friends and two men wrapped in cloaks like you who do not feel yourselves important.[35]

Second, arrogant demonstrations of piety referred to exaggerated details of ritual attire (Mt 23:5). Whereas Mark and Luke speak of "cloaks," the parallel in Matthew[36] speaks of the wearing[37] of "broad phylacteries" (signifying broad תפלין)[38] and long fringes (ציצית). These details, too, are mentioned in rabbinic criticism of Pharisaic "peacockery." Thus on the verse, "I further observed all the oppression ... behold the tears of the oppressed, with none to comfort them" (Eccl 4:1), Ecclesiastes Rabbah comments:

> R. Benjamin interpreted the verse as referring to hypocrites in regard to Torah [חנפי תורה]. People suppose that they can read the scriptures and the Mishnah, but they cannot. They wrap themselves in cloaks and put phylacteries on their heads. Of them it is written, 'Behold, the tears of the oppressed, with none to comfort them.' It is mine to punish, says God, as it is said: 'Cursed be they who do the work of the Lord deceitfully' (Jer 48:10).

The juxtaposition of demonstration of ceremonial piety on the one hand, and oppression of the underprivileged on the other, is thus clearly reflected in the rabbinic literature, too. Similarly, in interpreting the commandment against taking God's name in vain, Pesiqta Rabbati 22:5 states: "You are not to put on phylacteries and wrap yourself in your [fringed] cloak [טלית] and then go forth and commit transgression."

---

[35] EcclRab 1:9.

[36] For the equation of φυλακτήρια in Matthew with תפלין, see J. H. Tigay, "On the Term Phylacteries (Mt 23:5)," *HTR* 72 (1978) 45–52.

[37] For clarification of חנף in the sense of hypocrisy, cf. J. Barr, "The Background of 'Hypocrisy' in the Gospels," *A Tribute to G. Vermes*, ed. P. R. Davies and R. T. White (Sheffield, 1990), pp. 307–26.

[38] 111b, M. Friedmann ed. (Vienna, 1880).

The responsa of the Gaonic period includes an elaborated version of the intepretation of this commandment. To the ostentatious wearing of phylacteries and the fringed cloak, it adds the accusation of arrogating to oneself the first place at dinner, also mentioned in the Synoptic Gospels (Mt 23:6; Mk 12:39; and Lk 20:46).

> 'Do not take God's name in vain.' R. Simon said: 'If this refers to a false oath, this is superfluous because it has already been said: "you shall not swear falsely by My name" [Lev 19:12]. But what it means here is that you are not to wrap yourself in a cloak, cover yourself with the fringes, transgress the Torah in secrecy, presume to make the blessing first, open [the meal] first or take to portion first.'[39]

Making the phylacteries broad as an ostentatious sign of status, exactly as found in Mt 23:5, is mentioned in the testimony of R. Hai Gaon (10th century C.E.):

> It was the custom in the academy for the students to make their phylacteries small, not higher than a finger ... whereas the great Rabbis would make theirs some three fingers high, so that the students should not be equal to them.[40]

The term "hypocrites in regards to Torah" (חנפי תורה) from Ecclesiastes Rabbah (quoted above) is attested also in Leviticus Rabbah, interpreting Eccl 5:5: "'Do not let your mouth bring you into disfavor.' R. Benjamin interpreted this verse as referring to 'hypocrites in regard to Torah.'"[41]

Third, ostentatious behavior in tithing all kinds of petty things refers to observing minutiae of the Law, such as tithing mint, dill and cumin, while sinning against the great principles of the Law (Mt 23:23; Lk 11:47). This, too, has its parallels in Jewish Pharisaic lore, which accuses Esau of exactly the same behavior pattern. On Gen 25:28, "because hunting was in his mouth" [כי ציד בפיו], the Midrash com-

---

[39] J. Muller, *Teshuvot Ge'onei Mizrah u-Ma'arav* (Berlin, 1888), par. 132; cf. par. 171.
[40] Cf. J. H. Tigay (above, note 36).
[41] Margulies ed., p. 357.

ments: "He [Esau] used to ask his father, 'Does one give tithe from straw? Does one give tithe from salt or water?'"[42] In mouthing such questions, according to this interpretation, Esau "hunted" his father's esteem by pretending to be a very pious man.

Accusations of Pharisaic hypocrisy in the Gospels contain motifs identical with the accusations in the rabbinic sources reflecting Hillel's attitudes. These are: (1) not practicing what one preaches; (2) the wearing of ostentatious cloaks; (3) showing off one's phylacteries and fringes; (4) demanding the first place at dinner; and (5) tithing trivial things. All these are denounced in rabbinic literature, a fact which shows that such a critique was prevalent in Judaism at the time when Christianity began to take shape.

It appears that the critique of Pharisaic hypocrisy was a common phenomenon in Judaism of the first centuries of the common era. When the authors of the Synoptic Gospels wrote about Pharisaic hypocrites, they were using material that was widespread in Pharisaic lore itself, especially those of Hillel's imprint.

---

[42] Cf. GenRab 63:10, p. 693 (ed. Albeck) and note there.

HILLEL AND JESUS:
TWO WAYS OF SELF-AWARENESS

I

THE PRESENT CONTRIBUTION is based upon my two earlier studies about the outstanding personality of Hillel.[1] In the previous articles, I compared Hillel's self-awareness with that of Jesus. Here I want to pursue this approach with greater depth.

Both Hillel and Jesus were allies in an effort to remove all atavistic sediments from their Jewish heritage. They sought to render the Jewish message utterly humane. In fact, Jesus and Hillel are two major representatives of what I have come to call, "the new sensitivity in Judaism."[2] Hillel and his school have had a lasting impact upon early Jewish thought. Moreover, Hillel's influence is strongly felt in many facets of Jesus' theological and ethical teachings.

Some questions, however, remain: To what extent did Jesus rely upon Hillel and his school in developing his halachic positions? What decisions of halachah could Jesus have received from the more rigorous school of Shammai? Here I want to cite only one example of Hillel's clear influence upon the halachic teachings of Jesus.[3]

---

[1] See my two studies which were published in D. Flusser, *Judaism and the Origins of Christianity* (Jerusalem, 1988), "Hillel's Self-Awareness and Jesus," pp. 509–14, and "I am in the Midst of Them (Mt 18:20)," pp. 515–25. See also N. Glatzer, *Hillel the Elder* (New York, 1966); and E. E. Urbach, *The Sages* (Jerusalem, 1979), pp. 576–93.

[2] See D. Flusser, "A New Sensitivity in Judaism," *Judaism*, pp. 469–89.

[3] See D. Flusser, "Did You Ever See a Lion Working as a Porter?" (Hebrew), *The Bible and Jewish History: Studies Dedicated to Jacob Liver* (Tel Aviv, 1971), pp. 330–40. See also a summary of the article in *Immanuel* 3, (Winter 1973–74) 61–64.

It was told of Shammai the Elder: Whenever he found a fine portion he said: This will be for the Sabbath. If later he found a finer one, he put aside the second for the Sabbath, and ate the first; thus, whatever he ate, was meant for the honor of the Sabbath.

But Hillel the Elder had a different way, or all his works were for the sake of Heaven; he used to say: "Blessed be the Lord day by day."[4]

Hillel's behavior was dictated by his view that one shall praise God for the present time, because every day contains its own sanctity, as it is written: "Blessed be the Lord, day by day" (Ps 68:19). Jesus developed the same idea in a well-known and beautiful saying, "O you of little faith! Therefore do not be anxious, saying: 'What shall we eat,' or 'What shall we drink,' or 'What shall we wear?' For ... your heavenly Father knows that you need them all.... Therefore do not be anxious about tomorrow, for tomorrow will be anxious for itself. Let the day's own trouble be sufficient for the day" (Mt 6:25-34; see Lk 12:22-31).

In the Lord's Prayer (Mt 6:11), Jesus drew even a more radical conclusion from the opinion that the present day contains its own blessing. He taught his disciples to pray: "Give us *this day* our daily bread." Even when one prays, one is to pray for the food of the present day only. Luke (11:3) did not understand Jesus' Hillelite paradoxical formulation and rendered the original wording as follows: "Give us each day our daily bread."[5]

Jesus' critique for people of little faith who are anxious about

---

[4] See b.Beṣ 16a, quoting Ps 68:19; see Glatzer, p. 34.

[5] Jerome (commentary on Mt 6:11 and *Tractate on Ps cxxxv*) mentions that he found a variant reading of the text. In the Gospel according to the Hebrews, he found the expression, "Our bread for tomorrow" (in Hebrew, *mahar*, i.e., tomorrow) instead of the words "daily bread." "Therefore the meaning is, 'Our bread for tomorrow,' that is, for the future, 'give us today.'" See W. D. Stroker, *Extracanonical Sayings of Jesus* (Atlanta, 1989), p. 204; cf. P. Vielhauer and G. Strecker in W. Schneemelcher, *Neutestamentliche Apokryphen* I, *Evangelien* (Tübingen, 1987), p. 130, English translation, edited by R. McL. Wilson, *New Testament Apocrypha* (Louisville, 1991), rev. ed., vol. 1, p. 160. Jerome's Jewish-Christian gospel also did not grasp Jesus' Hillelite paradox in Mt 6:11. While it did not alter the wording "this day," the more original reading of "daily bread" was changed to the "bread of tomorrow." According to the Jewish-Christian gospel, one should pray today for tomorrow's food.

tomorrow belongs to a trend within rabbinic Judaism.[6] His words recall the saying of Rabbi Eleazar of Modiin: "If a man has food for the day, but says, 'What shall I eat tomorrow?' such a one is deficient in faith." And Rabbi Eliezer the Great said: "He who has yet bread in his basket, and says, 'What shall I eat tomorrow?' belongs to those of little faith."

In Jesus' saying, the expressions "tomorrow" and "those of little faith" also appear. This whole ideological complex forms a kind of explanation for Hillel's attitude towards the holiness of the present day.[7] It seems impossible to deny that this development somehow weakened Hillel's emphasis upon the actual divine presence in human life and activity. In other rabbinic sayings which are dependent upon the teachings of Hillel, we observe a similar weakening of his "existential" attitude. This peculiar existential element does not appear in Jesus' teaching or in his self-awareness.

On the other hand, one cannot deny that Hillel's stress on the present day in his blessings embraces a firm belief and an unrelenting trust in God. His interpretation of Ps 68:19 ("Blessed be the Lord, day by day") fits Hillel's creative exegesis of another verse in the book of Psalms:

Hillel the Elder used to say: "Bad news shall have no terror for him [i.e., the righteous man], because his heart is steadfast, trusting in the

[6] See my study noted above, "Did You Ever See a Lion Working as a Porter?" pp. 332–34; b.Soṭ 48b; and *Mekhilta d'Rabbi Ismael*, ed. H. S. Horovitz and I. A. Rabin (Jerusalem, 1960), p. 161 (on Ex 16:4). Compare also H. L. Strack and P. Billerbeck, *Kommentar zum Neuen Testament* vol. 1, (Munich, 1922), pp. 438–39; and W. D. Davies and D. C. Allison, *The Gospel According to Saint Matthew* (Edinburgh, 1988), vol. 1, pp. 646 and 654.

[7] For more details see my study, quoted above, "Did You Ever See a Lion Working as a Porter?" This whole complex is connected with a creative exegesis of Ex 16:4. When the miracle of the manna was announced, the people were commanded to go out "and gather each day that day's portion." B. J. Bamberger ("Philo and the Agaddah," *HUCA*, vol. 48 [Cincinnati, 1977], p. 171) aptly compares the saying of R. Eleazar in the Mekhilta with Philo, Leg. All. III, 164. The daily collection is understood as an expression of faith. "He that would fain have all at once," says Philo, "earns for himself lack of hope and trust [ἀπιστία], as well as a great lack of sense. He lacks hope if he expects that now only, but not in the future also, will God shower on him good things; he lacks faith [ἄπιστος], if he has no belief that both in the present and always the good gifts of God are lavishly bestowed on those worthy of them." This passage is important for the Jewishness of Mt 6:28-34.

Lord (Ps 112:7). He who is trusting in the Lord, bad news shall have no terror for him."[8]

According to Hillel, one who trusts in God becomes immune to bad news. It does not matter whether the bad news is true or not. Such a person cannot be "anxious about tomorrow" (Mt 6:34). A righteous person like this surely does not belong to those of little faith. So great is the power which is bestowed upon a person whose "heart is firm, trusting in the Lord." Hence, the character of the saying betrays both a touch of Hillel's unique genius and an affinity to Jesus' ethical message.

Our task here is to compare Jesus' high self-awareness with that of Hillel. However, at this point, I would like to include in the company of these two Jews a famous Greek; namely, Socrates. Socrates has often been compared with Jesus, but, as far as I know, never with Hillel.[9] There is even a parallel between these three men in the field of ethics. All three were outstanding teachers of mutual love. While both Jesus and Hillel belong to the "progressive" stream of Jewish humane ethics, Socrates was probably the founder of Greek humanism.[10]

There is something divine in the personality of all three. It should not be necessary to mention the "charismatic" side, not only of the "Christ of faith" but also of the historical Jesus. I will address this point more fully later. Regarding Hillel, there is a legendary account about a group of wise men who were assembled together in the upper chamber of Gadya's house in Jericho. On that occasion, a heavenly voice announced, "There is one man among you who is deserving that the Divine Spirit rest upon him but this generation is not worthy of it." Then all the eyes were fixed upon Hillel the Elder.[11]

---

[8] We quote the saying of Hillel from the MS Vatican 133. It is found in y.Ber 14b after the end of m.Ber 9:3. In the Babylonian Talmud (b.Ber 60a) there is a fusion between the end of m.Ber 9:3 and the saying of Hillel. The result is an improbable story about Hillel, who appears in the text as a kind of charismatic wonderworker.

[9] One time, Glatzer (p. 50) does mention Socrates in connection with Hillel.

[10] About the cognitive dissonance of Sophocles in connection with the traditional ethics, see A. Dihle, *Die Goldene Regel* (Göttingen, 1962), pp. 56–59. In a famous passage in his *Antigone* (verses 518-525), Sophocles shows how problematic the axiom is which teaches one to love friends and hate the enemy (Dihle, pp. 22–36). This reasoning is indirectly pertinent to the whole passage in Mt 5:43-48. By naming explicitly the tax collectors and the gentiles, Jesus characterizes the axiom as "vulgar ethics." See Hillel's saying in m.Ab 2:5, quoted below.

The evidence that Socrates had a markedly 'mystical' temperament is abundant. Plato tells of his curious 'rapts,' in one of which he stood spellbound for 24 hours in the trenches. The accounts of the philosopher's 'divine sign' tell the same story. This, according to Plato, was a voice often heard by Socrates from childhood. It forbade him to do things but never gave positive encouragement.[12]

In a rabbinic text, we find a story about how Hillel used to bring others near to the Torah:

> He stood in the gate of Jerusalem and met people going to work. He asked, 'How much will you earn to-day?' One said, 'A denarius,' the other said, 'Two denarii.' He asked them, 'What will you do with the money?' They gave answer, 'We will pay for the necessities of life.' Then he said to them, 'Why don't you rather come with me and gain knowledge of the Torah, that you may gain life in this world and life in the world-to-come?' Thus Hillel was wont to do all his days and has brought many under the wings of Heaven.[13]

To what extent should this story be considered authentic? Here it is even possible that the late rabbinic source was influenced by the method of Socrates.[14] No exact parallel to the story is to be found in the Gospels, but one cannot forget what is written in Lk 9:57-62 (Mt 8:19-22) about different people who were going to follow Jesus as disciples.

Is it possible that the story about Hillel's conversation with the passersby demonstrates his Socratic irony? That this attitude really existed in the words of Hillel is evident,[15] and we will cite further examples that illustrate it. I believe that one can speak about a kind of Socratic irony in Jesus' words, or at least in his humor.[16] In any case,

---

[11] See Glatzer, pp. 32-32, t.Soṭ 13:3, b.Soṭ 48b, and A. Büchler, *Types of Jewish-Palestinian Piety* (New York, 1968), p. 8, note 4.

[12] A. E. Taylor, "Socrates," in *Encyclopaedia Britannica* (Chicago, 1974), vol. 16, p. 1003.

[13] Glatzer, pp. 50-51, ARN A 27; B 26, ed. S. Schechter (New York, 1945), pp. 54-55.

[14] See e.g., Plato, *Apology of Socrates*, 29d-30b.

[15] Socratic irony can be seen in two stories about Hillel and his disciples in Leviticus Rabbah, chap. 34 (Glatzer, p. 36).

[16] See especially Jakob Jónsson, *Humour and Irony in the New Testament Illuminated by Parallels in Talmud and Midrash* (Reykjavik, 1965).

Jesus' debate about his authority (Mt 21:23-27) resembles the ironical tone of Socrates in Plato's *Apology*.

The irony of Socrates and of Hillel is a product of tension between their modesty and their self-awareness. A similar paradox can be detected in Jesus' basic character. His humility does not exclude his knowledge of the importance of his own person. At least according to the hymn in Mt 11:28-30,[17] which is the highest expression of Jesus' exalted self-awareness, Jesus says, "Take my yoke upon you and learn from me, for I am meek and lowly in heart."

Hillel's meekness manifested itself in his proverbial patience. His infinite forbearance for gentiles who wanted to become Jews caused them to became proselytes.[18] One of them said to Hillel, "If you can teach me the whole Torah while I stand on one foot, you can make me a Jew." Instead of becoming angry, Hillel summarized the Torah in one sentence by teaching the gentile the so-called Golden Rule.[19]

No less famous is another story about Hillel's patience.[20] Two men made a wager with each other. The one who could make Hillel angry would win the bet and receive four hundred *zuz*. One of the two was sure that he would win the wager. He chose the most inconvenient time to bother Hillel. On Friday afternoon, the time reserved for the preparation of the Sabbath, he came to Hillel's house to test the patience of the master. At regular intervals, he appeared on Hillel's doorstep to pose untimely questions for the wisdom of the sage: "Why are the heads of the Babylonians round?" he asked. Then he persisted with yet

---

[17] Mt 11:25-30 and Lk 10:21-22. The passage about Jesus' meekness (Mt 11:28-30) does not appear in Luke.

[18] Glatzer, pp. 74–76; b.Shab 31a.

[19] See my study quoted above, "A New Sensitivity in Judaism," pp. 478–80, and the additional note, p. 479; and H. W. Kuhn, "Das Liebesgebot Jesus als Tora und als Evangelium," *Vom Urchristentum zu Jesus, für Joachim Gnilka* (Freiburg, 1989), pp. 204–7. Incidentally, the expression "while standing on one foot" should not be taken literally. The same image appears in a poem of Horace, an older contemporary of Hillel; Horace, *Sat* 1.4.10. The verse is quoted as proverbial in A. Otto, *Die Sprichwörter der Römer* (Leipzig, 1890; reprint Hildesheim, 1965), p. 275. See also ARN (above, note 13), B 26, p. 53, where in the same story one reads, "all at once." Horace speaks about a poet who often dictated two hundred verses in an hour, "while he stood on one foot" (*stans pede in uno*).

[20] Glatzer, pp. 38–39; b.Shab 30b; ARN (above, note 11), p. 60 and A. Büchler, *Types* (above, note 10), pp. 10–12.

another question, "Why are the eyes of the Palmyreans bleared?" Finally he pestered Hillel with, "Why are the feet of the Africans wide?"

Hillel never lost his calm. He answered each question with great patience. After the third explanation, the man said to Hillel, "I have many more questions to put before you, but, I am afraid, you might become angry." But Hillel said, "Put forward any questions that you have to ask." Seeing that it was impossible to exhaust the master's patience, he asked him, "Are you the Hillel whom they call the prince of Israel?" "Yes," answered Hillel. The man said, "If that is so, I wish there may not be many like you in Israel." "Why, my son?" asked Hillel. "Because I have lost four hundred *zuz* through you." Said Hillel, "Watch out; Hillel deserves it that you lose four hundred *zuz*, or even eight hundred, and Hillel not be angry."

For our purpose, it was necessary to quote the whole episode about Hillel's patience. The story demonstrates not only Hillel's extreme forbearance, but also that he was not, as it might seem, a Babylonian "orthodox" who was little more than an awkward backwoodsman. On the contrary, Hillel was well-versed in a wide range of subjects which were of current interest for the popular culture of his day.[21]

Even more significant is the message of his final words. Hillel expresses a keen understanding of his own personal value and his high self esteem. Once again the story shows clearly that Hillel's meekness and his self-awareness are linked together. This is also the case with Jesus, although his sublime self-awareness possesses a distinct character of its own. Hillel was conscious of this paradox. He said, "My humiliation is my exaltation, my exaltation is my humiliation—it means, 'Who sits exalted humbles himself to see' (Ps 113:5b)."[22] In this regard, we must quote a parallel from the sectarian scrolls found in the caves at Qumran. The Essene author of the Thanksgiving Scroll (1QH 9.24-25) says about himself, "Thy rebuke of me has turned into gladness and joy

---

[21] Concerning the background of Hillel's words about the heads of the Babylonians, see M. Sachs, *Beiträge zur Sprach- und Altertumsforschung*, (Berlin, 1852), vol. 1, pp. 49–50.

[22] LevRab 1:5, Glatzer, p. 45; D. Flusser, "Hillel's Self-Awareness," *Judaism*, p. 512 and W. Bacher, *Die Agada der Tannaiten* (Strassburg, 1903, reprint, 1965), vol. 1, pp. 5–6.

... and the scorn of mine adversaries was turned into a crown of glory, and my failure into everlasting might."

The meaning of Hillel's saying is, if one humbles himself, in reality one is being elevated, and by exalting himself, one is being humiliated. The hidden theological implication of the apophthegm is expressed by the quotation of Ps 113:5b, where God himself speaks. But even if Hillel believes that the maxim can be applied to all, the saying itself, as many other sayings of Hillel, is at the same time a personal confession. It betrays the very nature of Hillel's proverbial meekness. It is rooted in his free decision to be meek and at the same time in his exalted view of himself.

Moreover it is not superfluous to stress that Hillel speaks about a human decision on a personal level to exalt or to humiliate himself. The saying does not refer to the divine intervention of God, who "makes poor and makes rich, who brings low and also exalts" (1 Sam 2:7). On the other hand, it was almost inevitable that Hillel's words about self-humiliation and exaltation would be interpreted as a truism about God, who humiliates the proud and exalts the humble.[23]

This new meaning already existed before the Gospels,[24] because the saying appears there in the form, "Everyone who exalts himself will be humbled, and the one who humbles himself will be exalted" (Lk 14:11, 18:14; Mt 23:12; cf. Mt 18:4 and Jas 4:10). This does not mean that Jesus was unacquainted with Hillel's dictum in its original wording. It seems certain that Jesus was familiar with Hillel's high self-awareness, because, as we will see, he made use of Hillel's proud sayings about himself in an effort to express his own exalted value.

We want now to discuss a saying of Hillel which has no parallel in the Gospels. The saying became part of a famous passage in Paul's Epistle to the Romans (12:8–13:7). I have shown elsewhere[25] that the

---

[23] See Bacher, *Agada*, p. 6, note 1; H. L. Strack and P. Billerbeck, *Kommentar*, pp. 774, 921; see especially D. Flusser, *Die rabbinischen Gleichnisse und der Gleichniserzähler Jesus* (Bern, 1981), pp. 94–96, 114, notes 95–96.

[24] M. Higger, ed., *The Treatises Derek Erez* (New York, 1935), chapter vii, 36, vol. 1, p. 146 (see the variants).

[25] About the whole passage and its Essene background, see D. Flusser, "A Jewish Source for the Attitude of the Early Church to the State," *Jewish Sources in Early Christianity* (Sifriat Poalim, 1979), pp. 397–401 (Hebrew). Concerning Rom 12:19-21, see my study, "Did You Ever See a Lion Working as a Porter?" pp. 122–24; and K. Stendahl, "Hate, Non-Retaliation and Love," *HTR* 55 (1962) 343–55.

whole passage in Romans originates from an Essene homily. Close parallels to Rom 12:8-13:7 appear especially in the Manual of Discipline from Qumran (1QS 9.21-26; 10.17-20; 11.1-2).

In order to appreciate the similar characteristics of these Essene texts and the passage in the Epistle to the Romans, I would like to point out some of the common wording from pertinent passages in these texts, which illustrates the spirit of their thought. First, however, let me draw attention to the final words of Rom 12:11.

According to the accepted reading, the believers are admonished: "Never flag in zeal, be aglow with the spirit, serve the *Lord.*" In another manuscript witness, however, an important variant reading has καιρῷ instead of κυρίῳ.[26] Such evidence is customarily referred to as *lectio difficilior.*[27] With the discovery of the Dead Sea Scrolls, this more difficult reading is practically certain. The passages in 1QS which parallel Rom 11:8-13:7 contain an exhortation to behave according to the "rule of each time."[28] The parallels appear in the Manual of Discipline (1QS 9.12-14,21-26; 10.16-20; 11.1-2). Here we will cite only some of these texts.

These are the statutes for the instructor for him to walk in them with everyone who lives, according to the rule of each time and the weight of each man, to do the will of God according to all that is revealed from time to time; and to learn all the wisdom which has been discovered in relation to the times and the law of the time.... These are the rules for the instructor in those times with respect to his loving and hating: Everlasting hatred for the men of perdition in spirit of secrecy, leaving to them property and toil of the hands like a slave for his master and meekness before him who lords it over him; to be a man

---

[26] See B. M. Metzger, *A Textual Commentary on the Greek New Testament* (London, 1975), p. 528, and U. Wilckens, *Der Brief an die Römer* (Neukirchen-Vluyn, 1982), vol. 3, p. 21. About the meaning of this reading, see O. Michael, *Der Brief an die Römer* (Göttingen, 1963), p. 304.

[27] See the pertinent definition in V. Taylor, *The Text of the New Testament* (New York, 1961), p. 4, "Of two other or more alternative readings, that one is more likely to be right which most easily accounts for the origin of the others."

[28] The next parallel is the Letter of Ignatius to Polycarp (3:1-2): "Especially for God's sake we must endure everything so that he may put up with us. Be more diligent (σπουδαῖος) than you are. Understand the times." Cf. also Mt 16:2-3; Lk 12:56.

zealous for the ordinance and its time, for the day of vengeance.... In
all that befalls him he will delight with willingness and save the will of
God he will take no pleasure.... I will praise Him when distress is
unlashed and I will sing His praise in the time of His salvation. I will
pay to no man the reward of evil; I will pursue him with goodness; for
with God is the judgment over all that lives and it is He who will
render to man his reward.... I will not grapple with the men of perdition until the Day of Revenge ... [I will] render meekness before the
haughty of spirit and with a broken spirit to the men of authority who
point the finger and speak of iniquity and are zealous for wealth.[29]

If one studies attentively the parallels in the Essene Manual of
Discipline, one can quickly discover the inner connection between the
command to be obedient to the law of the time in Rom 12:11 and the
ethical, political attitude the readers are encouraged to follow in Rom
12:8–13:7.

Now one question needs additional explanation: How did this
saying of Hillel which appears in Rom 12:15 happen to become
included in this "Essene" homily found in the Epistle to the Romans as
if it was an organic part of the entire homily itself? Its form in Paul's
epistle is, "Rejoice with those who rejoice, weep with those who
weep."

In the wording of Hillel, the saying appears in rabbinic literature
in the following text:

> Do not appear naked [among the dressed], neither dressed [among
> the naked].[30]
> Do not appear standing [among those who sit], neither sitting [about
> those who stand].

---

[29] I have followed here partly the translation of A. R. C. Leaney, *The Rule of
Qumran and Its Meaning* (London, 1966). Recently E. Qimron has published the text of
4QS 9.15–10.2 of the Manual of Discipline. Its text is practically identical with that of
1QS (see Qimron, in *Tarbiz* 60 [1991] 436.

[30] See Flusser, *Judaism*, p. XVI, nn. 7–8. Once I believed that the beginning of
the saying was not originally a part of Hillel's words because it is missing in the parallels from the Derek Erez tractate. Now I am less certain that the beginning of Hillel's
saying is a secondary addition because, as we shall see, Hillel regarded taking a bath as
a part of his *Weltanschauung* (LevRab 34; Glatzer, p. 36).

> Do not appear laughing [about those who weep], neither weeping [about those who laugh].
>
> As it is said [Eccl 3:4-5]: "A time to weep and a time to laugh, a time to embrace, and a time to refrain from embracing."[31]

The quotation from Ecclesiastes at the end of the saying elucidates the ethical background of the saying. One is called upon to obey the requirements of the present time and its circumstances. In other words, as it is written in Rom 12:11, one has to "serve the (present) time." Now we understand why a part of Hillel's saying[32] was inserted into the homily in Romans. The insertion probably happened already in the pre-Christian stage of the homily. Another important facet of understanding this development emerges from the comparison of the whole complex of motifs: One becomes aware of the strong links between Paul's epistle, Essene ideology, and Hillel's teachings.

We have quoted already the pertinent passages about the obedience of the Sect to the law of the Time from the Essene Manual of Discipline.[33] Two of these sources—the Essene Manual of Discipline and the homily in the Epistle to the Romans—betray the same ideological background for the well-known Essene doctrine which required

[31] See P. Billerbeck, *Kommentar*, vol. 3, p. 398. For Hillel's saying itself, see t.Ber 2:21 (S. Lieberman, *The Tosefta, Order Zeraim* [New York, 1953], p. 11); see also the commentary in M. Higger, *The Treatises Derek Erez* vol. 1, p. 221; *Masekhtot Zeirot* (Jerusalem reprint, 1950), p. 88; and M. van Loopik, *The Ways of the Sages* (Tübingen, 1991), pp. 120 and 271–72. See also Flusser, *Judaism*, pp. XIV–XV, and p. 522, note 36 there; and Glatzer, *Hillel*, p. 38. It has been suggested that Paul's famous words in 1Cor 9:19-23 were influenced by a Jewish motif as represented by our saying of Hillel (see H. Conzelmann, *Der erste Brief an die Korinther* [Göttingen, 1969], p. 189, esp. notes 19 and 21). This is possible because, as we have seen from Rom 12:15, Paul was certainly acquainted with this idea. On the other hand, Paul's tendency was completely different from what Hillel wanted to say. In adapting himself to the ways of other people, Paul wanted to win them for his gospel message: "For though I am free from all men, I made myself a slave to all, that I might win the more" (1Cor 9:19).

[32] Even if one does not accept the reading "serve the time" in Rom 12:15, it is sure that Rom 12:15 is dependent upon Hillel's saying and not taken from the similar verse in Sir 7:34: "Avoid not those who weep, but mourn with those who mourn." In contrast to Ben Sira, both Hillel and Paul (Rom 12:15) speak about rejoicing.

[33] See also my study quoted above, "A Jewish Source for the Attitude of the Early Church to the State," and D. Flusser, "The Sect of the Judaean Desert and its Beliefs" (Hebrew), *Zion* 19 (1954) 89–103, esp. p. 98; and D. Flusser, "The Social Message from Qumran," *Judaism*, pp. 112–14.

obedience to the governing authorities (see Josephus, *War* 2.140). The similarity between the description of the Essenes in the passage from Josephus and the final words of Paul's "Essene" homily (Rom 13:1-7) has already been recognized.

With the help of the Manual of Discipline from Qumran, one discovers that Essene pacifism and the requirement of obedience to the ruling authorities possess a distinctive character. Perhaps it is permitted to apply two Communist slogans to the Essenes' submissive attitude. The Essenes taught a "militant defeatism"[34] and "peaceful coexistence."[35] These concepts were originally based on an eschatological doctrine of predestination as well as an ideology of hatred. In the beginning, this chiliastic ideology created a longing for an apocalyptic war which would lead to the conquest of the whole world by the Essene Children of Light. This early stage is represented by the War Scroll from Qumran. When this hope failed, a new ideology was developed from the same old presuppositions. The Essenes did not renounce their doctrine of double predestination or their eschatological outlook of divine vengeance upon evildoers. On the other hand, because the *eschaton* lies in the future, it is forbidden to fight with the men of perdition until the Day of Vengeance. This is the secret of Essene pacifistic meekness and their doctrine of submission to the Law of the Time.

I venture that Hillel's emphasis upon pacifism and the urgency to decide here and now was influenced by the Essene requirements to obey the Law of the Time. We have already discussed the saying of Hillel in which he recommends appropriate behavior suitable for the practice of the people in accordance with the proper time and circumstance. As we have seen, the scriptural foundation of this saying is found in Eccl 3:4-5: "A time to weep and a time to laugh," etc. In such a context, appropriate conduct according to the rule of time is explicitly commanded in the Scripture. It is no wonder, then, that a reference to Hillel's saying was inserted in Rom 12:15 within an "Essene" homily (12:11) which teaches the people to "serve the (present) time."

---

[34] This term was coined by Lenin in order to justify the peace treaty between Soviet Russia, Germany, and its allies in the first world war (March 3, 1918).

[35] The term "peaceful coexistence" was used for the first time in 1952 by Stalin in an interview with an American journalist. In 1956, Nikita Khrushchev defined the meaning of this slogan.

On the other hand, one should not forget that neither Hillel nor Jesus accepted the Essene "militant pacifism," which was based upon a doctrine of hatred. This doctrine was decisively opposed to the very nature of these two Jewish teachers. They both preached universal and unconditional love. Their meekness was genuine, without any mental reservation. Unlike Hillel, Jesus did not even teach the doctrine of the Law of the Time, because his understanding of the "timetable" for the divine economy did not permit it.[36] Nevertheless, both Jesus and Hillel acknowledged the urgency to act now without delay. Like Hillel, Jesus stressed that "the harvest is plentiful, but the laborers are few" (Mt 9:37-38; Lk 10:2).

The uniqueness of Hillel's exceptional personality does not exclude the possibility of influence from outside, such as contact with the Essene concept of the Law of the Time, even if this idea took on another meaning within Hillel's philosophy. By its very nature, the idea of the urgency of the present time in the mind of Hillel forms a unity with the force of imminent action and the individual who has decided to act. In modern terms, one can speak about Hillel's "here and now" and his "I and Thou"—where the "I and the Thou" are here interchangeable. Or to use another anachronistic definition: Hillel's call for decision is that of an existentialist.

Here we will not mention all the sayings of Hillel. Rather, we will comment only on those which directly express his self-awareness or which are pertinent to it.[37] We have already quoted one of Hillel's profound personal sayings:[38] "My humiliation is my exaltation, my exaltation is my humiliation—it means: 'Who sits exalted, humbles himself to see' (Ps 113:5f)."

[36] About the messianic timetable of Jesus, see D. Flusser, "Die jüdische Messiaserwartung Jesu," *Das Christentum—eine jüdische Religion* (Munich, 1990), pp. 37–52.

[37] According to m.Ab 2:5, Hillel said, "Do not judge your neighbor until you come into his place." I believe that this is a fruitful conclusion which is based upon the Golden Rule, as quoted by Hillel himself: "What is hateful to you, do not do to your neighbor (b.Shab 31a). Billerbeck (above, note 6), pp. 441–43, connects Hillel's words about the judging of one's neighbor with Mt 7:1 and (and with Lk 6:37): "Judge not, that you be not judged." He cites other rabbinic materials as well. In any case, Hillel's words are far from the idea of divine recompense. In this respect, they are different from all other parallels.

[38] See above, p. 77.

This is not the only example where Hillel quotes a biblical verse in which the speaker in the text is God, but Hillel daringly applies it to himself, a humble human being. Another expression of Hillel's high self-awareness is included in the Sayings of the Fathers 1:14: "If I am not for myself, who is for me? And when I am for myself only, what am I? And if not now, when?" Here he stresses both the task of the person and the urgency of decision in the present moment. The saying of Hillel resembles the first part of Jesus' very personal words: "He who is not with me is against me, and who does not gather with me, scatters" (Mt 12:30; Lk 11:23). This similarity is not accidental, because the second half of Jesus' logion is a variant of another sentence uttered by Hillel.[39] This parallel saying forms a part of the chain of three phrases of Hillel:

> "It is time to act for the Lord; they have broken thy law" (Ps 119:126). You have to read: "they have broken thy law"—it is time to act for the Lord. And so says Hillel: "In a time when men scatter, gather![40] When there is not demand, buy then! In the place [where] there is no man, be there[41] a man!"[42]

Like his interpretation of Ps 112:7,[43] here also Hillel reverses the two halves of a biblical verse (Ps 119:126). With this change, he stresses the urgent need of uncommon personal action. The three short sentences work as shocks. In the rabbinic parallels to the saying, the first of them occurs in an expanded form: "In the time when men gather, scatter; in the time when men scatter, gather." While the longer form of the saying possesses profound meaning and can be interpreted with revealing content, I believe this expanded form was created for the sake of contrast and symmetry. The simpler form of the saying in *Sifre Zutta* fits the context far better, both in Hillel's exegesis of Ps 119:126 and in the two following sentences.

---

[39] See Billerbeck, *Kommentar*, pp. 635–36, and my study about Hillel's self-awareness, in Flusser, *Judaism*, pp. 510–11.

[40] For this reading, see Flusser, *Judaism*, p. 510, note 3.

[41] See the *apparatus criticus* in Sifre Zutta. The saying appears also in m.Ab 2:6.

[42] Sifre Zutta, *Pinchas*, ed. H. S. Horovitz (Leipzig, 1917; Jerusalem reprint, 1966), pp. 316–17.

[43] In y.Ber 14b. See above, note 8.

The whole unit is a reaction against a crisis in the study of the law. The law has become cheap and this is the best occasion to "buy" it. "In the place where there is no man, be there a man!" And in the time when the law is being broken (i.e., "scattered"), then "gather" it. The time is right to collect the oral tradition of the law and develop it. In the expanded form of the saying, these terms acquired a new meaning which does not suit their significance in the whole unit in *Sifre*.[44] It therefore seems doubtful that the longer form of the saying could be original.

I confess that the affinity between Hillel's saying and Jesus' words in Mt 12:30 and Lk 11:23 not only helped me to find the original version of Hillel's words in *Sifre Zutta*, but also paved the way for me to discover Hillel's high self-awareness. Then I was able to recognize that the original form of Hillel's saying, "In the time when men scatter, gather!" is close to "He who does not gather with me scatters" in Mt 12:30 (and Lk 11:23). Not only is there a similarity between the high self-awareness of Jesus and that of Hillel, Jesus also adopts Hillel's saying and changes it for his own use. These changes betray the distinctions between the two men: their basic character differences and aims.

The most significant change in the words of Jesus comes in the phrase "*with me.*" Hillel's high self-awareness was far removed from the conviction that only he was destined to stop the crisis and to create a new reality. Hillel spoke about himself and sometimes he appealed to the other ("I" *or* "Thou"). Jesus also called for action, but he was sure that only he was elected to perform this task. A movement of "revival" had begun in Israel. This revival is realized in the kingdom of heaven on earth. But now this movement must be centered around Jesus' person. Separate initiatives, independent from Jesus, would not gather but scatter. Here is yet another difference between Jesus and Hillel: while Hillel taught about the gathering of the increasing bulk of oral tradition pertaining to the Law, Jesus was concerned about the gathering of people who would respond to his call.[45]

The two most daring sayings of Hillel were pronounced, according to some sources,[46] during the Feast of Tabernacles:

---

[44] The enlarged form of the saying is duly discussed in t.Ber 6:24.

[45] On the meaning of "gathering" in the words of Jesus, see also Mt 23:37 (and Lk 13:34) and Jn 11:52.

[46] This is the case in b.Suk 53a and y.Suk 55b (both sayings). But see also

If I am here, all is here; if I am not here, what [or: who][47] is here? To the place that my heart loves, there my feet lead me; if you will come in my house, I will come in your house, but if you will not come in my house, I will not come in your house, as it is said (Ex 20:24): "In every place where I cause my name to be remembered I will come to you and bless you."

The first saying appears in the sources[48] also in an alternative form. In that version the logion is connected with the Feast of Tabernacles. On the occasion of the festival, Hillel was in the Temple and there declared: "If we are here, what [or: who] is here; if we are not here what [or: who] is here?" In both sources, the passage and the force of its argument are similar. The main point of the teaching stresses that, "If we are here (worshiping) what (or: who) is here?" Since God does not need human praises, "if we are not here, what (or: who) is here?"—because he does want the praises of human beings.[49]

While I am not convinced that these conclusions as transmitted represent Hillel's own exact words, it is plausible that they reflect more or less his thought. As a whole, the paradoxical saying itself fits admirably the character of Hillel. However, it is not probable that Hillel would have said "we" instead of "I," which is his more characteristic way of speaking. The original form must have been adapted to the description of the people worshiping in the Temple during the Feast of Tabernacles.

If we repeat Hillel's saying in its singular form, "If I am here *what* is here ...," then the second half of the logion is identical with its variant, "If I am here, *all* is here; if I am not here, what (or: who) is here?"[50] Even so, it is incredible that one of these two sayings was said

---

t.Suk 4:3 (only in regard to the second saying). In the other sources, no indication is given concerning what occasion Hillel uttered these sayings: ARN (above n. 11), p. 55, in both versions (the second saying before the first); Mekhilta (above, note 6), p. 234, on Ex 20:24, in the name of Rabbi Eliezer b. Jacob (the second saying).

[47] The Aramaic word *man* has both meanings; see M. Jastrow, *Dictionary* (New York, 1950), p. 727.

[48] See y.Suk 55b and ARN, p. 55, ARN B 27.

[49] In both sources one reads: "the praises of Israel."

[50] This form also appears in two sources: b.Suk 53a and ARN (above, note 11) A, p. 55.

by Hillel himself and the other was created only later on the basis of the first. Both sayings clearly have their own merits. The saying just now quoted is more daring than its partner. It is an extreme expression of the cosmic value of the human personality. The individual, as represented by Hillel himself, is, in a manner of speaking, the whole universe. All who know how the "historical" Jesus used to speak, will agree that he would not refer to himself in a similar way: he had other ways to express his high self-awareness. After the Cross the atmosphere changed.

It would be too easy to compare this saying of the Jewish sage with the cosmic extra-canonical Christ, as represented by a logion in an apocryphal Gospel: "Jesus said: I am the light which is over them all, I am the All. The All came forth from me, and the All has extended to me. Split a (piece of) wood; and I am there. Lift up the stone, and you will find me there."[51] Such a comparison, however, would be misleading. The external similarity between the apocryphal logion of Jesus and Hillel's astonishing saying is caused by the godlike nature of the supernatural Christ on the one hand, and Hillel's understanding that every single individual is created in the image of God on the other. Analysis of the two parallel sayings of Hillel shows that both teach his views concerning the mutual ties between the individual and society. This relationship between a person and the community appears in his famous declaration: "If I am not for myself, who is for me? And when I am for myself only, what am I?[52] And if not now, when?" (m.Ab 1:14).

At this juncture, I want to return to the other saying of Hillel, which we quoted earlier:[53]

To the place that my heart loves, there my feet lead me; if you will come in my house, I will come in your house, but if you will not come in my house, I will not come in your house, as it is said (Ex 20:24): "In every place where I proclaim my name[54] I will come to you and bless you."

---

[51] See GThom 77 and other extra-canonical parallels in W. D. Stroker, *Extracanonical*, noted above, p. 177; cf. also the quotations from Epiphanius, Ibid., pp. 177-78.

[52] Hillel also said, "Do not separate yourself from the community" (m.Ab 2:4).

[53] See above, note 46.

[54] Or: "cause my name to be remembered." In this biblical verse there is an

This saying is undoubtedly one of the more enigmatic words of Hillel. The main problem to be solved is evident. In the context of the Scripture, God is speaking in Ex 20:24. In the saying of Hillel, however, one must understand who the speaker is and to whom he addresses his invitation. There is no question that the speaker is Hillel himself and not God. We have already seen that Hillel does not hesitate to apply to himself biblical verses in which God speaks.[55] There is no evidence that Jesus used the same stratagem. Jesus did not apply Old Testament quotations of God's words to himself in order to express his unique ties with his heavenly Father. Hillel did not shrink from such an act. On the other hand, neither Hillel nor another Jewish sage would speak in the name of God.[56] Such an interpretation of Hillel's saying would be unrealistic.

We have demonstrated that God is not speaking in this saying, but rather Hillel himself. Hence the house to which people are invited to come must be the house of Hillel, or figuratively speaking, the sage's own sphere. While this much is clear, it is more difficult to resolve the question concerning whom Hillel invites: Does he ask God or his fellow human beings to enter his sphere? In any case, the saying is related to daily life. It begins with a proverb which says: "I go to the place where I like to go."

The proverb is followed by a rule of social behavior: "I visit your home only after you have visited me." Then, as scriptural proof, Hillel daringly adds a word which is said by God! If Hillel addresses God with his invitation, then the foreign house is in the sphere of God, the

---

important variant, namely "*You* proclaim" instead of the "*I* proclaim." The variant occurs in the Syriac translation, in the Targ. Jer., in Targum Neofiti, in Ms. A of the Samaritan Targum (see S. Tal, *The Samaritan Targum of the Pentateuch*, (part 1 [Tel Aviv, 1980], p. 307), as well as in some midrashim. See the work of S. Safrai in the present volume, notes 39 and 40. It is possible that Hillel used Ex 20:20[24] with this variant or interpreted the verse in this way.

[55] See also Bacher, *Agada*, p. 5, note 6.

[56] According to the synoptic Gospels, it is possible that Jesus did indeed speak once in God's name without an introductory formula. This may be the case in Mt 23:34: "Therefore I send you prophets." There is a parallel to this saying in Jub 1:12, where the speaker is God. Luke felt the anomaly (11:49). To avoid misunderstanding, he put an introductory formula before God's saying: "Therefore also the Wisdom of God said ..." In this case, Jesus did not speak as a Jewish sage, but rather as an apocalyptic prophet. See also below, note 84.

Temple, or some other place of worship or learning. This would evidently mean that if God will not enter our sphere, we will not enter his sphere. In such an unlikely case, it is difficult to escape the conclusion that Hillel was putting some kind of ultimatum before God.

Even in a less blasphemous form, the saying would mean: "If You will approach me, I will be able to approach You, but if You will not approach me, I will not be able to approach You." Such reasoning is unthinkable for a Jew as well as a non-Jew from this period of antiquity. Nor does such an interpretation fit the content of the proverbial introduction. Moreover, if the saying was spoken directly to God, it would be the only occasion in which Hillel addresses God in this way.

In conclusion, the best solution is to assume that here, as in the other sayings, we find Hillel's typical "I and Thou" construction, namely, the confrontation between two human beings. The two individuals described in the saying are not, of course, specific persons. As always in Hillel's teachings, the *dramatis personae* represent people in general. He wants each person to feel the force of his message.

To clarify the background of Hillel's words, we quote a saying from a collection of Zoroastrian apophthegms:

> They held this too: It is necessary to keep the door open to people. For when a man does not keep the door open to people, people do not come to his house. When people do not come to someone's house, the gods do not come in his house. When the gods do not come to someone's house, no fortune adheres to him. For people are after bread, gods are after people, and fortune follows the gods.[57]

The similarity between the Persian text and a saying of a Jewish sage is clearly not fortuitous. This is not the only instance where it is permitted to suppose influence from Persian religion and thought upon Judaism. The Persian saying expresses the idea that it is necessary to keep one's house open to people in order that the gods may enter in as well. The Persian sage does not refer to a place of worship or a temple, but to an ordinary house. Consequently, the Persian tradition supports

---

[57] *The Wisdom of the Sasanian Sages* (Denkard VI), translated by S. Shaked, *Persian Heritage Series*, no. 34 (Boulder, Col., 1979), No. 187 (p. 73); a parallel saying in E 10 (p. 191). See Flusser, *Judaism*, pp. 519–20.

our interpretation of Hillel's saying. Like the Zoroastrian teaching, Hillel invites the people to come into his own house.

We have also argued that it is difficult to believe that Hillel's partner in his saying is not a human being but God. Hence as a result of our study, the deeper meaning of Hillel's words has been made clearer: "I can act freely according to my inclination; if you are prepared to enter into my sphere, I will be prone to enter your sphere, but if you do not want to adapt yourself to me, I am not prepared to help you."

Our explanation of the saying does not eliminate all the difficulties, but it is far more plausible than any other solution. According to our understanding, Hillel is here more stubborn in his relationship with others than in his other sayings. But the same Hillel used to say, "One who does not add, ends,[58] and one who does not learn, deserves killing."[59] He also said, "In a place where there is no man, be there a man!"[60] This is a peculiar kind of meekness. Hillel's patience does not know any complacent compromise. Thus it is possible that he asked others to go half way towards him, which would enable him to meet them the rest of the way.

To throw more light on Hillel's words, it is worthwhile to compare them to Jesus' instructions to his disciples when he sent them out to proclaim the kingdom of heaven in Mt 20:12-14:

> As you enter the house, salute it. And if the house is worthy, let your peace come upon it; but if it is not worthy, let your peace return to you. And if any one will not receive you or listen to your words shake off the dust from your feet as you leave that house or town.

The house of Hillel's saying is more figurative and has a less literal meaning, but the paradox of the offer and acceptance (or nonacceptance) of the teaching is similar.[61]

We have tried to describe Hillel's high self-awareness as a unity between meekness and inner strength. He was sure that he was obliged not only to develop his proverbial patience, but also to open the way for

---

[58] I.e., his learning ends.
[59] m.Ab 1:13.
[60] See above, notes 39 and 40.
[61] See Flusser, *Judaism*, p. 520.

his natural boldness. He was convinced that it was a time of crisis and that immediate decision was urgent. So a right man in a right place was badly needed.

For our purpose it is important to repeat that Hillel's paradigmatic sayings appear either in the second person, so as to demand action from others, or in the first person. In the latter sayings, his own person is exemplary for all other people. In this way, Hillel shares the characteristic mistake of many a great man like him. A great individual who is at the same time humble, may think that any human being is able to perform on his same level of achievement, even though he himself is a gifted genius in comparison to others. In his open-mindedness towards others, Hillel resembles Socrates. Even his paradoxes have a pedagogical purpose. In any case, Hillel's opinion about human nature was closer to Socrates' than Jesus', who was less optimistic about it.

We have tried to describe the historical and psychological impulses which have molded Hillel's uncommon teachings. Did he have any philosophical justification for his high appreciation of human dignity? The following story illustrates the theological background of Hillel's opinion abut the dignity of man.

> Once when Hillel was taking leave of his disciples, they said to him: "Master, whither are you going?" He replied: "To do a pious duty." They said: "What is the pious duty which Hillel will do?" He replied: "To take a bath." They said: "Is that a pious duty?" He replied: "Yes. If the man appointed to the duty of securing and rinsing the statues of the king set up in the theaters and circuses is for that paid by maintenance, and, in addition, he is one of the government officials—how much more I,[62] who have been created in the divine image and likeness, have a duty to care for my body."[63]

The biblical assumption that *every* individual is created in the image of God is fundamental for Hillel's view concerning humans as individuals. The concept that the human is godlike is an important one

[62] "I" fits the context better than "we." See the *apparatus criticus* in Margoulies' edition.
[63] LevRab 34:3, ed. M. Margoulies (Jerusalem, 1958), p. 776; Glatzer (above, note 1), p. 36; Flusser, *Judaism*, p. 513, and Büchler, *Types*, p. 19.

in the doctrines of Hillel's followers, especially in the thought of Rabban Yoḥanan ben Zakkai and Rabbi Akiba. This is one of the roots of the "anthropocentric theocentrism" and the humanistic approach of the School of Hillel. Hillel could cherish his exalted self-awareness because it fit his humanistic theology.

Jesus not only embraced wholeheartedly Hillel's humane approach to other human beings, he also, in speaking about himself, incorporated in his message at least two of Hillel's sayings.[64] According to Mt 18:20, Jesus said: "Where two or three are gathered in my name, there I am in the midst of them." In an earlier study, I tried to explain why I am convinced that these are really the words of the "historical" Jesus. Evidently Jesus wanted to say that he is present among even the smallest number of people who meet together to deal with this message or his teaching. We have shown that there are two parallels among Hillel's sayings. The first parallel is: "If you will come in my house, I will come in your house, but if you will not come in my house, I will not come in your house." The other saying of Hillel is even more daring: "If I am here, all is here; if I am not here, what is here?" In this case, there is no essential difference between the content and tendency of the two sayings of Hillel and the words of Jesus in Mt 18:20. We have already argued[65] that the second saying of Hillel is so extremely daring that Jesus would not have expressed his self-awareness in such a way.

The second saying of Jesus which reflects Hillel's words is found in Mt 12:30 (and Lk 11:23): "He who is not with me, is against me and he who does not gather with me scatters." A parallel to the first part of the logion appears in Hillel's words from m.Ab 1:14: "If I am not for myself, who is for me?" As noted earlier, a close parallel to the second part of Jesus' words occurs in Hillel's saying: "In a time when men scatter, gather!"

Here we notice a basic difference between the self-awareness of Jesus and that of Hillel. Jesus makes an addition to the dictum of Hillel. Jesus mentions himself when he speaks about the gathering "*with me*." The "I" of Jesus is by no means identical with the "I" of Hillel. Hillel's "I" is interchangeable with his "Thou," and according to his theology

---

[64] See above, notes 42–45, 50; and D. Flusser, "I am in the Midst of Them," *Judaism*, pp. 515–25.

[65] See above, note 51.

of the godlikeness of each human being, it can be applied to everyone of us, while the "I" of Jesus expresses his own personal self-awareness and belongs exclusively to him. Therefore Jesus' sayings about himself lack the strong existential aspect of many of the important sayings by Hillel.

II

Before describing the differences between the aims of Hillel and Jesus, I am obliged to correct some common opinions about Jesus which are more or less independent from his sublime self-awareness. Does a free and well-informed research of the sources really confirm that Jesus was a "marginal Jew"?[66] I am not obliged to explain here the vested interests which foster this error. Can we take the "Jews" seriously in Jn 7:5, when they say about Jesus: "How does this fellow know Scripture when he has not studied?"

On one occasion, a serious scholar[67] was truly astonished when I said to him that Jesus' rabbinic training was superior to that of Paul. Reading Jesus' sayings without a thorough knowledge of Jewish, and especially of rabbinic sources, leads to wrong impressions. The wording is mostly very simple. Underneath the simple words of Jesus, however, runs another complex current of thought which is connected to the highest level of academic training. Thus, the unlearned crowd was able to enjoy the profound simplicity of Jesus on one level, while the intelligentsia of his day grasped the deeper meaning of his teachings, which were embedded in his manifold hints on a higher level. Jesus' distinctive manner of teaching was sophisticated.

Today this hidden texture of Jesus' preaching causes difficulties of understanding which did not exist during his day, because even a modern well-informed reader cannot catch all the associations which Jesus wanted to evoke in the heart of his hearers. Here it is necessary to

---

[66] J. P. Meier, *A Marginal Jew: Rethinking the Historical Jesus*. The Anchor Bible Reference Library (New York, 1991).

[67] R. Riesner, *Jesus als Lehrer*, WUNT, 2d series 7 (Tübingen, 1981). On the rabbinic learning in Galilee in the time of Jesus, see especially S. Safrai, "The Jewish Cultural Nature of Galilee in the First Century," in *The New Testament and Christian Jewish Dialogue, Studies in Honor of David Flusser, Immanuel*, 24/25 (Jerusalem, 1990), pp. 147–86.

discuss this common error about Jesus' erudition. The misleading view that the basic difference between "this hill-town boy from Lower Galilee"[68] and an outstanding Jewish sage is related to their education must be avoided. The difference between them is found in other areas.

Hillel was a leading figure among the Jewish sages. One may assume that he died in approximately 10 C.E. If so, it is possible that when Jesus was twelve years old, he met Hillel among the sages in the Temple area. The boy was sitting in the middle of the wise teachers of the law, listening to them and posing clever questions (Lk 2:46-47). It is true that the high self-awareness of Hillel has no parallel among other rabbinic scholars of his time. Jesus perhaps made use of Hillel's sayings when he was speaking about his own task, even if this task was by no means identical with that of Hillel. Both Jesus and Hillel wanted to initiate a radical change in their world, and this strong tendency is reflected in their proud sayings and acts. Their self-confidence, which was connected to their meekness, was an ideal premise for their enterprises. Both believed that their action was of vital importance for the whole future and that their personal initiative was a critical necessity. They sensed the urgency of the moment which demanded action without delay. For both of them, the "here and now" was crucial.

We have already quoted Hillel's sayings about the urgency of decision. In regard to Jesus, it is well-known how he called others to follow him immediately. His followers left all their possessions and their families in order to become his disciples. It is difficult to imagine that Hillel would have gained new disciples by using similar methods. While Jesus needed to create a movement in the midst of Israel, Hillel aspired to initiate a change which directly impacted the whole Jewish people.

Moreover, while Hillel was keenly conscious of his own personal value, he did not limit this view to himself alone, but stressed high esteem for human dignity in all people. Hillel viewed others in the same way that he viewed himself. Jesus on the other hand, recognized the unique importance of his own person and believed that he himself was indispensable for the realization of his plan. To use modern terminology: Hillel was *ante litteram* an existential philosopher, while Jesus was an incarnation of a Jewish "messianic" movement. On the other hand, it

[68] Meier, *Marginal*, p. 277.

is characteristic of Hillel that no saying about eschatology is known to have come from him. Evidently eschatology was not a major problem for Hillel.

The messianic scheme of Jesus is far from being an acute eschatology (*Näherwartung*), as it is often supposed.[69] On the contrary, Jesus decisively opposed any kind of apocalyptic chiliasm, even that of the Essenes, with which he was confronted by his meeting with John the Baptist. John announced, "Already the axe is laid to the roots of the trees; and every tree that does not produce good fruit is cut down and thrown in the fire" (Mt 3:10; Lk 3:9). John preached about the coming one, "His winnowing fork is in his hand, and he will clear his threshing floor and gather his wheat into the granary, but the chaff he will burn with a fire that never goes out" (Mt 3:12; Lk 3:17).

Jesus did not adhere to such a radical solution. His view was, "In gathering it [the weeds] you might pull up the wheat at the same time. Let them both grow together till harvest; and at the harvest time ... gather the weeds first, and tie it in bundles for burning; then collect the wheat into my barn" (Mt 13:30). In the eyes of Jesus, the present time is indeed different from the past because it belongs to a particular stage within the process of salvation. While this is true, the present is not viewed as the end times.[70]

Jesus introduced and modified the rabbinic concept of the kingdom of heaven, which was foreign to the eschatology of the Essenes and John the Baptist. John's importance for the history of salvation, however, was not denied by Jesus. On the contrary, Jesus said,

I tell you the truth, among those born of woman, there has not risen anyone greater than John the Baptist; yet he who is least in the kingdom of heaven is greater than he. From the days of John the Baptist until now, the kingdom of heaven has been forcefully advancing, and forceful men lay hold of it. (Mt 11:11-12)

John the Baptist marked the end of the preceding "biblical" era because "all the Prophets prophesied until John" (Mt 11:13). The pre-

[69] See my study, "Die jüdische Messiaserwartung Jesu."
[70] See the preceding note and "Jubelruf und selige Augenzeugen" in Flusser, *Gleichnisse*, pp. 265-81.

sent time is the era of the kingdom of heaven. Although John broke open the way for the kingdom of heaven, he himself did not belong to the new period, but rather fulfilled the role of Elijah as the precursor of the messiah.

The epochs of human history began with the biblical era before the time of John the Baptist. It led into the ministry of Jesus himself and the present period of the kingdom of heaven. This understanding of the division of human history forms the foundation for a true understanding of Jesus' "timetable of salvation." On the other hand, Jesus never connected the future coming of the Son of Man with a fixed or final stage in the spreading of the kingdom of heaven.[71] "For as the lightning flashes and lights up the sky from one side to the other, so will the Son of Man be in his day" (Lk 17:24 and Mt 24:37).[72]

Thus, Jesus' made a threefold division of the history of salvation. The first was the "biblical" period, which climaxed with the career of John the Baptist. The second period began with his own ministry, in which the kingdom of heaven is experienced as a present force when the good seed grows together with the weeds. The third period will be inaugurated with the coming of the Son of Man and the Last Judgment at a future time, which is unknown to anyone.[73] According to this scheme, we still live in the Middle Ages. The whole threefold scheme is not dissimilar to that of the early ecclesiastical sources in which the second era is a period of transition between the first and the second coming of Christ.[74]

This digression was indispensable in order to understand better what Jesus thought about his central task in history. His career was not

---

[71] See the important study of P. Vielhauer, "Gottesreich und Menschensohn in der Verkündigung Jesu" in *Aufsätze zum Neuen Testament* (Munich, 1965), pp. 55–91. I do not accept all the conclusions of the study. The author rightly points out on page 58 that in the synoptic sayings about the Son of Man, the kingdom of heaven is never mentioned. He is also correct when he says (p. 87) that in the rabbinic literature there is no organic connection between the kingdom of heaven and the concept of the messiah.

[72] Cf. Mk 13:32; Mt 24:36; and Acts 1:7. These sayings express the opinion of Jesus, although I am not sure that they are authentic.

[73] The vicarious offering on the cross does not signify a turning point in Jesus' eschatological scheme. In the meantime, see my "Christianity," in *Contemporary Jewish Religious Thought*, ed. A. A. Cohan and P. Mendes-Flohr (New York, 1988), pp. 62–63; and my "The Last Supper and the Essenes" in Flusser, *Judaism*, pp. 203–4.

[74] See, e.g., F. Graus, in K. J. Ploetz, *Grosse Weltgeschichte* (Darmstadt, 1986), p. 319.

confined to his earthly ministry, but he had a role to play in the eschatological future, as well. If I am correct, already the "historical" Jesus believed that at the end of time, he himself would appear as the eschatological divine judge, the coming Son of Man.[75] Such hopes of Jesus betray a self-awareness which was higher than modern scholars often suppose. One also sees this aspect of Jesus' personality when one takes seriously his authentic sayings concerning his task during his lifetime.

We have already observed[76] how Jesus applied two sayings of Hillel to himself (Mt 12:30 and Lk 11:23). In discussing this logion again at this point, I will focus on its broader setting in the Gospels. The saying is part of Jesus' answer to the accusation that he casts out demons by Beelzebul, the prince of the demons. He said, "If it is by the finger of God that I cast out demons, then the kingdom of God has come upon you" (Lk 11:20; cf. Mt 11:28).

The words "the finger of God" hint to Ex 8:15, where they describe one of the miraculous signs which preceded the redemption of Israel from Egypt. In the time of Jesus, a common Jewish opinion held that the messianic redemption will parallel the redemption of Israel from the Egyptian yoke. This idea is behind Jesus' words. When he casts out demons, he sees "the finger of God" and it is a messianic sign showing that "the kingdom of God has" already "come upon you." Thus the exorcisms of Jesus are a divine sign showing that the new era of the kingdom of heaven is already here.

In the metaphor which Jesus uses concerning the "strong man" who is overpowered by one who is stronger (Lk 11:21-22), Jesus is surely making his own indirect confession that he himself is the Redeemer.[77] Jesus is the stronger one who, by his exorcisms, frees

---

[75] See D. Flusser, "Jesus and the Sign of the Son of Man" in *Judaism*, pp. 526–34; and "Jewish Messianic Figures in Primitive Christianity" (Hebrew), *Messianism and Eschatology*, ed. Z. Baras (Jerusalem, 1983), pp. 103–34; esp. pp. 105–13, 115.

[76] See above, notes 39–41.

[77] We want now to quote the whole messianic metaphor in Lk 11:21-22: "When a strong man, fully armed, guards his own palace, his goods are in place. But when one stronger than he assails him and overcomes him, he takes away his armor in which he trusted, and divides his spoil." Mark (3:28) missed the "messianic secret" of the saying, and Matthew (12:29) follows Mark closely.

In a much earlier examination of the text, Alfred Plummer compared the saying with Isa 53:12 (*Gospel According to St. Luke*, ICC [Edinburgh, 1901], p. 303). In Isaiah, it is written that the Servant "shall divide the spoil with the strong." Already the

people from the sway of the strong one—the devil. After this hidden unveiling of his exalted task in the divine economy, Jesus quotes Hillel's words and adapts them for his own purposes: "He who is not with me is against me, and he who does not gather with me scatters" (Lk 11:23; Mt 12:30).[78] As we have seen, the "I" in both parts of the saying belongs exclusively to Jesus himself. Only he (and his adherents) is invested with the task to promote the kingdom of heaven. All who do not collaborate with him, virtually harm Jesus' activity, because instead of gathering *with him*, they scatter.

The lofty self-awareness of Jesus becomes evident from his way of speaking about himself.[79] One should not forget that even when speaking about God, Jesus made a distinction between himself and others. When addressing others and their relationship to God, Jesus would speak about "*your* Father," but he expressed his own specific connection with God by speaking about "*my* Father." He never referred to "our Father," except at the beginning of the Lord's prayer (Mt 6:9),

---

Greek translation interpreted the Hebrew as meaning that the Servant "shall divide the spoil *of* the strong." This interpretation of Isa 53:12 was not restricted to Hellenistic Judaism, because it is attested in the Aramaic Targum of the verse. The paraphrase there ("the riches of strong cities he shall divide as spoil") is based upon the assumption that the Servant "shall divide the spoil *of* the strong." The Aramaic paraphrase in the Targum shows that this interpretation of Isa 53:12 was known in the homeland of Jesus. He alludes to this tradition in Lk 11:21-22 and identifies himself with the Redeemer of Isa 53 (or at least with the person described in Isa 53:12). He interprets the "strong ones" of the biblical verse as singular: the strong one is now the devil, whose spoil is divided by the stronger one, i.e., Jesus.

It cannot be denied that such a hint regarding the exalted task of the speaker came from Jesus himself. The simple folk understood the saying in Lk 11:21-22 as a mere metaphoric illustration, while the learned bystanders who caught the dramatic hint of Isa 53:12, were obliged to ask themselves, "Who is the man Jesus?"

[78] This authentic saying stands in a certain tension with Lk 9:49-50 (and Mk 9:38-41): "He that is not against you is for you."

[79] Concerning some of the probable causes which explain why Jesus used the third person when he spoke about the Son of Man and the messiah, see Flusser, *Judaism*, pp. 93–98, and my Hebrew study quoted above, note 75, especially pp. 113–16. While Jesus spoke in the third person when he referred to the coming Savior, he implied nonetheless that he himself was the messiah. The main reason for using the third person relates to his sense that he had not yet fulfilled his messianic duty. From a strictly theological point of view, no man can be defined as messiah until he has accomplished fully the task of the anointed. So until the present, there can exist only messianic pretenders.

when he was teaching his followers how to pray, beginning with the words, "Our Father who art in heaven."[80] Jesus' personal unity with his heavenly Father evidently was based upon his own decisive experience. All his other attributes and activities were derived from this overwhelming feeling, probably including even his messianic consciousness.[81]

The strongest expression of this feeling of sonship appears in the short hymn in which Jesus speaks about his special relationship to God (Lk 10:21-22 and Mt 11:25-27):

> I thank thee, Father, Lord of heaven and earth, that thou hast hidden these things from the wise and understanding and revealed them to the simple; yea, Father, for such was thy gracious will. All things have been delivered to me by my Father, and no one knows who the son is except the father, or who the father is except the son and anyone to whom the son chooses to reveal him.

I have already analyzed this poetry of Jesus in another work.[82] Here only a few remarks will suffice. Until the discovery of the Dead Sea Scrolls, any real parallel for the literary *Gattung* of the hymn of Jesus was unknown. Now it is clear that this poetic form belongs to a type of Essene hymn contained in the Thanksgiving Scroll. The hymn of Jesus is similar in content, composed in the same free rhythm, and begins with the same formula ("I thank Thee") as do the majority of the thanksgiving hymns from Qumran. In addition, the Essene author of the hymns displays his own central task as an apocalyptic revealer of the mysteries of God, which were given primarily for the benefit of the simple ones. In contrast to Jesus, however, the composer of the Thanksgiving Scroll from Qumran never describes his peculiar connection with

---

[80] There are many reasons why this difference in Jesus' address to the heavenly Father cannot be considered a later dogmatic invention of the church. For instance, it surely would not have caused serious difficulties for Christian readers if Jesus would have spoken about *our* common Father. The "*my* Father" in his sayings therefore is of great significance.

[81] About Jesus as messiah, see below, note 86 (end), and especially the important contribution of M. Hengel, "Jesus der Messias Israels: zum Streit über das 'messianische Sendungsbewußtsein,'" in *Jesu: Messiah und Christos* (Tübingen, 1992), pp. 155–76.

[82] See Flusser, *Gleichnisse*, pp. 265–69 and 279–80.

God as that of a son to his father. In his proud saying, Jesus seems to have chosen the form of an Essene hymn because it partially fits his own aspirations, his high self-awareness, and even his own connection with God. In speaking about himself as the Son and about God as his heavenly Father, Jesus reveals the mystery of his own person.

We may conclude from all that has been observed up to now, that Jesus believed himself to be a son of God, but his filial relationship to God is not the same as that of other people who may be considered God's children (cf. Jn 10:31-36). Jesus' own sonship is of a different kind. This impression is confirmed by the parable of the wicked husbandmen (Lk 20:9-19; Mk 12:1-12; Mt 21:33-46), which Jesus pronounced in the shadow of his imminent death. The owner of a vineyard sent his servants, one after the other, to the tenants living on his land. He commissioned his servants with the task of collecting his share of the produce from the tenants. The tenants, however, thrashed his servants and sent them away empty-handed. Then the owner sent his own son to the tenants. They knew that his son was the heir of the vineyard and so they killed him. The vineyard in the parable is the house of Israel[83] and the servants who are sent to it are the prophets.[84] Since Jesus should be seen as the son, the parable is a further witness that he regarded himself as a prophet,[85] like many others who would have heard the story.[86] But the parable goes even further because it indicates

[83] See Isa 5:1-7.

[84] This commonplace is already attested in Jub 1:12: "And I shall send to them witnesses so that I might witness to them, but they will not hear. And they will persecute those who search out the Law." See also n. 56 above.

[85] See also, "Jewish Messianic Figures in Primitive Christianity" (Hebrew), pp. 116–20. Concerning the parable of the wicked husbandmen, compare also the treatment of B. H. Young, *Jesus and His Jewish Parables* (Mahwah, N.J., 1989), pp. 282–316.

[86] From the parable of the wicked husbandmen, it may appear that Jesus considered himself a direct successor in the chain of the prophets. However, it is by no means certain that Jesus rejected the view, common to the rabbinic Judaism and to Essenism, that biblical prophecy had ceased and would be renewed only by the eschatological prophet. A clear solution for this problem would have an important implication in the question of the self-awareness of Jesus. In any case, others believed that Jesus was indeed the prophet of the last days.

An account about it is contained in Lk 9:18 (Mk 8:27-28; Mt 16:13-14). The parallel in Lk 9:7b-8 (Mk 6:14b-15) is secondary and does not appear in Matthew. Once Jesus asked his disciples, "Who do the people say I am?" They answered, "Some say John the Baptist, others Elijah, others that one of the old prophets has risen." The popular belief that Jesus was John the Baptist resurrected from the dead (Mt 14:1-2; Mk 6:14; Lk 9:7) is well known. The Baptist was also believed to be Elijah who had

that Jesus regarded himself not only as God's messenger, but also as the only son of God. He was sure about this even during the end of his earthly ministry when he realized that he would soon die.

Thus, the main difference between the high self-awareness of Jesus and that of Hillel is found in the way that Hillel's proud sayings show him to be a representative of humanity. In contrast, Jesus acknowledged the unique importance of his own person in light of his special task. Hillel was an outstanding Jewish sage and thinker, while Jesus was a charismatic leader, healer, and—if it is permitted for me to say—a saint. Like Hillel, Jesus was sure that personal action here and now is of crucial importance. On the other hand, Jesus believed that only he himself could be the bearer of a messianic movement. He alone was responsible to his heavenly Father, who invested him with this task. In other words, evidently he came to the conclusion that he was the messiah. If I understand correctly the evidence contained in the Gospel narrative, he possibly even identified himself with the sublime judge of the last judgment: the Son of Man.

Similar to the character of Hillel, Jesus too possessed meekness as a complementary feature of his high self-awareness. Jesus did not like the focus of a "personality cult."[87] According to Mt 7:21 (cf. Lk

---

returned (see e.g., Mt 11:14). Behind the third opinion ("one of the old prophets has risen"), in its more original form, was an allusion to the text in Dt 18:15: "The Lord your God will raise up for you a prophet like me." Dt 18:15 was commonly understood as speaking about the eschatological prophet. In Acts 3:22 and 7:37 these words are applied to Jesus.

All these three opinions in Lk 8:18 are in reality three variants of *one* popular opinion about Jesus, namely, that he was the prophet of the last days, "the prophet who is to come into the world" (Jn 6:14). "A great prophet has arisen among us" (Lk 7:16). If this was what people believed at that time, all that followed after the discussion, is full of meaning. "And you," Jesus said. "Who do you say that I am?" Peter answered: "God's messiah" (Lk 9:20). It was Peter who acknowledged that his master was not only the prophet, but the messiah himself. Jesus' positive reaction to Peter's revelation (Mt 16:17-19) fits fully within the Judaism of Jesus' time. Further analysis of Lk 9:18-19, together with Mt 16:15-19, would show that it is extremely difficult to deny the historicity of the whole account. If the historicity of the account holds up, the messianic aspirations of the "historical" Jesus seem to be very plausible. See also Brad Young, "Messianic Blessings in Jewish and Christian Texts," in Flusser, *Judaism*, pp. 280–300.

[87] See my study, "Two Anti-Jewish Montages in Matthew," in Flusser, *Judaism*, pp. 554–58.

6:46), he said, "Not every one who says to me, 'Lord, Lord,' shall enter the kingdom of heaven, but he who does the will of my Father who is in heaven." Jesus opposed an empty "personality cult." He sought rather to call upon the people to do the will of God. The history of Christian churches has shown that his concern was justified. On the other hand, his warning also demonstrates how highly he was regarded among his followers.

Another saying (Lk 20:41-44; Mk 12:35-37a; Mt 22:41-46) indicates that Jesus himself was not opposed to being addressed as "Lord." He said, "How can one say that the messiah is the *son* of David? David himself declares in the book of Psalms (110:1): 'The LORD[88] said to *my Lord*, sit at my right hand.' David calls him '*Lord*.' How then can he be *his son*?" Jesus' disciples conformed to his wishes. In the Gospel of Luke, Jesus is commonly addressed by the outside world as Rabbi, but the inner circle—and those who asked him for help[89]—appealed to him always as "Lord." It is highly improbable that this differentiation was invented by a hypothetical and enigmatic Lucan theology.[90]

Having critically analyzed the synoptic materials, we now conclude that the majority of the New Testament christological motifs are attested to already in the high self-awareness of the "historical" Jesus himself.[91] The point of departure in our scrutiny of these sources was an objective evaluation of the texts and their literary development. Redaction criticism and linguistic analysis has guided our philological research. We have tried, as far as possible, to be independent from any positive or negative religious beliefs which might bias our results. The modern prejudice was already expressed by Voltaire.[92] He claims that

---

[88] Who will doubt that Jesus quoted the Hebrew Bible rather than the Septuagint? In the Hebrew text, the first "Lord" is God's name.

[89] See Lk 5:12; 7:6; 9:61; 18:41; 19:8.

[90] The present case is only one of many points where I have recognized the high historical importance of the Gospel of Luke.

[91] Significant exceptions are: the preexistence of Christ, the virgin birth, the atonement by Christ's death (see above, note 73), and the ascension. This incomplete list is concerned only with those sayings we do not recognize as the *ipsissima verba* of the historical Jesus. On the other hand it would be silly to deny, for instance, that the followers of Jesus really had the experience of the resurrected Lord, even if, as we believe, there was no clear hint of the resurrection of Christ in Jesus' authentic words.

[92] Voltaire, *Dictionaire philosophique*, ed. R. Naves, (Paris, 1967), pp. 111-12, s.v., "Christianisme."

Jesus was born under the Mosaic Law and fulfilled all its precepts. According to Voltaire, Jesus did not preach any message other than morals. He said nothing to the Jews that resembled Christology. This was accomplished later by the Church. Voltaire's line has been pursued by many Christian theologians—until today.[93]

Even before the discovery of the Dead Sea Scrolls, it was not easy to defend this view. The authors of the apocalypses do not really influence the picture, because those revealers of God's secrets lived in a distant, biblical past. The situation changed with the finds from Qumran. After all, the Teacher of Righteousness, the founder of Essenism, was an inspired person from recent history, "to whom God made known all the mysteries of the words of his servants the prophets" (1Qp Hab 7.4-5). While I do not believe that the author of the Essene Thanksgiving Scroll (1QH) was identical with the Teacher of Righteousness, I am convinced that as an inspired poet, the writer of these powerful hymns was a unique mediator of God's revelation to the community. "Through me thou has illuminated the faces of many and thou hast become mighty infinitely, for thou hast made known to me thy wondrous mysteries and by thy wondrous secret thou hast wrought mightily with me and thou hast acted wondrously in the presence of many for the sake of thy glory, and to make known thy mighty deeds to all the living" (1QH 4.27-29).

It should not be necessary here to repeat all the references made by Josephus concerning numerous false prophets in Judaea during the Roman period. The first century Jewish historian complained, "Deceivers and impostors, under the pretense of divine inspiration ... persuaded the multitude to act like madmen and led them into the desert under the belief that God would there give them signs of redemption" (*War* 2.258-260). This movement was crushed by Felix. About this time another curious movement led by a prophet of Egyptian origin was put down. The prophet escaped (*War* 2.261-263), but afterward in a case of mistaken identity, the apostle Paul was accused of being this man who had caused so much trouble (Acts 21:38). Later on, while the Temple was being destroyed, a certain prophet "had proclaimed to the people in the city that God commanded them to go up to the Temple court, to receive there the signs of redemption" (*War* 6.285-286). Sometime

[93] See Flusser, *Judaism*, pp. XX–XXI.

before this, when Fadus was governor of Judaea, a man called Theudas persuaded the masses to follow him to the Jordan River. "He stated that he was a prophet and that on his command the river would be parted and would provide them an easy passage." This strange movement was suppressed by the Romans. Theudas himself was captured and executed by the Romans (*Ant* 20.97-98).[94] As is well known, this same Theudas is mentioned in Acts 5:35-38, together with Judas the Galilean. In Acts, Theudas is described as the man who claimed "to be somebody." It is commonly accepted that Jesus himself warned his followers against such "chiliastic" movements, which were certainly prevalent during his day.[95]

We have mentioned all these phenomena in ancient Judaism in order to show that the specific high self-awareness of Jesus should not be viewed as an incomprehensible exception during the Second Temple Period. At that time, Judaism was by no means strictly a "realistic" religion of rationalism, as is often assumed. A "mythical" understanding of reality arose during this period, which is not identical with the religious outlook of the Old Testament. The fervent atmosphere in which Christianity was born also pervaded Pharisaic rabbinism, which certainly was not as rationalistic as it is often described. This mistake is still repeated today.[96]

Even if it became clear that Voltaire's strict severing of the "historical," simple, and unpretentious Jesus from the divine Christ of the church is unwarranted,[97] one cannot deny that this prejudice is based upon real, objective problems. The first problem is: How is it possible that the apocalyptic discourse from Lk 12:49-53 (cf. Mt 10:34-36) and

---

[94] A similar "chiliastic" movement among the Samaritans was instigated by a like prophet and was crushed by Pilate (*Ant* 18.85-87). On Jewish "false prophets" in the Roman period, see David Flusser, "Caiaphas in the New Testament," *Atiqot*, vol. 21 (Jerusalem, 1992), pp. 84–85.

[95] See Mt 24:22-26; Mk 13:21-23; Lk 17:23. See also I. H. Marshall, *Commentary on Luke* (Grand Rapids, 1979), pp. 659–60.

[96] See Flusser, *Judaism*, pp. XXI.

[97] This dichotomy was expressed in a far better way by G. E. Lessing, "Die Religion Christi," in *Gotthold Ephraim Lessings sämtliche Werke*, ed. K. Lachmann, F. Muncker, (Leipzig, 1902), vol. XVI, pp. 518–19; English translation in *Lessings' Theological Writings*, trans. H. Chadwick (Stanford University Press, 1957), p. 106. See also my article, "The Jewish-Christian Schism," reprinted in my collected writings, Flusser, *Judaism*, pp. 621–25.

the proud hymn from Mt 11:25-30 (Lk 10:21-22) were said by the same man who preached a strong moral message like the ethical teachings in the Sermon on the Mount? I believe that if we take into account the complexity of an exceptional creative personality, this problem does not really exist.

The second problem is far more serious. Nobody will deny today—even one who accepts the highest possible self-awareness of Jesus—the essential difference between the "historical" Jesus and the divine figure of Christ. The person of history called Jesus was quite different from the way he has been depicted in the epistles of Paul or in the Johannine writings, or the way he was later treated as an object of ecclesiastical dogmatics.[98]

There are basically three stages in the development of Christology. Its origin lies in the mythical elements of the Second Temple Judaism, some of which were connected with the figure of the messiah. Jesus' sublime self-awareness was nourished by this mythical atmosphere. He not only expressed his personal experience by messianic conceptions, but also by these mythical ones as well. After the cross, the early Christians not only interpreted the high self-awareness of Jesus and his earthly history in the way that they were understood by his first disciples, they also added to these teachings other Jewish mythical ideas to complete the picture. Thus Jewish contemporary meta-historical motifs influenced the Christology of the early followers of Jesus *twice*: once by the motifs which were accepted by Jesus himself, and later by meta-historical themes added after the cross. Sometimes it is difficult to distinguish between christological Jewish concepts, which were accepted during the whole process, and the *theologoumena*, or innovations, made by Jesus and/or the church. Even these new Christian motifs emerged well within the spirit of Judaism.

With this development, a whole cosmic drama came into existence. Its climax was reached in the tragedy of the cross.[99] Its significance is mainly responsible for the formation of the knot,[100] which

---

[98] On this point, see my two studies, "Messianology and Christology," Flusser, *Judaism*, pp. 245–79; and "The Jewish-Christian Schism," Ibid., pp. 621–25.

[99] See above, notes 73 and 91.

[100] The term was coined by Martin Buber, "Ragaz und Israel," *Pfade in der Utopia* (Heidelberg, 1985), p. 378, "Aber ich glaube ebenso fest daran, daß wir Jesus nie als gekommenen Messias anerkennen werden ... in das mächtige Seil unseres Messiasglaubens, das, an einen Felsen am Sinai geknüpft, sich bis zu einem noch

ties the other christological threads tightly together and becomes decisive for the Christian religious experience of most believers.[101] Nevertheless, all this later blossoming of Christology does not justify a disruption between the self-awareness of the "historical" Jesus and the heavenly Christ of the church. On the contrary, the high self-awareness of Jesus paved the way for the ecclesiastical image of Christ. It is unthinkable that an unassuming, local, idealistic rabbi could later become an object of divine honor.

III

The focus of our present study has been the high self-awareness of two Jewish men who lived approximately in the same period, namely, Hillel and Jesus. Hillel died when Jesus was a boy. Both men had great self-esteem and personal dignity. This high self-awareness was not the result of an excessive appreciation for themselves. Rather, it derived from their conviction that their missions possessed decisive importance. Thus their high self-awareness was linked to their proverbial meekness. It is no wonder, then, that Jesus was inclined to portray his personal involvement in the history of salvation with colors he borrowed from Hillel.

On the other hand, differences between the self-awareness of Jesus and that of Hillel are evident. Jesus believed that his heavenly Father had invested him with the highest possible mission. Hillel believed that the present was a time of crisis and that he must therefore act here and now. He thought that his person was somehow exemplary for the others. While Jesus' self-awareness was that of a charismatic leader, Hillel was an existentialist philosopher. It is easier to explain the self-awareness of Jesus than to discover the possible premises of Hillel's peculiar philosophy in the midst of ancient rabbinism, where he was an exception.

---

unsichtbaren, aber in den Grund der Welt gerammten Pflock spannt, ist kein Knoten geschlagen."

[101] Lk 24:13-35 (the Walk to Emmaus) visualizes how the tragedy of the Cross caused a serious cognitive dissonance in the hearts of Jesus' followers. They had hoped that "Jesus would crown his prophetic work by redeeming the people, i.e., by setting them free from their enemies and inaugurating the kingdom of God ... but their hopes had been dashed by his death. Nevertheless ... it was now the third day since his death, and nothing further had happened" (Marshall, above n. 96), p. 895.

I believe that the transformation of the high self-awareness of Jesus into the Christology of the church was far easier than is commonly accepted today. The belief in Christ became dominant in the Christian religious experience not only as a result of how the christological threads came together through belief in the vicarious sufferings of Christ and his resurrection, but also because the message of Jesus became relatively less important. Already in the New Testament period, far less emphasis was given to the ethical teachings of Jesus. This development seems to be connected with the christological transformation of Jesus.

Although Hillel's teaching transformed Jewish religious life, his rather radical philosophical approach to the genuine greatness of each person and his high esteem for individual human dignity has had only a minimal impact upon subsequent Jewish philosophy and religious thought. Hillel's daring views were evidently too uncommon. But what happened to the gospel of love preached by Jesus? It is not now my task to treat this question.

PART TWO

SOCIAL AND HISTORICAL STUDIES

ARCHAEOLOGY AND THE RELIGIOUS ETHOS OF PRE-70 PALESTINE

AT FIRST GLANCE, it seems strange to be looking for a link between archaeology and the religious ethos of ancient Palestine. Archaeology deals with the material culture, art, architecture, town planning, and epigraphic evidence of a particular site. It deals with mosaic stones, pottery, numismatics, and other small finds. It is placed within a political, social, or economic context, but rarely within a religious setting that might shed light on the institutions, beliefs, and practices of a particular society.

On the other hand, when one thinks of the religious ethos of a certain age, one automatically refers to various religious traditions preserved in literary sources. Nevertheless, and as I shall point out, archaeological finds clearly have some value in revealing certain aspects of a given society's religious ambience—its religious leadership, institutional frameworks, beliefs, and practices.[1]

When studying the archaeological remains of the Hellenistic and early Roman periods, several caveats are in order. In the first place, the archaeological material for pre-70 Palestine is woefully limited. Due to the large and growing population of the late Roman and Byzantine periods, the material remains from these centuries often obliterate, to a large extent or entirely, the remains of earlier periods. In both urban and rural settings, the culture of late antiquity was often built on and at times out of the material remains of earlier cultures.

Second, when material is discovered, the question arises as to how representative these finds are. As only a small percentage of pre-

---

[1] J. Charlesworth, *Jesus Within Judaism: New Light from Exciting Archaeological Discoveries* (Garden City, 1988), pp. 103–30.

70 Palestine has been uncovered in one form or another by the archaeologist's spade, we must be careful in assessing the extent and
normativity of the finds that have come to light.

Finally, we must consider the geographical distribution of the
finds. Whereas the remains of pre-70 Galilee are extremely meager,
those of Jerusalem—though far from what we would wish for—are
much more extensive in quantity, quality, and diversity. The same is the
case with regard to the finds of the Judean Desert area, such as Jericho,
Qumran, Masada, or any of the other fortress-palaces built by the Hasmoneans and Herodians during these centuries. Because of their relative
isolation, many of these sites are fairly well preserved. Yet, how indica-
tive they are of Jewish society generally—or even of upper class Jewish
society in this period—remains enigmatic.

The material to be discussed below may be divided into several
broad categories. The first comprises some of the more revolutionary
archaeological finds of the past generation or two. These finds have
called into question generally accepted assumptions about the religious
institutions and leadership of pre-70 Palestine. Archaeology alone is not
responsible for this reassessment. Often these issues also appeared independently on the agenda of scholars in various disciplines. Regardless
of their origin, quite a different appraisal of certain facets of religious
life in pre-70 Palestine has emerged than that prevalent in the nineteenth and in the first part of the twentieth centuries.

The Jerusalem Temple and its priestly leadership have often been
described as being in decline by the late first century C.E. The
politicization of the Temple from the time of the Hasmoneans onward,
the high-handed and sometimes-alleged contemptuous hiring and dis-
missing of high priests by Herod, as well as the corruption attributed to
the first-century Temple and priestly personnel have all contributed to
this assessment.[2] In fact, the prime sources at our disposal—the Dead
Sea scrolls, rabbinic literature, the New Testament, and the writings of

---

[2] Criticism of the high priest or of the priestly/Sadducean class is reflected in
Josephus *Ant* 13.11.1-3 (§§301-19); 13.13.5 (§§372-76); 13.14.2 (§§379-83); 18.1.4
(§§16-7); b.Pesaḥ 57a; and, of course, throughout the Dead Sea Scrolls. See also M.
Hengel, *The Zealots* (Edinburgh, 1989), pp. 210-13, 319-20; S. J. D. Cohen, "The
Significance of Yavneh: Pharisees, Rabbis, and the End of Jewish Sectarianism,"
HUCA 55 (1984) 43-45; M. Goodman, *The Ruling Class of Judaea* (Cambridge, Eng.,
1987), pp. 109-11, 124-25.

Josephus—give a rather negative evaluation of the priestly/Sadducean Temple leadership. However, archaeological excavations offer a somewhat different impression.

The first archaeological investigations of the Temple site area were undertaken by English archaeologists Warren, Wilson, and others in the nineteenth century. Since the Six-Day War in 1967, extensive excavations have been conducted on the southern and western sections of the Temple mount. The picture that has emerged is one which emphasizes the centrality, grandeur, and importance of the Temple (fig. 1).[3] The massive stones, monumental entrances, large plazas, series of streets abutting the Temple mount, as well as various architectural and epigraphical remains—the מקוואות miqvāʾôth (ritual baths) in the southern section of the Temple mount, along with the monumental staircase to accommodate large crowds—all point to the imposing nature of the site (fig. 2).

As a result, there has been a radical rethinking in the last half of the twentieth century about the functioning of the Temple in Jewish society. What was its importance, its attraction, and its significance for the Jewish population—not only in Jerusalem and Judea but also throughout Palestine and the Diaspora?[4] Temple concerns, such as the priests, purity, and the sacrificial cult, have been designated as central to the Jewish religious agenda of pre-70 Palestine[5]—so much so that the various sects and ideologies of the period all sought to define themselves in contradistinction to this central Jewish institution.[6]

Archaeology has also made a significant contribution to our knowledge of the synagogue of the Second Temple period. This pre-70

[3] B. Mazar, *The Mountain of the Lord—Excavating in Jerusalem* (Garden City, 1975); M. Ben-Dov, *In the Shadow of the Temple: The Discovery of Ancient Jerusalem* (Jerusalem, 1982), pp. 73–147; M. Ben-Dov et al., *The Western Wall* (Jerusalem, 1983), pp. 41–62.

[4] M. D. Herr, "Jerusalem, the Temple and Its Cult—In Reality and Consciousness—During Second Temple Times," *Jerusalem in the Second Temple Period: Abraham Schalit Memorial Volume*, eds. A. Oppenheimer et al. (Jerusalem, 1980), pp. 166–77 (Hebrew).

[5] G. Alon, *Jews, Judaism and the Classical World* (Jerusalem, 1977), pp. 146–234; B. Gärtner, *The Temple and the Community in Qumran and the New Testament* (Cambridge, Eng., 1965); E. P. Sanders, *Jewish Law from Jesus to the Mishnah* (London and Philadelphia, 1990).

[6] Cohen, "The Significance of Yavneh," pp. 45–48; idem, *From the Maccabees to the Mishnah* (Philadelphia, 1987), pp. 106–07.

institution has in the past been described as a Pharisaic institution which competed with a Sadducean-dominated Temple.[7] It was viewed primarily as a religious institution that emerged either in the late First Temple or early Second Temple period. It allegedly had a totally different liturgical agenda than that which had been known heretofore in Palestine. Yet, the three sites identified with relative confidence as pre-70 synagogues—Gamla, Masada, and Herodium—were all, in effect, communal meeting places with no noticeable religious significance.[8] None of these buildings was clearly oriented toward Jerusalem. None had a permanent place for a Torah shrine, none contained art indicating a religious ambience for the building, nor did any boast inscriptions identifying it as a holy site.

As the names בית כנסת (bêt kĕneset) and συναγωγή (synagōgē) commonly used in Palestine indicate, the synagogue there was primarily a place for congregating for a variety of communal purposes: social, political, judicial, legal, as well as religious. The focus of all these buildings was in the center of the room, with benches lining all four walls, resembling Hellenistic meeting places such as the βουλητήριον (boulētērion) and the ἐκκλησιαστήριον (ekklēsiastērion) (figs. 3a,b).[9]

In Jerusalem a synagogue probably had somewhat greater religious significance, since many communal needs were met in other ways. Those who founded synagogues there, especially Jews of the Diaspora, may have been more inclined to emphasize the institution's religious component, as was done throughout the Diaspora.[10] This seems to have been the case in the synagogue represented by the famous Theodotus inscription, which describes the synagogue as a place for Torah reading and study, and as a hostel for visitors from abroad (fig. 4).[11] The Theodotus inscription notwithstanding, archaeology

---

[7] See, for example, R. T. Herford, *The Pharisees* (London, 1924), pp. 88–103.

[8] See the articles of Ma'oz, Yadin, Gutman, and Foerster in *Ancient Synagogues Revealed*, ed. L. I. Levine (Jerusalem, 1981), pp. 19–41.

[9] Levine, *Ancient Synagogues*, pp. 20, 26, 44. On the possible influence of assembly halls as found at Dura on these synagogues, see pp. 26–29.

[10] L. I. Levine, "The Second Temple Synagogue: The Formative Years," *The Synagogue in Late Antiquity*, ed. L. I. Levine (Philadelphia, 1987), pp. 20–23; M. Hengel, "Proseuche und Synagoge," *The Synagogue: Studies in Origin, Archaeology and Architecture*, ed. J. Gutman (New York, 1975), pp. 27–54.

[11] L. Roth-Gerson, *The Greek Inscriptions from the Synagogues in Eretz-Israel* (Jerusalem, 1987), pp. 76–86 (Hebrew).

appears to point to a type of synagogue in the pre-70 era which was quite different from that which was to evolve during the centuries following the destruction of the Temple.

A third area affected by recent archaeological discoveries relates to the priests and Sadducees as a religious and political force in pre-70 Palestine. As is well known, these groups received either no press or very bad press in the sources that have come down to us from this period. Considered "the establishment," they were viewed critically by all other groups within the country and were accused of corruption, ignorance, estrangement from the populace, and haughtiness. These descriptions may well have had more than a kernel of truth but they should in any case be regarded as tendentious in nature.

Recent archaeological discoveries now offer us additional information about the priestly class. The results of the excavations on the western slope of Mt. Zion, as well as in Jericho (both first-century B.C.E. sites), ordinarily might not have aroused much discussion (fig. 5). However, the discovery of aqueducts passing through cemeteries at these sites[12] dovetails neatly with a dispute recorded in the Mishnah indicating that this very issue was a subject of dispute between the Pharisees and Sadducees.[13] The Sadducees claimed that the construction of an aqueduct through a cemetery was permissible, since the water flowing through it and through the cemetery retained its purity. The Pharisees objected to this practice. On the basis of the above archaeological finds, it is clear that this dispute was far from theoretical or academic, but in fact reflected a reality of the pre-Herodian or Herodian era—the very period when Hillel purportedly came to Jerusalem and assumed a leadership role among the Pharisees. If indeed this conclusion is accepted, and it appears to us more than reasonable, it would indicate that the Sadducees controlled the municipal politics in both Jerusalem and Jericho and that their halakhic decision was followed by those who were responsible for municipal services.

The extensive excavations carried out by the late Professor Nahman Avigad in the Jewish Quarter of the Old City (referred to by Josephus as the Upper City) have likewise shed a great deal of light on

---

[12] J. Patrich, "A Sadducean Halakha and the Jerusalem Aqueduct," *The Jerusalem Cathedra*, ed. L. I. Levine (Detroit, 1982) 2.25–39.

[13] m.Yad 4:7.

the priestly class.[14] There is now little doubt that this residential area was occupied largely by priests, both because they were representative of the upper class of Jerusalem society and because a special bridge had been constructed to allow their passage from the Upper City to the area of the sacred Temple precincts.[15] This fact has been dramatically confirmed by the discovery of a small stone weight in the Burnt House in the Jewish Quarter which bore the inscription, "Bar Qatros,"[16] the name of a high priestly family known to us from Josephus and rabbinic sources (fig. 6).[17]

The homes discovered in Avigad's excavations indicate a punctiliousness in their inhabitants' observance of religious norms. With all their lavishness, these homes were devoid of figural artwork, which was regarded as taboo by Jews during this era.[18] The large number of pools found in each home, many of which served as ritual baths, attests to the observance of purity laws by those living there.[19] The extensive use of stone utensils,[20] which were free from the danger of impurity, is also striking evidence for the religious scrupulousness of the local inhabitants. Any future assessment of the priestly class, and of the Sadducees in particular, must take these data into consideration (figs. 7,8,9).

* * *

A second major area where archaeology has made inroads in our understanding of pre-70 Palestine has to do with two sometimes-conflicting postures within Jewish society of the Greco-Roman period: parochialism

---

[14] N. Avigad, *Discovering Jerusalem* (Nashville, 1983), pp. 64–203.

[15] Josephus, *War* 1.7.2 (§143); *Ant* 14.4.2 (§§58–59); see also J. Simons, *Jerusalem in the Old Testament* (Leiden, 1952), pp. 364–69.

[16] Avigad, *Discovering Jerusalem*, pp. 129–31.

[17] See M. Stern, "Aspects of Jewish Society: The Priesthood and Other Classes," *The Jewish People in the First Century—Compendia*, eds. S. Safrai et al. (Philadelphia, 1976) 2.608.

[18] Avigad, *Discovering Jerusalem*, pp. 99–103, 144–46; R. Hachlili, *Ancient Jewish Art and Archaeology in the Land of Israel* (Leiden, 1988), pp. 65–83.

[19] Avigad, *Discovering Jerusalem*, pp. 139–43; R. Reich, "Mishnah, Sheqalim 8:2 and the Archaeological Evidence," *Jerusalem in the Second Temple Period: Abraham Schalit Memorial Volume*, eds. A. Oppenheimer et al. (Jerusalem, 1980), pp. 225–56 (Hebrew).

[20] Avigad, *Discovering Jerusalem*, pp. 165–83; cf. also Ben-Dov, *Shadow*, pp. 149–67.

and particularism versus universalism and cosmopolitanism. Archaeo-logical material conveys two distinct messages in this regard. On the one hand, discoveries of ritual baths and the absence of figural art indi-cate the degree to which Jewish society was different and separate from the surrounding culture. On the other hand, most archaeological discov-eries testify to the impact of the surrounding culture on Jewish practice. We will address each of these phenomena in turn.

Ever since the epochal studies of A. Büchler at the end of the last century and the beginning of this one, it has become clear that ritual purity was a central issue for Jewish sects of the late Second Temple period. His work has been continued by G. Alon, J. Neusner, and, most recently, by E. P. Sanders.[21] There is universal agreement among scholars that this indeed was a central issue in Jewish sectarianism, although there is disagreement about dating this phenomenon and the extent to which it was unique and determinant of Pharisaic behavior. The Dead Sea scrolls have confirmed the importance of this aspect of observance among Jewish sectarians.[22] Moreover, on the basis of literary material, we can date with confidence the appearance of these concerns with the rise of the Hasmonean dynasty somewhere near the mid-second century B.C.E. Such concerns remained focal, as evidenced in Hillel and New Testament traditions.

As archaeology has confirmed, the Qumran material as well as the various decisions taken by the early Pharisaic sages date from this period (fig. 10).[23] The earliest ritual baths were found at Gezer from the mid-second century B.C.E., and were followed by those at Qumran from the end of that century and the beginning of the first century B.C.E.[24] That this type of installation was revolutionary in Israel is con-

[21] Alon, *Jews*, pp. 146–234; Sanders, *Jewish Law*. See also A. Büchler, "The Levitical Impurity of the Gentile in Palestine before the Year 70," *JQR* 17 (1926–27) 1–81; J. Neusner, *The Idea of Purity in Ancient Judaism* (Leiden, 1973), pp. 32–71.

[22] See L. Schiffman, *Sectarian Law in the Dead Sea Scrolls* (Chico, Cal., 1983), pp. 215–16; idem, *The Eschatological Community of the Dead Sea Scrolls* (Atlanta, 1989), pp. 38–42.

[23] For Qumran material, see R. de Vaux, *Archaeology and the Dead Sea Scrolls* (London, 1973); *NEAEHL* 4.1235–41. For rabbinic material, see A. Gutman, *Rabbinic Judaism in the Making* (Detroit, 1970), pp. 40ff. Cf. also L. Ginzberg, *On Jewish Law and Lore* (Philadelphia, 1955), pp. 79–86.

[24] Reich, "Mishnah, Sheqalim 8:2 and the Archaeological Evidence," pp. 225–56 (Hebrew); idem, "Jewish Ritual Baths at Tel Gezer," *Qadmoniot* 15/58–59 (1982) 74–76 (Hebrew).

firmed by the fact that no such ritual baths have been found throughout the biblical or early Second Temple period. Ritual baths also appeared in the Hasmonean palaces of Jericho.[25] Later, in the Second Temple period, a large number were found in Jerusalem, especially in the Upper City and near the Temple entrances, as well as at Masada (fig. 11).[26]

A second indication of religious conservatism may be gained from Jewish art. Throughout the biblical and early Second Temple periods, Jewish art did not shrink from representing figural objects, although this was not necessarily a main motif. The cherubs over the ark of the Tabernacle, and later of the Temple; the lions surrounding Solomon's throne; the oxen holding the large basin in the Temple courtyard; the bronze serpent; and thousands of statuettes and figurines of fertility images found in Israelite sites—all attest to the use of figural art in the First Temple period.[27] Even in the Persian and early Hellenistic eras, figural representations appeared on the Yehud coins minted by the Jerusalem authorities in the fourth and third centuries B.C.E.[28] As late as the turn of the second century, representations of animals are featured on the facade of the palace (Temple?) of Hyrcanus the Tobiad in Irak el-Emir, located east of the Jordan River, and on the fountains there.[29]

With the advent of the Hasmoneans, this picture changed dramatically. For a period of three hundred years or so, down to the mid-second century C.E., the Jews appear to have studiously avoided any kind of figural representation, as is attested on their coins, mosaic floors, frescoes, lamps, and other small finds (figs. 12a,b).[30] The Jews

[25] E. Netzer, "Ancient Ritual Baths (Miqvaot) in Jericho," *Jerusalem Cathedra,* ed. L. I. Levine (Detroit, 1982) 2.106–19.

[26] In addition to Avigad, *Discovering Jerusalem,* pp. 139–43, and Reich, "Mishnah, Sheqalim 8:2 and the Archaeological Evidence," pp. 225–56, see also Ben-Dov, *Shadow,* pp. 150–53; Y. Yadin, *Masada* (New York, 1966), pp. 164–67.

[27] N. Avigad, *Beth She'arim* (Jerusalem, 1976) 3.275–77.

[28] Y. Meshorer, *Ancient Jewish Coins,* 2 vols. (New York, 1982) 1.13–34; U. Rappaport, "Numismatics," *Cambridge History of Judaism,* ed. W. D. Davies and L. Finkelstein (Cambridge, Eng., 1984) 1.25–31.

[29] *NEAEHL* 2.646–49.

[30] See Avigad, *Discovering Jerusalem,* pp. 99–103, 144–46; R. Hachlili, *Ancient Jewish Art,* pp. 65–83; M. Kon, "Jewish Art at the Time of the Second Temple," *Jewish Art: An Illustrated History,* ed. C. Roth; rev. ed., B. Narkiss (Jerusalem, 1971), pp. 51–64.

selectively borrowed motifs from the world around, but eschewed any kind of figural or pagan image.[31] Thus, the archaeological remains have confirmed the impression gained from the writings of Josephus, Philo, and other late Second Temple sources: the avoidance of such representations had become "normative" in Jewish society during this period.

* * *

If the archaeological material is clear and incontrovertible regarding the not inconsiderable degree of particularism in Jewish society in the above areas, it is likewise clear that Hellenistic influence was a serious social, cultural, and religious phenomenon at this time.[32] Many of the buildings in Jerusalem were drawn from Hellenistic models. For example, one of the towers built by Herod near his palace was an imitation of the Pharus lighthouse in Alexandria (fig. 13).[33] Moreover, Jerusalem boasted three of the main entertainment institutions prevalent in the Greco-Roman world: the theater, hippodrome, and amphitheater (fig. 14).[34] Even the Temple mount was constructed to resemble the typical Hellenistic-Roman τέμενος (temenos, sacred precinct) which could be found throughout the eastern Mediterranean at this time (fig. 15).[35]

Funerary remains in Jerusalem also indicate significant Hellenistic influence during this period. The funerary monuments in the Kidron Valley are typical of similar Hellenistic monuments. However, they lack any kind of imagery or statuary (fig. 16).[36] Even burial in ossuaries, which seems to have been the most widespread form of inter-

---

[31] A. Kindler, "The Hellenistic Influence in Hasmonean Coins," *The Seleucid Period in Eretz Israel*, ed. B. Bar-Kochva (Tel Aviv, 1980), pp. 289–308 (Hebrew).

[32] See most recently U. Rappaport, "The Hasmoneans and Hellenism," *Tarbiz* 60 (1991) 447–503 (Hebrew).

[33] Josephus, *War* 5.4.3 (§§166–69).

[34] Josephus, *Ant* 15.8.1 (§§267–76); see also Ben-Dov, *Shadow*, pp. 169–83; L. I. Levine, "Roman Rule," *History of Eretz Israel*, ed. M. Stern (Jerusalem, 1984) 4.61–70 (Hebrew).

[35] J. B. Ward-Perkins and M. H. Ballance, "The Caesareum at Cyrene and the Basilica at Cremna," *Papers of the British School at Rome* 26 (1958) 137–94. Cf. also G. Foerster, "Art and Architecture in Palestine," *The Jewish People in the First Century—Compendia*, eds. S. Safrai et al. (Philadelphia, 1976) 2.980.

[36] N. Avigad, *Ancient Monuments of the Kedron Valley* (Jerusalem, 1952; Hebrew).

ment in Jerusalem during the late Second Temple period, may have derived from the Roman practice of secondary burial of ashes in urns and similar stone chests.[37] Finally, the use of Greek in inscriptions from late Second Temple Jerusalem, where up to 35% were found in that language, attests to the widespread use of Greek in Jerusalem by both the native population and its Diaspora residents.[38]

Thus, archaeology clearly reveals conflicting attitudes in Jerusalem of the late Second Temple period regarding Hellenistic culture. One emphasized separation in ritual purity and differentiation from the norms of the surrounding society. Others integrated, adopted, and adapted regnant social and cultural currents.

How may one reconcile these two phenomena? One possibility is that as conflicting tendencies within Jewish society, they should be assigned to different classes, different religious groupings, different strata of society, or different geographical locations. However, it is also possible that these two phenomena are related to one another and that only when considered together do they enhance our understanding of the inclination toward the universalism of the Hellenistic world. This universalism not only invited imitation, but stimulated a surge towards particularism at the same time. Several studies over the last generation have indicated that particularism was often an expression of national and religious reassertion by subject groups to the dominant Hellenistic culture.[39]

A third possibility exists, one that views these conflicting tendencies as part of a complex situation which does not necessarily have to be assigned to different groups or different strata. The same people may have adopted Hellenistic practices in certain aspects of their lives while embracing particular Jewish modes of behavior in others. As we have noted above, the priests who lived in Jerusalem's Upper City adopted Greco-Roman patterns of decorating their houses. They imported many luxurious objects, such as glass vases from Anion of Sidon, even while eschewing figural representation and rigorously following laws of ritual purity (fig. 17). The same held true with artistic

---

[37] Levine, "Roman Rule," pp. 66–67.

[38] See J.-B. Frey, *CII*, vol. 2 (Rome, 1952).

[39] See, for example, S. Eddy, *The King is Dead* (Lincoln, Neb., 1961); J. J. Collins, "Jewish Apocalyptic against Its Hellenistic Environment," *BASOR* 220 (1975) 27–36.

representations generally. All the regnant motifs in Second Temple Jewish art were borrowed from the surrounding Greco-Roman culture, yet they were chosen selectively and carefully. Similarly, the use of ossuaries for secondary burial may well have been a Jewish adaptation of a foreign practice,[40] just as most motifs on these ossuaries were part of the artistic repertoire of the Hellenistic East.[41]

The same type of cultural synthesis is evidenced among the Pharisees as well, and specifically with regard to the Hillel traditions. On the one hand, Hillel is associated with all the areas of halakhic discourse that became normative among the Pharisees.[42] On the other hand, some rather significant steps associated with Hillel reflect a considerable degree of Hellenistic influence. To cite one example: Talmudic tradition associates with Hillel the adoption of hermeneutical rules of exegesis similar to those in usage among Stoics and others.[43] Whether the influence was limited only to terminology[44] or to the very methodology,[45] it is clear that the contacts between Jerusalem and Alexandria were rich and varied.[46]

In conclusion, it is universally recognized that archaeological discoveries have made an immense contribution to our understanding of the material dimension of Jewish society in pre-70 Palestine. Moreover, we suggest here that archaeology also plays a significant role in our knowledge of the cultural and religious dimensions of that society.

---

[40] Levine, "Roman Rule," pp. 66–67.

[41] See M. Avi-Yonah, *Oriental Art in Roman Palestine* (Rome, 1961), pp. 13–27.

[42] Gutman, *Rabbinic Judaism*, pp. 59–61.

[43] t.Sanh 7.11.

[44] S. Lieberman, *Hellenism in Jewish Palestine* (New York, 1950), pp. 47ff.

[45] D. Daube, "Rabbinic Methods of Interpretation and Hellenistic Rhetoric," *HUCA* 22 (1949) 239–64.

[46] On the influence of Alexandrian customs on Simeon b. Shetah's (early first century B.C.E.) changes in the *kĕtūbah*, see M. Geller, "New Sources for the Origin of the Rabbinic Ketubah," *HUCA* 49 (1978) 227–45. Cf. also E. Bickerman, "La chaîne de la tradition Phariséene," *RB* (1952) 44–54; M. Smith, "Palestinian Judaism in the First Century," *Israel: Its Role in Civilization*, ed. M. Davies (New York, 1956), pp. 67–73.

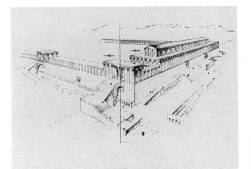

Fig. 1 Reconstruction of the Temple Mount, view from the southwest.

Fig. 2 Inscription originally located at the southwestern corner of the Temple Mount: "To the place of trumpeting to."

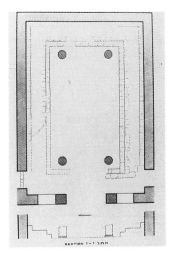

Fig. 3a Plan of synagogue at Herodium.

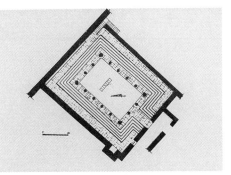

Fig. 3b Plan of synagogue at Gamla.

Fig. 4 Theodotus inscription found at Jerusalem.

Fig. 5 Route of Lower Aqueduct through the area of the graves on the western slope of Mount Zion.

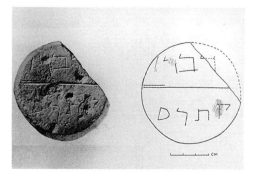

Fig. 6 Stone weight bearing Hebrew inscription: "[Of] Bar Kathros," found in Burnt House, Jewish Quarter, Jerusalem.

Fig. 7 Mosaic pavement found in Herodian House, Jewish Quarter, Jerusalem.

Fig. 8 Stepped and vaulted ritual bath in Jewish Quarter, Jerusalem.

Fig. 9 Assemblage of stone vessels from the Burnt House, Jewish Quarter, Jerusalem.

Fig. 10 Plan of Kh. Qumran, Phase 1.

Fig. 11 Miqbeh (ritual bath) in southern wall, Masada.

Fig. 12a A coin of Alexander Jannaeus depicting an anchor and the inscription: "Of Alexander the King."

Fig. 12b A coin of Judah Aristobulus depicting a cornucopia.

Fig. 13 Proposed reconstruction of three towers built by Herod near his palace; from the Holy Land model, Jerusalem.

Fig. 14 Herodian hippodrome and Temple Mount, view from the southwest; from the Holy Land model, Jerusalem.

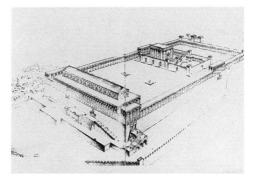

Fig. 15 Reconstruction of the Temple Mount, viewed from the southeast.

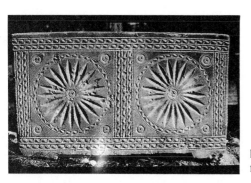

Fig. 16 Ossuary from Jerusalem, used for secondary burials.

Fig. 17 Glass pitcher made by Anion, found in Jewish Quarter excavations in Jerusalem.

6

APOCALYPTICISM IN THE TIME OF HILLEL AND JESUS

MODERN BIBLICAL SCHOLARSHIP has slowly come to appreciate the role of apocalypticism[1] in the piety of Jews and Christians before 70 C.E. Until fairly recently, apocalyptic literature and apocalypticism in the biblical world have been viewed with something of a jaundiced eye. Most scholars have accepted the change to a more positive evaluation of apocalypticism in biblical studies as an evolutionary process internal to the discipline. However, I would like to suggest that at least one external cultural factor may also have played a major part.

At the beginning of this century, after the great sifting of the modernist movement and the paradigm shift it brought about in scholarly disciplines, much of academic theology and religion acquired a bias that prized liberal religious views based on rational thought, a strong concern for ethics, and a broad and benificent humanism.[2] Modern liberalism had finally succeeded in establishing itself in many of the churches and most of the colleges and universities, but it was also

---

[1] I make no attempt here to define apocalypticism with any precision. It has often been maintained that intellectual abstractions like apocalypticism (or impressionism, humanism, feminism, conservatism, etc.) must be systematically defined with a precision approaching the mathematical before they can properly be used in scholarly discourse. I suggest such an approach represents a methodological black hole to be avoided. When dealing with the abstract and subjective, scholarship must tolerate some blurred edges if it is to speak at all. A good *general* description of apocalypticism may be found in P. D. Hanson et al., "Apocalypses and Apocalypticism," *ABD*, vol. I (New York, 1992), pp. 279–92.

[2] For the impact of modernism, see William R. Hutchison, *The Modernist Impulse in American Protestantism* (Cambridge, 1976) and Sydney E. Ahlstrom, *A Religious History of the American People* (New Haven, 1972), pp. 763○24, 904–15.

still wrestling with a strong conservative backlash.[3] As modernist liberals sought to overcome their conservative opponents, it became more and more difficult to distinguish conservative opponents from conservative theology. The understandable result was that modern liberals developed an intense aversion toward modern manifestations of literalism, supernaturalism, and apocalypticism. It was inevitable that their polemical situation, their own *Zeitgeist*, should prejudice their view of literalism, supernaturalism, and apocalypticism in the ancient world as well.[4] Thus, disdain for a supernatural worldview at the turn of the twentieth century translated into disdain for a supernatural worldview at the turn of the first century.

Though larger than biblical studies or theology, the modernist movement directly involved these disciplines and forced them to reevaluate themselves in terms of post-Enlightenment scientific developments and to distance themselves in self-defense from religious supernaturalism. One unfortunate casualty of the modernist controversy was any hope in the short run of friendly treatment for nonrationalist points of view, including apocalypticism. It also became more difficult to value positively historical figures, groups, or movements that held such views. Even those scholars who worked most closely with apocalyptic literature were sometimes unable to do so comfortably. T. W. Manson said of R. H. Charles that "he could never be completely at home in the world of the Apocalyptists. And this made it impossible for him to achieve that perfect understanding which demands sympathy as well as knowledge."[5]

After its traumatic collision with post-Enlightenment science, religion's first priority was damage control. For liberalism, that meant divesting itself of the supernatural and retrenching as best it could behind defensible ramparts of rationalism, ethics, and humanism. It was

---

[3] G. Marsden, *Fundamentalism and American Culture* (Oxford, 1980), pp. 171–75.

[4] A. Harnack's claim that apocalyptic writings were "an evil inheritance which the Christians took over from the Jews" (*History of Dogma* [London, 1894] 1:101) illustrates both the anti-apocalyptic and anti-Semitic biases of the time.

[5] *Dictionary of National Biography 1931–1940*, p. 170, cited in James Barr, "Jewish Apocalyptic in Recent Scholarly Study," *BJRL* 58 (1975) 32. Barr suggests that neither Charles nor Rowley could completely break away from the rationalism of contemporary scholarship in order to deal fairly with apocalypticism.

time for the social gospel and for demythologizing. In the liberal view, if religion were going to be respectable in the brave new world, it could have no taint of "superstition," that is, of any unscientific worldview. Apocalyptic elements like the periodization of history, the imminence of the kingdom of God, cosmic dualism, messianic expectation, and so forth, came to be identified in the universities with an anti-intellectual "fundamentalism."[6] This was due in part to heavy conservative use of the biblical apocalypses in defending against modernism. This perception inevitably, though unfairly, tainted scholarly evaluation of specifically apocalyptic thinking in the ancient world as well.[7] Behind much discussion of apocalypticism in the first half of this century was the unspoken conviction that "respectable" religion, "reasonable" religion (as judged by "modern" standards) had to be protected from any association with the irrational and the superstitious.[8] Many liberal theologians saw Albert Schweitzer's apocalyptic Jesus as a serious hazard to be resisted at all costs, for a Jesus tainted by apocalyptic would be a Jesus unfit for study or for worship.[9] In order to protect the Bible from apocalyptic contamination, more than one writer has argued that Daniel and Revelation are not apocalypses in the "usual" sense at all.[10]

The negative emotional value attached by liberal thinkers to literalism, supernaturalism, and apocalypticism is well evidenced by the animus that nonbiblical apocalypses evoked even in greatly respected scholars, who often viewed these apocalypses as unfit even for peripheral study during the first half of this century[11] and in some cases

---

[6] Cf. such liberal responses as Obadiah Holmes, "The Threat of Millennialism," *Christian Century* 38 (April 28, 1921) 10–13.

[7] See Marsden, *Fundamentalism*, p. 48. It was unfair because it imposed postscientific standards upon prescientific peoples and cultures.

[8] James Barr has already noted the impact of modern theological concerns on the study of apocalypticism in "Jewish Apocalyptic in Recent Scholarly Study," *BJRL* 58 (1975) 28–30.

[9] Hutchison, *Modernist*, p. 221, and W. Fenn, "Modern Liberalism," *American Journal of Theology* 17 (Oct 1913) 509–13.

[10] See the references in K. Koch, "The Agonized Attempt to Save Jesus from Apocalyptic," in *The Rediscovery of Apocalyptic* (SBT 2.22; Naperville, Ill., 1970), pp. 57–73 (also pp. 126–29).

[11] For example, R. T. Herford strongly disliked apocalypticism, referring to it as Esau to the Jacob of Pharisaism (*BJRL* 58 [Autumn 1975] 10). Louis Ginzberg blamed "the failure of some really great scholars to give us a true picture of the religious life of Israel at the time of the rise of Christianity" on their willingness to consider

even later.[12] Witness G. F. Moore's famous condemnation of the apocalypses: "It is a fallacy of method for the historian to make them a primary source for the eschatology of Judaism, much more to contaminate its theology with them."[13]

I. THE AGE OF HILLEL AND JESUS: AN AGE OF APOCALYPTICISM

Despite the cultural fallout of the modernist controversy, the evidence from antiquity remains what it is. Several scholars were able to separate that evidence from the biases of their own time and came to note the undeniable importance of apocalypticism for pre-70 Judaism and early Christianity. Since the discovery of the Dead Sea Scrolls at mid-century, and with the increased study devoted in the last two decades to the Pseudepigrapha of the Old Testament, it is no longer tenable to deny the apocalyptic *Zeitgeist* of the time of Hillel and Jesus, though stubborn resistance to it continues in some quarters.

From at least the postexilic period onward, ancient Judaism had become increasingly apocalyptic in its view of the cosmos.[14] By the time of Hillel and Jesus, apocalypticism had become an important, even fundamental, component in many of the main streams of Jewish thought. Assessing the role of apocalypticism is now generally agreed to be a necessary aspect of the study of pre-70 Judaism, including infant Christianity.

Most of the pre-70 literary evidence for Judaism and Christianity, as it is re-assessed in the light of the new evidence, reveals some degree

---

evidence from the apocalypses ("Some Observations on the Attitude of the Synagogue Towards the Apocalyptic-Eschatological Writings," *JBL* 41 [1922] 115). J. Bloch cites similar attitudes held by Montefiore and Schechter (*On the Apocalyptic in Judaism* [Philadelphia, 1952], pp. 132–33).

[12] G. B. Caird referred to apocalypses generally as "for the most part imitative and pedestrian," and to 1 Enoch as "justly called one of the world's six worst books," even as he tried to salvage the Revelation of John from the taint of apocalypticism in *The Revelation of St. John the Divine* (New York, 1966), p. 10.

[13] G. F. Moore, *Judaism*, Vol. 1 (New York, 1971), p. 127.

[14] See, for example, the research in J. H. Charlesworth, *The Pseudepigrapha and Modern Research with a Supplement* (Chico, 1981); J. J. Collins, *The Apocalyptic Imagination: An Introduction to the Jewish Matrix of Christianity* (New York, 1984); P. D. Hanson, *The Dawn of Apocalyptic* (Philadelphia, 1975); C. Rowland, *The Open Heaven: A Study of Apocalyptic in Judaism and Early Christianity* (London, 1982); and M. E. Stone (ed.), *Jewish Writings of the Second Temple Period* (Assen, 1984).

of influence by elements of apocalypticism. For example, with the advantage of hindsight, Flavius Josephus did not interpret events of the First Revolt apocalyptically, but rather sought to *hide* the apocalyptic views of the Jews from his audience. Nevertheless, his history provides several examples of how apocalyptic elements, particularly the messianic expectation, influenced Jewish thinking and shaped historical events before 70 C.E. Josephus describes in several places how "charlatans" and false prophets were able to play on popular eschatological expectations to precipitate political action against Rome.[15] He also informs us of the tremendous popular success of teachers like John the Baptist, known to us from the Gospels as an apocalyptic preacher.[16]

Some of the best evidence for apocalypticism in first-century Judaism comes from Qumran,[17] where multiple copies of the Book of Enoch witness the popularity of this grandfather of apocalypses. For instance, the War Scroll manifests a belief in the breaking in of the new age and the eschatological conflict of good and evil. Several documents manifest a cosmic dualism (e.g. 1QS 3.18-4.26) or the periodization of history (4Q180; 11QMel).[18]

Recently, J. H. Charlesworth has shown that Jewish folklore and folk traditions were an important part of the apocalyptic literature. The influence of myth (*Urzeit/Endzeit*, etc.) on apocalypticism has long been noted. If the apocalypses were a literature of the folk to any appreciable degree, as the presence of myth and folklore would indicate, then they could not have been far from the cultural mainstream.[19]

---

[15] E.g., *War* 2.259-64, 6.285-99, and 6.312-15. The Samaritans were similarly prone to such disturbances (e.g., *Ant* 18.85-87).

[16] *Ant* 18.116-19. I might point out here that Hillel and Jesus share the distinction of being ignored (or largely ignored, depending on one's assessment of the Testimonium Flavianum) by Josephus. Later Jews and Christians share the odd embarrassment of revering founders who were judged by this contemporary writer to have been of little or no historical importance.

[17] See, for example, John J. Collins, "Was the Dead Sea Sect an Apocalyptic Community?" in L. Schiffman (ed.), *Archaeology and History in the Dead Sea Scrolls* (Sheffield, 1990), pp. 25-51.

[18] John Collins has summarized well the apocalyptic elements found in the Dead Sea Scrolls in *The Apocalyptic Imagination*, pp. 115-41. See also F. García Martínez, *Qumran and Apocalyptic: Studies on the Aramaic Texts from Qumran* (Leiden, 1992).

[19] See most recently, J. H. Charlesworth, "Folk Traditions In Jewish Apocalyptic Literature," in Charlesworth and Collins (eds.), *Mysteries and Revelations: Apocalyptic Studies Since the Uppsala Colloquium* (Sheffield, 1991), pp. 91-113.

The books of the New Testament frequently reveal not only their own apocalyptic worldview, but occasionally that of the larger contemporary culture as well. For example, Acts 5:36-37 witnesses a certain popular messianic interest in the Galilee, just as Mark 11 and parallels do for Judaea. Recent interpreters of the apostle Paul have demonstrated that apocalypticism was fundamental to his theology,[20] and the Revelation of John is, of course, the premier Christian apocalypse.

The Apocrypha and Pseudepigrapha of the Old Testament also reveal the apocalyptic *Zeitgeist* of late Second Temple Judaism. Many of these documents date to the time of Hillel and Jesus. Many have a Palestinian Jewish provenance and they are indisputably apocalyptic. As G. W. E. Nickelsburg has summarized:

> We may properly use the term 'apocalyptic' to characterize the texts in *1 Enoch* [for example], because the claim to revelation or, indeed, the literary form that presents this claim, is not accidental to the text, but is essential to its world-view, or construction of reality. The authors' revelations are the salvific means by which the readers bridge and overcome the dualisms that are the very nature of reality as they understand and experience it."[21]

In other words, both the authors and their audience shared a profoundly apocalyptic worldview.

Thus, in the age of Hillel and Jesus, apocalyptic beliefs influenced and even precipitated key political events, generated a vast popular literature, reflected the lore of the folk, informed popular piety, and motivated several of the major sects, including infant Christianity. Therefore, it cannot be unfair to say that the age of Hillel and Jesus was an age of apocalypticism, or that apocalypticism was the *Zeitgeist* of that age.

---

[20] E.g., J. Christiaan Beker, *Paul the Apostle: The Triumph of God in Life and Thought* (Philadelphia, 1980), p. 181: "The apocalyptic worldview is the fundamental carrier of Paul's thought."

[21] G. W. E. Nickelsburg, "The Apocalyptic Construction of Reality in 1 Enoch," in Charlesworth and Collins (eds.), *Mysteries*, p. 62.

II. JESUS PROFOUNDLY INFLUENCED BY APOCALYPTICISM

There can no longer be any doubt that Jesus himself was profoundly influenced by apocalypticism. His declaration in the Gospel of Mark (1:15), "The time is fulfilled, and the kingdom of God is at hand," is a clear statement of the imminence of a new age in which God's rule will be established and in which this present aeon will find its end. Jesus' further pronouncement, a continual embarrassment to the later church, that "there be some of them that stand here, which shall not taste of death, till they have seen the kingdom of God come with power" (Mk 9:1 and parallels), further witnesses his belief in the imminent end of the world. Moreover, the phrase "come in power" is itself taken from the apocalyptic book of Daniel and reappears in such works as the Apocalypse of John, 4 Ezra, and 2 Baruch.

Jesus' belief in a Coming One or Son of Man—whether he understood this to be himself or not—is an expectation also found in apocalypses both earlier and later than Jesus.[22] Like the apocalypticists, Jesus has no interest in preserving the present social order; in fact, his utter pessimism and hostility toward it is clear. His hostility is expressed in woes upon the rich (Lk 6:24-25) and in his general disdain for the socially empowered. For Jesus, what would not transfer to the coming kingdom was not important. Jesus' historical dualism is clearly expressed in his belief in the two ages, utterly incompatible with each other, one of which was even then breaking in upon the other. Finally, Jesus looks forward to the eschatological purifying of the earth, which will then be inhabited by the meek.[23] Finally, Jesus may be describing an apocalyptic vision in Lk 10:18 where he reports having seen the fall of Satan like lightning from heaven.

Though the teachings of Jesus were clearly grounded in an apocalyptic worldview, Jesus himself was just as clearly *not* an apocalypticist in the narrowest sense. Apocalypse is a literary genre and there is no evidence that Jesus ever wrote at all beyond doodles on the ground. Certainly he never wrote an apocalypse, and writing is the

---

[22] 1En 1:9/Jude 14-15/4QEn^c 51. See also 2Bar 70-73; 4Ezra 13:29-40; TLevi 18:1-10; TJud 24:1-6; SibOr 3:49.

[23] Not all scholars agree. See e.g., R. Fuller, "Jesus, Paul, and Apocalyptic," *Anglican Theological Review* 71/2 (1989) 134–42; and M. Borg, *Conflict, Holiness and Politics in the Teachings of Jesus* (New York, 1984).

medium of apocalypse—a *sine qua non*. Jesus' medium was speech, rather than writing. His focus was proclamation, not publishing. Moreover, no apocalyptic vision is recorded in the New Testament in which Jesus plays the role of seer.[24]

The more than one hundred twenty aphorisms attributed to Jesus in the New Testament are remarkably free of apocalyptic elements. This works against any conclusion that Jesus was an apocalypticist in the radical sense.[25]

Also at odds with the usual apocalyptic viewpoint is Jesus' concern for the here and now, rather than the world above or the world to come. His apocalyptic pessimism toward the present world did not result in the usual detachment from present social concerns, but in a clear and surprising social activism. In this regard he shares with Hillel a concern for the poor and the oppressed. Although Jesus taught that the kingdom of heaven was at hand, the major significance of this fact was the preparatory changes it required of the converted—now and in *this* world. The critical time ($\kappa\alpha\iota\rho\delta\varsigma$) for Jesus was not the apocalyptic future but the determinative *now*. Jesus reflected no resigned fatalism. He did not wait patiently for a better world. Rather, he demanded that we change this one in anticipation of the one to come. Thus it would be a mistake to make Jesus a radical apocalypticist or the source of the apocalypticism of his world, but it would be an equal mistake to deny that Jesus fully accepted and operated within an apocalyptic worldview.

Early Christianity was heavily influenced by apocalypticism. Under the right circumstances, it later produced some sovereign apocalypses. But Jesus did not write them. Apocalypticism was the stream in which Jesus swam, but apparently it did not spring forth from him.

III. TRADITIONS OF HILLEL UNINFLUENCED BY APOCALYPTICISM

According to G. Boccaccini, apocalypticism in the late Second Temple period was not just one school of thought among others. Rather, it was

---

[24] Even though the transfiguration (Mk 9:2-10 and par.) and Jesus' reference to Satan's fall (Lk 10:18) should both be interpreted apocalyptically, by the time Christian apocalypses began to be written, casting Jesus as a seer would have constituted a theological demotion.

[25] My thanks are extended to D. Aune for this insightful observation.

"an expression of a wide cultural phenomenon that was spread well beyond the borders of Israel. The apocalypses witness not only a form but a content: they are the vehicles of a definitive 'world view.'"[26] That being the case, how did Hillel, a contemporary of Jesus, avoid being influenced by the same "wide cultural phenomenon" and the same "definitive world view?" The Hillel of tradition shows little influence from apocalypticism.[27] He shares neither Jesus' interest in the coming age and the eschatological kingdom of God nor his concern for the coming messiah. This tremendous difference cannot be dismissed merely as a distortion based on inadequate sources. As Nahum Glatzer observed, Hillel's "silence on messianism in a period in which it was a burning issue cannot be adequately explained by the paucity of our sources."[28] Why this absence of apocalypticism in Hillel?

First, it is possible that the ivory tower of the scholar protected Hillel from the same concerns that occupied the common folk. Apparently, Hillel's colleagues and associates were chiefly scholars like himself. Jesus was primarily a street preacher and an activist, rather than a scholar, although he was not unacquainted with the methods of the schools.[29] The New Testament indicates that Jesus' circle of friends was much different from that of the Pharisees. There would certainly have been a class difference between Jesus and his people on the one hand and Hillel and his people on the other. Different classes often have different interests and aspirations. Moreover, Galilee may have been less affected by the formal training and scholarship of the schools than Jerusalem.[30] Formal education may have made a difference in world-view. For example, we do not see much apocalypticism in the sages or in other intellectuals of the time such as Philo or Josephus, nor does it seem to have been common among the Sadducees.

---

[26] G. Boccaccini, "Jewish Apocalyptic Tradition: The Contribution of Italian Scholarship," in Charlesworth and Collins (eds.), *Mysteries*, p. 35.

[27] J. Neusner has clearly demonstrated the problem of the historical Hillel. While I make no attempt here to distinguish the Hillel of history from the Hillel of tradition, the difference between Hillel and the school of Hillel, a difference much like that between Jesus and the early church, should be noted.

[28] Nahum Glatzer, "Hillel the Elder in the Light of the Dead Sea Scrolls," in K. Stendahl (ed.), *The Scrolls and the New Testament* (London, 1957), p. 242.

[29] W. D. Davies, *Christian Origins and Judaism* (New York, 1973), pp. 20–21.

[30] R. Otto, *The Kingdom of God and the Son of Man* (London, 1943), pp. 13–15; but see also W. D. Davies, *Christian Origins*, pp. 20–21.

Second, Jesus was a Palestinian Jew and a Galilean. Hillel was a Judaean Jew of Babylonian origin. According to S. Safrai, Galilee may have provided a "hasidic fringe" to the Pharisaic movement, a more enthusiastic and conservative kind of Pharisee, just as it produced the extremist fringe of political Zealotism. Jesus the Galilean and his Galilean movement may have been a "hasidic" or "zealot" branch of an emerging Pharisaic Judaism, while Hillel and the "rabbinic" branch were going a different direction.[31]

Some scholars have suggested that there was no apocalypticism in Hillel because rejection of apocalypticism had always been a characteristic of the Pharisaic party.[32] But this is no longer tenable. The Pharisees originally supported both wars against Rome—wars fueled largely by popular apocalyptic fervor. And the school of Akiba was not hostile to apocalyptic concerns even after the disaster of 70 C.E. Even Johanan b. Zakkai still believed in the coming of the messiah.[33] Although certain aspects of apocalypticism lost their appeal in some circles after the First Revolt, apocalyptic messianism did not lose its credibility in the mainstream until after the Second.[34] Moreover, the continuance of apocalyptic motifs in 3 Enoch and the hekalot literature, in Jewish merkavah mysticism, in the later kabbalah, and even in the figure of Sabbatai Svi, works against the claim that apocalypticism was ever completely jettisoned, even after Bar Kochba.[35]

Although the halakhic literature contains remarkably little in it that could be called apocalyptic, the Mishnah's lack of apocalyptic material likely derives from its function, and does not necessarily define the entire thought world of the rabbis.[36] Though halakhah may be

---

[31] See the references in S. Safrai, *The Literature of the Sages* (Assen, 1987), p. 13, and notes 82–83.

[32] E.g., Bousset, Box, Charles, Herford, and Moore.

[33] b.Ber 28b. He identified the messiah with King Hezekiah (ARN 25).

[34] y.Taan 68d: "R. Simeon b. Johai taught: My teacher, R. Akiba interpreted, A star will come forth out of Jacob. Koseba came from Jacob. When Akiba saw him, he cried, This is the king-messiah. R. Johanan said, Grass will still be growing from your cheeks and the son of David will not have come."

[35] See J. Gruenwald, *Apocalyptic and Merkavah Mysticism* (Leiden, 1980); G. Scholem, *Major Trends in Jewish Mysticism* (New York, 1941); and W. D. Davies, "From Schweitzer to Scholem: Reflections on Sabbatai Svi," *JBL* 95/4 (1976) 529–58.

[36] As C. Rowland notes in *The Open Heaven*, p. 271; see also P. Henry, *New Directions in New Testament Study* (Philadelphia, 1979), p. 88, and W. D. Davies, *Christian Origins*, pp. 19–30. I am indebted to Prof. S. Safrai's observation in Jerusalem that "Halakah leaves little, if any, place for apocalypticism or mysticism."

remarkably free from apocalyptic influences, haggadic literature, produced and preserved by the same rabbinic Judaism as that which produced the halakhah, yields ample evidence of the continued popular influence of apocalypticism. The nonapocalyptic nature of halakhah simply reflects differences of genre and function, not differences of theology. As L. Ginzberg said, "It would be very difficult to prove the contention that the attitude of the apocalyptic authors toward the Torah was different from that taken by the Rabbis."[37] And at different ends of the spectrum, both G. F. Moore and J. Bloch allowed that the eschatology of the apocalypses is similar to that of the later rabbis.[38]

It was a mistake to attempt to find the sources of apocalypticism in Second Temple Judaism within a single sect, as its recognized presence in four of the five major sects now indicates. One can, on occasion, identify individual apocalypses as originating within one or another sect of Judaism, but not the apocalyptic worldview itself or apocalypses as a whole. Indeed, the *absence* of specifically sectarian concerns in the apocalypses indicates that they originated in the mainstream of Judaism, rather than in some sectarian backwater. To seek the fountain of apocalypticism in only one sect[39] is to adopt a reductionist view which cannot do justice to the pervasive influence of apocalypticism as a common cultural background to all the sects, including Pharisaism, before 70 C.E. Apocalypticism did not arrive all at once and fully dressed like Athena from the head of Zeus. It developed in mainstream Judaism over a period of centuries. Even if the apocalypticism of the twentieth century is principally associated with sectarian belief, we can no longer think of the apocalypses of Early Judaism and Christianity as a separate sectarian literature. Apocalypticism was not a limited sectarian aberration in the first century.

Finally, we cannot say with any certainty that the historical Hillel was *not* influenced in some degree by apocalypticism: all the traditions about him are controlled by the later rabbis and were filtered through their polemical situations.[40] If some small apocalyptic element existed in

---

[37] Ginzberg, "Some Observations," p. 134.

[38] Moore, *Judaism*, 2:285; and Bloch, *On the Apocalyptic*, p. 58.

[39] As, for example, does Bloch, *On the Apocalyptic*, p. 20 *et passim*.

[40] See J. Neusner, *Judaism in the Beginning of Christianity* (Philadelphia, 1984), pp. 63–88.

Hillel's thought, it would have been edited out in a later period. I suspect that Hillel, like other Jews of his day, may have prayed for the coming of the messiah, but the school that bears his name would never have preserved such information.

Still, it is extremely unlikely that Hillel was an apocalyptic teacher whose apocalypticism has merely been edited away. Schools may reinterpret their founders, but they seldom oppose them diametrically; so it must surely be accepted as a matter of historical probability that there are likely to be more continuities between Hillel and the school that bore his name than discontinuities, and therefore that Hillel did not likely hold an apocalyptic worldview.

Hillel's followers ultimately won out in Judaism because he had provided them in the first century with the only theology that could survive to the second. Only Hillel's method, his strategy for dealing with the crisis of his own time, proved serviceable for dealing with the crises of later times.

And what was the crisis of the first century B.C.E. to which Hillel the Elder provided only one of several answers? As in the modernist controversy of our own time, it was the challenge of new learning. The advantages of Greek thinking had presented themselves to Jewish intellectuals for two centuries, and though Hellenism was sporadically resisted, by the time of Hillel it had become necessary to match the rigors of Hellenistic thinking with a Torah scholarship that would be equally respected in a Hellenized environment.[41]

P. D. Hanson maintains that "political intrigue, military destruction, and *the imposition of the symbolic universe of Hellenism* created an overwhelming sense of alienation which called into question the viability of the dominant social and religious structures."[42] It was Hillel, according to tradition, who responded to that sense of alienation, to the intellectual challenge of Hellenism, and established "a new hermeneutic which broadened the range of interpretation and application of the Torah to everyday life."[43] Such everyday life, we must remember, was life in a Hellenized world.

---

[41] N. Glatzer also notes this crisis in Torah study in the post-Maccabean period in "Hillel the Elder in the Light of the Dead Sea Scrolls," pp. 232–34.

[42] P.D. Hanson, "Apocalypticism," in *IDBS* (Nashville, 1976), p. 33 [italics added].

[43] L. Ginzberg, "The Significance of the Halachah for Jewish History," in *On Jewish Law and Lore* (New York, 1955), p. 95.

To come full circle to my introduction, there was a modernist controversy of sorts still raging in Judaism in the first centuries B.C.E. Despite the military and political successes of the Maccabees, the new learning of Hellenism continued to exert intellectual pressure on Judaism. It increasingly presented Jews with a choice of accomodation and adaptation or of defiance and rejection.

The political challenge of foreign occupation and the intellectual challenge of the new learning forced Jews of the late Second Temple period to recognize that their traditional theological world was incompatible with contemporary reality. This is essentially the crisis of modernism. In response to it, liberals like Hillel adapted their theology to fit the contemporary reality, while conservatives rejected that reality as illegitimate and looked for eschatological vindication of their ideal— hence the characteristic pessimism of apocalypticism toward the evil of the present world and the expectation of a better world in which things are as they ought to be.

The choice presented to Judaism by the Hellenistic and Roman intellectual and political worlds was "fight or bend." The apocalypticists chose to fight on both levels; the sages chose to bend. This is the watershed of difference between them. There is no evidence that apocalypticists rejected the Law, just as there is ample evidence that Pharisaism continued to believe in the Messiah and the end time. But the apocalypticists chose with disastrous consequences to focus on the coming confrontation with the world, while the sages chose to focus on surviving and living in the world. Hillel saw that survival in the real world required adapting to the times and gleaning the benefits of Greek thinking. But the conservatives dug in their heels and damned both the new learning and the foreign world that produced it. This helps explain why apocalypticism was "a theology of martyrdom," as it has been called.[44] It may also explain the vengeful and uncompromising nature of apocalypticism in the land—it was usually born of a siege mentality.

In embracing the new learning, "modernists" like Hillel—an intellectual minority—sought to preserve the best of the old by synthesis with the best of the new. David Daube calls this strategy the "Judaizing of Hellenistic doctrines" in which Hillel and other rabbis

---

[44] I.e. by Beker, *Paul*, p. 136.

adopt Hellenistic ideas, yet they inject essentially Jewish notions into the material and thereby produce something which preserves the essentials of Jewish tradition but accomodates that tradition to prevalent Hellenistic doctrines.... The die-hards like the B'nai Bathyra who would have nothing to do with Hillel's 'new-fangled' Hellenistic approach were left by the wayside.[45]

Bickerman, Lieberman, Neusner and Smith have all noted the profoundly Hellenized character of Pharisaism after Hillel.[46]

Not only was the theory of the Pharisaic school that of a school of Greek philosopy, but so were its practices. Its teachers taught without pay, like philosophers; they attached to themselves particular disciples who followed them around and served them, like philosophers; they looked to gifts for support, like philosophers; they were exempt from taxation, like philosophers; they were distinguished in the street by their walk, speech, and peculiar clothing, like philosophers; they practiced and praised asceticism, like philosophers; and finally—what is, after all the meat of the matter—they discussed the questions philosophers discussed and reached the conclusions philosophers reached.[47]

In all of this Hellenizing, Hillel was motivated, as in the institution of the *prosbul*, with the "order [or 'preservation' or 'amelioration'] of the world." That is, he adjusted the outward demands of the Law to meet changing societal conditions.[48] He thus showed a concern for the present world and its necessities not shared by the apocalypticists. As a true modernist, he showed a willingness to sacrifice the ideal world of religious tradition for "the order of the world" (i.e., the present world of experience).[49] Judah Goldin observed

[45] D. Daube, "The New Testament and Rabbinic Judaism," *Liberal Jewish Monthly* 28 (1957) 8.

[46] Cf. Neusner, *From Politics to Piety* (New York, 1979), pp. 7–11.

[47] Smith, cited in Neusner, *From Politics to Piety*, p. 9.

[48] E.g., Giṭṭ 4:3.

[49] Hutchison defines modernism "first and most visibly" as "the conscious, intended adaptation of religious ideas to modern culture" (*The Modernist Impulse*, p. 2).

that after Hillel the "objective of social well-being" was reached "by adjusting traditional law and sacred Scripture to changing conditions."

The methodology passed on by Hillel was designed to "increase and discipline the possibilities for independent thought and thereby *liberalize* the Jewish mind." Of Hillel himself Goldin writes, "ethical zeal, love of learning, and sensitivity to social welfare ... were the recurring motifs of his life."[50] But again, these are precisely the values most highly prized by the liberals in our own modernist conflict—rationalism, ethicism and humanism. Thus, I insist that Hillel can be seen as a modernist liberal who "made new and important changes in the law" and "accomodated the law to the conditions of everyday life."[51]

This capacity to adjust was the greatest contribution of Hillel. After him, "for the order of the world," the sages could change their understanding of what the Law demanded according to circumstances, and yet remain faithful to the one whole Torah given to Moses on Sinai. In his own day, this allowed his followers to cope with the new learning of Hellenism. In a later time, the same principle would allow larger Judaism to cope with the loss of the Temple, the loss of sovereignty, and the loss of the land. While Hillel's modernism was only one of several answers to the challenge of Hellenism current in his own day, it proved to be the only concept of Torah that could survive the two revolts. For providing the means of adapting a fixed Torah to a changing reality, Hillel was eventually and deservedly recognized as a second Ezra.[52]

The outcome of the Second Revolt and the fate of R. Akiba sealed the fate of apocalypticism in subsequent Judaism. As J. Neusner has stated concerning messianic speculation, "In the aftermath of Bar Kokhba's debacle, silence on the subject [of the apocalyptic messiah] served to express a clarion judgment."[53] Apocalypticism survived in Christianity. Yet Chistian apocalypticism never faced the same crises as its Jewish counterpart, for Christian theology did not need the Temple or the land. Besides, Christianity ultimately vanquished its political opponents. After such an incredible victory it was not the failure of the

[50] Judah Goldin, "Hillel the Elder," *Journal of Religion* 26 (1946) 263 [emphasis mine].
[51] J. Neusner, *Judaism in the Beginning of Christianity*, p. 64.
[52] Glatzer, "Hillel the Elder," p. 244.
[53] J. Neusner, *Judaisms and Their Messiahs* (Cambridge, 1987), p. 275.

apocalyptic view but the success of *Heilsgeschichte* that caused the decline of apocalypticism in the Christian church.[54] Thus, ironically, while political defeat marked the nominal end of apocalypticism in Judaism, political victory marked the beginning of the same end in Christianity.

---

[54] Though, as in Judaism, it never did completely cease. See Norman Cohn, *The Pursuit of the Millennium* (Oxford, 1970^2).

WHO WERE THE PHARISEES?

SINCE THE DAYS of Abraham Geiger and Julius Wellhausen, the question of who the Pharisees really were has been hotly debated among scholars.[1] Among the more recent attempts to delineate the history, teachings, and functions of the Pharisees the ones by Neusner, Rivkin, Saldarini, and Mason are the most important.[2] Each of these authors has contributed in a special way to a better understandng of who the Pharisees were. Neusner is rightly credited with starting a new mode of critical inquiry into rabbinic texts. Rivkin helped delimit the extent of the material that may be used for defining the Pharisees. Saldarini has introduced social science models into the study of the first-century "sects." Finally, Mason has done a careful literary study of all the passages in Josephus that deal with the Pharisees.

---

[1] A preliminary version of this essay was published as "Chi erano i farisei? Un nuovo approccio a un problema antico," *Nuova Umanità* 75-76 (1991) 53-68. For the history of scholarship on the Pharisees, especially in Josephus, see S. Mason, *Flavius Josephus on the Pharisees: A Composition-Critical Study* (Leiden, 1991), pp. 1-39.

[2] J. Neusner, *The Rabbinic Traditions About the Pharisees Before 70*, 3 vols. (Leiden, 1971), has a full, though at times overly polemical, review of earlier literature (vol. 3, pp. 320-68); Neusner, *From Politics to Piety: The Emergence of Pharisaic Judaism* (Englewood Cliffs, N.J., 1973); E. Rivkin, "Defining the Pharisees: The Tannaitic Sources," *HUCA* 40-41 (1970) 205-49; Rivkin, *A Hidden Revolution: The Pharisees' Search for the Kingdom Within* (Nashville, 1978); A. J. Saldarini, *Pharisees, Scribes, and Sadducees in Palestinian Society: A Sociological Approach* (Wilmington, Del., 1988); Mason, *Flavius Josephus*. In addition, see A. Michel and J. Le Moyne, "Pharisiens," *DBSup* 7 (1966) 1022-1115; M. Pelletier, *Les Pharisiens: Histoire d'un parti méconnu* (Paris, 1990). D. B. Gowler, *Host, Guest, Enemy, and Friend: Portraits of the Pharisees in Luke and Acts*. Emory Studies in Early Christianity (New York, 1991); D. Goodblatt, "The Place of the Pharisees in First Century Judaism: The State of the Debate," *JSJ* 20 (1989) 12-30.

After over two decades of research, there is at least one assured result: we know considerably less about the Pharisees than an earlier generation "knew."[3] Evidently there are many more questions than answers. The crucial problems remain the usability and reliability of the various sources, the origin and history of the Pharisees, their teachings, and their relations to other contemporary groups, including rabbinic Judaism.

The complexity of these questions has led to divergent and contradictory answers. The question of who the Pharisees were and what we can know about them has never been as widely open as it is today—and this in spite of *and* because of considerable research efforts. This new situation is evident in a small volume by Stemberger, in which he shows how ill-founded many common assumptions about the Pharisees are, even though he is unable to offer a new coherent alternative picture.[4]

One means of finding out about the Pharisees that has hardly been exploited is a study of those individuals who either identified themselves or were identified by others as Pharisees. Their number is quite small, no more than a dozen in sources attested prior to the fourth century.[5] This is certainly not a representative sample of the whole

---

[3] Cf. L. Finkelstein, *The Pharisees: The Sociological Background of Their Faith*, 3rd ed. (Philadelphia, 1962); L. Finkelstein, *The Cambridge History of Judaism*, vol. 2 (Cambridge, 1989) pp. 229–77.

[4] G. Stemberger, *Pharisäer, Sadduzäer, Essener*, SBS 144 (Stuttgart, 1991).

[5] S. J. D. Cohen ("The Significance of Yavneh: Pharisees, Rabbis, and the End of Jewish Sectarianism," *HUCA* 55 [1984] 36, note 20) lists eleven of these. An apocryphal Gospel fragment (POxy 5.840.10–11) mentions "a certain Pharisee chief priest by the name of ...." Unfortunately, the reading of the name is extremely doubtful although the editors cautiously suggest Levi. This priest is described as having an argument with Jesus in the Temple area about purification requirements. Although preserved in only a copy of around 400 C.E., this text betrays an unexpectedly detailed acquaintance with some Jewish purity regulations (e.g., note the double stairway used for ritual baths). This fact however does not bestow historical probability on the incident recounted. See A. Büchler, "The New Fragment of an Uncanonical Gospel," *JQR* 20 (1908) 330–46; J. Jeremias, *Unbekannte Jesusworte*, 3rd ed. (Gütersloh, 1963), pp. 50–60. Another Pharisee, by the name of Arimanius or Arimanias, is mentioned in a gnostic text (ApocJn II.1.1.5-17; cf. Papyrus Berolinensis 8502 19.12). His question "[Where] is your master whom you followed?" addressed to John the son of Zebedee, sets the stage for the theological exposition of the tractate. Arimaius here seems to be a literary device more than a historical figure.

group in any given period, even less so for its entire history. Yet it might be profitable to try to treat the Pharisees not as a more or less amorphous collective, but as individuals who happened to be members of the same group. Through this approach we may find elements for verification or falsification of current theories about them. This limited study yields some negative as well as positive results that may be useful for the larger question as to who the Pharisees were, what they stood for, and what we can know about their connections with later rabbinic Judaism.

A first negative result is that only three or four of the sages studied by Neusner in his *The Rabbinic Traditions about the Pharisees Before 70* qualify for the present study. The others are not identified as Pharisees in ancient sources nor is it clear why they should be so identified today. Hillel and Shammai, for example, are explicitly connected with the Pharisees for the first time by Jewish-Christian sectarians cited in Jerome's commentary on Isaiah 8:14, written in the first decade of the fifth century.[6] Rabbinic literature never identifies any named individual as a Pharisee.[7] There is a growing awareness of the fact that the tannaitic sages were not necessarily either Pharisees or direct successors of the Pharisees, even though there are important lines of connection between Pharisees and later rabbis.[8]

My purpose here is not to deny that Hillel, Shammai, or other pre-70 rabbis were Pharisees, but to bring together the material about individuals explicitly associated with the group. This may provide a more secure foundation for affirmations about "the" Pharisees. It may also assist, incidentally, in calling into question stereotypical views of the group, whether favorable or unfavorable.

---

[6] Ad Isa 8:14: *Duas domus Nazaraei ... duas familias interpretantur, Sammai et Hellel, ex quibus orti sunt scribae et pharisaei* ("The Nazareans interpret the two houses [of Isa 8:14] as the two families, of Shammai and of Hillel, from whom the scribes and Pharisees originated") CCSL 73, ed. M. Adriaen (Paris-Turnhout, 1963), p. 116; *PL* 24.119. Cf. A. F. J. Klijn, "Jerome's Quotations from a Nazoraean Interpretation of Isaiah," in *Judéo-Christianisme: Récherches ... offertes ... à J. Danielou* (= *RSR* 60 [1972] 249-51). S. J. D. Cohen, "The Significance of Yavneh," pp. 52-53.

[7] On Judah ben Gedidyah, see below.

[8] E. P. Sanders, *Paul and Palestinian Judaism* (Philadelphia, 1977), pp. 60-62; J. Neusner, *Judaism: The Evidence of the Mishnah* (Chicago, 1981), pp. 70-71; S. J. D. Cohen, "The Significance of Yavneh," pp. 36-42; Stemberger, *Pharisäer*, pp. 40, 129-35.

1. The first individual who may be considered a Pharisee is a certain Eleazar. He is a key figure in the famous legend about the break between John Hyrcanus (135/4–104 B.C.E.) and the Pharisees, as recounted by Josephus (*Ant* 13.288-98). During a banquet given by Hyrcanus for his Pharisee friends, they find nothing about which to reproach him. Only Eleazar demands that he lay down the office of high priest. Hyrcanus is understandably upset and asks the Pharisees to determine the penalty for such arrogance. The Pharisees suggest to scourge Eleazar, but Hyrcanus considers such a light penalty an insult to his dignity. He therefore breaks relations with the Pharisees, whose pupil he was or had been,[9] and joins (*or:* sides with) the Sadducees. The whole story is quite legendary and not trustworthy as a historical source.[10] Eleazar is mentioned in conjunction with the Pharisees, but not clearly identified as one of them. If he was one, he is mentioned precisely because his disrespect for the high priest was exceptional.[11]

In the parallel story in the Babylonian Talmud (b.Kid 66a), the names as well as other details are different. Here it is Judah ben Gedidyah, an elder, who demands that King Yannai (!) renounce the high priestly office. The villain of the story is again a certain Eleazar (here identified as son of Poirah). It is not entirely clear, especially in light of Josephus, whether Judah ben Gedidyah is meant to represent *the* Pharisees' point of view.

2. The second person that concerns us here appears on the scene at the time of Herod the Great. Josephus calls him "Pollion the Pharisee." He and his disciple "Samaias" were honored by Herod for the assistance they had given him while he was still a commoner.[12] Because

---

[9] *Ant* 13.289. The MSS differ concerning the tense of the verb. The meaning of μαθητής in this context is unclear. On the one hand, it might be taken as an awkward way of saying that Hyrcanus himself was a Pharisee, as might also be inferred from *Ant* 13.296, according to which he abandoned the Pharisees for the Sadducees. On the other hand, Hyrcanus is clearly distinguished from "all the Pharisees" (*Ant* 13.292). The problem is foremost a literary one: What idea did Josephus and/or his source want to convey about Hyrcanus? It seems that at most he is presented as a pupil or supporter of the Pharisees, never as a member of the group.

[10] *Ant* 13.288-98; b.Kid 66a. Cf. J. Sievers, *The Hasmoneans and Their Supporters: From Mattathias to the Death of John Hyrcanus* (Atlanta, 1990), pp. 147-50.

[11] Cf. S. Mason, *Flavius Josephus on the Pharisees: A Composition-Critical Study* (Leiden, 1991), pp. 229-30.

[12] *Ant* 15.3-4, 370. Josephus is inconsistent in his report on the manslaughter trial of Herod. In *War* he says nothing of Pollion or Samaias. In *Ant* he first reports the intervention of Samaias (14.172-76), but later credits Pollion with it (15.4; cf. 370). In

of the similarity of names, Pollion and Samaias are often considered identical with Avtalyon and Shemayah of rabbinic literature.[13] When Josephus mentions Pollion and Samaias together, twice he calls only the former a Pharisee. One has to take this distinction seriously. That John Hyrcanus and Samaias are called disciples of Pharisees does not make them Pharisees.

In any case, according to Josephus, Pollion was an important person, a man with a following, who had assisted Herod. Because of this, he and his followers were exempted from a loyalty oath.[14]

It is possible that Pollion/Avtalyon was an authoritative representative of the Pharisees. According to *Ant* 14.172-76, his disciple Samaias was a member of the Sanhedrin, the only one spared by Herod. The roles of the two in relation to Herod are confused by Josephus. Much later, rabbinic tradition would call Avtalyon—and Shemayah—the two greatest men of their generation.[15]

3. The next person described by Josephus as a Pharisee is a certain Saddok (*Ant* 18.4), who, together with Judas the Galilean (*or:* the Gaulanite), founded the so-called Fourth Philosophy at the time of the census of Quirinus (c. 6 C.E.). Josephus says nothing else about Saddok, but charges that "the zeal which Judas and Saddok inspired in the younger element meant the ruin of our cause."[16]

With characteristic inconsistency, Josephus states first that the Fourth Philosophy had nothing in common with the other Jewish groups (*War* 2.118). Instead, later he asserts, "Concerning everything else they agree with the opinions of the Pharisees, except that they have an unconquerable passion for liberty" (*Ant* 18.23). Mason correctly points

---

Ant 15.3-4, the majority of the manuscripts assign the leading role to Pollion, while some harmonize the story with *Ant* 14, mentioning Samaias in his stead.

[13] m.Hag 2:2; m.Ab 1:10-11. L. Feldman, "The Identity of Pollio, the Pharisee," *JQR* 49 (1958–59) 53–62. Against this identification, cf. Neusner, *Rabbinic Traditions*, 1.159.

[14] *Ant* 15.370: συνέπειθε δὲ καὶ τοὺς περὶ Πολλίωνα τὸν Φαρισαῖον καὶ Σαμαίαν καὶ τῶν ἐκείνοις συνδιατριβόντων τοὺς πλείστους ὀμνύειν ("[Herod] tried to persuade also the people around Pollion the Pharisee and Samaias and most of those close to them to take the oath").

[15] b.Pes 66a. For other traditions attributed to them, see Neusner, *Rabbinic Traditions*, vol. 1, pp. 142–58.

[16] *Ant* 18.10 (trans. Feldman, LCL).

out that even in the *Antiquities*, "passion for liberty" is the main issue of this group. Similarities with the Pharisees in nondistinctive areas of teaching may tell us more about Josephus' attitude toward the Pharisees than about the actual closeness of the two groups.[17] Thus, Saddok is another Pharisee who is not representative of the group, even though Josephus admits (not in *War*, but in *Ant*) the Fourth Philosophy's indebtedness to Pharisaism. This does not in any way mitigate Josephus' negative—and biased—judgment about its founders.

In the numerous references to the Pharisees in the Gospels, few individual Pharisees are mentioned. Luke has Jesus dine on three occasions at the home of a Pharisee (probably each time a different one).[18]

4. Only the first one of these, Simon, is mentioned by name (Lk 7:40-44). Luke situates the story in Galilee. The name is probably introduced secondarily from Mark 14:3, even though Simon the Leper lived in Bethany near Jerusalem and is not called a Pharisee. Luke evidently wants to make the point that despite the tension and polemics, Jesus was in contact with several Pharisees.[19] All of them are portrayed as householders who are able to accommodate several guests at their homes.[20]

5. Nicodemus is the only other individual Pharisee in the Gospels. He appears only in John, first speaking with Jesus at night (3:1-15), then defending him, unsuccessfully, in the Sanhedrin (7:50-52). Finally, he participates in his burial (19:39). The historical reliability of this information is hard to assess, but aside from his problematic but enduring relationship with Jesus, Nicodemus is not a flat, stereotypical character, but a distinguished member of the ruling class (ἄρχων τῶν Ἰουδαίων; 3:1)—one who seeks truth and justice and offers compassion.[21]

---

[17] Cf. Mason, *Flavius Josephus*, pp. 282–85.

[18] Lk 7:36; 11:37; 14:1. Even more than in these banquet stories, the unnamed Pharisee in the parable of the Pharisee and the toll-collector (Lk 18:9-14) represents a type and not an individual.

[19] Many authors note that the historical basis of the Lukan banquet stories is not at all certain. Cf. G. Rossé, *Il Vangelo di Luca: commento esegetico e teologico* (Rome, 1992), p. 274, note 150; M. A. Powell, "The Religious Leaders in Luke: A Literary Critical Study," *JBL* 109 (1990) 93–110; J. T. Carroll, "Luke's Portrayal of the Pharisees," *CBQ* 50 (1988) 604–21.

[20] Cf. Lk 7:49; 11:45; 14:7.

[21] Cf. J. M. Bassler, "Mixed Signals: Nicodemus in the Fourth Gospel," *JBL* 108 (1989) 635–46. The so-called "Gospel of Nicodemus," also known as the "Acts of

6. Luke mentions two individual Pharisees in Acts: Paul (see below) and his alleged teacher, Gamaliel. Gamaliel is cited prominently on two occasions (5:34-39; 22:3). He is very important for the assessment of the Pharisaic movement, because he and his son, Simon ben Gamaliel, mentioned by Josephus, are the only persons unambiguously identified as Pharisees and cited in rabbinic literature. Thus, they are the only definite *personal* links between the Pharisees on one hand and the sages of rabbinic literature on the other. One has to bear in mind though that in the chain of tradition of m.Ab 1, Gamaliel and his son are listed after Hillel and Shammai, but without the usual formula "[they] received [the Torah] from them." This phrase appears again in m.Ab 2:8 in reference to Yoḥanan ben Zakkai, who "received from Hillel and Shammai." Abot de Rabbi Nathan, in fact, passes on to Yoḥanan ben Zakkai immediately after Hillel and Shammai.[22] Many scholars conclude, therefore, that Gamaliel and his son were inserted later into an existing text, perhaps to strengthen dynastic claims of the house of Judah the Prince.[23] The link between Gamaliel's family and the other sages is therefore more tenuous than is frequently assumed.[24]

Gamaliel is described in Acts as a Pharisee, a member of the Sanhedrin, and "a teacher of the law, held in honor by all the people" (5:34). His wise and tolerant attitude is expressed in the well-known statement, "If this plan or this undertaking is of human origin, it will dissolve: but if it is of God, you will not be able to dissolve them. You might even be found fighting against God!" (Acts 5:38-39). Luke can hardly have reconstructed an actual speech of Gamaliel at a closed-door session of the Sanhedrin. In fact, the anachronistic reference to the uprising of Theudas (5:36) shows that the speech was composed long after its dramatic date.[25] Here again—and even more than in Luke's Gospel—we find Luke's tendency to emphasize possible positive rela-

---

Pilate," is inspired by reminiscences of John's Nicodemus, but has no historical connection with him. Cf. *Apocrifi del NT*, vol. I/2, (Genova, 1981), p. 233.

[22] ARN A 14 (Schechter, p. 57).

[23] See, e.g., K. Marti and G. Beer, *'Abot (Väter)* (Giessen, 1927), p. 30.

[24] It may be that there was more than one prominent Gamaliel in the middle of the first century, because the high priest, Jesus, son of Gamaliel (*Ant* 20.213, 223), does not seem to have been a brother of his contemporary, Simon, son of Gamaliel. Perhaps Josephus reported the name of the high priest's father incorrectly.

[25] See Schürer-Vermes, *History*, Vol. I, p. 456, note 6.

tions between followers of Jesus and Pharisees.[26]

In rabbinic literature, it is not easy to distinguish traditions regarding this Gamaliel I (the Elder) from those of his grandson Gamaliel II. The traditions that may be assigned to Gamaliel I with some measure of confidence cover a great variety of topics.[27] Several of his decisions seem aimed at improving the position of women, especially in the case of widowhood or divorce. Gamaliel reportedly wrote letters regarding tithes and the intercalation of the calendar to various Jewish communities in Galilee, in the South, and in Babylon. In more than one story it is emphasized that he was unassuming and attentive to the opinions of others. He was rigorous, however, in not permitting use of the Targum of Job. Later it was asserted that "when Rabban Gamaliel the Elder died, the glory of the Law ceased and purity and abstinence (פרישות) died."[28] Thus both Luke and rabbinic literature paint a highly favorable image of Gamaliel as a man who stood up for the underprivileged and persecuted.

7. According to Acts 22:3, Paul was a student of Gamaliel. There are serious and well-founded doubts about this claim. What is beyond doubt, however, is that Paul—at least for some period of his life—understood himself as a Pharisee. In fact, the earliest known reference to a Pharisee is Phil 3:5-6, where Paul presents some of the principal elements of his earlier life, almost in the form of a brief resume:

---

[26] In some gnostic texts, Gamaliel is the name of an angel (cf. GEgyp III.2.57.6 and *passim*), whereas angelic names are usually easily distinguishable from human ones. In the Pseudo-Clementine *Recognitiones* (GCS 51, I.65.2 and *passim*), he is described as a secret Christian. An entire apocryphal Gospel, dating from the 5th or 6th century, is even attributed to Gamaliel (*Apocrifi del NT*, vol. I/2, pp. 346–66). He is also cited in other New Testament apocrypha. None of these texts adds any reliable and independent information about the historical Gamaliel.

[27] See Neusner, *Rabbinic Traditions*, 1.364–67, for a convenient but incomplete list of 26 traditions attributable to Gamaliel I. I. Konovitz (*Tannaitic Symposia*, Vol. 1: *R. Abba – Rabban Gamliel bar Yehudah ha-Nasi* [Jerusalem, 1967] pp. 269–74) cites 45 different traditions (in Hebrew/Aramaic), but omits some listed even by Neusner and includes others that refer to Yavneh and should therefore be attributed to Gamaliel II.

[28] m.Soṭ 9:15. פרישות is an abstract noun from the same verbal root as "Pharisee." Here it does not seem to indicate any connection with Pharisaism. This text is found in an appendix to the Mishnah tractate that contains material later than Judah the Patriarch, its main redactor. On the origin of the designation "Pharisee," see A. I. Baumgarten, "The Name of the Pharisees," *JBL* 102 (1983) 411–28.

circumcised	when eight days old,
of the people	(of) Israel,
of the tribe	(of) Benjamin,
a Hebrew of Hebrews;	
as to the law:	a Pharisee;
as to zeal:	a persecutor of the church;
as to righteousness under the law:	blameless.

Of the 99 references to Pharisees in the New Testament (Nestle-Aland, 26th ed.), this is the only one outside the Gospels and Acts. The Pauline corpus does not further mention Pharisees. Paul relates being a Pharisee to "the law," without further specification, but the context indicates that this identification should strengthen his credentials in the eyes of his audience.

Evidently he attributes to the Pharisees a particular view of or attitude toward the Torah. In Galatians 1:14 he gives the most extended description of his past. There he claims, "I advanced in Judaism beyond many among my people of the same age, for I was far more zealous for my ancestral traditions." Other Pharisees may not have agreed with this estimation,[29] but there is no doubt that Paul before his Damascus experience should be considered an authentic Pharisee.[30] It is clear that he means to emphasize the importance of Torah and of ancestral traditions in his understanding of Pharisaic Judaism. As was common among later rabbis, Paul did not occupy himself full-time with Torah study. Apparently he had learned a trade that enabled him to earn a living even during his missionary travels.[31]

Paul never explains who or what induced him to persecute the followers of Jesus, except that "as to zeal" he was "a persecutor of the church." He also does not state where and how he persecuted it. It seems unlikely that he did it in Jerusalem. Paul himself is silent about his place of origin and about a stay in Jerusalem before his conversion

---

[29] Josephus makes a similar claim for himself in *Life* 8–9.

[30] H. Maccoby's assertion (*Paul and Hellenism* [London and Philadelphia, 1991], p. 153) that "it was Jesus who was the Pharisee, and Paul the non-Pharisee" is interesting but unfounded. Maccoby thinks that Paul's knowledge of Pharisaic teachings was inadequate and thus that Paul could not have been a (good?) Pharisee. This approach begs the question: What were the criteria for belonging to the Pharisees?

[31] 1Thess 2:9; 1Cor 4:12; 9:6; cf. Acts 18:3.

experience. He only relates that even after his visit to Cephas in Jerusalem he was still "not known in person to the churches of Judea that are in Christ" (Gal 1:22). In his own writings, Paul offers little more explicitly autobiographical information concerning the time before the Damascus experience.[32]

Acts adds many more details about Paul's relation to the Pharisees. Much of this material reflects Luke's own interests. He has Paul state, "I am a Jew, born in Tarsus in Cilicia, but brought up in this city, educated at the feet of Gamaliel precisely according to our ancestral law, being zealous for God, just as all of you are today" (Acts 22:3). Luke underscores again Torah-observance and zeal as central elements of Paul's Pharisaism. He adds the word ἀκρίβεια, which is often used by Josephus in reference to the Pharisees' thoroughness and precision in interpreting the Torah.[33]

The most surprising assertion is made later, in a speech in his own defence, where Paul states, "Brothers, I am a Pharisee, a son of Pharisees" (Acts 23:6). Did Paul really remain a Pharisee? Was it possible to be a follower of Jesus and a Pharisee at the same time? For Luke, at least, the answer seems to be yes. On the occasion of the so-called Council of Jerusalem, he mentions "some believers who belonged to the school of the Pharisees."[34] As we noted before, Luke makes a point of emphasizing the closeness between (some of) the Pharisees and the early Christian community. According to Haenchen, Luke was convinced that the bridges between Pharisees and Christians had not yet been cut and that communion between them was still possible.[35] Even though Paul should be considered a *former* Pharisee (despite Luke's assertion to the contrary), Paul's own writings and Acts offer valuable information about some aspects of being a Pharisee.

---

[32] A. F. Segal, *Paul the Convert: The Apostolate and Apostasy of Saul the Pharisee* (New Haven, 1990), p. 26. For detailed discussions of Paul's Pharisaism, see M. Hengel and R. Deines, *The pre-Christian Paul* (London and Philadelphia, 1991), pp. 27–53; K. W. Niebuhr, *Heidenapostel aus Israel: Die jüdische Identität des Paulus nach ihrer Darstellung in seinen Briefen*, WUNT 62 (Tübingen, 1992), pp. 48–57, 108–9. I have not seen G. Carras, *Paul, Josephus and Judaism: The Shared Judaism of Paul and Josephus* (unpublished Oxford D.Phil. thesis, 1989).

[33] *War* 2.162; *Ant* 17.41; *Life* 191.

[34] Acts 15:5: τινες τῶν ἀπὸ τῆς αἱρέσεως τῶν Φαρισαίων πεπιστευκότες.

[35] E. Haenchen, *Die Apostelgeschichte*, 7th ed. (Göttingen, 1977), p. 615. Similarly, F. Mussner, *Apostelgeschichte*, Neue Echter Bibel (Würzburg, 1984), p. 138.

8. The only other writer who has generally been considered a Pharisee is Flavius Josephus. However, his membership in the group is at least as problematic as Paul's. He too is not forthcoming concerning his relationship to the group. He explicitly mentions his association with it only once, in his autobiography: "Being now in my nineteenth year I began to participate in public life (πολιτεύεσθαι), following (κατακολουθῶν) the school of the Pharisees, which is very close to the one the Greeks call the Stoic school."[36] The crux of the matter is the meaning of the two verbs indicated. Thackeray (LCL) and others take the former to mean "to govern one's life," but some scholars—most recently Mason—argue that one should translate "participate in public life." According to Mason, Josephus never claimed to have become a Pharisee, but rather only "followed" the Pharisees' political program so far as it was necessary to advance in public life.[37]

This hypothesis is interesting and would go a long way toward explaining Josephus' ambivalent or clearly negative remarks about the Pharisees. It is curious, however, that precisely in this context he compares the Pharisees to the Stoics. During the reign of Domitian, under whom Josephus most likely wrote these remarks (cf. *Life* 429), they represented a persecuted opposition. Even Mason admits that a point of comparison between Pharisees and Stoics is to be found in their teaching—specifically in their understanding of fate.[38]

Although Josephus does seem to adopt some Pharisaic doctrines, he does not write in a way one might expect of a member of the group.[39] Only twice does he refer to his own dealings with Pharisees. He reports that in the year 66, at the beginning of the revolt, he

---

[36] *Life* 12.

[37] Mason, *Flavius Josephus*, pp. 342–56.

[38] *Flavius Josephus*, p. 140; Mason struggles further with this question on p. 354, note 37.

[39] Free will and providence: *Ant* 16.398; cf. *War* 2.163; *Ant* 13.172; 18.13. See H. W. Attridge, "Josephus and His Works," in *Jewish Writings of the Second Temple Period*, ed. by M. Stone, CRINT, Section 2, Vol. II (1984), pp. 226–27. H. W. Attridge, *The Interpretation of Biblical History in the Antiquitates Judaicae of Flavius Josephus* (Missoula, 1976), pp. 178–79. S. Schwartz (*Josephus and Judaean Politics* [Leiden, 1990], pp. 172–208) points out how accurate Torah observance is a central theme of *Ant*, stated prominently in *Ant* 1.14. As we have seen, this is also central to Paul's Pharisaism. It is also one of the principal facets of later rabbinic Judaism. According to Schwartz, *Ant* is propaganda for this post-pharisaic type of Judaism.

"ventured out of the Temple and once more got together with the chief priests and the foremost Pharisees" (*Life* 21), to seek together with them, in vain, to avoid full-scale war.

The only other incident in which Josephus mentions several Pharisees is rather complex. He reports that at the request of John of Gischala, the Pharisee Simon ben Gamaliel induced the Sadducean high priest, Ananus, to send a four-man delegation (of whom three were Pharisees) to remove him, Josephus, from his office as a troop commander in Galilee. In the end, Josephus arrests two members of the delegation and then sends all four back to Jerusalem.[40] Certainly his relations with several Pharisees were not good at the time, even though they may have improved later, as his characterization of Simon ben Gamaliel in the same passage suggests.

9. Simon ben Gamaliel is described by Josephus as follows:

> a Jerusalemite, of a very prominent family, belonging to the school (αἵρεσις) of the Pharisees, who have the reputation of surpassing all others in their precision concerning the ancestral customs. This man was full of intelligence and reasoning power. By his practical wisdom he was able to straighten out troublesome situations. He was bound to John [of Gischala] by a longstanding and close friendship, whereas with me he was at odds at that time.   (*Life* 191–92)

It is unclear why Josephus has such words of appreciation for someone who tried to have him arrested. Mason sees here only Josephus' grudging admission of the well-known qualities of an adversary, whereas Cohen thinks that a reconciliation—evidenced by "at that time" (τότε)—must have taken place.[41] In any case, it is certain that Simon was a prominent person. His long friendship with John of Gischala, who is characterized by Josephus as an unscrupulous rebel leader from Galilee, is noteworthy.[42]

Simon, however, was well-connected in his native Jerusalem. He influenced the Sadducean high priest, Ananus, and his party to send the

[40] *Life* 191–332; cf. *War* 2.627–31.

[41] Mason, *Flavius Josephus*, p. 365. S. J. D. Cohen, *Josephus in Galilee and Rome* (Leiden, 1979), pp. 144–45.

[42] *War* 2.585 and passim.

delegation to remove Josephus from his post .[43] Apparently he led, together with Ananus, the opposition against the Zealots.[44] To the same circle belonged a chief priest, Jesus son of Gamalas,[45] sometimes identified with the high priest Jesus son of Gamaliel.[46] Even though our information about the personal and political connections between these men is incomplete, it is clear that the Pharisees as such did not form a party or represent a unified front as opposed to Sadducees or others.[47] Simon in particular was connected with priestly circles that included at least one Sadducee. He was influential, but did not hold a political decision-making position.

In the rabbinic texts that mention a Simon ben Gamaliel, we encounter the same difficulty as with his father; namely, that his name recurred in several generations of the same family. Most traditions concerning Simon ben Gamaliel are commonly assigned to his grandson, who was active in the second century. The main criterion for ascribing traditions to the elder Simon are explicit or implicit references to the existence of the Temple. Thus Simon ben Gamaliel I is credited with drastically reducing the price of doves for sacrifices.[48] In light of what we know from Josephus, it is highly doubtful that his teaching would have had an immediate and decisive impact as described in this instance.

Another brief story, reported with slight variations in three different sources, recounts how (during the feast of Sukkot) Simon used to

---

[43] (*Life* 193-96). Ananus is the only person called a Sadducee by Josephus (*Ant* 20.199) after John Hyrcanus' friend, Jonathan, almost two centuries earlier (*Ant* 13.293-98).

[44] *War* 4.159-60. The spelling of the name here is Symeon son of Gamaliel, but the identity of the person should not be doubted. Note that at least outwardly, John of Gischala sided for a while with Ananus and Simon (*War* 4.209-15).

[45] *Life* 193 and passim.

[46] *Ant* 20.213, 223. At one point, Schürer-Vermes (*History*, vol. 1, p. 431, note 5) distinguishes the two, but at another (vol. 2, p. 232) he considers them the same person, identifying them with Joshua son of Gamla and Ben Gamla. L. Feldman (*Josephus*, LCL, General Index, s.v. "Gamaliel") considers the high priest Jesus ben Gamaliel a brother of Simon, but distinguishes him from Jesus son of Gamalas. Josephus mentions his own friendship with Jesus son of Gamalas (*Life* 204), but does not hint at any family relationship between the latter and Simon.

[47] For a detailed study of the power relationships in Jerusalem, see M. Goodman, *The Ruling Class of Judaea: The Origins of the Jewish Revolt Against Rome A.D. 66-70* (Cambridge, 1987), esp. pp. 164, 183-87.

[48] m.Ker 1:7; see Neusner, *Rabbinic Traditions*, vol. 1, pp. 377-78.

juggle eight lighted torches and how no one could imitate this and other acrobatic acts of his.[49] Probably one would not expect to see a leading Pharisee in the role of popular entertainer. This may be one reason why the story was preserved.

Two additional traditions are attributed sometimes to him, sometimes to his father. One is about writing letters to various Jewish communities concerning the calendar and tithing, and the other is about blessing a beautiful Gentile woman.[50] The rabbinic material about Simon ben Gamaliel is not extensive. That almost no halachic decisions are preserved in his name is puzzling, given the importance attributed to him and especially to his family. Neusner suggests that the halachic material may have been suppressed because Simon was close to the school of Shammai, whose views were later overruled by those of the school of Hillel.[51] Although explanations of the paucity of traditions in his name are highly conjectural, the best one may be found in a saying attributed to Simon ben Gamaliel himself: "All my life I grew up among the Sages and have found nothing better for a person than silence. Not study is the most important thing but action; whoever indulges in too many words brings about sin."[52]

10-12. The three remaining known Pharisees all belong to the four-man delegation sent to depose Josephus. In his *Life* he introduces them as follows:

> They (Ananus and his entourage) decided to send men who were of different social classes, but of similar educational level. Two of them, Jonathan and Ananias, were lay people,[53] affiliated with the Pharisees (Φαρισαῖοι τὴν αἵρεσιν), the third one, Jozar (?), belonged to a priestly family, he too being a Pharisee; Simon, the youngest of them, was descended from high priests.
>
> (*Life* 197)

---

[49] See t.Suk 4:4; y.Suk 5:4; b.Suk 53a.

[50] Letters: t.Sanh 2:6; Midr. Tannaim to Deut 26:13; beautiful Gentile: y.AZ 1:9; b.AZ 20a.

[51] Neusner, *Rabbinic Traditions*, vol. 1, p. 387.

[52] m.Ab 1:17.

[53] δημοτικοί is translated by Thackeray (LCL) as "from the lower ranks." The term does have the connotation of "common" or "ordinary." Here, however, it seems to serve primarily to distinguish nonpriests from priests.

The story of this delegation takes up one third of Josephus' autobiography (*Life* 189-332), whereas in his earlier account he devotes only a few paragraphs to the whole episode (*War* 2.626-31). In the *War*, all four members are called "distinguished men, ... very capable speakers." The same passage differs from *Life* in other important details, including the delegates' names.[54] Our purpose here is not to analyze these passages in a detailed way, but to see what we can find out about these individuals as Pharisees.

10. The priest Jozar held a subordinate position in the delegation headed by Jonathan. From *War* 2.628 we learn that Joesdrus (= Jozar) was the son of a certain ΝΟΜΙΚΟΣ, either a man with a very unusual Greek name or a legal expert.[55] Jozar may be identical with the priest Jo(a)zar sent together with Josephus to Galilee (*Life* 29). Josephus accused this Jo(a)zar of unduly enriching himself through priestly tithes and bribes (*Life* 63, 73).

11. Both Ananias and Jonathan are characterized by Josephus as δημοτικοί. This expression implies nonpriestly status *and* lower social standing—especially in the eyes of Josephus, who prided himself on his priestly background. In the *War*, Ananias is identified as Σαδούκι, translated by Thackeray as "son of Sadok" (*War* 2.451, 628 [LCL]). Doubts about the appropriateness of this designation and its translation have been raised by Schlatter, who considered Σαδούκι a surname or

---

[54] τέσσαρας τῶν ἐπιφανῶν ἄνδρας ἔστειλαν, τόν τε τοῦ νομικοῦ (Νομικοῦ?) Ἰώεσδρον καὶ Ἀνανίαν Σαδούκι καὶ Σίμωνα καὶ Ἰούδην Ἰωνάθου, πάντας εἰπεῖν δυνατωτάτους (*War* 2.628).

[55] The word is taken as a personal name by most translators, but may also be a common noun: "learned in the Law," "scribe," "lawyer" (cf. K. H. Rengstorf, *et al.*, *A Complete Concordance to Flavius Josephus*, 4 vols. [Leiden, 1973-83], s.v. νομικός, although the preceding definite article makes this solution somewhat awkward (cf., however, Mt 13:55). In contrast to Lk (7:30; 11:45-52; 14:3), Josephus never connects Pharisees and νομικοί. J. Jeremias (*Jerusalem in the Time of Jesus* [Philadelphia, 1969], p. 234) assumes without further proof that both Jozar/Joezer and his father were scribes. *Nomikos* is a frequent personal name only in Byzantine times, but it is not listed in W. Pape and G. Benseler, *Wörterbuch der griechischen Eigennamen*, 3d ed., vol. 2 (Braunschweig, 1911). The father may have had a Greek name, whereas the son went by a Hebrew name. This phenomenon was somewhat rare, but it did occur. Thus, it is impossible to draw any conclusion about either Hellenization (Greek name?) or professional position (scribe/lawyer?) of Jozar's father.

title (Sadducee), mistakenly introduced here from *War* 2.451.[56] Could it be that Josephus in his earlier report meant to present a Pharisee as a Sadducee?

Ananias is treated by Josephus with great hostility. He is described as an evil and mischievous man who had no scruples about using religious pretexts to arrest Josephus (*Life* 290). In a separate incident, Ananias, along with others, was sent to negotiate the withdrawal of the Roman garrison from Jerusalem at the beginning of the war. They gave the Romans a pledge of security, but that pledge was broken as soon as they laid down their arms. The whole garrison, except its commander, was slain (*War* 2.451–53). If we take Josephus seriously, accounting for his personal polemics, it appears that certain Pharisees were actively involved in the revolt from the beginning. At the same time, some were, of course, trying to prevent war.[57]

12. According to the *Life*, where his name is mentioned fifty times, the delegation was headed by Jonathan. Josephus in fact quotes two letters he received from "Jonathan and those with him" (*Life* 217, 229). Josephus also accuses Jonathan of having used the occasion of the Sabbath service in the synagogue of Tiberias to incite the populace against him (*Life* 277, 302). It is difficult to gauge the veracity of these accusations, but they would suggest a preponderance of political over religious considerations.

In *War* 2.628, the last member of the delegation is Judas, son of Jonathan, instead of Jonathan himself. Grammatically, he appears here to be a brother of the Simon who, in *Life* 197, belonged to a high priestly family. The same Judas, son of Jonathan, appears alongside Ananias *Sadouki* in the garrison incident. It is difficult to decide which tradition to trust: Jonathan the lay-Pharisee of the *Life*, or Judas son of

---

[56] A. Schlatter, *Die hebräischen Namen bei Josephus* (Gütersloh, 1913), p. 93 (repr. in Schlatter, *Kleinere Schriften zu Flavius Josephus*, ed. by K. H. Rengstorf [Darmstadt, 1970], p. 205); cf. Cohen, *Josephus*, p. 224, note 88; J. Price, *Jerusalem Under Siege: The Collapse of the Jewish State 66–70 C.E.* (Leiden, 1992), p. 44.

[57] Josephus describes both the massacre of the Roman garrison and his meeting "with the chief priests and the foremost Pharisees" (*Life* 21) right after the murder of Menahem. Since he acknowledges that in their attempt to prevent a full-blown war "we professed to concur with their [i.e., the revolutionaries'] opinions" (*Life* 22), it is possible that Ananias was trying to collaborate with the revolutionaries to prevent worse from happening. But Josephus does not make this clear.

Jonathan and brother of Simon (of high priestly family?) and spokesperson for the rebels. Probably the detailed account in the *Life*, written to counter specific accusations by Justus of Tiberias (*Life* 336), should be given preference. The best argument in its favor would be if the letters from and to Jonathan (*Life* 217-18, 226-27, 229) could be shown to be genuine, but I doubt this is possible.

CONCLUSIONS

In our search through the different sources, we have been able to identify only a mere dozen individual Pharisees. They lived in a period of about two centuries and are not of sufficient number to draw any statistical conclusions. Due to the character of our sources, they cannot be presumed to constitute a representative sample. Of the twelve, two are known to have left to join other, conflicting groups (Saddok, Paul). The Pharisaic identity or even the historicity of several of the others is in doubt. Two are priests (Josephus, Jozar).[58]

All the Pharisees mentioned in Josephus—plus at least Nicodemus—are politically active, yet most often they represent a minority position or have to accept the authority of others. All except Paul (and Luke's Simon) are active in or coming from Judea. Pollion, Nicodemus, as well as Gamaliel and his son, Simon, exercise leadership functions. The last two represent the only case in which more than one member of a family is known as a Pharisee.[59] No woman—not Salome Alexandra nor even an unnamed woman—is ever called a Pharisee. This is not entirely surprising. Yet, though the Sadducees are even less well-known than the Pharisees, Sadducean women are mentioned in the Mishnah.[60] In no case do we have information about how one became a Pharisee, except for Josephus' problematic statement that he decided to follow them.

A question that imposes itself is why we know of so few individual Pharisees. A standard answer has been that "Pharisee" was not a

---

[58] On the Pharisee chief priest mentioned in POxy 840, see n. 5 above.

[59] See, however, Acts 23:6, where Paul is said to claim, "I am a Pharisee and a son of Pharisees."

[60] The term אשה פרושה at m.Soṭ 3:4, often rendered as "Pharisee woman," should be understood as "a woman who abstains" (from marital intercourse?); cf. E. Rivkin, "Defining the Pharisees," pp. 240–41. Sadducean women (more precisely, "daughters of Sadducees") appear in m.Nid 4:2 and elsewhere.

self-designation and that other terms, such as "sage" or "scribe," were normally used instead. It is clear that the term פרוש ("separated") was often used with negative connotations in Hebrew and Aramaic sources.[61] Yet it was used for self-identification by Paul and Josephus. Separation "from the majority of the peo[ple]" is also described as a voluntary act on the part of the writers of 4QMMT.[62] Though presumably Essenes, they advocate halakhic positions ascribed to the Sadducees in the Mishnah.[63] Thus, one cannot simply assert that "separate ones" (= "Pharisees") was necessarily a pejorative term.

In his entire work, Josephus mentions only two Sadducees and four Essenes. In the New Testament, only Acts 5:17 identifies a high priest (and his entourage) as Sadducean. As is well-known, Essenes are never mentioned in the New Testament or in rabbinic literature. Thus, of all the Jewish groups before 66 C.E. (with the exception of the followers of Jesus), the Pharisees have by far the highest number of known individual members!

In spite of these somewhat minimalist conclusions, I hope this prosopographical investigation can further the more general study of Pharisaism and of Second Temple Judaism in various ways. First, we must acknowledge that our knowledge about real-life Pharisees is extremely limited. Second, although a prosopographical approach can teach us little about Pharisaic teaching and observance, we do get glimpses into the life not of *the* Pharisees but of *some* Pharisees. Both negative and positive stereotypes are challenged by this look at individuals.

Third, although few generalizations are advisable, all the individuals studied were of some prominence. Many, however, found themselves in a minority position or had to bow to the authority of others.

Fourth, Neusner included in his ground-breaking study, *The Rabbinic Traditions About the Pharisees before 70*, more than fifty "Pharisees." Of these, only three or four are clearly identifiable as such. Some of those excluded from our list (e.g., Hillel, Shammai, Simon ben

---

[61] See Rivkin, "Defining the Pharisees," pp. 234–38.

[62] This text is quoted in E. Qimron and J. Strugnell, "An Unpublished Halakhic Letter from Qumran," *The Israel Museum Journal* 4 (1985) 10; see also now E. Qimron and J. Strugnell, eds., *Qumran Cave 4 V: Miqsat Ma'ase HaTorah* (DJD 10; Oxford, 1994).

[63] Qimron and Strugnell, "An Unpublished Halakhic Letter," p. 12.

Shetach) may well have been Pharisees, but their connection with the group is attested only in sources of the fifth century or later and can no longer simply be taken for granted.[64]

Fifth, the entire methodology for identifying a person, a doctrine, or a literary composition, as Pharisaic must change. In contrast to earlier generations, scholars today find themselves unable to attribute confidently *any* pre-70 document to a Pharisaic author.[65] Thus, to understand the Pharisees, we may first have to acknowledge that we know much less than we thought we did.

---

[64] It has often been assumed—and Rivkin ("Defining the Pharisees," pp. 214–20) has tried to demonstrate—that *all* the pre-70 sages were Pharisees. This claim does not stand up under critical scrutiny. See Stemberger, *Pharisäer*, p. 50.

[65] See J. H. Charlesworth in *OTP*, vol. 2, p. 642, on the Psalms of Solomon: "It is unwise to label these psalms as either Pharisaic or Essene." As a matter of fact, none of the documents included in *OTP* is labeled as Pharisaic in origin.

8

JESUS AND FACTIONALISM
IN EARLY JUDAISM:
HOW SERIOUS WAS THE FACTIONALISM
OF LATE SECOND TEMPLE JUDAISM?

THERE IS NOW a widespread consensus among students of late Second Temple Judaism and Christian origins on two points. The first point of consensus is that *Judaism was a diverse phenomenon in that period*; nor was any one of the different strands or interpretations of Judaism widely recognized as "normative" by Jews of the period.[1] Of course the word 'Ιουδαῖος was a meaningful concept (already in 2Mac 2:21; 8:1; 14:38) and identified a well marked-out range of religious conviction and practice.[2] And there was a "common Judaism" which was practised by the bulk of Jews living in the land of Israel.[3] Judging by its usage, the word 'Ιουδαῖος was a clear enough indicator of identity—certainly in ethnic terms, but also in religious terms,[4] even if the correlation of religious identity and ethnic identity caused problems (as now, so then!.

Whether as a matter of historical analysis it would be more accurate to speak of "Judaisms" (plural), rather than of "Judaism"

---

[1] See, e.g., G. W. E. Nickelsburg, "The Modern Study of Early Judaism," and G. G. Porton, "Diversity in Post-biblical Judaism," *Early Judaism and its Modern Interpreters*, ed. R. A. Kraft and G. W. E. Nickelsburg (Atlanta, 1986), pp. 1–30 and 57–80.

[2] See, e.g., Y. Amir, "The Term 'Ιουδαῖος (IOUDAISMOS): A Study in Jewish-Hellenistic Self-Identification," *Immanuel* 14 (1982) 34–41.

[3] E. P. Sanders, *Judaism: Practice and Belief 63 B.C.E.–66 C.E.* (London and Philadelphia, 1992).

[4] M. Casey, *From Jewish Prophet to Gentile God: The Origins and Development of New Testament Christology* (Cambridge, 1991), offers eight "identity factors" as constituting the self-identity of Second Temple Judaism (ch. 2). See also my *The Parting of the Ways between Christianity and Judaism* (London and Philadelphia, 1991) ch. 2 and pp. 143–46.

(singular) is a legitimate question.[5] There is also some dispute about the best way to describe and define the different subgroups within Judaism—whether as "sects" or "factions" or "schools"—how best, in other words, to translate Josephus's and Acts' term αἱρέσεις (Josephus, *Ant* 13.171; *War* 2.118; Acts 5:19; 15:5).[6] Nevertheless, the fact that late second Temple Judaism included such αἱρέσεις is not in question.[7]

The second point of consensus is on the status of Jesus and his immediate circle within first-century Judaism. There has been an increasing willingness in recent decades, from both the Jewish side and the Christian side,[8] to recognize not only the Jewishness of Jesus, but also the fact that *Jesus and the movement around him have to be reckoned within and as part of the wider, more diverse Judaism* of which we have just spoken ("the αἵρεσις of the Nazarenes" [Acts 24:5]).[9] The precise relation of Jesus to the Pharisees in particular is a matter of continuing controversy,[10] a controversy to which the present essay hopes to contribute. But that Jesus and his first followers can fairly be classified as one of the expressions of Judaism, or even as one of the Judaisms (plural) of the period is now much less controversial. Gone forever, one hopes, are the days when Judaism was seen *simpliciter* as the foil to Christianity, and therefore also to Jesus. Gone also, one hopes, such

---

[5] So, e.g., J. Neusner, et al., ed., *Judaisms and their Messiahs at the Turn of the Christian Era* (Cambridge, 1987); A. F. Segal, *The Other Judaisms of Late Antiquity*, BJS 127 (Atlanta, 1987).

[6] See the discussion in S. J. D. Cohen, *From the Maccabees to the Mishnah* (Philadelphia, 1987), pp. 125–27; A. J. Saldarini, *Pharisees, Scribes, and Sadducees* (Wilmington and Edinburgh, 1988/1989), pp. 70–73, 123–27; Sanders, *Judaism*, pp. 352–64.

[7] This is not to prejudge the importance of such sects in Second Temple Judaism, though it is a remarkable fact that such a high proportion of our sources from the period (second century B.C.E. to 70 C.E.) are sectarian in character.

[8] In this context I use the terms *Jewish* and *Christian* to denote not necessarily religious commitment or affiliation, but the perspective from which individual scholars have first approached these questions.

[9] See, e.g., J. H. Charlesworth, ed., *Jesus' Jewishness: Exploring the Place of Jesus in Early Judaism* (New York, 1991).

[10] Cf., e.g., H. Falk, *Jesus the Pharisee* (New York, 1985); E. P. Sanders, *Jesus and Judaism* (London, 1985), esp. "Pharisee" in the index; S. Westerholm, *Jesus and Scribal Authority* (Lund, 1978); M. J. Borg, *Jesus, A New Vision* (San Francisco, 1987), pp. 158–60; G. Stemberger, *Pharisäer, Sadduzäer, Essener* (Stuttgart, 1991), pp. 24–39.

too-simplistic or theologically overloaded claims as that of L. Goppelt, "that Jesus actually superseded Judaism at its very roots."[11] One of the main subjects of our consultation is Jesus *within* Judaism, and there is sufficient consensus on that point for us to proceed.

However, when we push behind this consensus, other, more specific, questions remain contentious. In particular, how did these different subgroups within Judaism view each other? How was Jesus viewed by them, and how did Jesus view them? The picture of different Judaisms (plural) is drawn from a modern social-historical perspective, a perspective sufficiently removed in time and historical context to be appropriately "objective." But what of the perspective from within? Would the talk of "different Judaisms" be recognized and accepted there? Or would at least some of the subgroups have regarded their own expression of Judaism as the only legitimate form of Judaism?

A widely agreed acceptance of a single "normative" Judaism there may not have been. But would each individual faction or sect or party not have acted on the assumption that their understanding and practice of Judaism was, in effect, "normative"? The history of sectarianism—whether religious, social, or political—certainly favors an affirmative answer to these questions. And if this is indeed the case, our specific question reemerges: What was the effect of these disagreements and of the accompanying polemic and vilification?[12] Do we have to speak, in effect, of mutually exclusive orthodoxies or orthopraxies—of one group disowning another to such an extent as to deny its status as or within Judaism—or merely of rhetorical thunderbolts and polemical fireworks? And where does Jesus stand in all this? How was he affected by such attitudes or such rhetoric?

---

[11] L. Goppelt, *Theology of the New Testament, Vol. I: The Ministry of Jesus and Its Theological Significance* (Grand Rapids, 1981), p. 97; cf. also J. Moltmann, *The Crucified God* (London and New York, 1974), p. 32. The discussion at this point has not been helped by Neusner's speaking of Christianity and Judaism as though they were two completely distinct entities (J. Neusner, *Jews and Christians: The Myth of a Common Tradition* [London and Philadelphia, 1991]). The claim is only effective in reference to Christianity and Judaism as they subsequently developed, not to Jesus. Though it reopens the old question of the relation between Jesus and Paul, we cannot enter into that here. Contrast, e.g., A. F. Segal, *Rebecca's Children: Judaism and Christianity in the Roman World* (Cambridge, 1986) and my *Partings*.

[12] For the fierceness of ancient polemic, see particularly, L. T. Johnson, "The New Testament's Anti-Jewish Slander and the Conventions of Ancient Polemic," *JBL* 108 (1989) 419–41.

The question has been posed for me particularly by the arguments of two scholars who have contributed more valuably than most to the larger discussions in this area. E. P. Sanders has continued to react against the much overdrawn and hostile portrayals by earlier scholarship of the Pharisees and of confrontation between them and Jesus. On the subject of impurity in particular, he maintains that their multiplication of rules about corpse impurity and midras impurity amount simply to "minor gestures towards extra purity."[13] He finds "no substantial conflict between Jesus and the Pharisees," or indeed "any substantial disputes between Jesus and *anyone*; that is, no dispute that goes beyond the normal range of disagreement." As with the disputes between the houses (of Hillel and Shammai), "neither seems to have regarded the other as *transgressing*, just as having a weak argument in favour of their own practice."[14] In my *Partings of the Ways*, I have questioned this view briefly.[15] Now I wish to develop a fuller critique of it.

The other position which I find it necessary to question is that of L. H. Schiffman. In his contribution to the *Jewish and Christian Self-Definition* volumes, Schiffman poses the issue which provokes my own interest at this point: "Why it is that Judaism, after tolerating sectarianism and schism for the entire length of the Second Temple period, elected to regard Christianity as another religion entirely?"[16] His attempt to resolve that issue, much as I find it helpful, raises our question in a sharp form. "Despite all the sectarian animus found in various texts from or about the Second Commonwealth period, even the most virulent never accuse the members of other groups of having left the Jewish community. Sinners they were, but Jews all the same." "Jewish status could never be cancelled, even for the most heinous offences against Jewish law and doctrine." "Heresy, no matter how great, was never seen as cutting the heretic's tie to Judaism."[17]

---

[13] E. P. Sanders, *Jewish Law from Jesus to the Mishnah: Five Studies* (London and Philadelphia, 1990), pp. 232–35.

[14] *Partings*, p. 300, note 19, citing first Sanders, *Jesus and Judaism*, p. 291, and then private correspondence.

[15] See *Partings*, p. 110, in particular, and below, note 36.

[16] L. H. Schiffman, "At the Crossroads: Tannaitic Perspectives on the Jewish-Christian Schism," *Jewish and Christian Self-Definition, Vol. Two: Aspects of Judaism in the Graeco-Roman Period*, ed. E. P. Sanders, et al. (London, 1981), pp. 115–56, esp. 115; cf. also *Who was a Jew? Rabbinic and Halakhic Perspectives on the Jewish-Christian Schism* (Hoboken, N.J., 1985), ch. 4.

[17] Schiffman, "Crossroads," pp. 116, 147, 152.

Was this in fact the case? When some subgroups held particular matters of Jewish belief and practice to be of special importance—indeed, of such importance as to constitute their separateness as a subgroup—how did they regard those who disregarded or sat light to these matters? Was it all a question of good liberal tolerance all round?

THE PROBLEM OF SINNERS

Our question can be focused quite simply and straightforwardly: How serious was it when one group called another group "sinners"? The question arises in connection with Jesus, of course, because he is remembered in Christian tradition as being criticised for consorting with "sinners" (Mk 2:16 pars.; Mt 11:19//Lk 7:34; Lk 15:1-2; 19:7). For what was he being criticized? To put the question another way: If he was reacting against some of his fellow Jews being designated "sinners," what was it he was reacting against? Was the designation of some Jews as "sinners" merely a harmless piece of name-calling, or a pious exhortation to repentance?

If designating some Jews as "sinners" was merely a harmless piece of name-calling, then Jesus' association with such sinners was little more than a mild social protest or else he hugely overreacted to criticism for his association with them. Or was the designation by some Jews of other Jews as "sinners" indeed more serious, as indicating complete rejection and condemnation of those so designated? In which case, was Jesus' response to them correspondingly radical?

The opinions of Sanders and Schiffman cited above suggest that it was all merely a matter of the rhetoric of polemic and argumentation, more than of fundamental disagreement and denunciation. But was not the whole issue a good deal more profound and its ramifications more far-reaching than that?

The obvious way to proceed is to examine the language used, what we might call the rhetoric of vilification—particularly the word *sinner*. Sanders has already done this in his *Paul and Palestinian Judaism*.[18] But much of the discussion there is oriented toward his own justified polemic against the classic Protestant denigration of Judaism.

---

[18] E. P. Sanders, *Paul and Palestinian Judaism* (London, 1977); see particularly "The Wicked" in the index.

When he turns to Jesus specifically, in *Jesus and Judaism*, his discussion is directed primarily against Jeremias and the equation of "sinners" with the *'amme ha'arets*. He fails to integrate his earlier insights.[19] For us, however, it is at the very heart of the matter that *sinners* was a term not only of moral repugnance directed against the blatant law-breaker ("the truly wicked" in Sanders' words),[20] but also a term of factional polemic.[21] That is to say, it was a term used by one group of Jews against other Jews who practiced their Judaism differently and who were thereby judged to be "sinners." The question which needs further clarification now is, "What did this rebuke or condemnation amount to?"

The basic term in Hebrew is, of course, רָשָׁע, with such near synonyms as חָנֵף and חַטָּא. The principal Greek renderings of these terms are ἁμαρτωλός, ἀσεβής, and ἄνομος.[22] The principal antonym, with which these terms—particularly the first—are frequently set in antithesis, is צַדִּיק, which is usually rendered into Greek by δίκαιος, with εὐσεβής a late alternative. But חָסִיד, which functions as a synonym for צַדִּיק (particularly in the Psalms, where it is usually rendered into Greek by ὅσιος), should also be considered.

The question, then, is simply, What did it mean for one Jew to use such negative terminology of another Jew? What did the exclusive claim to the epithet *righteous* mean for those from whom it was withheld? The evidence points to two answers: first in terms of what we

---

[19] *Jesus and Judaism*, ch. 6. For an earlier critique of Jeremias, see particularly, J. R. Donahue, "Tax Collectors and Sinners: An Attempt at Identification," *CBQ* 33 (1971) 39–61. Contrast, e.g., J. Gibson, "ΟΙ ΤΕΛΟΝΑΙ ΚΑΙ ΑΙ ΠΟΡΝΑΙ," *JTS* 32 (1981) 429–33.

[20] *Jesus and Judaism*, p. 210.

[21] J. D. G. Dunn, "Pharisees, Sinners and Jesus," *The Social World of Formative Christianity and Judaism: Essays in Tribute to Howard Clark Kee*, ed. J. Neusner, et al. (Philadelphia, 1988), pp. 264–89, reprinted in my *Jesus, Paul and the Law: Studies in Mark and Galatians* (London and Louisville, 1990), pp. 61–88, here 71–77; cf. also *Partings*, pp. 102–6. D. A. Neale (*None But the Sinners: Religious Categories in the Gospel of Luke*, JSNTSup 58 [Sheffield, 1991], pp. 68–75) shares Sanders' critique of Jeremias, but also fails to perceive the importance of the factional use of the term.

[22] It is a weakness of the *DNTT* article at this point that it subsumes the discussion wholly under the heading of "sin" and gives too little attention to the concept of the "sinner" as such (W. Günther, "Sin," *DNTT*, ed. C. Brown, vol. 3 [Exeter, 1978], pp. 577–83).

might call the "covenant significance" of the term *sinner* and its antithesis, *righteous*; and second in terms of the consequences envisaged within the Jewish biblical and post-biblical tradition for the "sinner."

SINNER AS A COVENANT-EXCLUDING TERM

Under this heading it is simplest to draw on work already done on this subject in a summary way.[23] These earlier findings can most simply be rehearsed in terms of covenant status.

It is significant that *sinner* could be used within biblical and post-biblical tradition, as reflected also in the New Testament, as equivalent to "Gentile" (Ps 9:17; Tob 13:8[6]; Jub 23:23-24; PssSol 1:1; 2:1-2; Lk 6:33 = Mt 5:47; Mk 14:41 and pars.; Gal 2:15). The Gentile was by definition a "sinner." The point is not that Gentiles were all criminals by nature. The point is rather that righteousness was defined in terms of membership of the covenant people, in terms of Israel's Torah. Gentiles (other nations) were by definition outside the people of Israel and consequently outside the law. They were literally "outlaws." Hence, such references to the Gentiles simply as "the lawless," as in WisSol 17:2, Acts 2:23, and 1Cor 9:21, and the talk of "lawless Gentiles" in 3Mac 6:9.

This covenant dimension of the term *sinner* becomes significant when we consider its use as a factional term within Judaism—that is, as a term used by some Jews of other Jews. For what it amounts to is *a denial of these other Jews' covenant status*. This is clear, for example, in 1 Maccabees, where the three terms of disparagement (*lawless, sinners*, and *ungodly*) are used both of Gentiles and of apostate Jews (1:10, 34; 2:44, 48, 62; 3:5-6, 8, 15; 6:21; 7:5, 9; etc.). From the perspective of the loyalist Jews, the Hellenizing Jews had forsaken the covenant and thus, to all intents and purposes, had become Gentiles.[24] Typical of the factional polemic that followed upon the Maccabean revolt was the description of those who disagreed with the writer's faction as behaving like Gentiles. To observe the wrong calendar was to "forget the feasts of the covenant and keep the feasts of the Gentiles" (Jub 6:35). The wrong faction controlling the Temple "left no sin undone, wherein they

---

[23] See above, note 21.

[24] See particularly D. Garlington, *"The Obedience of Faith": A Pauline Phrase in Historical Context*, WUNT 2.38 (Tübingen, 1991), pp. 91–102.

did not surpass the Gentiles" (PssSol 8:13). Cephas sitting light to the food laws and eating with Gentiles was "living like a Gentile" (Gal 2:14).

The same point becomes evident in the frequent antithesis of *sinner* and *righteous*. The contrast, of course, is typical of the Psalm passages cited below (Pss 1:5-6; 7:9; 34:21; 37:12-21, 32, 40; etc.), as of the Wisdom literature (Prov 10:2; 11:9, 31; 12:3, 13; etc.; Sir 12:4; 13:7; 16:13; 33:14; 41:5; WisSol 5:14-15).[25] But above all it is in 1 Enoch and the Psalms of Solomon in particular that the contrast gathers all the overtones and bitterness of factional dispute. In 1En 1–5 the "righteous/chosen" within Israel mark themselves off from the "sinners/impious" (1:1, 7-9; 5:6-7), where "sinners" are those who "have not persevered, nor observed the law of the Lord" (5:4). Clearly those behind the writing regarded themselves alone as faithful to the covenant. They alone were righteous and they regarded their fellow Jews whom they describe as sinners as effectively outside the covenant. The Psalms of Solomon are thoroughly marked by the attitude of those confident in their own covenant status—and equally confident that the opposing Jewish faction(s) were unacceptable to God.

Such attitudes and language, we may judge, are a particular expression of the Jewish community's recognition of the need to define and maintain its boundaries—not only to mark itself off from outsiders (Gentiles), but also by excluding or "excommunicating" members of the community who had deviated from its self-identifying norms. Such practice is attested for the early post-exilic community (Ezra 10:8; Neh 13:3). Though it is not otherwise well attested and is more characteristic of the sects of our period, W. Horbury has argued effectively that "the sects did not originate it [the practice of excommunication], but derived it from existing usage, within the common post-exilic inheritance of intense corporate loyalty to the covenant."[26]

---

[25] On the Sirach passages, see Garlington, *Obedience*, p. 55.

[26] W. Horbury, "Extirpation and Excommunication," *VT* 35 (1985) 13–38, here 30. For summary statements of the deviations/defections which warranted expulsion in the Old Testament, Dead Sea Scrolls, and rabbinic Judaism, see G. Forkman, *The Limits of the Religious Community: Expulsion from the Religious Community within the Qumran Sect, within Rabbinic Judaism, and within Primitive Christianity* (Lund, 1972), pp. 27–28, 59, 97–98.

None of this should surprise us: the sectarian attitude has always been marked by a self-confidence—or at least self-assertion of its own righteousness—and a denial of that righteousness to others. It is precisely the attempt to define righteousness more clearly and distinctively and to practise righteousness more completely and committedly which makes individuals form a sect. It is precisely their clearer definition of what righteousness involves in practice which creates the boundary which marks them off from others, including others who also seek to practise righteousness. And it is an inevitable corollary of that more precise definition and practice that those who do not agree with it should be judged as excommunicate, outside the boundary and unrighteous—in a word, "sinners." What the sectarian judges to be unacceptable to God he refuses to recognize or to practise. He calls it sin and those who practise it sinners.[27]

In short, the seriousness of designating a fellow Jew "sinner" was tantamount to *denying that person's status within the covenant and thus as recipient of God's saving righteousness.*

THE CONSEQUENCES FOR SINNERS IN JEWISH TRADITION

The seriousness of designating others as "sinners" is even more sharply felt when we consider how the biblical and post-biblical Jewish tradition describes the lot of the sinner and the sinner's eschatological prospects.

Classic examples of the sinner are provided by Israel's early history. The wickedness of the men of Sodom (Gen 13:13) became proverbial and their fate a standing warning of final judgment (Isa 3:9; Lam 4:6; TNaph 4:1; Mt 11:24//Lk 10:12; 2Pet 2:6; Jude 7). In punishment for their sin, Korah, Dathan, and Abiram "went down alive into Sheol ... and perished from the midst of the assembly" (Num 16). They are likewise recalled as a terrible warning (Ps 106:16-18; Ps-Philo 16:3-6), as also is the wilderness generation that perished as a result of sin (Num 32:14-15; CD 3.7-10). The famous Mishnah *Sanhedrin* 10 numbers these three cases, the men of Sodom, the generation of the wilderness,

---

[27] The same issue is posed within Christianity by an often too casual use of the term *sinner*. In fundamentalist groups "the saved" regard others (not least other Christians) as outside salvation. The logic of the theology even of less censorious conservative evangelical groups is that those who have not (yet) embraced the group's understanding of the gospel have not yet been reached by the gospel.

and the company of Korah as prime examples of those who have no share in the world to come (10:3).[28]

Other examples of the seriousness of sin and of the prospects for the sinner can be listed briefly:

With reference to those who sinned in the matter of the golden calf, the Lord says to Moses,

> Whoever has sinned against me, him will I blot out of my book.   (Ex 32:33)

> The [sinner] who turns away to serve other gods, and thinks he is safe though walking in the stubbornness of his heart is warned: 'The Lord would not pardon him, but rather ... the curses written in this book would settle upon him, and the Lord would blot out his name from under heaven.'[29]   (Deut 29:18)

Psalm 1 carries the classic contrast between the righteous and the sinners,

> who are like chaff which the wind drives away.
> Therefore the wicked will not stand in the judgment,
> nor sinners in the congregation of the righteous ...
> the way of the wicked will perish.   (Ps 1:4-6)

> The wicked shall depart to Sheol,
> all the nations that forget God.   (Ps 9:16)

> The wicked are doomed to destruction for ever.   (Ps 92:7)

> Let sinners be consumed from the earth,
> and let the wicked be no more.   (Ps 104:35)

> The Lord preserves all who love him;
> but all the wicked he will destroy.[30]   (Ps 145:20)

---

[28] See also E. E. Urbach, *The Sages: Their Concepts and Beliefs* (Jerusalem, 1979), pp. 462–63.

[29] For the use of חתא in D and P as necessarily leading to destruction, see K. Koch in *TDOT* 4.315.

Rebels and sinners shall be destroyed together,
and those who forsake the Lord shall be consumed.   (Isa 1:28)

Behold the day of the Lord comes,
cruel, with wrath and fierce anger,
to make the earth a desolation
and to destroy its sinners from it.   (Isa 13:9)

The wicked shall die in his iniquity [i.e., his life will not be saved].
                                        (Ezek 3:18-19 and 33:8-9)

As I live, says the Lord God, I have no pleasure in the death of the
wicked, but that the wicked turn from his way and live.   (Ezek 33:11)

Behold, the day comes, burning like an oven, when all the arrogant
and all evildoers will be stubble; the day that comes shall burn them
up, says the Lord of hosts, so that it will leave them neither root nor
branch.   (Mal 4:1)

The Lord's anger rests on sinners.   (Sir 5:6)

The ungodly will not be held guiltless as long as they live.   (Sir 9:11-
12)

The Most High hates sinners and will inflict punishment on the
ungodly.   (Sir 12:6)

The way of sinners is smoothly paved with stones,
but at its end is the pit of Hades.   (Sir 21:10)

When we move beyond the canonical and near canonical texts,
the picture is the same, except that as eschatological expectation
becomes steadily clearer, the consequences for the sinner can be defined
more sharply:[31]

---

[30] See also Neale, *Sinners*, pp. 82–83: "The over-riding theme in relation to the
'sinner' in the Psalms is that of condemnation" (p. 82). "The 'sinner' of the Greek
Psalms was completely beyond the pale of such restoration" (p. 86).
[31] "The 'sinner' is not portrayed as one for whom repentance and salvation are
possible" (Neale, *Sinners*, pp. 83–86). See also the earlier treatment of E. Sjöberg, *Gott*

He will destroy the wicked ones and censure all flesh on account of everything that they have done, that which the sinners and the wicked ones committed against him.   (1 En 1:9)

Hope not that you shall live, you sinners,
you who shall depart and die,
for you know for what [reason] you have been ready
for the day of great judgment,
for the day of anguish and great shame for your spirits

...

you shall have no hope of life.   (1 En 98:10-16)

Woe unto you, sinners, because of the works of your hands!
On account of the deeds of your wicked ones,
in blazing flames worse than fire, it shall burn.   (1 En 100:9)

You, sinners, you are accursed forever; there is no peace for you! (1 En 102:3)

They shall experience evil and great tribulation—in darkness, nets, and burning flame. Your souls shall enter into the great judgment; it shall be a great judgment in all the generations of the world. Woe unto you, for there is no peace for you!   (1 En 103:7-8)

Know now that whoever does plan evil against his brother will fall into his hand and be uprooted from the land of the living, and his progeny will perish from the earth.... He will be blotted out of the book of the discipline of mortal men, and not be recorded in the book of life, but rather in that which is appointed for destruction; and he will depart into eternal execration—so that their condemnation may be always renewed in hate and execration and wrath and torment and indignation, and in plagues and disease for ever.[32]   (Jub 36:9-10)

---

und die Sünder im palastinischen Judentum (Stuttgart, 1938), pp. 206–12.

[32] The term *sinner* is absent here, but the substance is the same.

[The Lord's judgment:] to repay sinners forever according to their
actions.   (PssSol 2:34)

The destruction of the sinner is for ever,
and he will not be remembered when [God] looks after the righteous.
This is the share of sinners forever.   (PssSol 3:11-12)

For the life of the righteous [goes on] forever,
but sinners shall be taken away to destruction,
and no memory of them will ever be found.   (PssSol 13:11)

The inheritance of sinners is destruction and darkness,
and their lawless actions shall pursue them below into Hades.
...
And sinners shall perish forever in the day of the Lord's judgment,
...
but sinners shall perish for all time.   (PssSol 15:10-13)

The broad gate is the gate of the sinners, which leads to destruction
and to eternal punishment.   (TAb 11:11)

The place of sinners, a most bitter place of punishment.   (TAb 13:12)

In the Dead Sea scrolls, the vocabulary of sin and vilification is
more diversified. Curses are called first on 'the men of the lot of Belial'
and then on the heads of the one who enters the Covenant in deceitful-
ness and in the stubbornness of his heart:

[Speaking of the men of the lot of Belial:] Be cursed because of all
your guilty wickedness! May He deliver you up for torture at the
hands of the vengeful Avengers! May He visit you with destruction by
the hand of all the Wreakers of Revenge! Be cursed without mercy
because of the darkness of your deeds! Be damned in the shadowy
places of everlasting fire! ...

[Speaking of the deceitful and stubborn covenanter:] His spirit shall be
destroyed without pardon. God's wrath and His zeal for his precepts
shall consume him in everlasting destruction. All the curses of the

Covenant shall cling to him and God will set him apart for evil. He shall be cut off from the midst of all the sons of light, and because he has turned aside from God on account of his idols and his stumbling-block of sin, his lot shall be among those who are cursed for ever.

(1QS 2.5-18)

From the early rabbinic period we need simply note again m.Sanh 10:1-4. Its firm opening statement, "All Israelites have a share in the world to come," is probably secondary.[33] It actually consists of a sequence defining different categories of persons (Jewish heretics) who have no portion in the world to come.[34] Also notable is the fierceness of the famous twelfth benediction, directed against Jewish *minim* and asking that they "be blotted out of the Book of Life and not be inscribed together with the righteous."[35]

The picture, then, could hardly be clearer. Sinners will be blotted out of the book of life. They will suffer eternal destruction: they will be burned up in everlasting fire. They have no hope of life. There is no peace for them. They are accursed for ever. They will perish for all time. They can look forward only to eternal punishment. They will have no place in the world to come. Of course this is the language of polemic, and in many cases the language of admonition and exhortation. The fearful prospect is held out before audiences in many cases to

---

[33] Schiffman, *Who was a Jew?* p. 90, note 1.

[34] Schiffman, *Who was a Jew?* p. 45, sees Sadducees or Hellenized Jews as the target of 10:1. He also cites t.Sanh 13:5: "But as to the heretics (*minim*), the apostates (*meshummadin*), the informers, the ʿ*apiqorsim*, those who have denied the Torah, those who have separated from the ways of the community, those who have denied the resurrection of the dead, and everyone who has transgressed and caused the public to transgress ..., Gehenna is shut in their faces (or 'before them'), and they are punished in it (Gehenna) for ever and ever" (p. 46). See also Sjöberg, *Sünder*, pp. 117–24.

[35] For discussion of the form of the twelfth Benediction, see, e.g., R. Kimelman, "*Birkat Ha-Minim* and the Lack of Evidence for an Anti-Jewish Prayer in Late Antiquity," *Jewish and Christian Self-Definition*, Vol. 2, ed. E. P. Sanders, et al. (London, 1981), pp. 226–44. In the same volume, E. E. Urbach argues that "what made a Jew a heretic was not slackness in observing the precepts, or even alienation from tradition, but the act of denying the election of the Jews," and that the sages "did not do so [erect fences and hedges around the Torah] for the purpose of self-isolation, but of self-affirmation" ("Self-Isolation or Self-Affirmation in Judaism in the First Three Centuries: Theory and Practice," *Jewish and Christian Self-Definition*, pp. 269–98, here, pp. 292 and 298).

stimulate repentance. It has been a millennia-old evangelistic strategy to call people sinners in order to turn them from their sin. Nevertheless, the fact remains that *to designate another as "sinner" in early Jewish tradition was to name that person as one who as such was disowned by God, and who, in status as a sinner, was liable to the fearful judgments illustrated above.*

When we consider together the conclusions of the last two sections, the result is even starker: there were Jews in the last two centuries of the Second Temple Period *who regarded other Jews as "sinners"* and therefore as *outside the covenant* and therefore also as *excluded from salvation.*

JESUS AND SINNERS

In the light of the above findings, what are we to make of the traditions that Jesus was criticised for consorting with "sinners"?

We should note at once that one cannot easily escape the sharpness of the issue. It is virtually impossible to deny that these traditions reflect criticism levelled against Jesus and/or his first disciples in pre-70 Palestine. The mutual supporting testimony of "Q" tradition with what is generally recognized as pre-formed material[36] in Mark (itself generally acknowledged to be the earliest Gospel) is too compelling.

Moreover, the fact that Mk 2:17 explicitly contrasts the "righteous" and "sinners" sets the exchange firmly in the context of the interfactional polemic between Jewish groups of the period. This interfactional polemic is reflected particularly in the Enoch traditions, the Psalms of Solomon, and the Dead Sea scrolls. In other words, it cannot be assumed that the "sinners" in question were the criminal class of first-century Palestine (as Sanders seems to have assumed). The language used indicates rather that same sectarian mentality which defined righteousness in its own terms (the sect would say, "in God's terms"), and which categorized as "sinners" other Jews who infringed that code of righteous praxis. That several of the criticisms leveled against Jesus on this score are attributed to Pharisees (Mk 2:16; Lk 15:1-2) provides confirmatory evidence, since in two of the documents just cited (Psalms

---

[36] See my "Mark 2:1–3:6: A Bridge between Jesus and Paul on the Question of the Law," *NTS* 30 (1984) 395–415, reprinted in *Jesus, Paul and the Law*, pp. 10–36.

of Solomon and Dead Sea scrolls), Pharisees or Pharisee-like groups seem to be on either side of that polemic—the self-styled righteous in one case, those attacked by the self-styled righteous in the other.[37]

It is true, on the other hand, that Mk 2:17 itself does not engage in such polemic. For Jesus to say that "those who are strong have no need of a doctor" and that he came "not to call righteous but sinners" is in itself no criticism of the righteous. On the contrary, the implication of the juxtaposed sayings is that the righteous are strong and in good health; that is, in good spiritual or religious health. Nevertheless, there is some significance in the way in which sinners and righteous are played off against each other at this point. The implication is that their standing relative to each other is altered, that sinners may be recipients of blessings which the righteous could justly have thought were for them alone. It is not that the righteous are any the less acceptable to God; it is rather that the corollary which the righteous drew (that those they regarded as sinners were therefore unacceptable to God) was wrong.

The point becomes clearer when we recall that the context of the saying (Mk 2:17) is that of table fellowship (Mk 2:15-17). The same is true of all the related references to Jesus' consorting with sinners in the Gospel tradition. The imagery evoked then by talk of a "call" by Jesus is that of an invitation or summons to a meal or banquet (as in Mt 22:3-4, 9; Lk 14:7-17, 24). On the one hand this fits well with a context of factional dispute, since, as is generally recognized, table fellowship was one of the clearest boundary lines which the subgroups at the time of Jesus drew round themselves.[38] On the other hand, it underlines the seriousness of what was at stake. For the meal table or banquet was an accepted image of the age to come, both for Jesus and for the Qumran community, at least (Lk 14; 1QSa).[39]

---

[37] I follow the usual view regarding those attacked in these documents. See, e.g., those cited in my *Jesus, Paul and the Law*, pp. 75-76.

[38] Sanders, *Judaism*, continues to question the still large consensus view of the Pharisees on this topic (see above, pp. 159-159), but he fails to ask why in a purity conscious society Pharisees were nicknamed "the separated ones," he fails to give enough weight to the evidence of the Gospels, and still he concludes that "when the Pharisee was pure he would not dine with an ordinary person ... [and] preferred not to dine with people who routinely had midras impurity" (p. 437).

[39] See further my "Jesus, Table-Fellowship, and Qumran," *Jesus and the Dead Sea Scrolls*, ed. J. H. Charlesworth (New York, 1993), pp. 254-72.

The saying of Jesus (Mk 2:17) begins thus to sound a more critical note. Sinners are recipients of Jesus' summons to the banquet of the new age and not the righteous! That presumably does not mean that the righteous are excluded from the banquet, nor does it deny that there are others to issue the invitation to the righteous. But when added to other similar sayings of Jesus, the critical note is reinforced. One thinks in particular of the role ascribed to the elder brother in the parable of the prodigal son. The father reassures him, "Son, you are always with me, and all that is mine is yours." But there is implied, nonetheless, a clear rebuke of his grudging and condemnatory attitude toward the younger brother. Still more critical is the saying of Mt 21:32 (though not directed against any specific group), that "the tax collectors and the prostitutes go into the kingdom of God before you." And equally critical are the parables already mentioned of those who would be the obvious recipients of invitations to the (messianic) banquet but who, for a mixture of reasons, refuse the summons (Mt 22//Lk 14).

The implication in every case is that sinners were being invited *despite* the righteous. Indeed, the attitude of the righteous toward sinners was in danger of putting them at a disadvantage in relation to participation in the heavenly banquet. The very strictures on table fellowship which were meant to reinforce or protect the righteousness which they assumed was alone pleasing to God were in danger of fencing *themselves* off from that very grace.

It is true that this more positive view toward sinners is not entirely distinctive within Jewish traditional talk of sinners. The sinner can return and find mercy (Isa 55:7). If he turns from his sins and keeps the law and does what is right, he shall live. The Lord has no pleasure in the death of the ungodly, but rather that he should turn from his way and live (Ezek 18:21-23, 27; 33:11). "Turn back, you sinners, and do right before him," prays Tobit; "Who knows if he will accept you and have mercy on you?" (13:6). The Qumran hymn writer rejoices that "there is hope for those who turn from transgression and for those who abandon sin" (1QH 6.6).

So too, the equation of Gentiles as sinners is not automatic or universal. In rabbinic Judaism, the positive regard for the righteous Gentile is well known.[40] However, the positive note in such sayings is

---

[40] See, e.g., G. F. Moore, *Judaism in the First Centuries of the Christian Era* (Cambridge, Mass., 1927) 1.279; 2.386.

present only insofar as the status of "sinner" is being or has been left behind. The positive attitude is toward the sinner who repents, toward the Gentile who is righteous.[41] In contrast, the invitation of Mk 2:17 is unqualified. To be sure, Lk 5:32 adds εἰς μετάνοιαν—"I came not to call the righteous but sinners *to repentance*"—but that may simply indicate that Luke understood *sinner* in a nonfactional way—as equivalent to *wicked* or *criminal*. In contrast, the earlier form of the saying in Mk 2:17 implies that *sinner* was used without qualification precisely because it was being understood as a factional antithesis to the self-styled "righteous."

In short, it is the way in which sinners are depicted as recipients of Jesus' invitation in unqualified terms, and the juxtaposition of sinners with righteous in clearly implied criticism of the attitude of the righteous towards the sinners, which marks out Mk 2:17 within Jewish tradition. With one notable exception, I can think of no close parallel in all the extensive Jewish talk of righteous and sinners, both biblical and postbiblical.[42] Elsewhere, *righteous* is an unequivocally positive category and *sinner*, when juxtaposed with *righteous*, is an unequivocally negative category.[43] The Jesus who said these words was taking a distinctive stand within that tradition against traditional and current usage and attitude.

CONCLUSIONS

The conclusions seem to be obvious and straightforward.

First, for one Jew to designate another as "sinner" was as serious a charge or condemnation as can be imagined within the context of

---

[41] See also Sjöberg, *Sünder*, ch. 5–8; Urbach, *Sages*, pp. 462–71.

[42] The exception is PrMan 8: "You, O Lord, God of the righteous ones, did not appoint grace for the righteous ones, such as Abraham, and Isaac, and Jacob, those who did not sin against you; but you appointed grace for me, who am a sinner." This represents a remarkable parallel to Mk 2.17, but it is equally remarkable for its distinctiveness within Jewish sources from the period prior to Jesus. (See the further discussion in Neale, *Sinners*, pp. 86–95.)

[43] See again the examples cited above. See also Neale, *Sinners*, p. 85: "From the second century B.C.E. to the turn of the era, strong literary evidence exists of a view of 'sinners' that is in basic harmony with the ideological representation of the 'righteous' and the 'sinners' in the Psalms. No restitution was contemplated for the 'sinner'; judgment was the only prospect."

Jewish tradition. For a "sinner" as such was living outside the law, outside the boundaries of the covenant. A "sinner" as such was liable to the total loss of all privileges and blessings which came from God through God's covenant to God's people. A sinner could look forward only to destruction and eternal punishment.

The issues which brought the denunciation of "sinner" upon the head of a Jew can therefore hardly be called "minor" matters, as Sanders implies. The very fact that *sinner* was used in such an exchange indicates that from the perspective of the one who so used it the matter was far from minor.[44] On the contrary, it had all the seriousness which *sinner* indicated. Nor does Schiffman's protest make much sense: "Sinners they were, but Jews all the same." For if they were "sinners" and as such debarred from the world to come, then what difference did it make that they were still Jews? If the religious definition of *Jew* is one who is a recipient of God's covenant and promises, then a "sinner" is no "Jew," or is merely an ethnic "Jew" (in name only).

The other obvious conclusion to draw from the above is that in Mk 2:17 Jesus was in effect protesting against the use of *sinner* in a factional way. He recognized the seriousness of the condemnation implicit in the use of the word—the seriousness, therefore, of the divisions within Judaism. That one group of Jews could thus deny covenant status, *Jewish* status, to other Jews, simply because the others disagreed with and ignored the distinctive features of their halakhah, was evidently something abhorrent to Jesus. Thus, this was also a protest against narrowing the grace of God, against an over-definition and over-restrictiveness in the understanding of God's will which made it necessary to condemn as "sinners" those who disputed those definitions by word or action. For Jesus the meal table symbolic of the messianic banquet was *not* reserved for the self-styled "righteous"; precisely as an expression of God's grace, it was open to those whom the righteous disparaged as "sinners."

Paul's defense of the further extension of that same grace to "Gentile sinners" (Gal 2:15-16) was simply an extension of the principle enunciated in Mk 2:17. Thus, Jesus' words and actions as

---

[44] As Kraft and Nickelsburg, *Early Judaism*, p. 18, point out: "In such instances, differences in interpretation and disputes about law are raised to the level of absolute truth and falsehood and have as their consequences salvation and damnation."

expressed in Mk 2:17 provide a challenge not only to Jewish tradition, but also to Jewish *and* Christian definition and practice ever since.

JESUS AND CYNICS IN FIRST-CENTURY PALESTINE:
SOME CRITICAL CONSIDERATIONS

INTRODUCTION

IN RECENT RESEARCH on the life and teachings of Jesus, particularly in the United States, a number of scholars have proposed that the historical Jesus can best be understood against the background of Jewish or Hellenistic *wisdom* traditions in preference to the earlier (and still dominant) emphasis on the contextual relevance of Jewish *apocalypticism*. One manifestation of this change in perspective is the view that the earliest form of Q (the hypothetical *Logienquelle* or Sayings Source reconstructed primarily on the basis of non-Markan parallels between Matthew and Luke) has a primarily sapiential character which was later overlayed by the addition of sayings with a prophetic and apocalyptic character.[1]

   There is, of course, no necessary connection between Jesus as a teacher of wisdom and Cynicism.[2] Nevertheless, some who have rejected the explanatory significance of apocalypticism for reconstructing the life and teachings of the historical Jesus have emphasized the similarities between Jesus and the Cynic sage, suggesting that Jesus was influenced by such figures. Burton Mack, for example, has made the following proposal:[3]

---

   [1] H. Koester, *Introduction to the New Testament* (2 vols.; Berlin and Philadelphia, 1982) 2.147–49; J. S. Kloppenborg, *The Formation of Q: Trajectories in Ancient Wisdom Collections* (Philadelphia, 1987).

   [2] Kloppenborg, for example, is careful not to assume that the earliest collection of wisdom speeches which he posits for Q represents authentic sayings of Jesus. He is also careful not to suggest that, despite the affinities between sayings in Q and Cynic *chreiai*, the Q community either imitated Cynics or borrowed or adapted their ideology (*Formation of Q*, 324).

   [3] B. L. Mack, *A Myth of Innocence: Mark and Christian Origins* (Philadelphia,

Jesus' use of parables, aphorisms, and clever rejoinders is very similar to the Cynics' way with words. Many of his themes are familiar Cynic themes. And his style of social criticism, diffident and vague, also agrees with the typical Cynic stance. Scholars have known about some of these similarities for some time.

But what do these "similarities" mean? Are they the result of the historical influence on Jesus and his followers of forms of Cynicism current in first century Palestine? Or are they phenomenological similarities with no historical connection—what Dominic Crossan calls "one of the great and fundamental options of the human spirit"?[4] Mack is clear on this issue, for he claims that the historical Jesus was influenced by the Cynic presence in first century Palestine. "The Cynic analogy repositions the historical Jesus away from a specifically Jewish sectarian milieu and toward the Hellenistic ethos known to have prevailed in Galilee."[5]

The scholar who has focused most intensely on the hypothesis of the connections between Jesus and the Cynics is F. Gerald Downing. In many articles and two major books,[6] Downing energetically argues that "the wealth of at least apparent 'parallels' between the Jesus tradition and *popular* Cynicism suggest that some kind of Cynic influence may well have been accepted by Jesus of Nazareth himself."[7] Here he suggests that Jesus consciously patterned his behavior and his teaching under the influence of Cynics. Elsewhere he shifts this argument slightly by claiming that early Christianity "looked like" popular Cynicism and that this similarity was both recognized and accepted by early Christian writers of the second century and later.[8] Despite what I regard as fatal weaknesses in many of Downing supportive arguments

---

1988), p. 68.

[4] J. D. Crossan, *The Historical Jesus: The Life of a Mediterranean Jewish Peasant* (San Francisco, 1991), p. 76.

[5] Mack, *Myth of Innocence*, p. 73.

[6] F. G. Downing, *Christ and the Cynics: Jesus and Other Radical Preachers in First Century Tradition* (Sheffield, 1988), and *Cynics and Christian Origins* (Edinburgh, 1992). The many articles written by Downing are listed in the bibliography of the latter book.

[7] Downing, *Cynics and Christian Origins*, p. 3.

[8] Downing, *Cynics and Christian Origins*, p. 302.

and proposals, it is important that interested scholars read his detailed arguments and draw their own conclusions.

RELEVANT ASPECTS OF CYNICISM

Cynicism is an abstract noun referring to the similarities scholars perceive among those ancients who claimed the designation "Cynic" (κυνικός, "like a dog," "canine"),[9] or were labeled "Cynics" by others, from the fourth century B.C.E. to the fourth century C.E. Cynicism is an extremely complex historical phenomenon, for the term *Cynic* was used in a variety of ways by those who lived in opposition to the norms and values of Greco-Roman culture, dramatized by unconventional appearance and behavior.

During the last two decades, the phenomenon of Cynicism has been subject to intensive scholarly investigation. Scholars know "less" about Cynicism now than a generation ago, in the sense that ancient sources are now being read from a more critical perspective so that the complexities and discontinuities involved in using the labels *Cynic* and *Cynicism* have been more fully recognized than previously. Though it is not possible in the present context to present a fully nuanced discussion of Cynics in antiquity, I will emphasize a number of features of ancient Cynics which must be taken into consideration when comparing Jesus and Cynics.

First, the center of gravity of Cynics was *freedom* or *liberation*, a concept captured by such terms as ἐλευθερία ("freedom") and αὐτάρκεια ("independence"),[10] though it is not really possible to speak of Cynic *termini technici* used consistently by most practitioners of Cynicism.[11] Cynics understood freedom in a primarily negative and practical way, i.e., freedom *from* care about food, clothing, home, marriage, children; freedom *from* legal, moral, political, intellectual, cultic, and social obligations; freedom *from* desires, emotions (ἀπαθεία),

---

[9] Since dogs were generally viewed in a pejorative way by the ancients, κυνικός appears to be a negative label affixed to early Cynics by those they criticized, perhaps in reference to the completely natural and unaffected way in which dogs behaved in public.

[10] A. M. Rich, "The Cynic Conception of Autarkeia," *Mnesonyne* 9 (1956) 23–29.

[11] F. G. Downing, *Cynics and Christian Origins* (Edinburgh, 1992), pp. 45–50.

ambitions; even freedom *from* life itself through suicide.[12] The Cynic lifestyle was based on a tradition which recognized physical asceticism, centering in the principle of αὐταρκεία, or "self-sufficiency," as the only means for realizing the full potential of human life.

Cynic asceticism is distinct from both Stoic asceticism of the soul and Christian asceticism based on the suppression of the body and the self so that the soul is enabled to concentrate exclusively on God.[13] For the most part Cynics did not theorize about their ascetic approach to freedom, while many prominent Stoics developed elaborate ethical theories to support their detachment from that which was not under their control. The aim of the Cynic was to live a life of virtue, τὸ κατ' ἀρετὴν ζῆν (Diogenes Laertius 6.104), but to regard the life of virtue and the life of the city with its established habits and norms as antithetical.

Cynics valued the simple life (Athenaeus *Deipn.* 4.156c–159d) and virtue (Athenaeus *Deipn.* 13.566e–571a), consciously enduring deprivation, pain, and suffering in order to be liberated from the constraints of ordinary living. According to Julian, the goal of Cynicism was ἀπαθεία, "freedom from emotion" (*Or.* 6.192A). He expresses a different aspect of this in *Or.* 6.193D, where he contrasts life according to nature and life according to culture:

> Now the end and aim of the Cynic philosophy, as indeed of every philosophy, is happiness, but happiness that consists in living according to nature and not according to the opinions of the multitude.

The hero Herakles, who lived in accordance with nature rather than culture and was apotheosized through suffering, was the exemplar of the Cynic mode of life.[14]

Second, Diogenes Laertius has little to say about the distinctive features of Cynicism in the Hellenistic period. Though he regards

---

[12] R. Höistad, *Cynic Hero and Cynic King* (Lund, 1948), pp. 15–16.

[13] The most important contribution to the subject of Cynic asceticism is M.-O. Goulet-Cazé, *L'ascèse cynique: un commentaire de Diogène Laërce VI 70–71,* Histoire des doctrines de l'antiquité classique, no. 10 (Paris, 1986).

[14] D. E. Aune, "Heracles and Christ: Heracles Imagery in the Christology of Early Christianity," *Greeks, Romans and Christians: Essays in Honor of Abraham J. Malherbe,* ed. D. L. Balch, E. Ferguson, and W. A. Meeks (Minneapolis, 1990), pp. 3–19.

Cynicism as a philosophical school, he is apparently unable to summarize the distinctive teachings of Cynicism, but chooses to underscore
the features which the Cynics and Stoics held in common (6.103–5):
(1) They emphasize ethics to the exclusion of physics and logic.
(2) They are opposed to subjects generally taught (e.g., geometry and
music). (3) The goal of life is to live according to virtue. (4) They eat
and dress simply; some are vegetarians and some drink only cold water.
(5) They despise wealth, fame, and noble birth. (6) Virtue can be taught
and once learned cannot be lost. (7) The wise man is worthy of love and
is a friend to his peers. (8) Nothing should be entrusted to fortune.
(9) Whatever is intermediate between virtue and vice is indifferent (ἀδιάφορα). In discussing individual Cynics, Diogenes emphasizes anecdotes which reveal their view of life. According to Malherbe,[15]

> What made a Cynic was his dress and conduct, self-sufficiency, harsh
> behaviour towards what appeared as excesses, and a practical ethical
> idealism, but not a detailed arrangement of a system resting on
> Socratic-Antisthenic principles.

Third, according to Diogenes Laertius (in agreement with ancient
thinking in general), a philosophical αἵρεσις follows a central principle
and has a coherent body of doctrines (Diogenes Laertius 1.20). Unlike
the other Hellenistic philosophical schools, Cynicism had no organiza-
tional structure and no central body of doctrine.[16] In the Hellenistic
period, there is no common body of doctrine to which would-be Cynics
had to subscribe. The term αἵρεσις, or "school" can be therefore used
of Cynicism only in the sense of "intellectual tradition." It is for this
reason that M.-O. Goulet-Cazé prefers to speak of individual Cynics
rather than "Cynicism" during the imperial period.[17]

   According to Varro, "Cynicism" was a term applied to a variety
of different philosophical positions whose only common denominator
was the Cynic mode of living (Augustine De civitate dei 19.1.2–3).[18]

---

[15] Malherbe, "Self-Definition among Epicureans and Cynics," pp. 49–50.
[16] M.-O. Goulet-Cazé, L'ascèse cynique: un commentaire de Diogéne Laerce
VI 70–71 (Paris, 1986), pp. 28–31.
[17] M.-O. Goulet-Cazé, "Le cynisme à l'époque impériale," ANRW, Part
II/36.4, 2817.
[18] See M.-O. Goulet-Cazé, L'ascèse cynique: un commentaire de Diogène
Laërce VI 70–71 (Paris, 1986), pp. 20–37.

Hippobotus, in a lost work entitled Περὶ αἱρέσεων, discussed nine philosophical schools, but ignored Cynicism, Elianism, and Dialecticism (Diogenes Laertius 1.19). The διάδοχαι ("successions") genre used by Diogenes Laertius in his presentation of the founder and subsequent major figures in the history of Cynicism is particularly problematic.[19] Though probably dependent on older διάδοχαι lists which postulated teacher-student relationships, the Cynic succession is filled with difficulties and is obviously fictitious.[20]

Diogenes terminates his discussion of the Cynics at about 200 B.C.E. for several reasons: (1) succession lists had fallen into disuse by the early first century C.E. and there were gaps in his information. (2) He wanted to emphasize the Greek, not the Roman character of philosophy. And (3) he and his contemporaries were primarily interested in the classical and early Hellenistic periods. The Greek doxographical tradition had a genius for creating order out of chaos. Further, Diogenes' interest in Cynicism, as in all other philosophical schools, was primarily limited to the Hellenistic period (ca. 450 to 200 B.C.E.), with the result that he entirely neglected the Roman imperial period. Julian, on the other hand, emphasizes the fact that Cynicism is a kind of philosophy (*Or.* 6.182C) which had no founder but was in fact a universal philosophy practiced before the time of Heracles (*Or.* 6.182C–D). In fact, claims Julian, it is unnecessary for Cynics to read books, or undergo the initiations common to neophytes entering other philosophical schools; they need only heed the two Delphic maxims "know yourself" and "falsify the common currency" (Julian *Or.* 6.187D–188A).

Despite the real or imagined historical connections which link the two "isms," however, Cynicism must be analyzed in terms of the specific ideas and lifestyles of those who identified themselves as Cynics as well as those who were identified as Cynics by others. Just as etymology is no infallible guide to the meanings of words down through

---

[19] On the succession-list form, see V. Egger, *Disputationis de fontibus Diogenis Laertii particula de successionibus philosophorum* (Bordeaux, 1881), pp. 32–63.

[20] Many of the problems relating to the intention, reliability and use of sources of Diogenes Laertius are discussed in J. Mejer, *Diogenes Laertius and His Hellenistic Background* (Wiesbaden, 1978), and "Diogenes Laertius and the Transmission of Greek Philosophy," *ANRW*, II.36.5, pp. 3556–3602. Diogenes tends to name sources when discussing biographical traditions, but omit them in doxographical sections.

centuries of usage, so the origins of a particular philosophical tendency such as Cynicism is no sure guide for the character of Cynicism as late as the first century C.E. The real issue is whether or not it is possible to speak of a Cynic view of the world which was widely shared among those who regarded themselves as Cynics.

Fourth, there was a widespread assumption in antiquity that Cynicism and Stoicism were closely related (Diogenes Laertius 6.104). Though there are certain links between Stoicism and various Cynics— and mutual influences between Stoics and Cynics during the late Hellenistic and early Roman periods—this problematic notion has been perpetuated in modern scholarship through the use of the compound adjective "Cynic-Stoic," which serves only to obscure the considerable differences between the two traditions.

Zeno, the founder of the Stoa, was reportedly a disciple of Crates the Cynic (Diogenes Laertius 7.2). At the time of Zeno (335–263 B.C.E.), Cynicism had the following two major characteristics:[21] (1) The wise person is distinguished from the fool in that the former attributes no value to anything at all except virtue. (2) The wise person will not accept what is conventional, but what is natural, κατὰ φύσιν (Diogenes Laertius 6.71).

Fifth, Cynicism was not a system of thought and behavior which remained constant throughout antiquity. While no historical system of thought and behavior can remain static for long, the unity of Cynicism lies in its countercultural posture, rather than its dogmatic tradition. The tendency among scholars until recently was to treat Cynicism after Diogenes synchronically—despite the paucity of evidence. The evidence is so sparse that even a diachronic treatment of Cynicism is extremely problematic. Thus, the views of individual Cynics, to the extent that they are known to us, are the proper focus of investigation.[22]

Sixth, there was an ancient debate concerning the identify of the founder of the Cynics. This debate continues among modern scholars. Some ancients regarded either Antisthenes or Diogenes as possible founders of Cynicism (Julian *Or.* 6.187C), though Oenomaeus of Gadara (a celebrated Cynic of the second century C.E.) observed that

---

[21] J. M. Rist, *Stoic Philosophy* (Cambridge, 1969), p. 62.
[22] See, for example, the study by M. Billerbeck, *Der Kyniker Demetrius: Ein Beitrag zur Geschichte der frühkaiserlichen Popularphilosophie* (Leiden, 1979).

"the Cynic philosophy is neither Antisthenism or Diogenism" (Julian *Or.* 6.187C). Since Diogenes Laertius considered Antisthenes the founder of Cynicism, he made a concerted effort to trace the characteristic features of Cynicism back to him. Julian thought that Cynicism was founded neither by Antisthenes nor Diogenes, but that it was a universal philosophy predating Heracles (*Or.* 6.182C–D). According to Dudley, Diogenes (not Antisthenes) was the real founder of Cynicism, for the relationship between Antisthenes and Diogenes was a fiction used by the Stoics to establish continuity between themselves and Socrates.[23]

One major distinction between Antisthenes and Diogenes and most of the Cynics following Diogenes, concerns their respective attitudes toward society. Though Antisthenes was critical of democratic politics, he remained within the framework of the ancient city (Athens). Diogenes and later Cynics, on the other hand, rejected the conventions of the city state. Yet Antisthenes and Diogenes were agreed in their rejection of the ancient heroic ideal of the glory which resulted in honor among their peers, in favor of an ἀρετή which consisted in good deeds.[24]

Seventh, Cynics strove for unconventionality in appearance and behavior. It is widely assumed that the uniform of the Cynic remained relatively constant throughout antiquity: a threadbare cloak (τρίβων), a leather pouch (πήρα), a staff (βακτηρία), and disheveled hair (Julian *Or.* 6.201A). The pouch and the staff, however, were widely used by travelers, and the worn cloak and disheveled hair were indications of involuntary poverty. These features were not always exhibited by those who considered themselves Cynics, nor were they restricted to such.

Eighth, Diogenes (404–323 B.C.E.) was the paradigmatic Cynic. Anecdotes attributed to him contributed to the ancient conception of how a Cynic should behave. He emphasized that the most important things in life were freedom of speech and freedom of action (Diogenes Laertius 6.69, 71). The wise man rejects the conventions of city life, i.e., the norms and values of Greco-Roman culture (Diogenes Laertius

---

[23] D. R. Dudley, *A History of Cynicism* (Hildesheim, 1967; originally published in 1937), pp. 1–16. That the relationship between Antisthenes and Diogenes was a fiction is also held by F. Sayre, *Diogenes of Sinope: A Study of Greek Cynicism* (Baltimore, 1938), who regards Crates as the founder of Cynicism.

[24] H. D. Rankin, *Anthisthenes Sokratikos* (Amsterdam, 1986), pp. 183–84.

6.38). The wise man is completely independent of others. His practice of masturbating in public dramatized the view that the demands of nature should be satisfied without recourse to others. He rejected conventional marriage, but thought that men and women could, if they wished, engage in sexual intercourse by mutual consent.

Many ancient authorities, however, correctly regarded Cynicism as an ἔνστασις βίου, "style of living" rather than a philosophy (Diogenes Laertius 1.19–20; 6.103; see Julian *Or.* 6.181D, 189B).[25] Much of our knowledge of Cynicism is based on doxographical traditions consisting largely of anecdotes or *chreiai* about prominent Cynics of the past, such as Antisthenes (ca. 446–366 B.C.E.),[26] Diogenes (404–323 B.C.E.), Monimus (4th century B.C.E.), Onesicratus (late 4th century B.C.E.), Crates (late 4th century B.C.E.), and others, preserved primarily in Diogenes Laertius, Book 6. These anecdotes were also assembled into collections and formed one of several types of ancient biography (e.g., Lucian *Demonax*). One did not need be a Cynic to enjoy reading or hearing witty, culturally critical, anecdotes told about one or another Cynic. In fact many of the themes of the Cynic anecdotes were part of ancient Greco-Roman sapiential traditions and not the exclusive province of the various practitioners of Cynicism.

Ninth, our knowledge of Cynicism during the imperial period is problematic.[27] Cynics wrote few if any philosophical treatises (Julian *Or.* 6.186B–C). Further, Cynicism of the first three centuries B.C.E. has been refracted through Stoic authors who tend to minimize the differences between the two schools of thought, or indeed to minimize the difference between individual Cynics.[28] The pseudepigraphic Cynic Epistles are the major primary sources for Cynicism in the early imperial period. Epictetus presents a highly Stoicized portrait the ideal Cynic (Arrian *Diss.* 3.22). Lucian presents an extremely negative portrait of Peregrinus (*De morte Peregrini*). Few Cynics from the imperial period are known; one of these is Cynulcus.[29]

---

[25] *Suida, s.v.* αἵρεσις; A. Adler, *Suidae Lexicon* (Leipzig, 1928–38) 2.177.

[26] Diogenes Laertius (6.15, 19) claims that Antithenes influenced both the Cynic and Stoic schools.

[27] The most comprehensive recent discussion of Cynicism during this period is found in Goulet-Cazé, "Le cynisme à l'époque impériale," 2720–2833.

[28] A. J. Malherbe, "Self-Definition among Epicureans and Cynics," *Self-Definition in the Greco-Roman World*, Vol. 3 of *Jewish and Christian Self-Definition*

PROBLEMATIC FEATURES OF THE HYPOTHESIS

The task of comparing ancient phenomena is an exceedingly complex undertaking in which differences as well as similarities must be taken into account. Even more problematically, such phenomena never exist in isolation but are part of a larger system. To do justice to the systemic context of phenomena, meaningful conclusions can be reached only as constellations of phenomena from two or more different systems are compared. For example, an emphasis in the teachings of Jesus (i.e., the *exemplum* of the birds who do not sow or reap yet are cared for by God) is presumably part of a larger perspective on the relationship between people and God in the teachings of the Matthaean Jesus, while parallel *exempla* in purportedly Cynic authors are aspects of their emphasis on freedom.

First, central to the program of exploring the similarities between Jesus and the Cynics is the methodologically thorny problem of assessing the significance of parallels. The most systematic presentation of such parallels has been compiled by F. Gerald Downing.[30] Downing lists (without comment, since he claims that the parallels speak for themselves), hundreds of parallels between the teachings of Jesus in the canonical Gospels and a wide array of literary testimonia supposedly drawn from Cynic sources. While isolated parallels are interesting from a phenomenological perspective, *only parallel structures of thought and behavior can be considered to have a possible historical or genetic relationship.* Masses of isolated parallels prove little, particularly when drawn indiscriminately from six centuries of real or imagined Cynic authors and historical reports about Cynics.

A further problematic feature is Downing's emphasis on the *teaching* of the Cynics in comparison with the *teaching* of Jesus. Since Cynicism was a style of living rather than a coherent body of doctrine, this emphasis on teaching tends to skew the essential character of

---

(ed. B. F. Meyer and E. P. Sanders; Philadelphia, 1982), pp. 48–49.

[29] R. F. Hock, "A Dog in the Manger: The Cynic Cynulcus among Athenaeus's Deipnosophists," *Greeks, Romans, and Christians: Essays in Honor of Abraham J. Malherbe,* ed. D. L. Balch, E. Ferguson, and W. A Meeks (Minneapolis, 1990), pp. 20–37.

[30] F. G. Downing, *Christ and the Cynics: Jesus and Other Radical Preachers in First Century Tradition* (Sheffield, 1988).

Cynicism. One would have thought that Downing's parallels would focus on such structurally central Cynic emphases as freedom (ἐλευθερία) and independence (αὐταρκεία), or even such concepts as frankness (παρρησία) or indifference (ἀδιάφορα)—but this he fails to do.[31] Downing's atomistic approach to the presentation of these parallels is inherently problematic, since many of them are simply common *topoi* with wide currency in the Greco-Roman world.

Even though the presentation of parallels in table form is atomistic, one would think it essential that the parallels adduced actually be drawn from Cynic sources. But the problem of determining which authors should be considered Cynics and which not, is extremely complicated. While some scholars have a very restricted list of ancients whom they consider Cynics, Downing casts his net as widely as possible.[32] Another problem is whether every utterance of an individual who claims to be a Cynic should be considered Cynic. Downing is confident about this: "the views a self-styled Cynic announces are Cynic."[33] However, Downing goes beyond this: "But we also allow as Cynic views expressed that are akin to those explicitly labelled as Cynic, even where no overt claim to Cynic commitment is made."[34] Downing therefore regards Musonius Rufus (ca. 30–100 C.E.) as a Cynic, a judgment which is methodologically problematic.[35]

The case of Dio Chrysostom, whom Downing with many others regards as having moved from Stoicism to Cynicism (or Cynic leanings), and then back to Stoicism again (in a late speech, *Or.* 34, he attacks Cynics), is more difficult and even more crucial.[36] Dio's orations provide Downing with a large number of parallels to the canonical Gospels. It has become increasing evident, however, that Dio was never

---

[31] In *Cynics and Christian Origins*, pp. 45–50, Downing admits that few if any of the catchwords attributed to Cynics occur widely enough in Cynic authors to be considered unimpeachably Cynic. What Downing does not admit is that these concepts are so widely used in the Hellenistic world that they cannot be associated exclusively with any specific intellectual tradition.

[32] This issue is fully and frankly discussed in Downing, *Cynics and Christian Origins*, pp. 26–56.

[33] Downing, *Cynics and Christian Origins*, p. 55.

[34] Downing, *Cynics and Christian Origins*, p. 55.

[35] Downing, *Cynics and Christian Origins*, pp. 69–70.

[36] This view, already espoused by Synesius in antiquity, was propounded by H. von Arnim, *Leben und Werke des Dio von Prusa* (Berlin, 1898), pp. 245, 464.

a Cynic. During Dio's banishment by Domitian (82–96 C.E.), his wandering, humble garb, and moralizing speeches were not exclusive characteristics of Cynics. Furthermore, his admiration of Diogenes, like his admiration of Herakles, Odysseus, and Socrates, was not the exclusive province of Cynics, but also characterized Stoics and others. Dio, like Epictetus, was probably a Stoic who admired the Cynic ideal while rejecting the impostors who claim the Cynic name.[37]

Second, to buttress his particular version of the Cynic hypothesis, Mack speaks of a "Hellenistic ethos" which "prevailed" in Galilee.[38] It is this Hellenistic ethos which Mack judges the necessary cultural context for supposing the presence of Cynic philosophers. After surveying the widespread use of Greek language, literature, and education in Palestine during the first century C.E., Martin Hengel argues that the older distinction between "Palestinian" and "Hellenistic" Judaism is no longer useful. He proposes that "Palestinian" Judaism should rather be designated "Hellenistic" Judaism.[39] Though there were enclaves of Hellenistic culture in the two major Hellenistic cities of Galilee—Sepphoris and Tiberias—and in the more northerly of the transjordanian cities of the Decapolis (e.g., Antiochia Hippos, Abila, Gadara, Pella, and Beth-Shean or Scythopolis),[40] no clear picture has yet emerged regarding the complex relationship between Jewish and Hellenistic cultural worlds in Galilee during the first century C.E. Hellenism was more in evidence in the cities of Palestine than in the countryside. Evidence suggests, in fact, that there was a tension between such Hellenistic cities as Tyre and the Galilean hinterland upon which it was dependent for its food supply.[41]

[37] C. P. Jones, *The Roman World of Dio Chrysostom* (Cambridge, Mass., 1978), pp. 45–55.

[38] Mack, *Myth of Innocence*, p. 68.

[39] M. Hengel, *The "Hellenization" of Judaea in the First Century after Christ* (London and Philadelphia, 1989).

[40] On these cities, see E. Stern, ed., *The New Encyclopedia of Archaeological Excavations in the Holy Land* (Jerusalem and New York, 1993) 4.1324–28 (Sepphoris), 4.1464–73 (Tiberias); 2.634–36 (Hippos), 1.1–3 (Abila), 3.1174–80 (Pella), 1.223–35 (Beth-Shean); on Gadara, see U. Wagner-Lux and K. J. H. Vriezen, "Gadarenes," *ABD* 2.866–68.

[41] G. Theissen, *The Gospels in Context: Social and Political History in the Synoptic Tradition* (Minneapolis, 1991), pp. 61–80.

Though Hengel's competent work on Hellenistic aspects of Judaism has often been used to argue for the syncretistic character of Judaism, Hengel himself makes it clear that the central features of Jewish faith remained distinctively within the traditional parameters of Israelite-Jewish tradition. There is, furthermore, no literary or archaeological evidence for a Cynic presence in first-century Galilee. Two famous Cynics, Menippus[42] and Oenomaus,[43] together with a Hellenistic poet with Cynic sympathies, Meleager,[44] were natives of Gadara (one of the more important Decapolis cities located 7.5 kilometers southeast of the Sea of Galilee). Menippus was a Phoenician who was sold as a slave to Baton in Pontus and later settled in Thebes. Some scholars have detected Semitic influence in the fragments of his writings which have survived.[45] Meleager was born in Gadara but grew up in Tyre and retired to Cos where he probably died. However, neither figure seems to have practiced the Cynic mode of life in Gadara. There is, finally, some late evidence for the awareness of Cynics on the part of rabbinic sages.[46]

Third, since the Greco-Roman norms and values to which the Cynics objected were focused in the social and political institutions of the ancient city-states, they were active almost exclusively in a urban environment. Even the Cynic practice of itinerant living was primarily a means of moving from one urban environment to another. The Jesus movement, on the other hand, was primarily rural; it even appears that Jesus consciously avoided the Hellenistic cities of Galilee and the surrounding regions. Dominic Crossan, who includes a dated synthetic presentation of Cynicism as part of the historical background for his major work on the historical Jesus,[47] is quite willing to entertain the pos-

---

[42] Menippus, early third century B.C.E. (Strabo 16.2.29), was a Phoenician or Syrian, according to Diogenes Laertius (6.99). On Menippus, see R. Helm, *PW*, 15.888–94; D. R. Dudley, *A History of Cynicism* (Hildesheim, 1967), pp. 69–74; L. Paquet, *Les Cyniques Grecs: Fragments et témoinages* (Ottawa, 1975), pp. 122–24.

[43] Oenomaus was early second century C.E. On Oenomaus, see Dudley, *Cynicism*, 162–70; J. Hammerstaedt, "Der Kyniker Oenomaus von Gadara," *ANRW*, II.36/4 (1990) 2834–65.

[44] Meleager flourished during the first century B.C.E. (*Anth. Graec.* 7.417–19).

[45] Martin Hengel, *Judaism and Hellenism* (2 vols.; Philadelphia, 1974) 1.84.

[46] M. Luz, "A Description of the Greek Cynic in the Jerusalem Talmud," *JSJ* 20 (1989) 49–60.

[47] Crossan's synthetic discussion of Cynicism is also problematic in that he used Bryan Wilson's sevenfold typology of millennarian movements to categorize Cynicism as an *introversionist* response to the world (*The Historical Jesus*, pp. 72–73;

sibility of Jesus as a "peasant Jewish Cynic," though he obviously does not use the term "Cynic" in the usual sense:[48]

> Greco-Roman Cynics, however, concentrated primarily on the marketplace rather than the farm, on the city dweller rather than the peasant. And they showed little sense of collective discipline, on the one hand, or of communal action, on the other. Jesus and his followers do not fit well against *that* background.

Here Crossan focuses on two major differences between Jesus and the Cynics, the primary setting of their activity (Jesus avoided cities, while Cynics were primarily urban) and the particular social context of their activity (Jesus played a central role in a socio-religious movement, while Cynics were convinced individualists).

Fourth, the Gospels are complex documents which contain authentic reminiscences of the teachings and activities of Jesus overlayed by the concerns of later forms of Christianity, including Palestinian Jewish Christianity, Hellenistic Jewish Christianity, and Hellenistic Gentile Christianity. Cynic influence would have become increasingly more likely with the Hellenization of the Jesus tradition.

Fifth, most New Testament scholars who discuss the relevance of the Cynics for understanding Jesus or early Christians depend upon syntheses of Cynicism formulated a generation or more ago which presuppose more unity and coherence in Cynicism than one can now safely assume.[49]

Sixth, the formal similarities between the *apophthegmata* of Jesus and the Cynic *chreiai* require discussion.[50] The relationship between the *apophthegmata*, or pronouncement stories, attributed to Jesus in the Synoptic Gospels, and the *chreiai* or anecdotes attributed to Cynic philosophers, has been the subject of some discussion.[51] After the

---

see B. Wilson, *Magic and the Millennium: A Sociological Study of Religious Movements of Protest among Tribal and Third-World Peoples* [New York, 1973], pp. 16–30). Since "Cynicism" (a designation for the common features of individual Cynics) is neither a social movement nor religious, the use of Wilson's typology is inherently problematic.

[48] Crossan, *The Historical Jesus*, p. 421.

[49] Major exceptions include F. G. Downing and A. Malherbe.

[50] Hengel, *Hellenization*, p. 44.

[51] The relevance of *chreiai* for understanding the form of certain sayings of Jesus presented within a brief narrative framework was emphasized by M. Dibelius, *Die Formgeschichte des Evangeliums*, 6. Aufl. (Tübingen, 1971), pp. 149–64.

aphorism, the *chreia* is the most frequently found literary form in the Synoptic Gospels. Klaus Berger has listed no less than 65 *chreiai* in the canonical Gospels.[52] The influence of the Greek *chreia* on rabbinic literature was explored earlier by H. A. Fischel.[53] While the use of *chreiai* was certainly not limited to Cynics, since they tend to center on conflicts in values, they proved to be appropriate vehicles for the Cynic critique of urban society generally.

There are differences as well as similarities between the Cynic *chreiai* and the *chreiai* of the Synoptic Gospels. First, *chreiai* in general, and the Cynic *chreiai* in particular, tend to be witty. This humorous element is almost completely missing from the *chreiai* attributed to Jesus. Second, the interlocutors in Cynic *chreiai* are either completely anonymous or famous people, such as Alexander the Great. The dialogue partners in the Synoptic *chreiai* tend to be stereotypical groups, such as Pharisees, Sadducees, and scribes. Even Jesus himself does not function as an individual sage so much as a representative of a group. The conflict, therefore, is not between the sage and society in general, but between two social groups. The conflict therefore functions as a means of defining social identity.[54]

CONCLUSIONS

In discussing the problems involved in attempting to use various kinds of testimonia about the Cynics in order to shed light on the distinctive character of the life and teaching of Jesus, several issues have emerged which make such a comparison extremely difficult.

First, the proposal assumes the influential presence of Cynics in Galilee during the early part of the first century C.E., perhaps even an adapted form of "Jewish Cynicism." No literary or archaeological evidence suggests any Cynic presence whatsoever in Galilee or even in the

---

[52] K. Berger, *Formgeschichte des Neuen Testaments* (Heidelberg, 1984), pp. 80–82.

[53] H. A. Fischel, "Studies in Cynicism and the Ancient Near East: The Transformation of a *Chria*," *Studies in Antiquity: Essays in Memory of Erwin Ramsdell Goodenough*, ed. J. Neusner (Leiden, 1968), pp. 372–411.

[54] Theissen, *Gospels in Context*, pp. 113–16.

Decapolis, nor for the presence or development of a hybrid type of "Jewish Cynicism."

Second, the Cynic protest against the political and social norms and values of Greco-Roman culture was possible only in the context of Greco-Roman cities. In contrast, the Jesus movement was primarily at home in a rural peasant context.

Third, Cynics did not belong to a "philosophical school" (αἵρησις) as that concept was normally understood in the ancient world. Diogenes Laertius presents a heavily fictional account of teacher-student connections based on ancient attempts to conceptualize "Cynicism" on analogy with the major philosophical schools. Even the attempt to provide Cynicism with a founder, on analogy with major philosophical schools, is problematic. It was an extremely diverse tradition with both intellectual and behavioral poles. This tradition was kept alive by the paradigmatic role played by Diogenes and other culturally marginal sages and was transmitted through anecdotes and biographies.

Fourth, "Cynicism" is so diverse throughout antiquity that it cannot be discussed adequately synchronically, but must be approached through the study of the thought and behavior of individuals who either considered themselves Cynics or were considered Cynics by others.

Fifth, the structural core of Cynic thought is the theme of *freedom*. This theme is characteristically expressed by frank speech, countercultural dress (typically pouch, staff, and ragged cloak), and behavior. The striking differences between Jesus and the Cynics become evident when the systemic structures of thought and behavior are compared. These differences are obscured when the proposed parallel material compared is atomized into individual themes and motifs.

Sixth, the roster of authors and testimonia assumed to be Cynic needs to be examined with extreme care. The comparative enterprise is vitiated if important authors such as Dio Chrysostom are assumed to be Cynics when in fact they probably were not. Furthermore, it cannot simply be assumed that every statement attributed to a supposed Cynic is characteristic of Cynicism.

Seventh, the hyphenated compound adjective "Cynic-Stoic" is problematic because it obscures the considerable distinctions between the two traditions.

Finally, the formal similarities between the anecdotes or *chreiai* attributed to Jesus and the Cynics are striking and deserve detailed study.[55]

[55] See also the following more recent discussions: K. Berger, "Hellenistische Gattungen im Neuen Testament," *ANRW* II.25/2 (1984) 1092–1110 (with an extensive bibliography); V. K. Robbins, "The Chreia," *Greco-Roman Literature and the New Testament*, ed. D. E. Aune (Atlanta, 1988), pp. 1–24; B. L. Mack and V. K. Robbins, *Patterns of Persuasion in the Gospels* (Sonoma, Cal., 1989).

JESUS AND HIS COMMUNITY:
BETWEEN ESSENES AND PHARISEES

INTRODUCTION

1. Pluralism in Second-Temple Judaism

The Judaism of the Second Temple period, and in particular the Judaism at the time of Jesus and the primitive church, was not monolithic in its religious attitude, but rather pluralistic. Although there were many different expressions of Judaism, the main religious outlooks were based on the three major Torah groups of that time as described by Flavius Josephus: the Sadducees, the Pharisees, and the Essenes (*War* 2.119-166; *Ant* 18.12-22).

A fourth group, the Zealots, issued from the Pharisees (*Ant* 18.23-25). They stood for a radical theocracy, which they strove to bring about by military means. Founded on the occasion of the census in the year 6 C.E., it was directed against the Roman overlords. The founders were the scholar Jehudah of Gamla and the Pharisaic Rabbi Zaddok (*Ant* 18.4). Led by the dynastic family of Jehudah of Gamla, their religious and often violent extremism led eventually to one disastrous debacle after another during the war against Rome: the fall of Galilee with the terrible slaughter of the inhabitants at the conquest of Gamla, the destruction of Jerusalem and its Temple, and finally, under the Gamlanite Eleazar, the fall of Masada.

The three major religious movements determined religious behavior during the two centuries before the destruction of Jerusalem. As Philipp Seidensticker has stressed, anybody active in religious life was somehow influenced by the one of the three groupings.[1] All three of

---

[1] "Die Gemeinschaftsform der religiösen Gruppen des Spätjudentums und der Urkirche," *SBFLA* 9 (1958/59) 94–198.

them considered the Torah as the supreme law, but each group had its own interpretation of the Law. The heart of their differences lay in the halakhah: how the Law should be observed in practical life. The calendar represented one major point of division. Detailed study of the Qumran scrolls has revealed this issue,[2] although Philo and Josephus had failed to mention it. That calendar controversies were a strong motif behind the Essene separation (cf. 1QpHab 11.4-8) is now confirmed by the halakhic letter of the Teacher of Righteousness (4QMMT), found in several copies in Qumran cave IV.[3]

Even though only the Pharisaic expression of Judaism survives in a modified form today, it is incorrect to classify this form as "normative Judaism" and the one professed by the Essenes as "sectarian." Most Qumran scholars have abandoned the practice of calling the Qumran Essenes a sect. At the time of the Second Temple all three movements were recognized forms of Jewish life.

The life of Flavius Josephus illustrates this "normative pluralism." He was the offspring of an aristocratic priestly family of Sadducees in Jerusalem (*Life* 1-6). He writes,

> At about the age of sixteen I determined to gain personal experience of the several sects [αἱρέσεις is not used here in a pejorative sense!] into which our nation is divided. These, as I have frequently mentioned, are three in number—the first that of the Pharisees, the second that of the Sadduccees, and the third that of the Essenes. I thought that, after a thourough investigation, I should be in a position to select the best. So I submitted myself to hard training and laborious exercises and passed through the three courses. (*Life* 9-10)

After undergoing training in these three groups, he even joined in the desert an ascetic by the name of Bannus (*Life* 11-12), whose way of life reminds us of John the Baptist. After three years of this, he decided to follow the Pharisaic halakhah (*Life* 12).

---

[2] Cf. the literature in J. A. Fitzmyer, *The Dead Sea Scrolls: Major Publications and Tools for Study* (SBL Resources for Biblical Studies 20; Atlanta 1990), pp. 180-82. My gratitude goes to Dr. Rainer Riesner (University of Tübingen) for some literary references and helpful criticisms.

[3] See now E. Qimron and J. Strugnell, eds., *Qumran Cave 4 V: Miqsat Ma'ase HaTorah* (DJD 10; Oxford, 1994).

2. The Proposed Thesis

In light of the above introductory remarks, which of these three religious groupings influenced Jesus and his community? As an answer to this question I propose the following thesis: The primitive Christian community on the Southwestern hill of Jerusalem lived in the proximity of the Essene quarter. There, next to the "Gate of the Essenes" (*War* 5.145), they had one of their three monastic centres, called כחלית in the Copper Scroll (3Q15 1.9-12; 2.13-15).

The personality most likely responsible for the close contacts between the groups was, in my opinion, James, "the brother of the Lord." Around him was an influential group of Jesus' relatives, who had come from Galilee. I hold that these relatives belonged to the Natzorean clan and had Essene leanings. This Natzorean clan had arrived from the Babylonian Diaspora around the year 100 B.C.E. Since Jesus felt that his kinsmen were trying to constrain him, he separated himself from them and formed in Capernaum his own group, which was built on the Pharisaic model. While in Capernaum, Jesus came closer to the Pharisaic teachings on the Torah and the halakhah, especially the one represented by the Bet Hillel. However, his attempted dialogue with the Pharisees led to many disputes and remained, in the final analysis, fruitless.

During his last months in Bethany beyond the Jordan and the Bethany near Jerusalem, Jesus was surrounded again by people with Essene sympathies. In those days, the Essenes and the Temple loyalists followed two different feast calendars. Jesus' Last Supper was a Passover meal held in a guesthouse of the Essene community on the Southwestern hill. The date was the Eve of Wednesday, when the Essenes celebrated their Passover Seder. During that night, Jesus was imprisoned. He was finally crucified on the Eve of the Passover (Saturday) as it was celebrated in the Temple.

I. JERUSALEM'S SOUTHWESTERN HILL

1. Mount Zion, the Cradle of Christianity

One of the best-proven facts of the Jerusalem topography, based on ancient traditions of the church fathers[4] and archaeological evidence,

---

[4] D. Baldi, *Enchiridion Locorum Sanctorum: Documenta S. Evangelii Loca Respicientia* (Jerusalem, [3]1982), pp. 473ff.

is the location of the primitive Christian community in Jerusalem. It is the Southwestern hill of the city, called today Mount Zion. There, next to the Benedictine Dormition Abbey, is the Cenacle and the so-called Tomb of David. The cenotaph of King David was put up there by the Crusaders because of a wrong interpretation of St. Peter's sermon on Pentecost (cf. Acts 2:29). In time it was also adopted by Jews and Moslems as the genuine site of David's Tomb. I have written on the architectural development of this area and its traditions elsewhere.[5]

2. The "Gate of the Essenes"

When in 1973 our Abbey on Mount Zion initiated a theological faculty for German-speaking theology students, both Catholic and Protestant, I was put in charge of teaching biblical archaeology and topography. At that time, my Abbot asked me to make a special study of the archaeology and traditions of Mount Zion.[6]

The findings in Qumran had polarized the entire world with regard to the monastery of the Essenes in the Judean desert. Possible points of contact between early Christians and Essenes were vigorously discussed. I took a special interest in a description by Josephus about the city walls of Jerusalem during the Roman War (66–70 C.E.). What caught my attention was this section:

> Starting at the same point [the Hippicus Tower] the wall, now facing west, proceeded in the other direction past a place called Bethso to the Gate of the Essenes (διὰ δὲ τοῦ Βηθσὼ καλουμένου χώρου κατατεῖνον ἐπὶ τὴν Ἐσσηνῶν πύλην) and thereafter, facing south, extended above the Fountain of Siloam. (War 5.145)

---

[5] "The Apostolic Synagogue on Mount Zion," *BAR* 17/3 (1990) 16–35, 60; "Die apostolische Synagoge auf dem Zion" in *Wege des Messias und Stätten der Urkirche: Jesus und das Judenchristentum im Licht neuer archäologischer Erkenntnisse*, R. Riesner, ed. (Studien zur Biblischen Archäologie und Zeitgeschichte 2; Gießen, [4]1994), pp. 287–326; "Archäologische Beobachtungen zum Jerusalemer Essener-Viertel und zur Urgemeinde" in B. Mayer, *Christen und Christliches in Qumran?* (Eichstätter Studien NF 32; Regensburg, 1992), pp. 89–113.

[6] "An Essene Quarter on Mount Zion?" in *Studia Hierosolymitana in onore di P. Bellarmino Bagatti I: Studi archeologici* (SBFCMa 22; Jerusalem, 1976), pp. 245–85 (also printed separately).

Some 700 feet south of the Cenacle on Mount Zion there is an old Protestant cemetery. After studying the ancient maps of Frederick J. Bliss' and Archibald C. Dickie's excavations in the nineties of the last century,[7] I guessed that the gate of Josephus must lie somewhere there. After obtaining permission of the owners and the Israeli Department of Antiquities, I started to search for the gate. Some twelve feet below the surface, I suddenly struck on a smooth slab of limestone in 1977, which turned out to belong to one of the sills of a gate complex of the ancient city wall.[8] I was later joined by the two Israeli archaeologists, Doron Chen and Shlomo Margalit. We were able to distinguish three super-imposed sills belonging to three different periods.[9]

After a thorough investigation, which took years of research, we were able to date the three sills. The upper one was of the Byzantine period, built probably by the workmen of the Empress Eudokia (around 450 C.E.), who had lived for some time in Jerusalem.[10] The middle sill, poorly shaped and made up of slabs collected from different sites, was from the period of the Aelia Capitolina and must have been a gate in a wall sorrounding Mount Zion, the so-called *murus Sion* of the Pilgrim of Bordeaux (333 C.E.).[11] The third and lowest sill was well built, but rather small in size for a city gate. It appeared to have been in use for a long time; the limestone slabs of the sill were well worn by passing of feet. The wings of the gate hinged on a post whose shoe was apparently of metal (judging from the shape of the socket which is still preserved). Underneath the gate we found a sewage channel, which was built of good material and which served as a channel for all later periods. The ceramic found underneath the threshold proved that this gate belonged

---

[7] F. J. Bliss, "Second Report on the Excavations at Jerusalem," *PEFQS* (1894) 243-57 (242-54); "Third Report on the Excavations at Jerusalem," *PEFQS* (1895) 9-25 (12); *Excavations at Jerusalem* (London, 1898), pp. 16-20, 322-24.

[8] B. Pixner, D. Chen, and S. Margalit, "Har Zijon" [Hebrew], *Hadashot Ark-heologiyot* 72 (1979) 28-29.

[9] B. Pixner, D. Chen, and S. Margalit, "The 'Gate of the Essenes' Re-Excavated," *ZDPV* 105 (1989) 85-95 and Plates 8-16; B. Pixner, "The History of the 'Essene Gate' Area," *ZDPV* 105 (1989) 96-104; R. Riesner, "Josephus' 'Gate of the Essenes' in Modern Discussion," *ZDPV* 105 (1989) 105-9.

[10] "Pilgrim of Piacenza," *Itinerarium* 25 (D. Baldi, *Enchiridion Locorum Sanctorum*, p. 469).

[11] *Itinerarium* 16 (Ibid. p. 474).

to the Herodian-Roman period. There was no doubt: this was the gate that Josephus called the "Gate of the Essenes" (*War* 5.145).

3. The Essene Quarter

There must have been a special reason for building such a city gate at the very edge of a precipice which led into the Gehinnom ravine and which could be reached only by climbing on foot the steep incline. One might think it was called the "Essene Gate" because the Essenes lived nearby and used it to reach their agricultural fields and their abodes in the desert. Actually, long before our excavations, several scholars had noted the description of Josephus Flavius and had concluded that the Essenes must have had their quarter close to Josephus' "Gate of the Essenes."[12] Such opinions were expressed by Emil Schürer,[13] Marie-Josèphe Lagrange,[14] and Otto Michel.[15] Gustaf Dalman pointed out that the purity regulations of the Essenes demanded

---

[12] Some have held that the names of gates refer *always* to localities outside the town. Thus, the Jerusalem "Gate of the Essenes" was the one through which the Essenes left the city to reach Qumran (B. Schwank, "Gab es zur Zeit der öffentlichen Tätigkeit Jesu Qumran-Essener in Jerusalem?" in B. Mayer, *Christen und Christliches in Qumran?*, pp. 115–30 [pp. 115–21]). But no such rule for the gates of Jerusalem in the different historical periods exists. Cf. R. Riesner, "Das Jerusalemer Essenerviertel: Antwort auf einige Einwände" in Z. J. Kapera, *Intertestamental Essays in honour of Józef Tadeusz Milik*. Qumranica Mogilanensia 6, vol. 1 (Kraków, 1992), pp. 179–86 (pp. 180–82). In a Qumran symposium, held at the Catholic University of Eichstätt (Germany) in October 1991, Professor Herbert Hunger (University of Vienna) pointed to the "Schottentor" in Vienna. It has its name after a convent of "Iro-Scottish" monks from the Middle Ages *inside* the town. A Jerusalem example is the Dung Gate which before 1967 was also known by local Arabs as *bab el-magharibe* "Gate of the Moors," leading to the living quarters of North African Arabs *inside* the city wall. Cf. B. Meistermann, *New Guide to the Holy Land* (London 1923), p. 213. In general it can be said that city gates named after a location point to the fact that roads from that gate led to that location, while gates named after a group of people indicate that such people dwelt in the vicinity of the gate.

[13] *Geschichte des Jüdischen Volkes im Zeitalter Jesu Christi*, vol. 2 (Leipzig, ⁴1907), p. 657–58 n. 5 (ET G. Vermes, F. Millar, and M. Black, *Emil Schürer: The History of the Jewish People in the Age of Jesus Christ*, vol. 2 [Edinburgh, 1979], p. 563 n. 5).

[14] *Le Judaisme avant Jésus-Christ* (Paris, 1931), p. 317.

[15] *De Bello Judaico: Der Jüdische Krieg: Griechisch und Deutsch*, vol. II/1 (Munich, 1963), p. 246 n. 41.

that they have a gate of their own.[16] Philipp Seidensticker wrote in 1958, "Surely there lived a group of Essenes in Jerusalem, since a gate was called after them, in whose vicinity they might have had a 'convent' of their order."[17] In the War Scroll of Qumran, mention is made of their "community in Jerusalem" (העדה ירושלים [1QM 3.10-11]). Given the strict purity regulations for the holy city (CD 12.1; 11QTemple 45.11; cf. Lev 15:18), this community must have been composed of celibate monks.[18]

To substantiate the opinion of such prominent scholars we examined the area around the Gate of the Essenes. This gave us a fairly clear idea about the position of the Jerusalem quarters of the Essenes,[19] which in their writings is called a "camp" (מחנה).[20] Some hundred fifty feet northeast of the gate are still thirty-six steps hewn into the rock, leading up to a small terrace in the corner of the city wall. This elevated rock ledge had been especially prepared for ritual washings.[21] Two stepped ritual baths can be seen there. One flight of steps has the typical hump separating (as in other Jerusalem baths and as in Qumran) the steps for the descent from those of the ascent.

Next to the baths are the remains of a (perhaps secret) entrance through the wall into the מחנה. In my opinion, this entrance is the "*manos*" מנוס (emergency exit) mentioned in the Copper Scroll of Qumran (3Q15 1.13-15). In an article on the Copper Scroll, I expressed the opinion that the seventeen first hiding places of treasures (3Q15 1.1-4.2) were located on or around Mount Zion.[22] These are the seventeen

---

[16] *Jerusalem und sein Gelände*. Schriften des Deutschen Palästina-Instituts 4 (Gütersloh, 1930), pp. 86–87.

[17] *SBFLA* 9 (1958/59) 129 [translation mine].

[18] Cf. B. Pixner, "The Jerusalem Essenes, Barnabas and the Letter to the Hebrews," in Z. J. Kapera, *Intertestamental Essays*, pp. 167–78.

[19] Cf. B. Pixner, "Das Essener-Quartier in Jerusalem," in *Wege des Messias*, pp. 180–207; and also R. Riesner, "Jesus, the Primitive Community, and the Essene Quarter of Jerusalem," in J. H. Charlesworth, *Jesus and the Dead Sea Scrolls* (New York, 1993), pp. 198–234.

[20] Cf. J. H. Charlesworth, *Graphic Concordance to the Dead Sea Scrolls* (Tübingen/Louisville, 1991), p. 392.

[21] Cf. B. Pixner, *Studia Hierosolymitana*, vol. 1, pp. 269–71; *Wege des Messias*, pp. 197–201.

[22] "Unravelling the Copper Scroll Code: A Study on the Topography of 3Q15," *RQ* 11 (1983) 323–66 (342–47). A growing number of scholars now holds that the Copper Scroll is a genuine Qumran document and not later folkloristic phantasy. Cf. B. Pixner, "Copper Scroll," *ABD*, vol. 1 (New York, 1992), pp. 1133–34.

that have the mysterious Greek letters, which refer probably to the names of the owners or supervisors of the hidden assets. Several of these hiding places fit perfectly the local conditions, which still can be traced today.

The above-mentioned ritual baths outside the city wall have, to my knowledge, only one real parallel, namely, Qumran. There, too, one can find a special *miqveh* (Locus 138) outside the monastic compound.[23] Such installations allowed the strict observers of the Torah to fulfill its command, "If any man among you is unclean by reason of a nocturnal emission, he must go out of the camp (אֶל־מִחוּץ לַמַּחֲנֶה) and not come into it again; towards evening he must take a bath and he may return to the camp at sunset" (Deut 23:11-12).

An additional ground for the Jerusalem double מקוה could have been that the Essene latrines were nearby, since the mysterious reference of Josephus to the *Bethso* near the Essene Gate can now be identified with the help of a passage in the Temple Scroll (11QTemple 46.13-16) as such an installation.[24] A rockhewn channel that used to carry "the water of purity" (1QS 5.13) runs from the מחנה to the double מקוה outside the city. Since this water should be touched only by full members (1QS 5.13ff; cf. 1QS 6.16-17; CD 10.10-13; *War* 2.137-142), this channel clearly points the way to the location of the Essenes' monastic center, namely to an area inside the ramparts of Jerusalem. This area is today part of the Greek Orthodox and the Dormition Abbey's gardens. In that very area we found several ritual baths, two of them quite large.[25] Their size seems to indicate that they served a whole community, rather than private individuals.

II. TWO NEIGHBORING COMMUNITIES ON MOUNT ZION

It should be of great interest to Christian scholars that such strong evidence exists that two religious communities lived next to each other on

---

[23] Cf. R. de Vaux, *Archaeology and the Dead Sea Scrolls* (Oxford, 1973), p. 9, and Plate XXXIX.

[24] As was first pointed out by Y. Yadin, "The Gate of the Essenes and the Temple Scroll" [Hebrew], *Qad* 5/3-4 (1972) 129–30 (ET in Y. Yadin, *Jerusalem Revealed* [Jerusalem, 1976], pp. 90–91).

[25] Cf. B. Pixner, *Studia Hierosolymitana*, vol. 1, pp. 271–73; *Wege des Messias*, p. 201.

Mount Zion from the year 30 C.E. (the commonly accepted year of the death of Jesus) to 70 C.E. (The Essenes seem to have vanished with the destruction of the Holy City.)

Were there any contacts between the two groups? Many scholars have remarked that the social structures of primitive Christianity and the Qumran Essenes were similar.[26] Even though Jesus himself was no Essene, nor were the apostles, some passages in the New Testament indicate possible points of contact.

1. Mutual Contacts

In Acts 6:7 it is said, "And the word of God increased; and the number of the disciples multiplied greatly and a large group of priests ($\pi o \lambda \dot{v} \varsigma$ $\tau \epsilon$ $\ddot{o} \chi \lambda o \varsigma$ $\tau \hat{\omega} \nu$ $\iota \epsilon \rho \dot{\epsilon} \omega \nu$) became obedient to the faith." Where did these Jewish priests come from? While the Pharisees were to a large extent lay people, the central core of the Sadducees and the Essenes was made up of *kohanim*. Since the aristocratic priesthood of the Sadducees were the sworn enemies and persecutors of the primitive church, scholars argued for a long time that this group of *kohanim* must have come from the Essene priestly class.[27]

It can also safely be presumed that the community of goods practised by the first Christians (Acts 2:44ff; 4:43ff) was influenced by the proximity of the Essenes,[28] for whom the sharing of all property was part and parcel of their establishment, especially inside their monastic section (1QS 1.7ff; 6.16ff; 7.6ff; *War* 2.122).

---

[26] Cf. S. E. Johnson, "The Dead Sea Manual of Discipline and the Jerusalem Church of Acts," in K. Stendahl, *The Scrolls and the New Testament* (New York, 1957), pp. 129–42, 273–75; H. Kosmala, *Hebräer, Essener, Christen: Studien zur Vorgeschichte der christlichen Verkündigung* (SPB 1; Leiden, 1959); W. S. LaSor, *The Dead Sea Scrolls and the New Testament* (Grand Rapids, 1962), pp. 368–78; K. Schubert, in J. Maier and K. Schubert, *Die Qumran-Essener* (München, 1973), pp. 127–37; R. Riesner, "Essener und Urkirche in Jerusalem," in B. Mayer, *Christen und Christliches in Qumran?*, pp. 139–55; O. Betz, "Kontakte zwischen Essenern und Christen," Ibid., pp. 157–75.

[27] Cf. H. Braun, *Qumran und das Neue Testament*, vol. 1 (Tübingen, 1966), p. 153.

[28] Cf. B. J. Capper, "'In der Hand des Ananias ...' Erwägungen zu 1QS VI,20 und der urchristlichen Gütergemeinschaft," *RQ* 12 (1986) 223–36; O. Betz, in B. Mayer, *Christen und Christliches in Qumran?* pp. 164–65.

That the first Jerusalem church followed such a practice is amazing. No general command of the Lord existed for such a practice, nor was it introduced elsewhere in the Christian churches. Even in Jerusalem it was soon abandoned. The reason why the community on Mount Zion made it part of their practice could well have been the influence of the social system of their neighbors, the Essenes. The Christians could not lag behind in "holiness." The fervor aroused by their conviction of living in the last days (Acts 2:17), which had seized both communities, might have been the stimulus for such singular behavior. Even so, the words spoken by Peter to Ananias and Sapphira ("While you still owned the land, was it not yours to keep, and after you had sold it, was not the money to do with as you liked?" [Acts 5:4]) suggests that the religious communism of these Christian Hebrews was voluntary, while that of the Essenes was obligatory on all full members.

The Christian Hellenists who lived all over the city apparently did not adopt such common ownership. That might also be why they complained that their widows were not taken care of as as well as those in the Mount Zion commune (Acts 6:1). The newly chosen Greek-speaking deacons were put in charge of the problem (Acts 6:2-6). Mary, the mother of Mark, for instance, in whose house the Greek-speaking used to gather for prayer, had a comfortable home of her own with a court that led to an outside gate (Acts 12:12ff).

Christian baptism may also have evolved from the baptismal practice of the Essenes and similar movements in the Jordan Valley.[29] Three stages of baptismal evolution can be observed. The first stage consisted in the ritual bathing for the forgiveness of personal transgressions, performed almost daily by the Essenes. They bathed by immersing themselves in "living water"—or at least sprinkling themselves with it (1QS 3.4ff). The second stage was the practice of John the Baptist, who acted himself as the Baptizer, immersing those who were ready to repent from their sins and to open their hearts for the messianic kingdom (Mk 1:4-5;

---

[29] Cf. O. Cullmann, "The Significance of the Qumran Texts for Research into the Beginnings of Christianity," in K. Stendahl, *The Scrolls and the New Testament*, pp. 18–32, 251–52 (pp. 21, 28–29); O. Betz, in B. Mayer, *Christen und Christliches in Qumran?*, pp. 158–60. For the history of the Baptist groups in the Jordan Valley, see J. Thomas, *Le mouvement baptiste en Palestine et Syrie (150 av. J.C.–300 ap. J.C.)* (Gembloux, 1935).

Ant 18.117). A further development was Christian baptism, administered as an initiation rite on those who accepted Jesus as the Lord and messiah (Acts 2:38). There can hardly be any doubt that in the early days of Christianity, some of the ritual baths still extant on Mount Zion were used for such purpose (cf. Acts 2:40).

During Luke's visit to Jerusalem (Acts 21:15ff), he may have had close contacts with the groups on Mount Zion. Although the word *Essenes* is never directly mentioned in the New Testament (nor in the Qumran scrolls), Luke may have had some knowledge of links with the Essenes. A key word used by him four times is εὐλαβής. Although there have been many suggestions explaining the derivation of the epithet *Essene*, the most likely one is that Ἐσσαῖος or Ἐσσηνός is the way Greeks would pronounce the Aramaic word חֲסָא. Its Hebrew equivalent is חָסִיד, "the pious one."

Luke used intentionally the language of the Septuagint for his double work. Three times the Septuagint uses for the word חָסִיד the expression εὐλαβής (Lev 15:31; Micah 7:2; Sir 11:17), and only one time the more common εὐσεβής (Sir 43:33). When Luke used εὐλαβής or εὐλαβεῖς for persons or groups he may well have meant "Essenes"; that is what they probably were. The four persons or groups mentioned as such are: (1) old Simeon (Lk 2:25) in the Temple, who, together with Hanna, "looked forward to the deliverance of Jerusalem" (Lk 2:38); (2) Ananias of Damascus (Acts 22:12), who baptized Paul and sent him off to some hiding place in Arabia where he spent some time, perhaps in the Batanea, before coming back to Damascus (Gal 1:17); (3) the Jewish pious men (Acts 2:5) who gathered in Jerusalem for the Feast of Pentecost (such a gathering may have been on the occasion of the Essene Pentecost, which was not celebrated in the Temple, but in their quarter on Mount Zion[30]; and finally, (4) the pious men who buried Stephen and mourned over him (Acts 8:2).

---

[30] Cf. B. Pixner, "Essener-Viertel und Urgemeinde," in *Wege des Messias*, pp. 327–34 (pp. 328–31); M. Delcor, "A propos de l'emplacement de la Porte des Esséniens selon Josèphe et de ses implications historiques, essénienne et chrétienne: Examen d'une théorie," in Z. J. Kapera, *Intertestamental Essays*, pp. 25–44 (pp. 35–42).

2. The Position of James, the Brother of the Lord

What sort of personality would have been responsible for the contacts between the primitive church and the Essene group? I would point to James, "the brother of the Lord" (Gal 1:19). After the execution of James, the son of Zebedee, and the flight of Simon Peter from Jerusalem (Acts 12:1-17), this James became the head of the church of Jerusalem.[31] In the liturgical calendar of the Catholic Church, he is usually still considered one of the twelve and is identified with James the son of Alphaeus (Mt 10:3; Mk 3:18; Lk 6:15; Acts 1:13). Nevertheless, scholarship today is agreed that he did not belong to the Twelve, but was rather what we might call the "sheikh" of the blood relatives of Jesus. He apparently was the oldest of Jesus' brothers and is mentioned several times in Luke's Gospel. He is called apostle because he was privileged with a special apparition of the Lord after the resurrection. According to the tradition received by Paul, the only two thus privileged were Simon Peter (Kephas) and James: "He (Jesus) appeared to Kephas, and then to the Twelve ..., then he appeared to James, then to all apostles" (1 Cor 15:7).

Neither of these two personal encounters with the risen Lord are described in the Gospels. But a trace of the apparition to James has come to us in a citation of Jerome from the Gospel to the Hebrews:

> When the Lord handed over the linen cloth to the priest's servant, he went to James and appeared to him. For James had made an oath to eat no bread after he had drunk the cup of the Lord until he saw him risen from those who sleep. Shortly thereafter the Lord said to him: "Bring a table here with bread." Straight away it [the Gospel] adds: He took the bread, spoke the blessing and gave it to James the Just and said to him: 'My brother, eat your bread, for the Son of Man is risen from those who are asleep."[32]

There may well be some truth in this Judeo-Christian tradition. Such an oath fits well the radical asceticism attributed to James. The

---

[31] Cf. B. Pixner, "Jakobus der Herrenbruder," in *Wege des Messias*, pp. 335–447.

[32] *De viris illustribus* 2; see A. F. J. Klijn and G. J. Reinink, *Patristic Evidence for Jewish Christian Sects* (NovTSuppl 36; Leiden, 1973), pp. 208–11.

words "after he had drunk the cup" would indicate that James, although not one of the Twelve, took part at the Last Supper. If so, I would not be surprised that it was he who made the arrangements for the Paschal meal of Jesus on Mount Zion. Someone outside the circle of the twelve must have done it in agreement with Jesus, since the two disciples coming from Bethany needed the pitcher carrier to guide them to the guesthouse (cf. Mk 14:12-16).

During the Council of Jerusalem, when the situation of the Gentile believers in Christ was up for consideration, it was James, besides Peter, who said the decisive word. It is revealing that he based his argument on the prophecy of Amos 9:11-12:

> After that I shall return and rebuild the fallen House of David; I shall rebuild it from the ruins and restore it. Then the rest of mankind, all the gentiles who are consecratred to my name, will look for the Lord, says the Lord who made this known long ago. (Acts 15:15-18)

Convinced of his and his brother's descent from the house of David, he saw in his own ascendency to the leadership of the mother church of Jerusalem the fulfillment of this prophecy. It is remarkable that this text from Amos was of great importance to the Qumran Essenes. We find it in the Damascus Document (CD 7.16) and also in the Florilegium from cave IV. The *pesher* to this citation is of special interest to our subject:

> The Lord declares to you that he will "build you a house. And after you (are dead,) I will elevate your seed and I will strengthen his throne for ever. To him I shall be a father and he shall be my son" [2Sam 7:1-14]. This is the branch of David (צֶמַח דָּוִיד), who shall rise up together with the Teacher of the Torah ... on Zion at the end of the days. As it is written: "I shall raise up the house of David, which has fallen" [Amos 9:11]. This fallen house I shall raise up in order to save Israel." (4QFlor 1.10-13)

Our thesis about the proximity of two religious movements on Mount Zion may explain another puzzling fact of the primitive church. How could someone from outside the intimate group of the Twelve become so highly regarded as to be entrusted with the leadership of the mother church? So highly was James esteemed that even Paul, when mentioning the three pillars of the Jerusalem church, puts him in first place: "So, James, Cephas, and John, these leaders, these pillars, shook hands with Barnabas and me as a sign of partnership. We were to go to the pagans and they to the circumcised" (Gal 2:9). After the flight of Peter from Jerusalem during the Passover celebration in 43 C.E., the Apostle John apparently stayed on in Jerusalem. It was not he who took over as head of the Jerusalem community, but James (cf. Acts 12:17). James's close relationship with Jesus was surely the major factor for his authority in the brotherhood of Jerusalem. The authority of the other apostles extended to the church at large.

The writings of the Qumran Essenes have revealed how intensive was their expectation of the messiah from the House of David. The recently published scrap of parchment from Cave IV paraphrasing Isa 11:1 adds new weight to this (4Q285). Geza Vermes of Oxford University translates the text (lines 2-5): "And there shall come forth a shoot from the stump of Jesse ... the Branch of David (צֶמַח דָּוִיד) and they will enter into judgement with ... and the Prince of the Congregation, the Branch of David, will kill him ... by strokes and by wounds."[33] James could claim to be a descendant of the royal Davidic dynasty. For people who set high value on such prophecies, James would have been more likely to arouse enthusiasm and trust than simple preachers like the apostles.

James's position in the community was in many ways identical to that of the "overseer" (מבקר) in the Essene community (cf. 1QS 6.12ff; CD 9.18ff). The exact equivalent is the Greek ἐπίσκοπος, which might actually derive from it.[34] As was the custom for the *mebaqqer*, James also appears during Paul's last visit in Jerusalem with his elders (Acts 21:18) and he speaks (according to Papyrus 74 and Codex Sinaiticus) of the assembly of the "many" (πλῆθος [Acts 21:22]), an equivalent to the הרבים in the Qumran writings.[35]

What made James even more acceptable was his ascetic lifestyle. He was such a faithful observer of the Torah that he received the

---

[33] "The 'Pierced Messiah' Text—An Interpretation Evaporates," *BAR* 18/4 (1992) 80–82 (81).

[34] Cf. the literature in H. Braun, *Qumran und das Neue Testament*, vol. 2 (Tübingen, 1966), pp. 328–32.

[35] Cf. J. H. Charlesworth, *Graphic Concordance*, p. 483.

epithet, "the Righteous" (ὁ δίκαιος; הַצַּדִּיק). Furthermore, his life showed extraordinary piety and integrity. Even if only part of what Hegesippus, the Judeo-Christian writer of around 180 C.E., relates is true, James must have been a very ascetic Jew.[36] "He was holy," says the writer, "from his mother's womb. He drank no strong drink, neither did he eat meat.... He wore no wool, but only white linen. And he would enter into the Temple alone, and be found there kneeling on his knees and asking forgiveness for the people" (HE 2.23.4-6).

It was James's staunch adherence to the Law and his holiness which earned for him the reverence of the people and which acted as a shield for his people. Eusebius calls him an "enclosure-wall of the people" (περιοχὴ τοῦ λαοῦ [HE 2.23.7]). Hegesippus (Ibid.) and Epiphanius[37] mention that people also gave him the name "Oblias (Ωβλίας), because the prophets announced him as such." This surely is an allusion to the prophetic words of Micah: "And you, Tower of the Flock, Ophel (עֹפֶל) of the daughter of Zion, to you shall be given back your former sovereignty, and royal power over the House of Israel. Why are you crying? Is there no king within you?" (Micah 4:8-9).

Hegesippus has his own version of the martyrdom of James (HE 2.23.10-19). He says there was alarm in Jerusalem because some people belonging to one of the seven sects were converted by the preaching of James to confess Christ (HE 2.23.8-9). Josephus relates that in the interregnum between the death of Festus and the arrival of Albinus, the high priest Ananus the younger, who belonged to the sect of the Sadducees, called the Sanhedrin into session, accused James of transgressing the law, and had him stoned to death (Ant 20.200). This happened in the year 62 C.E.

3. After James's Martyrdom

By his great authority, James, the Lord's brother, succeeded in holding together the different factions composing the church of Jerusalem. With his death a critical period began for the community of Jewish believers.

---

[36] Cf. J. Daniélou, The Theology of Jewish Christianity (London and Philadelphia, 1964), 370-71.

[37] AdvHaer 78.7.7. See A. F. J. Klijn and G. J. Reinink, Patristic Evidence, p. 196.

Hegesippus provides an ancient and important contribution to the understanding of the events that followed the disappearance of James.[38] Unfortunately, only short fragments of his monumental work of Memoirs (*Hypomnemata*) have come to us through quotations in the writings of Eusebius of Caesarea. Hegesippus relates that after the death of James, the surviving

> disciples of the Lord gathered in one place. They assembled with the blood relatives of the Lord, of whom many were still alive. Together they took council about who would be worthy to take the place of James. All unanimously considered Simeon, the son of Cleopha, the one mentioned in the Gospel [cf. Lk 24:18 and Jn 19:25], worthy to occupy the seat of bishop. He was a cousin of the Savior. (*HE* 3.11)

We are told that his father Cleopha was the brother of Joseph of Nazareth. In a parallel passage, Hegesippus says, "After James, called 'the Just' (ὁ δίκαιος), had, like the Lord, suffered martydom because he had proclaimed his doctrine, one of his cousins was elected, namely Simeon, the son of Cleopha, as bishop" (*HE* 4.22.4). From the literary sources it is not clear whether the election of Simeon Bar-Cleopha took place before or after the destruction of Jerusalem (cf. *HE* 3.11). It may well be that the initial election took place after the death of James and that it was later confirmed after the destruction of Jerusalem (70 C.E.) when the dispersed community returned from their places of refuge beyond the Jordan.[39] According to a tradition mentioned by the monk Alexander (540 C.E.), the location of Simeon's election was Mount Zion.[40]

The consequences of this election were very grave for the Jerusalem church. Hegesippus reports that a certain Thebutis, who had himself hoped to become bishop, refused to accept the election and started a rebellion. According to Hegesippus, this was the first time the unity of the church was ruptured, "which until then had been an untouched vir-

---

[38] Cf. L. Herrmann, "La Famille du Christ d'après Hégésippe," *RUB* 42 (1936/37) 387–94.

[39] Cf. B. Pixner, "Simeon Bar-Kleopha, zweiter Bischof Jerusalems," in *Wege des Messias*, pp. 358–64 (pp. 360–63).

[40] D. Baldi, *Enchiridion Locorum Sanctorum*, p. 486.

gin" (*HE* 4.22.4). Thebutis was therefore the first schismatic and became also the first heretic.

Who was Thebutis? He must have been a leading personality in the church so that he could consider himself a candidate for the bishopric. According to Hegesippus, he came originally from one of the Jewish sects (*HE* 4.22.5). In the enumeration of the seven Jewish sects, Hegesippus follows a novel sequence, based, as he says, on their attitudes toward the tribe of Judah and Christ. He begins with the Essenes, the most positively disposed toward them, and ends with the most extreme adversaries, the Pharisees (*HE* 4.22.7). From this we may conclude that Thebutis, previous to his acceptance of Jesus as messiah, may have been an important Essene personality.

The name Thebutis is completely unknown in the literature of this time—with one exception. Josephus mentions in his "Jewish War" a certain priest: Jesus, the son of Thebutis (*War* 6.387). After the fall of Jerusalem, the son of the *kohen* Thebutis produced some hidden treasures and with them purchased his freedom from the supreme commander Titus. Chronologically, this matches well the situation on Mount Zion. I am thus inclined to agree with former scholars that the Thebutis of Hegesippus and the Thebutis of Josephus are the same person.[41]

The son of Thebutis may have produced part of the treasure hidden near their Essene Quarter as described in the Copper Scroll of Qumran (3Q15 1.6–4.5). It is fascinating to see how well the valuables described by Josephus and the treasures enumerated in the Copper Scroll correspond. Even more amazing is that one of the hiding places (i.e., one of those on Mount Zion) was marked by the initials ΘΕ (3Q15 2.3-4), which could indicate that Thebutis was the one responsible for that area.[42]

If I am right, this offers a significant insight into the situation of the primitive church shortly before the outbreak of the great war against Rome (66–70 C.E.). The rebellion of Thebutis was directed against the influence of a circle of the Davidic families, which had been successful in having his rival, Simeon Bar-Kleopha, elected. Behind this rebellion may have been sharp discord between the Essene concept of leadership

---

[41] Cf. N. Hyldahl, "Hegesipps Hypomnemata," *StTh* 14 (1960) 70–113 (97).
[42] Cf. B. Pixner, *RQ* 11 (1983) 344–46.

and that of the Natzoreans, the blood relatives of Jesus. In the view of
the Essenes, the leadership role belonged to the *kohanim*. As shown in
the Temple Scroll, even the king of Israel was obliged to listen to the
advice and to receive the blessing of the priests (11QTemple 56.20-21;
58.18; 59.12-21). In their opinion, the same held true even for the
Davidic messiah (4QpIs[a] 161 22-24).

4. The Split in the Judeo-Christian Community

In this tension between the various groups in primitve Jewish
Christianity may lie the seed of the split between the Natzoreans and the
Essene-influenced Ebionites. The believers in Jesus the messiah, who
had come from traditionalist Essene Judaism, could not bear the thought
of the incarnation of a preexistent Son of God. This was the family
tradition of the Natzoreans.

Was Thebutis the main mover behind this split? Was his name
later forgotten and remained only vaguely known as Ebion (᾿Εβιών)
the first heretic and founder of the Ebionites (᾿Εβιωναῖοι) who had their
name from the Hebrew אֶבְיוֹנִים "the poor ones," an epithet also used by
the Qumran covenanters?[43] The Ebionites maintained that Jesus became
the Son of God because he was adopted as such by God during his baptism in the Jordan. Likewise they denied the virgin birth and said that
Jesus was born of Joseph and Mary. They also demonstrated a strong
anti-Pauline attitude. In a former study I tried to prove from Luke's
excellent knowledge of Jerusalem's topography that he had personally
visited Jerusalem, at the latest around 75 C.E.[44] There he discovered
among the circle of the Jesus family a haggadah written in Hebrew containing the story of Jesus' youth, as Mary might have told it to her family members (cf. Lk 2:19,51). He inserted it into his Gospel to counter
the Ebionite heresy. We find a similar reaction to the Ebionites in Matthew (Mt 1:18-25).

Since, in the view of the two evangelists, the conversion of large
segments of Essenes took such a heretical turn, the Essene influence on
Jesus and his family was passed over quietly. Typical of this is Matthew's treatment of the man in charge of the guesthouse where Jesus

---

[43] Cf. Epiphanius, *AdvHaer* 30:1-30:33; see A. F. J. Klijn and G. J. Reinink,
Patristic Evidence, pp. 174-93.
[44] "Lukas und Jerusalem," in *Wege des Messias*, pp. 372-81.

held the Last Supper. Matthew simply calls him "someone": "Go to so-
and-so (πρὸς τὸν δεῖνα) in the city" (Mt 26:18). This looks like a *dam-
natio memoriae* of an otherwise important personality. Could it have
been Thebuti himself? While the Natzorean branch of Judeo-Christianity
preserved a christology which was close to that of the universal church,
the large majority of Essene believers drifted gradually towards
Ebionism. They developed and survived for a long time east of the Jordan and in the Arab peninsula. Many of their doctrines lived on in
Islamic thought.[45]

5. *The Break with Rabbinic Pharisaism*

The catastrophy that befell Judaism with the fall of Jerusalem
brought about the end of a Jewish way of life, where different interpretations of the Law could live side by side. With the destruction of
the Temple and the end of the liturgical services there, Sadduceeism lost
its main basis and vanished. The Essenes, too, frustrated in their strong
eschatological expectation, were unable to survive the debacle. Their
centers in Qumran—whose original name had been "Sekhakha" (3Q15
4.13-5.14; cf. Josh 15:61-62 [סְכָכָה])[46]—and on Mount Zion had been
destroyed. The "War Between the Sons of Light and the Sons of
Darkness" had not gone the way they so ardently had hoped. The
monastic center (כחלית) which, according to my interpretation of the
Copper Scroll (3Q15 12.10-13), was located in Bashan (Batanea),[47] did
continue to exist, but could to a large extent have been absorbed by
Ebionism, which might explain the prevalence of Ebionite and Gnostic
groups in that area.[48]

The only expression of Judaism to survive was the Pharisaic
brand. In Jamnia the followers of the Pharisaic halakha gathered under
the leadership of Johanan Ben-Zakkai and reorganized the Sanhedrin.

---

[45] Cf. J. Magnin, "Notes sur l'Ébionisme: Dernières traces de l'Ébionisme
(Ébionisme et Islam)," *POC* 28 (1978) 220–48; R. Riesner, "Adolf Schlatter und die
Judenchristen Jerusalems," in K. Bockmühl, *Die Aktualität der Theologie Adolf Schlat-
ters* (Gießen, 1988), pp. 34–70 (pp. 67–68).

[46] Cf. O. Keel and M. Küchler, *Orte und Landschaften der Bibel 2: Der Süden*
(Zürich, 1982), p. 452.

[47] *RQ* 11 (1983) 350–53.

[48] Cf. H. J. Schoeps, *Theologie und Geschichte des Judenchristentums*
(Tübingen, 1949), pp. 270–77.

They felt the strong rivalry that came from the Judeo-Christian movement. What until then had been a tolerated expression of Judaism, so that these Messianic Jews continued to partake in the synagogue service, now had to be cut off radically. This was done by adding to the *shemoneh esreh* prayer the *birkat ha-minim* with special mention of the Notzrim (נצרים). Even though modern studies suggest that this Decree of Jamnia was not applied radically in all locations, it was doubtless the decisive event excluding the messianic Jews from worship in the rabbinic synagogues.

Where the Judeo-Christians were strong enough, they built their own synagogues. This was the case on Mount Zion, where the Last Supper room had become the meeting place of the messianic community (cf. Acts 1:13), and which, in 70 C.E., was demolished by the troops of Titus. On its ruins they built their synagogue after their return from Pella in the latter part of the first century.[49] Later it was called "the Mother of all the churches (μητὴρ παντῶν ἐκκλησιῶν—*mater ecclesiarum*)."[50]

There may have been two messianic synagogues in Nazareth, a Natzorean one at the site of the traditional house of Mary, and an Ebionite one where the Church of St. Joseph stands today.[51] It looks as if in Capernaum there existed a kind of symbiosis of Pharisaic and messianic Jews.[52] The latter used the house of Peter for eucharistic services while they continued to worship on shabbats in the common synagogue built by the centurion (Lk 7:5). Synagogue worship continued through the end of the fourth century, when it was reshaped into the magnificent synagogue seen there today.

This period of strong rivalry between Pharisaism and Christianity was also the *Sitz im Leben* in which the Gospels were written, where the bias of the authors against Pharisaism is clearly seen. The enemies of the community at the end of the first century are presented as enemies

---

[49] Cf. B. Pixner, *Wege des Messias*, pp. 303–05.

[50] This designation appeared first in an inscription in the church of St. Martin in Tours between 460 and 490 (D. Baldi, *Enchiridion Locorum Sanctorum*, p. 483, note 1).

[51] For a summary of the excavations, see B. Bagatti, *The Church from the Circumcision* (SBFCMi 2; Jerusalem, 1971), pp. 122–29.

[52] Cf. B. Pixner, "Rätsel um die Synagogen von Kafarnaum," in *Wege des Messias*, pp. 114–26.

already in the days of the Lord. Still, there were indeed some conflicts already between Jesus and some Pharisees, as we will see.

III. JESUS HIMSELF BETWEEN PHARISEES AND ESSENES

The similarities in the social structure of the primitive church and the Essenes have led many scholars to believe that the Essene movement could have had a strong influence on the Christian movement from its outset. This is even more apparent if my thesis is accepted that the two religious communities lived on Mount Zion side by side.

But what was the influence of Essenes and Pharisees on Jesus himself? I see in Jesus' attitude three stages of development: (1) he came from a family that had strong ties with the Essene movement; (2) he distanced himself from it, coming closer to the Pharisees during his stay in Capernaum, but he developed his own halakhah; (3) on his last journey to Jerusalem and in Jerusalem itself, there occurred once again a movement toward the Essenes.

1. The First Stage: Jesus' Essene-influenced Family

In the much-discussed question on the meaning of "the brothers of the Lord," I favor the oldest tradition, which we find in the Protevangelium of James (ProtJames 9:2; 17:1-2; 18:1) and the earliest church fathers.[53] This position is still held by the oriental churches, namely, that the four named brothers of Jesus and the unnamed sisters (Mk 6:3) were children of Joseph from a first marriage.[54] According to this tradition, Joseph was a widower. Mary, his second wife, helped him bring up his children and had one child of her own.

I do not think Jerome was right when he introduced a new notion suggesting that his "brothers" were in reality cousins of Jesus, a view which became the prevalent one in the Catholic Church. Joseph was from Nazareth, where his brother, Cleopha also lived. Cleopha was

---

[53] Cf., e.g., Clement of Alexandria, *Adumbratio in epistula Iudae* (*GCS* 17, pp. 206-7; cf. Epiphanius, *AdvHaer* 29.4.3); Hippolytus of Rome, *De benedictione Moysis* (*TU* 26:1a, p. 59); Origen, *CommJn* I 4 (*GCS* 10, p. 8); Eusebius, *HE* 2.1.2; Epiphanius, *AdvHaer* 28.7.6 (*GCS* 25, pp. 319-20).

[54] Cf. now also R. J. Bauckham, *Jude and the Relatives of Jesus in the Early Church* (Edinburgh, 1990), pp. 19-32.

married to another Mary. Their son Simeon was the second bishop of Jerusalem.

Judging from the excavations done by the Franciscan archaelogist, Bellarmino Bagatti, Nazareth was a small village of some 120 to 150 inhabitants.[55] Bagatti told me personally that there was apparently a gap in settlement between 700 and aproximately the year 100 B.C.E. No Persian, Syrian, or early Hellenistic pottery was found. This phenomenon is found in many Galilean sites. After the deportation (732 B.C.E.) by Tiglat-Pileser III, (cf. 2Kgs 15:29), Galilee became for six hundred years a pagan country (גליל הגוים [Isa 9:1])—up to the conquest by the Hasmoneans (*Ant* 13.318-319).

Around 100 B.C.E., a completely new group settled in this abandoned mountain village. Who were they and where did they come from? I propose this theory: they belonged to a Davidic clan which came from the Babylonian diaspora.[56] Part of it settled down in Kochaba ("star village"; cf. Num 24:17) in the Batanea. A small branch inhabited a vacant site that had belonged to the tribe of Zebulon. They were from the tribe of Judah and called themselves the "Natzoreans" from the conviction that they were the bearers of the Isaian prophecy : "A shoot springs from the stock of Jesse, a scion (נֵצֶר) thrusts from his roots" (Isa 11:1). After them the village was named Nazareth ("star village"). Julius Africanus, writing soon after 200 C.E. on the genealogies in the Gospels, informs us about the original settlements of the relatives of Jesus:

> Among them [the keepers of genealogies] were the already mentioned 'Lord's people' (δεσποσύνοι), so-called because of their relationship with the Savior's family. Originating from the Jewish villages of Nazara and Kochaba (Ναζάρων καὶ Κωχάβα), they spread out over the rest of the country. (*HE* 1.7.14)

I suspect that these Natzoreans, while in Kochaba beyond the Jordan, had contact with Essene groups which had been living there since

---

[55] *Excavations in Nazareth I: From the Beginnings till the XIIth Century.* SBFCMa 17 (Jerusalem, 1969).

[56] Cf. B. Pixner, "Die Batanäa als jüdisches Siedlungsgebiet," in *Wege des Messias*, pp. 159–65.

their flight to the "Land of Damascus" (CD 7.15ff). In the Thanksgiving Hymns, the word נֵצֶר stands for a commmunity (1QH 6.15; 8.6,10).[57]

Another clue regarding which Torah party the Natzoreans were inclined may be derived from their relationship with John the Baptist. According to an ancient tradition, Jesus' mother, Mary, was a Davidite,[58] even though she was also related to the priestly house of John the Baptist, possibly from her mother's side (Lk 1:5,36). In light of a passage in the Temple Scroll (11QTemple 53.16-54.3) it may be that, as some church fathers thought,[59] Mary made a voluntary vow of virginity (cf. Lk 1:34).[60] Ancient tradition holds that she was born in Jerusalem, near the Bethesda pools,[61] mentioned also in the Qumran Copper Scroll (3Q15 11.11-14). We can assume that Mary was a frequent visitor in the priestly house where John was born. Of him it is said that from his childhood on "he lived out in the wilderness until the day he appeared openly to Israel" (Lk 1:80). Since his first activity was close to Qumran and other Essene hermitages in the Jericho area, it is reasonable to conclude that he came from that movement or at least was close to its spirit.[62] But at a certain moment he must have left it to start his own ministry, which, contrary to Essene practice, was open to all.

How close the thinking of John must have been to the Essenes can also be deduced from the reply given by Jesus when a delegation came to him from the imprisoned baptist: "Go and tell John what you see and hear: The blind see; the lame walk; lepers are cleansed; the deaf hear; the dead are raised; the poor are evangelized" (Lk 7:22 cf. Isa 61:1-2). These words are so similar to those found in Qumran on a just-published fragment from Cave IV (4Q521) that they could not have failed bringing to John's memory words familiar to him since his youth

---

[57] Cf. B. Gärtner, *Die rätselhaften Termini Nazoräer und Iskariot*. Horae Soederblomianae 4 (Uppsala, 1957), pp. 5–36.

[58] ProtJames 10:1; Ignatius, *To the Ephesians* 18:2; Justin, *DialTrypho* 45:4.

[59] Gregory of Nyssa, *In diem natalem Christi* (*PG* 46, pp. 1140ff); Augustine, *De sacra virginitate* 4 (*PL* 40, p. 398); *Sermo* 291:5 (*PL* 38, p. 1318).

[60] Cf. B. Pixner, "Maria im Hause Davids," in *Wege des Messias*, pp. 42–55.

[61] D. Baldi, *Enchiridion Locorum Sanctorum*, pp. 720ff.

[62] Cf. W. H. Brownlee, "John the Baptist in the Light of Ancient Scrolls," in K. Stendahl, *The Scrolls and the New Testament*, pp. 33–53, 252–56; O. Betz, in B. Mayer, *Christen und Christliches in Qumran?*, pp. 159–64.

(cf. Lk 1:78) in the desert: "The Lord shall visit the pious (חסדים) and the righteous (צדיקים) shall he call by name.... He shall release the prisoners, make the blind see.... He shall heal the wounded and resurrect the dead [and to] the poor announce glad tidings" (lines 5,8,12).[63]

After his baptism, Jesus spent several months in the fellowship of John. Living close to John in "Bethany beyond the Jordan," he met his first disciples (Jn 1:28-42). During this period Jesus' newly acquired disciples came and went just as they had with John. Some were with Jesus during the first Passover feast in Jerusalem (Jn 2:13-17). The cleansing of the Temple must have stirred up many passions, pro and contra. This courageous act of Jesus must have made a deep impression on the Jerusalem Essenes, who considered the Temple defiled by the activities of an illegal priesthood. This seems to be behind the remark of the Fourth Gospel: "Now when he was in Jerusalem at the Passover feast, many believed in his name, when they saw the signs which he did; but Jesus did not trust himself to them, because he knew all men and needed no one to bear witness of man; for he himself knew what was in man" (Jn 2:23-24). In trying to analyse these words of the Gospel, there is a possibility that an offer of support was made by certain anti-Temple elements. Such an offer Jesus refused to accept.

Then something took place which changed the course of events. John the Baptist was put into prison. Jesus recognized that the time had come for him to start on his own: "He left Judea and departed again for Galilee" (Jn 4:3). Soon he broke with his own clan in Nazareth (Lk 4:16-29). Their Essene-oriented outlook was too narrow and restrictive for his message.[64] They wanted to use the thaumaturgic power they noticed in him for their own purpose. Jesus had no intention of putting himself at the disposal of their ambitions: "Physician, heal yourself; what we have heard you did in Capernaum, do here also in your own country" (Lk 4:23). The quarrel finally degenerated into a vehement attempt at lynching this recalcitrant kinsman of theirs. The expulsion from the village also meant expulsion from his own clan.

---

[63] R. H. Eisenman, "A Messianic Vision," *BAR* 17/6 (1991) 65.
[64] Cf. B. Pixner, *Wege des Messias*, pp. 336–39.

2. The Second Stage: Contacts with Pharisees in Capernaum

The violent reaction of his Natzorean clan was the end result of an ongoing alienation from his own kinsmen in Nazareth. Jesus' choice of Capernaum (Lk 4:31) might have had something to do with it. Capernaum was under the influence of the Pharisees. There Jesus adopted Pharisaic views and a corresponding lifestyle. Capernaum was one of the key towns in Galilee.[65] Shortly before 100 B.C.E., Galilee had been conquered by the Hasmoneans and made a part of their commonwealth. Six hundred years of Gentile occupation had left its mark. Not much was left of Israelite traditions. During the first century B.C.E., those Gentiles who wished to stay in the land of Israel were forced to adopt the religion of the land (*Ant* 13.318). Other Jews had returned from the diaspora. So at the time of Jesus the majority of Galileans were Jews of only the second or third generation. It was the great merit of the Pharisaic preachers to come to Galilee, occasionally all the way from Jerusalem (cf. Lk 5:12), in order to introduce to these people the traditions of the fathers. This may be why, whenever Jesus went to towns and villages, he found scribes and Pharisees there. They would teach the people on sabbaths in the synagogues or gather them in the *bet ha-midrash*, where many discussions took place. (Surely there was one in Capernaum, even though the one shown there is of a later date.)

The Essenes, on the other hand, gathered only in selected groups of similar-minded people (1QS 6.6-8). They did not bother to instruct the common folk. They often lived in villages of their own.[66] Nazareth may have been one of them.

Capernaum was special. Not far from Capernaum was Gamla, the birthplace of Zealotism. Lying like an aerie on top of a rock, it spread its influence over the surrounding villages on the lake. Zealotism was an offshoot of the Pharisees, founded by the scribe Jehuda of Gamla (*War* 2.433) and the Pharisaic Rabbi Zadok (*War* 2.11). Herod Antipas, the friend of Rome, considered their radical theocracy—which was directed against the Romans—very dangerous. So he had placed a military garrison in the border town Capernaum, headed by a centurion (Mt 8:5; Lk 7:1-2). Capernaum became the town of choice for Jesus (Mt 9:1). Following the customs of the Pharisees, he formed around himself

---

[65] Cf. S. Loffreda, *Recovering Capharnaum* (Jerusalem, 1985).

[66] Cf. Philo, *Apologia pro Iudaeis* 1 (Eusebius, *PE* 8.6); Josephus, *War* 2.24.

the group of twelve (Mk 3:13-19). It looked like a Pharisaic *haburah*, with him as the rabbi (cf. Jn 1:38).

Already before his return to Galilee he had made contact in Jerusalem with eminent Pharisees. One of them was Nicodemus (Jn 3:1ff). As with his friend, Joseph of Arimathea, he belonged to the Sanhedrin (Jn 19:38-39). Another member of the Sanhedrin was the Pharisee Gamaliel the Elder (cf. Acts 5:34). He adhered to the school of Hillel and was the leading exponent of the more liberal and humane interpretation of the Law. During his secret colloquiums with people like them, Jesus was not only the teacher. He also got to know a lot about Hillel's halakhic teaching. These contacts continued in Capernaum.[67] He was an invited guest in the home of Simon the Pharisee (Lk 7:36). It was Pharisees who warned him about the intrigues of Herod Antipas (Lk 13:31ff). When, during the month of Adar in early spring, messengers passed through Capernaum to collect from every adult Jew the contribution for the Temple cult, Jesus obliged, although he did not feel an obligation to do so (cf. Mt 17:24-27). The Essenes certainly refused to pay for a cult that they considered illegal.

Much has already been written about traces of the halakhic teachings of Pharisees and Essenes in the Gospels. Jesus took from everywhere what seemed to him to be best and added much of his own. Like the Pharisees, he upheld the sacredness of the Law of Moses ("Not one iota will pass" [Mt 5:18]). It was during his stay in Capernaum that he developed his own halakhah.

One episode seems to confirm that during his stay in Capernaum he distanced himself from the practice of his own Natzorean family. In chapter 7 John speaks of Jesus' brothers coming to him and begging him to go with them up to Jerusalem for the Feast of Tabernacles. They tried to remind him not to neglect "his disciples" in Judea (Jn 7:2-3). Obviously, they were referring to the "many who believed in his name" (Jn 2:23) during the Passover feast. We have already seen that many of these early believers may have come from the ranks of the Essenes. Now the brothers were going up to Jerusalem to the Essenes' Feast of Tabernacles, which, as we know since the discoveries in Qumran, was

---

[67] Since other contributors to this volume have dealt with the subject of the possible influence of Hillel on Jesus' teaching, I will not address the matter yet again.

always celebrated on Wednesday and usually fell before the date of the Temple feast.[68] They were following the solar calender observed by the Qumran Essenes and other similar religious groupings.

With this in mind we read the reply of Jesus: "The right time (καιρός) for me has not yet come; for you any time is right.... You go to the feast. I am not going up to this feast (εἰς τὴν ἑορτὴν ταύτην) because for me the right time has not yet come" (Jn 7:6-8). Jesus wanted to indicate that he was no longer following the *kairos*, i.e. the appropriate time of the calendar of his family,[69] but that he observed, together with the apostles, the feast as celebrated in the Temple. So the brothers went to Jerusalem for Sukkoth on their own. This feast was not celebrated in the Temple area, but, it can be presumed, on the southwestern hill of the city, where the Essenes had their quarters. Jesus also went—when his *kairos* was right—up to Jerusalem but he joined the worshipers in the Temple area (Jn 7:14).

Finally, the attempt made in Capernaum to enter into dialogue with the Pharisees ended without success. The disputations became ever more acerbic and left on both sides bitter feelings of enmity (cf. Mk 2:1ff). Pressure from tetrarch Herod Antipas also became increasingly dangerous. Warned that the tetrarch Herod—Jesus calls him "that fox" (Lk 13:32)—wanted to kill him, Jesus "went away from Galilee and entered the region of Judea beyond the Jordan" (Mt 19:1; Mk 10:1).

3. The Third Stage: Essene Contacts of the Last Days

"Judea beyond the Jordan" ('Ιουδαία πέραν τοῦ 'Ιορδάνου) was not, as it is sometimes taught, Perea (Περαία).[70] Jesus left Galilee to get out of the danger zone of Antipas. Perea was a territory administered by the same Antipas. Perea is never called Judea. Flavius

---

[68] Cf. S. Talmon, "The Calendar of the Covenanters of the Judean Desert," in *The World of Qumran from Within* (Jerusalem, 1989), pp. 147-85.

[69] The word *kairos* is also used in this sense in the Septuagint version of the Book of Daniel in a vision that may have been alluding to Antiochus Epiphanes (175-167 B.C.E.), who played a very destructive role in Jewish life. It speaks of the arrival of the fourth king, who will change the set times (καιροί) and the laws (Dan 7:25).

[70] Cf. R. Riesner, "'Bethany Beyond the Jordan' (John 1:28): Topography, Theology and History in the Fourth Gospel," *TB* 38 (1987) 29-63; B. Pixner, "Bethanien jenseits des Jordan," in *Wege des Messias*, pp. 166-79.

Josephus once speaks of Batanea as a region belonging to Judea (*War* 3.54-58). The ruler of that area was the mild and peace-loving Philip (*Ant* 18.106-107). Jesus experienced there a period of quiet activity: "And again crowds gathered around him, and again he taught them, as his custom was" (Mk 10:1; cf. Jn 10:40-42).

This ancient land of the tribe of Manasseh lay on the pilgrim route to Jerusalem (*Ant* 17.26). After it was conquered by the Hasmoneans (1Mac 5:9ff; *Ant* 12.330ff), it attracted all kinds of refugees from the East and South.[71] Based on my interpretation of the Copper Scroll (3Q15 8.1-10.4), I believe that this area on the Yarmuk was probably also "the Land of Damascus" mentioned in the Damascus Document (CD 6.15,19; 7.15,19; 8.21; 19.34; 20.12) as a refuge of the Qumran covenanters.[72]

During Jesus' stay in that region, he spoke on the subjects of marriage, divorce, and celibacy (Mk 10:2-12). In the matter of marriage and divorce, Jesus seems to favor the halakhah of the Essenes (cf. 11QTemple 57.17-19; CD 4.20-21). The presence of Essene monks in the area makes him utter the phrase about the "eunuchs for the kingdom of God" (Mt 19:12). On his way to Jerusalem we also have from Jesus the words recorded by Luke: "For the children of the world are more astute in dealing with their own kind than are the children of light" (Lk 16:8). Professor David Flusser of the Hebrew University of Jerusalem is convinced that by the "children of light" Jesus referred to the Essenes.[73]

From "Bethany beyond the Jordan" (Βηθανία πέραν τοῦ Ἰορδάνου [Jn 1:28]), i.e. the Batanea, Jesus went up to Jerusalem and to his death. During his last days in the Jerusalem area, he dwelt mostly in Bethany near Jerusalem (cf. Mk 11:11-12; Lk 19:29; Jn 12:1). With the discovery of the "Temple Scroll," we now understand better the composition of Bethany's inhabitants.[74] Yigael Yadin, who published the scroll, thought Bethany was one of the three villages mentioned in it, where the Essenes kept people who were not ritually clean enough to

---

[71] Cf. B. Pixner, *Wege des Messias*, pp. 161-65.

[72] *RQ* 11 (1983) 350-53.

[73] "Jesus' Opinion about the Essenes," in *Judaism and the Origins of Christianity* (Jerusalem, 1988), pp. 150-68.

[74] Cf. B. Pixner, "Bethanien bei Jerusalem—eine Essener-Siedlung?" in *Wege des Messias*, pp. 208-18.

visit the Holy City and its Temple.[75] In that scroll the Essenes could find this order given by God: "And you shall make yourself three separate places to the East of the city, to which the lepers and sufferers of execration ... should come" (11QTemple 46.16-17). Yadin thinks that Simon the leper, mentioned in Mk 14:3 ("And while he was in Bethany in the house of Simon the leper"), may have been one of these Essene sufferers of leprosy, to whom Jesus went with his disciples for a meal.[76] Jesus also felt very close to a family of friends living in Bethany, Lazarus, Mary, and Martha (Jn 11; cf. Lk 10:38-42). It strikes us that here Lazarus is living with two celibate sisters. This seems to indicate a lifestyle that was practically unknown in Pharisaic or Sadducean circles, but was common to the Essenes.[77]

Living in such Essene surroundings, it is not surprising that Jesus chose to celebrate his Passover meal according the Essene calendar. Here may lie the solution to a puzzle that has been intriguing exegetes for a long time.[78] According to the synoptic Gospels, the Last Supper of Jesus was a Passover meal (Mk 14:12; Mt 26:16; Lk 22:15); for the evangelist John it was a meal before the Passover feast (Jn 13:1). According to John, the trial of Jesus took place before Passover; according to the Synoptics, it followed it. In John's view: (1) The high priests and the scribes "did not go into the Praetorium themselves so as not to be defiled and made unable to eat the passover" (Jn 18:28); (2) Pilate recalls that he was prepared to release a prisoner for Passover (Jn 18:39-40). (3) Good Friday was "Preparation Day ($\pi\alpha\rho\alpha\sigma\kappa\epsilon\upsilon\acute{\eta}$) and to prevent the bodies from remaining on the cross during the sabbath—since that sabbath was a day of special solemnity" (Jn 19:31)—the burial took place that evening.

In 30 C.E., when Jesus was crucified, the Temple Passover was on a sabbath. It was extremely important for Johannine Christology to point out that Jesus died (as the Lamb of God) while the lambs were slaughtered in the Temple (cf. Jn 19:36). The meal in the house of

---

[75] *The Temple Scroll I: Introduction* (Jerusalem, 1983), p. 305.

[76] *The Temple Scroll: The Hidden Law of the Dead Sea Sect* (London, 1985), pp. 176–77.

[77] Cf. also B. Schwank in B. Mayer, *Christen und Christliches in Qumran?* p. 129.

[78] Cf. R. E. Brown, *The Gospel According to John (XIII-XXI)* (New York, 1966), pp. 555–56.

Simon the leper, as John sees it, had already taken place "six days before Passover" (Jn 12:1), while for the Synoptics it was "two days before Passover" (Mk 14:1). The Synoptics and John have two different Passovers in mind; for the first, it began on the eve of Wednesday, for the other, on the eve of Sabbath.

Two pericopes in the Gospel that are somehow related could have originated in some Essene circles of the primitive church. One is the story of Jesus mounting the donkey in Bethphage. With the simple reminder, "The master needs it" (Mk 11:3), the disciples are permitted to get hold of the donkey. Who had prepared the way? Did Jesus have friends in Bethphage? The other fascinating story is how the two disciples of Jesus were looking for the place for Jesus' Passover meal. As mentioned above, I have a strong suspicion that James, the brother of the Lord, was somehow involved in its preparations. Jesus must have been staying somewhere in or near Bethany when the disciples asked him where they should prepare the passover meal. Jesus

> said to them: 'Go into the city, and a man carrying a jar of water will meet you; follow him, and wherever he enters, say to the lord of the house: The Teacher says, where is my guest house, where I am to eat the Passover with my disciples? And he will show you a large upper room furnished and ready ($\xi\tau o\iota\mu o\varsigma$); there prepare for us.' And the disciples set out and went to the city, and found it as he had told them; and they prepared the passover. (Mk 14:13-16)

To localize the site of the Passover, it is important to remember that it had to be eaten in the city proper—somewhere near the Temple. It is not my aim to analyze here the text cited above.[79] Rather, I wish to pose a few questions and suggest some answers: (1) Where could a Jerusalemite find a good supply of water? The only spring in the city was the Gihon spring. At that time, its waters passed through the Hesekiah tunnel to Siloam. (2) A man carrying a water jar would immediately have attracted the attention of the apostles. Those who know the customs of the Orient know that water jars are carried on the head by women. Why here a man? Was it a type of man who had no

---

[79] Cf. B. Pixner, "Das letzte Abendmahl Jesu," in *Wege des Messias*, pp. 219–28.

woman he could send? Could he have been an Essene monk? (3) The disciples would find the upper room "prepared" for Passover. This meant that the room had been cleansed of all leavened bread. It was the hosts' duty to provide for it, not the guests, who would be unfamiliar with the whereabouts of the leavened bread. The ceremony of the removal of all breadcrumbs is always performed on the "Day of Preparation," the 14th of Nisan. In John's Gospel the "Day of Preparation" (Jn 19:31) is what is known now as Good Friday. For the owners of the Last Supper room, it must have been much earlier. Since they were Essenes, as we surmise, it was on Tuesday, because they were using the solar calendar of the Book of Jubilees.

During his stay in Capernaum, Jesus was inclined to use the calendar of the Temple, as we have seen. However, Jesus was coming from Bethany, an Essene-influenced community, and going to Mount Zion, where the Essene calendar prevailed. It is therefore not surprising that Jesus and his disciples adapted themselves to their customs.[80] So both are right, the Synoptics, with their view that the Last Supper meal was a Passover, and John, with his view that Jesus died on the (official) Eve of Passover.

The archaeological findings and the Qumran studies of the last several years have given added credence to the theory proposed by the late Professor Annie Jaubert of the Sorbonne, who first put forward this solution,[81] since then also adopted by others.[82] In her view, the trials of

---

[80] There are some interesting parallels between the Essene sacred meals (1QS 6.4-5 cf. 1QSa 2.11-22), the daily meals of the primitive community in Jerusalem (Acts 2:46), and Jesus' Last Supper. Cf. K. G. Kuhn, "The Lord's Supper and the Communal Meal at Qumran," in K. Stendahl, *The Scrolls and the New Testament*, pp. 65-93, 259-65.

[81] "La date de la dernière Cène," *RHR* 146 (1954) 140-73; *La date de la Cène, calendrier biblique et liturgie chrétienne* (EBib; Paris, 1957 [ET: *The Date of the Last Supper* (New York, 1965)].

[82] E.g. B. Schwank, "War das letzte Abendmahl am Dienstag der Karwoche?," *Bibel und Kirche* 13 (1958) 34-44; M. Black, "The Qumran Calendar and the Last Supper," in *The Scrolls and Christian Origins: Studies in the Jewish Background of the New Testament* (BJS 48; Chico, 1983), pp. 199-201; E. Ruckstuhl, *Chronology of the Last Days of Jesus: A Critical Study* (New York, 1965); "Zur Chronologie der Leidensgeschichte," in *Jesus im Horizont der Evangelien* (Stuttgarter Biblische Aufsatzbände 3; Stuttgart, 1988), pp. 141-218; "Zur Frage einer Essenergemeinde in Jerusalem und zum Fundort von 7Q5," in B. Mayer, *Christen und Christliches in Qumran?*, pp. 131-37.

Jesus—both the religious one before the Sanhedrin and the civilian one before Pilate—lasted three days.

She found this confirmed in ancient traditions.[83] In the years after Jesus' death, the Judeo-Christians commemorated in Jerusalem the events of his passion by fasting on Wednesday ("When the bridgroom is taken away" [Mk 2:20]) and on Friday, when he died (cf. Did 8:1). On Saturday night they celebrated with great jubilation the resurrection of Christ, expecting his return during that night's vigil. Some churches in Asia Minor followed the Johannine tradition and celebrated on the 14th of Nisan with the rabbinic Jews. The following of two different traditions[84] led to a serious split in Christendom, the so-called Easter date quarrel (*HE* 5.23), which was not resolved until the Council of Nicea (325 C.E.).

CONCLUSION

Jesus gathered together what he considered to be the best in the different Torah schools of his time, added to it his own teaching, and so formed the gospel message which was to reshape the face of the earth. He acted "like a scribe"—using his own words—"who like a housemaster brings forth from his treasure things new and old" (Mt 13:52). Jesus made use of the rich treasure of the Jewish nation that religious scholars had collected during long years of work. The Passover meal on Mount Zion was to crown his deeds and his message. On this southwestern hill of Jerusalem, the first community continued his work. This hill rising above the Gehinnom valley became the cradle of Christianity and the point of departure for the evangelization of the world. Even before the Byzantine period, at the beginning of the 4th century, the historian Eusebius of Caesarea (265–340 C.E.), picking up a Judeo-Christian tradition, could proclaim: "It is a fact that [the law of the gospel went forth] from Jerusalem and the adjoining Mount Sion, on which our Saviour and Lord often made his stay and issued many teachings."[85]

---

[83] *Didascalia Apostolorum* 5.12-18; Epiphanius, *AdvHaer* 51:26; Victorinus of Pettau, *De fabrica mundi* 3 (*CSEL* 49, p. 4).

[84] Cf. J. Daniélou, *The Theology of Jewish Christianity*, pp. 343–44.

[85] *DE* I 4 (D. Baldi, *ELS*, pp. 473–74).

JESUS' SOCIOECONOMIC BACKGROUND

THE RISING INTEREST in the past twenty years in the sociological investigation of the Bible results from the insight that the history presented in its pages was not only religiously but also socio-economically influenced. To fail to appreciate those factors in the study of biblical history is to miss the richness of interpretive possibilities. One of the earlier advocates of the new methodology, H. Kreissig, lamented works that fail to distinguish Jews of the Second Temple period both religiously and socially "as if they had been a homogeneous mass who lived only from religion."[1]

Scholars who have studied the socioeconomic conditions of Herodian Palestine have concurred with Kreissig's complaint. S. Freyne has produced a description of Galilee from Alexander to Hadrian which seeks to understand it as a peasant society. R. A. Horsley and J. S. Hanson have attempted to understand the Jewish rebellion as a class conflict between the rural peasants and the urban elite. S. Applebaum, A. Ben-David, and D. E. Oakman emphasize the economic plight of the agricultural worker. B. Malina has described peasant categories and values in New Testament period Palestine to make us aware of the otherness of this society.[2]

---

[1] Kreissig, *Die sozialen Zusammenhänge des judäischen Krieges* (Berlin, 1970), p. 89. Cf. more recently J. H. Charlesworth, *The Old Testament Pseudepigrapha and the New Testament* (Cambridge, 1985), esp. pp. 19–23.

[2] Freyne, *Galilee from Alexander to Hadrian* (Wilmington, Del., 1980); Horsley and Hanson, *Bandits, Prophets, and Messiahs* (Minneapolis, 1985); Applebaum, "Economic Life in Palestine" in S. Safrai and M. Stern, *The Jewish People in the First Century* (Assen/Amsterdam, 1974–76) Vol. I.2, pp. 631–700; Oakman, *Jesus and the Economic Questions of His Day* (Lewiston/Queenston, 1986); Ben-David, *Talmudische Ökonomie* (Hildesheim, 1974); Malina, *The New Testament World: Insights from Cultural Anthropology* (Atlanta, 1981).

Jesus lived under conditions typical of ancient agrarian societies. To understand him in this background is to add new contours to the investigation. He not only dialogued with numerous religious groups, he interacted with certain socioeconomic classes. His parables were not only imbued with theological insights, but with economic content as well. His lifestyle did not simply reflect the necessities of itinerant preaching, it also resulted from conscious socioeconomic choices.

This essay seeks to place Jesus in his Galilean, socioeconomic environment by answering two questions. What was the socioeconomic environment structure of Galilee during the tetrarchy of Antipas? From which socioeconomic rung did Jesus come? First we will sketch the structure of Galilean society. Then we will review what evidence exists for Jesus' own socioeconomic origins.

THE ECONOMIC STRUCTURE OF GALILEAN SOCIETY

Greco-Roman Society

The economic structure of Galilean society was essentially similar to the rest of the Mediterranean world. The agrarian economies of the ancient empires followed remarkably familiar patterns. Therefore we can benefit from insights gained from studies of Greek and Roman societies. The works of eminent classical scholars can be especially valuable in putting the Galilee of Herod Antipas in its historical and economic setting.[3]

The same holds true for using sociological models. Although one must be cautious in applying sociological theories to the study of ancient society, some interesting insights can nevertheless result from such attempts. If the sociological model has been informed by ancient sources and is judiciously eclectic in its selection of modern sociological

---

[3] E.g., M. Rostovtzeff, *The Social and Economic History of the Roman Empire* (Oxford, 1957); G. E. M. de Ste. Croix, *Class Struggle in the Ancient Greek World* (Ithaca, N.Y., 1981). A. H. M. Jones, *The Greek City from Alexander to Justinian* (Oxford, 1940); idem., *Cities of the Eastern Roman Empire* (Oxford, 1971); R. Mac-Mullen, *Roman Social Relations* (New Haven, 1974); P. Brunt, *Italian Man Power* (Oxford, 1971); J. M. Frayne, *Subsistence Farming in Roman Italy* (London, 1979); P. Garnsey, ed., *Non-slave Labour in the Greco-Roman World* (Cambridge, 1980); K. D. White, *Roman Farming* (London, 1970); M. Grant, *A Social History of Greece and Rome* (New York, 1992); G. Alföldy, *Die römische Gesellschaft* (Wiesbaden, 1986).

theory, we can be reasonably assured that we are not guilty of merely molding the past to fit the present. On the other hand, to ignore sociology or anthropology is surely to invite ethnocentrism. The work of G. E. Lenski[4] meets these criteria well.

Our structuring of Galilean society is heavily dependent on economic standing, as was Lenski's in his work on agrarian societies in general. Some of the categories important to theologians may not even be mentioned.

Galilee had Gentiles from various geographical and ethnic backgrounds in addition to the majority of Jews (Strabo 16.2.34). But for the purposes of this socioeconomic classification, these variations are often irrelevant. A well-to-do merchant is about on the same level regardless of his or her ethnic origins. Likewise, a poor day laborer suffered the same plight whether he or she was a Jew, a Phoenician, an Arabian, or a Greek.

Society in the ancient empires was divided into urban and rural. G. Alföldy and many other historians have noted this condition.[5] The rural population in the eastern Roman empire generally maintained its native language and customs[6] whether Coptic in Egypt,[7] Lycaonian or Celtic in Asia Minor,[8] or Aramaic in Syria and Palestine.[9]

---

[4] G. E. Lenski, *Power and Privilege* (New York, 1966). Cf. J. D. Crossan, *The Historical Jesus: The Life of a Mediterranean Jewish Peasant* (San Francisco, 1991), pp. 44f., who also has used Lenski's work as a check against viewing Jesus' world through uninformed, ethnocentric spectacles. Crossan writes: "One can obviously debate Lenski's master-model in whole or in part, but I accept it as a basic discipline to eliminate the danger of imposing presuppositions from advanced industrial experience on the world of an ancient agrarian empire." The descriptions of Roman social structure by J. Gager (*Kingdom and Community* [Englewood Cliffs, N.J., 1975], pp. 93–113), and Alföldy (*Die römische Gesellschaft*, p. 10), based on legal standing, are also helpful. But Lenski's analysis is more socio-economically nuanced.

[5] Alföldy, *Die römische Gesellschaft* (Wiesbaden, 1986), p. 10.

[6] De Ste. Croix, *Class Struggle*, pp. 10, 13; Rostovtzeff, *Social and Economic History*, pp. 193, 343; R. MacMullen, *Roman Social Relations* (New Haven, 1974), p. 46.

[7] MacMullen, *Roman Social Relations*, p. 46; A. H. M. Jones, *The Greek City from Alexander to Justinian* (Oxford, 1940), p. 293.

[8] Jones, *Greek City*, p. 290; Acts 14:11.

[9] Schürer-Vermes II, p. 26: "The prominence of Aramaic at every level as the main language of Palestinian Jewry is now solidly backed by evidence." The same was true for the native languages of North Africa, Britain, Gaul, Spain, and others. See Rostovtzeff, *Social and Economic History*, pp. 193f; Jones, *Greek City*, pp. 290f; P. Brunt, *Social Conflicts in the Roman Republic* (New York, 1971), pp. 170–72. For

On the other hand, in the cities, people spoke Greek. Many were literate and most were in touch with the great institutions and ideas of Greco-Roman society. This was especially true of the aristocrats, but to some extent even of the urban poor, according to De Ste. Croix, since the urban poor may have "mixed with the educated" in some way.[10] Such mixing could take place in Galilean cities not only in synagogues but in theaters, amphitheaters, and hippodromes, as well as in the courts of justice.[11] Thus even the urban poor had different cultural experiences from those of the rural peasants. As L. White has observed, for medieval agrarian societies, "cities were atolls of civilization ... on an ocean of primitivism."[12]

This description of ancient society, while typical for classical historians, should be modified somewhat for Lower Galilee. In the first place, E. Meyers has shown that Greek made strong inroads into that region.[13] Thus the linguistic differences between urban and rural areas, so marked in other parts of the empire, were less striking—though still existent—in Lower Galilee. Second, D. Edwards has argued persuasively for economic reciprocity and cultural continuity between urban and rural areas of Lower Galilee.[14] Yet Edwards also indicates that even in this region there were cultural differences between urban and rural.[15] We do not need to posit a radical cultural gulf between city

---

Aramaic as the nearly exclusive language of Upper Galilee, see E. M. Meyers, "Galilean Regionalism as a Factor in Historical Reconstruction" *BASOR* 221 (1976) 93–101.

[10] De Ste. Croix, *Class Struggle*, p. 13.

[11] See Schürer-Vermes, Vol. II, pp. 46, 48, 54f. As the authors say (p. 55), even though Josephus (*Ant* 15.268) declared that theaters and amphitheaters were alien to Jewish custom, "it should not be assumed that the mass of the Jewish population did not frequent them." On the benefits for the urban proletariat of living in the city, see Jones, *Greek City*, p. 285. See J. A. Overman, "Who Were the First Urban Christians?" *SBL 1988 Seminar Papers* (Atlanta, 1988), pp. 160–68, for a description of the cities of Galilee and their public institutions.

[12] White quoted in de Ste. Croix, *Class Struggle*, p. 10.

[13] Meyers, "Galilean Regionalism as a Factor in Historical Reconstruction," p. 97.

[14] Edwards, "First Century Urban/Rural Relations in Lower Galilee: Exploring the Archaeological and Literary Evidence," *SBL 1988 Seminar Papers* (Atlanta, 1988), pp. 169–82.

[15] See Edwards, "First Century Urban/Rural Relations in Lower Galilee: Exploring the Archaeological and Literary Evidence," p. 176: "While ideological tensions may have existed between rural and urban inhabitants ..."; and on p. 179 he allows that there were in Lower Galilee "rural areas that were largely conservative,

and country to appreciate that living in the one was not the same culturally as living in the other.

The natural result of different cultural experiences was a sense of superiority on the part of the urbanite over the country peasant. Lenski shows that in agrarian societies in general, the urban elite viewed peasants as subhuman.[16] M. Rostovtzeff observed that city residents in the Roman empire regarded the farmer as an inferior, uncivilized being.[17] R. MacMullen writes that the urbanite regarded the peasant as an "unmannerly, ignorant being."[18]

Palestine

Did this attitude prevail in Palestine? L. Finkelstein maintained that all the residents of Jerusalem, both wealthy and poor, agreed in their contempt for the provincials (country peasants).[19] One detects such contempt in Josephus, a Jerusalemite. He has the high priest (*War* 4.239, 241) refer to the Zealots—many of whom came from the rural districts of Palestine[20]—as "slaughtered victims" and "offscourings." G. Cornfeld's translation captures the tone of these words: "the dregs and scum of the whole country."[21] Whether these words are the high priest's or Josephus's own words, they represent words of someone from the elite urban class describing the lower rural classes. Josephus himself calls the Zealots "slaves, rabble, and bastards," which Cornfeld renders, "slaves, the dregs of humanity and bastard scum."[22]

Although Josephus is somewhat later than the time of Jesus and Antipas, these same attitudes likely prevailed in the early first century

---

Aramaic speaking enclaves."

[16] Lenski, *Power and Privilege*, p. 271.

[17] Rostovtzeff, *Social and Economic History*, p. 192.

[18] MacMullen, *Roman Social Relations*, p. 32; see also Jones, *Greek City*, pp. 295f.

[19] Finkelstein, *The Pharisees* (Philadelphia, 1962), p. 24. For Palestine, see also S. Applebaum, "Judea as a Roman Province: the Countryside as a Political and Economic Factor," *ANRW* II.8, pp. 370f; and G. Theissen, *Sociology of Early Palestinian Christianity* (Philadelphia, 1978), pp. 47–58.

[20] This conclusion is convincingly argued by Horsley and Hanson, *Bandits*, pp. 220-23. See, e.g., *War* 4.135, 419-39, 451.

[21] Cornfeld, *Josephus: The Jewish War* (Grand Rapids, 1982), p. 227.

[22] *War* 5.433; p. 388 of his edition.

C.E. Such attitudes were common in antiquity. Further, although Josephus likely had an apologetic purpose in blaming the Jewish war on rural riffraff, the way he discredited his scapegoats is instructive. He attacked them in these passages as much on socioeconomic grounds as on any other.

We have no direct evidence that such an attitude prevailed in Galilee itself. Perhaps the urban snobbery was less pronounced in Lower Galilee because of the greater economic reciprocity between city and village. But we should probably not conclude that it did not exist at all in that region.[23] It is unlikely that Lower Galilee escaped the kind of urban prejudice that was common in the Greco-Roman world.

Ancient agrarian societies tended to be structured around two groups: the takers (i.e., the elites) and the givers (i.e., the large class of rural peasants). The total make-up of these societies was complex, consisting of several socioeconomic classes and subgroups—as we will attempt to establish below—but these other classes were oriented toward one of the two main groupings listed above.

The socioeconomic distance between these two classes was typically enormous. As Lenski notes, "One fact impresses itself on almost any observer of agrarian societies, especially on one who views them in a broadly comparative perspective. This is the fact of the *marked social*

---

[23] Second-century C.E. rabbinic statements about the Galilean ʿam hāʾareṣ (people of the land) should caution against such a conclusion. Disparaging comments about the עַם הָאָרֶץ may reflect not only religious, but also social differences. The עַם הָאָרֶץ are called בּוּר in Hebrew, which means uncultured or mannerless (cf. M. Jastrow, *A Dictionary of the Targumim, the Talmud Babli and Yerushalmi, and the Midrashic Literature* [2 vols.; London, 1895-1903; repr. New York, 1950], 1:148). They are consistently represented as ignorant and unteachable. Their wives are "like reptiles." See G. F. Moore, *Judaism* (Cambridge, 1954) Vol. I, p. 60; Vol. II, pp. 72f, 157; and G. Vermes, *Jesus the Jew* (London, 1973), pp. 54f. Cf. also E. E. Urbach, "Class Status and Leadership in the World of the Palestinian Sages," *Proceedings of the Israel Academy of Sciences and Humanities* 2 (1968) 71, where Rabbi would open his storehouses during the famine but not for the עַם הָאָרֶץ; and J. H. Heinemann, "The Status of the Laborer in Jewish Law and Society in the Tannaitic Period" *HUCA* 25 (1954) 267. Although the עַם הָאָרֶץ were a religious designation and not a social class, as A. Oppenheimer, (*The Am Ha-aretz* [Leiden, 1977] pp. 18–21) argued, most of them were rural residents. See Finkelstein, *The Pharisees*, pp. 24f, 754–61; and S. Zeitlin, "The Am Haaretz: A Study in the Social and Economic Life of the Jews Before and After the Destruction of the Second Temple," *Jewish Quarterly Review*, N.S. 23 (1932) 45–61.

inequality."[24] The extent to which Galilee fits or deviates from a typical agrarian society must now be demonstrated.

The Elites of Galilee

The elites of Galilee consisted of Herod Antipas and his family, as well as certain other wealthy families. They almost always lived in urban centers as absentee landlords and government officials. Their wealth derived from the surpluses of the peasants in the form of taxes or rents on land.

At the top of Galilean society stood Antipas, the tetrarch, and his family. Antipas evidently received an annual income of 200 talents (*Ant* 17.318) both from taxes and from his large estates in Perea, on the Great Plain, and in Galilee.[25] His family exceeded all other members of the elite class not only in political power but also in wealth. Because these political overlords enriched their top government officers and other friends with large land grants,[26] commanded the army, and levied taxes, their power over even other aristocrats was enormous.

Another social group within the elite class was the group of non-noble aristocrats. They were called elders (Mk 15:1, Acts 4:5), leaders (*Life* 194), first men (*Life* 9, 185; Mk 6:21), notables (*War* 2.318, 410), powerful ones (*War* 2.316, 411), those first in rank and birth (*Ant* 20.123), and honored men (m.Yoma 6:4). These men and their families were the nonpriestly and nonroyal members of the elite class who, because of their wealth, influence, and achievements, were leaders of their communities. Some were local magistrates (*War* 2.237=*Ant* 20.123; *Life* 134; cf. *Life* 246, 278)[27] and some apparently had to assist

---

[24] Lenski, *Power and Privilege*, p. 210. Emphasis is Lenski's.

[25] For Perea, see *Life* 33 where the estate at that time belonged to Crispus, one of Agrippa I's former prefects. For the Great Plain, see *Life* 119 where there is reference to an estate there of Berenice, Agrippa II's sister. These lands then were passed down to members of the Herod family. For Galilee, see *Ant* 18.252 and H. W. Hoehner, *Herod Antipas* (Cambridge, 1972), p. 70. See additionally, D. A. Fiensy, *The Social History of Palestine in the Herodian Period: The Land is Mine* (Lewiston/Queenston/Lampeter, 1991), pp. 21–73; and J. H. Charlesworth, *Jesus Within Judaism* (New York, 1988), pp. 139–48.

[26] As did Herod the Great to Ptolemy of Rhodes (*War* 1.473, 667, 2.14-16, 24, 64) and Agrippa I to Crispus (*Life* 33).

[27] J. Jeremias, *Jerusalem in the Time of Jesus*, trans. F. H. Cave and C. H. Cave (Philadelphia, 1969), p. 224.

the tax farmers in collecting the taxes (*Ant* 20.194; *War* 2.405).[28]
We clearly find nonnoble aristocrats in Tiberias. Josephus says
(*Life* 32-39) there were three groups in Tiberias at the outbreak of the
war: a group of the most insignificant persons; a group led by Justus;
and the respectable citizens. In the latter group were Julius Capellus;
Herod, son of Miaris; Herod, son of Gamalus; and Compsus, the son of
Compsus. T. Rajak[29] surmises that the first man listed by Josephus was
a Roman citizen, judging by his name and that the next two are from the
Herodian family. She also notes that Compsus's brother Crispus was the
former prefect of Agrippa I (*Life* 33). These men are clearly from the
upper class of Tiberias.[30]

Apparently this social group also existed at Sepphoris. We do not
possess information about the leaders of Sepphoris from the Herodian
period, but the later rabbinic material about Sepphoris indicates a class
of aristocrats. A. Büchler[31] affirmed that these leading citizens were
called "the great ones," "the great of the generation," and "Parnasim"
(i.e., leaders or managers). These great ones were large landowners. In
a Talmud passage quoted by Büchler, a sage from the third century C.E.
distinguishes three social classes based on wealth: the landowners, the
peasants (עַם הָאָרֶץ), and the "empty ones" (i.e., the poor).[32] Probably
every town of good size had its wealthy and influential citizens, such as
John of Gischala (*Life* 43-45)[33] or Simon of Gabara (*Life* 123-25).

It is important to emphasize that ancient agrarian societies, with
poor agricultural technology, could support only a small group of elites.

---

[28] Jeremias, *Jerusalem*, p. 228; S. W. Baron, *A Social and Religious History of the Jews* (New York, 1952), Vol. I, p. 274; J. S. McLaren, *Power and Politics in Palestine* (Sheffield, 1991), pp. 204-6.

[29] T. Rajak, "Justus of Tiberias," *Classical Quarterly* N.S. 23 (1973) 345-68. Cf. H. G. Kippenberg, *Religion und Klassenbildung im antiken Judäa* (Göttingen, 1978), pp. 129f.

[30] M. Goodman, *State and Society in Roman Galilee* (Totowa, N.J., 1983), p. 33, seems correct that Mk 6:21 refers to the aristocrats of Galilee. This reference probably pertains more specifically to Tiberias.

[31] A. Büchler, *The Political and Social Leaders of the Jewish Community of Sepphoris in the Second and Third Centuries* (London, 1909), pp. 7-10.

[32] b.Hull 92a; Büchler, *Political and Social Leaders*, p. 35. The comments of S. S. Miller, *Studies in the History and Traditions of Sepphoris* (New York University, Ph.D., 1980), pp. 141-71, are also interesting in this connection.

[33] See U. Rappaport, "John of Gischala: From Galilee to Jerusalem," *JJS* 33 (1982) 479-93.

The surplus was simply too meager. J. H. Kautsky's statement accurately assesses what was typical:

> The Aristocracy can be initially defined simply as consisting of those in an agrarian economy who, without themselves engaging in agricultural labor, live off the land by controlling the peasants so as to be able to take from them a part of their product. Of course, only a small percentage of the population can be aristocrats, because each peasant produces only a relatively small surplus and the average aristocrat consumes far more than a peasant.[34]

Thus the elite groups, although highly significant in wealth and power, were only a very small percentage of the population.

R. MacMullen, G. Alföldy, and R. Rillinger estimate that the upper classes of the Roman empire (the senators, knights, and decurions) comprised no more than one per cent of the total population.[35] One would expect this percentage roughly to hold true in Galilee, for the nature of agrarian societies, as Kautsky observed, prevented a large elite class.

The Retainers

The class termed by Lenski[36] "the retainers" stood between the elite and the peasants. Lenski maintains that most agrarian societies have employed retainers to mediate between the common people and the ruling class. Lenski suggests that retainers deflected some of the hostility of the lower classes toward the elite, since the peasants and small craftsmen could never be sure whether their trouble comes mainly from the retainers or from higher up.

---

[34] J. H. Kautsky, *The Politics of Aristocratic Empires* (Chapel Hill, N.C., 1982), pp. 79f.

[35] MacMullen, *Roman Social Relations*, p. 89; R. Rillinger, "Moderne und zeitgenössische Vorstellungen vor der Gesellschaftsordnung der römischen Kaiserzeit" *Saeculum* 36 (1985) 302; G. Alföldy, *Römische Sozialgeschichte* (Wiesbaden, 1975), p. 130. Cf. Lenski, *Power and Privilege*, p. 228, who gives a similar figure for other agrarian societies.

[36] Lenski, *Power*, pp. 243–48. Lenski estimates the average number of retainers for agrarian societies at 5% of the population (p. 245).

The retainers administered the financial and political affairs of the upper class and enforced their goals. For this service, says Lenski, they "shared in the economic surplus." That is to say, they were elevated economically above the ordinary mass of people. As with nearly all social distinctions, however, the line between the lower aristocrats and upper retainers was fuzzy, as was the line between the lower retainers and upper peasantry.

Tax collectors were obvious examples of retainers, whether one speaks of the small tax farmers—who F. Herrenbrück[37] maintains were mainly responsible for collecting the revenue—or of toll collectors. John, the tax collector, who resided at Caesarea (*War* 2.287), Zacchaeus, the chief tax collector, who lived at Jericho (Lk 19:1-10), and Levi of Galilee (Lk 5:29) belonged to this class. The first two examples indicate that the retainers could become quite wealthy.

We should also expect the estate overseers or bailiffs to have played a significant role in Galilean society. The office of bailiff was known all over the empire.[38] These important officials are mentioned twice in Lk (12:42-48; 16:1-8). The example in Lk 16:1-8 of the dishonest bailiff is especially revealing. Here we see the far-reaching authority the bailiff exercised over his master's economic affairs. Since bailiffs could be either slaves or freedmen,[39] the slaves referred to in Mk 12:2 and Mt 24:45 are probably also bailiffs.[40]

In spite of the lowly origins of many of the bailiffs, their skills at administration must have made them invaluable to absentee landlords. Columella (first century C.E.) described at length the characteristics both the bailiff and his wife should possess (11.1.3-29, 12.1.1-6). They must be of sober and nonindulgent dispositions and must work hard. They

---

[37] F. Herrenbrück, "Wer waren die 'Zöllner?'" *ZNW* 72 (1981) 178-94. Cf. M. Stern, "The Province of Judea," S. Safrai and M. Stern, *The Jewish People in the First Century*, Vol. I.1, pp. 308-76.

[38] For the Latin term *vilicus*, see A. H. M. Jones "Colonus" in *OCD*. For the Greek term οἰκονόμος, see *LSJM* and O. Michel, "οἰκονόμος," *TDNT*. For the Hebrew terms איקונומוס and סנטר, see Jastrow. For the wide distribution of the Greek term, see E. Ziebarth, "Oikonomos" *PW* XVII, 2, Col. 2118f. For the terms in the rabbinic literature, see LevRab 12; PesRab 10; b.Shab 153a; t.BMeṣ 9:14; t.Beṣ 4:9; t.BB 3:5; m.BB 4:7.

[39] Jones, "Colonus."

[40] Michel, "οἰκονόμος," *TDNT*.

must by example and by use of authority ensure that everyone does a full day's work.[41]

The third type of retainer is the judicial magistrate, whom S. Freyne finds in *War* 21.571 and Lk 12:58 (= Mt 5:25).[42] Lk 18:2 may also refer to this official. They evidently judged legal disputes and served in nearly every town of any size. To these officials we should also add soldiers, both Roman and Herodian.[43] The lower officials of the royal court would also be retainers.[44]

The governing class and their retainers stood over the lower classes both in the urban centers and in the country. They extracted rents and taxes, the "surplus," from the peasantry and others and they lived mostly in the cities, usually in wealth and luxury.

Rural Peasantry

Most of the population in ancient agrarian societies belonged, as Rostovtzeff affirmed, to the rural peasantry.[45] MacMullen suggests, for example, that 75% of the people of ancient Italy were peasants.[46] De Ste. Croix accepts the figure of L. White, the medievalist, who estimated that ten people were needed in the country to produce enough food to enable one person to live away from the land. The latter figure agrees with sociologists of agrarian societies.[47] In light of the works of J. A. Overman and D. R. Edwards[48] on the urbanization of Upper

[41] Cf. Cato, *Agr.* CXLIIf.

[42] See Freyne, *Galilee*, p. 198. These local judges appear also in the rabbinic literature. See b.Shab 139a and E. E. Urbach, "Class-Status and Leadership," p. 67.

[43] For Roman soldiers, see Mt 8:5-13. For Herodian soldiers, see *Ant* 18.113f.

[44] See Jeremias, *Jerusalem*, pp. 88–90, for a description of these officials.

[45] Rostovtzeff, *Social and Economic History*, p. 346.

[46] MacMullen, *Roman Social Relations*, p. 253.

[47] De Ste. Croix, *Class Struggle*, p. 10; L. White, "Die Ausbreitung der Technik 500–1500," in *Europäische Wirtschaftsgeschichte: Mittelalter*, ed. C. M. Cipolla and K. Borchardt, Bd. 1 (Stuttgart, 1978), p. 92. See also G. Sjoberg, *The Preindustrial City* (Glencoe, Ill., 1960), p. 83. Sjoberg affirms that no more than 10% of agrarian populations usually lived in cities. Sometimes it was less than 5%. Lenski's figure is similar (*Power and Privilege*, p. 199).

[48] Overman, "Who were the First Urban Christians?" *SBL 1988 Seminar Papers* (Atlanta, 1988), pp. 160-68; Edwards, "First Century Urban/Rural Relations in Lower Galilee: Exploring the Archaeological and Literary Evidence," *SBL 1988 Seminar Papers* (Atlanta, 1988), pp. 169-82.

Galilee, we may wish to incline somewhat toward MacMullen's lower figure, but we should still conclude that the rural, agricultural workers comprised by far the majority of the population in first-century Galilee.

The agricultural workers included small freeholders, tenant farmers, day laborers, and slaves. The small freeholders (see t.Pe'a 2:2) were generally subsistence farmers, though some may have been somewhat more prosperous. A survey of farm plots from ancient Galilee indicated that they ranged from 1 to 15 acres, with most of them being around 4 acres.[49] These farm sizes are in line with the survey of Samaria done by S. Dar.[50] As A. Ben-David has concluded, that size farm is only large enough for a subsistence at best[51] if the peasant had a large family of 6 to 9 people. Still, Freyne is probably correct that the small freeholders of Galilee do not appear, in Josephus's references to them, to have been starving, but earned their living with little or no margin for error.[52]

There is ample evidence—literary,[53] inscriptional,[54] and archaeological[55]—that many large estates existed in Herodian Palestine, just as they certainly existed in other parts of the Roman empire.[56] Large estates needed a pool of cheap labor. Hence, they were worked by varying combinations of tenant farmers, day laborers, and slaves.

If Jesus' parables are descriptions of ordinary life in Galilee, then Galilee too had its share of workers on large estates. As J. Herz, M. Hengel, and J. H. Charlesworth have demonstrated,[57] the parables of

---

[49] B. Golomb and Y. Kedar, "Ancient Agriculture in the Galilee Mountains" *IEJ* 21 (1971) 136–40.

[50] S. Dar, *Landscape and Pattern* (Oxford, 1986), pp. 46, 60–76; cf. esp. p. 262.

[51] Ben-David, *Talmudische Ökonomie*, p. 44.

[52] Freyne, *Galilee*, pp. 193f, 208.

[53] See the collected evidence in Fiensy, *Social History*, pp. 21–73.

[54] Cf. the Hefzibah inscription. See Y. H. Landau, "A Greek Inscription Found Near Hefzibah" *IEJ* 16 (1966) 54–70.

[55] See especially Dar, *Landscape and Pattern*, pp. 230–45.

[56] See MacMullen, *Roman Social Relations*, p. 6; P. A. Brunt, *Social Conflicts in the Roman Republic* (New York, 1971), p. 34; M. I. Finley, *The Ancient Economy* (London, 1973), p. 99.

[57] Herz, "Grossgrundbesitz in Palästina im Zeitalter Jesu" *PJ* 24 (1928) 98–113; Hengel, "Das Gleichnis von der Weingärtnern Mc 12:1-12 im Licht der Zenonpapyri und der rabbinischen Gleichnisse" *ZNW* 59 (1968) 1–39; J. H. Charlesworth, *Jesus Within Judaism*, pp. 139–48.

the Wicked Tenants (Mk 12:1-12), the Rich Fool (Lk 12:16-21), the Laborers in the Vineyard (Mt 20:1-15), the Tares (Mt 13:24-30), the Prodigal Son (Lk 15:1-32), and others[58] describe conditions on large estates with tenants, day laborers, and slaves. Furthermore, there were quite likely imperial estates in Galilee (*Life* 71-73), as well as Antipas' own large holdings.[59]

Thus we may conclude that estates large enough to support an absentee urban landlord and his family[60] did exist in Galilee in the first century C.E. The corollary of this conclusion is that there were people working these estates who often lived in extreme poverty.

The tenant farmer[61] (אריס) farmed a small section of the land-lord's estate and paid him a percentage of the harvest, anywhere from 25% to 50% (m.Pe²a 5:5, t.BMeṣ 9:11). Day laborers and hirelings were very poor workers who found work especially at harvest time (t.Maas 2:13, 2:15; t.BMeṣ 7:5f; m.BMeṣ 7:4-7:7; m.Pe²a 5:5). Agricultural slaves, though probably less numerous than in other parts of the empire, did exist in Galilee (Mt 13:27; Lk 17:7).

Although agriculture was clearly the most important form of rural livelihood, it was not the only form. There were also shepherds. Some of the shepherds undoubtedly owned their own flocks. Others were day laborers or slaves (Lk 17:7; Jn 10:11f) who tended the flocks of large estate owners or the collected village flocks.

The socioeconomic standing of the rural people of Galilee proba-bly ranged from the comfortable (those with more than sufficient land) to the subsistence level (those with little or no margin for error in the year's crops) to the destitute (poor day laborers and beggars).

---

[58] See also the large sums of money and produce mentioned. These indicate large estates (cf. Lk 16:1-12; Mt 25:14-30; Lk 7:41-43; Mt 18:21-31; and Mk 10:17-22). Freyne is correct, however, to caution against placing too much emphasis on the parables alone in determining socio-economic conditions. See *Galilee*, pp. 165f.

[59] See A. Alt, *Kleine Schriften* (München, 1959), p. 395; Rostovtzeff, *Social and Economic History*, p. 664, note 32; and Hoehner, *Herod Antipas*, p. 70.

[60] One usually required at least 50 acres to live as an absentee landlord. See K. D. White, *Roman Farming* (London, 1970), pp. 385-87.

[61] Other forms of tenancy were probably land entrepreneurs, according to Ben-David, *Talmudische Ökonomie*, p. 63. Cf. S. Krauss, *Talmudische Archäologie* (Hildesheim, 1966), pp. 109f.

Village and Urban Trades

Others lived in the cities and towns besides the absentee landlords: merchants, artisans, and urban day laborers. Wealthy merchants
eventually entered the aristocratic class. The smaller merchants include
what J. Jeremias called the "retail traders" and those who engaged in
either foreign or local trade on a small scale.[62]

One of the major Galilean export items was fish. The Sea of Galilee contained many varieties of fish edible for both Jews and Gentiles
(*War* 3.508, 520; m.AZ 2:6). These fish were pickled or salted (Strabo
16.2.45; m.AZ 2:6; m.Ned 6:4) and then sold all over Palestine. Many
were involved in this trade, from the fishermen—who could be day
laborers (Mk 1:19-20)—to the owners of the fishing boats and the merchants who marketed the fish. Josephus could allegedly round up 230
boats on the Sea of Galilee (*War* 2.635). The Gospels also attest to a
thriving fishing trade (Mk 1:16-17, Mt 4:17-22, Lk 5:11).[63]

There were also cloth industries in Galilee. Linen, grain, and
olive oil were exported.[64] Pottery was also an important item of trade.
The pottery of Kefar Hanania and Kefar Shichin were especially famous
(m.Kel 2:2; b.BMeş 74a; b.Shab 120b) and were sold all over Galilee
and the Golan.[65] The distribution required for such trade would have
required an active mercantile class.

Just below the merchants in socioeconomic status were the
artisans or craftsmen. These workers were able, because of their skills,
to demand a higher wage than the ordinary unskilled day laborer, yet
they were usually not as comfortable as the merchants. The crafts in the
ancient world included making leather products, cloth products, and
pottery. Carpentry, masonry, and metal working were also prominent.[66]
All of these trades are attested in the sources for Palestine as well.[67]

---

[62] Jeremias, *Jerusalem*, pp. 35–51, 100.

[63] See Hoehner, *Herod Antipas*, p. 67; W. H. Wuellner, *The Meaning of
Fishers of Men* (Philadelphia, 1967), pp. 45–63; K. W. Clark, "Sea of Galilee" *IDB*
Vol. II, p. 349.

[64] See Hoehner, *Herod Antipas*, p. 68; and Edwards, "First Century
Urban/Rural Relations in Lower Galilee," p. 175.

[65] See D. Adan-Bayewitz, "Kefar Hananya, 1986" *IEJ* 37 (1987) 178f; and
Adan-Bayewitz and I. Perlman, "The Local Trade of Sepphoris in the Roman Period"
IEJ 40 (1990) 153–72.

[66] See H. Michell, *The Economics of Ancient Greece* (Cambridge, 1957), pp.
170–209.

[67] J. Klausner, *Jesus of Nazareth* (London, 1925), p. 177, lists over forty

Historians agree that most artisans worked hard, but were able to earn just enough to live simply.[68] They were not usually wealthy but neither were they starving. However, craftsmen could attain a level of affluence if their skills were especially in demand[69] or if they could afford slaves to mass-produce their goods.[70] Archaeology has discovered a family of well-to-do artisans in Palestine as well: the family of Simon the temple builder, buried in Tomb I on Givat ha-Mivtar, north of Jerusalem.[71] This was a family of craftsmen which did hard manual labor but attained enough financial success to afford both a tomb in a rather high-priced area[72] and ossuaries.[73]

Artisans did not enjoy a high social standing among the Greeks or the Romans. Herodotus (fifth century B.C.E.) writes that the Egyptians and other foreigners regarded craftsmen as low on the social scale and that the Greeks also accepted this attitude (2.167). Aristotle (fourth century B.C.E.) allows that some of the crafts are necessary for a society

---

trades.

[68] A. Burford, *Craftsmen in Greek and Roman Society* (New York, 1972), pp. 138–43; C. Mossé, *The Ancient World at Work* (New York, 1969), p. 79; R. Hock, *The Social Context of Paul's Ministry* (Philadelphia, 1980), p. 35. Dio Chrys., *Or.* 7.112f, says that those who know a trade will never worry about a living. Lucian, *Dial. Meret.* 6.293, says that as long as Philenus the smith was alive, his family had plenty of everything. In b.Sanh 29a the Talmud says that as long as one knows a trade he need have no fear of famine. T.Kid 1:11 compares knowledge of a trade to a vineyard with a wall around it. Did 12:3f assumes that a person without a craft may need financial assistance. Cf. also G. Glotz, *Ancient Greece at Work* (New York, 1976), p. 359, who notes that craftsmen at Delos earned twice as much per day as unskilled laborers in the fourth and third centuries B.C.E.

[69] Burford, *Craftsmen*, p. 141; Hock, *Social Context*, p. 34, cites the case of Tryphon the weaver (POxy 2.264), who earned enough to buy his own half of a three-story house.

[70] Mossé, *The Ancient World at Work*, pp. 90f, refers to three famous and affluent tanners in classical Athens.

[71] This tomb and its contents are described by V. Tzaferis, "Jewish Tombs at and near Givat ha-Mivtar, Jerusalem" *IEJ* 20 (1970) 18–22; N. Haas, "Anthropological Observations on the Skeletal Remains from Givat ha-Mivtar" *IEJ* 20 (1970) 38–59; J. Naveh, "The Ossuary Inscriptions from Givat ha-Mivtar" *IEJ* 20 (1970) 33–37.

[72] See P. Smith and J. Zias, "Skeletal Remains from the Late Hellenistic French Hill Tomb" *IEJ* 30 (1980) 115. They note that this was an expensive area to purchase a tomb.

[73] Tzaferis, "Jewish Tombs" p. 30, indicates that only the well-to-do could afford ossuaries.

(*Pol.* 4.3.11-12; cf. Plato, *Resp.* 2.396b-371e). Nevertheless, he regards the artisans as inferior beings. Artisans are much like slaves (*Pol.* 1.5.10) and they, the day laborers, and the market people are clearly inferior to other classes, even farmers (*Pol.* 6.2.7; 7.8.2).

Xenophon (fourth century B.C.E.) has Socrates denigrate the artisans. In some cities, says Socrates, they cannot be citizens (*Oec.* 4.1-4). The same attitude can be found in later Greek authors, such as Dio Chrysostom (first century C.E.; see *Or.* 7.110), Lucian of Samosata (second century C.E.; see *Fug.* 12f), and Celsus (second century C.E.; see Origen, *c. Cels.* 6:36). Important Roman authors, such as Cicero (first century B.C.E.; see *Off.* 1.42 and *Brut.* 73) and Livy (first century B.C.E.; see 20.2.25)[74] also reflect this attitude, though Cicero also admits that artisans are useful to the city (*Rep.* 2.22).

This attitude stemmed from the effect some of these trades had on the body, disfiguring it or making it soft because of a sedentary life (Socrates in Xen, *Oec.* 4.1-4; Dio Chrys., *Or.* 7.110). In addition, an artisan was not considered an adequate defender of his city in contrast to a peasant farmer (Socrates in Xen., *Oec.* 4.1-4). We must bear in mind, however, that this was the attitude of the elite toward artisans, not the attitude of the artisans themselves or of other classes.

The same attitude seems not to have prevailed among Palestinian Jews. The rabbinic sources extol both manual labor (m.Ab 1:10; ARN B XXI, 23a) and teaching one's son a craft (m.Kid 4:14; t.Kid 1:11; b.Kid 29a). Artisans often receive special recognition (m.Bik 3:3; b.Kid 33a) and many of the sages were artisans. Josephus also seems to have regarded artisans highly. He praises their skills in building the Temples (*Ant* 3.200, 8.76), sacred vessels (*Ant* 12.58-84), and towers (*War* 5.175). He never refers to artisans using the pejorative term "mechanical workers."[75]

---

[74] See especially Hock, *Social Context*, pp. 35f; Burford, *Craftsmen*, pp. 29, 34, 39f; and MacMullen, *Roman Social Relations*, pp. 115f.

[75] For rabbinic sages as artisans, see A. Büchler, *Economic Conditions of Judea after the Destruction of the Second Temple* (London, 1912), p. 50; Klausner, *Jesus of Nazareth*, p. 177; H. Strack and P. Billerbeck, *Kommentar zum Neuen Testament aus Talmud und Midrasch*, Vol. II (München, 1924), pp. 745f. For further citations on the rabbinic view of craftsmen, see Krauss, *Talmudische Archäologie*, Vol. II, pp. 249–51. For the pejorative connotation of the term βάναυσος, see *LSJM* and MacMullen, *Roman Social Relations*, p. 138, and the citations given by each.

It is also interesting that Origen (third century C.E.), the Christian scholar of Alexandria, tried to deny that Jesus was a carpenter (*c. Cels* 6.36). Justin (second century C.E.) on the other hand, although he was also a Christian philosopher-apologist, was quite willing to admit that Jesus had been a carpenter and maintained that he had made yokes and ploughs (*Dial. Trypho* **88**.8). Justin grew up in Samaria, the semi-Jewish region between Judea and Galilee, and evidently did not have the Greek elitist view regarding artisans.

In addition to the craftsmen, who were associated both with the urban centers and small villages, there were also in the cities the unskilled day laborers. Some were burden bearers, others messengers, and others working assistants to artisans. Some were paid to be watchmen over children, over the sick, even over the dead. One can even find reference to manure gatherers and thorn gatherers.[76] Their lack of skills made these persons less capable of earning a living.[77]

Unclean and Degraded Classes

Below all the above classes existed, according to Lenski, the unclean and degraded classes. They were found both in the city and the countryside and consisted of people "inferior to that of the masses of common people" due to occupation, heredity, or disease.[78]

The occupations which were scorned were, among others, prostitutes, dung collectors, ass drivers, gamblers, sailors, tanners, peddlers, herdsmen, and usurers.[79] Those groups inferior to the common people, due to heredity, included mainly those born illegitimately. M.Kid 4:1 lists a hierarchy of births ranging from priests to the lowly four: bastards, Gibeonites, those that must be silent when reproached

---

[76] See Krauss, *Talmudische Archäologie*, Vol. II, pp. 105f, and the copious references cited there.

[77] See D. Sperber, "Costs of Living in Roman Palestine" *Journal of the Economic and Social History of the Orient* 8 (1965) 248–71. Sperber shows that skilled labor usually received greater wages than unskilled (see p. 250f). Cf. also Glotz, *Ancient Greece at Work*, p. 359, who notes that craftsmen at Delos in the fourth and third centuries B.C.E. earned twice as much per day as unskilled workers.

[78] Lenski, *Power and Privilege*, pp. 280f.

[79] Lk 7:37-39, Mt 21:31. See the rabbinic lists of unacceptable occupations: m.Kid 4:14; m.Keṭ 7:10; m.Sanh 3:3; b.Kid 82a; b.Sanh 25b. See also Jeremias, *Jerusalem*, pp. 303–12.

about their origins, and foundlings. The Hebrew word usually translated *bastard* (מַמְזֵר) does not refer to any illegitimate child. This person is the child of an adulterous or incestuous union (as defined by Lev 18 and 20). Bastards could not "enter the congregation of the Lord" (Deut 23:3).[80] That is, they could not intermarry with Israelites.

The second of this lowly four was a descendant of the Gibeonites whom Joshua (Josh 9:27) made Temple slaves. According to later rabbinic law (b.Yeb 78b), they were also excluded from the Israelite community.[81] The third person must be silent when reproached about his descent because he does not know who his father was (m.Kid 4:2).[82] The foundling is a child taken up from the street whose father and mother are unknown (m.Kid 4:2).[83]

Mishnah Yebamoth 4:13 indicates that records were kept of one's ancestry. Rabbi Simeon ben Azzai (second century C.E.) reports that he found a family register in Jerusalem which indicated that a certain person was a bastard. The precise definitions of these terms were debated by the sages, but the stigma attached to them was not. It "marked every male descendant ... forever and indelibly."[84] One Mishnaic passage, for example, demands that an Israelite who marries a bastard or Gibeonite be scourged (m.Mak 3:1).

Another category of those scorned are those included in the unclean and degraded class due to disease. We should think here especially of the lepers, who seem to have abounded in Palestine.[85] Such people were declared unclean by a priest (Lev 13:11, 25) and had to remain apart from everyone else, crying out from a distance, "Unclean!" (Lev 13:45f). Lepers lived a life of social ostracism.

The Expendables

At the very bottom of the social structure, according to Lenski, were the "expendables." This group consisted of "criminals, beggars,

---

[80] L. N. D. Dembitz, "Bastard," in *JE*.

[81] See Jastrow, p. 943, נתין.

[82] Jastrow, p. 1637, שְׁתוּקִי.

[83] Jastrow, p. 89, אסופי. B.BMeṣ 87a says a man should not marry a foundling.

[84] Jeremias, *Jerusalem*, p. 342. For his definition of these terms, see pp. 337–44.

[85] See Mk 1:40; 14:3; Lk 17:12; m.Meg 1:7; m.MK 3:1; m.Soṭ 1:5; m.Zeb 14:3; *LAB* 13:3; 5ApocSyrPss 155 (see *OPT* II, p. 629). The word seems to have been used for infectious skin diseases in general. See J. Zias, "Death and Disease in Ancient

and underemployed itinerant workers." Lenski remarks concerning this class: "Agrarian societies usually produced more people than the dominant classes found it profitable to employ." Lenski estimates, based on statistics from Europe from the sixteenth to the eighteenth century, that in most agrarian societies, about five to ten percept of the population were in this class.[86]

First in the list of expendables were the bandits. Hengel was one of the first scholars to describe bandits in Palestine in sociological terms. Banditry was a problem throughout the Greco-Roman world in the time period we are considering. The ranks of bandits were swollen by runaway slaves, deserting soldiers, and impoverished peasants.[87] One sociologist, E. J. Hobsbawm, has described the phenomenon of banditry in agrarian societies generally as "a primitive form of organized social protest."[88] This thesis has been taken up most recently by R. Horsley and J. S. Hanson in their work on Palestine in the first century C.E.[89]

That banditry in the ancient world was rooted in social and economic factors is hardly deniable.[90] We also find examples in Palestine of banditry originating in poverty and hardship. But we must be cautious about attributing to bandits the Robin Hood heroic stature that Horsley and Hanson describe.[91] They attempt to show that bandits often enjoyed the support and protection of the peasant villagers and were even their heroes. Their two examples are Hezekiah and his men, who were executed by Herod the Great (*Ant* 14.168), and Elezar ben Dinai, to whom the Galileans turned to get justice on a group of Samaritans for murdering some Jewish pilgrims (*Ant* 20.118-36; *War* 2.228-31).

Horsley and Hanson point out that the execution of Hezekiah and his men brought a storm of protest. But those protesting in the case of

---

Israel" *BA* 54 (1991) 147-69.
[86] Lenski, *Power and Privilege*, pp. 281-83.
[87] Hengel, *The Zealots*, trans. D. Smith (Edinburgh, 1989), pp. 33f.
[88] E. J. Hobsbawm, *Primitive Rebels* (New York, 1965), p. 13.
[89] Horsley and Hanson, *Bandits*.
[90] See R. MacMullen, *Enemies of the Roman Order* (Cambridge, 1966), pp. 255-68; B. D. Shaw, "Bandits in the Roman Empire" *Past and Present* 102 (1984) 3-52.
[91] Horsley and Hanson refer to the bandits of Palestine as "Jewish Robin Hoods" (*Bandits*, p. 74).

Hezekiah were the relatives of those slain and their protest was primarily against Herod's summary execution of these men without trial. Even the Sanhedrin, certainly no lover of bandits, was appalled by Herod's handling of the matter (*Ant* 14.165-67). Furthermore, Josephus writes that they sang Herod's praises in the villages and cities because in getting rid of Hezekiah, he had granted security and peace to the region (*Ant* 14.160). Josephus may be stretching the truth here in presenting the viewpoint of the urban elite rather than the peasant villager, but it is also possible that many peasants honored bandits as much from fear as from hero worship and that there was general relief when Hezekiah was executed.

In the case of Eleazar ben Dinai, the peasants turned to him as a last resort only after Cumanus dallied about giving them justice. The Mishnah, on the other hand (m.Soṭ 9:9), remembers ben Dinai as a murderer. Perhaps he was a local hero or even a "freedom fighter" or Zealot,[92] but this is hardly provable.

Even if one could produce a few examples of bandits as social protesters representing the will of the common people, it would not change the verdict on banditry in general. Bandits were generally considered objects of dread and animosity in the Jewish sources. They were dangerous, ruthless criminals who preyed on innocent people. The rabbinic sources, Josephus, and the New Testament all reflect this attitude.[93]

Beggars also appear frequently in Palestine. They are lame (Acts 3:2; Jn 5:3; m.Shab 6:8; Lk 16:20) or blind (Jn 9:1; Mt 21:14; Mk 10:46) and sit along the roadside in the country (Mk 10:46) or along the streets and alleys in the city (Lk 14:21). A favorite place for beggars was the Temple (Acts 3:2), since almsgiving was considered especially meritorious when done there.[94]

In conclusion to the first part of this essay, the numerical difference between rich and poor was enormous. Perhaps only about 1%

---

[92] H. Bientenhard, *Sota* (Berlin, 1956), pp. 153–55, regarded Eleazar ben Dinai as a Zealot freedom fighter.

[93] See, e.g., Mk 14:48; Lk 10:30; Jn 10:1; 2Cor 11:26; m.Shab 2:5; t.Taan 2:12; m.BMeṣ 7:9; *War* 2.253; 4.135; 406; *Ant* 14.159; 17.285, 256. Some authors in antiquity romanticized the brigand and pirate leaders as heroic figures. However, the bandits also caused untold hardship on the general population. See Hengel, *The Zealots*, pp. 25–34.

[94] Jeremias, *Jerusalem*, pp. 116f.

of the population belonged to the elite class. What percentage of the population lived in extreme poverty? We can only estimate based on statistics from other societies. MacMullen notes that in Europe in the fourteenth and fifteenth centuries, one-third of the population lived in "habitual want." According to MacMullen, the person living in "habitual want" "devoted the vast bulk of each day's earnings to his immediate needs and accumulated no property or possessions to speak of."[95]

MacMullen estimates that the poor consisted of about one-third of the Roman empire. This figure may be somewhat out of line for Antipas's Galilee, but probably not by much. The figure includes not only many of the expendables, but most of the day laborers among the urban and rural workers—and probably many of the tenant farmers. Most of the rest lived more or less also in poverty, but at least had their physical needs met. The average peasant or artisan was very poor compared to the elite classes, but was not destitute and did not live in habitual want.

WHERE DID JESUS FIT?

Where did Jesus fit into the socioeconomic structure of Galilee? Many scholars in the past have pictured Jesus as coming from the poorest rung of Galilean society.[96] Others have added to Jesus' supposed poverty the dimension of social or political activism.[97] Still others maintain that

[95] MacMullen, *Roman Social Relations*, p. 93.

[96] See A. Plummer, *The Gospel According to Luke* (New York, 1901), pp. 32, 65. But Plummer adds astutely: "Neither here (Lk 2:24) nor elsewhere in the New Testament have we any evidence that our Lord or His parents were among the abjectly poor." See W. Manson, *The Gospel of Luke* (New York, 1930), pp. 20f; H. Branscomb, *The Teachings of Jesus* (New York, 1931), pp. 213f; J. W. Bowman, *Jesus' Teaching in its Environment* (Richmond, Va., 1963), p. 27; R. Batey, *Jesus and the Poor* (New York, 1972), p. 5. P. H. Furfey, "Christ as TEKTΩN," *CBQ* 17 (1955) 215, also concludes that Jesus was poor, but like most people of his day.

[97] R. von Pöhlmann, *Geschichte der sozialen Frage und des Sozialismus in der antiken Welt*, Vol. II (München, 1925), pp. 467–73; A. Mayer, *Der zensierte Jesus* (Olten, 1983), pp. 21–45. There are other recent studies of Jesus from this perspective, but one cannot discern how the authors view Jesus' socio-economic background. See, e.g., A. Trocmé, *Jésus et la Révolution Non-violente* (Geneva, 1961); J. H. Yoder, *The Politics of Jesus* (Grand Rapids, 1972); P. Hollenbach, "Liberating Jesus for Social Involvement" *Biblical Theology Bulletin* 15 (1985) 151–57; D. E. Oakman, *Jesus and the Economic Questions of His Day*; R. Horsley, *Jesus and the Spiral of Violence* (San Francisco, 1987).

Jesus came from a middle class background.[98] At least one scholar has claimed for Jesus membership in the wealthy class.[99] Many scholars either assume that Jesus was poor or place too much emphasis on a few verses in the Lucan birth narrative which are capable of various interpretations.[100] Others unwisely use economic terms ("middle class") that are appropriate only for industrial society.

To understand Jesus' socioeconomic origins, we must explore what it meant for Jesus to be an artisan in ancient Galilee. Next we should look for any hints in the Gospels themselves about Jesus' background.

We should consider it probable that Jesus was a τέκτων, or carpenter. This assertion is found only in Mk 6:3, while in the parallel passage in Mt 13:55 he is called "the son of the carpenter." Nevertheless, the historical probability that Jesus was a carpenter remains high. All the major Greek manuscripts—except one[101]—and many of the early versions have the reading: "Is not this the carpenter?"[102] Furthermore, these words are found in a text describing Jesus' rejection at his home town, a narrative unlikely to have been invented by the early church. Third, the passage in Matthew ("Is not this the son of the carpenter?")—even if one were to argue that it is more accurate or authentic—actually supports the meaning of Mark, since fathers usually taught their craft to their sons.[103] Thus, we should conclude that Jesus came from the artisan class.[104]

---

[98] M. Hengel, *Property and Riches in the Early Church*, trans. J. Bowden (Philadelphia, 1974), p. 27; and J. P. Meier, *A Marginal Jew* (New York, 1991), p. 282.

[99] G. W. Buchanan, "Jesus and the Upper Class" *NovT* 7 (1964) 195–209.

[100] Scholars point especially to the offering paid by Mary (Lk 2:24), which seems to be that of a poor person. But we must be cautious about the meaning of *poor*. What might seem poor (i.e., destitute or nearly so) to moderns could have been quite average to ancients. At most, this offering indicates only that Jesus' family was not wealthy at that time.

[101] Papyrus 45 from the third century C.E. has the text of Mk 6:3 read like that of Mt 13:55.

[102] See B. M. Metzger, *A Textual Commentary on the Greek New Testament* (London/New York, 1971), pp. 88f; and C. E. B. Cranfield, *The Gospel According to St. Mark* (Cambridge, 1963), pp. 194f. But for an opposing view, see V. Taylor, *The Gospel According to St. Mark* (Grand Rapids, 1966), pp. 299–301.

[103] Burford, *Craftsmen*, p. 82; Klausner, *Jesus of Nazareth*, p. 178.

[104] The Aramaic term for carpenter sometimes is used in the Talmud meta-

Carpentry in Greco-Roman Society

As a carpenter,[105] Jesus would have been skilled in fashioning wood products, such as furniture, tools, agricultural implements, water wheels for irrigation, scaffolding for houses, and perhaps even ships.[106] He would have known and used a wide assortment of tools, including axes, chisels, drills, saws, squares, hammers, and plumb lines.[107] His skills would have been not unlike those of carpenters of one hundred years ago.

What sort of business would a carpenter in Galilee in the first century C.E. have done? The traditional concept is of a simple village carpenter who made mostly yokes and ploughs for the local peasantry.[108] According to this view, he would seldom, if ever, have left the village.

The Greek historian Xenophon describes the work of a village carpenter and then compares it to the life of an artisan in a large city (evidently in a shoe factory):

> For in the small cities the same people make chairs, doors, ploughs, and tables, and many times this same person even builds (houses) and he is contented if in such a way he can get enough employers to feed himself. It is impossible for a man skilled in many things to do all of them well. But in the big cities because many people need each trade, one skill can support a person. And many times (one needs) not even a complete skill, but one makes men's shoes, another women's (shoes).

---

phorically of a scholar (see Vermes, *Jesus the Jew*, pp. 21f) even as the Greek word for carpenter was occasionally used for any master of an art, such as a gymnast, poet, or physician (see *LSJM*). But the term in Mk 6:3 clearly is not used in that sense. Mark's point is that because Jesus was only a carpenter, the residents of Nazareth refused to listen to him. Otherwise the passage makes no sense.

[105] Gk.: τέκτων; Heb.: חרשׁ; Aram.: נגרא; Lat.: *faber*.

[106] See C. C. McCown, "'Ο ΤΕΚΤΩΝ," in S. J. Case, ed. *Studies in Early Christianity* (New York/London, 1928), pp. 173–89; Furfey, "Christ as ΤΕΚΤΩΝ"; and H. Blümner, *Technologie und Terminologie der Gewerbe und Künste*, Vol. II (Leipzig, 1879), pp. 311–47.

[107] See C. U. Wolf, "Carpenter" *IDB*, Vol. I, p. 539; and Burford, *Craftsmen*, pp. 39f.

[108] This is, e.g., Furfey's view ("Christ as ΤΕΚΤΩΝ," p. 213) and Klausner's (*Jesus of Nazareth*, p. 233). Most recently, S. S. Miller, "Sepphoris, the Well Remembered City" *BA* 55 (1992) 74–83, argues for this view.

It is possible for someone to support himself by merely stitching shoes.
One divides (the parts), another only cuts out shoe pieces, and another
of these workers does nothing but putting the pieces together.   (Xen.,
Cyr. 8.2.5)

The differences between village artisans and city artisans could be
great not only in terms of job description but also in terms of economic
comfort. The traditional understanding of Jesus' background has been
that of the small village artisan described by Xenophon. But did Jesus'
skill as a carpenter ever take him out of the village and into the city,
where he learned about and participated in urban culture? If so, could
his urban employment have elevated his economic status? Was Jesus a
village woodworker or did he also work in the building trade?

Traveling Artisans

Since S. J. Case,[109] an alternate view has existed regarding Jesus'
background. Although Nazareth was probably a small village, it stood
only three or four miles from Sepphoris, one of the largest cities in
Galilee. Case suggested that Jesus as a youth had worked in the
reconstruction of Sepphoris and later in the construction of Tiberias.
Sepphoris had been destroyed by the Romans in 3 B.C.E. and was then
magnificently rebuilt by Antipas (*Ant* 18.27). Since it would take many
years to reconstruct a city such as Sepphoris, Case reasoned that a carpenter's family could have found important and lucrative work there for
a sustained period of time. R. Batey has more recently taken up Case's
thesis and supported it from his own work on the excavation of Sepphoris.[110]

That artisans in antiquity would travel from their home villages to
work on large construction projects is well known. It is also quite

[109] *Jesus: A New Biography* (New York, 1968), pp. 199–212.
[110] See the following publications by Batey: "Is Not This the Carpenter?" *NTS*
30 (1984) 249–58; "Sepphoris: An Urban Portrait of Jesus" *BAR* 18 (1992) 50–62;
Jesus and the Forgotten City (Grand Rapids, 1992), esp. pp. 65–82. For Sepphoris, see
also E. M. Meyers, E. Netzer, and C. L. Meyers, "Sepphoris 'Ornament of all
Galilee'" *BA* 49 (1986) 4–19; E. M. Meyers, E. Netzer, and C. L. Meyers, *Sepphoris*
(Winona Lake, Ind., 1992); and J. Strange, "Sepphoris" in *ABD*, Vol. V (New York,
1992), pp. 1090–93. For the history of Sepphoris, see Miller, *Studies in the History and
Traditions of Sepphoris*.

plausible that Jesus and his family worked in other towns in Galilee, such as Tiberias, which began construction somewhere between 18 and 23 C.E.[111] They may even have worked in Jerusalem.

There are clear examples in the Mediterranean world of artisans' traveling to distant building sites. Building temples and other public works almost always required importing craftsmen from surrounding cities. There was a general shortage of craftsmen in the building trades—carpenters, masons, sculptors—especially from the fourth century B.C.E. on. This shortage necessitated that craftsmen travel from city to city. A. Burford cites, for example, the case of the city of Epidauros in Greece which, to build the temple of Asclepius (c. 370 B.C.E.), imported masons, carpenters, and sculptors from Argos, Corinth, Athens, Paros, Arcadia, and Troizen. Argos itself had to hire Athenian masons to complete its long walls in 418 B.C.E. Athens also needed carpenters and masons from Megara and Thebes to rebuild its walls in the 390s B.C.E.

According to Burford, this shortage of craftsmen was especially acute in the Roman period. The cities of North Africa, Asia Minor, Persia, and Palmyra imported craftsmen for their building projects. The local artisans contributed what they could. Burford affirms, "For unusual projects such as public works, no city, not even Athens, had a sufficiently large skilled labor force to do the job by itself."[112]

Since this was the case throughout the Mediterranean world, we should expect that in Palestine in the Herodian period artisans from surrounding cities and villages were used for large building projects. This expectation is confirmed by a passage in Josephus. Josephus relates that Herod the Great (ruled 37 to 4 B.C.E.) made the following preparations to build his Temple in 20 B.C.E.: "He made ready 1000 wagons which would carry the stones. He gathered 10,000 of the most skillful workers … and he taught some to be masons and others to be carpenters" (*Ant* 15.390).

---

[111] For the date in which construction began on Tiberias, see Overman, "Who were the First Urban Christians?" p. 163.

[112] Burford, *Craftsmen*, pp. 62–67; quote on p. 63. See also Burford, "The Economics of Greek Temple Building" *Proceedings of the Cambridge Philological Society* 191 (1965) 21–34, in which he emphasizes the mobility of the ancient craftsmen: "Certainly, when there was a demand for them, skilled craftsmen were automatically at a premium…. The mobility of skilled craftsmen in the ancient world thus offset the perennial shortage of skilled men in any given city" (p. 31).

Josephus' description of Herod's collection and training of carpenters and builders in preparation for building his Temple implies
there was a shortage of artisans in Jerusalem for this massive construction project. Furthermore, according to Josephus (*Ant* 20.219f), the
completion of the Temple, which did not occur until the procuratorship
of Albinus (62–64 C.E.), put 18,000 artisans out of work. Although
Josephus's figure may be somewhat exaggerated,[113] the construction of
the Temple required a large force of artisans throughout most of the
first century C.E.

The evidence from Josephus confirms that an extensive public
works project like building the Temple required recruiting and importing—and even training—artisans from distant cities and employing them
over long periods of time. The construction of Sepphoris and Tiberias
must have required a similar contribution of skilled labor. Given the
urbanization of Lower Galilee—e.g., Sepphoris, Tiberias, Magdala,
Capernaum, and Scythopolis[114]—and also of the Tetrarchy of Philip—
Caesarea Philippi and Bethsaida Julius—one can well imagine that an
artisan in the building trade would be in demand. Since such was the
case in the Greco-Roman world in general, causing artisans to move frequently from job to job, we should expect the same to have been true in
Galilee. It is even possible that Jesus and his family worked on the
Temple in Jerusalem from time to time.[115]

Batey asserts that carpenters were necessary for construction of
public works. This construction included the erecting of scaffolding and
forms for vaults, cranes, and ceiling beams.[116] Batey's assertion is confirmed not only by the examples from classical Greece listed above, but

---

[113] A colossal project such as Herod's Temple surely required a very large
force of craftsmen. Burford notes, for example (*Craftsmen*, p. 62), that the tiny
Erechtheum in Athens needed 100 craftsmen to complete its final stages in 408 B.C.E.
These included 44 masons; 9 sculptors; 7 woodcarvers; 22 carpenters, sawyers, and
joiners; 1 lathe worker; 3 painters; 1 gilder; and 9 laborers and other unspecified
workers.

[114] Overman, "Who Were the First Urban Christians?"

[115] D. E. Oakman, *Jesus and the Economic Questions of His Day*, pp. 186–93,
argues that Jesus' social contacts with people in Jerusalem indicate that he was there
many times before his ministry began. Oakman points to Jesus' friends in Bethany (near
Jerusalem, Mk 14:3; Lk 10:38–42; Jn 11:1) and to the owner of the upper room (Mk
14:12–16).

[116] Batey, *Jesus and the Forgotten City*, pp. 68–82.

also by Josephus. He celebrates the importance of carpenters for building Solomon's Temple (*Ant* 7.66; 7.340; 7.377), Zerubbabel's Temple (*Ant* 11.78), and Herod's Temple (*Ant* 15.390). They also figure prominently in building city walls (*War* 3.173).

Therefore, we can say with certainty that there were several continuous and massive building projects during Jesus' youth and early adulthood. Second, we can be reasonably confident that these projects necessitated the services of skilled carpenters from distant cities and villages. Jesus and his extended family could easily have worked in Sepphoris, Tiberias, in other Galilean cities, and even in Jerusalem. Opportunities were there for this family to have experienced urban culture and to have risen to the same level of economic comfort as the artisan family of Simon the temple builder.

Jesus' Standard of Living

But establishing that the possibility was there to have attained a modest level of economic comfort does not, of course, prove that Jesus' family did so. Are there any indications in the Gospels that Jesus came from an upper-level artisan family as opposed to a poor village artisan family?

Buchanan has noted[117] that Jesus is found among well-to-do people rather often. He called to be his disciples James and John, sons of Zebedee, a fishing merchant who was wealthy enough to employ day laborers (Mk 1:19f). Levi, the tax collector, hosted a banquet for Jesus—in which they reclined at table[118]—and became a disciple (Mt 9:9-11). A certain man "of the rulers of the Pharisees" invited Jesus to dine with him (Lk 14:1-6). Jairus, ruler of the synagogue at Capernaum, and a certain unnamed Roman centurion approached him (Mk 5:22f; Mt 8:5). Zaccheus, the chief tax collector, also gave a meal for Jesus (Lk 19:1-10). Lazarus (or Simon the leper) hosted a banquet

---

[117] Buchanan, "Jesus and the Upper Class," pp. 205f. Buchanan argues on the basis of 2Cor 8:9 that Jesus came from a wealthy family: "He became poor even though he was rich." But Buchanan's reasons for concluding that these words refer to the historical Jesus' socioeconomic status are less than compelling.

[118] Reclining while eating was a Greek practice which the Romans and others adopted. It was usually a sign of status and wealth to eat a meal while reclining on a couch. Poor people usually ate sitting upright or on mats. See E. Badian, "Triclinium" *OCD*. See also Mt 22:10f; 26:7; Mk 6:26; Jn 12:2.

for Jesus in Bethany (Mk 14:3; Jn 12:2). Joanna, the wife of a court official of Antipas, was a disciple of Jesus (Lk 8:3). Nicodemus, said to be a member of the Sanhedrin, was a disciple of Jesus in secret (Jn 3:1f; 7:50; 19:39). Finally, Joseph of Arimathea, who buried Jesus' body and was a disciple, is described as a member of the council and wealthy (Mk 15:43; Mt 27:57).

That Jesus could so easily move among these wealthier people suggests some experience in similar social situations and an earlier association with people of some economic means. Further, given the common urban snobbery toward the village peasants, one may reasonably wonder if a simple village carpenter would ever be the guest of such people as those listed above.

It does not follow from these texts, however, that Jesus was himself wealthy or a member of the elite class. He was only in a position to have known such people. An itinerant artisan who had experience in urban environments working for wealthy patrons could easily have become familiar with such people.

Some commentators have sought to find in Jesus' teachings evidence of his urban and/or wealthy background. This evidence is, however, not convincing. Some argue that his neutral position toward Rome and his willingness to associate with all types of people prove Jesus' association with Sepphoris and other cities.[119] Others find in his use of the term *hypocrite* (a Greek theatrical term) a familiarity with the theater at Sepphoris and in his parables about kings firsthand observation of Antipas.[120] Still others believe that the banking and judicial system of Sepphoris informed Jesus' parables.[121] Buchanan even believes that Jesus' parables betray a wealthy background. Those parables which speak of enormous wealth (Mt 18:32-35), the investment of large sums (Mt 25:14-30), or the business practices of a large estate (Lk 16:1-9) indicate a familiarity with the affairs of the rich, maintains Buchanan.[122]

---

[119] Cf., e.g., Case, *Jesus*, pp. 206–10.

[120] Batey, *Jesus and the Forgotten City*, pp. 83–104, 119–34. Cf. B. Schwank, "Das Theater von Sepphoris und die Jugenjahre Jesu" *Erbe und Auftrag* 52 (1976) 199–206.

[121] Schwank, "Das Theater von Sepphoris."

[122] Buchanan, "Jesus and the Upper Class," pp. 204f. Buchanan states: "It is an impressive fact, however, that there are very few teachings of Jesus that reflect lower class associations" (204).

These items are certainly suggestive, but S. S. Miller[123] is wise to caution against accepting them as evidence. If one has already established that Jesus was well-acquainted with Sepphoris, for example, then one could rightly argue that this background lies behind Jesus' actions and teachings. But it is difficult to use the argument the other way around. One can get illustrations (parables) from many sources (travelers, folk tradition, etc.), so Jesus need not have observed, for example, Antipas in speaking about kings. Nor does it follow that he visited the theater because he used the word *hypocrite*.

On the other hand, Miller's assertions about where Jesus concentrated his ministry geographically need some adjustment. Miller affirms that Jesus preached primarily at "Nazareth, Nain, Cana and especially in the Sea of Galilee area, Capernaum, Chorazin and Bethsaida. Noticeably missing are allusions to visits to Sepphoris and Tiberias."[124]

But Jesus is reported to have preached in his home village of Nazareth only once (Mt 13:53-58; Mk 6:1-6; Lk 4:16-30) and this effort met with opposition. The clear impression is that Jesus never preached there again. Likewise, there is only one reference to Jesus' being in Nain (Lk 7:11) and two references to his presence in Cana (Jn 2:1; 4:26). One hesitates to say these places were Jesus' ministerial focuses.

It does appear that Jesus concentrated on the Sea of Galilee basin. He is portrayed as living in and preaching mostly in Capernaum, which was, however, not a "rural town," but a thriving fishing-business town with a population of 12,000 to 15,000.[125] The Gospels describe his ministry in Bethsaida and Chorazin, two other large towns, in the same terms as Capernaum (Mt 11:21-23 = Lk 10:13-15). Jesus quite likely preached also in Magdala, a city Josephus said had 40,000 residents (*War* 2.608), since one of his most important disciples was Mary from Magdala (Mt 27:56, 61; Mk 15:40, 47; 16:1, 9; Lk 8:2; 24:10; Jn 19:25; 20:1, 18). Thus Jesus is often found in the cities and large towns of Galilee. He made preaching tours in the country side in Lower Galilee, but concentrated mainly on the area around the Sea.

---

[123] Miller, "Sepphoris, the Well Remembered City."

[124] Miller, "Sepphoris, the Well Remembered City," p. 79.

[125] See Overman, "Who Were the First Urban Christians?" p. 162. Miller, "Sepphoris, the Well Remembered City", p. 79, calls Capernaum a rural town.

It is true that the Gospels never expressly place Jesus in Sepphoris or Tiberias. Miller affirms that this silence indicates that these cities played no significant role in either Jesus' youth or ministry.[126] Overman and Batey suggest that Jesus intentionally avoided these cities because of the danger there from Antipas and his officials.[127]

There is, however, at least one hint that Jesus preached in Tiberias. Joanna, the wife of Chuza, one of Antipas' bureaucrats, became a disciple of Jesus (Lk 8:3). As an official of Antipas, Chuza and his family would have lived in Tiberias. Joanna could have heard Jesus preach and teach in nearby Magdala or some other city, but her presence among Jesus' disciples suggests that we should keep an open mind about whether Jesus ministered in Tiberias, the capital of Galilee. And if he preached in Tiberias without the Gospels' recording it, why not also in Sepphoris?

Arguments from silence regarding geography in the Gospels should be made with great caution. These are theological works that emphasize cities and towns with symbolic importance, such as Cana, where Jesus performed his first miracle (Jn 2:1). Thus a village which Jesus visited only once or twice may be highlighted in the Gospels because something significant happened there. Conversely, an urban center which he often visited might be seldom or never mentioned because little or nothing happened of theological importance there. If Sepphoris and Tiberias were unimportant to Jesus' ministry, we may understand their omission from the Gospels. It is likely that the large Gentile populations in these two cities would have been unimpressed with a preaching artisan. All we can really say about the silence in the Gospels regarding these two cities is that the authors never expressly place Jesus there. Anything more than that is not convincing.

CONCLUSION

We may say in conclusion that Jesus lived in an agrarian society that tended to be divided culturally into urban and rural, with the overwhelming majority of the population being rural. If the bias which prevailed throughout the ancient Greco-Roman world also existed in

---

[126] Miller, "Sepphoris, the Well Remembered City," p. 81.

[127] Overman, "Who were the First Urban Christians?" pp. 167f; Batey, "Sepphoris: An Urban Portrait of Jesus," p. 56.

Palestine, the urban residents viewed the rural peasants as inferior beings. Jesus, an artisan who probably was often in urban environments, might not have been considered with the same eye of urban snobbery. Yet he had other cultural and social barriers. Artisans were usually disdained by the elitist Greeks and Romans; the Gentile residents of the urban centers of Galilee would not have paid him much attention. On the other hand, Jews seem to have had much more respect for craftsmen.

Jesus was probably not economically destitute before his ministry. We should expect that he and his brothers worked at hard manual labor but did not want for the necessities of life. The massive building projects of Palestine—especially in Galilee—should have provided ample opportunity for work. It is even possible that his family was rather comfortable, like that of Simon the temple builder. Certain texts in the Gospels may incline us in that direction.

But in the eyes of the elite, Jesus would still have been poor. Compared to their luxurious lifestyle, he must have lived very simply and humbly. The socioeconomic distance between Jesus and the elite classes—even if he did come from a comfortable artisan family—was enormous.

THE RELATIONSHIP OF PAUL TO JESUS

INTRODUCTION

IN CERTAIN CIRCLES of scholarship it is considered axiomatic that Paul had no or little interest in the life and teachings of Jesus. The argument is that Paul knew little about Jesus of Nazareth and that he was disinterested in Jesus' deeds and teachings. Paul may have sat at the feet of Gamaliel, but never at the feet of Jesus. Instead, Paul preached only the death and resurrection of Christ the Lord. In this interpretation, the "Christic acid" of Paul's theology has dissolved the historical Jesus of Nazareth.[1]

In recent years, a number of scholars have reassessed more favorably the relationship between these two first-century Jewish luminaries, emphasizing strongly the continuity between them. Representing a wide variety of scholarship and methodologies, these investigations are dismantling older categories and presuppositions and replacing them with interpretations that more accurately reflect the historical and sociological realities of the first-century Palestinian Jesus Movement.[2]

These studies have challenged the paradigm of discontinuity on several fronts. The assumptions of form criticism have been questioned by scholars who herald tradition itself as the locus of the transmission of Jesus material from the moment of utterance through the Gospel

---

[1] Victor Paul Furnish, "The Jesus-Paul Debate: From Baur to Bultmann," *BJRL* 47 (1965) 342–81.

[2] David L. Dungan, *The Sayings of Jesus in the Churches of Paul: The Use of the Synoptic Tradition in the Regulation of Early Church Life* (Philadelphia, 1971); Dale C. Allison, "The Pauline Epistles and the Synoptic Gospels: The Pattern of the Parallels," *NTS* 28 (1982) 3–32; A. J. M. Wedderburn, "Paul and Jesus: Similarity and Continuity," *NTS* 34 (1988) 161–82.

authors.[3] Despite its lingering presence and influence, the Tübingen chasm separating Pauline from Jerusalem Christianity has been challenged by investigations of Paul's letters—including Galatians—focusing on the historical and socio-political factors conditioning the occasional nature of the correspondence.[4] These studies recognize the letters' situational and polemical nature, which account in part for Paul's characteristic use of Jesus' sayings and his remarks about the Jerusalem apostles. Recent genre and media analyses provide insights regarding the importance of the letter *qua* letter on Paul's words.[5] Such studies of Pauline rhetoric help modern denizens of the prevailing "textual culture" to appreciate how Paul's references and allusions to the spoken words of Jesus were heard and understood by his audience when his letters were read aloud to them.

This essay will examine the above themes in an effort to emphasize the continuity between Paul and Jesus, primarily with regard to Paul's knowledge and use of traditional material about Jesus. We will identify and respond to major objections to a Paul-Jesus model which displays Paul's positive interest in Jesus. We will also respond to the Tübingen specter, recently revised by Gerd Lüdemann (1983), which severed Paul from the Jerusalem apostles, from Jesus' family, and ultimately from Jesus himself.[6]

Secondly, we will apply findings in media and genre studies to the perplexing question of the paucity of explicit citations of Jesus sayings and stories in Paul's letters. The conditional nature of the Pauline letters as polemical responses to crisis situations will be related

---

[3] Birger Gerhardsson, *Memory and Manuscript: Oral and Written Transmission in Rabbinic Judaism and Early Christianity* (Uppsala, 1964); *The Origins of the Gospel Traditions* (Philadelphia, 1979).

[4] Hans J. Schoeps, *Paul: The Theology of the Apostle in the Light of Jewish Religious History* (Philadelphia, 1961); Walter Schmithals, *Paul and James* (London, 1965), pp. 71–72; J. Phillip Arnold, *Jewish Christianity in Galatians: A Study of the Teachers and Their Gospel* (Rice University Dissertation, 1991).

[5] Walter Ong, *Interfaces of the Word: Studies in the Evolution of Consciousness and Culture* (Ithaca, 1977); *Orality and Literacy* (New York, 1982); *The Presence of the Word: Some Prolegomena for Cultural and Religious History* (New Haven, 1967); Werner Kelber, *The Oral and Written Gospel* (Philadelphia, 1983); Kevin B. Maxwell, *Bemba Myth and Ritual: The Impact of Literacy on an Oral Culture* (New York, 1983).

[6] Gerd Lüdemann, *Opposition to Paul in Jewish Christianity* (Philadelphia, 1989).

to Paul's selective use of Jesus material. This essay seeks to illumine the positive role the traditions and sayings of Jesus had for Paul.

REVIEW OF RESEARCH

A brief review of the research will highlight the hermeneutical issues and clarify their implications for the study. The wedge driven between Pauline Christianity and Jerusalem Christianity by F. C. Baur in his 1831 study, "Die Christuspartei," also severed Paul from Jesus of Nazareth.[7] Baur maintained that Paul had no need for Jerusalem Christianity and its connection to the historical Jesus because Paul enjoyed direct access to the resurrected heavenly Lord from whom he had received his gospel by revelation. Since Paul's letters contain few direct references to Jesus' life and teachings, Baur reasoned that the apostle was indifferent to the historical Jesus. Heavenly revelations from the risen Christ made obedience to Jerusalem's traditions and stories about Jesus irrelevant. Although attacked by his enemies and modified by his Tübingen heirs, Baur's wedge between Pauline Christianity and the Jerusalem apostles continues to deter efforts to find continuity between Paul and Jesus.[8]

In the wake of Baur's bifurcation of earliest Christianity, other scholars magnified the chasm between Paul and Jesus. Several studies of the "Damascus Road" experience portrayed Paul's conversion as a rejection of the Jewish religion and an acceptance of a liberating gospel with a universal mission. It was claimed that the "religious genius" of Paul freed him from the constraints of Judaism and enabled him to create a new faith.[9] Since Jesus belonged within Judaism, the distance between Paul and the Nazarene increased.

The apogee of this approach was reached in William Wrede's *Paulus* in 1904.[10] Writing under the influence of Baur and the Tübingen school, Wrede conjectured that prior to his "conversion," Paul believed in *Christ* while denying *Jesus*! How could this be? Wrede explained that

---

[7] Ferdinand Christian Baur, "Die Christuspartei in der korinthischen Gemeinde," *ZTK* 5 (1831) 61–206.

[8] Lüdemann, *Opposition*, pp. 44–52, 97–104, 112–15.

[9] Furnish, "Debate," pp. 342–81.

[10] ET, William Wrede, *Paul* (London, 1907).

the pre-Christian Paul "already believed" in a heavenly Christ.[11] Paul identified this celestial Christ on the Damascus road with the resurrected Lord Jesus. Later, in his preaching and letters, Paul urged believers to enjoy mystical participation in the heavenly risen Christ. Wrede concluded that Paul had no interest in the Jesus who trod the roads of first-century Palestine. As a result of such studies, Paul appeared to be a "solitary genius" disconnected not only from Jesus, but also from the Jerusalem church, including James, Peter, and Judaism itself.[12]

In order to relocate Paul within Judaism and Christianity while maintaining his supposed distance from Jesus, Wilhelm Heitmuller and Rudolf Bultmann explained Paul's supposed deemphasis of Jesus by placing the apostle within the Hellenistic wing of Christianity. They argued that this division of Christianity had no real interest in the historical Jesus. By placing Paul within this milieu, an historical context could be posited for him while accounting for his assumed indifference to the life and teachings of Jesus.[13]

Although Bultmann concurred that the incarnation, death, and resurrection of Jesus as the messiah were crucial for Paul, the "eschatological and ethical preaching of the historical Jesus plays no role in Paul."[14] Bultmann insisted that Paul made

---

[11] *Ibid.*, pp. 151–53. Paul may well have speculated about intermediary figures, such as wisdom. Had Paul been zealous for such esoteric Jewish traditions? His familiarity with wisdom speculation and Adam figures in 1 Corinthians may suggest a prior interest in such "Jewish Christology." But Wrede is wrong to assume that Paul's Christ obviated the historical Jesus (cf. 1Cor 13:9-11; Gal 4:1-3; A. Segal, *Paul the Convert: The Apostolate and Apostacy of Saul the Pharisee* [New Haven, 1990]).

[12] Furnish, "Debate," pp. 342–81.

[13] Wilhelm Heitmuller, "Zum Problem Paulus und Jesus", *ZNW* 13 (1912) 320–37; Rudolf Bultmann, *Faith and Understanding* (New York, 1969), p. 221. Some scholars construe 2Cor 5:16 to mean that Paul rejected the historical Jesus in favor of the heavenly Christ. But Paul means that his present understanding of Jesus differs from his pre-Christian view in that he now recognizes Jesus for who he is, the promised Christ. A qualitative change (2Cor 5:17) has occurred in his *perception*. See Dieter Georgi, *The Opponents of Paul in Second Corinthians* (Philadelphia, 1986), pp. 253–54, note 160, esp. pp. 276–77. Also Bultmann, *Theology*, I, p. 238; "The Significance of the Historical Jesus for the Theology of Paul," ET in *Faith and Understanding*, I (London, 1966), p. 241.

[14] Bultmann, "The Primitive Christian Kerygma and the Historical Jesus" in *The Historical Jesus and the Kerygmatic Christ Essays on the New Quest of the Historical Jesus*, ed. by Carl E. Braaten and Roy A. Harrisville (New York, 1964), p. 20.

no effort toward communicating with Jesus' disciples or the Jerusalem Church for instruction concerning Jesus and his ministry.... All that is important for him in the story of Jesus is the fact that Jesus was born a Jew and lived under the law and that he had been crucified.[15]

For Bultmann, the Pauline "Christ of the kerygma has, as it were, displaced the historical Jesus."[16]

Günther Bornkamm also supported the view that Paul had no interest in the historical Jesus. In his 1969 *Paul*, Bornkamm states:

Never does he make the slightest effort to expound the teachings of the historical Jesus. Nowhere does he speak of the rabbi from Nazareth, the prophet and miracle-worker who ate with tax collectors and sinners, or of his Sermon on the Mount, his parables of the Kingdom of God, and his encounters with Pharisees and scribes. His letters do not even mention the Lord's Prayer.... The Jesus of history is apparently dismissed. Paul himself never met him.[17]

In response to this negative assessment of Paul's relation to Jesus, a counterattack was launched from the very beginning by scholars who saw continuity between Paul and Jesus. As early as 1858, Heinrich Paret responded to Baur's position with an article which sought to demonstrate Paul's dependence on and interest in Jesus.[18] Paret anticipated many of the arguments which were to be advanced by those who rejected the alleged dichotomy between Jesus and Paul. He attempted to show that passages from Paul's letters do, in fact, evince knowledge of the life and teachings of Jesus. He defended the relatively small quantity of Paul's references to the historical Jesus by differentiating Paul's letters from his original missionary preaching, which, Paget believed, contained much traditional Jesus material.[19]

See David B. Capes, "Tradition From Jesus to Paul" p. 8, a 1984 unpublished study at Southwestern Baptist Theological Seminary.

[15] Bultmann, *Theology of the New Testament* (2 vols; New York, 1951–1955), vol. I, p. 188.

[16] Bultmann, "Primitive," p. 30.

[17] Günther Bornkamm, *Paul* (New York, 1969), pp. 110, 238.

[18] Furnish, "Debate," pp. 342–81.

[19] *Ibid.*

More recently, recognition of Paul's positive relation to Jesus has emerged in the work of such scholars as W. D. Davies, Krister Stendahl, Birger Gerhardsson, David Dungan, and J. D. G. Dunn.[20] Davies concluded in 1948 that twenty-five instances occur in Paul's letter where Jesus' teachings are woven into traditional material (1 Cor 11:23, 15:3). He found six instances where Paul refers to a collection of Jesus sayings similar to Q. Coupled with Davies' conclusion that Paul is best understood against the backdrop of first-century Judaism, these observations underscored the continuity between the apostle and Jesus.[21] Since both figures belonged to an early form of rabbinic Judaism, the Tübingen dichotomy between Paul the Hellenist Jew and the earliest Palestinian Jewish Christians was mitigated.[22]

The growing insistence on viewing both Paul and Jesus in light of their Jewish background received significant support from the Scandinavian School, which included such scholars as Aston Fridrichesen, Stendahl, and Gerhardsson.[23] These scholars argued that first-century Christians purposely used professional techniques developed in the rabbinic schools to maintain and transmit the teachings of Jesus.

Stendahl concluded in his 1954 work on Matthew that Matthew was produced by a learned Christian school whose members were trained in the rabbinic art of tradition transmission.[24] In favor of continuity in transmission, Stendahl wrote:

> There may therefore be an unbroken line from the School of Jesus via the 'teaching of the apostles,' the 'ways' of Paul (I Cor. 4:17), the basic teaching of Mark ... the more mature School of John to the rather elaborate School of Matthew with its ingenious interpretation of the Old Testament as the crown of its scholarship.[25]

---

[20] W. D. Davies, *Paul and Rabbinic Judaism: Some Rabbinic Elements in Pauline Theology* (London, 1965). K. Stendahl, *The School of St. Matthew and Its Use of the Old Testament* (Philadelphia, 1968); Gerhardsson, *Memory*; *Origins*; D. Dungan, *Sayings*; J. D. G. Dunn *Unity and Diversity in the New Testament: An Inquiry into the Character of Earliest Christianity* (London, 1990); Peter J. Tomson, "The Halakhic Jesus Traditions in Paul and Their Implications for His Christology," a paper presented at the Society of Biblical Literature Annual Meeting, San Francisco, 1992.

[21] Davies, *Paul*, pp. 136–49.

[22] *Ibid.*, pp. 2–16.

[23] Dungan, *Sayings*, pp. xxvi–xxix.

[24] Stendahl, *School*, pp. 13–35.

[25] *Ibid.*, p. 34.

In his 1961 *Memory and Manuscript*, Gerhardsson presented evidence that the primary focus for the transmission of tradition lay not in the worship of the church, but in the act of transmission itself. The use of specific terms in Paul's letters which denote the careful preservation of traditional material indicates that Paul himself contributed to the safekeeping of Jesus material.[26]

In 1971, Stendahl's student David Dungan produced a monograph, *The Sayings of Jesus in the Churches of Paul*, supporting major assertions of Gerhardsson and the Scandinavian School. Dungan maintains that Paul not only was aware of the historical Jesus, but also played a significant role in the careful preservation of traditional material about Jesus.

Dungan based his study on two important Pauline references to the teachings of Jesus: 1 Corinthians 7:10-11 (Jesus' word against divorce) and 1 Corinthians 9:14 (Jesus' word establishing support for apostles.)[27] Paul refers to Jesus' command against divorce as authoritative and binding in 1 Corinthians 7. He carefully distinguishes the words of Jesus from his own in such a way as to show his high regard for Jesus' instructions. When he draws implications from Jesus' words, Paul is cautious to point out that he is not quoting Jesus (1Cor 7:12). Paul does this not because his own words *lack* authority for his churches, but because Jesus' words are qualitatively of higher value. Thus, Paul's use of Jesus' words demonstrates that they played an important role in the Pauline churches. From Paul's appeal to the teachings of Jesus, Dungan concludes:

> Paul stands squarely within the tradition that led to the Synoptic gospels, and is of one mind with the editors of those gospels, not only in the way he understands what Jesus (the Lord) was actually commanding in the sayings themselves but also in the way he prefigures the Synoptic editors' use of them.[28]

---

[26] Cf. 1Cor 11:23; 15:3. Gerhardsson contends that Jesus taught his followers to memorize his words after the fashion of the rabbis. These words and deeds were carefully preserved in oral and written form and were passed down through the apostles to Paul and others, eventually culminating in the Gospels. See Gerhardsson, *Memory*, pp. 288–323; *Origins*, pp. 27–41.

[27] Dungan, *Sayings*, pp. 3–131.

[28] *Ibid.*, p. 139.

Since the appearance of Dungan's work, other scholars have also determined that Paul used and passed on traditional Jesus material, some of which may have come from Jesus himself. One of the more recent and perceptive studies is that of Dale Allison, Jr. In 1982, Allison concluded that Paul not only alluded to individual sayings of Jesus, but had access to more Jesus material with which he was quite familiar.[29] Allison shows that Paul was aware of and used Jesus material which later found its way to Luke 6:27-38, Mark 9:33-50, and elsewhere. This material concerns Jesus' missionary instructions, Sermon on the Plain, community ethics, and passion.[30]

Allison also observes that Paul's conscious and deliberate use of these Jesus traditions in cluster reveals a pattern which evinces his knowledge of blocks of traditional Jesus material (Rom 12-14, 1Thes 4-5, 1Cor 11:23-24). He argues that Paul "delivered" this material to his congregations when he founded the communities. That explains why Paul often presupposes that his audience already knows important facts about Jesus—such as his relation to David (Rom 1:3); his Jewish mother (Gal 4:4); his betrayal (1Cor 11:23); the "night" (1Cor 11:23); the paschal supper (1Cor 11:23-24); and apocalyptic prophecy (1Thes 4:15-16). With Dungan, Allison presents a strong case that Paul was an important part of a transmission tradition which had a keen interest in preserving the stories, deeds, and words of the historical Jesus.

PAUL'S USE OF JESUS TRADITIONS

The "continuity consensus" forged by Davies, Dungan, Gerhardsson, Allison, and others is based on textual evidence from Paul's letters as well as reasonable inferences from them. This body of evidence is three-fold.

First, Paul taught more material that is contained in his preserved letters. He states that he had "delivered" important traditions which he had "received" (1Cor 11:23 and 15:3). His references to esoteric subjects indicates that he presupposes his audience's prior knowledge of a traditional interpretation he had given them. Paul's use of such terms as

---

[29] Allison, "Epistles," pp. 3-32.
[30] *Ibid.*, esp. p. 15.

παραλαμβάνειν, παραδιδόναι, παραδόσεις, and παρέδωκα indicates a
technical usage which implies his role in a transmission tradition which
receives, preserves, and passes on Jesus material. This transmission was
not limited to his original missionary preaching, but was continued by
Paul and his coworkers between the founding of the congregations and
his writing to them.

Second, Paul "received" these traditions from other Christians
who instructed him. This is not to negate his statement that the revelation of the gospel was "not from a human source" (Gal 1:12), but
recognizes the fact that Paul also received Jesus material from others.
His sources for this material were not limited to Hellenistic circles outside of Palestine, but included the Jerusalem "pillars"—James, the
brother of Jesus, the apostles Peter and John (Gal 1:18; 2:9)—and family members who "were in Christ before" Paul (Rom 16:7).

Third, some of these traditions about Jesus are specified and discussed in Paul's letters and contain detailed data about Jesus. They
demonstrate Paul's awareness and careful use of information about the
historical Jesus, including Jesus' Davidic origins (Rom 1:3); birth (Gal
4:4); Jewish mother (Gal 4:4); circumcision (Gal 4:4); observance of
Torah (Gal 4:4); teaching of disciples (1Cor 11:23); apocalyptic interests (1Thes 4:15-16); emphasis on an ethic of love and nonresistance to
evil (Gal 5:14, 6:2; Rom 12:14,17, 21; 13:8-10); recognition of marriage (1Cor 7:10); awareness that his disciples would preach a distinct
message (1Cor 9:14); words about financial gain for his disciples (1Cor
9:14); institution of an "eucharistic supper" and that this service took
place at night (1Cor 11:23-24); betrayal at night (1Cor 11:23); Lord's
Prayer (Gal 1:4; Col 3:13); and his disciples' failure to watch (1Thes
5:6; Rom 13:11,12; Col 4:2).

Most of these examples have received detailed analysis. Victor
Furnish, for example, thinks they hold little value as evidence for Paul's
use of Jesus traditions. He advises caution and restraint in identifying
allusions to Jesus' words and refers to the "relative sparsity of direct
references to or citation of Jesus' teachings in the Pauline letters."[31]

Allison and Fjärstedt argue that some of these instances show
Paul's knowledge and use of entire *blocks* of traditional Jesus material

---

[31] Furnish, *Theology and Ethics in Paul* (Nashville, 1978), p. 55; *Jesus
According to Paul* (Cambridge, 1993), p. 40.

from which these individual allusions are taken.[32] J. D. G. Dunn writes:

> It would appear then that Paul is able at these points to draw on quite an extensive tradition about Jesus, and to assume that his converts were also familiar with it.... This suggests in turn that the traditions which Paul passed on when he first established a new church ... included a fair amount of tradition about Jesus.[33]

The continuity between Jesus and Paul is further clarified by scholars who find similarities in the teachings of Jesus and Paul, particularly in theology and soteriology. Even Bultmann, who denied Paul's interest in the historical Jesus, noted similarities in the messages of Jesus and Paul. He and others found parallels in their their relative freedom from any external code and their mutual recognition of the centrality of love as the cardinal virtue.[34]

In a 1988 article on this issue, A. J. M. Wedderburn claimed continuity between Paul and Jesus on two grounds. First, he argued that both presented a prophetic critique of the Law. Second, both openly accepted "outsiders." Jesus received "sinners" and the "unclean;" Paul included the "ungodly" and Gentiles.[35]

Citing Eberhard Jüngel, F. F. Bruce discusses several themes shared by Paul and Jesus. He underscores their mutual emphasis on the primacy of God's grace and the importance of faith. He compares Paul's teaching on justification by faith with Jesus' parables about the kingdom of God. Both sound a strongly eschatological note which proclaims that the old aeon of Law gives way to a new age of faith. "In all of this Paul saw more clearly than most of his Christian contemporaries into the inwardness of Jesus' teaching."[36]

---

[32] Allison, "Epistles," p. 6, refers to B. Fjärstedt *Synoptic Traditions in I Corinthians: Themes and Clusters of Theme Words in I Corinthians 1-4 and 9* (Uppsala Dissertation, 1974).

[33] Dunn, *Unity*, p. 68.

[34] Bultmann, *Existence and Faith* (New York, 1960), pp. 189-95.

[35] Wedderburn, "Continuity," pp. 174-75.

[36] F. F. Bruce, *Paul Apostle of the Heart Set Free* (Grand Rapids, 1984), pp. 95-105.

CONTINUITY VERSUS DISCONTINUITY

Some scholars seem reluctant to accept and integrate these findings into their understanding of Paul and Jesus.[37] What are the primary reasons for their resistance to the proposition that Paul knew and valued traditions of Jesus? Two major questions remain unsettled. First, how radical was the discontinuity between Paul and Jerusalem Christians, including Jesus? Second, why would Paul only *allude* to Jesus sayings if he had access to so many? In order to establish more fully the positive relation of Paul to Jesus, it is imperative to confront and treat these two crucial issues.

Tübingen Reexamined

Although criticized and modified, Baur's wedge between Paul and the apostles retains a powerful place in contemporary scholarship, especially in view of its 1983 revival by Gerd Lüdemann.[38] Baur's severing of Paul from the Jerusalem "pillars" (James, Peter, and John) became the first step in separating Paul from Jesus. The likelihood that Paul acquired traditions about the historical Jesus rises in proportion to the closeness of his relation—theologically and geographically—to Jesus' brother, James, and to the original disciples, Peter and John.

Any theory which severs Paul from Jesus and his disciples stands or falls on how one understands Paul's remarks in the letter to the Galatians about the Jerusalem community and its "pillar" apostles, James, Peter, and John. It is in Galatians that Paul distances himself from Jerusalem and publicly rebukes Peter in Antioch when the latter was persuaded by "the men from James" (2:12) to separate from fellowship with uncircumcised Gentiles.

Only by reading Galatians into Paul's other letters could the Tübingen school claim that the Jerusalem "pillar" apostles are Paul's opponents throughout his correspondence. Paul's letters nowhere identify his "opponents" as Jesus' family or apostles.[39] Outside Galatians, Paul approvingly cites both Peter and James as Christian witnesses to

---

[37] See Calvin J. Roetzel, *The Letters of Paul: Conversations in Context* (Atlanta, 1975), pp. 33–37. Furnish, *Theology*, pp. 51–67.

[38] Lüdemann, *Opposition*, pp. xv–32, 38–39, 113–15.

[39] E.g., Paul never identifies the rival apostles in 2Cor 12:11.

the resurrection (1Cor 15:1-5). Earlier in 1 Corinthians, Paul expresses no regret that Peter had ministered to the Corinthian congregation (9:5). And the "brothers of the Lord" are singled out as examples of acceptable Christian conduct (9:5). In none of these letters does Paul identify his "opponents" as Jesus' family or apostles—not even in Galatians.

Paul and Jerusalem

It has been argued that Paul's statements in the autobiographical section of Galatians confirm his disinterest in traditions about the historical Jesus, since there he denies that he received his gospel "from a human source" (1:12).[40] He was content to receive heavenly revelations from the risen Lord.

It is certain that Galatians 1:12-13 intentionally creates space between Paul and the Jerusalem Christian leaders, but what is Paul's reason for distancing himself? Is it to sever himself from the historical Jesus? Is it to demonstrate that he has no regard for the words and deeds of Jesus? By no means! Paul was simply seeking to certify that his authority to preach his gospel about Jesus to the Gentiles was not dependent on the Jerusalem leadership.

The issue under debate in the letter concerns the source of Paul's authority for his apostolic mission to Galatia and the Gentile world, not his interest in Jesus traditions or his Christian fellowship and theological agreement with the Jerusalem "pillars." The "opponents" in Galatia attacked Paul's gospel-mission to the Gentiles and assigned him a subordinate role to the Jerusalem leadership. In response to their defamation of his gospel, authority, and character, Paul asserts the divine origin of his mission to the Gentiles and his equality with the Jerusalem apostles. The distance Paul establishes in Galatians does not reflect theological disparity between Paul and Jerusalem nor his disinterest in Jesus. Rather, it authenticates the validity, authority, and freedom of his Gentile apostolate.[41]

---

[40] Bultmann, *Theology*, I, p. 188.

[41] H. D. Betz, *Galatians: A Commentary on Paul's Letter to the Churches in Galatia* (Philadelphia, 1979), pp. 98–99, 229; W. Schmithals, *Paul and the Gnostics* (Nashville, 1972), pp. 29–32; Arnold, *Jewish Christianity*, pp. 89–95; J. D. G. Dunn, "The Relationship Between Paul and Jerusalem According to Galatians 1 and 2," in *Jesus, Paul and the Law: Studies in Mark and Galatians* (Louisville, 1990) pp. 108–28.

After establishing that his authority to preach his gospel was not dependent on Jerusalem, Paul shows that the content of his gospel revelation is fully compatible with that preached by Jesus' own brother and disciples. Paul asserts the similarity of his gospel message to that of the Jerusalem leaders in Galatians 2:6-9. His gospel tradition was fully acceptable to the Jerusalem "pillars"; they "added nothing." In fact, they offered him full fellowship and treated him as an equal.

In Galatians 1:18-19 Paul verifies that he spent two weeks with Peter and visited with James. Did Paul visit or discuss with Peter the site of the crucifixion, the "empty tomb," the paschal supper, or the betrayal? Dunn writes that the use of ἱστορῆσαι in 1:18 indicates that Paul visited Peter to get information from him "no doubt primarily background information about the ministry of Jesus while on earth."[42] Here was an excellent opportunity for Paul to acquire traditions—oral or written—which he would later "deliver" to his Gentile churches (cf. 1Cor 15:1-5)!

The "False Brothers" and the "Pillars"

To validate Baur's theory, some scholars identify the "false brothers" of Galatians 2:4 (and/or the Galatian "opponents" of Paul) with the pillar apostles of 2:9.[43] However, such an identification is not found in the Galatian text. The "false brothers" and the Galatian opponents were theologically to the right of the pillars. This wing of the Jesus Movement was Torah-observant and believed that the Law provided eschatological life in the Spirit for both Jews and Gentiles. As a third force in the early Jesus Movement, this Jewish-Christian tradition insisted on Gentile obedience to the Torah—the repository of power and revelation.[44]

---

[42] Ibid., pp. 108-10.

[43] See Lüdemann, Opposition, pp. 1-63, 97-103, for a review of Tübingen interpretations.

[44] Charles H. Cosgrove, The Cross and the Spirit: A Study in the Argument and Theology of Galatians (Macon, 1988), pp. 38-52; Arnold, Jewish Christianity, pp. 130-48, 202-42. The Galatian Torah-observant "teachers" must not be reduced to mere "legalists" who sought to merit "right-standing" before God by works of the Law. Instead, they represent a Jewish Christianity which regarded the Torah as the sacred path leading the observant Christian to greater degrees of the Spirit and its charismatic revelations. The debate in Galatians is over how one receives the Spirit ("righteousness" as eschatological life), not how one is juridically justified. Paul claims that faith brings the Spirit. The teachers answer that the Torah channels it (Gal 3:3-

If this line of interpretation is correct, at least three circles of influence existed in the early Jesus Movement around 50 C.E. On the right were the "false brothers" who demanded that Titus (2:3) and other Gentile converts be circumcised and take on the "yoke of Torah" (understood positively), or (as Paul would say) come "into bondage" under the Law (2:4). On the left were the Paulinists (1:1) who insisted that Gentile converts were free from the Law and were "not compelled to be circumcised" (2:3). Occupying a middle ground were the pillars—James, Peter, and John—who acknowledged that Gentiles were free from the Law (2:6,9), but encouraged Jewish believers to maintain some Torah observances.

The Jerusalem meeting described in Galatians 2 resulted in an accord between the pillars and Paul in which the pillars "added nothing" (2:6) to Paul's Law-free gospel. Rather, they acknowledged Paul's right to preach his gospel to the Gentiles and gave Paul and Barnabas "the right hand of fellowship" (2:9). By averring that the pillars supported his mission, Paul implies that the "false brothers" failed to convince the pillars of the need for Gentiles to observe the Jewish Law.

Even if Paul prejudiced the account in his favor, we cannot believe that the pillars sided with the "false brothers" in demanding Gentile obedience to the Law. Some kind of accord was reached between the Paulinists and the pillars regarding the Gentile mission. The text affirms that this accord recognized Paul's right to continue his Law-free gospel to the Gentiles, requiring only that he "remember" the Jerusalem poor. The existence of the accord shows that the left wing and center of the Jesus Movement had by 50 C.E. evolved through debate and discussion into a cooperative fellowship (2:9).

Although Paul does not report how the "false brothers" reacted to the agreement between the pillars and the Paulinists, we must not assume that the Torah-observant "false brothers" agreed to the accord. The text does not include them in the agreement between the pillars and the Paulinists. From 2:5 we infer that the "false brothers" and Paul reached no agreement whatsoever. Their Galatian allies—the teachers of the Torah opposing Paul—are cursed for preaching a false gospel

5,14,21).

(1:8,9). Had the "false brothers" compromised their Law-abiding position and dropped their demand for circumcision, Paul would surely have informed the Galatian audience! The absence of such information indicates that the "false brothers" rejected the accord. Believing that their interpretation of the Christian gospel was correct, these members of the early Jesus Movement continued to demand of Gentiles obedience to the Law despite the opinion of Paul and the pillars.

The Antioch Episode

Recognizing the apparent implausibility of considering the pillar apostles as part of the right-wing "false brothers" at the time of the accord around 50 C.E., Lüdemann believes that James *later* joined the anti-Pauline Law-abiding wing represented by these "false brothers" and the Galatian "opponents." For support of his theory, Lüdemann argues that James' ascendancy to power *increased* during Peter's absence. With Peter away from Jerusalem after the conference, James's conservative tendency toward a Torah-observant theology converged with the "right-wing" circle of the "false brothers" to form a strong Law-abiding Jerusalem community. Lüdemann believes that it was this circle, under James' leadership, which later instigated the Antioch episode discussed in Galatians 2:11.[45] The text states:

> But when Cephas [Peter] came to Antioch I opposed him to his face, because he stood condemned. For before *certain men came from James* [τινας ἀπὸ Ἰακώβου] he ate with the Gentiles; but when they came, he drew back and separated himself, fearing the circumcision party [τοὺς ἐκ περιτομῆς].

Lüdemann argues that the Jerusalem visitors demanded Gentile obedience to circumcision and other Jewish laws.[46] They persuaded Peter and certain Paulinists to repudiate Paul's gospel and conform to the circumcision party of James and the nomists. In this way, Lüdemann attempts to explain how the apparent agreement between the pillars and Paul in 2:9 broke down. This permits Lüdemann to oppose the Jewish

---

[45] Lüdemann, *Opposition*, pp. 38–39. "The incident at Antioch must therefore be classified as an anti-Pauline action on the part of James the Lord's brother."
[46] *Ibid.*

Christians and the maverick Paul with his Gentile congregations and and to maintain essential discontinuity between Paul and Jesus.

If Lüdemann is correct, James must later have thrown his support behind the "right wing" of the Jesus Movement represented by the "false brothers" and Galatian "opponents." Paul's opponents would then consist of his Galatian foes, the "false brothers," and the pillar apostles! This provocative interpretation would align the earliest followers of Jesus against Paul, an interloper with little or no historical or theological connection to Jesus or the original followers or family members of Jesus—James, John, Peter, and "the twelve."

If Lüdemann's interpretation stands, one must suspect that the teachers' gospel tradition was more similar to that of the earliest Jesus tradition than was Paul's. If the pillars, the "false brothers," the "men from James," and the teachers all agreed that faithfulness to Jesus required obeying the Law, why should Paul be believed? Paul freely admits that he was not one of the original followers of Jesus. Was the Torah teachers' gospel more faithful to or continuous with Jesus's teaching than Paul's gospel was? Lüdemann's claim that James broke his earlier accord with the Paulinists does not have a strong basis in the Galatian letter. Peter's absence from Jerusalem does not account for James' disavowal of the accord made with Paul and Barnabas.

There are important reasons to reject Lüdemann's explanation of James' theological position. First, the Galatian passage does not state that James disagreed with the Paulinists nor that James changed his opinion. Galatians 2:9 says that James, Peter, and John agreed with the Paulinists and sealed the accord with the "right hand of fellowship." Second, Lüdemann's only evidence from Galatians of a change in James' position is his connection with those who "came from James" to Antioch (Gal 2:12). This is insufficient reason to believe that James reneged on his agreement with Paul and sided with the Jewish-Christian "false brothers."

Since Paul implies that James did not side with the "false brothers" at the time of the Jerusalem accord, it is unlikely that the persons who came to Antioch in 2:12 implemented James' official orders to impose the Law on the Paulinist congregation in Antioch. Paul would hardly have implicated James in the Antioch episode in 2:12 after citing him for support in 2:9!

Several alternative interpretations of the passage in 2:12 more effectively explain the presence of the Jerusalem visitors. The text does not specify that the people "from James" represented his theological viewpoint or had his official authorization to impose the Law.[47] The visitors may have been Law-abiding associates of James without being an official delegation sent by him. Thus, their insistence that Gentiles be Law-observant may not represent the position of James and the moderate leadership reflected in 2:9.

The interpretation that best explains the Antioch episode focuses attention on *why* the people from James urged the Antioch congregation to observe the Law. This explanation takes into account the agreement between James and Paul in 2:9 as well as the visitation from Jerusalem.

Galatians 2:12 states that Peter refused to eat with the Gentile Christians and "separated himself" from them—"fearing the circumcision." This signifies that the visitors from Jerusalem, as well as Peter, Barnabas, and others discontinued table fellowship with the Gentiles because they feared further persecution from *non-Christian* Jews who zealously protected their Jewish customs and identity. We must not assume that "circumcision" ($\tau o\grave{v}\varsigma\ \grave{\epsilon}\kappa\ \pi\epsilon\rho\iota\tau o\mu\tilde{\eta}\varsigma$) refers to Christians who are Jews.[48] Three times in 2:7-9 the same term refers specifically to non-Christian Jews. Paul never uses the term to denote Jewish Christians; he employs it only to specify non-Christian Jews. Thus, Paul believed that Peter and Barnabas feared persecution (Gal 6:12) from non-Christian Jews—not from James, from the visitors, or from the Jewish *Christian* circumcision party!

Jewett, Schmithals, and Dunn argue that the Antioch episode must be understood in view of the socio-political crisis at the time.[49] Zealot unrest and Jewish nationalism were rising to fever pitch during this period. Cordial relationships with the Jewish community in Jerusalem were necessary for Christian survival. In order to maintains such relationships, James permitted associates from Jerusalem ("the men from James") to travel to Antioch to ensure the cooperation of the Antioch Jewish and Gentile Christians in avoiding any pretext for persecution. That Peter and certain Paulinists quickly cooperated indicates that they did not consider the issue a theological one nor did it signify a

---

[47] Discussed in Schmithals, *James*, p. 67, note 12.

[48] See the correct analysis in Schmithals, *James*, p. 66.

[49] Robert Jewett, "The Agitators and the Galatian Congregations," *NTS* 17 (1971) 196–218; Schmithals, *James*, p. 66; Dunn, "The Incident at Antioch (Gal. 2:11-18)." In *Law*, pp. 129–82.

rejection of the accord. It was a matter of expediency—an impromptu action expressing flexibility and cooperation with Jerusalem in the face of the threat of renewed persecution from some non-Christian Jews zealous for the Law and Jewish nationalism.

Paul does not attack Peter and his sympathizers for theological errors or for preaching a "false gospel." He accuses them of hypocrisy (2:13) in the face of persecution.[50] What to Paul was hypocrisy was to Peter and certain Paulinists a spirit of cooperation and compromise. They cooperated with the Jerusalem community in an effort to alleviate possible persecution. There is no evidence of theological disagreement over the Law between Paul and Peter in Antioch.

We cannot conclude that fundamental differences existed between Paul and James on the issue of Gentile obedience to the Torah. The accord made by James, Peter, John, and Paul was not rejected in principle in Antioch. To relieve the threat of persecution, James requested that Antioch suspend table fellowship between Jewish and Gentile Christians. Several of the Paulinists agreed with this pragmatic program. For Paul, this compromise was hypocritical and originated from cowardice. Paul's fearlessness and bravado resulted in his "defeat" at Antioch and, according to tradition, later contributed to his capture and death.[51]

We cannot concur with the Tübingen school, ranging from Baur to Lüdemann, that James underwent a transformation of theology—or began to enforce "latent" Torah-observant policies on Gentiles—once he gained more power in the absence of Peter. The Antioch episode is better understood as a cooperative effort on the part of the Jerusalem community under James and the Antioch congregation to be less offensive to non-Christian Judaism. Paul's protest does not reflect a fundamental opposition between Paul's gospel and James's gospel. Within a few years Paul writes positively of Peter and Barnabas as well as of James.[52] Paul continues to honor his part of the original accord to provide a collection for the "poor" in Jerusalem.[53]

---

[50] Schmithals, *James*, pp. 71–72.

[51] Acts 20:22–28:30; cf. 2Tim 4:6-8.

[52] 1Cor 3:22; 9:5,6; 15:5-7; cf. Col 4:10.

[53] 1Cor 16:1-4; 2Cor 8:2-4; 9:3-15; Rom 15:25-28. Some hold that James and the Jerusalem church rejected the collection. They believe Luke failed to mention this rejection because he intended to downplay its evidence of tension between Paul and Jerusalem. But Luke may have had other reasons for not reporting that Paul delivered a

What is the significance of this interpretation for our understanding of James and his relationship to Paul's opponents? And what of Paul's relation to Jerusalem and Jesus? Since James is not to be identified with the "false brothers" nor with a Gentile Law-observant gospel tradition, we cannot believe that the Galatian opponents authentically represent James or his circle. The Galatian teachers' alternative gospel is *not* the same gospel preached by James, Peter, John, or Paul. Instead, the Galatian teachers and the "false brothers" belonged to an independent nomist tradition in the Jesus Movement which insisted on Torah obedience for Jews and Gentiles.

From this analysis we conclude that the alleged dichotomy between Paul and the Jerusalem "pillars" did not exist. No significant theological gap existed between Paul and these members of Jesus' disciples and family. The Jerusalem Christian community valued Jesus' life and teachings as a vital part of its gospel proclamation. Jesus' family and disciples—James, Peter, John—found Paul's gospel compatible with theirs. Thus, it is reasonable to conclude that Paul's gospel included—not excluded—a significant place for the deeds and teachings of Jesus.

Why Paul Alludes to Jesus Sayings

The second major barrier to accepting Paul's continuity with the historical Jesus concerns Paul's apparent lack of direct citations of Jesus' sayings in his letters. Paul refers to the words of Jesus in his letters in three ways. He uses two direct citations (1Cor 11:24,25), a few explicit references (1Cor 7:10; 9:14; 11:23; 1Cor 14:37; and 1Thess 4:15-16), but over two dozen *allusions* as enumerated by Davies.[54] Why does Paul almost always only *allude* to Jesus' sayings? In the words of Albert Schweitzer: "If so many utterances of Jesus are hovering before Paul's mind, how comes it that he always merely paraphrases them, instead of quoting them as sayings of Jesus and thus sheltering

---

large amount of money to Jerusalem on the eve of the Jewish revolt against Rome. Even if the collection did not fall into the hands of Jewish Christians sympathetic to the Zealots, Luke would have wanted to avoid the perception of such a possibility. In Acts 24:2,5,12 sedition is part of the accusation leveled against Paul. Paul explains that the collection had nothing to do with sedition in 24:17-18 (*Contra* Lüdemann, *Opposition*, pp. 59-60; *pace* Dunn, *Unity*, pp. 256-57).

[54] Davies, *Paul*, pp. 136-49.

himself behind their authority?"[55] Dungan concluded that it was simply "Paul's characteristic way to *cite* sayings of the Lord by doing so allusively."[56] But *why* was this "Paul's characteristic way"? Since this question has not been answered adequately, it is often raised in an effort to resist the evidence amassed by Davies, Dungan, Gerhardsson, and Allison that Paul knew and preserved Jesus material.[57]

We offer two responses for consideration. The first is indebted to the media and rhetoric studies of Walter Ong and others on the nature of oral discourse and the letter genre.[58] The second concerns the nature and diversity of the Pauline "opponents" against which the various letters were written.[59] An examination of these two issues provides important insights into *why* Paul's letters do not cite the words of Jesus more directly and more often.

Media, Genre, and Rhetoric

The disinterest of Schweitzer, Bultmann, Bornkamm, and Furnish in media studies impaired their ability to appreciate the significance of the letter medium upon the content of Paul's writing. Recent studies by Ong, Kelber, and Maxwell have examined how the specific medium in which words are cast shapes the content of the message.[60] Certain media are more conducive than others for carrying and expressing particular messages. The medium which carries the oral or written word helps shape the communication.

The function of the letter genre for Paul and for other Christian writers of the first century was not to tell stories or cite the words of Jesus. Paul used the specialized function of the letter genre to maintain contact with his scattered congregations and to remind them of his love

[55] Dungan, *Sayings*, p. xxiv. Paul often alludes to and cites from scripture. However it is questionable whether the use of an ancient *written* text can be compared to the rhetorical use of an oral sayings tradition of recent origin. See Ellis, *Paul's Use of the Old Testament* (Grand Rapids, 1957).

[56] Dungan, *Sayings*, p. 149.

[57] Roetzel, *Letters*, p. 33; Bornkamm, *Paul*, pp. 109–12; Furnish, *Theology*, pp. 51–67.

[58] Ong, *Interfaces*; Kelber, *Oral*; Maxwell, *Myth*.

[59] Ellis, "Paul and His Opponents," in *Christianity, Judaism, and Other Greco-Roman cults: Studies for Morton Smith at Sixty*. ed. J. Neusner (Leiden, 1975).

[60] Ong, *Interfaces*; Kelber, *Oral*; Maxwell, *Myth*.

for them, his authority over them, and his instructions for them. He did not write treatises, gospels, or collections of sayings.[61]

Instead, Paul used the letter genre as the medium through which to manifest his "apostolic parousia" to the congregations.[62] Through this vehicle, Paul reminded his audience that he delivered blocks of traditions to them when he was physically present among them. He recalled specific items within these traditions to their memory by indirect references and allusions. The letters often promise an imminent visit when he would personally (orally) expound and expand his written solutions to the congregations, if needed.[63] "The subsequent reading of his letters in the primitive Christian communities would then have been the occasions for full exposition and expansion of the sketch of material in the letter."[64]

The letter genre conditioned the written content by imposing upon it certain limitations. In not listing the sayings of Jesus, citing his parables, or narrating stories about Jesus, Paul is showing respect—consciously or unconsciously—to the letter genre. Paul's references to Jesus are limited to the confines of this medium and are characterized by rhetoric appropriate to it, including indirect references and allusions.

Ong has contrasted the oral-aural world with the textualized world in which moderns live. It is often difficult for modern readers to transcend the bias toward textuality and participate in the dynamic, living world of rhetoric and orality. To demand that Paul use "direct quotations" if he really knows Jesus sayings imposes anachronistic categories of textuality on the realm of rhetoric in which the preacher Paul lived.

Rhetoric has its own high standards for measuring competence and artistry. It produces techniques and strategies which facilitate its oral and written performances. Mnemonic devices, such as alliteration, assonance, cadence, repetition, indirectness and allusions, play a central

[61] William G. Doty, *Letters in Primitive Christianity* (Philadelphia, 1973), pp. 21–68; William A. Beardslee, *Literary Criticism of the New Testament* (Philadelphia, 1970).

[62] Robert W. Funk, "The Apostolic Parousia: Form and Significance." In *Christian History and Interpretation: Studies Presented to John Knox*, ed. W. R. Farmer, C. F. D. Moule, and R. R. Niebuhr (New York, 1967).

[63] *Ibid.*, pp. 249–68.

[64] Douty, *Letters*, p. 46.

role. Attempts to control the rhetorical moment by the imposition of static forms common to textuality disrupts the oral event, deadening it and freezing its inherent dynamic. The standards and strategies of Paul's rhetoric must be recognized and respected in their own right.

Paul's allusions stimulate his audiences' memory and engage them more dynamically in the communication event. When his words were eventually spoken to a listening audience, Paul's presence was generated and experienced by the hearers. In this way, in line with the rhetorical cannons of his chosen medium, Paul actually does—*contra* Schweitzer—shelter himself behind the authority of the words of Jesus.

Polemics and Situation

The second response to why Paul hesitates to explicitly quote Jesus' words concerns the situational and contextual nature of the letters. It is no coincidence that a frequency analysis of his correspondence reveals a greater number of references to Jesus' words and traditions in 1 Corinthians than in Galatians. The former contains at least a dozen references, whereas Galatians has perhaps two—a difference disproportionate to the size of the letters. Since both letters are clearly polemical, the difference in frequency may be related to the context— the polemical situation.[65]

1 Corinthians: Opponents and Jesus Sayings

An analysis of 1 Corinthians by James Robinson and others indicates that the crisis addressed by Paul included the use or "misuse" of a Jesus sayings tradition by the opponents in Corinth.[66] Birger Pearson correctly identified this opposition as realized eschatologists (the "spiritual ones") who enjoyed the realized kingdom through a Law-free gospel which emphasized the role of the Spirit and the importance of wisdom.[67] Such a gospel liberated the "spiritual ones" to enjoy an antinomian existence freed from the normative structures of life found under the Torah or in the Christian community. As evidence of their

[65] Davies, *Paul*, pp. 136–49.

[66] James M. Robinson, "Kerygma and History in the New Testament," in *Trajectories through Early Christianity* (Philadelphia, 1971), pp. 20–70, esp. pp. 40–46.

[67] Birger A. Pearson, *The Pneumatikos-Psychikos Terminology in I Corinthians* (SBLDS 12; Chico, Cal., 1973).

realized eschatological life in the spirit, the "spiritual ones" experienced charismatic gifts such as healings, glossolalia, and prophecy. Robinson traces such theological interests on a trajectory from Jewish wisdom speculation through Q to the Gospel of Thomas and the Pirqé 'Abot—all of which highlight the central importance of wisdom sayings independent of historical narrative context. In Corinth, Paul encountered "opponents" who cited free-floating Jesus sayings in a manner similar to Q and the Gospel of Thomas.[68]

Paul finds himself in the awkward position of having to defend his gospel traditions against sayings of Jesus. Paul encountered opponents in Corinth who knew and used Jesus sayings to support their insistence on financial support from the Corinthians. So Paul attempted to contextualize these disembodied oral citations in his text. Once embedded in the structure of his letter, the oral dynamic and power of the free-floating words will be quieted and brought under contextual control. Paul uses the Jesus of his inherited tradition to silence the Jesus of the opposing tradition.

In several important references to the words of Jesus in 1 Corinthians, Paul displays a concern with the "misuse" of these sayings. In response to his opponents' use of what may be Jesus' recognition of celibacy in his "eunuchs of the kingdom" saying, Paul agrees that marriage is not for all (7:8). But Paul quickly qualifies their use of this saying by restricting celibacy to those who possess a special "gift." Next, he agrees with Jesus' command against divorce, but permits some exceptions. In 9:14 he admits that Jesus' words teach that those who "proclaim the gospel should get their living by the gospel," but Paul confesses that he does not do it (9:15). In 13:2 Paul alludes to Jesus' saying that mountain-moving faith is a possibility for his followers, but Paul counters that one could have such faith as Jesus described and be "as nothing."

In this way, the Corinthian situation influenced Paul's selection and use of sayings of Jesus—both in the manner and frequency of use. Finding himself in an awkward situation where the opposition were also citing the words of Jesus, Paul carefully positioned the words of Jesus in a written *context* which, he believed, was faithful to the Jesus tradi-

---

[68] Robinson, *"History"* pp. 56–57; *LOGOI SOPHON. On the Gattung of Q*, in *Trajectories*; pp. 71–113.

tion he received. The polemical situation conditioned and limited Paul's use of Jesus sayings in this letter. Realizing that little was to be gained by escalating the battle over the exact meaning of Jesus' words, Paul shifted to the theological and ethical significance of Jesus' death and resurrection (1Cor 1, 11–12).

Galatians: Opponents and Jesus Traditions

The polemical nature of Paul's letter to the Galatians also accounts for his stance toward Jesus material. Paul encountered Jewish-Christian teachers of the Torah as his "opponents." According to their "other gospel," Gentile converts to Jesus had to submit to the Jewish rite of circumcision, obey selected portions of the Torah, and observe the sabbath and other holy days (6:12; 4:10). These Torah teachers cited the scriptural examples of Abraham and Moses as models for Gentile proselytes to follow (2:6-19). And Jesus was a primary role model.

After examining the role and function played by Jesus' life and teachings for the Galatian teachers, we will investigate Paul's response to their Jesus traditions. This inquiry will account for Paul's apparent disregard for Jesus' words in Galatians and thus illumine Paul's use of Jesus material.

The Galatian teachers apparently proclaimed that Jesus taught his followers—both Jews and Gentiles—to submit to circumcision and obey the Torah. The teachers elevated Jesus to a central and exemplary role. That the teachers advocated a positive role for Jesus can be seen from 1:7, where the teachers are said to "pervert" the gospel message about Jesus. They are not accused of rejecting Jesus, nor of denying him, as are the unbelievers in 1 Thessalonians 2:15. The letter nowhere denounces the teachers or the Galatians for rejecting Jesus. Rather, the letter argues that the teachers preached a "different gospel" about Jesus.

Indications of the type of Jesus traditions propagated by these Christian teachers are found in 4:4 and 5. The passage says, "But when the time had fully come, God sent forth his son, born of woman born under the law: to redeem those who were under the law." Galatians 4:4-5 has long been regarded as a repository of pre-Pauline traditional material about the role and function of Jesus.[69]

---

[69] Betz, *Galatians*, pp. 205-6, ns. 38, 40.

E. Schweizer and others have analyzed the Pauline redaction and use of the tradition.[70] These studies indicate that 4:4 contains pre-Pauline material, whereas most of 4:5 consists of Pauline redaction and interpretation. The ideology of the traditional material was not conducive to Pauline thought—especially in the argument here. According to this passage, a Jewish woman gave birth to a Jewish son who was subject to circumcision and the Law of Moses and was sent by the God of Israel to free those in bondage (4:4,5). Such an understanding of Jesus fits best with the teachers' advocacy of Torah-obedience.

Why would Paul introduce a tradition that undercut his point? Such an admission would seem the last thing Paul would want to attribute to the Christ who frees believers (5:1,2; 6:15) from the Law. Yet, we find interjected into Paul's polemic against the Law the statement that Christ was subservient to the Law from the moment of his birth "under the law." The close association of Jesus' birth and his obedience to the Law suggests that Jesus was circumcised at birth in conformity with the Torah, which required the rite be performed on the correct calendar date after birth. Paul's apparent confirmation that Jesus was obedient to the Law—including circumcision—creates the difficult quandary that he forbade for the Galatians exactly what Jesus practiced!

It is difficult to believe that Paul was the first to supply this information to the Galatians, since it tends to subvert his own position. It is much more likely that the teachers informed the Galatians of the tradition that Jesus obeyed and taught his followers to keep the Law.

Galatians 4:4

The tradition encountered and reworked in 4:4 and 5 used the phrase ὑπὸ νόμον to communicate their positive valuation of the Law. Paul is at pains to reinterpret the tradition in a way that is compatible with his Law-free gospel. His rhetorical strategy conditioned the audience earlier in the letter to respond to the phrase "under the law" with a negative assessment. The letter's previous pejorative use of similar phrases such as "under the curse" (3:10), "under the curse of the law" (3:13), "under sin" (3:22), "under a custodian" (3:25) prepares the reader for the pejorative use in 4:4 and 5. Thus, the

---

[70] Eduard Schweizer, "υἱός," *TDNT*, (10 vols., Grand Rapids, 1964–1976), vol. VIII, pp. 363–92.

teachers' positive phrase, ὑπὸ νόμον, is repetitively tainted by Paul with the negative connotations of burden, curse, prison, and finally slavery.

Upon learning in 4:4 that Jesus was "born under the law," the reader regrets it. Paul does not reject or deny the historicity of this tradition, but argues in 4:5 that Jesus' life and death "under the law" redeems Jews and Gentiles from the Law. In a concerted effort to reinterpret the teachers' positive assessment of Jesus' obedience to the Law, Paul refashions "under the law" by reprogramming his Galatian audience to hear the phrase rather negatively. The language in 4:4-5 corrects the role Jesus enjoyed in the teachers' tradition as a Jew subject in all matters to the Law.

The teachers had profitted from a Jesus tradition which portrayed him as a teacher of the Law. They used or introduced the phrase "under the Law" and the remaining elements of the tradition in 4:4 as support for their understanding of Jesus. The tradition served their purpose by describing Jesus as one who remained obedient to the Torah throughout his life.

The teachers also profitted from the tradition describing Jesus as "born of a woman" (4:4). This part of the tradition drew attention to the particularity of Jesus' human birth from a Jewish woman and the legal necessity of circumcision eight days after his birth. It identified him as a recipient of the covenant and placed him alongside Abraham and Moses as obedient to the Torah. For the teachers, the rite of circumcision was the common denominator between the Abrahamic covenant, Sinai, and Jesus' gospel.

In the teachers' traditions about Jesus, his gospel ratified the original covenant. Consequently, there was no severance of the "old" covenant from the "new" gospel of Jesus in the teachers' gospel. Their gospel preserved the seamless continuity of *Heilsgeschichte*.

Galatians 6:2

Since Jesus was subject to the Law, it is plausible to assume that for the teachers of the Law, Jesus himself played the role of Teacher of the Law. The phrase "the law of Christ" (τὸν νόμον τοῦ Χριστοῦ) in 6:2 supports this interpretation.[71] This un-Pauline phrase appears only once

---

[71] Donald Allen Stoike, *"The Law of Christ:" A Study of Paul's Use of the Expression in Galatians 6:2.* (Dissertation, School of Theology at Claremont, 1971.)

and seems contradictory in a polemic against the Law. Throughout the letter Paul has reiterated that those in Christ do not need to be circumcised, obey the Law, or be "under the law." Yet in 6:2, he commands his readers to fulfill "the law of Christ!" Since Paul does not portray Jesus as a teacher of the Law, the phrase strikes a discordant note.

Paul is likely quoting the phrase "law of Christ" as a slogan of the teachers' theology.[72] First, the notion appears only here in Paul's writings. Second, some non-Pauline Christian traditions considered Jesus Christ to be a teacher of the Law—for example, the second-century Jewish-Christian *Kergymata Petrou*.[73] Third, the teachers combined Law-keeping with obedience to Christ. Fourth, the teachers contrasted their model of Jesus Christ, "born under the law," with Paul's lawless Christ, the "agent of sin" (2:17; 4:4). As Betz says, had the concept of the "law of Christ" been part of Paul's gospel proclamation and teaching, he would have introduced it earlier in the letter and it would appear in other letters. It is also probable that he would have argued in 1:7-8 against a "different law of Christ," not against a "different gospel." We concur with Betz that "the law of Christ" reflects the teachers' understanding of Jesus' teaching.

Even if Paul did not take "the law of Christ" from the teachers' vocabulary, it nevertheless expresses the teachers' understanding of Jesus Christ as a teacher of the Law. Its effective use by Paul presupposes that the Galatian nomists regarded Jesus as one who taught obedience. In Galatians, Paul's gospel does not portray Jesus as one who must be *obeyed*, but as the crucified and resurrected Lord in whom one believes.[74] Paul used the image of Christ as a Law-giver in 6:2 because he believed it would be understood by his readers, which implies that his audience was favorably disposed to understanding Jesus as a teacher of the Law. Paul recognized this familiarity and constructed or borrowed a phrase which resonated with his audiences' under-

---

[72] Cf. Betz, *Galatians*, pp. 300–1.

[73] For the *Kerygmata Petrou*, see "Pseudo-Clementine Literature" in *Ante-Nicene Fathers*, vol. VII (Buffalo, 1886), pp. 75–360; G. Strecker, "The *Kerygmata Petrou*" in *New Testament Apocrypha*, vol. II, ed. Edgar Hennecke and Wilhelm Schneemelcher (Philadelphia, 1965), pp. 102–11. For the "Book of Elkesai," see *NTA* II, pp. 745–50. The Christian tradition represented by the Gospel of Matthew also portrays Jesus as a teacher of the Law (cf. 5:2,17-20).

[74] Gal. 1:1; 2:20; 3:13; 6:14,17.

standing. Betz concludes: "The unique position of the notion of law of Christ makes it most likely that it is used here polemically."[75]

The teachers had brought to the Gentiles their Jesus traditions, including his teachings as the "law of Christ." The "law of Christ" complemented previous revelations and covenants. Their Jesus was a circumcised, Torah-observant teacher who ratified the covenant. For the teachers, the "law of Christ" affirmed obedience to the Torah, especially circumcision and the Jewish festivals (4:10). The teachers' understanding of Jesus was consistent with their gospel, which compelled submission to the covenant and Torah. The teachers' gospel proclaimed a Jesus whose birth, life, and teachings elucidated and exemplified the Torah.

Jesus' teachings about the Law may have represented the primary hermeneutic for their alternate gospel. Since the teachers were Jewish *Christians* who proclaimed a gospel about Christ, his Torah-observant life and his messianic law conditioned the content of their gospel. As the messianic teacher, Jesus' interpretation of the Law determined the applicability and significance of the Torah for his followers. Davies writes:

> It is fundamental to recognize that a messianic movement inevitably had to come to terms with the law.... Despite the firmly entrenched doctrine that the law was perfect, unchangeable, and eternal, some expected that Elijah would be a messianic forerunner who would explain obscurities in the law, that in the Messianic Age or in the Age to Come difficulties in the law would be explained, that certain enactments *would cease* to be applicable, and that there would be *changes in the commandments*.[76]

Although the teachers insisted on obedience to the Law, they may not have required obedience to all 613 commands of the Torah nor to its many oral interpretations. The teachers distilled from the Torah two primary pillars: circumcision, by which the obedient become "sons of Abraham" (3:7); and the sacred calendar, through which celebrants participate in the "Israel of God" (6:16). These laws established the realm of

---

[75] Betz, *Galatians*, pp. 300–1.
[76] Davies, *Jewish and Pauline Studies* (Philadelphia, 1984), p. 101.

holiness and purity delineating the sacred from the profane. The teachers informed the Galatians that obedience to these laws incorporates them into the people of God. For the teachers, Jesus' teachings—the "law of Christ"—contained all that was necessary to "complete" or "perfect" (3:3) the soteriological quest. His teachings established the hermeneutic by which the Torah is to be understood and obeyed.

Paul's Response

In view of this understanding of the Teachers' gospel, is it any wonder that Paul does not cite Jesus' teachings about the Torah? Apparently, Paul believed that Jesus observed the Torah and that his words about the Torah were generally positive. Paul could find few words of Jesus to support his case. No words from Jesus would prove his position that Gentiles do not need to be circumcised and obey Torah to be part of God's people.[77] Jesus did not address the difficult issue facing Paul: Must Gentile converts be circumcised and observe the Torah?

Paul knew his cause would be lost if he based his case on the example and words Jesus spoke to Torah-observant Jews in Palestine. And he respected the Jesus tradition too much to "create" sayings to prove his point. So he shifted the ground of debate from the teachers' traditions about Jesus to the eschatological significance of Jesus' death and resurrection. Paul argues that in the "new creation" there is no need for Gentiles to adopt Torah observances which belong to a different aeon (1:4; 6:16). Now that the new aeon has introduced the power of faith, the "custodian" is no longer needed (3:4). This Pauline shift from the historical Jesus to the eschatological Christ is a significant hermeneutical move on Paul's part.

Yet Paul is not content to leave the historical Jesus entirely in the hands of his Galatian opponents. His collection of Jesus material contained at least one reference which could substantiate his case and save his gospel: "For the whole law is fulfilled in one word: you shall love your neighbor as yourself" (5:14). Here Paul cites Jesus' teaching on the intent of the Torah (ἐν ἑνὶ λόγῳ) and applies it to the issue at hand.

---

[77] Cf. Dungan: "The reason Paul did not appeal to any sayings of Jesus in support of his stand on the Torah was because there weren't any" (*Sayings*, p. 150, note 2).

From Jesus' teaching on the purpose of the Torah, Paul moves to the controversial conclusion that if Gentiles serve one another in love, they have fulfilled the Torah—despite their lack of circumcision and observance of all 613 commandments.

Paul, Jesus, and Hillel

In citing this quotation in 5:14, Paul may be indebted to Leviticus 19:18 and the similar dictum of his predecessor Hillel. But the striking association of fulfilling the law with the love command clearly resonates with the sayings tradition of Jesus (Matt 22:34-44; 5:17). Paul's reference does not simply restate or derive solely from Leviticus. Furthermore, the phrase "but through love be servants one of another" in the previous verse echoes the servant images used by and of Jesus in the Gospels. In 6:2 Paul again calls upon the Gentiles to serve one another: "Bear one another burdens and so fulfil the law of Christ." This reformulation of the love command, first given in 5:14, is called the "law of Christ" in 6:2. As the old law is fulfilled by love, so is Jesus' new law.[78]

Paul's citation of the "law of the Christ" in 6:2 confirms that he has Jesus' teaching in mind—not primarily Leviticus or Hillel's—in 5:14 where he cites the "one word" of love. Against the many words of Jesus which the teachers cite to support the Torah, Paul cites what he considers the single most important utterance Jesus made which could be applied to the issue of Gentiles and the Torah: Jesus' statement about the underlying intentionality of the many commandments of Torah. Desperate to counter the teachers' effective use of Jesus' words, Paul focuses on the one word of love as the primary hermeneutic for the many words. Paul believed that Jesus' teachings confirmed his halakhah for Gentiles.

Paul, Jesus, and Hillel all emphasized the love ethic as the basis and intent of Torah observance. Paul expresses in Galatians 5:14 and 6:2 a close affinity with the dictum traditionally assigned to Hillel: "What is hateful to yourself do not to another; that is the whole law, all the rest is commentary."[79] This interpretive tradition contrasts with

[78] Kelber, *Oral*, p. 155; B. H. Brinsmead, *Galatians—Dialogical Response to Opponents* (Chico, Cal., 1982), pp. 178–81; Bruce, *Paul*, p. 110.
[79] See Jacob Neusner, *The Rabbinic Traditions About the Pharisees Before 70* (Leiden, 1971), p. 338, for a critical study on Hillel's words in b.Shab 31a.

other first-century Jewish schools. As Paul battled his Galatian
opponents and the "false brothers," so Jesus clashed with the Essenes
and Hillel with the Shammaites over the purpose and intention of the
Torah. While important differences remain, these three Jewish interpreters—Hillel, Jesus, and Paul—seem to have agreed that the love ethic
was crucial to fulfilling the Torah. For Paul, this interpretation of the
Torah became the principle through which Gentiles fulfilled the Law
(Gal 5:14, 6:2).

Paul believed that he was in a line of tradition that extended back
to Jesus' "law of Christ" and perhaps through Gamaliel to Hillel.[80] In
view of his possible connection with Gamaliel, Paul may have been
trained as a Hillelite, especially since rabbinic sources closely associate
Gamaliel with Hillel. Paul's letters do reflect teachings associated with
Hillel's school. For instance, it is generally accepted that Hillel urged a
more open and inclusive approach to Gentiles than did Shammai or the
Essenes.[81] Indeed, some have concluded that prior to his Christian call,
Paul was already on a Gentile mission as a Hillelite Jewish missionary.
Hengel writes: "We have to give serious consideration to the possibility
that, before he became a Christian, the Hillelite Paul was committed to
a Jewish mission."[82] At any rate, Paul's openness to Gentiles and flexi-
ble approach to the Torah may indicate that in his pre-Christian period,
Paul was associated with Jewish circles around Hillel and Gamaliel in
Jerusalem.

Contexts and Situations

From our investigation into the reasons which prompted the writing of 1 Corinthians and Galatians, we have determined that the polemical situations account to a large degree for Paul's use or nonuse of Jesus
material. In 1 Corinthians he cites more of this material than he does
elsewhere—much more than in Galatians. Paul does this because in 1
Corinthians he confronts opponents who used sayings of Jesus to sup-

---

[80] Acts 22:3 states that Gamaliel was Paul's teacher prior to his Christian calling. Recent scholarship avers the plausibility of such a connection between Paul and
Gamaliel (cf. Martin Hengel, *The Pre-Christian Paul* [Philadelphia, 1991], pp. 27–39).

[81] *Ibid.*, pp. 28, 43–53, esp. n. 157.

[82] Hengel, "Die Ursprunge der christlichen Mission," *NTS* 18 (1971–72) 23.
See also Gal 5:11.

port their emphasis on wisdom, freedom, miracles, and "apostolic rights" to financial gain. In this situation, Paul found himself resisting the "misuse" of Jesus sayings. He was able to contextualize the sayings in such a way as to remain true, in his opinion, to their original intent on the lips of Jesus.

Paul introduces his own Jesus material in 11:23-24 to support his effort to teach the Corinthians to live in community as members of the "body of Christ," instead of in discord as independent antinomians. These words of Jesus confirm Paul's understanding of servanthood. Paul's appeal to Jesus' words and teachings in a traditional formula underscores the high esteem in which he held Jesus material.

But in Galatians a radically different situation occurred which precluded Paul's citing the words of Jesus, except in 5:14. In this context, Paul encountered a Law-observant tradition which lay claim to Jesus' example and words and affirmed the importance of the Torah. Confronted by the life and words of a Torah-observant Jesus, who never addressed the difficult issues brought about by a successful Gentile mission, Paul remained silent. He did utter one word of Jesus in 5:14 which, he hoped, would answer those who advocated circumcision.

We conclude that the extent and manner of Paul's use of Jesus traditions varies from letter to letter, depending on the polemical situation and theological context. The occasional character of the correspondence conditioned Paul's use of the Jesus material in his possession and which he had previously delivered to his audience. This material remained authoritative for Paul, but his task was a hermeneutical one.

CONCLUSION

Continuity between Jesus and Paul has been supported by several important studies in recent years. Our examination of Paul's letters has confirmed his interest in and use of Jesus traditions. Our rebuttal of Lüdemann's revision of the Tübingen theory delineated its flaws and urged its rejection in light of the diversity of the Jesus Movement, which included the "spiritual ones" of Corinth and the "false brothers" in Jerusalem. Our reconstruction argues for unity in fellowship and gospel between Paul and the Jerusalem pillar apostles. It can no longer be maintained that Paul had no opportunity or motivation to acquire traditions about the historical Jesus.

The letter genre was not the medium conducive for carrying Jesus' voice. The rhetorical device of allusion served Paul well as a means of recalling to his audience's memory important traditions about Jesus. The specific occasion for which Paul's letters were written determined, in part, the quantity and kind of Jesus sayings Paul used. This varied from one occasion to another, depending on the nature of the opposition Paul encountered.

For Paul, the "Christic acid" did not dissolve the historical Jesus. Instead, Paul's interest in and continuity with Jesus is confirmed. Paul's positive relationship to the historical Jesus is evinced by his *transmission* of traditional material about Jesus, his *application* of these traditions to the needs of Gentile converts, and his *defense* of these traditions against opposing Jesus traditions which represented "another Jesus" and a "different gospel."[83] Medium, genre, and rhetorical strategies affected both in quantity and kind the nature of Paul's transmission of the Jesus traditions he had inherited from Jerusalem and other sources in the Palestinian Jesus Movement.

[83] 2Cor 11:4; Gal 1:6.

PART THREE

THE SAYINGS OF HILLEL AND JESUS

THE SAYINGS OF JESUS AND ARCHAEOLOGY

TODAY IT IS a simple, scholarly consensus that no ancient document can be interpreted apart from its historical, geographical, and social context.[1] Although the foregoing assertion is widely accepted, the role of archaeology in developing the social and historical context is hardly recognized in the field of New Testament studies. This is true whether the critic is developing some point in the chronology of Paul's life or whether she is attempting a new view of the "historical Jesus."

COMMON ERRORS IN NEW TESTAMENT SCHOLARSHIP

Recent historical Jesus research scarcely mentions archaeology at all, even in contexts where the Temple is under discussion, or the nature of travel narratives in the Gospels, or in discussions of dining practices. This is true specifically of Dominic Crossan's interesting work and of John Meier's two volumes, but also of most current commentaries on the Gospels or historical Jesus investigations—with certain clear exceptions.[2] This amounts to a tacit admission that historical Jesus research is not historical at all, but something else.

---

[1] This paper was first read at the Hillel and Jesus Symposium in Jerusalem on June 8, 1992. It benefited from the comments and criticisms of the participants there, then benefited further from comments from Professor T. R. W. Longstaff of Colby College, Professor T. McCollough of Centre College, and others. In revised form it was then read in the New Testament Archaeology Seminar at the Society for New Testament Studies Annual Meeting in Madrid, Spain, on July 29, 1992. It has benefited greatly from comments and discussion at that seminar. I thank the members of that seminar for their lively and penetrating conversation, particularly the conveners, R. R. Batey of Rhodes College and R. Oster of Harding Graduate School of Religion.

[2] Cf. J. D. Crossan, *The Historical Jesus: The Life of a Mediterranean Peasant* (San Francisco, 1991); J. Meier, *A Marginal Jew:Rethinking the Historical Jesus* (New York, 1991) and *A Marginal Jew: Rethinking the Historical Jesus*, Vol. II (Mentor,

In this essay we will look at an assertion in historical Jesus research that appears to be a conclusion based on an examination of the topography or ancient road system of lower Galilee. When this statement is treated as a testable hypothesis and compared to its empirical context, it turns out *not* to be based on available archaeological evidence. In this case "the empirical context" refers to the topographical situation of ancient Galilee.

In his third Shaffer Lecture at Yale Divinity School in 1991, E. P. Sanders made several critical remarks about recent historical Jesus research.[3] Sanders was at pains to refute the speculations of F. Gerald Downing and Burton Mack that placed Jesus among the Cynic philosophers.[4] One of Mr. Sanders' points was that the villagers of Galilee were quite place-bound and could not have visited a population center, such as Sepphoris, on any regular basis and could not therefore have encountered Cynic philosophers—if indeed there were any in Galilee. He goes so far as to assert that "it would have taken about half a day to get from Nazareth to Sepphoris and half a day to get back."[5] How does Mr. Sanders know this?

In the past nine years of surveying and excavating at Sepphoris, several athletes and others from the University of South Florida Excavations at Sepphoris have traveled on foot from Nazareth to Sepphoris, some across country and some on the modern roads. The trip takes from 45 minutes for the joggers to two hours for the sightseers. It is highly unlikely that the ancient road was much different from the modern route to Sepphoris from Nazareth, but it hardly matters. The journey started at the southwest edge of ancient Nazareth, judging from the position of the tombs of the Herodian period, which demarcate the ancient village.[6]

Message, and Miracles) (New York, 1994). For exceptions, cf. J. H. Charlesworth, *Jesus Within Judaism* (New York, 1988); J. H. Charlesworth, ed., *Jesus and the Dead Sea Scrolls* (New York, 1992).

[3] E. P. Sanders, "Jesus: His Religious 'Type.'" *Reflections* [Yale Divinity School Magazine] (1992) 4–12. Third Shaffer Lecture.

[4] F. G. Downing, *Jesus and the Threat of Freedom* (London, 1987); Downing, *Christ and the Cynics: Jesus and other Radical Preachers in First Century Tradition* (Sheffield, 1988); B. Mack, *A Myth of Innocence: Mark and Christian Origins* (Philadelphia, 1988).

[5] Sanders, "Jesus: His Religious 'Type,'" p. 5, col. 2b.

[6] In 1991, I described the distance as "about one and one-half hour's walk," to allow for mothers with young children. See J. F. Strange, "Two Aspects of the Development of Universalism in Early Christianity: The First to the Fourth Centuries," in *Religion and Global Order*, eds. R. Robertson and W. R. Garrett, Religion and the

If we err, we err in making the modern trip too long, not too short. In any case, Mr. Sanders' remark fails when tested against the actual topographical context.[7]

It is also useful to note the travel summaries of the Byzantine and later Christian pilgrims provided by John Wilkinson.[8] Wilkinson notes that a traveler on a donkey or on foot could expect to travel about two and one-half miles per hour. That seems slow compared to our walkers.

It is a simple matter to test and refute the hypothesis of a half-day requirement to travel on foot from Nazareth to Sepphoris. It is remarkable that scarcely anyone thinks to test such assertions in the field. Whether the rest of Mr. Sanders' argument necessarily falls is another matter, but the failure of this tested hypothesis does call into question the force of the argument, particularly if one of its main points collapses.

Other points in Mr. Sanders' argument may also be amenable to field testing, such as the assertion that there were no Roman soldiers in Galilee in the first half of the first century C.E., or that knowledge of the Greek language in Galilee was severely limited, not to mention direct knowledge of Greek customs and culture.[9]

Political Order IV (New York, 1991). For a detailed discussion of Nazareth, see C. Kopp, *The Holy Places of the Gospels* (New York, 1963), pp. 49–86. See also B. Bagatti, *Excavations at Nazareth: From the Beginnings till the XII Century* (Jerusalem, 1969), Fig. 3, p. 28. The most detailed map is probably in C. Kopp, "Beiträge zur Geschichte Nazareths," *The Journal of the Palestine Oriental Society* XVIII/3-4 (1938) 187–228, and plate XLIV; map on p. 193.

[7] Parenthetically, I may add that one of our volunteers walked from modern Nazareth to Tiberias in sandals. The trip took six hours, or roughly half a day.

[8] J. Wilkinson, *Palestine Pilgrims Before the Crusades* (Warminster, 1977), pp. 16–20.

[9] For the opinion that three legions of Roman soldiers were stationed in Judea (and therefore also Galilee) from 4 B.C.E. (and four legions from the time of Tiberius and perhaps late in Augustus' reign), see E. Schürer, *The History of the Jewish People in the Age of Jesus Christ*, rev. and ed. G. Vermes, F. Millar, and M. Black, Vol. 1 (Edinburgh, 1973), p. 362, note 42. For an alternative view of the extent of Greek in Galilee during the same period, see E. Schürer, *The History of the Jewish People in the age of Jesus Christ*, rev. and ed. G. Vermes, F. Millar, and M. Black, Vol. 2 (1979), pp. 74–80. See also p. 77, note 257. For the penetration of Greek culture in general, see *Ibid.*, Vol 2, pp. 1–80.

In any case, archaeology as excavation, or as surface survey, or even as interpretation of material culture is capable of advancing historical knowledge when it tests historical and other kinds of hypotheses.[10] If historical Jesus research does not develop hypotheses we as scholars can test against both literary and archaeological evidence, then these hypotheses do not relate to anything in particular. Such research becomes an exercise in a vacuum in which scholars develop a kind of private code by which they communicate private thoughts. Their research no longer relates to the wider hermeneutical enterprise of conventional historical scholarship.

"NEW WORLD" ARCHAEOLOGY AS SOCIAL ARCHAEOLOGY

The context of the sayings of Jesus includes anything archaeology may unearth that contributes to the reconstruction of the social world of those sayings. But archaeology as archaeology is not the context of the document. After all, archaeology as we understand it and practice it is a modern discipline and thus a component of the modern world. So the question about the archaeological context of the Sermon on the Mount, for example, makes no sense, because the Sermon on the Mount has no archaeological context.

The proper question may be, What are the worlds of social structures and social relations in which the teachings of Jesus were first uttered, then remembered, framed, transmitted, and recorded? The corollary question is, What role does archaeology play in the reconstruction of those worlds?

Our reconstructions rely upon information from literature, numismatics, epigraphy, ostraca, and any other written materials, plus a full and detailed analysis and synthesis of what we can understand of that world *from the patterns detected in archaeological evidence.*

Note the phrase "the patterns detected in archaeological evidence." This is the new element in current archaeology. Archaeologists are not finished once everything that has been excavated is recorded in a catalog and published. Rather, archaeology is a serious intellectual enterprise in which archaeologists look earnestly for recurring patterns

---

[10] J. F. Strange, "Some Implications of Archaeology for New Testament Studies," in *What has Archaeology to do with Faith?* ed. J. H. Charlesworth and W. P. Weaver (Philadelphia, 1992), pp. 23–59, esp. p. 29.

of distribution in artifact scatters. Such patterns comprise the *logos*, the footprint that reveals social reality to the probing archaeological mind. From this footprint we infer the social identity, status, relative wealth, and many other social factors of the one who trod here.[11]

Before we proceed, we must also address what archaeology is *not*, for inappropriate understandings of archaeology have impeded the dialogue for some years. We speak here of archaeology inappropriately conceived both by archaeologists and by New Testament scholars.

Archaeology today is not simply the recovery of artifacts. It most decidedly is not merely exposing monuments to the air or mining the earth for objects of art. Nor is it a matter of recovering "interesting things" from the debris of ancient cities. It may accomplish these things proximately while pursuing its final goals, but such excavation, such "pot-hunting," is not archaeology.

Rather, archaeology in its most sophisticated form formulates historical, economic, or social hypotheses based on reading both the archaeological record and the literary record. Archaeology advances knowledge and understanding by testing these hypotheses—else it is not archaeology. In other words, archaeology in general—and New Testament archaeology in particular—draws conclusions that are continually subject to revision, as is true of all historical scholarship of the ancient world. In contrast, many excavation reports in the past have been little more than catalogues of the architecture and the objects. Many archaeologists today would not recognize this as archaeology in any modern sense.

In the past, many archaeologists focused upon architecture, stratigraphy, and pottery, but were not interested in the reconstruction of ancient social realities. Some archaeologists even appeared disinterested in correlating their finds with ancient literature, but spoke of architecture, subsistence patterns, city planning, or statistical analyses of space. In many areas today, however, archaeology includes the new goal of correlating their finds with ancient literature. This new goal puts it in position to make a substantial contribution to exegesis of the New Testament in general and of the sayings of Jesus in particular.[12]

---

[11] The most seminal statement of the purposes of social archaeology are still found in C. Renfrew, *Approaches to Social Archaeology* (Cambridge, 1984), pp. 10–14.

[12] Note the recent attempts to use texts in New World archaeology: B. J. Little, ed., *Text-Aided Archaeology* (Boca Raton, Fl., 1992).

In other words, the goal of social archaeologists is to reconstruct past social systems and relations.[13] Archaeology makes available by excavation the physical evidence for past human activity and values—perhaps even human thought.[14] Archaeology then further makes available a reconstruction of past behaviors and values, which, taken in sum, provide us with a snapshot of the values, economics, social organization and relations, aesthetics, and daily religion of the ancient people who left the debris. These reconstructions provide important information different from that found in literary texts. After all, literary texts tend to focus on atypical individuals, those who "make history," while archaeology provides information from the activities of people and groups who may go unmentioned or unnoticed in literary texts.[15]

We build up views of an ancient world incrementally, slice by slice, from small steps in interpretation of archaeological data. The process is primarily analytic and scientific, but also heuristic and intuitive. It requires a powerful, informed, and practiced imagination.[16]

Archaeology provides its own metaphor for understanding how its theoretical approach operates. The metaphor is stratigraphy. At Level I, the most humble and least useful theoretical level, lies archaeology as illustration. At this level of research, the archaeologist produces an example of something mentioned in the New Testament or in a sayings context, such as a cup or a scroll, or perhaps the Temple mount in Jerusalem.

Level 2, the second theoretical level, is much more important to exegesis. At this level we find reconstruction of a *practice* mentioned in the New Testament. Two examples are covering the head while praying or prophesying in public in a Pauline context and dining with an important person in a Gospels context.[17] What distinguishes this level from the

[13] Renfrew, *Approaches to Social Archaeology*, p. 3.

[14] C. Renfrew, *Towards an Archaeology of Mind: An Inaugural Lecture Delivered Before the University of Cambridge on 30 November 1982* (Cambridge, 1982).

[15] J. F. Strange, T. R. W. Longstaff, and D. E. Groh, *Excavation Manual for Area Supervisors* (Tampa, Fl., 1992), p. 1.

[16] The foregoing synthesis has profited greatly from I. Hodder, *Reading the Past* (Cambridge, 1986).

[17] R. E. Oster, "Use, Misuse, and Neglect of Archaeological Evidence in Some Modern Works on 1 Corinthians (1 Cor. 7,1-5; 8,10; 11,2-16; 12,14-26)" *Zeitschrift für die neutestamentliche Wissenschaft* 83/1-2 (1992) 52-73; K. Dunbabin, M.D., "Triclinium and Stibadium," in W. J. Slater, ed., *Dining in a Classical Context* (Ann

first is that we are now inferring ancient values and stereotypical behaviors. The text is to be read in context with these values and behaviors.

At Level 3, the third and most sophisticated theoretical level of archaeology, we find the reconstruction of the social world of the sayings of Jesus or of various layers within the traditions of the New Testament.

The concerns of the Roman period archaeologist over the past five decades have been dominated by the lowest theoretical level: illustration. As a result, historical Jesus scholars have had little use for Palestinian archaeology, aside from the question of the impoverished theoretical stance of said archaeology.

Historically, archaeological interest in architecture, to cite one example, was confined to reconstructions on paper that served New Testament scholars primarily at Level 1: illustration. For example, some scholars used the putative first-century synagogue finds at Capernaum, Gamala, Herodium, and Masada to introduce the student of the Gospels to one detail in "New Testament background studies"; namely, what the term *synagogue* might mean in certain Gospel texts (figs. 18-21). These treatments were often woefully inadequate in interpreting these finds. For example, the announcement in the Israeli press in 1991 that a Hellenistic synagogue had been uncovered was used in one scholarly conference to press the case that the word *synagogue* in the New Testament always refers to a specific type of architecture.[18] But more recently it appears that the discovery in question was merely a large, bare room, perhaps of the late second century B.C.E., which may or may not have cultic associations. The debate still rages.

Today the archaeologist's interest in any architecture, not just synagogue architecture, includes at least three other concerns.[19] First,

---

Arbor, Mich., 1991), pp. 121–48.

[18] A novel solution to the problem of first century synagogues in ancient Israel is provided by Z. U. Ma'oz, "The Synagogue in the Second Temple Period," *Eretz Israel* 23 (1992) 331–44 [Hebrew] and English summary pp. 157*–58*. "Synagogues were not built in Israel before the time of Herod, when they were erected only in the major urban centers and district capitals; synagogues were not built in villages prior to the destruction of the Second Temple" (p. 157*).

[19] A fresh attempt to interpret ancient and modern architecture and built space in "existential" categories is found in C. Norberg-Schulz, *Meaning in Western Architecture: Selected Essays* (New York, 1980). See esp. chap. three, which is devoted to Roman architecture.

what is the function of the building in terms of the economics, values, and aesthetics of the community that built and used it? What function does this building serve in the religious ritual, social organization, or social relations of the community? What does this building reveal about the economics of the locality, the region, and the province in which it was built? What does it reveal about the values of the people in relation to their environment or their attitudes about social status and group identity? What about its aesthetics? In what way does it relate to the religion of these people? What social organization is revealed by analysis of the uses of this building in ancient society?

Second, what does the organization and use of the internal and external spaces of the building tell us about local economics, values, and so forth?[20] Precisely how is space organized within the building? How many people are expected to make use of this space? What will they be doing? Is it public space, private space, or something in between? Is the space organized by categories other than public and private, such as formal and informal?[21] Are there gender or other social issues in the use of this space?

Third, how does the building fit into the total organization of space we call "village," "town," or "city"? What is the role of this building in terms of conscious or unconscious "city planning" in antiquity? How does it relate to structures around it? Is it in high, middle, or low prestige space within the town? Does it follow the geometry or organization of the city's layout, or is it somehow anomalous?[22]

We ask analogous questions of texts. First, how does this text reflect the values, economics, aesthetics, religion, and social organization and relations of its ancient community? To what extent are these

---

[20] For an analysis of sacred, public space, see J. R. Branham, "Sacred Space under Erasure in Ancient Synagogues and Early Churches" *The Art Bulletin* 75/3 (1992) 375–94. O. Grün, E. Engelstad, and I. Lindblom, *Social Space: Human Spatial Behaviour in Dwellings and Settlements* (Odense, Denmark, 1992). The contributions focus on domestic space and site planning rather than public space.

[21] For analyses of modern architectural space which appear useful for the study of ancient spaces, see S. M. Low and E. Chambers, eds., *Housing, Culture, and Design: A Comparative Perspective* (Philadelphia, 1989). See especially chapters 13 and 17.

[22] In New World archaeological theory, the above set of questions coincides with what is called "middle-range theory." See P. Kosso, "Method in Archaeology: Middle-Range Theory as Hermeneutics," *American Antiquity* 56(4) (1991) 621–27.

expressions implicit and to what extent explicit within the text? Second, how does the internal organization or genre of the text reflect its setting in terms of these five categories? Third, how does this text "fit" into its wider textual context? How does it relate to the texts before and after it?

Another issue needs to be addressed in any attempt to understand the divorce of archaeology from historical Jesus studies. There is a structural imbalance between New Testament Studies and Old Testament Studies. Where in New Testament Studies is there a corollary to "History of Israel" or "History of Israelite Religion" in Tanakh or Old Testament Studies? Who routinely reads primary New Testament period archaeological reports in order to mediate knowledge of the archaeological world to New Testament historians and New Testament exegetes?

To benefit from archaeological research, the Gospels scholar must believe that the Gospel writings mediate *time* and *space* in some real, observable sense. If there is no empirical correlate with the internal world of the sayings of Jesus or to a New Testament writing—either to the world of its authorship or to the world of its characters—then no relationship can exist between the two fields of inquiry.

On the other hand, correlation of archaeological evidence with historical Jesus research does not rest upon a specific view of the historicity of the Gospels. There is latitude for interpretation here, just as there is in all historiography.

HOW ARCHAEOLOGY INFORMS HISTORICAL JESUS RESEARCH

We will now turn to some specific examples of the kind of information that archaeology affords historical Jesus research. Exegetes have available to them different information that is both valuable and necessary to their enterprise.

First, we must give up the view that Galilee is a bucolic, isolated area with poor communication and with no major cities. It is still not clear why Shirley Jackson Case of the University of Chicago could not persuade a generation of scholars that the presence of Sepphoris in the middle of lower Galilee necessarily modified the received view of that region.[23] Sepphoris is now all the more clearly a major city with Hel-

---

[23] S. J. Case, *Jesus: A New Biography* (Chicago, 1927).

lenistic and earlier history and with vital Roman connections since 55
B.C.E.

Second, we must give up the view that there is a sharp distinction
between city dwellers and the peasants in the countryside. Not only did
absentee landlords live in cities, as many have suggested, but farmers
also lived there. They left at dawn, when the city gates are opened, to
tend their fields in the territory of the city.

Third, Sepphoris itself had a theater from the time of Antipas
(fig. 22). Furthermore, Zev Weiss and Ehud Netzer of Hebrew University uncovered during the 1992 season of excavations at Sepphoris a
Roman street with side columnations, a discovery that leaves little doubt
about the Roman character of the city. In our own excavations, we have
been uncovering a major market building. This building is some 40
meters broad and was furnished with mosaics.[24] Its founding may date
from the death of Herod the Great after the destruction of the city by
Varus. If so, it was surely an imposing sight in the first century C.E.,
and it would have been visible from Nazareth as one came up over the
top of the Nazareth fault from the ancient village on the two-hour walk
to Sepphoris.

"A city on a hill cannot be hid." From almost every point in
lower Galilee—except to the immediate west and to the east on the
downhill drop to Tiberias—this city was visible on its hilltop. If it were
only 300 acres in extent, it could hardly have dominated the setting in
lower Galilee more.

Ancient Galilee was densely settled with small villages and localities, all of which depended in an economic, if not political sense, on
the cities of Tiberias and Sepphoris from 21 C.E. In the surveys of the
University of South Florida Excavations at Sepphoris, we have located
two such dependent villages within 1.5 kilometers of Sepphoris. One of
these lies to the southwest of Sepphoris and one of these to the north.

---

[24] J. F. Strange, D. E. Groh, and T. R. W. Longstaff, "Sepphoris (Zippori),
1987," Notes and News, *Israel Exploration Journal* 38/3 (1988) 188–90; idem,
"Sepphoris (Zippori), 1988," Notes and News, *Israel Exploration Journal* 34 (1984)
51–52; J. F. Strange and T. R. W. Longstaff, "Sepphoris (Zippori)—Survey, 1984,"
Notes and News, *Israel Exploration Journal* 34 (1984) 269–70; idem, "Sepphoris (Zippori), 1985 (II)," Notes and News, *Israel Exploration Journal* 35 (1985) 297–99; idem,
"Sepphoris (Zippori), 1986 (II)," Notes and News, *Israel Exploration Journal* 37/4
(1987) 278–80.

We identify the one to the north as ancient Shikhin.[25] Surely others are waiting to be discovered and recorded.[26]

The point is that proximity breeds familiarity. That is, the village inhabitants of Galilee can see Sepphoris, if not Tiberias, almost in their backyards. Furthermore, these two cities offered important services to these villagers, one of which was market day. We all know the importance of market day for the exchange of goods and services, but also for news, gossip, and other social transactions.

One of the striking discoveries of David Adan-Bayewitz in his dissertation research is that the everyday pottery manufactured at the village of Kefar Hananya, hardly ten Roman miles from Sepphoris, has turned up in every corner of Galilee and even in the Golan Heights.[27] This pottery comprises nearly 75% of the daily pottery in use at ancient Sepphoris. Another 10% of the pottery, mostly in the form of storage jars and cooking pots, was manufactured at Shikhin, the small village we identify with a ruin 1.5 kilometers north. A final small amount in the form of storage jars was manufactured at an ancient site today called Nahf, which stands east of Acco-Ptolemais and west of Rama.[28]

That the source of everyday pottery can be identified by neutron activation analysis and that it is to be found in Galilee and across the Jordan is arresting and important, for it implies the presence of a dense trade network across the Galilee and beyond. For several centuries, the people of three small villages in Galilee manufactured most of the com-

---

[25] J. F. Strange, D. E. Groh, and T. R. W. Longstaff, with a contribution by D. Adan-Bayewitz, "University of South Florida Excavations at Sepphoris: The Location and Identification of Shikhin," Part 1 and Part 2, accepted by the *Israel Exploration Journal*.

[26] See the maps in M. Avi-Yonah, *Gazetteer of Roman Palestine*. Qedem 5 (Jerusalem, 1976), maps 1, 2, and 4, pp. 106–7, 109. I count forty-two identified villages in the city territory of Sepphoris, whose territorial outline is not shown in this book. For the city territories of Sepphoris and Tiberias, see Fig. 1 of this chapter and idem, *The Holy Land from the Persian to the Arab Conquest*, rev. ed. (Grand Rapids, 1977), p. 134.

[27] D. Adan-Bayewitz, "Kefar Hananya, 1988," Notes and News, *Israel Exploration Journal* 37 (1987) 178–79; D. Adan-Bayewitz and I. Perlman, "The Local Trade of Sepphoris in the Roman Period," *Israel Exploration Journal* 40/2–3 (1990) 153–72; D. Adan-Bayewitz, *Common Pottery in Roman Galilee: A Study of Local Trade* (Bar-Ilan Studies in Near Eastern Languages and Culture; Ramat Gan, 1993).

[28] Oral communication from D. Adan-Bayewitz.

mon wares in use in ordinary houses from Acco to Qatsrein and from Meiron to Nazareth.

The implications of this archaeological datum are astounding. The village people of Galilee did *not* live in isolation, but in a local trade network alive with possibilities for exchange—not only the exchange of goods and services, but also of ideas. Itinerant Jewish peddlers moved from village to village, from town to town, sharing the latest in ceramic or clothing fashions and discussing much more than the weather. We need not posit itinerant Cynic philosophers, only traveling salesmen.

A similar archaeological datum may be deduced from certain finds in our squares at Sepphoris. We find not only coins minted as far away as Bithynia in Pontus, but also fragments of the goods themselves that originated in exotic and far-away places. To name only one example, fine red ceramic wares manufactured in eastern Italy are well-represented in the first-century deposits of Sepphoris. This need not imply that tradesmen visited Sepphoris directly from Italy, but it does suggest that Sepphoris—and therefore Galilee—participated in a major Roman trade network of international dimensions. The local trade network was enmeshed in the international network.

At this point it may be useful to discuss again the significance of the putative Early Roman building we have been uncovering beside the major north-south street (perhaps even a cardo as suggested by Netzer and Weiss) on the east side of Sepphoris. One can discuss this building in a preliminary fashion by following, where possible, the order of questions about architecture proposed above.

The simplest interpretation of Field V building is that it is a market. If this is so, then this building served as a central place for major economic and social transactions for the city of Sepphoris.

The building was beautifully appointed and decorated throughout its history, which tends to confirm that it occupied a central place in the consciousness of the city. It was a highly valued edifice, for the citizens of Sepphoris spent sums of money plastering it, painting its plaster, covering its façade with sheets of marble, and installing beautiful floors. That such a building was built at all implies a planning body, the βουλή of the city. On the other hand, there must also have been a bureaucracy that collected rents, saw to its maintenance, and cleaned its drains when necessary. This building served as a focal point for governmental bureaucracy as well as for social relations of all sorts.

The space inside the building appears to be organized into three main areas: A row of shops on either side of the main axis, a gathering area on the west side of the building between the two rows of shops (perhaps near the main entrances), and a large roofed, but open, area in the center of the building surrounded by a rectangle of columns.

We cannot say much about these three areas, and what we can say must be very tentative. But we do see shops in a line with back rooms on either side of the main axis of the building. We may have a dozen shops on each side of the market. This was surely a place of high traffic for dense crowds of shoppers on market days, which would explain the many repairs to the floors in this area. It also helps us understand the black bands in the mosaic, ostensibly to direct traffic from space to space within the building.

There is no hint anywhere of differentiation of visitors by sex or social status, though the beautiful decoration of the building itself suggests prestige space. The large size of the building and its placement next to major streets within Sepphoris suggests that this was public space.

Second, the space at the west end of the building, where the main entrances are located, is furnished with a beautiful mosaic floor with at least one garden spot about ten by twenty Roman feet, itself surrounded by columns. The garden spot is reminiscent of Vitruvius' dictum about providing restful and pleasant places for crowds of businessmen.[29]

In the third and fourth century, the images in the floor mosaic were not distinctively Jewish, pagan, or Christian. In other words, members of any of these three groups could shop here without being confronted by the symbols of the other religions. We cannot yet say whether this was true of the first-century floors.

The large roofed area in the center of the building may have provided space for the daily transactions of the population so that they did not need to stand and talk in the weather. On the other hand, in the fourth century three kinds of artifacts occur in this rectangle of columns in surprising numbers: coins, small nails, and fragments of glass vessels.

In the squares excavated along the west row of columns we found directly upon the mosaic floor and in the first ten centimeters of debris

[29] Vitruvius, *On Architecture*, V.1.5 (on the basilica).

washed onto the floor after the abandonment of the building, more than 200 bronze coins, dating mainly from the mid-fourth century. These correlate well with the nearly 100 bronze and iron nails about six centimeters long found in the same layer.

The simplest explanation is that wooden furniture was erected here, perhaps stalls, and that a brisk trade was carried on. Since this is late in the history of the building it seems unlikely that this activity was carried on in this very spot for several hundred years. On the other hand, it does not indicate that in all periods the citizens of Sepphoris and visitors to the city required special, public space devoted to a high level of economic activity. Furthermore, the archons of the city were willing to spend large sums to make this highly attractive.

What about the glass? Much of it is window pane glass; the rest is of bottles, jars, jugs, glass lamps designed for suspension in a bronze frame, and unguentaria. Glass vessels correlate well with the perfume industry, but also with the drinking of wine and other recreation drinks in daily social life. The social dimension here should not be missed.

This building appears to fit into the city's total organization of space, the "city planning" of Sepphoris, as a major element at the intersections of two primary streets and two side streets. It is surrounded by streets on all four sides. These streets separate it from all other structures. Two of them are well-paved, which implies high traffic. One of these streets, the proposed cardo, runs roughly southwest in the general direction of the fruitful wadi that even today provides the course of the road to modern Tsippori and to the ancient city. This street, when it turns into a road outside the city, would direct us to the road that connects us with ancient Yaphia and Nazareth.

A side street on the north side of the market proceeds up the hill of Sepphoris to the stage area of the theater. Another side street on the south side proceeds up the hill to form a tangent with the curve of the theater near its entrance. The main street on the west side of the market is well-paved with large stone blocks. The paving dates to the first century C.E., judging from the material in its make-up. The side street on the north is paved with finely crushed limestone, which helps us to understand it as a side street.

In other words, this building fits well into the geometry of the city plan of ancient Sepphoris. It is not an anomaly, but helps us deduce the plan, at least on the east side of the city. It gives us the working hypothesis that the city blocks or insulae on the east side were in multiples of 40 x 60 meters.

The foregoing analysis makes clear what we now know that we could not have known without archaeological excavation: We are now in a much better position to understand how news and gossip got around in Roman Galilee. Specifically, we now know that in Sepphoris there stood an example of Roman period planning and building for economic management. One of the results of this planning and building was that in effect an informal communication center was built. This institution, more than just a building, encouraged and expected crowd participation, human interaction, and group impact. Those who came to participate in economic and other human interactions went away changed by those economic and social transactions. From a Roman point of view, the hope may have been that they would come away better citizens for their interactions here, ever more deeply committed to Roman ideals, including that of law and order.

All of the above discussion needs to be factored into an understanding of the setting of the sayings of Jesus. It does no good to assert that the people of Galilee were place-bound in the face of such evidence. Neither does it suggest that the Galileans were gadabouts who visited a different village every day. What it does open for us is the possibility of demonstrating the plausibility of the geographical, political, religious, and cultural settings of the sayings of Jesus. It does not answer the question of historicity itself, but then neither does it deny that historicity. Again it is a question of opening up our scholarship to new dimensions of interpretation, dimensions uncovered by such archaeological data.

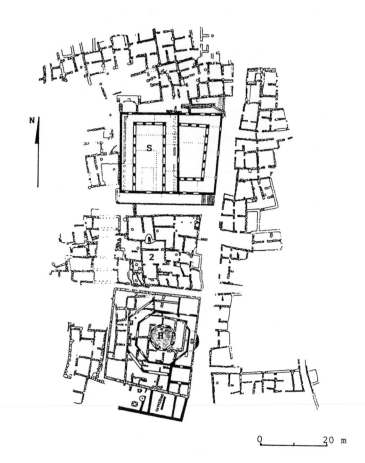

N

0   20 m

Fig. 18 Capernaum. Excavations in the Franciscan property.
S=Synagogue; 2=Insula No. 2; H=Octagonal church over house.

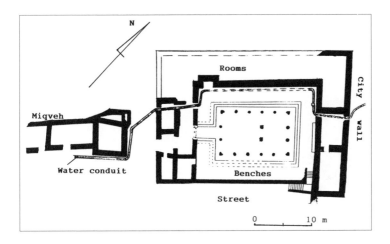

Fig. 19a The Synagogue of Gamla as seen in 1993 .
Fig. 19b The Synagogue of Gamla (After Zvi 'Uri Ma'oz, 1992).

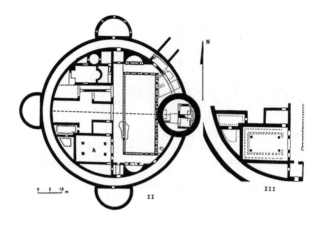

Fig. 20 Herodium. I: General map of the area with Lower Herodium in the north. II: Plan of the fortress-palace A: Triclinium III. Enlargement of the triclinium after its transformation. Three rows of masonry benches were added along the walls. By analogy with Masada, it may be considered that the fighters of the First Revolt (66–70 C.E.) made the addition. (After G. Foerster and E. Netzer)

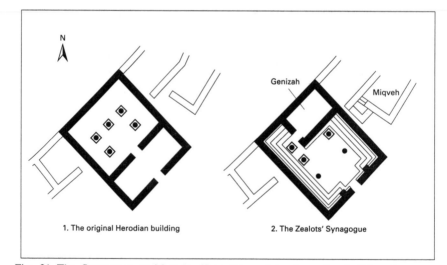

Fig. 21 The Synagogue at Masada. How the zealots changed a building into a synagogue.

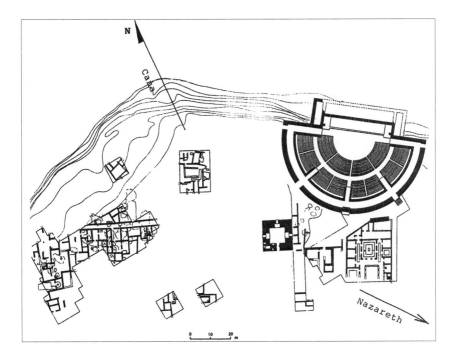

Fig. 22 Sepphoris. Excavations at the end of 1992. The theater may date from the first century C.E. and could have been built by Herod Antipas, but the large mansion in the south dates from the third century. Cana is six and a half miles in the north, and Nazareth three and a half miles in the southeast.

SAYINGS AND LEGENDS
IN THE HILLEL TRADITION

SAYINGS AND LEGENDS are two well-established genres in Gospel studies. Before examining them in connection with the Hillel tradition, one should define them in the context of rabbinic literature. In this preliminary discussion, sayings may be defined as single utterances or collections of sayings not accompanied by a story or a legend.[1] The sayings under discussion may be divided into four categories.

A TYPOLOGY OF HILLEL SAYINGS

A. Sayings attributed to Hillel himself. The obvious example is naturally m.Ab 1 and 2,[2] but also collections in Abot de Rabbi Nathan (ARN).[3]

B. Utterances not attributed to Hillel, from which one or more saying is incorporated into a story or legend about Hillel the Elder. Two cases may be discerned in the literature:

B.1. A list of sayings concerning the abrogation of Sabbath prohibitions in cases of danger to life (פקוח נפש דוחה שבת). Here a saying apparently in the name of R. Nathan[4] concludes the story of how the poor young Hillel joined the school in Jerusalem.[5]

---

[1] Y. Fraenkel, דרכי המדרש והאגדה (Jerusalem, 1991), pp. 396–404; notes on p. 661.

[2] 1:12-14; 2:4-7.

[3] A 12 (Schechter, pp. 48, 54, 55), B 24 (Schechter, p. 48); B 27 (Schechter, pp. 54–55).

[4] Mekhilta de R. Ishmael, Ki Tisa 1 (Horovitz, p. 341] on: אך את שבתותי תשמורו (Ex 31:13); and (p. 343] on: ושמרו בני ישראל את השבת (31:16); t.Shab 15:16, though the saying is missing in the Tosefta. See also Midrash haGadol to Exodus (p. 669); Yalkut to Ex 31:13; Lekah Tov to Ex (p. 101).

[5] b.Yoma 35b.

B.2. Various documents and situations that are not to be included in the general release of debts at the end of the seventh year (the first sentence of m.Shevi'it 10:3 [פרוזבול אינו משמט] is the last item in a list beginning in 10:1). Details of the story, such as when and why the release was decreed, will naturally be discussed below.

C. Individual sayings attributed to Hillel found in rabbinic literature. R. Tanhuma bar Abba quotes Hillel's saying, הגבהתי השפלתי השפלתי הגבהתי, as a Midrash to Proverbs 25:7.[6] When Ben Azai elaborates on the same saying of Hillel, he continues by quoting Hillel's words.[7] Thus an utterence unknown in early Tannaitic literature nonetheless found its way to the tradition of Hillel's life.[8]

D. Certain sayings, otherwise unknown and possibly hidden in existing stories and legends, authored by Hillel.

In the following discussion we retain the analytical order outlined above without losing track of other literary connections between the stories in the Hillel tradition.

A. SAYINGS ATTRIBUTED TO HILLEL

The first six examples are all part of the first category of sayings.

One could consider the various stories and legends in the passages in ARN as one literary phenomenon. Among other methods,[9] ARN adopted this one,[10] namely elaborating the sayings of Hillel and reworking them into legends regarding his individual study and life.[11] We find in both versions four examples, all of which open with the same formula: מעשה בהלל הזקן (a story about Hillel the Elder). We introduce them here through the saying cited in ARN.

---

[6] ExRab 45:5.

[7] LevRab 1:5.

[8] On the traditions of this saying, see S. Safrai in this volume.

[9] כיצד is a noticeable literary method of openings in version A (Schechter, pp. 2, 18, 19, 21, 27 (bis), 33, etc.). ש.. or זו/זה.. is the opening literary expression found in B (Schechter, pp. 2, 18, 23, 27, 28, 29, etc.; but see also in A, pp. 14, 34, and others), or וכן אתה מוצא.. (Schechter, p. 18).

[10] A variant on this literary device is to introduce stories concerning other personalities with the saying of Hillel: Aharon (A,B; Schechter, pp. 48–52), Eunomos the Gardi and Rabban Gamaliel (B; Schechter, p. 49), the righteous man from Beith Rama (A,B; Schechter, p. 56), Belshazar (B; Schechter, p. 56), R. Joshua (B; Schechter, p. 56).

[11] Cf. Schechter, pp. 54–55.

1. ומקרבן לתורה *(Bring them near to the Torah.)*

In Version B, this saying[12] serves as the occasion to describe the "habit" of Hillel to sit at the gate of Jerusalem and engage in philosophical or moral discussions with the working passersby, trying to direct them to engage in the study of Torah.[13] "Thus did Hillel all his life, until he brought them under the wings of heaven."[14] Hillel is depicted as having lived up to his own saying.

2. אם אני כאן הכל כאן *(If I am present, all are present.)*

In ARN A,[15] the legend incorporating the saying לפום צערא אגרא (reward is according to effort)[16] reflects Hillel's persistence of acting according to his convictions and motivating people to the right way of Torah.[17] The continuous behaviour is the manifestation of the saying, "If I am here, all are here." Hillel's very presence in the market provided the impetus for the edification of others. Once as Hillel was discussing market prices, one of the merchants retorts with Hillel's own saying[18] that "rewards are according to effort." In this legend, the saying carries a realistic connotation rather than a moralistic one, though the entire story has a deeper spiritual meaning.

Intermediate Conclusions I

Both of the stories above cast Hillel in the mold of the Greek teacher and philosopher Socrates,[19] thus emphasizing even more the

---

[12] m.Ab 1:12.

[13] This is a recurring theme in Hillel stories (cf. n. 17).

[14] ARN B 26 (Schechter, p. 54).

[15] ARN A 12 (Schechter, p. 55).

[16] In a saying form, those two sayings are combined without a legendary content in ARN B 27 (Schechter, p. 55).

[17] See above, note 13.

[18] See below, note 21.

[19] Demetrius of Byzantium says that Socrates used to discuss moral questions in workshops and in the marketplace (Diog. Laer. 2.20), The story is that Socrates met Xenophon in a narrow passage and started a conversation on foods. As a result of the encounter, Xenophon became his pupil (2.48). Diogenes explains that Socrates did not travel, but rather spent his time arguing with everyone under all circumstances (2.22). See also N. Glatzer, *Hillel the Elder* (New York, 1957), p. 51. See also the discussion by S. Robinson in this volume.

literary function of the sayings within the legends. Hillel is depicted as the famous philosopher, but those legends in return stress that he was the great teacher of the humble people in the streets.[20]

3. לפום צערא אגרא (Reward is according to effort.)

This saying appears in a short collection of Aramaic sayings of Ben Bag Bag in Abot 5:22.[21] It is also quoted in both versions of ARN,[22] along with the other sayings of Hillel.[23] It was incorporated in the answer of the corn merchant to Hillel. One pays according to the distance the merchandise is carried. Once again in a similar moral sense, the saying is incorporated in a dialogue. But this time it appears in Hillel's answer to a donkey driver from Jerusalem who was sneering at Hillel, the pilgrim from Babylon:[24] לפי הדרך הוא השכר, אמר לו: לא יהו שכר רגלי כשכר בהמה? (The reward is according to the length of the way, and he continued: Do not my feet deserve, at least, a reward similar to that of a donkey?). The saying is incorporated in Hebrew[25] and the conclusion repeats it in Aramaic: הוא שהיה הלל מקיים, לפום צערא אגרא (Thus Hillel fulfilled [the saying,] "Reward is according to effort"). Once again we have here a conscious attempt to view Hillel's life in light of a saying attributed to him.[26]

4. דאנן בה מן בה מן בה ואין אנן לית בה מן בה (If I am here, all is here; if I am not here, who is here?)

This saying is quoted in a list of sayings[27] and serves as an opening for a story (מעשה) about Hillel. The saying appears in a con-

---

[20] A. H. Weiss, דור דור ודורשיו (Wilna, 1911), pp. 150–53.

[21] For a brief discussion on the development of the saying and its traditions, see J. Goldin, "The End of Ecclesiastes: Literal Exegesis and its Transformation," in *Studies in Midrash and Related Literature* (New York, 1988), pp. 4–6.

[22] Schechter, p. 55.

[23] For a discussion of this double tradition, see B. Z. Bacher: אגדות התנאים, Vol. 1 (Jerusalem, 1882), p. 7.

[24] B 27 (Schechter, pp. 55–56).

[25] The rabbinic tradition is aware that Hebrew and Aramaic are intertwined in the Hillel tradition. ועוד ה' (A; Schechter, p. 55); אף הוא אומר בלשון בבלי ארבעה דברים דברים היה אומר בלשון הבבליים (B; Schechter, p. 56). Bacher sees here a connection with Hillel's Babylonian origins. See Bacher, אגדות התנאים, p. 8.

[26] For a similar story not connected with the saying, see b.Hag 9b; W. Bacher, אגדות התנאים, p. 6.

[27] In Aramaic, ARN B 27 (Schechter, p. 55); in half Hebrew, half Aramaic,

versation between Hillel and some people he observes celebrating the intermediate days of Sukkot. The saying also appears in the dialogue. Hillel directs the first half of the saying toward those who arrogantly assume an air of importance in light of their participation in the Temple festivities. The second half is Hillel's consolation, once they took to heart his previous rebuke.[28]

In ARN, each half of the saying is quoted as an opening heading and explained with the story. Hillel himself is supposed to approach both groups with a differnt Midrash: first a Midrash on Job 25:3 and later a Midrash on Psalm 22:4. In y.Sukkah, the saying is part of the words of Hillel in both occasions.

Hillel includes here the Midrash as well as the appropriate part of his saying in Aramaic in somewhat different wording:

הלל הזקן, כד הוה חמי לון עבדין בפחז, הוה אמר לון: דאנן הכא מאן הכא, ולקילוסן הוא צריך? והכתיב אלף אלפין ישמשוניה וריבוי ריבוון קדמוהי יקומון. כד הוה חמי ולון עבדין בכושר הוה אמר די לא נן הכא מאן הכא, שאף על פי שיש לפניו כמה קילוסין חביב הוא קילוסין של ישראל יותר מכל. מה טעם? נעים זמירות ישראל.

Hillel the Elder, when he saw them acting arrogantly, used to say to them: If I am here, who is here? They were discouraged and said: Does He need their praise? Is it not written that thousands of thousands serve him, and tens of thousands stand in front of Him?[29] When he [Hillel] saw them lagging behind,[30] he used to say to them: If I am not here, who is here? Even though he has many praises before him, Israel's praise is his favorite. Why? Pleasant is the singing of Israel [2Sam 23:1].

Thus, in both versions of the story, we encounter the saying functioning in two different literary positions.[31]

ARN A 12 (Schechter, p. 55).

[28] ARN B 27 (Schechter, p. 55); y.Suk 5:4 (55b–c).

[29] In ARN, this statement is supported with Job 25:3.

[30] In ARN: שנשבר לבם (that their heart broke).

[31] See above No. 3: לפום צערא אגרא.

5. ‫למקום שלבי אוהב לשם רגליי מוליכות אותי, אם אתה תבוא לביתי, אני‬
‫אבוא לביתיך, אם אתה לא תבוא לביתי, אני לא אבוא לביתיך‬ *(To where my
heart loves, my feet lead me. If you will come to my house, I will come
to yours; if you do not come to my house, I will not come to your
house.)*

This example belongs to the traditions of *Simhat Bet hashoeva*
and Hillel. The Mishnah[32] mentions the dancing with torches of the
‫חסידים ואנשי מעשה‬ (the righteous and men of deeds). The Tosefta[33]
elaborates and identifies some famous dancers as well as the context of
their songs, Hillel among them.[34] It supposedly recalls the exact words
of Hillel's songs.[35]

These two sayings of Hillel are appended with a biblical
prooftext: ‫למקום שלבי אוהב לשם רגליי מוליכות אותי. אם אתה תבוא‬
‫לביתי, אני אבוא לביתיך, אם אתה לא תבוא לביתי, אני לא אבוא לביתיך, שנ'‬
‫בכל המקום אשר אזכיר את שמי אבא אליך ובירכתיך‬ (Ex 23:1).[36] It would
seem that a short list of sayings was included to expand and enrich the
story. This context gives a specific meaning to all sayings having to do
with Temple/God/human relations.[37] The tradition converted Hillel's
sayings into texts for his songs in the Temple. In the Tosefta, only two
sayings were handled this way; in later Amoraic tradition, three and
possibly even four.

6. ‫על דאטפת אטיפוך, וסוף מטיפיך יטופון‬ *(Since you caused others to
drown, you have been drowned yourself; and the end of those who
drowned you is to be drowned.)*

---

[32] m.Suk 5:4

[33] t.Suk 4:2-5.

[34] t.Suk 4:3.

[35] There are scholars that read the tradition as the original background for the
sayings, A. H. Weiss, ‫דור דור ודורשיו‬ (Wilna, 1911), p. 151. B. Z. Bacher, ‫אגדות‬
‫התנאים‬, Vol. 1 (Jerusalem, (1882), p. 4; N. Glatzer, *Hillel the Elder* (New York,
1957), p. 39; M. Z. Fuchs, ‫שמחת בית השואבה‬ *Tarbiz* 55 (1985) 173-207.

[36] b.Suk 53a includes three of Hillel's sayings and adds the above mentioned
saying (cf. n. 15): ‫אם אני כאן הכל כאן, ואם איני כאן מי כאן?‬ This Babylonian tradition
includes also the Mishnaic short story m.Ab 2:6 well attested in the manuscripts.

[37] For a similar interpretation—though not in a 'Hillel' story—see ARN A 12
(Schechter, p. 55), ARN B 27, for ‫למקום שלבי אוהב‬ (to a place that my heart likes). As
can be seen in the text cited above, the relationship between God and humanity implied
in the phrase ‫אם תבוא לביתי‬ (if you come to my house) is not to be understood in the
cultic sense.

The Mishnah introduces this saying with a short story designed to provide a narrative context. Hillel said it on the riverbank upon seeing a skull floating in the water. One might assume that the close relation betweeen the saying, the story, and the presumed occasion implies a concrete situation.[38] However, one might argue exactly the opposite in light of the unrealistic flavor of the story itself and its artificial proximity to the saying.[39]

We will support the second approach with one more tradition concerning the saying in relation to R. Joshua.[40] Here once again, R. Joshua was walking along, saw a floating skull on the water, and told it the same moral lesson. In this strange story, similar to that of Hillel, the narrator was not careful to place R. Joshua at a source of water, but he does cite the same saying, after providing a tenuous framework for it.[41] As on other occasions, the saying seems to aquire new story settings, even with a different rabbinic personality.

B. SAYINGS NOT ATTRIBUTED TO HILLEL

At this point we pass on to the second category, namely, sayings not explicitly attributed to Hillel that are incorporated in the Hillel stories.

7. פרוזבול אינו משמט ([A loan secured by] a prozbol[42] is not cancelled [by the Seventh Year]).[43]

This Halachic statement is followed in the Mishnah[44] with a

---

[38] Thus Y. Fraenkel, דרכי האגדה והמדרש (Jerusalem, 1991), p. 401. Fraenkel maintains that such occasions stimulated Hillel to create sayings on the spot and that its transmission in story form was meant to encourage others to make up sayings in a like manner. Fraenkel quotes H. Fischel, *Story and History* (Bloomington Ind., 1969), pp. 59–88.

[39] D. Flusser, משלי ישו והמשלים בספרות חז"ל in יהדות ומקורות הנצרות (Tel Aviv, 1979), pp. 157–58.

[40] ARN B 27 (Schechter, p. 56).

[41] Schechter, ad loc., wonders if there is a copyist error in the tradition.

[42] Danby transliterates with an interpretation in his Appendix I, A Glossary of Untranslated Hebrew Terms (p. 795, note 34): Hillel enacted the rule of the Prozbol, which was a declaration made before the court of law by a creditor, and signed by witnesses, to the effect that the loan in question would not be remitted under the terms of the Seventh Year law.

[43] The translation according to Danby.

[44] m.Shevi 10:3.

seemingly personal experience of Hillel and its midrashic implication: Hillel saw that the people were not complying with the written Torah (Deut 15:9). Therefore he instituted the Prozbol, a document that effectively canceled the release of debts at the end of the Seventh Year. The doubled use of Scripture in this rabbinic learning is rather impressive, but beyond the scope of this study.[45] The personal story involved here ties this Halachic Mishnah with the present paper.

One cannot argue that we have here a unique case in the Mishnah,[46] but one is required to include this case in the framework of sayings and legends of Hillel. We could infer that the single Halachic statement once appeared without the accompanying story. Thus it is quoted in the Talmud.[47] It is possible that the accompanying Midrash on Deuteronomy or even the personal overtone played a role in establishing the ruling on Prozbol, but the literary form in the Mishnah places this Mishnah within the scope of this study. The Hillel story is, quite possibly, secondary and derivative. Thus, though the so-called saying here is not presented as a saying of Hillel, it is nevertheless an utterance that is manifested in a life story of Hillel.

8. חלל עליו שבת אחת כדי שישמור שבתות הרבה *(Desecrate one Sabbath for him, so that he will observe many more Sabbaths.)*

This saying occurs in the name of R. Nathan[48] in a Tannaitic collection of Midrashim on פקוח נפש (saving life),[49] and elsewhere in a comparison between any living baby and the dead King David. The latter was a separate saying, possibly in the name of R. Simeon b. Gamaliel.[50] Thus, in the Tannaitic tradition, the author or first sage to

---

[45] J. Neusner, "From Exegesis to Fable in Rabbinic Traditions about the Pharisees," *JJS* 25 (1974) 263–69. He considers the exegetical part of the Mishnah the earliest in the development of the Hillel story. Concerning the "new" approach of teaching and decision-making in Hillel's teaching, see the discussion of S. Schwartz in this volume.

[46] Cf. m.RH 4:1; m.ʿEduy 1:12-14; m.Ber 2:5-7, and many others.

[47] y.Shevi 10:2 [39c].

[48] b.Yoma 85b: R. Simeon b. Menasia; y.Yoma 8;5 [45b]: אית דבעי מימר.

[49] Mekhilta de R. Ishmael, Ki Tisa 1 (Horovitz, p. 341). For a similar, but shorter, collection without this saying: t.Shab 15:16. See also G. Porton, *The Traditions of Rabbi Ishmael* II (Leiden, 1977), pp. 136–37.

[50] This saying may be seen as operating in two different ways. On the one hand, it could be a logical conclusion: one desecrates the Sabbath for a newly born living baby, but once King David is dead, one should not desecrate the Sabbath in his

pass on the saying is ambiguous, but the form is rather clear. It is either a single Midrash on Ex 31:16 or was incorporated within a chain of midrashim on the the subject of *Piquah Nefesh*. Its literary life as a Midrash saying is well attested.

The first part of the saying[51] in the affirmative form[52] is the final concluding sentence in the legend concerning the begining of Hillel as a student in the school of Shema'aya and Abtalion.[53] The identity of the author or sentence in the story is once more ambiguous. It is introduced with, "They said" (אמרו). This could have been said by the people present on the occasion within the narrative, but it could also be a more technical expression for a conscious quotation or rather Tannaitic quotation.[54] Thus, we have in this saying, which was incorporated in the late legend about Hillel,[55] a similar phenomenon of saying and legend, though from different origins.[56] One might even go so far as to speculate that Hillel was the author of the saying.

C. SAYINGS IN RABBINIC LITERATURE ATTRIBUTED TO HILLEL

In category C, there are three examples of individual sayings of Hillel.

9. ואהבת לרעך כמוך, זה כלל גדול בתורה (*Love your neighbor as yourself, this is a great rule of the Torah*).

This specific formulation is preserved in the tradition in the name of R. Akiba. The negative formulation, on the other hand, appears in

---

honor. On the other hand, it could be a prooftext: one desecrates the Sabbath for a newly born living baby as the Torah said (b.Shab 154b).

[51] No other version attested in Mss. For the recycling of Hillel sayings in parts, see D. Flusser in this volume.

[52] For grammatical verbal changes, see n. 82 below.

[53] b.Yoma 35b. See n. 76 below.

[54] See Y. N. Epstein, מבוא לנוסח המשנה (Jerusalem, 1948), pp. 726–53, esp. p. 752.

[55] S. Safrai, "Tales of the Sages in the Palestinian Tradition and the Babylonian Talmud," *Studies in Aggadah and Folklore Literature, Scripta Hierosolymitana* 22 (1971) 209–32. S. Safrai, "ארץ," מעשה חכמים במסורת הארצישראלית ובתלמוד הבבלי, ישראל וחכמיה בתקופת המשנה והתלמוד (Jerusalem, 1983), pp. 161–80.

[56] All the names to which this saying has been attributed belong to the school of Hillel and its adjuncts.

ARN B in the name of R. Akiba[57] and in the Babylonian tradition in the name of Hillel.[58] Thus in the Baylonian version, the saying is found within a lengthy story or legend about the patience of Hillel the Elder as a teacher toward possible converts. This saying clearly existed in wisdom and ethical literature long before Hillel.[59] Considering the rather early traditions in early Jewish sources, I am inclined to include it in this section of the discussion as a possible saying of Hillel as well.[60] Be that as it may, here again we encounter a case of a famous popular saying incorporated within a story about Hillel as a scholar in Jerusalem. מאי דשניא עלך becomes the first instruction in Torah study, as if created within that context, be it for Akiba or Hillel. Within the legend, כלל (rule) is taken to mean the first principle, on which all further study should accumulate—or possibly the beginning of the learning process.[61]

10. הגבהתי השפלתי השפלת הגבהתי (My uplifting is my lowering, and my lowering is my uplifting.)

This saying appears within a later presentation and interpretation in the words of Simeon b. Azai. It already existed in a form of Midrash attached to Psalm 113:5-6.[62] This saying was developed in a variety of forms in rabbinic traditions,[63] one of which is of concern in the present essay. We encounter the saying in the concluding remarks of the Babylonian Talmud. It appears there as part of the attempt to reason with the Halachic evidence. Its claim is that Halacha eventually follows the Hillel school, "since both of them [the decrees of both schools] are the words of the living God, what was the merit of the school of Hillel?"[64] This discussion is concluded with three moral remarks, one of which is the saying under discussion:[65]

---

[57] ARN B 26 (Schechter, p. 53).

[58] b.Shab 31a.

[59] Cf. P. Alexander in this volume.

[60] Thus B. Z. Bacher, אגדות התנאים, vol. 1 (Jerusalem, 1882), p. 3; cf. also D. Flusser, התורה בדרשה על ההר, in יהדות ומקורות הנצרות (Tel Aviv, 1979), p. 228. But see the discussion of P. Alexander in this volumes.

[61] For a similar interpretation, see m.Ab 6:1 and many equivalents; the oppening of Didache; and many others.

[62] LevRab 1:5; see also ExRab 45:5.

[63] See S. Safrai in this volume.

[64] b.ʿErub 13b.

[65] For the possibility that all three statements are Hillel's sayings, see D. Flus-

[It] comes to teach you that:

a. He who lowers himself, the Blessed be He lifts him up, and he who lifts himself up, the Blessed be He lowers him.

b. He who courts greatness, greatness alludes him, and he who tries to escape greatness, greatness courts him.

c. He who urges the hour [or opportunity],[66] the hour pushes him, and he who shies away from the hour, the hour [or opportunity] presents itself[67] to him."[68]

Granted, the saying is formulated here in a different grammatical form, but it preserves the original vocabulary.[69] In this context, the saying is manifested in the behavior of the school, rather than in the life of Hillel himself. One should understand the entire passage as a social fulfillment of the master's saying among his disciples. From a literary perspective, the saying is incorporated in the school teaching as an inherent part of its social and religious[70] self-understanding.[71]

11. משמועה רעה לא יירא *(Let one not fear bad news [Ps. 112:7].)*

The Babylonian Talmud relates a story opening with the formula מעשה בהלל הזקן (a story of Hillel the Elder) concerning premonition

---

ser in this volume.

[66] שעה.

[67] Lit: stands.

[68] For a different version: b.Ber 64a.

[69] For similar grammatical changes, see b.Ned 55a; ARN A 11 (Schechter, p. 46); ExRab 45:5; Midrash Mishlei 20:3; PesRab 14:6. Ma'ase Rav Kahana 6 (Wertheimer, p. 306). Midrash R. Akiba on the תגין (letters), ch. 17; on 'ע,' see Wertheimer, p. 475.

[70] God is added in the saying in this context. The saying is understood in the realm of divine reward and punishment. For another reworking of this saying in a similar vein, as well as other traditions of Hillel, see S. Safrai in this volume.

[71] The saying is read as a proclamation of behavior for another list of personalities in late Amoraic literature. See Pirqé de R. Eliezer 51:1 (Abraham and Nimrod), Agadot Bereshit 29:1 (Pharoah, Abraham, the sons of Eli the priest, Samuel, Hannah, the nations). From a literary perspective of the tradition, it is interesting that E. E. Urbach reads this saying as the motto of Hillel's life history and personal conduct (*The Sages* [Jerusalem, 1969], p. 529 [in Hebrew]).

and absolute trust in Divine security.[72] The Jerusalem Talmud recognizes as Hillel's saying only the quotation from Psalms,[73] in connection with the Mishnah[74] that a prayer to save one from harm when the clamor is already audible is a prayer in vain. The Jerusalem Talmud states that one should have the trust to assume it is not his private calamity. The Babylonian Talmud turns it into a story manifesting Hillel's deep faith.[75] In the Jerusalem Talmud, we encounter an additional literary factor; namely, the saying of Hillel is the concluding sentence.[76]

Intermediate Conclusions II

Apparently we have found here traces of a literary development of the Hillel tradition. It is not surprising to find similar ideas attached to different sayings. Thus, "to bring people under the divine wings" appears in connection with מקרבן לתורה (#1), as well as with אם אני כאן (#2). Likewise, the same saying recurs in more than one Hillel story אם אני כאן הכל כאן in #2 and #4 and #5, or לפום צערא אגרא in #2 and #3.

The sayings that appear in the stories exhibit a variety of literary functions. They are the opening key words in some stories, particulary in the ARN legends #1–4 and in #7 as well. They are part of the story dialogue, either as the words of Hillel himself (#3, 4, 5, 6, 9, and 11; or the words addressed to him (#2 and 8). And finally, they serve as a summary of the story in light of Hillel's saying, a conscious recognition of the literary character of the legend (#8, 10, and 11).

But the real benefit of this approach would emerge if one could identify an existing story about Hillel as one that adapts a saying and consequently identify the saying as possibly a genuine saying of Hillel. We hope to do this in the following and last example in this paper.

12. הוי זהיר ברוחך (Guard your spirit.)

[72] b.Ber 60a.

[73] y.Ber 9:4 [14b].

[74] m.Ber 9:3.

[75] N. Glatzer, *Hillel the Elder* (New York, 1957), p. 34. On this saying and its development, see J. Neusner, "From Exegesis to Fable in Rabbinic Traditions about the Pharisees," *JJS* 25 (1974) 263–69. See also an article of Safrai and Flusser in the near future in *Tarbiz*.

[76] For similar literary structure, see examples (#8) and (#10) and n. 53 above.

This statement occurs once in the literature in the series of stories about Hillel the Elder and his limitless patience. The series bears all the signs of a balanced and well-structured literary work. On one side, we have three encounters of nonsensical pseudo-ethnographical questions,[77] which arise as a result of a wager to see if Hillel's renowned patience can be compromised. On the other side, we have three encounters comparing Hillel's and Shammai's respective attitudes toward tiresome future converts. The series concludes with a sentence summing up the entire passage.[78] The quotation under discussion, הוי זהיר ברוחך, could serve as the title to the entire series of these six encounters, but in all versions it occurs in the first part of the series—in the discussion between Hillel and his interlocutor. In all versions, it is an utterance of Hillel himself directed toward his interlocutor. Nonetheless, it carries different meanings in the various versions.[79]

In the Babylonian Talmud, tractate Shabbath, Hillel addresses his partner and says in the final sentence of this part: הוי זהיר ברוחך, כדי הוא הלל שתאבד על ידו ארבע מאות זוז וארבע מאות זוז והלל לא יקפיד! (Guard your spirit! Hillel is worthy for you to lose on his account twice four hundred Zuz, and he will not get angry.) The expression is here taken to mean, "Do not be angry," or, "Contain yourself and do not curse me." In this version, this is the summary of all three encounters: Hillel stands for sublime patience.

In ARN A, a similar expression comes at the beginning of the last dialogue, where we find Hillel encouraging his interlocutor to go on with his tiresome questions:

> He [the opponent] said to him: "Let there not be more like you in Israel!" He [Hillel] said to him: "Be careful, contain yourself (הוי זהיר ברוחך). What is it that you want to ask?"

In other words, do not curse Israel, but rather ask your question. Both versions present similar contents and context, but altered literary posi-

---

[77] ARN B has an additional, so-called zoological question, as well as a slightly different end to the first part.

[78] ARN, pp. 60–62; b.Shab 31a. Despite noticeable variants, the general structure is preserved.

[79] P. Alexander points a similar phenomenon in the Golden Rule. See his essay in this volume.

tions and emphases. In ARN A, the competition money plays a lesser role and the concern is about patience in Israel.

In the third version,[80] the formula is altered somewhat[81] to הזהר ברוחך and occurs no less than four times in each of the irritating questions, rather as a refrain. Hillel encourages the question and the opponent claims to have forgotten his question. To this Hillel responds, הזהר ברוחך. (Here we should read it as, "Gather your wits.") Only then is the question finally asked. ARN B deviates from the balanced structure of the series, but maintains the tradition that this expression, in which we discern a "saying," is part of the literary structure.

All three versions give the utterance a prominent position in the story, albeit different meanings in their immediate contexts, which indicates that the expression existed independently prior to all the legends. Could the expression be considered a "saying" within a legend?

We have observed previously[82] that linguistic variation is a literary feature of sayings. In this saying, we find the unusual hortative form (הוי) interchanging with the regular imperative (הזהר). The use of הוי reminds one immediately of the well-known saying attributed to Hillel: "Be (הוי) of the disciples of Aaron."[83] Even though this grammatical feature cannot be considered conclusive proof, it is an exciting possibility, since this would be one more saying that expresses Hillel's general philosophy; namely, self-awareness and personal responsibility.

CONCLUSIONS

In all twelve examples, we attempted to trace the distinctive literary dynamics of the various sayings. We also attempted to follow their recycling in stories and legends about Hillel the Elder and the house of Hillel. This literary criticism, or form criticism, naturally questions the historicity of the various elements in those stories.[84] In the last case, however, the dynamics have returned us to a possibile reconstruction of Hillel's teachings. The legendary or even mythic character of the stories

---

[80] ARN B.

[81] The auxiliary form הוי is omitted. See discussion below.

[82] See #3, 8, and 10 above.

[83] m.Ab 1:12.

[84] See Y. Dernburg, משא ארץ ישראל (St. Petersburg, 1896), ch. 11, pp. 92–101; Y. Fraenkel, דרכי המשנה (Berlin, 1923), pp. 37–39.

has been recognized in past research.[85] Nonetheless, the literary approach need not ignore the historical possibilities in such stories. Rather, it illuminates one more angle or it may offer clearer insight into the combination of historical facts and legendary presentations.[86]

[85] Y. Dernburg, משא ארץ ישראל (St. Petersburg, 1896), p. 95. J. Neusner, From Exegesis to Fable in Rabbinic Traditions about the Pharisees, *JJS* 25 (1974) 263–69.

[86] For a similar argument, see the essay by C. Evans in this volume.

THE SAYINGS OF HILLEL:
THEIR TRANSMISSION AND REINTERPRETATION

THE SAYINGS OF Hillel in the haggada are relatively numerous in comparison to those of other sages from the generations that preceded the destruction of the Second Temple. Hillel's sayings are more numerous than those of his contemporary adversary, Shammai, and far more so than those of other sages who preceded the destruction of the Temple. From most of them we have only one three-part saying found in Pirqé ʾAbot. Nevertheless, even though Hillel's sayings are not that numerous, they are quoted in a number of places in different contexts, interspersed into the sayings of sages from various generations and interepreted in a variety of ways.

The purpose of this study is to point out the manner in which some of Hillel's sayings were transmitted and how they were understood and interpreted in the course of generations. We shall examine whether they were interpreted and understood according to the meaning that emerges from the earliest sources and contexts or whether they were occasionally reinterpreted in such a way as to reduce their significance, treating their message more simplistically and adapting them to the opinions of later sages.

I

In ʾAbot 1:13, we learn sayings of Hillel, among them: ודלא מוסיף ייסוף (He who does not add will perish.)[1]. In the Babylonian Talmud at the end of the tractate Taʿanit and in Baba Batra 121b, the Gemara deals

---

[1] This is the reading in Kaufmann. Many recensions read: יסוף. Many versions, especially of the Mishna read: יאסף, evidently under the influence of the interpretation in the Babylonian Talmud. Cf. below.

with the nature of the festivity on the fifteenth of Ab, establishing that on that day "the power of the sun declines." It adds: "And from now on he who adds, adds and he who adds not, will be gathered,[2] what is gathered?[3]—Rav Joseph taught: his mother will bury him." Clearly this text and Rav Yosef understood that one must increase his study from the fifteenth of Ab on, since the nights begin to increase and the days to decrease and one must add "nights to days" (Rashi). Whoever increases his study time, from night to day, "will add life to his life" (Rashi), but whoever "adds not, will be gathered." That is, he will die young "and his mother will bury him." Some of the interpreters of the Mishnah in ʾAbot interpret the saying of Hillel in light of the passage in Taʿanit and its parallels, whether they mention Rav Yosef explicitly or not.[4]

This saying also appears in ARN in both its versions. Version A (Chapter 12, fol. 28a) includes this saying in a list of sayings under the heading, "And he also said four things in the Babylonian language." Version B (Chapter 27, fol. 28b) includes it under, "And five more things he said in the Babylonian language."[5] In both versions we read ודלא מוסיף פסיד (and he who does not increase loses). The point of Hillel's threat of punishment in ARN is not that whoever does not increase his study will die young and his mother will bury him. Rather, it is that if he does not increase his study, he will lose and his study will be harmed, as the continuation of the passage implies: "It will cause the first to be forgotten" (Version A); or "in the end he will forget" (Version B).

The expression יסוף should be understood as "it will be reduced" (i.e., his learning will be reduced). The first part of the saying is interpreted in ARN A as follows: "How is this? It teaches that if a person learns one tractate or two tractates or three tractates and does not increase them." ARN B has: "To teach you that anyone who learns one

---

[2] To this point the passage is identical in LamRab, Petiḥta 35, (fol. 18b). In all the manuscripts of Taʿanit, Baba Batra, and early authorities (ראשונים): ואסף. However in LamRab: יסוף. Cf. ed. Malter, p. 146.

[3] יאסף appears in all the versions of the Babylonian Talmud.

[4] For example, see the commentaries attributed to Rashi, Maimonides, Meiri, Mahzor Vitri, Itzhak of Toledo, Bahye ibn Paquda, and others.

[5] The order differs between the two versions. In Version B, a saying is added: ודשמש ולא מקיים חייב קטלי קטילין (and whoever makes use, but does not fulfill, deserves to die.)

passage of the Torah (if he does not continue to) study, but does not study, his end will be to forget." From the context it is unclear whether this means that whoever learns one passage must review the passage or whether he should learn other passages. Since ARN is interpreting Hillel's words "he who does not add," it is more reasonable to take them to mean that the student must add to what he has learned.

At any rate, according to both versions, the addition that Hillel demands is not one of time—an addition of the hours of the day—but an addition of study itself. The expression יסוף or יסוף[6] does not mean he will die, but that his learning will decrease. From the Mishnah itself it is clear that the intention is not to threaten punishment of death on whoever does not increase his study, since this punishment is intended for those who do not study at all: "And he who does not study deserves to die." However, we may question whether the increase called for is to add "a tractate or two or three tractates" or "a passage of the Torah."

It seems more reasonable to interpret Hillel's saying on the obligation to increase as meaning to increase by making new interpretations of the Torah. Thus, whoever does not add to the Torah, his Torah will decrease. There are many examples in the teachings of the Tannaim that one must be innovative in the study of Torah. Rabbi Yehoshua asked the sages who came from Yavne, "What new discovery did you make in the House of Learning today?" When the visiting sages answer him politely that they had nothing new, Rabbi Yehoshua says to them, "It is impossible for the house of learning to be without any novelty."[7]

In ʾAbot 2, Mishnah 8, Rabban Yohanan ben Zakkai recounts the praises of his disciples. He calls Rabbi Eliezer ben Hyrcanus "a cemented cistern which loses not a drop."[8] But he says Rabbi Elazar ben Arakh is like "an overflowing spring"[9]—according to one interpretation, "making innovations on his own."[10] According to the plain text of the Mishnah, Rabban Yohanan ben Zakkai regarded Rabbi

[6] See above, note 1.
[7] t.Soṭ 7:9; y.Soṭ 3 (18d); y.Hag 1 (75d); b.Hag 3a; Mekhilta Bo, 15:58; ARN A 18 (34a). Even Eliezer ben Hyrcanus, who was not one of the outstanding innovators, asks the sages who come to him, "What new thing did you learn in the house of learning today?" (m.Yad 4:3).
[8] Cf. both versions of ARN (A 14 29b; B 29, Ibid.) on the Mishnah.
[9] Ibid.
[10] Cf. the commentary of Rabbi Yonah of Gerona.

Eliezer ben Hyrcanus, "the cemented cistern," as the first among his disciples: "If all the sages of Israel were in one scale of the balance and Eliezer ben Hyrcanus in the other, he would outweigh them all." But the Mishnah offers another tradition as well: "Abba Shaul said in his name, If all the sages of Israel, together with Eliezer ben Hyrcanus, were in one scale of the balance, and Elazar ben Arakh, in the other scale, he would outweigh them all."

According to ARN B, "Abba Shaul used to say in the name of Rabbi Aqiba who said in his name, "he did not say [that], but 'if all the sages of Israel would be in one scale of the balance and Eliezer ben Hyrcanus with them, [nevertheless] the finger of Rabbi Elazar ben Arakh would outweigh them all.'" From the continuation of the Mishnah it appears that Rabban Yohanan ben Zakkai regarded Rabbi Elazar ben Arakh as his primary disciple.

In Mishnah 9 it says that Rabban Yohanan ben Zakkai said to his disciples, "Go forth and see which is the good way to which a man should cleave." And he also said to them, "Go forth and see which is the evil way that a man should shun." Regarding the answers of these two disciples, he says, "I approve the words of Elazar ben Arakh, for in his words yours are included." In the continuation of the Mishnaic passage that tells of Rabban Yohana ben Zakkai's preference for the opinion of Rabbi Elazar ben Arakh, ARN A tells that upon the death of the son of Rabbi Yohanan, his disciples came to comfort him, but he refused their consolation "until Rabbi Elazar ben Arakh entered; when he saw him he said to his servant: Take a vessel and come after me to the bathouse, for he is a great man and I cannot stand [against] him."

From the traditions on the explication of מעשי מרכבה (the chapters of the chariot) by Rabbi Elazar ben Arakh before Rabban Yohanan ben Zakkai we may conclude that he was indeed the foremost disciple. The traditions related in the Tosefta, Mekhilta de Rabbi Shimon ben Yohai, and the Talmuds[11] relate the things which the outstanding disciples recited. Rabban Yohanan ben Zakkai gives Rabbi Elazar ben

---

[11] t.Hag 12:1-2; y.Hag 2 (77b); b.Hag 14b; Mekhilta de R. Shimon Bar Yohai, pp. 158–59. The passage was printed in Hoffman's edition of the Mekhilta according to the Cambridge manuscript published by Schechter in *JQR* (1904) 443–45. In the Tosefta and the Mekhilta, only Rabbi Elazar ben Arakh is mentioned. In the Talmuds, the story was expanded and the other disciples of Rabban Yohanan also discussed the "chariot." Cf. D. J. Halperin, *The Falls of the Chariot* (Tübingen, 1988), pp. 13–17.

Arakh the highest praise: "Happy are you, Abraham our father, that Elazar ben Arakh is your descendent," and according to the Mekhilta, Rabban Yoḥanan ben Zakkai testified regarding him, "If all the sages of Israel would be in one scale of the balance and Rabbi Elazar ben Arakh in the other, he would outweigh all of them." The Mekhilta gives no indication of a second version or a different opinion.

One may presume that the tradition giving Rabbi Eliezer ben Hyrcanus as the foremost disicple developed after Rabbi Elazar ben Arakh failed to accompany Rabban Yoḥanan ben Zakkai and his companions to Yavne and "his name declined in Torah" (ARN A), or "his name declined in wisdom" (ARN B).

To summarize this point, Rabbi Elazar ben Arakh, "the overflowing spring," was held in the highest esteem by Rabban Yoḥanan ben Zakkai, who himself also reinterpreted and added new insights to the Torah. Even though he was his disciple, he was, as his teacher, said, "father of wisdom and father of generations."[12]

The crucial point in interpreting this saying of Hillel is the fact that the verb *add* refers to the words of Torah, meaning that the individual expands the words and adds to the written words from the oral. In Tosefta Megilla (2:41) we learn,[13] "Rabbi Yehuda says: He who translates a verse literally is a deceiver and, he adds, is a blasphemer." *Add* here means expands the verse beyond that which is written, which may not be done when translating the Torah in a public reading. Likewise, Tosefta Berakhot (4:18)[14]: "A story of four old [scholars] who were sitting in the gatehouse of Rabbi Yehoshua ... and they were discussing that which Rabbi Aqiba had taught them ... they added on their own." Similarly Tosefta Shabbat (8:4)[15]: Rabbi Aqiba and Munbaz disagreed over a point of law. Munbaz explained his view and "Rabbi Aqiba said to me: 'I add myself to your words,'" and he added an additional reason to reinforce his dissenting opinion. In Mishnah Kilaim, the tractate opens with those categories which are not considered *kilaim* (forbidden injunction) when planted together. The various kinds of vegetables are listed in Mishnayot 1–3, but "Rabbi Aqiba added to them garlic and

---

[12] ARN B 14 (29a).

[13] The baraita appears in b.Kid 49a with certain differences.

[14] For a midrash of Hillel like this baraita, cf. Beth Hamidrash, part 5, p. 95.

[15] Similarly in b.Shab 62b.

wild garlic" and other pairs, which are like the kinds the Mishnah listed.

A few additional examples from the halakhic midrashim and from the Talmud will suffice. At the beginning[16] of the Mekhilta of Rabbi Ishmael, Rabbi Aqiba interprets scripture and concludes that God spoke to Moses by the merit of Israel, regarding which Ben Azzai says: "I am not responding to my teacher's words, but adding to them, and not only with Moses did he speak by virtue of Israel, but with all the prophets." In Sifre Beha'alotkha,[17] Rabbi Aqiba presents an interpretation regarding which "Rabbi Shimon ha-Teimani said: 'I am not annuling Rabbi Aqiba's words but adding to them.'" In the Babylonian Talmud (b.Ber 46a) the blessing to be recited by a guest in the grace after meals on behalf of a host is given, and it says that Rabbi [Yehuda ha-Nasi] added words. In the Jerusalem Talmud (y.Soṭ 9 [23a]), this principle is given as an idiom: "Like a man who says I add this to the words of my teacher."

Hillel's saying demands that an individual seek new insights and add to the teaching he recevies, and he that does not add to his Torah, his Torah decreases, but in ARN the saying was already taken technically, as if to say that one should add tractates or review a Biblical passage. According to the interpretation of the Amora Rav Yosef, this demand was understood as a demand to add time to one's study and the term יסוף was taken to mean a threat of capital punishment: יאסף. In other words: Hillel's noble demand that one add insights to what he learns was reinterpreted mechanically in terms of quantity, time and punishment.

Hillel's saying in 'Abot 2, Mishnah 7: "the more Torah, the more life" should also be interpreted along these lines. Usually this is taken to mean that he who studies Torah will attain added years of life, as it says in Proverbs 3:2: "For length of life is with me, and years of life will be added to you." However, the group of expressions in this Mishnah (the more flesh, the more worms; the more property, the more anxiety, etc.) does not provide rewards and punishments, but describes the state of the world as Hillel saw it. More Torah here means adding to Torah, increasing the Torah, increasing it itself, adding and creating.

---

[16] Masekhta de Pisḥa, Ch. 1, p. 5.
[17] Paragraph 103, p. 101.

"More life" refers to the words of Torah, which live forever, as the expression appears in Tosefta Sota and the parallel passages quoted above.[18]

"Innovation in the house of learning" and "words of Torah that are fruitful and multiply" are like saplings that bring "life to the world," and in the language attributed to a *"bat qol"* (echo) speaking of the controversy between Beth Shammai and Beth Hillel, לו ואלו דברי אלהים חיים.[19] This does not mean "both these and those are the words of the living God." The word חיים is not a description of God—which would be out of place in this context—but a characterization of the words of Beth Shammai and Beth Hillel. The teaching here is that even though they are in disagreement, the words of both are divine and alive. The same expression appears in a different place regarding a dispute between Amoraim, of which the Holy One, Blessed be He, says, "Both these and those are living words of God."[20] Clearly, God is not characterizing himself, but the good quality of the dispute.

This saying of Hillel is also expressed in the teaching of Jesus on the growth and expansion of those who already have.[21] As in the teaching of Paul[22] and the Western church fathers, it is adapted and applied to the kingdom of heaven and faith rather than study.[23] However, the kingdom of heaven may not have originally appeared in Jesus' saying and the parallel to Hillel may have been greater. That is, Jesus may be expanding the idea from study of Torah and creativity in Torah through study to a life of Torah in general.[24]

II

In Leviticus Rabba, Chapter 1, p. 16, we read: Rabbi Levi opened [his exposition on] scripture [thus]: "For it is better that he should say to

[18] See note 7 above.
[19] y.Ber 1 (72b) and parallel passages; b.'Erub 13b and parallel passages. Cf. also m.Yoma 35b.
[20] M.Giṭṭ 6:2.
[21] Matt. 13:12; 13:32,29; Mark 4:55; Luke 8:10. Cf. B. T. Viviano, *Study as Worship* (Leiden, 1978), pp. 24–25.
[22] Eph. 4:15 and additional places.
[23] Cf. Viviano (note 21 above and note 25 below).
[24] D. Flusser, *Judaism and the Origin of Christianity* (Jerusalem, 1988), pp. 263–335; 379–80.

you 'Come up here,' than move you down to make room for a nobleman" (Prov 25:7). Rabbi Aqiba taught in the name of Rabbi Shimon ben Azzai: Distance yourself two or three places from your place and sit; descend so that they tell you to ascend, but do not ascend so that they tell you to descend; it is better that they tell you ascend, ascend and do not say to you descend, descend. Hillel said: השפלתי היא השפלתי, הגבהתי, הגבהתי היא השפלתי (my humbling is my exaltation, my exalta- tion is my humbling). What is the proof? "Who sets his throne so high, but deigns to look down so low" (Psalms 113:5-6). In this midrash, the saying of Hillel is connected to the saying of Ben Azzai that it is better for a man to humble himself and merit being exalted. Rabbi Levi related the sayings of these two sages to the opening verse of Leviticus: "And the Lord called Moses"—Moses humbled himself and the Lord called him and exalted him.

In Midrash Tanḥuma[25] on this verse, the first part of the same homily is quoted in the name of Rabbi Tanḥum. It states that one should remove himself two or three seats from his place, but without the addi- tion of Hillel's homily:

> This is what scripture means when it says: 'For it is better that he should say to you "Come up here," than, "Move you down to make room for a nobleman."' Rabbi Tanhum says: 'Distance yourself two or three places so that they say ascend, and do not ascend, so that they not say to you: "Descend." ... Likewise Moses did not ascend until the Holy One—Blessed Be He—called him. And He called Moses.'

One the other hand, we find this homily opens with Hillel's saying in Shemot Rabba (Chapter 45): "Rabbi Tanḥuma Bar Abba opened [his exposition of scripture thus]: 'For it is better that he should say to you 'Come up here,' than 'move you down.' Hillel says: My humbling is my exaltation, my exaltation is my humbling. It is better that they tell him go up higher and not say to him go down lower."

Even though in some midrashim Hillel's saying is tied to the idea that it befits a man to take a back bench, these are in fact two separate sayings. This is clear since the homily on the verse in Proverbs and the first verse of Leviticus appears without Hillel's saying. We find this

---

[25] TanYash 1; ed., Buber, par. 2.

saying twice in ARN and once in the Babylonian Talmud without any reference to Hillel's saying. In ARN[26] we read an expansion of Shemaya's saying "Despise authority" (ARN B 10): "Rabbi Yose says: Descend above and ascend below—If a man demotes himself he is elevated and if he elevates himself he is demoted."[27] In chapter 25 (Version I only) among the sayings of Ben Azzai we read, "He used to say, 'Descend two or three steps and sit'; it is better for them to tell you ascend than to tell you descend, as it is said: 'For it is better that he should say to you "Come up here," than move you down to make room for a nobleman' (Proverbs 25:7)."

The tradition in the Babylonian Talmud ('Erubin 13b) is a special case. It presents the story mentioned in the Mishnah (m.Suk 2:7) according to which elders of Beth Shammai and elders of Beth Hillel went to visit Rabbi Yohanan ben Hahorani. The passage concludes that Beth Hillel gained the privilege to have the halakha conform to their view "because they are compromising and self-effacing ... and not only that, but they also put the words of Beth Shammai before their own words." It continues: "In order to teach you that whoever humbles himself, the Holy One Blessed Be He exalts him and whoever exalts himself, the Holy One Blessed Be He humbles." This idea is found in a partial fashion in several places, especially the emphasis that whoever lowers himself, the Holy One Blessed Be He lifts him up.[28]

Hillel's saying does not deal with banquet etiquette or how to reach a nobler position respectfully or how to undertstand divine providence. The saying stands on its own and teaches that the seeking of aggrandizement is in itself degradation, but the degradation one seeks for oneself is in itself elevation: "My humbling is my exaltation, my exaltation is my humbling." In the characteristic manner of Hillel, the idea is not presented as an abstraction, but in the first person. He applies it, as it were, to himself. This saying does not deal with reward and punishment, but with a religious idea in ethics and philosophy: Humiliation itself is one's exaltation, just as exaltation itself is one's humiliation. Teachers and homilists linked Hillel's saying to verses that

---

[26] A 11 (23b); B 22 (23b).

[27] Transcribed on the basis of ARN B, which is clearer.

[28] Derekh Eretz Zuta, Ch. 9 (Higger, Tractate Yirat Het, p. 80); b.'Erub 54a; b.Sanh 17a; Midrash Hillel Beit Hamidrash, part. 5, p. 91), and elsewhere.

speak of appropriate religious behavior (Proverbs) or verses that have a religious character and speak of the ways of the divine providence (Psalms).

The connection between Hillel's saying and appropriate behavior at a banquet appears already in the New Testament in a tradition regarding Jesus' actions and teaching. In Luke 14:1-13 we read that Jesus was invited to a Sabbath dinner in the home of one of the leading Pharisees. First, he healed a sick person on the Sabbath. When he saw how they chose to sit at the head of the table, he told them a parable (vss. 7-10) much like the words of Rabbi Aqiba in the name of Ben Azzai, ending with an expression very close to Hillel's saying. But instead of putting it in the first person, he says: "For everyone who exalts himself will be humbled, and whoever humbles himself will be exalted" (vs. 11).[29] As in the rabbinic tradition, the idea is found in the New Testament alone without reference to the parable of the dinner, but as a conclusion to the homily in Luke 18:14 and Matthew 23:12.[30]

To summarize: Already in earliest times the saying of Hillel was added to sermons on behavior at banquets and behavior in general, but by virtue of this context, its meaning was reduced and it came to teach how a man should reach a nobler place. But the primary reduction of the saying is in the reduction of one's personal responsibility toward oneself and the reduction of the significance of pride and humility.

III

In Tosefta Sukka (4:3)[31] we read: הלל הזקן אומר: למקום שלבי אוהב לשם רגליי מוליכות אותי, אם אתה תבוא לביתי אני אבא לביתיך אם אתה לא תבוא לביתי אני לא אבא לביתיך שנאמר 'בכל המקום אשר אזכיר את שמי אבא אליך וביירכתיך'. (Hillel the Elder said: To the place my heart loves, my feet lead me; if you come to my house I will come to your house, if you

<hr/>

[29] Strack and Billerbeck present many sources in their commentary, some of them relevant to the issue (Vol. II, 203–7). But they refer neither to Hillel's saying nor to the parable of the banquet and its explication.

[30] Also in the New Testament we find the idea that God raises the humble or those who humble themselves (cf. Matt. 5:19; 18:4).

[31] This passage appears in a partial form in Mekhilta, end of Yitro, p. 243 in the name of Rabbi Eliezer ben Yaaqov. Also partially in ARN among the sayings of Hillel. Cf. ARN A 12 and B 27 (fol. 28a).

do not come to my house, I will not come to your house, as it says: "In every place where I cause my name to be mentioned, I will come to you and bless you" (Exod 20:21).

This *baraita* is one of those that tells about what happened in the Temple during the Tabernacle celebrations of *simḥat beit hashoeva*. One may presume that its content refers to the Temple. Thus we find explicitly in the Babylonian Talmud (b.Suk 53a): It is learned: they said of him of Hillel the Elder that when he rejoiced at the celebration of the drawing of the water he said, if I am here everyone is here; if I am absent, who is here?[32] To the place my heart loves my feet lead me;[33] if you come to my house I will come to your house, if you do not come to my house I will not come to your house as it says: "In every place where I cause my name to be mentioned, I will come to you and bless you" (Exod 20:24).

Who is the subject of the two sayings—God or Hillel? Who says, "If I am here ...?" and who says, "If you come to my house ..."? Rashi interpreted the passage to mean that Hillel said these things in God's name: "He would preach to the masses in the name of the Holy One Blessed be He that they not sin—If I am here everyone is here (i.e., as long as I desire this house and my presence dwells in it, its honor is sustained and everyone will come here); but if you sin, I will remove my presence and who will come here?" And indeed we find in some versions of the Talmud: "And also the Holy One Blessed Be He says: if you come to my house, etc."[34] But this is only hyper-correction[35] and in the primary texts, God is not mentioned as the speaker (e.g., in Ms. Munich and the fragments of the Sheiltot):[36] "He used to say, etc." The Tosafists ("If I am here") write: [Rashi] wrote in his commentary that Hillel said this in the name of the Holy One Blessed be He, but in the

---

[32] This saying is found among the sayings of Hillel in ARN A without the context of *Simḥat Beit Hashoeva*.

[33] Regarding the text in the Babylonian Talmud, cf. Lieberman's commentary on the Tosefta, pp. 887–88.

[34] Cf. Ms. Munich B; Ein Ya'aqov, first edition; Aggadot Hatalmud, Kad Haqemah, item "'Azeret" (Ed. Chavel, p. 296) and elsewhere. Cf. Diqduqei Hasoferim, p. 172, note 6.

[35] As S. Lieberman correctly pointed out in *Tosefta Kifshuṭah*, Part 4 (New York, 1962), p. 888.

[36] *Tarbiz* 6 (1935) 493.

Jerusalem Talmud, it is clear that he said it about himself and does he
need to praise himself, etc." The Tosafists disagree with Rashi regarding the saying, "If I am here ...," but they agree regarding the saying,
"If you come to my house ...": "And who said, 'If you come to my
house I will come to your house?' That could only be the Divine
presence, which may be expounded from the scripture: 'In every place
where I cause my name to be mentioned, I will come to you and bless
you.'"[37]

In both versions of ARN, Hillel's words were interpreted in this
way. In version A 12, fol. 28a, we read:

> He used to say: if you come to my house, I will come to your house.
> To the place my heart loves my feet lead me. If you come to my house,
> I will come to your house. How is that so? These are people who go
> morning and evening to synagogues and houses of learning—the Holy
> One Blessed be He blesses them for the world to come, as it says: 'In
> every place where I cause my name to be mentioned, I will come to
> you and bless you.

Version B has:

> He used to say: If you come to my house, I will come to your house—
> these are Israel who leave their threshing floors and their winepresses
> and go up to Jerusalem on three pilgrimages and the Holy One Blessed
> be He returns to them and blesses them as it says: 'I will come to you
> and bless you.'

In both versions, the words are taken to mean that God makes his
blessing conditional on Israel's coming to his house: If you come to my
house, I will come to your house and bless you. But in Version A, the
expression applies to synagogues and houses of learning and in Version
B to the Temple in Jerusalem.[38]

---

[37] Lieberman accepts this interpretation and regards the view of the Tosafists as
the plain meaning of the text.

[38] The two different interpretations of בכל מקום already appear in the Mekhilta
Masekhta de baHodesh, Ch. 11, p. 243: בכל מאום וגו־ שאני נגלה עליך בבית הבחירה
וכוליה. However below: מכאן אמרו כל עשרה בני אדם שנכנסין לבית הכנסת שכינה
עמההם ... ומנין אפילו שנים ... ומנין אפילו אהד שנאמר בכל המקום אשר אזכיר את שמי אבוא
אליך. Hillel's saying appears in the Mekhilta in the name of Rabbi Eliezer ben Yaaqov.

However, in no case do the sages speak in God's name in the name of the divine presence. This is the style and language of the prophets. The sages speak to the people or to God, but never in his name. The sages express their opinion with the help of scripture or without it, but they never speak for God. If they wish to repeat something God has said, they preface it with: המקום אומר (the everlasting says), or אומרת השכינה (the divine presence says) and similar expressions.

The verse, "In every place where I cause my name to be mentioned," should not be interpreted regarding anything but a person, since God does not mention his own name, but people do mention it.[39] God promises in this verse that in every place where his name is mentioned, he will come and bless. The same verse forbids the making of gods of silver and gold and demands that "you make for me an altar of earth," promising that "in every place where I cause my name to be mentioned, I will come to you and bless you."[40]

During the tabernacle celebrations, when everyone is singing before God, Hillel says to God: If you come to my house, that causes your presence to abide, I will be able to come to your house, but if you do not come to my house and do not cause your presence to abide in the house which we have built in your honor, then we will not come to the house of the Lord, but to a house of stone and wood.

There is no reason whatsoever to presume that in the tradition in the Tosefta, which gives two sentences in the first person, Hillel is speaking of himself in one sentence and on behalf of God in the other.

---

[39] Cf. especially the commentary by A. B. Ehrlich in *Mikra Kifshutto*, p. 174. At the beginning of his comments, he writes, "It seems to me that Rabbenu Yona already said in one of his books that this 'I will cause my name to be mentioned' means you will mention." In Rabbenu Yona's commentary on the Torah, there is no gloss on this verse. I do not know where or whether he made such a comment.

[40] Onkelos avoids translating the word אזכיר. Likewise Yonatan translates: בכל אתרא דאישרי שכינתי ואנת פלח קדמי. However, he stresses the human's actions. The "Jerusalem translation" reads as if the verse said, תזכיר (i.e., בכל דתדכרו). Similarly, Neophyte translates, adding: די תדכרון ית שמי בצלו. Likewise in the Syriac and Samaritan translation, Ms. A (Ed. Tal, p. 307). In the translation of Saadia Gaon: רשות להזכיר את שמי. In Midrash Shmuel on 'Abot 3:7, in the name of Rabbi Yom Tov ben Avraham-Ashvili: יש אומרים אזכיר כמו תזכיר. In the Ms. Or Beaphela (Torah Shelema, p. 165), אל תקרי אזכיר אלא תזכיר.

Likewise the baraita in the Babylonian Talmud. It contains three sentences:

(1) If I am here ...
(2) To the place which I love ...
(3) If you come to my house ...

Since Hillel is obviously speaking of himself in the first two sentences, he must be speaking of himself in the third sentence as well.

These sayings may sound daring and even arrogant when addressed to God and have been interpreted not according to their plain meaning. But although there is a remarkable religious strength in the words of Hillel, there is no arrogance. The interpretation of "if you come to my house" as something said by God involves a reduction of the image: God requests that we come to his house and promises that he will return the favor to the one who comes to his house and come to that person's house. In this way, an exalted saying turns into petty bargaining.

HILLEL AND SCRIPTURE:
FROM AUTHORITY TO EXEGESIS

IN DISCUSSING HILLEL'S use of Scripture, we must always distinguish between the historical Hillel and later accretions to his image.[1] There are also various exegetical difficulties. In the materials we shall discuss below, however, neither of these problems is too difficult or crucial. More daunting is the paucity of materials: of the 105 pericopae mentioning Hillel assembled by Professor Jacob Neusner in his *The Rabbinic Traditions about the Pharisees Before 70* (vol. 1, chapters 9-10), only one-third (35) include any biblical verses at all. Of those, barely half impute the citation of Scripture or any reflection upon it to Hillel himself.

Moreover, the best-known statements of Hillel are remarkably nonbiblical, even anti-biblical. Thus, in the central rabbinic repository of his apothegms, the Mishnaic tractate *Ab*, we find no quotations of Scripture or allusions to verses. We do find—as only rarely among the statements of these "fathers"—the usage of the vernacular and nonbiblical language, Aramaic (1:13; 2:7). We also find a nonbiblical genre— paradox (1:14), a rhetorical genre which reappears elsewhere among Hillel's apothegms.[2]

In a similar way, according to a famous story (b.Shab 31a), when Hillel was asked to summarize the Torah in one rule, his response is an Aramaic rendition of the Golden Rule negatively formulated—"don't do to others what is hateful to you"—not the scriptural "love your neighbor

---

[1] I would like to acknowledge the insights contributed by my friend, Paul Mandel, as well as the special usefulness of J. Neusner's groundbreaking work, *The Rabbinic Traditions about the Pharisees Before 70*, 3 vols. (Leiden, 1971).

[2] See, *inter alia*, t.Ber 2:24 and 7:24; t.Suk 4:3, ed. Zuckermandel (pp. 5, 17, 198); b.Suk 53a.

as yourself" (Lev 19:18). Correspondingly, in the collection of his legal disputes with Shammai, recorded in m.ʿEduy 1:1-3, no verses or exegesis are cited. As the topics themselves suggest and as the parallel texts show, none seems to have been involved.[3]

The nonbiblical orientation of Hillel's teaching is confirmed by the observation that of the four legal opinions for which he is most famous in rabbinic tradition, two consist of innovations allowing the circumvention of scriptural law. First, Hillel allowed debts not to be voided by the sabbatical year despite Deut 15:2-3. Second, he allowed houses in walled cities to return to their original owners despite their inability to fulfill the scriptural demand that they repurchase them from the current titleholders (Lev 25:29-30).[4]

As for Hillel's other two famous legal views, one (discussed below, Part I) is Hillel's affirmation that the Paschal sacrifice should be offered even when the eve of a Passover falls on a Sabbath. He tried to justify this opinion on the basis of scriptural exegesis, but carried it only by an appeal to tradition. Hillel's other famous legal view, concerning the proper consumption of the Paschal sacrifice, is never presented as exegesis, but rather as a practice which corresponds to the plain sense of a verse (Ex 12:8/Num 9:11)—a claim later contested by no less a sage than R. Johanan. Hillel's practice made its way into the

---

[3] According to t.ʿduy 1:1 (ed. Zuckermandel, p. 454), neither Hillel's nor Shammai's opinion is based on a biblical verse; only "the Sages'" opinion is said to have rested on Num 15:20. For an attempt to derive Hillel's and Shammai's opinions too from differing exegesis of that same verse, see A. Schwarz, *Die Erleichterungen der Schammaiten und die Erschwerungen der Hilleliten: Ein Beitrag zur Entwicklungsgeschichte der Halachah* (Vienna, 1893), pp. 26–29. The suggested interpretations are so abstruse, however, that it is difficult to accept them without more explicit evidence. They are not in the Yerushalmi, despite the medieval source Schwarz quotes (see B. Ratner, *Ahawath Zion We-Jeruscholaim, Traktate Terumoth und Challa* [Vilna, 1904], pp. 126–27 [in Hebrew]). Otherwise, no verses are suggested as the basis for the disputes between Hillel and Shammai. Cf. below, note 33.

[4] For the main texts, see, for the former, m.Shevi 10:3, m.Giṭṭ 4:3, and SifDeut 113 (ed. Finkelstein, pp. 173–74); for the latter, m.ʿArak 9:4 and SifLev, SifBehar 4:8 (ed. Weiss, p. 108d). Cf. below, note 42. In general, on the two enactments, see the recent discussion by I. Ben-Shalom, "Hillel the Elder: His Personality and Accomplishments on their Contemporary Background," *Leaders and Leadership in Jewish and World History*, ed. I. Malkin and Z. Tzahor (Jerusalem, 1992), pp. 117–21 (in Hebrew).

Passover liturgy (haggadah) merely as an appendix, a reminiscence unsanctified by any benediction.[5]

The proper conclusion from this is that Hillel is to be considered a sage of the oral tradition. Just as Josephus characterizes the Pharisees as the virtuosos of the "tradition of the fathers" and the Law (not of Scripture),[6] and the same emerges from such texts as Mark 7 and the comparison of Gal 1:14 and Phil 3:5. So too, what is characteristic of Hillel's teachings, whether ethical or legal, is that they stand on his authority and that of his teachers in the Pharisaic tradition—but *not* on that of Scripture. Indeed, this insistence on the importance and even primacy of the Oral Law is underlined in the famous story of the Gentile who came to Hillel to convert but wanted only to learn the Written Law.[7] The point of Hillel's trick, which demonstrated that one needs to depend on teachers even to be able to read, is that the Oral Law has primacy.

However, two groups of traditions—the ones which aim to depict Hillel's rise to prominence—show him dealing with Scripture in a very direct way. These warrant special discussion here. In Part I, we shall study the traditions which refer to the legal topic(s) "on account of which Hillel came up [i.e., immigrated to Palestine] from Babylonia." That is, it is said that the resolution of legal problems was the reason for Hillel's immigration. These traditions should be understood in light of the third-century statement (b.Suk 20a) that the Torah had been forgotten in Palestine. Thus, a Babylonian—explicitly compared to Ezra—was needed to restore its knowledge. As the written Torah—the Pentateuch—cannot be forgotten,[8] this characterization of the need for

---

[5] See b.Pes 115a and S. Lieberman, *Tosefta Ki-Fshutah*, 10 vols. (New York, 1955–1988), vol. 4, p. 510 (in Hebrew); cf. Neusner, *Rabbinic Traditions*, vol. 1, pp. 257–58, 280–81.

[6] Josephus, *War* 1.5.2 §110; 2.8.4 §162; *Ant* 13.10.6 §297; 13.16.2 §408; *Life* 38 §191. See also *War* 2.17.3-4 §§411–17, *Ant* 18.1.3 §12 (for the contrast here with the Sadducees, who follow Scripture alone, see G. Baumbach, "The Sadducees in Josephus," *Josephus, the Bible, and History* [ed. L. H. Feldman and G. Hata; Detroit, 1989], pp. 177–78) and *Ant* 20.9.1 §201 (for the identification of these legalists as Pharisees, cf. A. I. Baumgarten, "The Name of the Pharisees," *JBL* 102 [1983] 413–14, note 9). In general, cf. idem, "The Pharisaic Paradosis," *HTR* 80 (1987) 63–77.

[7] b.Shab 31a; ARN A 15 (ed. Schechter, p. 61).

[8] Cf. the rabbinic phrase, "It is rolled up and deposited in a corner and whoever wishes to study it can come and study" (b.Kid 66a).

Hillel's interpretation refers to the Oral Torah; or rather, to the combination of the Oral Torah and Scripture. The same conclusion underlies the other group of traditions, discussed in Part II, concerning the debate about the Paschal sacrifice on Sabbath. These claim that some sages ("the sons of Bathyra") appealed to Hillel because they themselves had forgotten the relevant law, and made him their leader (Nasi) after he showed his knowledge of it.[9] Nevertheless, the topics "on account of which Hillel came up from Babylonia" all deal with Scripture, as does the debate about the Paschal sacrifice. The relationship between Scripture and the Oral Law thus requires investigation.

I. "ON ACCOUNT OF THIS HILLEL CAME UP FROM BABYLONIA"

The notion that Hillel came up from Babylonia on account of some halachic issue or issues is found in three passages in rabbinic literature. Two of them, in the Tosefta and Sifra, deal only with an issue concerning leprosy. The third, in the Yerushalmi, deals with that issue and two others. We will deal first with the leprosy issue.

The laws of Leviticus 13 entrust to priests the diagnosis of leprosy and give them full authority to quarantine for two successive weeks persons suspected of being afflicted by it and to proclaim them impure due to it. They also had authority to proclaim them pure after being cured of it or after being determined never to have had it. But what if the priest errs and declares an afflicted person pure or vice versa? According to our sources, the answer was supplied by Hillel on the basis of Lev 13:37, "He is pure, and the priest shall declare him pure."

t.Neg 1:16 (ed. Zuckermandel, p. 619)

(a) If a priest declared a pure man impure or an impure man pure and

---

[9] It is noteworthy that the sages in question may well have been of Babylonian origin. It is not said that they appointed Hillel "Nasi" *simpliciter* but, rather, "Nasi over them." That is, the discussion and appointment may have been within a limited framework. The implications cannot be pursued here. Cf. Ben-Shalom, "Hillel the Elder" 116; H. Albeck, "The Sanhedrin and its President," *Zion* 8 (1942/43) 166–67 (in Hebrew); and E. Nodet, *Essai sur les origines du Judaïsme, de Josué aux Pharisiens* (Paris, 1992), pp. 230–36.

he handled [i.e., inspected] him (ונזקק לו[10]) at the end of the week [of quarantine], (b) [then,] despite the fact that he declared the impure man impure, or the pure man pure, he did nothing. (c) [For] of impurity it [Scripture] says "he is impure and the priest shall declare him impure" and of purity it says "he is pure and the priest shall declare him pure" [Lev 13:37]. And this is one of the things on account of which Hillel came up from Babylonia.

SifLev, Tazria 9:16
(ed. Weiss, pp. 66d-67a; Ms. Vatican 66, p. 275)

(a) "He is pure" [Lev 13:37]. Perhaps [one might infer that] he [the previously quarantined man] may simply depart and go his own way—therefore [i.e., to exclude that inference] it says, "and the priest shall declare him pure" [Lev 13:37]. (b) But from "and the priest shall declare him pure," perhaps [one might infer that] if the priest said of an impure man "pure" he would be pure—therefore it says "he is pure and the priest shall declare him pure." On account of this thing Hillel came up from Babylonia.

y.Pes 6:1,33a

On account of three things Hillel came up from Babylonia. (a) "He is pure"—perhaps [one might infer that] he may simply depart and go his own way, therefore it says, "and the priest shall declare him pure." (b) If "and the priest shall declare him pure," perhaps [one might think that] if a priest said of an impure man "pure" he would be pure—therefore it says "he is pure and the priest shall declare him pure." On account of this Hillel came up from Babylonia.

---

[10] Zuckermandel's edition reads here נזקק (without the opening copula), but that edition (according to p. 478) is based upon the Vienna manuscript which, like other witnesses, in fact reads *with* the copula (see J. Krengel, "Variae Lectiones zur Tosefta," *MGWJ* 45 [1901] 28; S. Lieberman, *Tosefeth Rishonim* [4 vols.; Jerusalem, 1936–1939], vol. 3, p. 167 [in Hebrew]). This point is important. *Without* the copula, נזקק is a directive that the priest should reexamine the man, as six times in the preceding paragraph of the Tosefta (association with which probably caused Zuckermandel's error). *With* the copula, all of paragraph (a) becomes the case ruled upon by paragraph (b). The text without the copula is in any case difficult: How could the law impose an obligation on someone to know that the priest had erred?

(Two other matters follow here in y.Pes and will be discussed below.) The Tosefta refers to a man who has been diagnosed incorrectly. That is, a priest declared someone pure when he was impure or vice versa. Then, after a week, the same priest inspected the man and correctly diagnosed him. The law rules that such a priest "did nothing."

There are two radically different understandings of this law. One understanding, offered in the classic eighteenth-century rabbinical commentaries, was followed by the modern German commentator on this tractate.[11] It construes the law to treat someone who has been wrongly pronounced impure and quarantined. If, at the end of the week, he is reexamined and symptoms are found and so he is found to be impure, then, in order to meet the biblical demand of two weeks' quarantine, he must be quarantined for *two* weeks. The first week, since it was mistakenly imposed, does not qualify. It is of the first imposition of quarantine that paragraph (b) speaks when it rules that the priest "did nothing."

The other explanation, apparently suggested by S. Lieberman,[12] is that the priest's error at the first examination disqualified him from engaging again in such diagnosis. So if he does again examine the man, his judgment lacks legal validity even if it is correct. The man who was first wrongly declared impure and then rightly so is therefore still pure, for of the two proclamations, the first was wrong and the second was made by a priest who had been disqualified from such practice. Thus, in terms of legal consequences, throughout the affair, the priest "did nothing."

It seems clear that the latter interpretation is preferable. The classical one reads more into the laconic statement, "he did nothing." Only

---

[11] See D. Pardo, *Ḥasdei David*, 4/2 (Jerusalem 1970/71), p. 15 (in Hebrew); R. Elijah of Vilna's commentary on the Tosefta, printed after Tractate Niddah in the standard Vilna (Romm) edition of the Babylonian Talmud; and W. Windfuhr, *Ahilot/Negaim* (*Die Tosefta* 6/9 = Rabbinische Texte 1/15; Stuttgart, 1959), p. 358, note 101.

[12] Lieberman's formulation (above, note 10) is so telegraphic that it is difficult to be certain: "It means that although at the end of the week the sore is like the priest said, since at first he [the priest] did not properly declare him impure his [second] statement, '[he is] impure', has no effect and he is pure" (my bracketed supplements—D.R.S.). Lieberman is followed by J. Neusner, *A History of the Mishnaic Law of Purities* (SJLA 6; 22 vols.; Leiden, 1974–1977), vol. 6, p. 58. However, Neusner's translation of וגונק is misleading. Its sense emerges clearly from the preceding passage in the Tosefta.

by removing it from its context can it apply to the first examination instead of the second one. Moreover, according to that interpretation, it is nearly impossible to make the prooftexts, quoted in paragraph (c), support the statement of paragraphs a–b. On Lieberman's interpretation, however, the words "he did nothing" apply to everything the priest did (both examinations). And the point of the prooftexts is that a man is first of all pure or impure: the priest's statement only certifies that situation. Thus, it is of no value if wrong.

Furthermore, while it is *possible* that a man who had been wrongly declared pure might go back for an examination a week later, it is much more likely that he would not. How should he know the first diagnosis was wrong and why should he look for trouble? Thus, the first interpretation, which is concerned basically with the status of the man suspected of leprosy, discusses only one of the two cases described in paragraph (a); namely, the man who had wrongly been declared impure. It cannot apply the apodosis ("he did nothing") to anything concerning the case of the man who was objectively impure but first declared pure. This limitation of the classical interpretation, explicitly noted by one of its exponents (R. Elijah of Vilna), impugns its acceptability.

Lieberman's explanation, in contrast, focuses on the status of the priest, who is, after all, the grammatical subject of the law. This interpretation applies equally well to both errors mentioned in paragraph (a): whether the priest declared a pure man impure or an impure man pure, he loses his license. Understood this way, the law better fits its Toseftan context. The preceding paragraph says that while usually the same priest is to conduct the successive weekly examinations, he is to be replaced if he is sick or dies. Thereafter, on this interpretation, our text gives another case in which the original priest is to be replaced.

We conclude that the point of this Toseftan law, said to be the reason for Hillel's move to Palestine, is that leprosy decisions by priests are invalid if they conflict with nature, and priests who make such proclamations are to be disqualified from further practice. This point should be emphasized, in contrast to other versions which state that the natural situation is not by itself enough. We will deal further with these other versions below.

On either interpretation, the use of Scripture in part (c) seems quite primitive. This is, in fact, no exegesis, but only the citation of two half-verses. Moreover, the text cited with regard to impurity does not exist. The phrase, "He is pure and the priest shall declare him pure," is found in Lev 13:37, but no biblical verse reads, "He is impure and the priest shall declare him impure." (The closest candidate is in Lev 13:44, where the text is different and there is no quarantining.)

Thus, the exegete seems to have been working from memory, which fooled him in this case. Or perhaps the exegete had a free-wheeling notion of the biblical text or of the task of the exegete. The statement, "He is pure and the priest shall declare him pure," may have been taken to imply a parallel statement about impurity, much as the author of CD 5.7-11 thought the biblical prohibition of marriage with aunts (Lev 18:13) implied a prohibition of marriage with uncles.

The two other rabbinic works which cite this tradition, the Sifra and the Talmud Yerushalmi, contrast with the Tosefta on three counts: they are clear, they are balanced, and they include explicit exegesis. First, they address directly the validity of objectively wrong diagnoses. None of the ambiguity engendered by the Tosefta's reference to two successive examinations remains. Second, they expand Hillel's statement via symmetry: where the Tosefta had insisted only that a priest cannot overrule nature, they add the insistence that nature cannot do without the priest. Finally, in support of this teaching they do not confine themselves to quoting verses, extant or otherwise. They quote Scripture and subject it to explicit exegesis. They point out the apparent implication of each of two clauses of Lev 13:37 and note the contradiction between the implications: one clause implies that reality is enough, while the other implies that the priest's declaration is enough. They resolve it by concluding that Scripture insists on both reality and declaration.

The version in the Sifra and the Yerushalmi is thus an improvement in every way. It is clear, it quotes real texts, and it makes a neatly symmetric point through explicit exegesis dealing at the second-story level of the contradicting implications of two halves of the same verse. A historian should suspect that the Toseftan version is nearer the beginning, nearer Hillel himself. The Tosefta represents here an early stage, when the statement of principle was important but biblical grounding was not, and when there was no concern to be fair to the priest. The Toseftan version is content to point out the superiority of reality to the priest and says nothing of reality's need to be certified by the priest.

One can well imagine sages and priests (Pharisees and Sadducees?) arguing this point in Hillel's day, but not in those of the later rabbis, when there was hardly any priestly opposition.[13] According to the Tosefta, the point of Hillel's opinion is that the declarations of the priests have no independent constitutive effect. Priests are like doctors, who diagnose, and whose diagnoses may be disproven by the natural facts. They are not like judges, whose rulings have independent authority.[14] This contrasts squarely with the sages' opinion of the efficacy of their own declarations in matters of law in which they claimed competence. Whether with regard to calendrical determinations or to law in general, they claimed that their own declarations had constitutive effect and were valid—even if objectively wrong.[15] Note, in particular, the round statement in m.Bek 4:4: When a sage sits in judgement and errs in that he "declared the pure impure or declared the impure pure, that which he did is done" (although he may or may not have to reimburse the damaged party). This is exactly the opposite of "he did nothing" said by the rabbis of the priests in such circumstances.

One can also imagine priests wishing to claim the same constitutive authority for themselves, both on general principles of party politics and on specific exegetical grounds: Deut 17:8ff., upon which the sages depended,[16] opens by referring to the priests as judges (v. 9).

---

[13] For competition between the sages and priests, see, in general, S. A. Cohen, *The Three Crowns: Structures of Communal Politics in Early Rabbinic Jewry* (Cambridge, 1990), esp. pp. 147–78. After the destruction of the Second Temple (70 C.E.), it is difficult to find evidence for priestly claims for authority as priests. Cf. D. R. Schwartz, *Studies in the Jewish Background of Christianity* (WUNT 60; Tübingen, 1992), pp. 54–55, note 49.

[14] For the following discussion, see my essay, "Law and Truth: On Qumran/Sadducean and Rabbinic Views of Law," *The Dead Sea Scrolls: Forty Years of Research*, ed. D. Dimant and U. Rappaport (Leiden and Jerusalem, 1992), pp. 229–40.

[15] For the most resounding statements of this, see m.RH 2:8–3:1a; b.BMeṣ 59b; and the next note.

[16] See SifDeut 154 on Deut 17:11 (ed. Finkelstein, p. 207; parallels cited in note *ad locum*): "'Do not depart to the right or left from the law they tell you'—even if they show you that right is left and left is right, obey them." The paraphrase of Deut 17:10-11 in the *Temple Scroll* (56.4) adds that the judges' decisions must be "out of the Torah scroll" and "true." Thus, 11QTemple seems to polemicize against the rabbinic view that the decisions by competent authorities are *eo ipso* valid.

So whatever the sages claimed for themselves on the basis of that scriptural text should also be granted to the priests. By insisting that the validity of priests' declarations derived from Lev 13, not from Deut 17, and was thus limited by reality, Hillel was defending a monopoly the sages were claiming.

The cardinal importance of the point in partisan debates is reflected by the statement that it was this which motivated the watershed-like immigration of Hillel to Palestine. In a later generation, that point was a dead horse which needed no beating: no partisan politics existed to prevent sages from symmetrically completing the exegesis by asserting that the priest's declaration too is a *sine qua non*—as we see in the Sifra and the Yerushalmi.

***

In the Yerushalmi, the account of the leprosy issue is concluded by the statement, "On account of this Hillel came up from Babylonia." Nevertheless, two more issues are then added, thus completing the three on account of which he is said to have immigrated to Palestine.

This arrangement of the text is suspicious and engenders doubt about whether these two issues were actually handled by Hillel. So does the fact that the details of Hillel's exegesis here are elsewhere attributed to later sages.[17] Nevertheless, these two will help us formulate the Yerushalmi's picture of Hillel as opposed to that in the Tosefta.

> One text says, "and you shall sacrifice the *Pesach* [paschal sacrifice] to the Lord your God, sheep and cattle" [Deut 16:2], and one text says, "you shall take from the sheep and from the goats" [Ex 12:5]. How can this be? Sheep for the *Pesach* and sheep and cattle for the *ḥagigah* [offering].

---

[17] See W. Bacher, *Die Agada der Tannaiten* (2 vols.; 2d ed.; Strassburg, 1903), vol. 1, pp. 2–3, note 4; I. Gafni, *The Jews of Babylonia in the Talmudic Era* (Jerusalem, 1990), pp. 75–76 (in Hebrew). Similarly, with regard to Hillel's most famous colleague, it has been shown that the original tradition about "three things which Shammai the Elder expounded" (SifDeut 203 [ed. Finkelstein, p. 239]) did not include any scriptural prooftext. One was added, along with some exegesis, by a later sage. See M. D. Herr, "The Problem of War on the Sabbath," *Tarbiz* 30 (1960–61) 249–52 (in Hebrew); E. E. Urbach, "The Derasha as a Basis of the Halakha and the Problem of the Soferim," *Tarbiz* 27 [1957–58] 176, note 35 (= idem, *The World of the Sages: Col-*

One text says, "Six days shall you eat unleavened bread" [Deut 16:8] and one text says, "Seven days shall you eat unleavened bread" [Ex 12:15]. How can this be? Six [days] from the new [grain] and seven from the old [cf. Lev 23:14].

Here we have simple exegesis. The problems are obvious, screaming contradictions between biblical verses, and the solutions are just as simple: harmonization by fiat. No attempt is made to justify the resolution of the problems or to prove the assigning of the conflicting elements to different situations.

Following the above text, the Yerushalmi concludes somewhat theatrically with the following flourish:

And he explained and caused to agree and went up [immigrated to Palestine] and received the law [ודרש והסכים ועלה וקבל הלכה].

The meaning of this rhythmic phrase has been enthusiastically debated. For our purposes, it is enough to deal with the word והסכים, which we rendered "he caused to agree." Some have affirmed that, as elsewhere, it means, "He caused an opinion to agree with the tradition," or, "He agreed with the tradition" (even before he heard it). However, in the two cases which precede this summary comment, no tradition is mentioned. In context, the comment means that in each case, Hillel caused the two biblical verses to agree; i.e., to stop contradicting one another.[18] This is precisely what Hillel did in the case concerning leprosy, where the two halves of Lev 13:37 are first shown to imply contradicting conclusions and then the contradiction is resolved by

---

lected Studies [Jerusalem, 1988], p. 60, note 35 [both in Hebrew]).

[18] The first interpretation is that of Schwarz, Erleichterungen, pp. 18–19. The second is Bacher's: Die Agada, p. 2 and idem, Die exegetische Terminologie der jüdischen Traditionsliteratur (2 vols; Leipzig, 1905), vol. 1, p. 133. For the third, which we have adopted, see A. Geiger, "Sadducäer und Pharisäer," Jüdische Zeitschrift für Wissenschaft und Leben 2 (1863) 48: "er deutete und glich (die streitenden Verse) aus." In yet another interpretation, M. Friedmann argued that Hillel "agreed" to become Nasi. See his somewhat detailed discussion of the traditions about the things "on account of which Hillel came up from Babylonia" in Sifra: Der älteste Midrasch zu Levitikus (Breslau, 1915), pp. 7–8 (in Hebrew). For further literature, see Gafni, Jews of Babylonia, pp. 74–75, note 90.

insisting on both. The contradiction in that case is more subtle, for it is only implicit and has first to be exposed. Nevertheless, all Hillel is said to have done was point out a contradiction and resolve it by fiat.

Thus, the Yerushalmi characterizes Hillel as one who attempted to resolve crass contradictions within the Pentateuch. However, we have so far seen Hillel to be largely unconcerned and unfettered by Scripture. The major exception—the ostensible reason for his immigration—concerned an issue which was apparently of importance in the sages' competition with the priests. To explain this exception, we suggest that it was necessary to supply a scriptural proof because proof from Pharisaic tradition, or the personal authority of a Pharisaic sage, would not impress priests, given the polemic framework we have posited for Hillel's contention that the priest's declarations are conditioned upon reality.

Later rabbinic tradents, however, were less interested in the sectarian issue and more interested in scriptural exegesis. Their predilections are reflected in the Sifra amd Yerushalmi, which make the exegesis explicit and complete it, as it were, by adding the symmetric conclusion that reality must be confirmed by the priests. Additionally, the Yerushalmi underlines its view of Hillel's statement as exegesis by adding to it two other cases of exegetical resolution of simple contradictions. The partisan lawyer has become an exegete of Scripture.[19]

We turn now to the other major tradition which shows Hillel arguing directly on the basis of Scripture. Here, too, the tradition itself and an associated debate in the context where it is recorded show that although the rabbis tried to make Hillel stand within their exegetical tradition, his own approach was in fact something quite different.

II. HILLEL'S JUSTIFICATION FOR THE OFFERING OF THE PASCHAL SACRIFICE ON THE SABBATH

The tradition about Hillel's justification for the offering of the paschal sacrifice on the Sabbath results from another conflict between biblical laws. This time it was not a literal contradiction, but rather a question

---

[19] On the Yerushalmi's interest in supplying law with scriptural justification, cf. J. Neusner, "Accomodating Mishnah to Scripture in Judaism: The Uneasy Union and Its Offspring," *Backgrounds for the Bible* (ed. M. P. O'Connor and D. N. Freedman; Winona Lake, Indiana, 1987), pp. 39–53.

of precedence.[20] On the one hand, the Fourth Commandment and other Pentateuchal texts forbid work on the Sabbath, and slaughtering is a type of work. On the other hand, Ex 12:6 explicitly required the slaughtering of the first *Pesach*, the paschal sacrifice, on the fourteenth of Nisan for the first Passover, and Num 9:2-3 applies the first Passover's rules to to all subsequent years. If the fourteenth of Nisan falls on the Sabbath, which rule takes precedence? According to our sources, the Sons of Bathyra[21] put the question to Hillel. He answered that the *Pesach* should indeed be offered and defended this opinion in a number of ways.

Like those traditions said to have motivated Hillel's immigration to Palestine, this tradition appears in various parts of rabbinic literature. In the Tosefta, again, we find the most primitive version:[22]

Once the fourteenth (of Nisan) fell on the Sabbath. They asked Hillel the Elder: "Does the *Pesach* override the Sabbath?"

(a) He said to them, "Do we then have only one *Pesach* in the year which overrides the Sabbath? We have more than three hundred *Pesachs* in the year and they override the Sabbath!" All of the [people in] the Temple-court gathered about him. He said to them, "The *Pesach* is a public sacrifice and the *Tamid* [perpetual daily offering] is a public sacrifice; just as the *Tamid* is a public sacrifice and overrides the Sabbath, so too the *Pesach* is a public sacrifice and overrides the Sabbath."

(b) Another thing: Of the *Tamid* it is written "[to sacrifice to Me in] its appointed time" [Num 28:2] and of the *Pesach* it is written "its

---

[20] For a study of the didactic and literary aspects of these traditions, see J. Fraenkel, "Hermeneutic Problems in the Study of the Aggadic Narrative," *Tarbiz* 47 (1977/78) 149-57 (in Hebrew). Other, more historically oriented literature, is listed by Ben-Shalom, "Hillel the Elder," p. 116, note 61; add Nodet, *Essai*, pp. 226-36. In our discussion, we will study only the opening sections of these traditions, which deal with Hillel's proof that the *Pesach* should be brought on the Sabbath. In the sequel, which addresses the specific question as to how the knives could be brought, there is no reference to Scripture—a point which is itself of interest (cf. below, note 33).

[21] See n. 9.

[22] Text according to Lieberman's edition, t.Pes 4:13-14, p. 165. Only insignificant differences exist in Zuckermandel's edition (4:1-2, p. 162).

appointed time" [Num 9:2 or 9:3]; just as the *Tamid*, of which it says "its appointed time," overrides the Sabbath, so too the *Pesach*, of which it says "its appointed time," should override the Sabbath.

(c) And there is also an argument from *qal vaḥomer (a minori ad majus)*: Since the *Tamid*, for [the omission of] which one is not liable to [the severe penalty of] excision, overrides the Sabbath, is it not logical that the *Pesach*, for [the omission of] which one is liable to excision, should override the Sabbath?

(d) "And furthermore, I have received from my teachers [the teaching] that the *Pesach* overrides the Sabbath."

Here, four arguments are adduced, of which the first three are based upon a comparison between the *Pesach* and the *Tamid*. The first and the third are based on the *laws* concerning these two sacrifices and apply the law of *Tamid* to *Pesach* via analogy (a) or argument *a fortiori* (c). The second argument (b), in contrast, is based on a comparison of the *texts* concerning these sacrifices. The fourth argument is from tradition.

Of these arguments, only the first and the fourth are clearly said to be Hillel's. (Note the expressions, "He said" and "I have received"). In contrast, the second is introduced by "another thing," which is a standard formula for introducing extraneous material. This second argument is indeed found elsewhere in tannaitic literature as an innovation of a later rabbi which was disputed by one of his contemporaries.[23] Thus, this second argument is probably not to be counted among ones historically offered by Hillel. Excluding it also eliminates the disjointedness noted in the separation of two arguments from law by one from text. Elimination of the verbal analogy leaves Hillel three arguments, none of which is based upon text. Two are based upon law and one upon tradition.

This should be emphasized, since later versions of the story in the Palestinian and Babylonian Talmuds clearly attribute to Hillel all the arguments. Rather than eliminating the argument from text, each of those other versions inserts order in its own way.

---

[23] Mekh, *Bo* 5 (ed. Horovitz-Rabin, p. 17); SifNum 65, 142 (ed. Horovitz, pp. 61, 188).

In y.Pes 6:1,33a, each of the arguments is formally classified. While the Tosefta named only the *qal vahomer* (*a minori ad majus*), the comparison with public sacrifices in the Yerushalmi is technically called a *heqqesh* ("analogy") and the argument from the shared use of "its appointed time" is given its technical name, *gezerah shavah*. Moreover, the disjointed presentation in the Tosefta, in which the two arguments from law are separated from the one from text, is replaced by a more logical order, in which the two from law are followed by the one from text. Finally, Hillel's arguments are the object of sustained interest. They are said to have been refuted by codisputants who took up his (again named) arguments in turn and showed they were not watertight,[24] thus explaining why Hillel had to bring his final argument, the appeal to tradition.

Both the Tosefta and the Yerushalmi insist that the final, clinching, argument was from tradition. The Yerushalmi underlined that point by undermining all the other arguments. This brings us back to our starting point—the Pharisaic sage who argues from tradition. However, both versions show an attempt to use arguments based upon exegesis of the biblical text: the Tosefta inserts one argument from the biblical text and the Yerushalmi attributes all the arguments to Hillel, gives them names, and debates their validity. Thus, from the Tosefta to the Yerushalmi, we see movement from an original story concerning an exponent of tradition toward one concerning an exegete.

This development continues in the Babylonian version of the story, where there is no argument at all from tradition.[25] Indeed, whereas the Yerushalmi has the Sons of Bathyra begin the debate by asking Hillel whether he has "heard" whether the *Pesach* overrides the Sabbath, the Babylonian version has them ask him whether he "knows." Correspondingly, although Hillel is invited to respond because he was the student of Shemaiah and Abtalion, he carries his point by virtue of arguments alone (the *gezerah shavah* [here unnamed] and the *qal*

---

[24] They showed that the *Pesach* and the *Tamid* are not totally comparable and that the *Pesach*, notwithstanding the more severe punishment for its omission, is not in all respects more weighty a sacrifice than the *Tamid*.

[25] Cf. b.Pes 66a. The Babylonian version of the story also omits the comment which, according to the Yerushalmi, introduced the arguments offered in rebuttal of Hillel's arguments: "Is there any profit from a Babylonian?!" But that point of partisan editing is another matter. Cf. Gafni, *Jews of Babylonia*, p. 75.

vaḥomer [so denominated]). These are allowed to stand. There is no need for an appeal to tradition received from his teachers, and none is made.[26] The sage who tries to argue from law or text but falls back upon tradition has been replaced by one who successfully argues by recognized exegetical methods.[27]

III. TWO OTHERS LIKE HILLEL, AND THEIR REMAKING

This replacement of argument from tradition by argument from exegesis is usually associated with the name of R. Akiba, who so developed exegesis that he became capable of reading virtually all traditions back into Scripture. But R. Akiba, who was martyred ca. 135 C.E., flourished about a century later than Hillel. A great deal of water went under

---

[26] More precisely, in the Babylonian Talmud's discussion *after* the story, the fact of Hillel having received a tradition is redirected from the law itself (as in the Tosefta and the Yerushalmi) to the exegetical device. In consonance with a reaction against wild usage of the *gezerah shavah*, Hillel is said to have received this one from his teachers. In contrast, the plain sense of the other versions of the story is that he received from them the law but not the supporting arguments. See Lieberman, *Hellenism in Jewish Palestine* (Texts and Studies 18; New York, 1950), p. 54, note 58; cf. M. Chernick, "Internal Restraints on *Gezerah Shawah*'s Application," *JQR* 80 (1989/90) 281, note 51.

[27] In a further development of this tendency, another tradition—found in t.Sanh 7:11 (ed. Zuckermandel, p. 427), SifLev, introduction para. 7 (ed. Weiss, p. 3a–b), and ARN A 37 (ed. Schechter, p. 110)—even claims that Hillel used seven named hermeneutic rules when arguing before the Sons of Batyra. This is an apparent reference to the same *Pesach*/Sabbath debate. Although the sources preserve only three such arguments, it is usually asserted that Hillel used all seven (see, in general, D. Patte, *Early Jewish Hermeneutics in Palestine* (SBLDS 22; Missoula, Montana, 1975), pp. 109–15). Doubts are usually expressed only as to (a) whether Hillel invented the rules (a notion which Schwarz [*Erleichterungen*, p. 36, note 1], for example, terms a "*gewaltiger Irrthum*"; see also S. Lieberman, *Hellenism*, p. 54), and (b) whether Hillel knew them by their technical names (cf. Lieberman, Ibid., pp. 61–62).

It seems unlikely that Hillel used these formal arguments. Most of them are not cited, the arguments have not been preserved, and one of the most elementary ones, the *gezerah shavah* (shared usage of "its appointed time"), seems, as we have noted, to be of non-Hillelic, probably post-Hillelic, origin. On the other hand, I would hesitate to go as far as L. Ginzberg, who asserts that Hillel in fact gave no argument apart from tradition. See his "The Relation Between the Mishnah and the Mekilta," *Studies in Memory of Moses Schorr, 1874–1941* (ed. L. Ginzberg and A. Weiss; New York, 1945), pp. 85–86 (in Hebrew). Cf. also J. Goldin, "Hillel the Elder," *JR* 26 (1946) 269, note 48; and Neusner, *Rabbinic Traditions*, vol. 3, pp. 98–99.

the bridge during that fateful century. In our attempt to assess Hillel's own approach it is both fortunate and interesting that the Palestinian and Babylonian Talmuds bring our story about Hillel's arguments concerning sacrificing the *Pesach* on the Sabbath in connection with a Mishnah reporting a sharp confrontation between R. Akiba and a notoriously conservative colleague, R. Eliezer ben Hyrcanus.[28] It is likely that this account in m.Pes 6:1-2 can help us flesh out the difference between Hillel's approach to Scripture and that which was to sweep the field a century later.

m.Pes 6:1-2

These things for the *Pesach* override the Sabbath: slaughtering it, sprinkling its blood, scraping its entrails and washing its fat. But roasting it and washing its entrails away do not override the Sabbath. Hoisting it, and bringing it from outside the [Sabbath] limit and cutting off its wart do not override the Sabbath; R. Eliezer says they do override [the Sabbath].

(I) R. Eliezer said: "Is it not logical, for if slaughtering, which is forbidden [on other Sabbaths] as *melachah* [biblically forbidden work], overrides the Sabbath, these labors, which are forbidden [only] due to *shevut* [rabbinic Sabbath prohibitions], should they not override the Sabbath?!"

(I/A) R. Joshua said to him: "Let the [laws of the] festival prove [that *shevut* need not be allowed when *melachah* is allowed], for they allow *melachah* on it but forbid *shevut* on it."

(I/A/1) R. Eliezer said to him, "What is this, Joshua?! What proof can one bring from that which is allowed to what is commanded?" [That is, the fact that the rabbis forbade *shevut* labors in order to do something which is merely allowed need not imply they would forbid *shevut* labors in order to do something such as the *Pesach*, which is required by law.]

---

[28] On Eliezer, see J. Neusner, *Eliezer ben Hyrcanus: The Tradition and the Man* (SJLA 3; 2 vols.; Leiden, 1973); Y. D. Gilat, *R. Eliezer ben Hyrcanus: A Scholar Outcast* (Ramat Gan, Israel, 1984). Cf. below, notes 50-51. On the Mishnaic text we focus upon, see Neusner, esp. vol. 1, pp. 122-27; Gilat, esp. pp. 266-71.

(I/B) R. Akiba replied and said, "Let sprinkling [of purifying water—Num 19:12] prove [that *shevut* need not be allowed when *melachah* is allowed], for it is commanded [to purify those affected by death-impurity], and is only forbidden as *shevut*, but [nevertheless] does not override the Sabbath [even when the eve of Passover falls on a Sabbath]. So you [Eliezer] should not be surprised about these [labors] which, although they are commanded and are only forbidden as *shevut*, do not override the Sabbath."

(I/B/1) R. Eliezer said to him, "But I would argue about that case [too], for if slaughtering, which is forbidden as *melachah*, overrides the Sabbath, should not sprinkling, which is only forbidden as *shevut*, override the Sabbath?"

(I/B/1/i) R. Akiba said to him, "Or vice versa: Just as sprinkling, which is [only] forbidden as *shevut*, does not override the Sabbath, is it not logical that slaughtering, which is forbidden as *melachah* [which is more sever than *shevut*], should not override the Sabbath?"

(I/B/1/i/a) R. Eliezer said to him, "Akiba, you have uprooted that which is written in the Torah, [namely], 'in the evening, at its appointed time' [Num 9:3]— [which means] whether on weekday or Sabbath."

(I/B/1/i/a/α) He [R. Akiba] said to him, "Rabbi, bring me an 'appointed time' for those [labors] similar to the one for slaughtering."

II. R. Akiba enunciated the rule, that any labor [for the *Pesach*] which can be done on the eve of the Sabbath does not override the Sabbath; slaughtering, which cannot be done on the eve of the Sabbath [for Scripture specifically requires it on the fourteenth of Nisan], overrides the Sabbath.

This discussion tacitly takes as its point of departure the point, made by Hillel in the traditions discussed in Part II, that the *Pesach* may be slaughtered on the Sabbath. The question for these Jabnean sages is whether the permit extends to ancillary labors required for the preparation of the sacrifice.

R. Eliezer holds that once the major prohibition is suspended, the minor ones are too, much as a lawyer might hold that a seizure warrant empowers the police to search, even if that is unspecified, for searching is necessary for seizing and constitutes a lesser infringement of rights. R. Akiba, in contrast, holds that just as special scriptural authorization was necessary to exclude the slaughtering of the *Pesach* from the normal Sabbath prohibition of work, so, too, special scriptural sanction is needed for the other labors. Since R. Eliezer is unable to "bring" (cite) any such other sanctions, those other labors remain forbidden by the usual Sabbath prohibitions.

Two points are important here. The first is that R. Akiba did not win this argument. He only asserted his own starting point, that one always needs scriptural support for law. R. Akiba's demand of scriptural support for the permission of the ancillary labors was made according to his own presumption. R. Eliezer never claimed to have or need such scriptural support. Rather, R. Eliezer claimed to deduce the law by *qal vaḥomer* from the law pertaining to slaughtering. R. Akiba wanted text; R. Eliezer offered logic applied to law. In this Mishnah, R. Eliezer begins with law and cites text (I/B/1/i/a) only when R. Akiba maneuvers him into it, whereupon R. Akiba insisted upon a strict interpretation of the text.[29] As suggested above, we see here the Hillel-like

---

[29] Here we must raise a problem of text and interpretation. We have assumed that R. Akiba's point is that, in contrast to slaughtering, there is no scriptural *text* requiring the ancillary labors to be done on the fourteenth of Nisan. The text R. Eliezer cited refers to slaughtering alone. However, the text R. Eliezer is said to have cited, בין הערבים במועדו, is apparently taken from Num 9:3, the third and fourth words (תעשו אתו—"ye shall do it [the *Pesach*]") having been omitted. This text refers so generally to the "doing" of the *Pesach* (see also v. 2) that one wonders how R. Akiba can assert that it applies to slaughtering alone. Perhaps the answer is an unstated *gezerah shavah* with בין הערבים in Ex 12:6, which refers only to slaughtering.

In the absence of evidence for such a *gezerah shavah*, some commentators suggest that the text of the Mishnah is wrong and that R. Eliezer cited only במועדו, alluding to Hillel's original *gezerah shavah* (so, *inter alia*, the "*Tossefot Yomtov*" commentary by Y. T. Lipmann Heller, *ad loc*). This claim has influenced some printed editions of the Mishnah, despite the manuscripts' support for reading Num 9:3. This, however, still leaves us wondering how the reference of Num 9:2-3 came to be limited to slaughtering. It also raises the question of how בין הערבים crept into the text.

Another possibility is that R. Akiba did not assert that Num 9:2-3 refers to

approach being passed by, if not defeated, by the Akiban insistence upon Scripture.

This bypassing is illustrated by a second point of interest. This Mishnaic debate pushes the issue back to its roots and R. Eliezer is made to supply the source of the permission of slaughtering the *Pesach* on the Sabbath. However, all he is made to cite (I/B/1/i/a) is Scripture-cum-exegesis, based, as is the *gezerah shavah* attributed to Hillel, upon the biblical usage of "in its appointed time" in connection with the *Pesach* (Num 9:3). Hillel's two arguments based on the comparison of the *laws* of the *Tamid* to that of the *Pesach* and his appeal to the tradition from Shemaiah and Abtalion have all fallen by the wayside. Even the *gezerah shavah* attributed to Hillel has been replaced by a bit of Akiban exegesis: R. Eliezer's justification of slaughtering on Passover results not from the repetition of the same phrase in verses about the *Tamid* and the *Pesach*, but, from the presence of ostensibly "superfluous" language in the latter—a typically Akiban way of arguing. R. Eliezer has been made to defend Hillel's approach in a court where all the rules and tools are Akiban.[30]

***

The situation is similar to that of R. Ishmael, a contemporary competitor of R. Akiba's. Although he already represents a move to explicit and refined scriptural exegesis on a wide scale, he still insisted on reading Scripture plainly, as a rule, as if it were human speech. He would complain about those who, as he is said to have put it, "tell the Scripture 'Be quiet until I interpret.'"[31]

---

slaughtering alone. Rather, he thought it refers to all labors associated with the *Pesach* for which there is a fixed time. But since slaughtering has a fixed time and the disputed *shevut* labors do not, he concludes that they may not be done on the Sabbath. But R. Akiba's language, "Rabbi, bring me an 'appointed time' for those [labors] similar to the one for slaughtering," seems to indicate that R. Eliezer had cited one for slaughtering. Unless we amplify or correct the text (as above), all that R. Eliezer has quoted is the general statement of Num 9:2-3.

[30] For Eliezer's affinity with Hillel in this debate, see Neusner, *Eliezer*, vol. 1, p. 126.

[31] SifLev, *Tazria* 13:2 (ed. Weiss, p. 68b). On R. Ishmael as an exegete of Scripture, see the survey in G. Porton, *The Traditions of Rabbi Ishmael* (SJLA 19; 4 vols; Leiden, 1976–1982), vol. 4, pp. 160–211. (See esp. pp. 205–9 on the contrast with Akiba.) Porton sees less of a contrast than that frequently found in the literature, such as the works he cites at p. 184, note 197; see also L. Finkelstein, *Akiba: Scholar,*

For example, Akiba and Ishmael discuss in b.Sanh 51b the application of Lev 21:9, "And a daughter of a priest who profanes herself by playing the harlot profanes her father; she shall be burnt in fire." In this discussion, Ishmael uses only logical arguments from related laws to show that it applies to betrothed daughters of priests alone, while Akiba preferred to depend upon a verbal analogy (*gezerah shavah*) with Deut 22:21, where "her father" also appears, to show that Lev 21:9 does not apply to unattached women. So far, there is no argument, just different methods. But then Akiba goes on to ascribe to the opening copula of Lev 21:9 the function of subsuming married daughters of priests under the terms of this law (as opposed to other adulterous married women, who are covered by Lev 20:10—strangulation).

R. Ishmael, who preferred to ignore opening conjunctions, as in human speech generally, is said to have responded heatedly to Akiba: "Just because you interpret '*and* a daughter' instead of 'a daughter' should we take this one out and burn her?!"[32] But the Akiban steamroller could not be stopped, and the Babylonian Talmud blithely goes on to ask, a few lines later, what R. Ishmael did with that opening copula. Of course, it supplies an answer.

Just as R. Eliezer in the mishnaic discussion of the *Pesach*, so, too, another conservative has thus been remodeled along Akiban lines. Though different, both are reminiscent of Hillel and the way he was domesticated into an exegete, as we have seen. And so, too, with regard to Hillel's disciples, "the House of Hillel," we may note with Neusner, finally, "a tendency of ʿAqibans to contribute supporting exegetical materials for Hillelite opinions, even to formulate in the names of the Houses disagreements on the application of ʿAqiban principles."[33]

Saint and Martyr (New York, 1936), pp. 308–12.

[32] There is a pun here. "Take her out" is used both of execution (cf. Gen 38:24-25) and—as explicit a few lines earlier in the Talmud's discussion—of the exegetical "exclusion" of the married daughter of a priest from the basic rule of Lev 20:10, which prescribes strangulation for married adulteresses. (Lev 20:10 leaves the mode of execution unspecified. In such cases the rabbis imposed strangulation, whether due to its swiftness or because it leaves the body intact.

[33] Neusner, *Rabbinic Traditions*, vol. 2, p. 98; cf. also pp. 40–42. A. Guttmann expressed surprise at the fact that, despite Hillel's exegetical activity, according to the *Pesach*/Sabbath debate and the sources cited in n. 27, there is little evidence for such by the first generations of his disciples. Most of what is attributed to them is actually of Akiban or later origin. See his *Rabbinic Judaism in the Making: A Chapter in the His-*

IV. FROM EXEGESIS TO FABLE?

So far we have based our case for the limited significance of Scripture for Hillel upon an examination of legal opinions attributed to him. We have showed that Scripture rarely figures in them, especially in their earlier versions. Later tradents tended to supply his opinions with scriptural underpinning.

We will now fill out the picture briefly with a discussion of *narratives* about Hillel, along with some relevant comments by Professor Neusner in *The Rabbinic Traditions about the Pharisees Before 70.*[34] Neusner argued that the exegesis preceded the stories. In contrast, we have argued above, in connection with Hillel's legal opinions, that the opinion usually preceded the exegesis. We shall now review the evidence concerning the stories. There is some overlap.

In y.Ber 9:3,14a, the *law* is stated that if a man coming home from a trip hears an outcry in the town, he is not allowed to pray that it

---

tory of the Halakhah from Ezra to Judah I (Detroit, 1970), pp. 74–75, 95–99. However, rather than explaining this with Guttmann as a result of opposition or changed circumstances, one might simply infer that the point of departure is faulty, as we have suggested; cf. above, note 27. Note also E. E. Urbach's insistence ("The Derashah" 181–82 [= *World of the Sages*, pp. 65–66]) that the arguments between Pharisees and Sadducees do not concern biblical exegesis and E. Nodet's recent verdict (*Essai*, p. 6) that *"la tradition rabbinique, dans ses couches les plus anciennes, n'exhibe aucun fondement scriptuaire."*

[34] Neusner also presented several of his arguments in "From Exegesis to Fable in Rabbinic Traditions about the Pharisees," which deals only with Hillel materials. This article appeared in *JJS* 25 (1974) 263–69.

Neusner's point of departure here is an analogy to the parallel between the exegesis in Acts 2:33-34 and the story in Mk 12:35-37. He follows B. Lindars' argument that the latter developed out of the former (cf. *New Testament Apologetic: The Doctrinal Significance of the Old Testament Quotations* [Philadelphia, 1961], pp. 45–47). Lindars' argument is that Mark's assumption that David would not call his own descendant "my lord" depends on Acts' demonstration that Ps 110 alludes to Jesus. But even if Mark depends on some prior tradition that Ps 110 has David referring to a superior being, that tradition need not be the Christian one reflected in Acts 2. The Melchizedek text from Qumran, published after Lindars wrote, shows the pre-Christian currency of such an assumption. Cf. D. Flusser, *Judaism and the Origins of Christianity* (Jerusalem, 1988), pp. 186–92, 301–5. For criticism of Lindars, see D. M. Hay, *Glory at the Right Hand: Psalm 110 in Early Christianity* (SBLMS 18; Nashville/New York, 1973) pp. 106–7. In any event, the rabbinic evidence must be judged on its own.

not be in his house, for "he who petitions about the past, lo, this is a vain prayer" (m.Ber 9:3). But he is allowed to say, "I am sure that these are not in my house." Then follows the comment, "Hillel says: 'From a bad report he shall not fear,'" i.e., a passage from Ps 112:7, adduced either as a comment on the law or as an alternate text recommended to the returning traveler. In the parallel in b.Ber 60a, in contrast, there is a *story* according to which a returning Hillel once heard an outcry in the city and said, "I am sure that these are not in my house." There then follows the comment, "Of him Scripture says: 'From a bad report he shall not fear.'"

Professor Neusner comments, "This is a standard example of the transformation of a Hillel-exegesis into a Hillel-narrative."[35] However, there is no exegesis in either version; only the citation of a verse. Nor, secondly, is it at all clear that historically the use of the verse should be ascribed to Hillel. That is, it is not clear that the Palestinian version is the more primitive of the two. The Babylonian version is presented as a tannaitic tradition (*baraita*, introduced by תנו רבנן), while the Palestinian version does not claim to be tannaitic. Rather than assuming that scriptural exegesis has been fleshed out into a story, it is more economical an assumption that a story about a pious man, Hillel, who voiced without scriptural help his confidence in God, has been improved by later tradents who preferred to bring Scripture into the story, even into Hillel's mouth.[36]

In his general conclusions, Neusner claims that "transformation of Hillel-exegesis into Hillel-narrative" is "standard." He cites four more cases under the heading, "From Exegesis to Chria."[37] By this he

[35] *Rabbinic Traditions*, vol. 1, p. 294.

[36] In his *JJS* article, p. 265, Neusner writes: "I take it for granted that the *baraita* came later than, and is based upon, the Palestinian Talmudic tradition, which is not given a tannaitic attribution. The word-for-word correspondences make this virtually certain, and the movement from an anonymous to a named teaching seems to me decisive evidence that the Babylonian depend upon the Palestinian." While it must be granted that a *baraita* in the Babylonian Talmud *might* preserve a text later than a non-*baraita* in the Palestinian Talmud, the rebuttal of the presumption that a *baraita* is tannaitic must in each case be shown, not taken for granted. Word-for-word correspondences can, by their very nature, cut either way.

[37] Vol. 3, pp. 42–43. This heading indicates the influence of H. Fischel. See Neusner, *Rabbinic Traditions*, vol. 3, pp. 330–32; and *Essays in Greco-Roman and Related Talmudic Literature* (ed. H. A. Fischel; New York, 1977), esp. pp. 451–53 (Fischel on Hillel and *chriae*.)

means cases in which "an anonymous exegesis is accompanied by a terse chria, or biographical apophthegm (*sic*), in which a named master acts out the exegesis." However, as the exegesis in these cases is anonymous, it is not clear why one should assume that the sage has been made to act out the exegesis. Perhaps the exegesis has been supplied in order to supply the sage's practice with scriptural support.

Concerning *aggadic* (nonlegal) materials, Neusner notes that "no exegesis of Scripture produces a nonlegal story about an event or a master."[38] Why should it have been different concerning legal materials? In any case, examination of the five cases Neusner assembles under "From Exegesis to Chria" shows that the first is irrelevant (the exegesis which the Shammai story illustrates is *not* anonymous; it is attributed to him) and we have already dismissed the fifth (about the trusting traveler). This leaves three. In the first, there is no exegesis, and in the other two, the story likely preceded the exegesis:

1. In the traditions about how Hillel wrapped together all the paschal foods in order to fulfill Ex 12:8/Num 9:11, he is never said to have cited the verse.[39] It is to be assumed, of course, that he intended to fulfill the biblical command, but no exegesis is offered—or needed—to derive his practice from the verse.

2. In the several early reports about Hillel's institution of the *prosbul*, the fundamental exegesis limits the erasure of debts to those which are "yours" (Deut 15:3) and allows for the innovation of a way to avoid the law by fictively depositing one's debts with the court. This exegesis is anonymous. It is attributed to Hillel only in the late *Midrash Tannaim*.[40] All we need posit here is a story about a sage who did what he assumed needed to be done—doing what he assumed God would want done—in order to help the poor. Later tradents added the exegesis and eventually put it into his mouth.

Neusner cites m.SheviʾPit 10:3 in this connection.[41] But m.SheviʾPit 10:3 says that Hillel ordained the *prosbul* when he saw that people were abstaining from charitable loans because they did not want them to be cancelled by the sabbatical year. The Mishnah characterizes their behav-

[38] Vol. 3, p. 64.

[39] For a synopsis of these texts, see Neusner, *Rabbinic Traditions*, vol. 1, pp. 280–81.

[40] See ed. Hoffmann, p. 80. For the other texts, see above, note 4.

[41] *Rabbinic Traditions*, vol. 3, p. 42.

ior as a violation of Deut 15:9, but (a) it does not attribute the citation to Hillel; (b) it cites the verse without exegesis; and (c) there is no way this verse, or any other verse, could generate the *prosbul*.[42]

3. According to another story, Hillel supplied a horse and a slave to an impoverished aristocrat, thus fulfilling the requirement in Deut 15:8 to supply the poor "all that he lacks."[43] However, Hillel is never said to have cited the verse. The verse is not cited at all in the Yerushalmi. The Sifre, the Tosefta, and the Babylonian Talmud do cite the verse, along with exegesis, illustrated by a story about Hillel, who did what the exegesis says he should—just as in all three sources, the proper behavior is illustrated by a story about some supercharitable Galileans. As in the preceding case, it is more convincing that stories about pious people caring for the poor were secondarily supplied with biblical support.[44]

Thus, in narrative, as in legal opinions, it is most reasonable to conclude that the historical Hillel, who did what he did because he thought it should be done, has been domesticated into a rabbinic Hillel who did what he did because Scripture said it should be done.

V. CONCLUSION

We have examined Hillel's use of Scripture as illustrated by the two central complexes of halachic scriptural exegesis linked to his name and by the use of Scripture in narratives about Hillel. We have seen that his approach to Scripture was governed by its content, not by its text.

To the limited extent Hillel drew conclusions from the biblical text or based laws upon it, he did so directly on the basis of a plain

[42] Cf. Neusner's *JJS* article (above, note 34) 266–69. Here, he argues that two versions regarding Hillel's innovation circulated independently. One derived it exegetically and one attributed it to the sage's independent authority. According to Neusner, the latter was preferred for political reasons by R. Judah the Prince, who therefore included it in his Mishnah (m.Giṭṭ 4:3). Neusner does not discuss m.Shevi 10:3 here. It would be strange if the contrary tendency were expressed in the same context elsewhere in the Mishnah.

[43] SifDeut 116 (ed. Finkelstein, p. 175); t.Pe'a 4:10 (ed. Zuckermandel, p. 23; ed. Lieberman, p. 58); y.Pe'a 8:8,21a; b.Keṭ 67b.

[44] As Neusner points out (*Rabbinic Traditions*, vol: 1, p. 286; *JJS* [above, note 34] 265–66), the Babylonian story develops the preceding versions by making Hillel even more heroic. But that does not mean that the whole story is late, leaving only the exegesis early.

reading of it. With texts which posed no problem, there was no need for exegesis, as with Ex 12:8/Num 9:11. But Hillel did not have to search the Scriptures for the answers to all problems which arose. Contrary to Ben Bag-Bag (m.Ab 5:22) and Akiba, Hillel did not assume that everything was to be found in it. Rather, the same type of common sense approach which limited his reading of Scripture also allowed for rulings based on tradition or on his own authority, as illustrated by his famous decrees concerning the noncancellation of debts in the sabbatical year and the return of houses in walled cities. These rulings departed radically from the letter of the biblical law in order to achieve what Hillel— as any plain reader of Scripture—took to be its basic, charitable purpose.

In other words, if scribes—*sopherim*—directed their attention to the details of Scripture (cf. b.Kid 30a), Hillel did not teach "as one of the scribes"; he taught either directly out of Scripture, or on the basis of tradition, or, most characteristically, "as one who had authority."[45] But as we have seen, as soon as a century later, in Jabneh, the main approach of rabbinic Judaism had become one which sought to anchor all divine law in Scripture. It would not be audacious to suggest that an important reason for the triumph of this textually bound approach in Judaism was the secession from Judaism of a religion whose founder, like Hillel, had preferred the other one.

The same reaction is indicated in the remarkable refusal of the Jabnean rabbis to accept instructions from what they all admitted to be God's voice calling out of heaven[46] and their willingness even to excommunicate R. Eliezer for abiding by it (b.BMeṣ 59b). Here too, as in the *Pesach* dispute, R. Eliezer seems to follow an older approach, one typically Hillelite: the doctrine that the halachah always follows the School of Hillel was said to rest on a voice out of heaven;[47] just as a

---

[45] The precise sense of the contrast in Mk 1:22 between teaching as scribes and teaching with authority has not been satisfactorily resolved. I venture to suggest the above distinction; cf. A. W. Argyle, "The meaning of *exousia* in Mark I: 22,27," *ExpTim* 80 (1968/69) 343. Recent discussions about the "scribes," of whom not much is known, include A. J. Saldarini, *Pharisees, Scribes and Sadducees in Palestinian Society* (Edinburgh 1988), esp. ch. 11, and Schwartz, *Studies*, pp. 89–101.

[46] On the instrumentality of heavenly voices, see the interesting discussion in Lieberman, *Hellenism*, pp. 194–99.

[47] Cf. b.ʿErub 13b and parallels.

heavenly voice was said to have acclaimed Hillel worthy of the Holy Spirit,[48] the Hillelites also accepted evidence concerning a heavenly voice;[49] and a Hillelite opinion also allows a woman to remarry on the basis of such a voice's testimony that her husband was dead.[50]

Here, then, we have Hillelites and the conservative Eliezer finding authentic and normative expressions of God's will outside of Scripture. Put otherwise, we see Hillelites and Eliezer allowing God to reveal his will as he chooses and accepting it as binding—something quite reasonable for religious persons, so long as their considerations are not affected by second thoughts about what such willingness to accept new divine intervention might lead to.[51] However, voices out of heaven and teaching on one's own authority had everything to do with the rise of Christianity in the first century. Thus, by the second century, they too were taboo for rabbinic Jews.

As any Catholic or Anabaptist can tell you, listening to voices from within or from heaven and allowing the Bible to be read in the vernacular are a lethal combination. They can wreak havoc with stable religion. And by the second century, between the destruction of the Second Temple and the rise of Christianity, there was enough havoc in Judaism and the rabbis were dearly in need of stability.[52] The rabbis

---

[48] Cf. t.Soṭ 13:3 (ed. Zuckermandel, pp. 318–19) and parallels.

[49] Cf. t.Nez 1:1.

[50] Cf. m.Yeb 16:6; b.Yeb 122a. R. Eliezer is said to have been a *shammuti* or *shammati* (e.g. b.Shab 130b), a term which is often taken to mean "Shammaite." Hence, he is often ascribed to the school which competed with the Hillelites. But both the general validity of that interpretation of the term and that ascription are denied by A. Guttmann, *Studies in Rabbinic Judaism* (New York, 1976), pp. 163–74 (= *HUCA* 28 [1957] 115–26), a study unmentioned by Gilat in his more positive review of the same subjects in *R. Eliezer*, pp. 462–73. Whatever the verdict on these points, Eliezer's opinion here is explicitly that of the Hillelites. See Neusner, *Rabbinic Traditions*, vol. 2, pp. 221–22.

[51] Similarly, in m.Ber 4:3–4 we find R. Eliezer defending spontaneous prayer against the attempts of his colleagues to dictate a fixed liturgy. R. Eliezer defends the normative significance of voices from within, something just as reasonable for religious persons as voices from heaven, so long as one need not worry about schismatics. According to the Mishnah, R. Eliezer's Jabnean colleagues simply ignored him.

[52] This is true, regardless of whether one views Jabneh as a place where unanimity was imposed by an authoritarian leadership or as one where a "grand coalition" subsumed differing trends under a common umbrella, as argued by S. J. D. Cohen, "The Significance of Jabneh: Pharisees, Rabbis, and the End of Jewish Sectarianism," *HUCA* 55 (1984) 27–53.

claimed with Akiba against R. Ishmael that "the Bible does not speak in human language," but "all is in it"; not even voices from heaven can interfere with it. By carrying those claims, the rabbis ensured that a rabbinic class would be endowed with a monopoly on the interpretation of God's will. Only the rabbis would be capable of reading the book they now proclaimed to be in a language accessible only to scholars (like Latin) and not the vernacular. This monopoly would allow for stability.

Hillel's way gave voice to tradition but also allowed considerable authority to such uncontrollable sources as voices from within and above, along with some input from a reasonable reading of Scripture the way any layperson would. This way had to go. All that remained of it was his name, which the later rabbis used now and then to supply a prestigious precedent for their own methods.

JESUS AND THE GOLDEN RULE

ANY COMPARISON OF Hillel and Jesus must address, sooner or later, the problem of the Golden Rule. Both Hillel and Jesus are credited with having quoted the Rule and both are said to have used it in rather similar situations as a summary of the law. This apparent agreement between these two influential Palestinian Jewish teachers from the turn of the eras is striking and merits close investigation. Obvious questions arise. Are the traditions which attribute the Rule to Hillel and to Jesus reliable? What does the Rule mean and who was its author? What is involved in the claim that the Rule is the sum of the law? Does the Rule throw any light on first-century Judaism or on the relationship between Judaism and Christianity? We shall try to answer some of these questions in the present essay. But first we must define the Rule itself.

The Golden Rule is not a fixed form of words, but a proposition which can be expressed in a variety of ways. The origins of the term are surprisingly obscure. Though it was probably first attached to the saying in Mt 7:12, "All things whatsoever ye would that men should do to you, do so even to them" (KJV), it was rapidly extended to cover all other forms of this moral maxim. It is commonly quoted, both in everyday speech and in literature, not in its classic Matthean wording, but in shorter, crisper versions, such as, "Do as you would be done by."[1]

---

[1] The epithet "golden" expresses the value, excellence, or utility of the Rule (cf. Golden Mean, Golden Section, Golden Number, Golden Age). The designation "Golden Rule" was first applied to Mt 7:12, for it is there, not in the parallel in Lk 6:31, that the excellence of the maxim is implied ("for this is the law and the prophets"). This use of the term is apparently modern. The earliest example cited is Gibbon, *Decline and Fall of the Roman Empire*, chap. 54, footnote: "Calvin violated the golden rule of doing as he would be done by." The usage is, however, anticipated by Isaac Watts in 1741 ("that golden principle of morality which our blessed Lord has given us") and by R. Godfrey in 1674 ("that Golden Law do as you would be done

The fact that the Golden Rule embraces a range of verbally different utterances, which are thought of as expressing the same basic idea, means that it is defined primarily in terms of concepts. Thus, in tracing its history, we are tracing the history of an idea. We should be in no doubt at the outset of our inquiry that this will complicate matters, since the history of an idea is much more difficult to unravel than the transmission of a stable and distinctive form of words.

THE GOLDEN RULE, THE HISTORICAL HILLEL, AND THE HISTORICAL JESUS

What evidence do we have for linking the Hillel and the Jesus of history with the Golden Rule? In the case of Hillel, it is much weaker than has sometimes been supposed. There is only one text in the whole of classic rabbinic literature which attributes the saying to him, namely, Babli Šabbat 31a. This simple fact should give us pause for thought. The Babylonian Talmud was redacted at least five hundred years after the time of Hillel. We should be extremely wary of basing deductions regarding the historical Hillel on so late a source.

This caution is amply reinforced by an analysis of the literary context in which the attribution is found. To clarify the range and depth of the problems concerning the historicity of the attribution, we must set out the relevant text in full. The language of the passage is, for the most part, simple, elegant Hebrew. But certain words and phrases (indicated in the translation by underlining) are in Aramaic.

> (A) Our Rabbis taught (*tānû rabbānan*): A man should always be gentle like Hillel, and not impatient like Shammai.

---

by"). For R. Recorde in 1542 "the Golden Rule" referred, not to Mt 7:12, but to the mathematical rule of proportions, the rule of three; cf. *Oxford English Dictionary*, 2d ed., VI, p. 656, *s.v.* "golden." Attempts to trace the term back to the Renaissance or the Middle Ages (see A. Dihle, "Goldene Regel," *Reallexikon für Antike und Christentum*, XI [Stuttgart, 1981], col. 930) are purely speculative. The designation of the maxim in Mt 7:12 as "the Golden Rule" probably originated in England. From there it passed over to Germany and France. See L. J. Philippidis, *Die "Goldene Regel" religionsgeschichtlich untersucht, Inaugural-Dissertation zur Erlangung der Doktorwürde der Hohen Philosophischen Fakultät der Universität Leipzig* (Leipzig, 1930), pp. 11–15.

(B) It once happened (*ma'aseh be*) that two men made a wager with each other, saying, "He who goes and makes Hillel angry shall receive four hundred zuz." One of them said, "I will make him angry."

That day was the Sabbath eve and Hillel was washing his head. The man went, passed by the door of Hillel's house, and called out, "Is Hillel here? Is Hillel here?" Hillel robed, went out to him and said, "My son, what do you seek?" "I have a question to ask," said he. "Ask, my son," he said to him. He asked, "Why are the heads of the Babylonians round?" "My son, you have asked a great question," said he. "It is because they do not have skillful midwives."

The man departed, tarried awhile, returned, and said, "Is Hillel here? Is Hillel here?" Hillel robed, went out to him, and said, "My son, what do you seek?" "I have a question to ask," said he. "Ask, my son," he said to him. He asked, "Why are the eyes of the Palmyrenes bleary?" "My son, you have asked a great question," said he. "It is because they live in sandy places."

The man departed, tarried awhile, returned, and said, "Is Hillel here? Is Hillel here?" Hillel robed, went out to meet him, and said, "My son, what do you seek?" "I have a question to ask," said he. "Ask, my son," he said to him. He asked, "Why are the feet of the Africans wide?" "My son, you have asked a great question," said he. "It is because they live in watery marshes." The man said, "I have many questions to ask, but I am afraid that you may become angry." He robed, sat before him, and said, "Ask all the questions you have to ask." He said, "Are you the Hillel whom they call the Nasi of Israel?" "Yes," he said. "If that is so," said he, "may there not be many more like you in Israel!" "Why, my son?" asked he. "Because I have lost four hundred zuz through you," complained he. "Control yourself!" he answered. "It is better that you should lose four hundred zuz on account of Hillel, and a further four hundred zuz, than that Hillel should lose his temper."

(C) Our Rabbis taught (*tānû rabbānan*): Once (*ma'aseh be*) a certain heathen came before Shammai and asked him, "How many Torahs do you have?" "Two," he replied, "the Written Torah and the Oral

Torah." The heathen said, "I believe you about the Written Torah, but not about the Oral. Make me a proselyte on condition that you teach me only the Written Torah." Shammai scolded him and angrily ordered him to get out.

When he went before Hillel, he made him a proselyte. On the first day Hillel taught him 'âlef, bêt, gîmel, dālet. The following day he reversed the order of the letters. The heathen protested, "But yesterday you did not teach them to me thus." "Must you not rely upon me in this matter?" Hillel replied. "Then rely on me with respect also to the Oral Torah."

(D) On another occasion it happened (šûv maʿaśeh be) that a certain heathen came before Shammai and said to him, "Make me a proselyte on condition that you teach me the whole Torah while I stand on one foot. Shammai drove him out with the builder's cubit which was in his hand. When he went before Hillel, he made him a proselyte. He said to him, "What is hateful to you, do not do to your neighbor. That is the whole Torah. The rest is commentary. Go and learn!"

(E) On another occasion it happened (šûv maʿaśeh be) that a certain heathen was passing behind a school and heard the voice of a teacher reciting, "And these are the garments which they shall make: a breast-plate and an ephod" (Ex 28:4). Said he, "For whom are these?" "For the high priest," said they. The heathen said to himself, "I will go and become a proselyte, so that I may be appointed a high priest." So he went before Shammai and said to him, "Make me a proselyte on condition that you appoint me high priest." Shammai drove him out with the builder's cubit which was in his hand.

When he went before Hillel, he made him a proselyte. Hillel said to him, "No one is appointed king who does not know the arts of government. Go and study the arts of government!" So he went and read. When he came to the words, "The stranger that comes nigh shall be put to death" (Num 1:51), he asked Hillel, "To whom does this verse apply?" "Even to David, king of Israel," was the answer. Thereupon the proselyte reasoned a fortiori, "If the words, 'The stranger that comes nigh shall be put to death,' are applied in Scripture to

Israel, who are called sons of the Omnipresent, and whom in his love
he designated, 'Israel, my firstborn son' (Ex 4:22), how much more do
they apply to a mere proselyte, who comes with his staff and his bag!"
So he went before Shammai and said to him, "Could I ever have been
eligible to be high priest? Is it not written in the Torah, "The stranger
that comes nigh shall be put to death"? He went before Hillel and said
to him, "O gentle Hillel, may blessings rest on your head for bringing
me under the wings of the Shekhinah!"

(F) Some time later, when the three proselytes met in one place, they
said, "Shammai's impatience nearly drove us out of the world, but Hillel's gentleness brought us under the wings of the Shekhinah!"

This unusually long pericope is clearly demarcated by the inclusio
of the superscription (section A) and the subscription (section F). The
purpose of the unit is to illustrate, by a series of exempla (*ma'asîm*), the
proposition that "a man should always be gentle like Hillel and not
impatient like Shammai." The exempla fall into two groups, the first of
which is represented by section B, and the second by sections C, D, and
E—a fact signalled by the repetition of *tānû rabbānan* at the beginning
of section C. Section B concerns Hillel alone, whereas sections C, D,
and E are structurally similar, they contrast Hillel and Shammai, and
they are linked by the theme of conversion. All the individual anecdotes
may once have existed independently, but they have been marshalled
here into an effective and coherent unity.

There can be little doubt that this pericope was not composed by
the redactor of the Babli, but was taken over by him more or less intact
from tradition. Evidence for this may be found not only in the formula
tānû rabbānan, which shows that he claimed the material was Tannaitic
in origin, but also in the strange fact that the pericope bears absolutely
no relationship to the Mishnaic lemma to which it is now attached. It
cannot have been generated or influenced by the lemma, but must have
come as a block from elsewhere.

Two similar blocks of material are, in fact, found in ARN A 15
and B 29. They are completely at home there. Large narrative structures, such as we have here, are comparatively rare in rabbinic literature, but are characteristic of ARN. Moreover, the pericope is attached
in ARN to an appropriate lemma from Mishnah Abot: "Be not easily

angered." It is not inconceivable that this lemma generated the pericope. The versions of the pericope in ARN A and B differ considerably from each other and from the version in b.Šab. The Babli version is much closer to that in ARN A and is most plausibly explained as a reworking of it.[2]

Interestingly, section D of the Babli version (the story of Hillel and the Golden Rule) is absent from the ARN versions, though it would have been totally appropriate to the ARN context. The conclusion seems unavoidable: section D is a post-ARN intrusion into the pericope. We can only speculate about its origins, but it is surely rather curious that a similar story is told in ARN B 26 about Aqiba. It seems likely that the Babylonian redactor of the tradition, whether deliberately or through faulty memory, transferred the Aqiba story to Hillel.

Tradition-historical analysis of the pericope suggests the late and unhistorical character of the anecdote about Hillel and the Golden Rule. The style of the pericope points in the same direction. The unit reflects the unmistakable elements of hagiography and is most plausibly dated to a time when Hillel and Shammai belonged to the distant past and had been reduced to stereotypes—the former to a paragon of scholarly virtue, the latter to his foil. The stereotypical nature of section A is particularly strong. There Hillel is depicted as playing the age-old role of the sage who is able to answer conundrums and riddles.

Thus, the case against the historicity of the tradition is very strong. But nothing can be conclusively proved. There will doubtless always be some who will remain unmoved by the kind of argument just advanced and who will invoke the rabbis' extraordinary powers of

---

[2] Sections A and B of the pericope are paralleled in the late sources Kallah Rabbati 10:3 and Sefer Ha-Maʿaśiyyôt 84 (ed. M. Gaster, *The Exempla of the Rabbis* [New York, 1968], pp. 55f). Section E is paralleled in SefMaʿas 31 (Gaster, p. 23). The intrusion of Aramaic into the predominantly Hebrew text is puzzling. The fact that the Golden Rule itself is quoted in Aramaic is easily explained: Aramaic seems to have been the language in which the maxim was current in rabbinic circles.

The form of the maxim is close to that found in the Book of Tobit (4:15). Though it is still an open question whether Tobit was composed originally in Aramaic or in Hebrew, Jerome knew only the Aramaic. This suggests that by the Amoraic period, the Aramaic text had prevailed in Palestine. Some older writers assume that Hillel was consciously quoting Tobit, but it is more likely that the maxim had entered general parlance. More puzzling is the fact that some of the narrative framework is in Aramaic. This phenomenon occurs in all three recensions of the pericope.

memory to argue that this Talmudic unit contains early, reliable tradition, and may even preserve the Aramaic *ipsissima verba* of Hillel. What of it if a similar story is told of another early authority? Could not both Hillel and Aqiba have cited the Golden Rule?

In the last analysis, such views cannot be decisively refuted, historical scholarship is not a matter of proof, or even of argument, but of judgment. Having weighed all the evidence, I can only conclude that there are no good historical grounds for stating that Hillel himself ever cited the Golden Rule; he cites it only in later rabbinic fiction.

The evidence that Jesus quoted the Golden Rule is much stronger. The Rule is found both in the Sermon on the Mount (Mt 7:12) and in the Sermon on the Plain (Lk 6:31). It is not possible here to do justice to the complex source- and redaction-critical problems raised by the comparison of these two texts. It must suffice to present Fitzmyer's plausible conclusion:

> Despite the many differences in the two sermons, there is a basic similarity in them which makes one argue for a nucleus sermon that was inherited by 'Q' and that the two evangelists have reworked each in his own way. The similarities are such that they suggest that the tradition preserved something of an extended sermon delivered by Jesus towards the beginning of his ministry.[3]

The Golden Rule belongs to the "nucleus sermon."

Though the substance of the Rule in both Gospels is patently the same, the exact wording differs. The differences may be displayed graphically as follows:

Matthew: πάντα οὖν ὅσα ἐὰν θέλητε ἵνα ποιῶσιν ὑμῖν οἱ
Luke: καθὼς θέλετε ἵνα ποιῶσιν ὑμῖν οἱ

Matthew: ἄνθρωποι, οὕτως καὶ ὑμεῖς ποιεῖτε αὐτοῖς
Luke: ἄνθρωποι, ποιεῖτε αὐτοῖς ὁμοίως

Of the variants here, the Matthean πάντα οὖν is probably secondary. The Matthean οὕτως and the Lukan ὁμοίως may both be sec-

[3] J. A. Fitzmyer, *The Gospel According to Luke*, vol. I (AB; New York, 1981), p. 627.

ondary, since both words are characteristic of their authors. The resumptive adverb is not strictly necessary, though it improves the style in Greek. In comparison to the Matthean ὅσα ἐάν, the Lukan καθώς is, on the face of it, more likely to be original. Thus behind the two versions may stand the formulation, καθὼς θέλετε ἵνα ποιῶσιν ὑμῖν οἱ ἄνθρωποι, ποιεῖτε αὐτοῖς, which each Gospel writer has styled in his own distinctive way.[4] There is no problem retroverting this statement into Aramaic, the vernacular of Jesus, and the language in which the Golden Rule apparently circulated among Palestinian Jews.[5]

There is an indirect line of argument which lends some support to the view that the tradition of Jesus' use of the Golden Rule is sound. It would be a truism to say that the concept of love plays an important part in early Christian teaching. This stress on love is found in diverse early Christian texts. It is so ubiquitous that it is reasonable to suppose that it reflects something in the teaching of Jesus himself. More specifically, evidence suggests that Jesus laid great store in the Love Command of Lev 19:18 and that the early Christian writers remembered this fact and pondered upon it. In Gal 5:14 Paul asserts that the whole law is fulfilled by keeping the Love Command. In Gal 6:2 he picks up this idea again in the following terms: "Bear one another's burdens, and so fulfil the law of Christ." Could the "law of Christ" here refer in an historical sense to the law which Christ himself established as the most fundamental of all the laws, namely, the Love Command? Paul returns to this theme in Rom 13:9, where he claims that all the other commandments are summed up in the sentence, "You shall love your neighbor as yourself." James, writing from a different standpoint, also stresses the importance of the Love Commandment. It is "the royal law": "If you really fulfill the royal law, according to the Scripture, 'You shall love your neighbor as yourself,' you do well" (Jas 2:8). The Gospels of Matthew (22:34-40) and Mark (12:28-34) take up the same refrain.

---

[4] On the redactional problems, see W. D. Davies and D. C. Allison, *The Gospel According to St. Matthew*, vol. I (ICC; Edinburgh, 1988), p. 688; I. H. Marshall, *The Gospel of Luke* (Exeter, 1978), p. 261.

[5] G. Dalman, *Jesus-Jeshua: Studies in the Gospels*, trans. P. P. Levertoff (London, 1929), p. 226, offers the following retroversion: *kol ma de-ʾattun baʿayin de-yaʿbedun lekhon bene nasha hakheden ʾuph ʾattun hawon ʿabedin lehon.* In the light of our discussion of the redaction of the saying, we may refine this to *kema de-ʾattun baʿayin de-yaʿbedun lekhon bene nasha hawon ʿabedin lehon.* See further, T. W. Manson, *The Sayings of Jesus* (London, 1949), pp. 18-19.

This agreement is impressive and points to a very early element of Christian tradition, probably deriving from Jesus' himself. But as we shall see below, the Golden Rule tended to be regarded in early Judaism as simply a variant of the Love Command. Indeed, it is noteworthy that Paul in Rom 13:10 glosses the Love Command with what sounds like an echo of the negative form of the Golden Rule: "love does no wrong to a neighbor." Consequently, the Golden Rule fits snugly into Jesus' teaching and is consonant with his emphasis on the centrality of the Love Command.

We are left, then, with an asymmetry in our evidence. That Jesus cited the Golden Rule is well-attested and highly probable. That Hillel quoted it cannot absolutely be ruled out, since we are in no position to assert such a negative. But there is no reliable evidence that he did. The conclusion is unavoidable: there is no logic in comparing and contrasting how the historical Hillel and the historical Jesus used the Golden Rule. The Rule may enlighten us as to the teachings of Jesus, but it cannot enlighten us as to the teachings of Hillel.

ORIGINS AND ORIGINALITY OF THE GOLDEN RULE

We turn now to the question of the originality of the Golden Rule. For the sake of argument, we will lay aside the foregoing reservations and assume that Hillel and Jesus did indeed quote the Golden Rule. Would the formulations of either teacher have been original to them? Does the Rule mark a breakthrough in religion or ethics? Would the Rule be of any use in defining what was distinctive in the teaching of either Hillel or Jesus?

The answer to all these questions must be an emphatic negative. The Golden Rule is found long before the time of Hillel and Jesus. It was so widespread in the ancient world that if either Hillel or Jesus did use it, they would have been citing an ethical commonplace which, however true it may be, cannot in their day be seen as enunciating an original or distinctive moral principle. Indeed, in both the Christian (Mt 7:12) and the Jewish sources (b.Šab 31a), any claim to originality is explicitly denied. The Rule is offered as a summation of age-old teaching—a point too often ignored by Christian commentators.

In its classic formulation, the Golden Rule is not found in the Hebrew Bible nor in the literature of the ancient Near East. The common view, argued at length by Dihle,[6] is that it was formulated in the Greek world and from there passed over into Jewish writings in the Hellenistic period. If we set aside Diogenes Laertius' attribution of the Rule to Thales (LEP 1.36), the reliability of which must be in serious doubt, then the earliest allusion to it in the Mediterranean world is in the *Histories* of Herodotus. Herodotus (3.142) depicts Maenandrius as telling the Samians: "It is known that I have sole charge of Polycrates' sceptre and dominion; and it is in my power to be your ruler. But, so far as in me lies, I will not do myself that which I account blameworthy in my neighbor."

Another echo of the Rule may be detected in Herodotus' report of Xerxes' reply to the Spartan emissaries (7.136). The obliqueness of these two early references is noteworthy. It suggests that already in the time of Herodotus the Rule was a commonplace. Further references to it occur later in the writings of Isocrates, and from then on it is fairly widespread in both Greek and Latin literature.[7]

The earliest Jewish attestation of the Rule is probably in the collection of wisdom sayings which constitute the teaching of Tobit (frequently dated around 200 B.C.E.): "Take heed to yourself, my child, in all your works, and be discreet in all your behavior. And what you [yourself] hate, do to no one." Another early reference (c. 150 B.C.E.) is Aristeas 207:

> The king received the answer with great delight and looking at the next guest said, 'What is the teaching of wisdom?' He replied, 'As you wish no evil to befall you, but to partake of every blessing, so you should act on the same principle toward your subjects, including wrongdoers, and you should mildly admonish the noble and the good. For God draws all men to himself in his mercy.'

The application here of the Golden Rule specifically to the relationship between a ruler and his subjects may reflect its frequent use in political

---

[6] A. Dihle, *Die 'Goldene Regel': Eine Einführung in die Geschichte der antiken und frühchristlichen Vulgärethik* (Göttingen, 1962). See further the valuable review by D. A. Russell in *Gnomon* 35 (1963) 213–5.

[7] For a list of references, see Dihle, *Goldene Regel*, pp. 85–102; cf. his summary article in *Reallexikon für Antike und Christentum*, vol. XI, cols 933–36. Further, Philippidis, *Goldene Regel religionsgeschichtlich untersucht*, pp. 42–55.

contexts in earlier Greek writers.[8]

Although chronology appears to favor the view that the Golden Rule passed over from the Greek world into Judaism, it would be wrong to be too dogmatic on this point. This cultural transfer—if transfer it be—should be evaluated with great care. The Greek culture from which the Jews may have borrowed the Golden Rule was not an autonomous entity, cut off from the general culture of the Levant and the ancient near east.

The absence of the Rule in the surviving literature of the ancient Near East may be accidental. A version of the Rule is found in the Armenian Wisdom of Ahiqar.[9] Its presence there may, of course, be due to Christian influence. On the other hand, the Armenian version at this point may preserve early Ahiqar material not attested in the other recensions. It is hard to tell. Moreover, it should be borne in mind that the date of Tobit is by no means certain. If, as has been argued, Tobit was composed in the Persian period, then the Greek origin of the Golden Rule loses its force.[10]

The earliest attestation of the Rule may be in the Analects of Confucius (551–479 B.C.E.): "Tsze-Kung asked, saying, 'Is there one word which may serve as a rule of practice for all one's life?' The Master said, 'Is not reciprocity such a word? What you do not want done to yourself, do not do to others'" (Analects 15:23).[11] If the attribution to Confucius is historically accurate, this reference effectively destroys any simple diffusionist model for the spread of the Golden Rule, for how on this model could we explain the occurrence of the Rule in Greece (Herodotus) and China (Confucius) at roughly the same time. The Rule is found in many cultures—a fact noted already by Voltaire: "La raison universelle qui contrebalance les passions ... imprimie cette loi dans tous les coeurs: ne fait pas ce que tu ne voudrais

---

[8] Herodotus 3.142; Isocrates, *Nicocles* 49 and 61; *To Nicocles* 24; *Panegyricus* 81; cf. Cassius Dio 52.34.

[9] "Son, that which seems evil unto thee, do not do to thy companion; and what is not thine own give not to others" (F. C. Conybeare, J. R. Harris and A. S. Lewis, *The Story of Ahiqar* [London, 1898], p. 34). The absence of obvious verbal echoes here of the Gospels is noteworthy.

[10] See C. A. Moore, "Tobit," *ABD*, vol. VI (New York, 1992), p. 591, for a recent survey of the problem of the date of Tobit.

[11] Trans. J. Legge, *The Chinese Classics*, vol. I (Hong Kong, 1960), p. 301.

pas qu'on te fit."[12] To suggest that there is something quintessentially Hellenic about the Rule—in that it seems to imply that the human, or self, is the measure of things (cf. Protagoras in Plato, *Theaetetus* 160D)—would be grossly to overinterpret it.

Furthermore, even if the Rule was borrowed from the Greeks, it was easily domesticated within Judaism. The ease of this domestication is a direct reflection of the fact that the ideas contained in the Rule were not alien to Judaism. Though none of its precise formulations are found, the substance of the Rule was attested. As we have already hinted, the so-called Love Command of Lev 19:18 ("You shall love your neighbor as yourself") appears to have played a central role in this process of domestication. The Golden Rule seems to have been treated as a comment on—or restatement of—this commandment. A few examples will illustrate this phenomenon.

(1) Lk 6:31 quotes the Golden Rule, but the commentary on the Rule in Lk 6:32-38 seems to be formulated with reference to the Love Command. We noted above that early Christian literature sometimes defines the *summum ius* in terms of the Love Command (Rom 13:9) and sometimes in terms of the Golden Rule (Mt 7:12). It is unlikely that these were two mutually exclusive or contradictory points of view. Rather the Golden Rule and the Love Command would have been seen simply as alternative statements of the same principle.

(2) Did 1:2: "The way of life is this: first of all, you shall love the God who made you, and secondly your neighbor as yourself. And all things whatsoever you would not befall yourself, neither do to another." In the juxtaposition here of the Love Command and the Golden Rule, the latter is intended to throw light on the former.

(3) TarJon to Lev 19:18: "You shall not take revenge, nor shall you bear a grudge against the children of your people, but you shall love your neighbor [*ḥābēr*]. What you hate for yourself, you shall not do to him." Note how here the Golden Rule functions specifically to clarify the sense of כָּמוֹךָ in the original Hebrew.

(4) A possible fourth example of the equation of the Golden Rule with the Love Command may be implicit in b.Šab 31a. It is paradoxical that the Gentile who asks Hillel to summarize the whole Torah while he

---

[12] Voltaire, "Essai sur les moeurs et l'esprit des nations" (1765), in *Oeuvres Complétes*, vol. IV (Paris, 1784), p. 289.

stands on one foot is answered with a maxim—the Golden Rule—which is not actually found in the Torah. Perhaps the point is that Hillel, in trying to draw the Gentile under the wings of the Shekhinah, cunningly chooses to summarize the Torah in terms of a principle the Gentile would readily recognize.

Is there behind this passage a doctrine akin to that enunciated by Paul in Rom 2:14-15: "When the Gentiles who have not the law do by nature the things contained in the law, they are a law unto themselves, even though they do not have the law. They show that the work of the law is written in their hearts"? Is Hillel appealing to an innate, God-given moral sense in the Gentile?[13] This may be pressing the text too hard. One thing is certain: the text makes no sense if the Golden Rule is not a reasonably satisfactory statement of the essence of the Torah. Such a use of the Golden Rule as a summary of the Torah is best explained by supposing that it is being taken as a restatement of the Love Command. Elsewhere in rabbinic literature the Love Command is cited as the *summum ius* (GenRab 24:27; SifQed 4:12 [ed. Weiss 89b]; y.Ned 9:3 [41 c. 36-38]). This is not contradictory to Hillel's view in b.Šab 31a, since the rabbis, like the early Christians, may have seen the Golden Rule and the Love Command as different formulations of the same fundamental principle.

Treating the Golden Rule as a reformulation of the Love Command helps to resolve some of the linguistic ambiguities of the Love Command and favors a universalizing interpretation of it. The Love Command is surprisingly ambiguous. Does כָּמוֹךָ modify וְאָהַבְתָּ ("and you shall love your neighbor in the same manner as you love yourself"), or does it qualify רֵעֲךָ ("and you shall love your neighbor who is like yourself")? And what is meant by רֵעֲךָ? Does it mean, "your fellow Jew?" Or, "your friend but not your enemy"? Or, "your fellowman or woman, whoever they may be"? All these interpretations are found in

---

[13] Cf. J. Jeremias: "Hillel benutzt offensichtlich die stoische Lehre vom ἄγραφος νόμος (vgl. Röm. 2,14), wenn er die G.R. für das göttliche Urgesetz erklärt" ("Goldene Regel," *Die Religion in Geschichte und Gegenwart*, vol. II [Tübingen, 1958], col. 1688). Cf. also Jeremias, "Paulus als Hillelit," *Neotestamentica et Semitica: Studies in Honour of Matthew Black*, E. E. Ellis and M. Wilcox, eds. (Edinburgh, 1969), p. 89f. On the "unwritten law" in Judaism, see I. Heinemann, "Die Lehre vom ungeschriebenen Gesetz im jüdischen Schrifttum," *HUCA* 4 (1927) 149-71.

early Jewish tradition. But the Golden Rule seems to sit easiest with the view that כָּמוֹךָ expresses the manner of the love and that the love command should be given a universal reference.

Although the Golden Rule may have been used to formulate the universalizing interpretation, it would be going too far to suggest that it generated the universalizing interpretation. The early Jewish sages were perfectly capable of following their own strong moral sense and of reaching such a universal interpretation without the help of the Golden Rule.

The indications are, then, that the Love Command played a major part in domesticating the Golden Rule in Judaism. But it is by no means the only maxim in early Jewish literature to express the principle of reciprocity which lies at the heart of the Rule. Even if we confine ourselves to the rabbinic corpus, we can find there numerous sayings which can be seen simply as applications of the Rule to concrete situations. The following will illustrate this point:

(1) "Let the honor of your friend [ḥābēr] be as dear to you as your own honor" (m.Ab 2:10).

(2) "Even as a man looks out for his own home, so should he look out for the home of his fellow. And even as no man wishes that his own wife and children be held in ill repute, so should no man wish that his fellow's wife and his fellow's children be held in ill repute" (ARN A 16).

(3) "Let your neighbor's property be as dear to you as your own" (m.Ab 2:12).

(4) "If you do not want a man to take what is yours, do not take what is his" (ARN B 30).

(5) "If you do not wish to be slandered, do not slander another" (ARN B 29).

(6) "If you do not want a man to hurt you or what is yours, then you too should not hurt him" (ARN B 26).

(7) "Do a kindness that one may be done to you. Attend a funeral that people should attend your funeral; mourn for others so that others should mourn for you; bury so that others should concern themselves with your burial; act benevolently so that benevolence should be done to you" (EcclRab 7.2.5; cf. t.Meg 4(3):16; t.Keṭ 7:6; y.Keṭ 7:5 [31b.54]).

There can be no denying that the sentiments expressed by the Golden Rule were thoroughly at home in early Judaism. Even if the Rule was borrowed from outside, it found a ready acceptance in Jewish circles.

A final, thorny question needs to be addressed regarding the originality of the Golden Rule. Hillel quotes the Rule in its negative form ("Do not do to others what you would not want them to do to you"), Jesus in the positive ("Do to others as you would want them to do to you"). Is there a significant difference between these two formulations?

Christian writers have commonly asserted that there is. They have argued that the positive form is much superior to the negative in that it contains a positive injunction to love one's neighbor, whereas the negative does not. Some have gone so far as to assert that Jesus was actually the first to use the positive form. On this view a gap opens up between Hillel and Jesus. Hillel may well have been citing an ethical commonplace, but Jesus was not. One nineteenth-century Christian writer puts the case thus:

The merest beginner in logic must perceive that there is a vast difference between the negative injunction, or the prohibition to do to others what is hateful to ourselves, and the positive direction to do unto others as we would have them do unto us. The one does not rise above the standpoint of the Law, being as yet far removed from that love which would lavish on others the good we ourselves desire, while the Christian saying embodies the nearest approach to absolute love of which human nature is capable, making that the test of our conduct to others which we ourselves desire to possess.[14]

[14] A. Edersheim, *The Life and Times of Jesus the Messiah*, vol. I (London, 1906), pp. 535–36.

There are a number of reasons why this position is untenable. In the first place, it is not true that Jesus was the first, or the only one, to formulate the Rule in its positive form. Aristeas 207 combines both the negative and the positive forms: "As you wish that no evil should befall you, but to partake of every blessing, so you should act on the same principle toward your subjects, including wrongdoers." According to Diogenes Laertius (5.21), Aristotle, when asked how we should act toward our friends, replied, "As we would they should act toward us." Even if this logion is not genuinely Aristotle's, it is unlikely that Diogenes, or his source, was influenced by Christian texts. Christian influence can equally be ruled out in 2En 61:2, where we have, in effect, a positive version of the Golden Rule: "That which a person makes request for from the Lord for his own soul, in the same manner let him behave toward every living soul." However, it is intriguing that the majority of the instances of the Golden Rule in both Jewish and pagan authors in antiquity are in the negative form.

Second, even if the concept of generosity of action toward others is not expressed explicitly in the negative form of the Golden Rule, that concept itself is not alien to Judaism. The performing of acts of loving-kindness (*gemîlût ḥasādîm*) is as much a part of Jewish as of Christian ethics. To imply otherwise is absurd. The positive injunction to love one's fellows is found not only in the Hebrew Bible, in the Love Command and its parallels (e.g., Lev 19:34), but in rabbinic literature as well: "Hillel says: 'Be of the disciples of Aaron, loving peace and pursuing peace, loving mankind and drawing them to the Torah'" (m.Ab 1:12; cf. ARN A and B, ad loc.). "If Israel would but look closely at what their father Jacob said to them (cf. Gen 49:28), no nation or kingdom could dominate them. What did he say to them? Accept upon yourselves the kingdom of heaven, vie with each other in the fear of heaven, and act toward each other with loving-kindness."[15]

Third, if the difference between the two formulations is so obvious and so important, it is surprising that more was not made of it in antiquity. As we noted earlier, Paul in Rom 13:10 seems to echo the negative form. The negative form is found in the Gospel of Thomas (Logion 6) and is common in the church fathers, despite the fact that the

[15] SifDeut §323 (Finkelstein ed., p. 372).

two occurrences of the Rule in the New Testament are positive.[16] This indifference toward nuancing the forms continued down through the Middle Ages to the philosophers of the seventeenth and eighteenth centuries, such as Hobbes, Locke, and Kant. The philosophers show little interest in the Rule and seem unaware of any profound differences between its positive and negative versions.[17]

Only in the nineteenth and twentieth centuries do Christian writers begin to insist on the superiority and originality of the positive form. The context of the assertion was polemical. It was part of a concerted attempt to maintain—in the face of the new historical-critical approach to the Bible—the traditional claim that Christianity was distinct from and had transcended its Jewish origins. Some Jewish writers replied in kind. Aḥad Ha-Am, for example, urged the superiority of the negative form, arguing that the positive formulation stands in direct contradiction to the moral basis of Judaism, since it deprives man of an objective moral value.[18]

---

[16] See Dihle, "Goldene Regel," *Reallexikon für Antike und Christentum*, vol. XI, cols. 938–39.

[17] Locke, *Essay on Human Understanding*, Book 1, chap. 3, §4 (ed. Nidditch, 1975, p. 68) quotes the Rule in its positive form: "... that most unshaken Rule of Morality, and foundation of all social Virtue, That one should do as he would be done unto...." Hobbes, *Leviathan*, Part I, chap. 15 (ed. Oakeshott, 1955, p. 103) quotes it in the negative: "... to leave all men inexcusable, they [the laws of nature] have been contracted into one easy sum, intelligible even to the meanest capacity; and that is, Do not that to another, which thou wouldest not have done to thyself." Kant, *Grundlagen zur Metaphysik der Sitten*, chap. II (Gesammelte Schriften, Band IV, Berlin, 1903, p. 421) restates the Rule in a more rigorous form: "Handle so also ob die Maxime deiner Handlung durch deinen Willen zum algemeinen Naturgesetze werden sollte." For a useful survey of the use of the Rule in medieval and modern times, see Heinz-Horst Schrey, "Goldene Regel III. Historisch und ethisch," *Theologische Realenzyclopädie*, vol. XIII (Berlin, 1984), pp. 575–78.

[18] Aḥad Ha-Am's powerful critique deserves to be quoted at some length: "Christian commentators point proudly to the positive principle of the Gospels: 'Whatsoever ye would that men should do to you, do ye even so to them' ... and thereby disparage Judaism, which has only the negative principle of Hillel: 'What is hateful to thyself do not unto thy neighbour.' Mr. Montefiore debates the matter, and cannot make up his mind whether the positive principle really embraces more in its intention than the negative, or whether Hillel and Jesus meant the same thing. But of this at least he is certain, that if Hillel's saying were suddenly discovered somewhere in a positive form, the Jews would be 'rather pleased' and the Christians would be 'rather sorry.'... But if we look deeper, we shall find that the difference between the two doctrines on this point is not one of more or less, but that there is a fundamental difference between their views as to the basis of morality. It was not by accident that Hillel put his principle in the

Finally, the Rule is too imprecise a principle to bear much philosophical weight. It should not be overnuanced. Despite its sophisticated linguistic form, it is unsophisticated in content. As Dihle rightly
saw, it is not a philosophical principle, but a piece of Vulgärethik.[19]
Philosophers have never been much interested in it. What little
philosophic interest has existed in the twentieth century has been
provoked by the theological debate. Bultmann put his finger on the
philosophical weakness of the Rule when he said that it "embodies the
morality of an naive egoism."[20]

To make one's own ego—its needs and desires—the standard of
one's actions toward others is clearly fraught with danger. The philosopher L. J. Russell stated the problem boldly when he argued that

> the rule as its stands gives no hint of the kind of person it is desirable
> you should be, if you are to be trusted to carry it out. It authorizes the

---

negative form; the truth is that the moral basis of Judaism will not bear the positive
principle. If the positive saying were to be found somewhere attributed to Hillel, we
should not be able to rejoice; we should have to impugn the genuineness of the
'discovery' which puts in Hillel's mouth a saying opposed to the spirit of Judaism. The
root of the distinction lies here also, as I have said, in the love of Judaism for abstract
principles. The moral law of the Gospels beholds man in his individual shape, with his
natural attitude towards himself and others and asks him to reverse this attitude, to substitute the 'other' for the 'self' in his individual life, to abandon plain egoism for
inverted egoism. Altruism and egoism alike deny the individual as such all objective
moral value, and make him a means to the subjective end; but egoism makes the 'other'
a means to the advantage of the 'self,' while altruism does just the reverse. Now
Judaism removed this subjective attitude from the moral law, and based it on an
abstract, objective foundation, on absolute justice, which regards the individual as such
as having moral value, and makes no distinction between the 'self' and the 'other.'...
Just as I have no right to ruin another man's life for my own sake, so I have no right to
ruin my own life for the sake of others. Both of us are men, and both our lives have the
same value before the throne of justice." See: "Judaism and the Gospels (1910)," *Ten
Essays on Judaism by Achad Ha-Am*, trans. L. Simon (New York, 1973), pp. 235–36.
The original Hebrew can be found in the essay, "'Al šetê ha-se'ippîm" ("Halting
Between Two Opinions") in *Kol Kitbê Aḥad Ha-'Am* (Tel Aviv, 1947), p. 374. For
Claude Montefiore's views on the Golden Rule, see his *Synoptic Gospels*, vol. II
(London, 1917), pp. 119–20, and his *Rabbinic Literature and Gospel Teaching*
(London, 1930), pp. 150f. Cf. also I. Abrahams, *Studies in Pharisaism and the
Gospels*, First Series (Cambridge, 1917), pp. 18–29.

[19] Dihle, *Goldene Regel*, pp. 30–40.

[20] R. Bultmann, *The History of the Synoptic Tradition*, trans. J. Marsh (Oxford,
1963), p. 103.

quarrelsome person, who loves to be provoked, to go about provoking others, and the person who hates friendliness and sympathy to be cold and unsympathetic in his dealings with others; it authorizes the man who loves to find himself in a network of intrigue and sharp dealing, to deal with others habitually in this way.[21]

Norms of behavior should transcend the self and have some sort of universality. This problem was noticed early on by Christian commentators. The Old Latin translates Mt 7:12 "Whatsoever good things ..." (*omnia ergo quaecumque vultis ut faciant vobis homines bona, ita et vos facite illis*). The addition is significant and attempts to introduce an objective moral standard. In his commentary on the Sermon on the Mount, Augustine argues that a distinction should be drawn between "desiring" and "wishing." He claims that a man, however much he may desire it, cannot will or wish for himself anything which is not good.[22]

Two popular nineteenth-century Christian commentaries illustrate two other ploys for getting round the problem. One urges that

the precise sense of the maxim is best referred to common sense. It is not, of course, what—in our wayward, capricious, grasping moods— we should wish that men would do to us, that we are to hold ourselves bound to do to them; but only what—in the exercise of an impartial judgment, and putting ourselves in their place—we consider it reasonable that they should do to us, that we are to do to them.[23]

Another proposes that the self envisaged in the Rule is not any or every self, but the purified, redeemed self:

---

[21] L. J. Russell, "Ideals and Practice (I)," *Philosophy* 17 (1942) 110.

[22] Augustine, *De Sermone Domini in Monte secundum Matthaeum* 2.74 (Patrologia Latina XXXIV, col. 1303): "Intelligendum est ergo plenam esse sententiam et omnino perfectam, etiam si hoc verbum [bona] non addatur. Id enim quod dictum est, *quaecumque vultis*, non usitate ac passim, sed proprie dictum accipi oportet. Voluntas namque non est nisi in bonis: nam in malis flagitiosisque factis cupiditas proprie dicitur, non voluntas. Non quia semper proprie loquuntur Scripturae, sed ubi oportet ita omnino proprium verbum tenent, ut non aliud sinant intelligi."

[23] D. Brown, *A Commentary, Critical, Experimental and Practical, on the Old and New Testaments*, ed. R. Jamieson, A. R. Fausset and D. Brown, vol. III (Grand Rapids, Mich., 1976), pp. 47f.

There is, of necessity, an implied limitation. We cannot comply with all men's desires, nor ought we to wish that they should comply with ours, for those desires may be foolish and frivolous, or may involve the indulgence of lust or passion. The rule is only safe when our own will has been first purified, so that we wish only from others that which is really good. Reciprocity in folly is obviously altogether alien from the mind of Christ.[24]

All this special pleading serves only to highlight the deficiencies of the Rule and the dangers of pressing it too hard. Theologians and philosophers can nuance the Rule to their hearts content, but the fact remains that it is a popular saying and should not be asked to bear the weight of a theological or philosophical system. If Jesus' positive formulation of the Golden Rule marked a profound moral breakthrough, then it is very odd that no one—whether theologian or philosopher—seems to have spotted the fact till the nineteenth century.

THE GOLDEN RULE AS THE *SUMMUM IUS*

Our analysis leads inevitably to the conclusion that the Golden Rule is of no use whatsoever in comparing the historical Hillel and the historical Jesus. The evidence that Hillel quoted the Rule is shaky in the extreme. Even if he did, he would only have uttered a maxim which would have sprung readily to the lips of any street-corner moralist in antiquity. There are better grounds for believing that Jesus quoted the Rule, but his positive formulation of it is not so innovative as has often been claimed.

The fact remains that Jewish and Christian tradition claim that Hillel and Jesus quoted the Golden Rule and that both teachers proposed that the Rule could be seen in some sense as a summation of the law. This striking agreement calls for explanation. It suggests that there is a valid and illuminating comparison to be made, not between the historical figures, but between the images of those figures which have been projected by the religious communities which they have influenced. We can legitimately compare and contrast the traditions about Hillel with

---

[24] E. H. Plumptre, *A New Testament Commentary for English Readers*, ed. C. J. Ellicott, vol. I (3d ed., London [c. 1881]), p. 41.

the traditions about Jesus. A comprehensive comparison cannot be undertaken here. We will content ourselves with trying to clarify what might be meant in both traditions by asserting that the Golden Rule is the *summum ius*.

In b.Šab 31a the Gentile asks Hillel to teach him the whole Torah while he stands on one foot. Clearly he wants Hillel to sum up the Law, to put it in a nutshell. Hillel obliges by quoting the Golden Rule and by claiming that it is "the whole Torah." The implication appears to be that the Rule is the fundamental principle which underlies the whole Torah: the rest of the Torah is but "commentary" (*pērûš*) on the principle, which draws out its meaning and applies it to concrete situations. The analogy of text and commentary to explain the relationship between the Golden Rule and the Torah is suggestive but vague.

In ARN B 26, however, the language is more precise. There the Golden Rule is described as "the great principle (כלל גדול) of the whole Torah." *Kelāl* is a technical term in rabbinic literature for a general principle underlying a series of concrete rulings. M.Keṭ 3:9 provides a simple example:

> If a man said, 'I have seduced the daughter of such-a-one,' he must pay [compensation for] indignity and blemish on his own admission, but he does not pay the [prescribed] fine.

> If a man said, 'I have stolen,' he must repay the value on his own admission, but he does not make double or fourfold or fivefold restitution.

> [If he said], 'My ox has killed such-a-one,' or 'the ox of such-a-one,' he must make restitution on his own admission.

> [If he said], 'My ox has killed the bondman of such-a-one,' he does not make restitution on his own admission.

> This is the general principle (*zeh ha-kelāl*): whosoever must pay more than the cost of damage does not pay on his own admission.

Here the kelal clearly has the function of stating succinctly the principle embodied in the bill of particulars.

The *kelāl* in m.Keṭ 3:9 is of limited scope and will cover only a limited bill of particulars. However, once one has started looking for *kelālîm*, the question of ever more comprehensive principles naturally arises. Faced with a number of limited *kelālîm*, one could ask if there is a more general *kelāl* which would embrace them all. These second-order *kelālîm*, of wider application, appear to be called "great principles" (*kelālîm gedôlîm*) in rabbinic literature.[25]

There is no logical stopping place on this road till one has asked the ultimate question of whether there is a single "great *kelāl*" underlying the whole Torah. This is clearly the issue in ARN B 26. It is also the issue in GenRab 24:7 (cf. SifQed 4:12 [ed. Weiss 89b]), where Ben Azzai states that the creation of man in God's image (Gen 5:1) is the "great principle" of the Torah, whereas Aqiba claims that the Love Command (often identified, as we have seen, with the Golden Rule) has that status. The context and the parallels with b.Šab 31a and ARN B 26 indicate that the dispute is not about *a* great principle, but about the greatest principle of all.

This search for the ultimate principle of the Torah is vividly illustrated by b.Mak 23b–24a:

> R. Simlai, when preaching, said: Six hundred and thirteen precepts (*miṣvôt*) were communicated to Moses, three hundred and sixty-five negative (corresponding to the days of the solar year), and two hundred and forty-eight positive (corresponding to the number of a man's limbs). ...

> David came and based them upon eleven [precepts], as it is written: "Lord, who shall sojourn in your tent, who shall dwell in your holy mountain? (1) He who walks uprightly, and (2) does righteousness, and (3) speaks the truth in his heart. (4) He who has no malice on his tongue, (5) nor wrongs his fellow, (6) nor tells tales against his neighbor; (7) in whose eyes a reprobate is despised, (8) but who honors

---

[25] See, for example, m.Shab 7:1, "A great principle have they laid down concerning the Sabbath [*kelāl gādôl 'āmerû*]." The *kelāl* which follows appears to embrace virtually all the complex Sabbath legislation. Likewise, when in b.BQam 46a the principle that "the burden of the proof lies with the plaintiff" (cf. m.BQam 3:11) is described as a "great principle of jurisprudence" (*kelāl gādôl ba-dîn*), the *kelāl* in question is clearly of a high order of generality.

those who fear the Lord. (9) He who swears to his own hurt, and does not change; (10) he who does not put out his money to usury, (11) nor takes a bribe against the innocent. He who does these things shall never be moved" (Ps 15:1-5). ...

Then Isaiah came and based them upon six, as it is written: "(1) He who walks in righteousness, and (2) speaks the truth; (3) he who scorns to enrich himself by extortion, (4) and who keeps his hands clean from bribes; (5) who stops his ears against talk of murder, and (6) shuts his eyes against looking at evil" (Isa 33:15).

Then Micah came and based them upon three, as it is written: "The Lord has told you, O man, what is good, and what it is that the Lord requires of you: only (1) to act justly, (2) to love mercy, and (3) to walk humbly with your God?'" (Mic 6:8). ...

Again Isaiah came and based them upon two, as it is written: "Thus says the Lord: (1) Keep judgment, and (2) do righteousness" (Isa 56:1).

Then came Amos and based them upon one: "Thus says the Lord, Seek me and you shall live" (Amos 5:4).

To this R. Naḥman b. Isaac objected: [Might not the sense be,] seek me by observing the whole Torah and [thus] live? Rather, Habakkuk came and based them all upon one [precept], as it is written: "The righteous man shall live by his faith" (Hab 2:4).

Interest in the underlying principles of the Torah is not confined to rabbinic texts. It surfaces also in Philo. Philo distinguishes between the Decalogue and the "special laws" (i.e., the concrete miṣvôt, including the ritual laws and the laws of kašrût). He argues that the latter may be subsumed under the former: "We must not forget that the Ten Words are summaries of the special laws which are recorded in the sacred Books and run through the whole of the legislation" (De Decalogo 154; cf. De Specialibus Legibus 1.1).

We find similar concerns in early Christian texts. In Mark 12:28ff a scribe asks Jesus, "Which is the first commandment of all?"

Jesus replies, "Hear, O Israel: the Lord our God, the Lord is one; and you shall love the Lord your God with all your heart, and with all your soul, and with all your mind, and with all your strength" (Deut 6:4-5). He then goes on to add that the second commandment is, "You shall love your neighbor as yourself" (Lev 19:18). *First* here is probably to be taken in a hierarchical sense: which law contains the first and fundamental principle of the Torah underlying all the other laws? The parallel in Mt 22:34ff speaks of the whole law and the prophets "depending" on the commandments to love God and to love one's neighbor. The sense appears to be that the former are derived from, or give expression to, the latter.

Gal 5:14 uses slightly different language: "The whole law is fulfilled in one word, 'You shall love your neighbor as yourself.'" Rom 13:8-10 introduces the notion of a single law as the "summation" of the rest of the laws:

> He who loves his neighbor has fulfilled the law. The commandments, 'You shall not commit adultery, You shall not kill, You shall not steal, You shall not covet,' and any other commandment, are summed up in this sentence, 'You shall love your neighbor as yourself.' Love does no wrong to an neighbor; therefore love is the fulfilling of the law.

In Mt 7:12 (though not in Lk 6:31) the Golden Rule is given as the essence of the Torah: "for this is the law and the prophets." A similar idea may lie behind the Western text of Acts 15:29, where the negative form of the Golden Rule is inserted. The purpose of the interpolation may be quite simple. The context is concerned with the question of what commandments of the Torah should Gentile converts be required to observe. The interpolator wished to suggest that if they kept the Golden Rule, they would, in effect, be observing the whole Law. He could have quoted as effectively the Love Command, but perhaps, as in the story of Hillel in b.Šab 31a, the Golden Rule was deliberately chosen as the "Gentile" version of this command.

Many of the *kelālê ha-Tôrāh* are propositions drawn from the Bible. They may, indeed, themselves be biblical *misvôt*. In this case, some laws of the Torah would be more universal and fundamental than others and may lie behind the more concrete and specific pieces of legislation. But it also appears permissible to formulate independent principles not explicitly stated in the Bible through extrapolation from the concrete laws. No obvious distinction is drawn between these two types of *kelālîm*: the "nonbiblical" *kelāl* is treated as being as valid as the "biblical" *kelāl*.

The search for the *kelālê ha-Tôrāh* is linked to the long-running debate within Judaism concerning the "reasons for the commandments" (*taʿamê ha-miṣvôt*). It is natural to ask why a given piece of legislation has been enacted. What is its purpose? One answer to this question is that the specific law gives concrete expression to a moral or rational principle. If one pursues the *kelālê ha-Tôrāh* to a sufficiently high level of abstraction, then almost inevitably one will identify them with moral propositions, since only moral propositions have a sufficiently universal and abstract character to embrace a wide variety of different, concrete laws. On this view, the reason for a given commandment is simply to apply the moral principle in the everyday world. Thus a view of the Torah emerges in which it is seen to comprise both eternal, universal truths, and the working out of those truths in the form of specific legislation.

The potential for radicalism in this position is obvious. It opens the way for the argument that what is important is not the concrete law but the eternal truth. The concrete law is valid only insofar as it successfully expresses—under the conditions of space and time—the underlying universal principle. If it fails to do this, then it should be abolished or modified. Thus the *kelālîm* can be used as a platform for a radical critique of the legislation. Some early Christian writers seem drawn to this position,[26] but, not surprisingly, it held few attractions for the Rabbis.

The words used by Hillel in b.Shab 31a, in which the *kelāl* is compared to the text and the remaining legislation to the commentary, *could* be given a radical twist. Nevertheless, halakhists would reject drawing radical conclusions from such an haggadah. A more normative halakhic view would be that the concrete halakhot are primary, the *kelālîm* secondary. That is, the halakhot are the "text," the *kelālîm* the

---

[26] For example, the argument in Mk 2:23-27 appeals to a *kelal* ("the Sabbath was made for the benefit of humanity") and plays it off against a concrete (Pharisaic) ruling that plucking ears of corn on Sabbath constituted forbidden work (cf. b.Šab 73a-b).

"commentary." The direction of the critique must always be from the halakhot to the *kelālîm*, not vice versa.[27]

There is also a significant tendency among halakhists to resist the idea that every *miṣvāh* must have a moral or rational basis. Some *miṣvôt*, such as the laws of the Red Heifer, have no such basis, but must nevertheless be obeyed.[28] The authority of the *miṣvāh* lies not in its morality or rationality, but in its fundamental character as a *ius divinum*.

CONCLUSION

Comparing the historical Hillel and the historical Jesus is a questionable exercise. Comparing the traditions regarding these two great teachers is not. As we have seen, such comparison can be illuminating and can draw out the nuances of both traditions. At the end of our analysis, the overriding feeling is one of astonishment at the convergence of the two traditions. Christians have commonly regarded Jesus' teaching on love as the heart of the gospel. Yet similar ideas are found in rabbinic literature. Here, arguably, is a significant community of belief, which imparts substance to the notion of a Judeo-Christian tradition.

---

[27] B.Kid 34a: *ʾên lemēdîn min ha-kelālôt va-ʾafîlû bemāqôm še-neʾemar bô ḥûṣ* ("no inference may be drawn from general rulings, even where an exception is actually specified"). Cf. also y.Ter 1:2 (40 c. 36): *lêt kelālîn de-Rabbî kelālîn* ("the general statements made by Rabbi are not general statements"). Cf. Paulus, *Digest* 50.17.1: Regula est, quae rem quae est breviter enarrat. Non ex regula ius sumatur, sed ex iure quod est regula fiat. Per regulam igitur brevis rerum narratio traditur, et, ut ait Sabinus, quasi causae coniectio est, quae simul cum in aliquo vitiata est, perdit officium suum.

[28] This is the point of the story about Yoḥanan ben Zakkai and the Red Heifer in Pesiqta deRab Kahana 4:7.

JESUS AND THE DEAD SEA SCROLLS[1]

AS A SUCCESSOR of Franz Delitzsch and as director of the Institutum Judaicum Delitzschianum (1988-1993), I would like to consider briefly the little essay on "Jesus and Hillel" Franz Delitzsch published in 1865-66[2] in several expanded editions and which was translated into Hebrew by Jechiel Lichtenstein in 1894.

Delitzsch began with the similarities and common features in Jesus and Hillel (note the order!) and examined the traditions concerning three issues: (1) How did Hillel and Jesus become great teachers? (2) What were the teachings of Hillel the Babylonian and Jesus the Nazarite? and (3) How are we to understand the tradition about the meekness of Hillel and Jesus?

Unlike other Christian scholars who depicted Jews or representatives of Judaism (e.g., the Pharisees) in a derogatory way, Delitzsch portrayed Hillel favorably—but only in order to show how much superior Jesus is in comparison to him.

> Therefore we let Hillel's people lament at Hillel's grave: 'Alas, the meek, the pious, the pupil of Ezra'—but we praise the patient, the innocent slaughtered lamb of God.... Hillel is dead and belongs as a representative of an old system of laws to the past, but Jesus lives.[3]

From such a religiously motivated starting point—which had above all a function in mission—neither the person of Hillel nor that of Jesus could

---

[1] See now the magnificent volume edited by J. H. Charlesworth: *Jesus and the Dead Sea Scrolls* (New York, 1993).

[2] *Jesus und Hillel: Mit Rücksicht auf Renan und Geiger verglichen*, Franz Delitzsch (Erlangen, 1866).

[3] *Jesus und Hillel*, p. 39; Hebrew, p. 44.

be aptly described. This was an unhistorical approach to both. The sayings attributed to Hillel or Jesus were taken uncritically as historical. After all, does the *topos* of "meekness" really lend itself to a historical-critical conclusion?

Delitzsch's essay was written in part as a response to Geiger, who had made Jesus a pupil of Hillel's. "Jesus was a Pharisee who walked in the ways of Hillel. There was no new thought in him. But Hillel represents—and the word will not desecrate but ennoble him—the appearance of a real reformer."[4]

It is striking that Delitzsch blamed Geiger for allowing his view of Jesus to be shaped by or dependent upon his view of Hillel. He did not realize that his own view of Hillel was heavily dependent upon his own demeaning of Hillel in comparison to Jesus.

What comparison *are* we able to achieve? Where are the limits and where the errors? In this essay I will suggest several underlying principles that may make such a comparison fruitful.

I am not suggesting that we look for allusions to Jesus or for early Christian doctrines or personalities in early Jewish literature, especially of that kind that aims at discovering Jesus or representatives of early Christianity in the Dead Sea Scrolls. Nor am I suggesting that we focus on the much more interesting question of "Jesus in Talmudic literature." Instead, we should simply ask in a paradigmatic way how Jesus' person, doctrines, and destiny are to be seen in the light of early Jewish literature.

It is immediately evident that we must establish some limitations on the scope of this inquiry. We will limit the investigation chronology to the lifetime of Jesus, taking into consideration texts coming with certainty from the time before 70, such as the Dead Sea Scrolls.

Despite all the controversial questions concerning the Dead Sea Scrolls, we may say with certainty that the finds of the Dead Sea represent the most encompassing library we know from the Second Temple Period. They surely do not represent what everybody knew, but to a large degree, what many or some could have known.

Even without clear historical connections between Jesus and the Qumran community, even though there is strangely no explicit allusion in the New Testament literature to the Qumran community, we must

---

[4] *Jesus und Hillel*, p. 7.

take into account the sort of literature and theological thought that was common in early Jewish times.

We will not address the difficult question of whether Jesus and his followers had connections with the Qumran Essenes and their literature. We will, however, inquire about the "picture" of first-century Judaism reflected in the library with its variety of texts, most of them not special texts of the Qumran Essenes. The library certainly does represent the variety of early Jewish literature.[5]

To approach this question, we will consider several examples, beginning with the nature of theological understanding.

God as King in the Shiroth ʿolat ha-shabbath[6] and Jesus' Gospel of the Kingdom of Heaven[7]

In 4QŠirot ʿolat haššabbat, the frequent use of God as *mèlèk* and of his *malkut* is striking. These songs speak of God's present kingdom in the heavenly realm. But this present kingdom does not contrast with the eschatological hope for God's kingdom on earth, but in a special way represents and anticipates this coming kingdom. In exhorting the angels to praise, the community already takes part in the heavenly service. This idea corresponds to the idea of the community with the angels, as we know from the Hodayot and other texts (e.g., 1QH 3.19-23).

The expectation of the coming of God's kingdom on earth corresponds to the present reign of God in heaven. This evidently sheds light on the Lord's Prayer: "Your will shall be done—as it is already done in heaven (by the angels), it shall be done on earth" (cf. Mt 6:12; not reflected in Luke).

---

[5] We must also leave to one side whether somebody like Jesus could have had access to such a literature. The question is not whether Jesus actually studied the texts in Jerusalem or Qumran, but what a Galilean Jew could have "learned." This question of study was treated by Shmuel Safrai in his contribution to the Compendia Rerum Judaicarum ad Novum Testamentum: *Education and the Study of the Torah*, Vol II, pp. 945-70.

[6] Cf. *Songs of the Sabbath Sacrifice: A Critical Edition*, C. A. Newsom (Atlanta, 1985).

[7] See A. M. Schwemer, "Gott als König und seine Königsherrschaft in den Sabbatliedern aus Qumran," M. Hengel and A. M. Schwemer, eds, *Königsherrschaft und himmlischer Kult im Judentum, Urchristentum und der hellenistischen Welt* (Tübingen, 1991), pp. 45-118.

The concept of the *malkut* of God in 4QŠirot ʿolat haššabbat opens a better understanding of the presence and the future of God's kingdom in the proclamation of Jesus. Moreover the description of the heavenly service in 4QŠirot ʿolat haššabbat is very important for understanding the heavenly service in Hebrews and Revelation, and in another way for the Hekhalot literature.

Exactly 100 years ago, the 29-year-old Johannes Weiß[8] wrote in his booklet, *Die Predigt Jesu vom Reiche Gottes*, that "das Reich Gottes nach der Auffassung Jesu eine schlechthin überweltliche Größe ist, die zu dieser Welt in ausschließlichem Gegensatz steht."[9] Weiß was, of course, opposing German *Kulturprotestantismus*, which saw in the development of civilization the fulfillment of God's kingdom on earth. At the same time he realized the transmundane character of Jesus' view in terms of apocalyptic expectations.

We now realize, however, the correspondence of God's kingdom in heaven with the present participation of humanity in the praise of that kingdom and the anticipation of that coming kingdom in the present praise.

The Self-Consciousness/Self-Awareness of the Teacher of Righteousness and of Jesus[10]

The question of the self-consciousness (or "self-awareness," as Prof. Flusser has taught us to say) of the Teacher of Righteousness and of Jesus has been treated often. Here, too, Christian scholars are in danger of fatal hermeneutics. In order to draw a brilliant picture of Jesus, they show the inferiority of the Teacher of Righteousness or show the Teacher in a positive way only to portray in all the more dazzling colors the sublime self-awareness of Jesus!

The self-consciousness of an authorized teacher becomes more obvious if 4QMMT represents a letter of the Teacher of Righteousness. The claim with which this leader of the community criticizes an opposing group and their leader reveals the conviction of a divine mission and the correctness of the Teacher's own way:

---

[8] See H. Merkel, "Die Gottesherrschaft in der Verkündigung Jesu," *Königsherrschaft*, pp. 119–61, especially 120–21.

[9] "The kingdom of God is, in Jesus' understanding, a totally transmundane entity in contradictory opposition to this world."

Remember the kings of Israe[l and consider their deeds, that whoever of them ... respected [the Tor]ah was delivered from distresses. And these were seekers of the Torah and guilt [was pardoned]. Remember David, that he was a man of honour [and] he [too] was delivered from many afflictions and was pardoned. Moreover, we have written to you some of the precepts of the Torah which we regard as for your benefit and for that of your people. For [we have seen that] with you is wisdom and knowledge of Torah. Consider all these and seek from Him that He confirm your counsel and put away from you the evil plans and counsel of Belial so that you may rejoice at the end of time as you find that some of our words are true, and it shall be reckoned to you as righteousness when you do what is upright and what is good before Him, for your wellbeing and that of Israel.[11]

As they interpreted the Torah, Jesus and the Teacher of Righteousness acted as authorized teachers. The Teacher of Righteousness led his people in the way of God's heart (see CD 1.11). Both had a prophetic consciousness (see, concerning the Teacher of Righteousness, 1QpHab 7.1-8). The Teacher was fulfilling his mission immediately before the impending end and only his community would be saved in the final judgment. Those entering the covenant and repenting would be atoned for and saved. The Teacher of Righteousness also knew the sinfulness of humanity, as well as God's grace. As eschatological preachers with prophetic self-consciousness, both were God's messengers in this final phase of time.

Of course, there were differences. First, the Teacher of Righteousness had a priestly descent and self-consciousness. In his community, cultic categories determined daily life and worship and served as rules for admission and exclusion (see esp. 1QSa 2.3-9). Purity was also a presupposition for the community with the angels.

---

[10] See G. Jeremias, *Der Lehrer der Gerechtigkeit* (Göttingen, 1963).

[11] For text and translation, see "An Unpublished Halakhic Letter from Qumran," E. Qimron and J. Strugnell, in *Biblical Archaeology Today: Proceedings of the International Congress on Biblical Archaeology* (Jerusalem, 1984), pp. 400-7; "An Unpublished Halakhic Letter from Qumran," E. Qimron and J. Strugnell, in *Israel Museum Journal* 4 (1985) 9-12; see also *The Qumran Chronicle*, Appendix A, No. 2 (Cracow, 1990); see also now E. Qimron and J. Strugnell (DJD 10; Oxford, 1994).

Second, Jesus shared with sapiental and apocalyptic literature the use of the "Gattung" *makarismos* (beatitude).[12] In fact, Jesus was often portrayed as a sapiential teacher. He used the *makarismos* in both ways: as a single *makarismos* (e.g., Matt 11:6) and in a series (e.g., at the beginning of the Sermon of the Mount, Matt 5:3-11).

Not long ago, few makarisms were known from the finds of the Dead Sea. But the recent opening of the scrolls to all scholars has led to new publications and a careful rereading of the source material.[13]

Puech has recently tried again to solve a long-known problem: What is the relationship between the numbers of the makarisms in Matthew 5:3-11 (total of nine) to those in Luke 6:20-22 (total of four plus four woes)? The *opinio communis* is that Luke has preserved the original number and that the additional material in Matthew consists of extensions relying mostly on the Old Testament. Puech, on the other hand, holds that the number in Matthew was original because it reflects the pattern of seven (or eight) series he finds represented in 4Q525. However, this text preserves only five makarisms (see the following text). Thus, this text and Puech's conclusions do not overthrow New Testament studies. Nevertheless, the text is a fine example of sort of poetry in Jewish literature reflected in the New Testament makarisms.

The following is Puech's text according to Viviano's English translation:[14]

Column I
  [Words (or Proverbs) of David (or of Solomon son of David), which he spok]e (or [wrot]e) by the wisdom God gave to him [to ... to acquir]e wisdom and disci[pline,] to understand [...] to increase kn[owledge or wisdom] ...

---

[12] The parables should also be noted. Most striking, of course, is Jesus' parabolic way of speaking, which can be understood only in the light of early Jewish literature.

[13] E. Puech, "Un hymne essénien en partie retrouvé et les Béatitudes, 1QH V,12 - VI,18 (= col. XIII - XIV,7) et 4Q Béat," *RQ* 13 (1988) 59-88; E. Puech, "4Q 525 et les péricopes des Béatitudes en Ben Sira et Matthieu," *RB* 98 (1991) 80-106; B. T. Viviano, "Beatitudes Found Among Dead Sea Scrolls," *BAR* 18 (1992) 53-55, 85.

[14] "Beatitudes," p. 55.

Column II

    [Blessed ...

    [Blessed ...

    [Blessed ...

    [Blessed ...

    [Blessed is he who speaks truth] with a pure heart and who does not slander with his tongue.

    Blessed are those who cling to his statutes and who do not cling to her ways of perversity.

    Blessed are those who rejoice because of her and who do not spread themselves in the ways of folly.

    Blessed is he who seeks her with pure hands and who does not go after her with a deceitful heart.

    Blessed the man who has attained Wisdom and walks in the law of the Most High and applies his heart to her ways, who cherishes her lessons and ev[e]r rejoices in her corrections, but who does not repel her in the pain of [his] misfortune[s?] (or in the distress of tri[al?]) and in bad times does not abandon her, who does not forget her [in days of] terror and in his humility of soul does not reproach [her].

Column III

    Thus he thinks always of her and in his misfortune he meditates on [the Law (?) during al]l his existence on it [he reflects (?) and keeps it (?)] before his eyes, in order not to go in the ways o[f the wicked (?)/folly/impiety (?) and ...] his/her/its [...] together and his heart burns for her [... and a crown of pure] gol[d (she) will place on] his [he]ad and with kings she [will make him] si[t down ... and ... by] his scepter on [... and amon]g brothers he will deci[de ...] And now, (my) sons, listen to me [and] do not re[fuse the words of my mouth, ...]

This text combines Torah and Wisdom (see Sir 24; Deut 4:6; 4Q185). Comparison with the makarisms in the Sermon on the Mount reveals some special traits: (1) 4Q525 is sapiential, not apocalyptic; and (2) Unlike Matthew and Luke, 4Q525 contains no paradoxical reversion of reality.

On the other hand, they have in common a future perspective and the last of the makarisms exceeds the others in dimension and forms in this way a conclusion with a special importance.

FINAL REFLECTIONS ON METHODOLOGY

The famous criterion of New Testament scholarship that we can find authentic Jesus tradition only where a saying cannot be derived from Judaism or from the needs of the early church has proven more and more fruitless. This criterion is perhaps nothing more than a specialized form of Christian anti-Judaism.

However, the reverse is also of little help: that authentic Jesus tradition exists only where it can be derived from early Judaism. This would bring us back to the apologetic position of Geiger: "Einen neuen Gedanken sprach er [Jesus] keineswegs aus."[15] The responsibility of historians of early Judaism and Christianity is simply too important to solve such questions by simple rules like those.

The literature of Early Judaism as represented by the Dead Sea Scrolls presents a range of personalities and doctrines. In this literature we can find analogies relating to the self-consciousness and the doctrine of Jesus. This relationship enriches our knowledge and does not diminish Jesus' originality and individuality.

However, if we are to understand the prophet of Galilee in the context of early Jewish literature, we must realize that studying or describing Hillel with the intention of commending Jesus by way of contrast is historically and morally mistaken. May this symposium serve to begin the process of correcting this common fundamental flaw in the hermeneutics of Christian theology which has historically prevented Christians from an unprejudiced approach to Judaism.

[15] "In no way did Jesus ever express a genuinely new thought."

RECONSTRUCTING JESUS' TEACHING:
PROBLEMS AND POSSIBILITIES

IN MANY QUARTERS a new mood of optimism has emerged regarding the possibility of recovering the teaching and activities of the historical Jesus.[1] The older assumptions of form criticism that the early church invented much, if not most, of the dominical tradition[2] is now called into question.[3]

The assumption that tradition was created to meet needs and answer questions faced by the early Christian communities is seen to be in

---

[1] Cf. E. P. Sanders, *Jesus and Judaism* (Philadelphia, 1985), p. 2: "The dominant view today seems to be that we can know pretty well what Jesus was out to accomplish, that we can know a lot about what he said, and that those two things make sense within the world of first-century Judaism.... This is not the result of a rapid increase in knowledge, but rather of a shift in attitude." See also H. Schürmann, "Zur aktuellen Situation der Leben-Jesu-Forschung," *Geist und Leben* 46 (1973) 300–10. Several recent studies seem to bear this out; cf. B. F. Meyer, *The Aims of Jesus* (London, 1979); W. R. Farmer, *Jesus and the Gospel: Tradition, Scripture, and Canon* (Philadelphia, 1982); B. D. Chilton, *A Galilean Rabbi and His Bible: Jesus' Use of the Interpreted Scripture of His Time* (Good News Studies 8; Wilmington, 1984); M. J. Borg, *Jesus a New Vision: Spirit, Culture, and the Life of Discipleship* (San Francisco, 1987); R. A. Horsley, *Jesus and the Spiral of Violence: Popular Jewish Resistance in Roman Palestine* (San Francisco, 1987); J. H. Charlesworth, *Jesus within Judaism* (Anchor Bible Reference Library; New York, 1988); B. Witherington, *The Christology of Jesus* (Minneapolis, 1990); J. D. Crossan, *The Historical Jesus: The Life of a Mediterranean Jewish Peasant* (San Francisco, 1991); M. de Jonge, *Jesus, The Servant-Messiah* (Shaffer Lectures; New Haven, 1991); J. P. Meier, *A Marginal Jew: Rethinking the Historical Jesus. Volume One: The Roots of the Problem and the Person* (Anchor Bible Reference Library; New York, 1991).

[2] As seen in M. Dibelius, *From Tradition to Gospel* (London, 1971), and esp. R. Bultmann, *The History of the Synoptic Tradition* (Oxford, 1971).

[3] Cf. R. Riesner, *Jesus als Lehrer: Eine Untersuchung zum Ursprung der Evangelien-Überlieferung* (WUNT 2.7; Tübingen, 1981; 3rd ed., 1988).

need of major qualification. After all, there were many issues that vexed the early church, to which Jesus offered no word of clarification. These include spiritual gifts, church officers, various doctrines, and, more importantly, teaching that speaks to the Gentile problem. If dominical tradition was freely created, as many form and redaction critics once assumed, then why did not teachings attributed to Jesus arise that might have resolved some of these controversial issues? The inference that should be drawn from this observation is that early Christian communities were not given to the creation of dominical tradition.[4]

In my judgment, the challenge faced by those engaged in Jesus research lies not so much in the task of identifying tradition that originated with Jesus, but in ascertaining what the tradition originally meant.[5] Even if all agreed that the bulk of the tradition goes back to Jesus, the much greater problem of its interpretation remains. Not only has the tradition been edited, paraphrased, adapted, and applied to new contexts by early Christian tradents and by the evangelists themselves, much of the tradition simply has no context at all. Even the literary context supplied by the evangelists is often of little or no help. One need only think of sayings material common to Matthew and Luke (i.e., "Q"), which appears in widely different contexts in these two Gospels. The following passages should illustrate this problem.

John's prophetic utterance, "You brood of vipers, who warned you ...?" (Matt 3:7-10 // Luke 3:7-9) offers a clear example of the discrepancies in contextualization that interpreters encounter. In Matthew, these sharp words are addressed to "many of the Pharisees and Sadducees," while in Luke they are addressed to "the multitudes." Knowing to whom John spoke these words is important in order to form an accurate interpretation of them. Fortunately, in this case we have in Josephus a third witness. The Jewish historian tells us that John was

---

[4] *Pace* M. E. Boring, *Sayings of the Risen Jesus* (SNTSMS 46; Cambridge, 1982). For a better assessment, see D. E. Aune, *Prophecy in Early Christianity and the Ancient Mediterranean World* (Grand Rapids, 1983), pp. 153–88.

[5] Dibelius (*From Tradition to Gospel*, p. 255), speaking in reference to Luke's Parable of the Pounds, rightly admitted: "We do not know the original references of numerous parables." To a certain extent, the same can be said with respect to Hillel research. Much of the material attributed to this early sage may well be authentic, but allowance must be made for the editing, adapting, and contextualization of it. The picture our sources have left behind is a filtered one.

popular with the multitudes, but a threat to Herod Antipas (*War* 18.5.2 §116-19; cf. 18.5.4 §136; Mark 6:17-29). It is likely, then, that John's harsh criticism was originally uttered against Israel's rulers, rather than against the people themselves. In this case, Matthew's contextualization is probably closer to the original historical setting.[6]

The contextualization of Jesus' Parable of the Lost Sheep (Matt 18:12-14 // Luke 15:3-7) provides another helpful example. In the Matthean context, the parable contributes to Jesus' teaching that his followers are to seek after those who have wandered astray from his community (i.e., the ἐκκλησία; cf. Matt 18:17). His disciples are to be forgiving and to seek reconciliation, as the subsequent material teaches (cf. Matt 18:15-22,23-35). But in the Lucan context, the parable explains why Jesus associates with sinners; that is, with those who are not (yet) part of his community (cf. Luke 15:1-2). He hopes to reclaim those who are lost to Israel. In Luke's context, Jesus' critics—in this instance, Pharisees—are challenged for expressing disapprobation over his outreach to Israel's religious and social outcasts. According to Luke, Jesus is not talking of bringing people into *his* community, but rather of bringing people back into believing Israel. In this case, it is likely that the Lucan usage is closest to the original application, for it coheres with Jesus' orientation to Israel, as opposed to Gentiles (cf. Mark 7:27).[7]

The modest task of the current study is to underscore the need to reexamine Jesus' teaching in a manner that is more sensitive to the first-century Palestinian context.[8] The essay is divided into two parts. The

[6] So K. H. Rengstorf, *Das Evangelium nach Lukas* (NTD 3; Göttingen, 1969), p. 55; E. E. Ellis, *The Gospel of Luke* (NCB; Grand Rapids, 1974), p. 89; J. A. Fitzmyer, *The Gospel According to Luke I-IX* (AB 28; Garden City, 1981), p. 467. Fitzmyer comments that the epithet, "brood of vipers," seems to apply more readily to the Matthean audience.

[7] Cf. G. Schneider, *Das Evangelium nach Lukas* (2 vols., Gütersloh/Würzburg, 1977) 2.324-25; J. Lambrecht, *Once More Astonished: The Parables of Jesus* (New York, 1981), pp. 37-42. The Matthean missionary directive to "go nowhere among the Gentiles ..., but go rather to the lost sheep of the house of Israel" (Matt 10:5-6; cf. 15:24) faithfully interprets Jesus' *modus operandi*, at least early in his ministry. There is, of course, the distinct possibility that this saying did originate with Jesus and has been added by the Matthean evangelist to material drawn from Mark. It is not likely that Matthew would have invented such a saying, given the conclusion of his Gospel, in which the risen Christ commands his apostles, by way of contrast, to go to the Gentiles and to make disciples of them.

[8] Cf. G. Theissen, *Sociology of Early Palestinian Christianity* (Philadelphia, 1977); E. Bammel and C. F. D. Moule (eds.), *Jesus and the Politics of His Day* (Cam-

first part will briefly treat what I regard as the most important problem that interpreters face in determining the nature of Jesus' teaching. The second part of the study will offer a few suggestions related to the possibilities of recovering Jesus' teaching. Here we shall examine two parables that illustrate both the problems and the possibilities in reconstructing the teaching of Jesus.

PROBLEMS IN RECONSTRUCTING JESUS' TEACHING

One of the major reasons why form critics assigned so much of the Jesus tradition to the early church was because the original *Sitz im Leben* was not properly understood. The interpretation the early church gave to Jesus' teachings was frequently and often uncritically assumed to be the original point of the teachings. (By "early church" I refer both to the generation that preserved the Jesus tradition and eventually published the Gospels and to subsequent generations that interpreted the Jesus tradition as it is now found in the Gospels.) Since these teachings, understood this way, reflected the concerns and perspectives of the early church, it was concluded (*a là* the criterion of dissimilarity) that the teachings originated with first generation Christians and not with Jesus.[9]

The two parables treated in this paper illustrate this problem. Because these parables (as well as others) have been understood in the sense of Church versus Israel, and in some instances in an anti-Semitic sense, scholars have questioned their authenticity. It is, of course, rightly assumed that the historical Jesus was not anti-Semitic in any sense of the term. His polemic could at times be harsh, his criticism scathing (cf. Matt 23), but it is highly unlikely that he had repudiated

---

bridge, 1984); R. A. Horsley, *Jesus and the Spiral of Violence: Popular Jewish Resistance in Roman Palestine* (San Francisco, 1987) S. Freyne, *Galilee, Jesus and the Gospels* (Philadelphia, 1988); D. E. Oakman, *Jesus and the Economic Questions of His Day* (Studies in Bible and Early Christianity 8; Lewiston, 1988); B. J. Malina and R. L. Rohrbaugh, *Social-Science Commentary on the Synoptic Gospels* (Minneapolis, 1992). The latter item is an indispensable tool for Jesus Research.

[9] Both pre-Gospel and post-Gospel generations of Christians interpreted the Jesus tradition in their own terms and according to their needs. The form critics rightly detected these tendencies, but erred in frequently assuming that these tendencies argue for the inauthenticity of the tradition.

his Jewish heritage or that he ever offered criticism against his own people for being Jewish.

Although disagreements in many particulars do exist, the consensus of recent scholarship is that Jesus hoped for Israel's restoration.[10] What Jesus wanted for Israel was pretty much what most first-century Jews wanted. How this restoration was to be achieved was no doubt a matter of debate, but that restoration of one sort or another was desired was widely held. For this reason, scholars assume that parables that seem to hold to a Gentile or anti-Israel perspective are inauthentic.

Any investigation of Jesus' teaching naturally begins with his parables. This is the case not only because the Gospels assert that this was Jesus' customary manner of teaching (e.g., Mark 4:2,33-34), but also because the parables are widely regarded as the most reliable part of the dominical tradition.[11] Recent work in rabbinic parables and first-century Palestine has made important contributions to the study of Jesus' parables.[12] This work will be taken into consideration in the balance of the present study.

[10] Cf. Sanders, *Jesus and Judaism*, pp. 77–119, 335–40; Borg, *Jesus*, pp. 125–49; de Jonge, *Jesus, the Servant-Messiah*, pp. 55–75.

[11] One recalls J. Jeremias' famous dictum (*The Parables of Jesus* [rev. ed., New York, 1963], p. 11): "The Parables are a fragment of the original rock of tradition." Recent studies have confirmed this positive assessment; cf. P. B. Payne, "The Authenticity of the Parables of Jesus," in R. T. France and D. Wenham (eds.), *Studies of History and Tradition in the Four Gospels* (Gospel Perspectives 2; Sheffield, 1980), pp. 329–44; B. B. Scott, "Essaying the Rock: The Authenticity of the Jesus Parable Tradition," *Forum* 2/3 (1986) 3–53; C. L. Blomberg, *Interpreting the Parables* (Downers Grove, 1990). *Pace* Jeremias, Scott ("Essaying the Rock"; idem, *Hear Then the Parable: A Commentary on the Parables of Jesus* [Minneapolis, 1989], pp. 17–19), J. D. Crossan (*Cliffs of Fall: Paradox and Polyvalence in the Parables of Jesus* [New York, 1980], pp. 18–27), and others prefer to speak of the *ipsissima structura* ("the very structure itself"), rather than the *ipsissima verba* ("the very words themselves").

[12] K. E. Bailey, *Poet and Peasant: A Literary-Cultural Approach to the Parables in Luke* (Grand Rapids, 1976); idem, *Through Peasant Eyes: More Lucan Parables* (Grand Rapids, 1980); R. M. Johnston, "The Study of Rabbinic Parables: Some Preliminary Observations," *SBLSP* 15 (1977), pp. 337–57; D. Flusser, *Die rabbinischen Gleichnisse und der Gleichniserzähler Jesus* (2 vols., Bern and Frankfurt am Main, 1981); B. H. Young, *Jesus and His Jewish Parables: Rediscovering the Roots of Jesus' Teaching* (New York, 1989); H. K. McArthur and R. M. Johnston, *They Also Taught in Parables: Rabbinic Parables from the First Centuries of the Christian Era* (Grand Rapids, 1990); D. Stern, *Parables in Midrash: Narrative and Exegesis in Rabbinic Literature* (Cambridge, Mass., 1991). The progress in recent years is quite evident when one compares the older works with it; cf. W. O. E. Oesterley, *The Gospel Parables in the Light of Their Jewish Background* (London, 1936).

The two parables with which we are concerned are the Parable of
the Prodigal Son and the Parable of the Pounds. Both of these parables
are found only in Luke. Because these parables do not enjoy multiple
attestation,[13] their authenticity is established with greater difficulty and
will have to be demonstrated on other grounds (such as dissimilarity to
early Christian themes and tendencies). For our purposes, they will
make good test cases. The texts follow:

Parable of the Prodigal Son (Luke 15:1-3,11-32; RSV)

Now the tax collectors and sinners were all drawing near to hear him.
And the Pharisees and the scribes murmured, saying, 'This man
receives sinners and eats with them.' So he told them this parable. ...

And he said, 'There was man who had two sons; and the younger of
them said to his father, "Father, give me the share of the property that
falls to me." And he divided his living between them. Not many days
later, the younger son gathered all he had and took his journey into a
far country, and there he squandered his property in loose living. And
when he had spent everything, a great famine arose in that country,
and he began to be in want. So he went and joined himself to one of
the citizens of that country, who sent him into his fields to feed swine.
And he would gladly have fed on the pods that the swine ate; and no
one gave him anything. But when he came to himself he said, "How
many of my father's hired servants have bread enough and to spare,
but I perish here with hunger! I will arise and go to my father, and I
will say to him, 'Father, I have sinned against heaven and before you;
I am no longer worthy to be called your son; treat me as one of your
hired servants.'" And he arose and came to his father. But while he
was yet at a distance, his father saw him and had compassion, and ran
and embraced him and kissed him. And the son said to him, "Father, I
have sinned against heaven and before you; I am no longer worthy to

---

[13] Crossan (*The Historical Jesus*, pp. xxxi–xxxiii, 257, 410) attaches great
importance to the criterion of multiple attestation. He states (p. 257): "My methodological discipline in this book forbids the use of single attestations for reconstructing
the historical Jesus." True to his methodology, Crossan does not take into account
either parable considered in this paper.

be called your son." But the father said to his servants, "Bring quickly the best robe, and put it on him; and put a ring on his hand, and shoes on his feet; and bring the fatted calf and kill it, and let us eat and make merry; for this my son was dead, and is alive again; he was lost, and is found." And they began to make merry.

'Now his elder son was in the field; and as he came and drew near to the house, he heard music and dancing. And he called one of the servants and asked what this meant. And he said to him, "Your brother has come, and your father has killed the fatted calf, because he has received him safe and sound." But he was angry and refused to go in. His father came out and entreated him, but he answered his father, "Lo, these many years I have served you, and I never disobeyed your command; yet you never gave me a kid, that I might make merry with my friends. But when this son of yours came, who has devoured your living with harlots, you killed for him the fatted calf!" And he said to him, "Son, you are always with me, and all that is mine is yours. It was fitting to make merry and be glad, for this your brother was dead, and is alive; he was lost, and is found."'

Parable of the Pounds (Luke 19:11-27)

He proceeded to tell a parable, because he was near to Jerusalem, and because they supposed that the kingdom of God was to appear immediately. He said therefore, 'A nobleman went into a far country to receive a kingdom and then return. Calling ten of his servants, he gave them ten pounds, and said to them, "Trade with these till I come." But his citizens hated him and sent an embassy after him, saying, "We do not want this man to reign over us." When he returned, having received the kingdom, he commanded these servants, to whom he had given the money, to be called to him, that he might know what they had gained by trading. The first came before him, saying, "Lord, your pound has made ten pounds more." And he said to him, "Well done, good servant! Because you have been faithful in a very little, you shall have authority over ten cities." And the second came, saying, "Lord, your pound has made five pounds." And he said to him, "You are to be over five cities." Then another came, saying, "Lord, here is your pound, which I kept laid away in a napkin; for I was afraid of you, because you are a severe man; you take up what you did not lay down, and reap what you did not sow." He said to him, "I will condemn you out of your own mouth, you wicked servant! You knew that I was a severe man, taking up what I did not lay down and reaping what I did not sow? Why then did you not put my money into the bank, and at my coming I should have collected it with interest?" And he said to those who stood by, "Take the pound from him, and give it to him who has the ten pounds." (And they said to him, "Lord, he has ten pounds!") "I tell you, that to every one who has will more be given; but from him who has not, even what he has will be taken away. But as for these enemies of mine, who did not want me to reign over them, bring them here and slay them before me." '

Because these parables are singly attested and have been understood as allegories of the early church, each implying that the gospel will be rejected by Jews, but accepted by Gentiles,[14] some modern biblical interpreters have assumed that they are creations of the early church.[15] It is to be admitted, of course, that the evangelist Luke understood them in an allegorical manner. For him, the Parable of the Prodigal Son probably did point to the inclusion of Gentiles, on the basis of repentance, into the church. The Parable of the Pounds evidently was understood in part as an explanation of the Parousia's delay (as 19:11 seems to indicate) and in part as teaching on rewards and punishment

---

[14] For example, see J. M. Creed, *The Gospel According to St. Luke* (London, 1930), p. 197. In reference to the Parable of the Pounds, Creed (p. 235) says that the disloyal citizens are "the Jews, who refused Christ as their king." See also T. W. Manson, *The Sayings of Jesus* (London, 1949), p. 317.

[15] See Dibelius, *From Tradition to Gospel*, p. 255; Bultmann, *History of the Synoptic Tradition*, pp. 176, 195-96; J. T. Sanders, "Tradition and Redaction in Luke XV. 11-32," *NTS* 15 (1969) 433-38; idem, "The Parable of the Pounds and Lucan Anti-Semitism," *TS* 42 (1981) 660-68; L. Schottroff, "Das Gleichnis vom verlorenen Sohn," *ZTK* 68 (1971) 27-52; W. Schmithals, *Das Evangelium nach Lukas* (Zürich, 1980), p. 165; J. Drury, *The Parables in the Gospels* (London/New York, 1985), p. 142; M. Goulder, *Luke: A New Paradigm* (JSNTSup 20; Sheffield, 1989), pp. 609-14; H. Räisänen, "The Prodigal Gentile and His Jewish Christian Brother [Lk 15,11-32]," in F. Van Segbroeck et al. (eds.), *The Four Gospels 1992* (F. Neirynck Festschrift; 3 vols., BETL 100; Leuven, 1992) 2.1617-36; V. Fusco, "'Point of View' and 'Implicit Reader' in Two Eschatological Texts [Lk 19,11-28; Acts 1,6-8]," in F. Van Segbroeck et al. (eds.), *The Four Gospels 1992*, 2.1677-96, esp. 1687-91. For a survey of the opinions, see J. A. Fitzmyer, *The Gospel According to Luke X-XXIV* (AB 28a; Garden City, 1985), pp. 1084-85, 1228-33.

(as the exchanges with the servants imply; cf. esp. v. 26). But Luke's application, of course, does not necessarily reflect the parables' original meanings.

Recently a few scholars have detected the presence of anti-Semitism in these parables. Jack Sanders believes that the Parable of the Prodigal Son intends to disparage the Torah-observant Jew (represented by the older son) and to show that the Christian gospel is to go to repentant Gentiles (represented by the prodigal son).[16] Sanders regards the Parable of the Pounds as the most offensive example of anti-Semitic sentiment in the synoptic tradition. According to his interpretation, the parable is an allegory about Jesus who has gone to heaven and who will return to reward his faithful servants and destroy his fellow "citizens" (i.e., the Jews) for having rejected his kingship.[17]

What I hope to demonstrate in the present study is that many interpreters have uncritically and perhaps even unconsciously accepted elements of precritical interpretation of these parables, interpretation which was often anti-Judaistic (i.e., against Judaism as a religion) and, alas, at times anti-Semitic (i.e., against the Jewish people).[18] Sanders

---

[16] J. T. Sanders, *The Jews in Luke-Acts* (Philadelphia, 1987), pp. 108–9, 197–98.

[17] Sanders, *The Jews in Luke-Acts*, pp. 61–62, 208–9, 317; cf. idem, "The Parable of the Pounds," p. 667. Whatever one's position is regarding the authenticity or inauthenticity of these Lucan parables, I do not think they reflect anti-Semitism; cf. C. A. Evans, "Is Luke's View of the Jewish Rejection of Jesus Anti-Semitic?" in D. D. Sylva (ed.), *Reimaging the Death of the Lukan Jesus* (BBB 73; Frankfurt am Main, 1990), pp. 29–56, 174–83; idem, *Luke* (NIBC 3; Peabody, 1990), pp. 234–35, 286. For a better assessment of Luke's attitudes to the Jewish people, see D. L. Tiede, *Prophecy and History in Luke-Acts* (Philadelphia, 1980); R. L. Brawley, *Luke-Acts and the Jews: Conflict, Apology, and Conciliation* (SBLMS 33; Atlanta, 1987); M. Salmon, "Insider or Outsider? Luke's Relationship with Judaism," in J. B. Tyson (ed.), *Luke-Acts and the Jewish People: Eight Critical Perspectives* (Minneapolis, 1988), pp. 76–82, 149–50.

[18] In his *Commentary on the Harmony of the Gospels*, John Calvin interprets the older son of the prodigal son parable as "a type of the Jewish people." The Parable of the Pounds, he thinks, "seems to be rebuking the Jews in particular." Origen, one of the church's earliest commentators, was a bit more even-handed in his interpretation, believing that the citizens who hated the nobleman of the Parable of the Pounds "are perhaps Israel who disbelieved him, and perhaps the Gentiles who disbelieved him" (*Comm. Matt.* 14.12 [on Matt 25:14-30]). More typical, however, was the interpretation of Cyril of Alexandria (PG 72.876) and Theophilactus (PG 123.1029), who saw in the destruction of Jerusalem the punishment that was to be meted out to the king's disloyal citizens.

and others have assumed that the anti-Judaistic/anti-Semitic understanding of these parables is original to the parables and therefore the parables cannot go back to Jesus himself. But I suspect that we have not understood the parables in their original context.[19]

POSSIBILITIES OF RECONSTRUCTING JESUS' TEACHING

For the moment let us assume that the Parable of the Prodigal Son and the Parable of the Pounds were uttered by Jesus. Let us assume futhermore that the allegorizing interpretation of Christian versus Jew or Church versus Judaism is secondary and was not part of the original meaning. Do these parables make sense in the setting and context of Jesus' life and ministry? I think they do, as the following comparative study should make evident.

The Parable of the Prodigal Son

There are several indications that support the claim that this parable is a unified whole[20] and derives from the historical Jesus.[21]

---

[19] I wonder if we should not think carefully about what is frequently assumed. Are we to believe that a Jewish movement, centered around a Jewish personality, some of whose followers thought might be Israel's messiah, a movement competing for the minds and hearts of the Jewish people, and sensing the need to explain itself in terms of the Jewish Scriptures would, in one generation, mutate into an anti-Semitic religion? (See the critical discussion of Luke, John, and Hebrews with regard to this question.) On theoretical grounds alone I find this proposition odd and questionable. Perhaps it would be more prudent to ask ourselves if we have correctly understood these materials in the first place. For a collection of studies that attempts to do this, see C. A. Evans and D. A. Hagner (eds.), *Anti-Semitism and Early Christianity: Issues of Polemic and Faith* (Minneapolis, 1993).

[20] Cf. Bultmann, *History of the Synoptic Tradition*, p. 196; Manson, *The Sayings of Jesus*, p. 285. Sanders ("Tradition and Redaction in Luke XV. 11-32," pp. 433–38) argues that vv. 24-32 were not part of the original parable, but his conclusion has been refuted; cf. J. Jeremias, "Tradition und Redaktion in Lukas 15," *ZNW* 62 (1971) 172-89; J. J. O'Rourke, "Some Notes on Luke xv. 11-32," *NTS* 18 (1971–72) 431-33; C. E. Carlston, "Reminiscence and Redaction in Luke 15:11-32," *JBL* 94 (1975) 368–90.

[21] The authenticity of the parable is accepted by C. H. Dodd, *The Parables of the Kingdom* (London, 1935), p. 120; Manson, *Sayings of Jesus*, p. 285; Jeremias, *Parables of Jesus*, pp. 128–32; I. Broer, "Das Gleichnis vom verlorenen Sohn und die Theologie des Lukas," *NTS* 20 (1973–1974) 453-62, esp. p. 461; Carlston, "Reminiscence and Redaction," pp. 385–87; R. Pesch, "Zur Exegese Gottes durch Jesus von Nazaret: Eine Auslegung des Gleichnisses vom Vater und den beiden Söhnen (Lk 15,11-32)," in B. Casper (ed.), *Jesus: Ort der Erfahrung Gottes* (B. Welte

First, the Jewishness of the parable is quite evident, as is seen in several details. A Palestinian audience would have understood well the danger of famine.[22] The degradation implied in feeding swine would have been sensed by a Jewish audience especially, for whom these animals are unclean (Lev 11:7-8; Deut 14:8). A later rabbinic saying, "Cursed is the man who raises pigs" (b.BQam 82b; cf. m.BQam 7:7: "No Israelite may raise pigs anywhere"),[23] likely reflects the sentiments that would have been held by Torah-observant Jews of Jesus' time.

When the younger son is forced to eat the "pods"[24] fed to the swine, he finally repents (vv. 16-17). This detail parallels the rabbinic saying, "When Israelites are reduced to eating carob-pods, they repent."[25] The expression, "he came to himself" (v. 17), is apparently Jewish.[26] The son's words of repentance derive wholly from Jewish prayers and piety.[27] The son's determination to return to his father parallels another rabbinic saying: "When a son [abroad] goes barefoot [through poverty] he remembers the comfort of his father's house" (LamRab 1:7 §34; attributed to "the Palestinian rabbis"). The son's confession that he has sinned "against Heaven," instead of "against God," reflects Jewish respect for God and his name.[28] Unlike the Mat-

---

Festschrift; Freiburg, 1976) 140–89, esp. p. 150; H. Weder, *Die Gleichnisse Jesu als Metaphern. Traditions- und redaktionsgeschichtliche Analysen und Interpretationen* (FRLANT 120; Göttingen, 1978), p. 254; K.-W. Niebuhr, "Kommunikationsebenen im Gleichnis vom verlorenen Sohn," *TLZ* 116 (1991) cols. 481–94, esp. col. 492, note 32; and apparently most commentators.

[22] According to J. Jeremias (*Jerusalem in the Time of Jesus* [Philadelphia, 1969], pp. 140–44) there were at least ten famines in Palestine from 169 B.C.E. to 70 C.E.

[23] As an insult to Diocletian, the emperor is said to have been a swineherd in his youth (y.Ter 8:10; GenRab 63.8 [on 25:24]).

[24] I.e., the bitter, coarser wild carob, not the *ceratonia siliqua*, which is the sweeter, more wholesome variety; cf. Bailey, *Poet and Peasant*, pp. 172–73.

[25] Cf. LevRab 13.4 (on Lev 11:2); 35.6 (on 26:3); SongRab 1:4 §3; attributed to the Tanna Aha.

[26] Cf. TJos 3:9; b.Shab 104a; b.Sanh 102a. However, whether it is the equivalent of "he repented" is debated; cf. Bailey, *Poet and Peasant*, pp. 173–75.

[27] Cf. PrMan 8-14; Sir 17:24-25, 29; Wis 11:23; Jub 5:17-18.

[28] *Heaven* is a common substitute for *God* in 1 Maccabees (cf. 3:18,60). In rabbinic literature, "heaven" appears absolutely (b.BMeṣ 37a) and frequently in various pat phrases, e.g., "kingdom of heaven" (b.Ber 13b; cf. Matt 3:2; 5:3, *passim*); "fear of heaven" (m.Ab 1:3), "honor of heaven" (b.Ber 13a); "by the hand of heaven" (b.Ber 33b); and "the name of heaven" (m.Ab 4:4).

thean evangelist, the Lucan evangelist does not avoid using *God*. The appearance of *Heaven*, therefore, argues against Lucan composition.

The scene of reconciliation between son and father (v. 20) is probably indebted to language from the scene of reconciliation between Jacob and Esau. Fearing what lies ahead, Jacob, according to targumic tradition, confesses to God: "I am not worthy" (Neof, Gen 32:11).[29] But the errant Jacob is well received: "Esau ran to meet him [Jacob], and embraced him, and fell on his neck and kissed him, and they wept" (Gen 33:4; cf. 29:13; 46:29, where Joseph and Jacob are reunited; and Tob 11:9-15, where a father and mother receive with joy a returning son). There are other allusions to Scripture.[30] In the time of Joseph there is a great famine (Gen 43:1). Pharaoh places a ring and a robe on Joseph (Gen 41:41-42). Just as the father of the parable exclaims, "My son was dead and is alive again" (Luke 15:24, 32), Jacob is told, "Your son Joseph is alive" (Gen 45:26). The generous treatment of the repentant son (robe, ring, sandals, and fatted calf) also reflects biblical language and the customs of first-century Palestine.[31] The father's exclamation that his son had been dead reflects the Jewish view of people cut off socially and spiritually as "dead": "Four are regarded as dead: the leper, the blind, he who is childless, and he who has become impoverished"[32] (GenRab 71.6 [on 30:1]; cf. ExRab 5.4 [on 4:19]; Matt 8:22 // Luke 9:60: "Leave the dead to bury their own dead").[33]

Second, there are several generic Jewish parallels. One thinks of the Parable of the King's Errant Son:

> This can be compared to the son of a king who took to evil ways. The king sent a tutor to him who appealed to him saying, 'Repent, my

---

[29] The Hebrew reads: "I am too small." "I am not worthy" also appears in Tg. 1 Chr 17:16 and the midrash on Gen 32:11 in GenRab 76:5. On targumic diction in the Jesus tradition, see Chilton, *A Galilean Rabbi*, pp. 90–111.

[30] O. Hofius, "Alttestamentliche Motive im Gleichnis vom verlorenen Sohn," *NTS* 24 (1977–78) 240–48; Drury, *Parables in the Gospels*, pp. 144–46; Goulder, *Luke—A New Paradigm*, pp. 611–12.

[31] See Bailey, *Poet and Peasant*, pp. 184–86; Fitzmyer, *Luke X–XXIV*, p. 1090.

[32] Trans. H. Freedman, "Genesis," in H. Freedman and M. Simon (eds.), *Midrash Rabbah* (10 vols., London and New York, 1983) 2.657.

[33] For relevant background, see K. H. Rengstorf, *Die Re-Investitur des verlorenen Sohnes in der Gleichniserzählung Jesu: Luk. 15,11-32* (Köln, 1967).

son.' The son, however, sent him back to his father [with the message], 'How can I have the effrontery to return? I am ashamed to come before you.' Thereupon the father sent back word, 'My son, is a son ever ashamed to return to his father? And is it not to your father that you are returning?'" (DeutRab 2.24 [on Deut 4:30]; attributed to R. Meir, ca. 150 C.E.)[34]

The parable is used to illustrate God's paternal love for Israel and his ever-willingness to receive back the repentant sinner. The point of the parable is completely in agreement with the Parable of the Prodigal Son. Other parables that should be considered include the Parable of the King's Youngest Son (SifDeut §352 [on Deut 33:12]), the Parable of King's Twelve Sons, one of whom the king loved more (GenRab 98.6 [on 49:8]), the Parable of the Repatriated Prince who according to one version returned to his "inheritance" (SifDeut §345 [on Deut 33:4]) and according to another was met halfway by his father (Pesiq. R. 44.9),[35] and finally the Parable of the Father who divided his inheritance among his sons (b.Kid 61b, attributed to Rabbi Hanina ben Gamaliel, ca. 120 C.E.).[36]

---

[34] Trans. J. Rabbinowitz, "Deuteronomy," in Freedman and Simon (eds.), *Midrash Rabbah*, 7.53.

[35] These parables are anonymous. For recent discussion of them and what relevance they may have for the interpretation of Jesus' parables, see McArthur and Johnston, *They Also Taught in Parables*, pp. 83, 78–79, 194–95.

[36] A letter from a prodigal son to his mother provides a delightful real-life parallel (papyrus 846, Berlin Museum; Fayûm, 2d century C.E.): "Antonis Longus to Nilus, his mother: Many greetings. I pray continually that you are in good health. I make intercession for you daily to the Lord Serapis. I wish you to know that I had no hope that you would go up to the metropolis. For this reason I did not enter the city. But I was ashamed to come to Caranis, because I walk about in rags. I have written to you, because I am naked. I beseech you, mother, be reconciled to me. Furthermore, I know what I have brought upon myself. I have been chastened, even as is necessary. I know that I have sinned. I heard from Postumus, who met you in the vicinity of Arsinoë and inopportunely told you everything. Do you not know that I had rather been maimed than know that I still owe a man an obol? ... Come yourself! ... I have heard that ... I beseech you ... I almost ... I beseech you ... I wish ... not ... to do otherwise, ... to his mother, from Antonius Longus, her son." Although the last lines are fragmentary, the gist of the letter is quite clear. The son of Nilus admits, "I have sinned," just as the prodigal son of Jesus' parable confesses (Luke 15:18,21). For Greek text and discussion, see A. Deissmann, *Light from the Ancient East* (New York, 1922), pp. 187–92.

Third, the Parable of the Prodigal Son coheres significantly with Jewish law. According to Deut 21:15-17, a man is to assign to his oldest son a double portion of his inheritance, even if he loves his youngest son more. The Parable of the Prodigal Son apparently presupposes this legislation, including the practice of dividing the inheritance before death (cf. Sir 33:19-33, which counsels against this practice, thus implying that it was not unheard of; cf. b.BMeṣ 75b: One of those who cry out and are not answered is "he who transfers his property to his children in his lifetime"). Note also that the older son refers to the prodigal as "this son of yours" (v. 30), rather than "my brother," possibly implying that they were only half-brothers (which provides the point of departure in Deut 21:15-17).

The passage that immediately follows is concerned with the "stubborn and rebellious son" (Deut 21:18-22). If a son fails to heed his parents and lives a dissolute life ("a glutton and drunkard"), he is liable to trial and stoning. This passage is interpreted in m.Sanh 8:1-5 and further discussed in b.Sanh 68a–72a. According to m.Sanh 8:1, a rebellious son is one who gorges himself with meat and wine, and so is a glutton and drunkard. According to m.Sanh 8:3, a rebellious son is one who "steals from his father and eats it in the domain of strangers." In the *gemara*, one rabbi interprets this to mean stealing "from the money set aside for his father and mother" (b.Sanh 71a). The rebellious son who is convicted, but flees, is regarded as "dead" (b.Sanh 71b).

But why put to death the rebellious son? Why such a harsh penalty? Rabbi Yose the Galilean explains:

> Did the Torah decree that the rebellious son shall be brought before Beth din and stoned merely because he [was a glutton and drunkard? No.] But the Torah foresaw his ultimate destiny. For at the end, after dissipating his father's wealth, he would [still] seek to satisfy his accustomed [gluttonous] wants but being unable to do so, go forth at the cross roads and rob.[37]

---

[37] B.Sanh 72a; cf. SifDeut §218 [on 21:18]; §220 [on 21:21]; y.Sanh 8:7), trans. J. Schacter and H. Freedman, "Sanhedrin," in I. Epstein (ed.), *The Babylonian Talmud* (18 vols., London, 1978) 12.488. Yose's comment interprets m.Sanh 8:5: "A stubborn and rebellious son is condemned because of [what he may become in] the end: Let him die innocent and let him not die guilty."

The parallel passage in SifDeut §218 (on 21:18) reads: "Just because he has squandered his father's money, do you say that a stubborn and rebellious son should die?"[38] Implicit here is the view that one sin leads to another, eventuating in destruction and damnation (cf. m.Ab 4:2). Therefore, stoning the rebellious son, while he is still relatively innocent, is an act of mercy.

Without assuming that all of the above halakhic tradition had come to expression in the early part of the first century, it is fair to say that the prodigal son of Jesus' parable could easily have qualified as a "rebellious son." Although he has not literally stolen from his father, he has taken what should have remained in his father's possession during his lifetime. He has, in effect, taken his food and consumed it with strangers in a foreign country. He has certainly squandered his father's property. The rapid consumption of this wealth may well have been due in part to gluttony and drunkenness. The anger expressed by the older son is consistent with the precepts of Deut 21:18-22 and aspects of their interpretation in the rabbis. He likely viewed his brother as deserving punishment, not restoration.

Where the parable coincides with the rabbinic halakhah in a significant way is in the outcome. Stoning was required, it was believed, to cut short a life of sin that would surely result in damnation. Such harsh punishment was to be meted out in view of the son's presumed "destiny." But if the son *repents*, everything is changed. The younger son of Jesus' parable may have set out upon a path that initially looked as though it would end in destruction, but his repentance wiped the slate clean. He may have departed from his home in a spirit of arrogance and rebellion, but he returned chastened and contrite. His father rightly and not unexpectedly forgave him. In short, the son's repentance changed his destiny. There is nothing in Jesus' parable that is inconsistent with the rabbinic tradition.

Fourth, several details argue specifically against viewing the Parable of the Prodigal Son as a creation of the early church. The sins of the youngest son are best understood in Jewish perspective, not Gentile perspective. He requests his share of the inheritance in advance and

---

[38] Trans. R. Hammer, *Sifre: A Tannaitic Commentary on the Book of Deuteronomy* (Yale Judaica 24; New Haven and London, 1986), p. 229. Hammer (p. 466, note 8) notes that Vatican ms. 32 omits this passage.

leaves home, evidently showing little concern for the welfare of his father or family (contrast the expression of filial loyalty in Matt 8:21 // Luke 9:59: "Let me first go and bury my father"; cf. Tob 4:3; 6:14). His action would have been understood as clearly out of step with the command to honor one's parents (Exod 20:12; Lev 19:3; Deut 5:16), certainly as this command was understood in early Judaism (e.g., Mek. on Exod 20:12 [Baḥodesh §8]: "Honoring father and mother is very dear in the sight of [God] .... For he declared that honoring them is like honoring him";[39] DeutRab 6.2 [on 22:6]: "The honoring of parents is the weightiest [of the commandments]"), and the Jewish sense that sons were obligated to maintain their parents (Philo, Decal. 23 §111–20: "May not humans, who take no thought for their parents, deservedly hide for shame and reproach themselves for their neglect of those whose welfare should necessarily have been their only or primary care ...?"; cf. b.Keṭ 49b–50a).

Indeed, requesting his portion of the estate, which he then sells, could imply that the youngest son regarded his father as dead.[40] The feeling might have been mutual, in view of the father's later exclamation: "My son was dead and now is alive again" (v. 24, cf. v. 32). Evidently the youngest son travels to a Gentile region, further implying that he has abandoned the land of Israel itself, as well as his parents. By attaching himself to a Gentile and feeding his swine, the hearer is probably to assume that this son did not observe the sabbath or Jewish food laws.[41] His immoral conduct (vv. 13,30: "devoured your living with harlots") would be especially offensive to Jewish sensitivities.

In short, beyond the act of repentance itself (which in Jewish thought occupies a place as prominent as that in Christianity),[42] nothing praiseworthy can be said of the youngest son. He hardly appears to be a

---

[39] The tradition is ancient, as seen in Philo, Decal. 23 §119: "For parents are the servants of God ... he who dishonors the servant dishonors also the Lord."

[40] G. Bornkamm, *Jesus of Nazareth* (New York, 1960) p. 126; D. O. Via, *The Parables: Their Literary and Existential Dimension* (Philadelphia, 1967), p. 169; Bailey, *Poet and Peasant*, p. 165.

[41] Jeremias, *Parables of Jesus*, p. 129.

[42] The prominence and importance of repentance are amply documented in the Apocrypha and Pseudepigrapha (Sir 44:16; Wis 11:23; 12:10; PrMan 8, 13), the rabbinic literature (m.Ab 4:17; m.Yoma 8:8; b.Yoma 86a; b.Ned 39b), and the liturgy of the synagogue (Amidah §5); cf. J. Behm, *TDNT* 4.989–99.

self-serving portrait of a gentilizing Christian community. Of greater significance is the observation that the older son scarcely paints a negative picture of the Torah-observant Jew. As the celebration for the younger son's return gets under way, it is noted that the older son is laboring in the field (v. 25). We learn that he has for many years faithfully served his father and has never disobeyed him (v. 29). There is not the least hint of criticism here.[43] On the contrary, the older son has fulfilled the obligation to care for his parents. Even more importantly, his father assures him that he is "always with" him and that "all" that the father has is his (v. 31).[44] The older son's only fault is his failure to rejoice over his brother's repentance. In every other sense he is a model of fidelity.[45]

In what sense do these details denigrate Judaism, assuming that the older son is supposed to represent Jews and the younger son Gentiles? They do not. Such a reading makes little sense. Moreover, there is no christological point to the parable. In fact, there is nothing distinctively Christian about it.

In short, if the Parable of the Prodigal Son had been created to illustrate the moral superiority of the youngest son over that of the older son, it must be judged a failure. If it had been created to illustrate that the Christian message will be accepted by Gentiles and rejected by Jews, it is confusing and inconsistent. If it had been created to promote anti-Semitism, it is an incredible failure; for the older son is left in full

---

[43] *Pace* Bailey, *Poet and Peasant*, pp. 193-203. In my judgment, Bailey and others read too much between the lines. I do not think that the parable is about two lost sons; nor is the older son (*pace* J. D. M. Derrett, "Law in the New Testament: The Parable of the Prodigal Son," *NTS* 14 [1967-1968] 56-74, esp. pp. 72-74) modeled after the various older-son villains of the Old Testament.

[44] It is important to note that Philo defines "the elder" as the one who is faithful and wise, while "the younger" is foolish and rebels against God (Abrah. 46 §274; Quaest. Gen. §65 [on 4:7]).

[45] Cf. F. Bovon, "The Parable of the Prodigal Son, Luke 15:11-32, First Reading," in Bovon and G. Rouiller (eds.), *Exegesis: Problems of Method and Exercises in Reading* (Pittsburgh, 1978), pp. 43-73, esp. p. 61. Blomberg (*Interpreting the Parables*, pp. 178-79) rightly comments that neither son is a perfect role model: the younger son was foolish, selfish, inconsiderate, and disloyal, but at least had the sense to repent; the older son was faithful and upright, but was unwilling to forgive; cf. C. H. Talbert, *Reading Luke: A Literary and Theological Commentary on the Third Gospel* (New York, 1988), pp. 150-51. The true model is the father, who is forgiving and accepts the shortcomings of both sons.

possession of all that the father has! On the contrary, it is more likely that the parable is authentic and that it had nothing to do with a comparison between Christians and/or Gentiles, on the one hand, and Jews, on the other.

In this instance, it is probable that the context into which the Lucan evangelist placed the parable is true to it original intent. The point of the parable in its present context is to provide an answer to the Pharisees who criticized Jesus for associating with "sinners" (Luke 15:1-2). The point is that the Torah-observant Jew should rejoice when the sinner sees the error of his ways and seeks reconciliation. The position, indeed, the priority of the Torah-observant Jew is in no wise diminished or threatened. Jesus' parable amounted to an intramural admonition in a manner that closely parallels rabbinic debate. He spoke as one Jewish religious authority to another.[46]

The Parable of the Pounds

The Parable of the Pounds bears an uncertain relationship to the Matthean Parable of the Talents (Matt 25:14-30). It is not clear that the Matthean and Lucan parables are redacted versions drawn from Q, their common non-Marcan source (though a large number of commentators think so).[47] Nevertheless, the similarity of these parables makes their comparison both necessary and fruitful. Of more importance is the presence of the theme, found only in Luke's version, of the nobleman who is rejected by his subjects (cf. vv. 12, 14, 24a, 27).

It is probable that these details represent fragments of another parable[48] and not allegorical embellishments by the Lucan evangelist or

---

[46] Räisänen ("The Prodigal Gentile," p. 1621) doubts the authenticity of the parable because of the total absence of eschatology. This is hardly a compelling objection. In my judgment, the importance of the presence or absence of eschatology, which sometimes is treated as a criterion of authenticity (e.g., C. E. Carlston, "A Positive Criterion of Authenticity?" *BR* 7 [1962] 33–44, esp. p. 34), has been exaggerated. In his conclusion, Räisänen (p. 1636) admits that Luke worked with traditional material.

[47] Dodd, *Parables*, p. 146; S. Schulz, *Q. Die Spruchquelle der Evangelisten* (Zurich, 1972), pp. 288–98; Fitzmyer, *Luke X–XXIV*, p. 1230. For a convenient summary of the options and opinions, see J. S. Kloppenborg, *Q Parallels* (Sonoma, 1988), p. 200. For a recent demural from the common view that the Matthean and Lucan versions ultimately go back to a common parable, see Blomberg, *Interpreting the Parables*, pp. 219–21.

[48] V. Taylor, *The Formation of the Gospel Tradition* (London, 1935), p. 105; Jeremias, *Parables*, p. 59; M. Zerwick, "Die Parabel vom Thronanwärter," *Bib* 40

earlier Christian tradents (for reasons which will become clear shortly).[49] What we have to do with here, then, are two parables, not one. But were these parables combined by Luke or by the tradition before him? The context in which the Parable of the Pounds is found may provide the answer to this question.

The stewardship theme of the parable continues the preceding theme of the proper use of wealth (19:1-10), while the theme of the rejected king anticipates Jesus' triumphal entry and proclamation as king (19:28-40). This linking function of the Parable of the Pounds is a strong indication that Luke did indeed combine the parables.[50] In this form, the parable presents Jesus as Israel's king (cf. Luke 1:32-33) and at the same time explains why his kingship is not yet nationally recognized (cf. Acts 1:6-7; 2:36; 3:18-21; 4:24-28).

We have to consider what both parables (i.e., [1] the man who entrusted money and [2] the throne claimant) meant in Jesus' time and setting. Both probably originally depicted a tyrant outraged at his servant who did not engage in profiteering and at his citizens who rejected him as their king. The tradition prior to Luke understood both of these

---

(1959) 654-74; Ellis, *Luke*, pp. 221-22; F. D. Weinert, "The Parable of the Throne Claimant (Luke 19:12, 14-15a, 27) Reconsidered," *CBQ* 39 (1977) 505-14; D. L. Tiede, *Luke* (ACNT; Minneapolis, 1988), p. 323.

[49] Bultmann (*History of the Synoptic Tradition*, pp. 195-96) regarded these details as "an allegory of the departure and return of Jesus." L. C. McGaughy ("The Fear of Yahweh and the Mission of Judaism: A Post-Exilic Maxim and Its Early Christian Expansion in the Parable of the Talents," *JBL* 94 [1975] 235-45) thinks the parable as a whole is a Christian moral based on the saying in v. 26. Scott (*Hear Then the Parable*, p. 223) also views this material as Lucan embellishment. For discussion of the options and arguments, see Fitzmyer (*Luke X–XXIV*, p. 1231), who also leans this way. E. Schweizer (*The Good News According to Luke* [Atlanta, 1984], p. 293) notes that the throne claimant fragments are un-Lucan in style.

[50] Manson (*Sayings of Jesus*, p. 313) and Jeremias (*Parables*, p. 59) think the parables of the stewards and the nobleman were combined in the tradition and not by Luke himself because the evangelist does not "conflate in this way." Nevertheless, there is evidence elsewhere that Luke did combine related traditions: Mark 1:2-8 with Q (cf. Matt 3:7-10) and L material (cf. Luke 3:10-14) to expand John's preaching (Luke 3:1-17); Mark 6:1-6a with L material (cf. Luke 4:17-21[?],25-27,28-30[?]) to create the Nazareth sermon (Luke 4:16-30); Mark 1:16-18 with L material (cf. Luke 5:4-9) to create the miraculous catch of fish and the call of the disciples (Luke 5:1-11); Mark 6:7-13, Q (cf. Matt 11:20-24), and L material (cf. Luke 10:17-20) to create the sending of the seventy (Luke 10:1-20).

parables in a spiritualized sense. That is, the servants parable came to be understood as a stewardship parable (Jesus will reward his faithful disciples), while the citizens parable came to be understood christologically (Jesus has been rejected by his own people). Luke understands the combined parable as teaching that while Jesus is away, to be recognized as king only later, not immediately,[51] his followers are to be faithful stewards, knowing an accounting will have to be given.

Most interpreters have concluded that the parable of the man who entrusted money derives from Jesus, but many have expressed doubts about the throne claimant materials.[52] Although these materials suit the evangelist's theology and redaction well[53] and so might be viewed as produced by the evangelist himself, there are reasons why they too should be regarded as deriving from a *Sitz im Leben Jesu*. In the discussion that follows, both components of Luke's parable will be treated together.

First, as a whole, the Parable of the Pounds reflects recent Palestinian history, specifically paralleling Archelaus's attempt to gain his father's kingdom.[54] The nobleman went to a far country (v. 12), just as Archelaus went to Rome (*Ant* 17.9.3 §219); the nobleman hoped to receive a kingdom ($\beta \alpha \sigma \iota \lambda \epsilon i \alpha$) and to return (v. 12), just as Archelaus hoped (*Ant* 17.9.3 §220: $\beta \alpha \sigma \iota \lambda \epsilon i \alpha$); the nobleman left household instructions to his servants (v. 13), just as Archelaus did (*War* 2.2.1 §14, §19; *Ant* 17.9.3 §219, 223); the nobleman's citizens hated ($\mu \iota \sigma \epsilon \hat{\iota} \nu$) him (v. 14), just as Archelaus' subjects hated him (*War* 2.2.3 §22; *Ant* 17.9.4 §227: $\mu \hat{\iota} \sigma o \varsigma$); an embassy ($\pi \rho \epsilon \sigma \beta \epsilon i \alpha$) is sent after the nobleman

---

[51] *Pace* L. T. Johnson, "The Lukan Kingship Parable (Lk. 19:11-27)," *NovT* 24 (1982) 139–59. For a critique of this view, see J. T. Carroll, *Response to the End of History: Eschatology and Situation in Luke-Acts* (SBLDS 92; Atlanta, 1988), pp. 100–3.

[52] For a succinct discussion, see Scott, *Hear Then the Parable*, pp. 221–35.

[53] See D. L. Tiede, *Prophecy and History in Luke-Acts* (Philadelphia, 1980), p. 79; C. H. Talbert, *Reading Luke: A Literary and Theological Commentary on the Third Gospel* (New York, 1988), pp. 177–79.

[54] Scott (*Hear Then the Parable*, p. 223) demurs, saying that "the identification of Archelaus is both distant and unnecessary." I have to disagree for two basic reasons. First, about twenty years after the exile of Archelaus, Jesus began his ministry. This hardly qualifies as "distant." Second, the parallels are simply too numerous and too close to be dismissed. To claim that the identification of Archelaus is "unnecessary" begs the question. The presence of the parallels demands explanation, whether contemporary hermeneutics find them necessary or not.

(v. 14), as one was sent after Archelaus (*Ant* 17.11.1 §300: πρεσβεία); the citizens petitioned the foreign country against the nobleman's rule (v. 14), just as the envoys petitioned against Archelaus (*Ant* 17.11.1 §302); the nobleman slaughtered (κατασφάζειν) his citizens who opposed him (v. 27), just as Archelaus had done before his journey (*Ant* 17.9.5 §237, 239: σφάζειν); the nobleman received the kingdom (v. 15), just as Archelaus was given half of his father's kingdom (*War* 2.6.3. §93; βασιλεία); when the nobleman returned as ruler (v. 15; *Ant* 17.13.1 §339), he collected his revenues (vv. 15-19), just as Josephus notes that Archelaus was to receive 600 talents as his yearly tribute (*Ant* 17.11.4 §320). And finally, when the nobleman returned, he settled accounts with those who had opposed him (v. 27), just as Archelaus "did not forget old feuds" (*War* 2.7.3 §111), but settled with his opponents, such as Joazar the high priest, for having supported the rebels (*Ant* 17.13.1 §339). Since Herod Antipas also traveled to Rome to press his claim to the throne, and was also opposed, his experience loosely fits the experience of the parable's nobleman. But it is Archelaus who offers the closest match.[55]

The Jewishness of the parable is seen at many other points. The command to "do business" is consistent with Jewish diction, which in this case employed the Greek loan word πραγματεία (cf. GenRab 100.10 [on 50:22][56] and Tanḥuma on Exod 21:1–24:18 [Mishpatim §9][57]), whose verbal cognate (πραγματεύομαι) appears in Luke 19:13. Putting money in a σουδάριον ("napkin" or "scarf") also parallels Jewish diction, which employed the Latin loan word *sudarium* (cf. b.Keṭ 67b[58] and m.BMeṣ 3:10[59]) and is the word used in Luke 19:20. The noble man's condemnation of the servant who did not engage in

---

[55] Although there are several parallels, including some vocabulary, I do not think that the Archelaus parallels were drawn from Josephus' *Jewish War* (2.2.1-7 §14–38; 2.6.1-3 §80–100), whose publication probably preceded that of Luke's Gospel by only a few years, principally because there are a few significant points of divergence. *Antiquities*, of course, was probably published after the Lucan Gospel.

[56] "Rabbi Yohanan ben Zakkai engaged in business [עשה פרגמטיא] forty years ...."

[57] "Take from me a loan of one hundred thousand, and do business [ותעשה פרגמטיא] with it ...."

[58] "Rabbi Abba used to wrap money in his scarf [בסודריה] ...."

[59] "If someone gives money to another for safe keeping, and he wraps it up in his scarf [בסודרו] ..." (so Rashi).

business, "out of your own mouth I shall condemn you," closely parallels the words of a king in one of the rabbinic parables (NumRab 16.21 [on 14:2][60]).

One might wonder, of course, if it is likely that Jesus or any Jew of the first century would have referred to one of the Herods as a εὐγενής ("noble man"). As it turns out, approximate usage can be documented. In the LXX, εὐγενής translates גָּדוֹל. We have an example in Job 1:3: "That man [i.e., Job] was the most noble [εὐγενής = גָּדוֹל] of the men of the east." Josephus actually uses the word in reference to Herod's son, Alexander (*War* 1.26.2 §522).[61] In the rabbinic writings, גְּדוֹלֵי רוֹמִי appears in the sense of "Roman noble men" (b.AZ 18a).[62] Thus, the use of εὐγενής in the Lucan parable coheres with Jewish diction.

Second, several generic parallels again point to a Jewish origin. Probably the closest parallel is Rabbi Yose the Galilean's parable of the King's Workmen (Midr. Prov. 16:11):

> A parable. To what may this be likened? To a king of flesh and blood who had a garden in which he built a tall tower. He showed affection for the garden by assigning workmen to it, and ordered them to busy themselves with its cultivation. The king thereupon ascended to the top of the tower, from which he could see them but they could not see him .... At the day's end the king came down and sat in judgment upon them, saying, 'Let the tillers come forward and receive their wages, let the hoers come forward and receive their wages,' [and so on, until] there remained only those workmen who had done no work at all. The king asked, 'These, what did they do?' They answered, 'They emptied full vessels into empty ones.' 'What benefit is there for me in their emptying full vessels into empty ones?' asked the king, adding, 'Let those who have done my work receive their wages, but those who did

---

[60] "I shall pass upon you the sentence which you have uttered with your own mouth. It shall be to you as you have said."

[61] See also *Ant* 16.3.1 §69. Josephus normally uses εὐγενής in reference to Jewish nobility. On one occasion he refers to "the blood of (Roman) nobles" (*War* 4.11.4 §647).

[62] Lit. "nobles [or great ones] of Rome." M. Jastrow (*A Dictionary of the Targumim, the Talmud Babli and Yerushalmi, and the Midrashic Literature* [2 vols.; London, 1895–1903; repr. New York, 1950] 1.211) translates, "Roman dignitaries."

not do my work, let them be taken out and executed, for they have rebelled against my command!'[63]

Also worthy of note is the Parable of the King's Steward (ARN A 14:6; attributed to R. Eleazar ben Arak, ca. 90 C.E.) and the Parable of the Wife's Stewardship (SongRab 7:14 §1). In the former, the steward frets over the deposit left in his charge. In the latter, the faithful wife adds to the money her husband entrusted to her when he departed on a journey. The Parable of the Two Administrators (Mek. on Exod 20:2 [Baḥodesh § 5]; attributed to R. Simon ben Eleazar, ca. 170 C.E.), the Parable of the King's Daughters (SongRab 4:12 §1; attributed to R. Joshua ben Levi, ca. 220-240 C.E.), and the Parable of the Reliable Bailee (SifDeut §357 [on 34:5]) also bear some similarities. Finally, the Parable of the King's Two Servants (Yalqut Shimeoni on Deut 6:4) offers a few parallels. The king goes away, leaving his palace and garden in the care of two servants. One servant loves the king and labors diligently. The other fears the king and so does nothing. When the king returns, he generously rewards the first servant.

Third, there are certain details in both components of the Parable of the Pounds that point to a setting in the context of Jesus' ministry. A gentilizing church would likely not make use of the Aramaic loan word מָנֶה (usually translated "pound"). Moreover, this denomination would be a small amount of money to the relatively more affluent and literary audience for which the Matthean and Lucan Gospels were probably written (compare Matthew's "talents"—a much larger amount of money). However, it would seem large to a marginalized peasant audience,[64] the type of audience Jesus had. The nobleman's large profits reflect the profiteering that went on in first-century Palestine.[65] When the "good" servant is told that because he had been "faithful in little" he would have "authority over ten cities" (v. 17), we have a possible parallel with rabbinic thought: "Before God confers greatness on a man he first tests him by a little thing and then promotes him to greatness"

---

[63] Translation from B. L. Visotzky, *The Midrash on Proverbs* (Yale Judaica 27; New Haven and London, 1992), p. 82.

[64] Scott, *Hear Then the Parable*, p. 224.

[65] cf. J. D. M. Derrett, "Law in the New Testament: The Parable of the Talents and Two Logia," *ZNW* 56 (1965) 184-95, esp. p. 190. The enormous profits of the parable are undoubtedly hyperbolic.

(ExRab 2.3 [on 3:1]). The slaying of the citizens who had opposed the nobleman's bid for kingship reflects biblical language (cf. 1Sam 15:33) and parallels the language in the rabbinic Parable of the King's Workmen.

Fourth, several features of the Parable of the Pounds make little sense if interpreted along traditional lines. Commentators have usually assumed that Jesus intended his hearers to understand that the heroes of the parable are the servants who have increased their master's money. These servants are models for Jesus' followers: "no disciple can miss the point that active stewardship is expected."[66] Commenting on the Matthean version, one commentator explains: "All of this constitutes an appeal to good works as demonstrating the reality of professed discipleship."[67] The servant who hid his master's money and did not even lend to bankers for interest is understood to be a poor model: "Thus the parable closes on a threatening note concerning the punishment Jesus will mete out to disciples who falsify their profession by failing to do good works."[68] The lesson, another recent commentator tells us, is "to be profitable at all costs and by all means."[69] In essential agreement with this line of interpretation, but expressed more in existentialist terms, Brandon Scott believes that "the third servant's image of the master deprives him of a future, for it freezes the servant in fear."[70]

The traditional interpretation ignores the biblical principles and economic realities by which the majority of Palestinians in Jesus' day lived. The first problem is a general one. The wealthy and grasping nobleman of the parable would hardly have been looked up to as a hero or role model, but would have been viewed with distrust and contempt. Joshua ben Sirach's sentiments would surely have reflected the views of most of Jesus' agrarian hearers: "A rich man will exploit you if you can be of use to him" (Sir 13:4); and, "A merchant can hardly keep from wrongdoing, and a tradesman will not be declared innocent of sin" (Sir

---

[66] D. L. Tiede, *Luke* (ACNT; Minneapolis, 1982), p. 323. See also Evans, *Luke*, pp. 284–87; Fitzmyer, *Luke X–XXIV*, pp. 1232–33.

[67] R. H. Gundry, *Matthew: A Commentary on His Literary and Theological Art* (Grand Rapids, 1982), p. 505.

[68] Gundry, *Matthew*, p. 510.

[69] C. F. Evans, *Saint Luke* (TPI New Testament Commentaries; London/Philadelphia, 1990), p. 667.

[70] Scott, *Here Then the Parable*, p. 234. Scott cites Via, *Parables*, p. 119.

26:29). There are clear indications that Jesus held to a similar view. In Luke's Sermon on the Plain he says, "Woe to you who are rich!" (Luke 6:24). In reference to the money changers and merchants in the Temple, Jesus says, "You have made [the Temple] a den of robbers" (Mark 11:17), while in the Johannine version he says, "Take these things away; you shall not make my Father's house a house of trade" (John 2:16). Elsewhere Jesus teaches his disciples to "lend, expecting nothing in return" (Luke 6:35). In a related saying that some regard as independent and perhaps authentic, Jesus says, "If you have money, do not lend it at interest, but give it to one from whom you will not get it back" (Gospel of Thomas §95). In Luke's Parable of the Great Banquet (Luke 14:15-24) the wealthy refuse the summons and so will not taste of the banquet. According to another version, Jesus added, "Businessmen and merchants will not enter the Places of my Father" (Gospel of Thomas §64).[71] Remember, too, the Parable of the Rich Man and Lazarus (Luke 16:19-31).[72]

There is, therefore, every indication that Jesus shared, at least in large measure, the peasant view of wealth and the wealthy. The traditional interpretation of the parable, unconsciously informed by western capitalist assumptions (as Richard Rohrbaugh[73] is so correct in pointing out), assumes that the nobleman, even if strict and demanding, is in the right and that his servants have been rewarded or punished in a just manner. The traditional interpretation, however, has not realistically taken into account peasant assumptions regarding wealth. As Rohrbaugh and Bruce Malina point out,

---

[71] Crossan, *The Historical Jesus*, p. 261

[72] Of course, Jesus can make use of villains to make his point. As an illustration, one thinks of the dishonest steward (Luke 16:1-8). Jesus' disciples are to draw lessons of prudence from the example of this steward, but his prudence does not in any way mitigate the moral shortcomings of his character. Jesus' disciples are not to become dishonest. The same is true in the case of the unjust judge who grudgingly vindicates the importunate widow (Luke 18:1-8). Although the parable compares him to God, the judge is still unjust and is hardly exemplary. This kind of argument is "from the minor to the major" (e.g., Matt 7:11: "If you then, who are evil, know how to give good gifts to your children, how much more will your Father in heaven give good things to those who ask him!").

[73] R. L. Rohrbaugh, "A Peasant Reading of the Parable of the Talents/ Pounds: A Text of Terror?" a paper read in New Orleans at the 1990 annual meeting of the Society of Biblical Literature. For a briefer version, see Malina and Rohrbaugh, *Social-Science Commentary*, pp. 389—91.

if the parable is taken as a description of the way the kingdom of God functions, it is bitter news indeed for peasant hearers. It would confirm all of their worst fears: that God (and Jesus) operates in exactly the same demanding, exploitive, grasping manner as the overlords who daily forced them to produce more and more for elite coffers— rewarding those who did so (thereby exploiting their neighbors) and taking away the livelihood of those who did not.[74]

Two other specific problems arise as well. The first has to do with the "nobleman." He is hated by his subjects who do not want him to reign as king over them (Luke 19:14). He expects exorbitant profits, he is a "severe" man, he reaps the fields of others, gathers the grain that others have threshed, and has no scruples about usury (Luke 19:21-22). Moreover, he is merciless (Luke 19:27). At the very least this is a hard-nosed businessman (or ruler) who does not observe the Law's express prohibition against the practice of usury (cf. Exod 22:25; Lev 6:2; Ps 15:5) and how this law was interpreted in the first century (cf. Josephus, *Apion* 2.27 §208). It is more probable that the picture is worse. This man is apparently an oppressive gouger and a thief. In any case, it is hard to imagine how an agrarian audience, for the most part peasants,[75] could have heard this parable (or these parables) and understood the businessman/nobleman in a favorable sense.[76] The presence of details drawn from the life of the hated Archelaus only renders the traditional interpretation more problematic. The presence of these details argues for the authenticity of the throne claimant parable, for it is hard to understand why an early Christian would have created a parable whose principal character is modeled after Archelaus.

The second problem has to do with the actions of the servants. The first two double their master's money. In the minds of first-century peasants, such margins of profit were not fair, but could only take place

---

[74] Malina and Rohrbaugh, *Social-Science Commentary*, p. 389. See also Horsley, *Spiral of Violence*, p. 14.

[75] Oakman (*Jesus and the Economic Questions of His Day*, p. 207) describes Jesus' ministry thus: "Jesus appealed, apparently without strong moral prerequisites, to the many disenfranchised rural poor and stood for their interests."

[76] This point is well taken by Rohrbaugh, "A Peasant Reading"; cf. Malina and Rohrbaugh, *Social-Science Commentary*, pp. 390–91.

through high interest rates, excessive returns from tenant farmers, taxation, or outright theft. However these profits were obtained, the peasants knew it would be at their expense.[77] The third servant neither cheated anyone, nor made a profit at anyone's expense. He kept his master's money safe and returned it to him. Although guiltless in the eyes of the peasants and above reproach with regard to rabbinic halakhah,[78] this servant is "worthless" in the eyes of his master and is punished.

For these reasons, one may well wonder if the parable as we now have it in the canonical Gospels has been misunderstood. Eusebius wondered this also. Commenting on the Matthean version of the parable, he discusses the different perspective found in the Gospel of the Nazoreans (GNaz §18; cf. Eusebius, *Theophania* 22 [on Matt 25:14-15]):

> But since the Gospel in Hebrew characters which has come into our hands enters the threat not against the man who had hid [the talent], but against him who had lived dissolutely—for he [the master] had three servants: [a] one who squandered his master's substance with harlots and flute-girls, [b] one who multiplied the gain, and [c] one who hid the talent; and accordingly [c'] one was accepted (with joy), [b'] another merely rebuked, and [a'] another cast into prison—I wonder whether in Matthew [25:26-30] the threat which is uttered after the word against the man who did nothing may refer not to him, but by epanalepsis to the first who had feasted and drunk with the drunken [cf. Matt 24:48-49].

The parable of the Gospel of the Nazoreans seems to be a combination of the Parable of the Talents (Matt 25:14-30) and the Parable of the Wicked Servant (Matt 24:45-51; Luke 12:45-48), with possible influence from the Parable of the Prodigal Son (Luke 15:11-32). But what is interesting here is Eusebius' suggestion that perhaps the word of rebuke (b') was originally uttered against the man who made huge profits (b), while the man who hid his master's money (c) was accepted (c').

---

[77] See Oakman, *Jesus and the Economic Questions of His Day*, pp. 37–91.

[78] Dodd (*Parables*, p. 150) rightly suggests that the third servant "expected to be commended for his caution and strict honesty."

424 RECONSTRUCTING JESUS' TEACHING

I would propose that the history of the parable ran something like this: First, Jesus told two parables, one about a man and his servants to whom he entrusted money (Luke 19:13,15b-25 // Matt 25:14-28) and the other about a nobleman who sought a throne (Luke 19:12,14-15a,27). How these parables were understood by their original hearers will be considered shortly.

Second, the parable of the man who entrusted money was allegorized, with the assumption that Jesus was the "man" and the disciples the "servants." The original point of the parable was lost. The parable came to be understood as teaching a lesson on Christian stewardship. Those who are productive and fruitful will be rewarded, those who are not will be punished. A Jewish saying ("to every one who has more will be given") was added to the parable (Luke 19:26 // Matt 25:29) to make this interpretation clear.[79]

Third, the Lucan and Matthean evangelists accept the stewardship interpretation, but heighten the eschatological implications. Luke accomplishes this by introducing the parable with v. 11 ("because they supposed that the kingdom of God was to appear immediately"); and Matthew by adding v. 30 at the parable's conclusion ("cast the worthless servant into outer darkness").

Fourth, Luke fuses the parable of the man who entrusted money with the parable of the throne claimant. In Luke's fused version the "man" ($\check{\alpha}\nu\theta\rho\omega\pi\sigma\varsigma$) becomes the "nobleman" ($\check{\alpha}\nu\theta\rho\omega\pi\acute{o}\varsigma$ $\tau\iota\varsigma$ $\epsilon\grave{\upsilon}\gamma\epsilon\nu\acute{\eta}\varsigma$). He did this for the reasons suggested above.

What could these parables have meant to a Palestinian peasant audience? Why would Jesus tell parables whose principal characters are non-Torah-observant, despised tyrants? In what sense does such persons model Jesus? In what sense are the servants who work for this man and assist him in his oppressive activities models for Jesus' followers? These questions are severely problematic if we attempt to answer them within the parameters of the traditional interpretation of these parables.

Perhaps this is not what Jesus originally intended. Following the lead of Eusebius's discussion of the form of the parable in the Gospel of the Nazoreans, it is possible that Jesus' original hearers assumed that the man and his servants who profitted most were the true villains, not

---

[79] Scott, *Hear Then the Parable*, p. 224: the verse gives "the narrative a parenetic point, underscoring the servant's action."

the servant who hid the money. Jesus may have originally told his parable to illustrate how *not* to be a master and how *not* to be servants. The same may have been true in the case of the throne claimant parable. The Archelaus-like figure, who is hated and merciless, may not have been intended to model Jesus, but to contrast with Jesus. In other words, in their original context, again remembering the worldview and assumptions of an agrarian peasant society, the parables may well have underscored grim realities of the present world, *in contrast to the kingdom whose approach Jesus has announced.*

This idea coheres with his teaching elsewhere (Mark 10:42-44):

> You know that those who are supposed to rule over the Gentiles lord it over them, and their great men exercise authority over them. But it shall not be so among you; but whoever would be great among you must be your servant, and whoever would be first among you must be slave of all.

In its original context, the parable may have presented a contrast between Jesus' style of kingship and that of the Herodian dynasty. The latter was known for its oppression and ruthlessness. But Jesus offered a new understanding of kingship and kingdom and expected his followers to adopt it as well.

It is not difficult to see how the original point of the parables came to be confused with teaching concerned with stewardship and responsibility (cf. Matt 24:45-47; Luke 12:35-38; 17:7-10). The servant who is wise and faithful, doing what he is expected to do, such as treating the members of the master's household properly (or not profiteering at his neighbors' expense) will be rewarded. It is possible, then, that the theme of reward drew these parables together, so that the servants of the oppressive master and nobleman came to be interpreted much as the servants of the other parables. Whereas the latter were held up as worthy models, the former were not.

CONCLUSION

The Parable of the Prodigal Son and the Parable of the Pounds have proven to be interesting illustrations of the major problem that attends analysis of Jesus' teaching. Both of these parables were likely understood by the Lucan evangelist as allegories that shed light on problems that vexed the church of his day. The Prodigal Son, it was believed, taught Jewish Christians to be accepting of Gentile Christians and so made an important contribution to ecclesiology. The Pounds warned Christians to be diligent and faithful stewards, while the Throne Claimant additions warned the Jews of impending judgment for rejecting their King. These parables in combination contributed to christology and eschatology.

It is highly unlikely that Jesus would ever have intended these parables to mean these things. But this likely fact does not mean that the parables were themselves generated by the early church. Bereft of their original setting and context, the parables, by virtue of their meta-phorical and symbolic nature, were easily recontextualized and made to speak to new issues and questions. The challenge those in Jesus Research must meet is in recognizing these secondary applications and not confusing them with the original points scored by the parables.

It is hoped that the discussion of the two (or three) parables con-sidered in this essay has clarified some of the difficulties faced by those engaged in Jesus Research. Whether or not the above interpretations are accepted, the principal point is surely compelling: namely, that better contextualized interpretation will identify authentic material and present a more accurate picture of Jesus of Nazareth.[80]

[80] I would like to record my appreciation for Professor James H. Charlesworth, who not only edited the present volume, but organized and convened the symposium. Our stay in Jerusalem was made pleasant and stimulating because of his generosity and hard work.

HILLEL AND JESUS ON PRAYER

INTRODUCTION

PRAYER IS THE most basic religious act of all, the very food of faith. Academically, it has been the object of endless phenomenological, psychological, political, and literary scrutiny.[1] The various forms of its expression have been the object of debate and conflict. In the twentieth century, the classic work which established the terms of the debate is the book *Prayer*, by Friedrich Heiler, of 1918. Heiler set up a dichotomy between two different forms of prayer: the mystical and the prophetic. He then proceeded to play them off against one another at great length. Let us cite a few paragraphs:

> The difference between mystical and prophetic prayer is manifest in every way: in motive, form, and content, in the conception of God and in the relation to God implied in the standard of prayer. Mystical prayer has its roots in the yearning of the devout person for union with the Infinite; prophetic prayer arises from the profound need of the heart and the longing for salvation and grace. Mystical prayer is artificially prepared through a refined psychological technique of meditation; the prophetic petition breaks forth spontaneously and violently from the subconscious depths of the religious soul that has been deeply stirred. Mystical prayer is silent, contemplative delight; prophetic prayer a passionate crying and groaning, vehement complaining and

[1] For example, F. Heiler, *Prayer* (Oxford, 1932; Germ. orig., 1918); W. James, *The Varieties of Religious Experience* (New York, 1902); J. Daniélou, *Prayer as a Political Problem* (New York, 1967); J. Heinemann, *Prayer in the Talmud: Forms and Patterns* (Studia Judaica 9; Berlin, 1977); H. G. Reventlow, *Gebet im Alten Testament* (Stuttgart, 1986); M. Greenberg, *Biblical Prose Prayer* (Berkeley, 1983).

pleading. Mystical prayer is a passing out of oneself, an entering and sinking into the Infinite God; prophetic prayer is the utterance of the profound need that moves the inmost being.

Mystical prayer is a weary climbing by degrees to the heights of vision and union with God; prophetic prayer a stormy assault upon the Father's heart. Mystical prayer represents advances in a straight course, continuous progress, purification, enlightenment, union; prophetic prayer comprises inner transformation, radical revolution; anxious fear and eager longing pass over into serene trust and the joy of calm surrender. The God of the mystic is the Infinite One, the *summum bonum*, in whom the mystic is completely absorbed; the God of prophetic prayer is the living Lord, to whom the worshiper is bound with every fibre of his being, the kind Father to whom he clings in absolute trust and confidence.

Mystical prayer is the consuming of self in the flame of God's love, dissolving into the glow of the Infinite, melting into the stream of the Immeasurable; prophetic prayer is a mighty wrestling with a challenging and commanding God. Mystical prayer is the passing away in desire for the divine Loved One and then again a blessed tranquillity and ecstatic delight in the tender embrace of the heavenly Bridegroom; prophetic prayer is humble reverence before the majesty of the eternal King and Lord, a timorous pleading of the guilt-laden soul before the stern Judge, a heartfelt, trusting approach of the child to the loving Father. Mystical prayer is something totally new as compared with that of primitive man: the complete detachment from one's ego, absorption in the *summum bonum*; in prophetic worship primitive prayer reappears, greatly refined, it is true, and ennobled, but yet with all its original force of passion and *naivete* and its dramatic vitality. Like primitive prayer, prophetic petition is essentially the expression of need, desire for salvation and blessing; it is belief in a God who will hearken and aid.

Yet both types, despite all these differences, reveal a final common quality. All mystic prayer is a rising to the highest good; all prophetic prayer finds its culmination in the desire for the coming of the Kingdom of God, that is, the realization of all spiritual values. Here it dif-

fers strikingly from primitive prayer, for like mystical devotion it is
directed not to a fleeting, temporary good, but to an ultimate, supreme
good. Nevertheless, there exists here an essential distinction. The end
of the latter is a static final good; that of the former, a vital, dynamic
magnitude, the Kingdom of God. The final good which the mystic
seeks is beyond all concrete reality, beyond all manifoldness, the
"One," "the Only"; that towards which prophetic piety looks, which
controls and permeates all reality, manifests itself in multiplicity, 'God
who is all in all' (1Cor 15:28).[2]

Thoughtful readers will wonder whether such a dualistic scheme
is quite plausible. Do not yearning and longing have something in common? Both weary climbing and stormy assault imply hard effort. The
delights of union strangely resemble serene trust and the joy of calm
surrender. The Infinite One, if not dead, must be the same as the living
Lord. The apparent conflict between spontaneity and set, formal prayer
had been overcome by Sigmund Mowinckel in 1953:

> In the development of religion, the liturgical or ritual prayer has
> played a greater role than "free prayer." In Israel we see remarkably
> little free prayer outside of cultic occasions and unconnected with a
> cult place even with the prophets; basically it occurs to a marked
> extent only with Jeremiah, and to some extent with Amos. But it can
> be present and lie hidden even under a rigidly prescribed life of prayer,
> as is the case with the fixed times of prayer and the prescribed for-
> mulas of Islam. Precisely Islam shows how the believer can add his
> own private prayers to the prescribed confession and laudative *salat*.
> We see the same in Judaism, from Samuel's mother Hannah, who
> made use of the worship of the festival service to 'pour out her heart
> before the Lord,' to the publican in the parable (Luke 18:13), who
> when the time for prayer came, could produce nothing better than his
> 'God, be merciful to me a sinner.'

The fixed forms constitute no barrier—indeed they are often of help.
Even a spontaneous or private prayer can find expression in the prescribed forms of prayer in the service; it has often proved true that what

---

[2] Heiler, *Prayer*, pp. 283-85.

the individual feels in his heart can be better expressed in that than in his own words. Many in the course of time have become increasingly thankful for the help of a life of prayer, which goes to show that one can elicit private and personal prayers from the very order of the service.[3]

While true, this tilts too far in the opposite direction. Moshe Greenberg has summarized well further nuances since Mowinckel and added his own contribution: "There is something between set ritual prayers and free invention; it is ... patterned prayer speech."[4] In other words, spontaneity arises from a tradition of technique.

But Heiler's dualism must be seen in a still broader context. The reader cannot be spared a little intellectual history. Sixteen years before Heiler's work on prayer, an even more fundamental work had appeared: William James's *Varieties of Religious Experience*. James was born a Protestant, though an independent one. In this work he makes his famous distinction between two religious types: the once-born, healthy-minded type whose religious experience is a harmonious development, and the twice-born, sick soul whose experience is marked by a decisive, even violent, conversion followed by a new birth. James classified Jesus as a once-born; Paul and Luther as twice-born.

This step threatened Lutheran theologians, notably the Swedish archbishop, Nathan Söderblom. Söderblom was engaged at the time in a massive program of modernism which provoked resistance in the Church of Sweden. To protect his right flank, Söderblom invoked the figure of Luther. Against James, Söderblom argued that Luther was not a sick soul but a prophetic figure of willful self-assertion as opposed to personality-denying mystics. This is where Heiler's distinction originated, as Heiler himself admits.[5]

Heiler felt the need to adopt this apologetic distinction because he was a young Munich Catholic in (understandable) rebellion against the practical prohibition of living theological thought by the sweeping papal condemnation of modernism (1907). There was no place in the church of that time for a man like Heiler. So he took the road to Uppsala, made

---

[3] S. Mowinckel, *Religion und Kultus* (Göttingen, 1953), p. 121.

[4] Greenberg, *Biblical Prose Prayer*, pp. 41–45.

[5] Heiler, *Prayer*, p. 135.

Söderbløm his patron, and made a new career for himself as a semi-Protestant (until Vatican II). The force of circumstances led him to accept Söderbløm's alternative distinction in place of James' better-founded one.[6]

The point of this excursion into the history of concept formation is to clarify the terms in which the academic discussion of prayer takes place. To peek ahead to our conclusions, both Hillel and Jesus can be categorized, so far as our information permits, as once born, healthy-minded types in Jamesian terms and both have their mystical as well as prophetic moments, to use Heiler's terms, in that both are at once lovers of and wrestlers with God. Of course, such binary sets do not exhaust the possibilities of conceptual clarification, but more of this later.

The topic of prayer according to Hillel and Jesus is a beautiful one. The difficulty is that while we know a good deal about the teaching and practice of Jesus on prayer—and even more is written about it—we know comparatively little about Hillel on prayer. As a result, I will interpret my brief rather broadly to include not only traditions attributed to Hillel directly but also school debates between Beth Hillel and Beth Shammai. I will also report on recent Israeli scholarship on some aspects of Jewish prayer that may be useful for students who live outside Israel. Similarly, in regard to Jesus, I intend to include a report on some recent studies on the fatherhood of God in both testaments as well as studies on the origin of the eucharistic prayer.

HILLEL AND HIS SCHOOL ON PRAYER

Schools Debate

In m.Ber 1:3 the following debate between the schools (lit., "houses") of Hillel and Shammai is recorded:

A. Beth Shammai say: In the evening all should recline, when they recite [the Shema'], but in the morning they should stand up, for it is written, When you lie down and when you get up (Deut. 6:7).

[6] G. Lanczkowski, s.v. "Heiler, Friedrich," *TRE* 14.638-41; H. Rollmann, "Evangelical Catholicity: Friedrich von Hügel, Nathan Söderbløm and Friedrich Heiler in Conversation," *The Downside Review* 100 (1982) 274-79; for discussion of Heiler's distinction, see L. Bouyer, *Christian Mysticism*, trans. I. Trethowan (Edinburgh, 1990), pp. 2-3, 179, 207, 263-64.

But Beth Hillel say: They may recite it every one in his own way, for
it is written, When you are away (Deut. 6:7). Why then is it written,
When you lie down and when you get up? [It means] the time when
men usually lie down and the time when men usually rise up.

B. Rabbi Tarfon said: I was once on a journey and I reclined to recite
[the Shema'] in accordance with the words of the School of Shammai,
and so endangered my life because of the robbers [there]. They said to
him: You deserved to be declared guilty since you transgressed the
words of Beth Hillel.[7]

The mishnah may be divided into two parts, a legal lemma (A),
and a story (B) of Rabbi Tarfon's experience in the matter. The legal
debate illustrates the Shammaites' effort to fulfill the biblical text in its
details, as part of the general Pharisaic and later rabbinic goal of trying
to do the will of God in all the details of daily life. The Hillelite
counter-position adopts a remarkably broad policy of letting everyone
recite the normative prayer *in his own way*. They interpret the biblical
verse under discussion (Deut 6:7) as giving only rough guidelines for
the individual worshiper. There seems also to be a shift from a concern
for posture (or space, Beth Shammai) to a concern for time (Beth Hillel).

---

[7] C. Albeck, *Mishnah*, vol. 1, Seder Zeraim (Jerusalem, n.d.), pp. 14–15; H.
Danby, *Mishnah* (Oxford, 1933), p. 2; J. Neusner, *The Rabbinic Traditions about the
Pharisees before 70*, Part II, *The Houses* (Leiden, 1971), pp. 41–42. The translation is
my own, with an eye on these earlier translations. On Hillel the Elder, out of the
abundant literature, it will suffice to refer to a small selection where further references
are given: N. N. Glatzer, *Hillel the Elder: The Emergence of Classical Judaism* (New
York, 1956; rev. 1966); E. Schürer, *The History of the Jewish People in the Age of
Jesus Christ*, vol. 3, rev. G. Vermes *et al.* (Edinburgh, 1979), pp. 363–67; H. L.
Strack and G. Stemberger, *Introduction to the Talmud and Midrash* (Edinburgh, 1991),
pp. 71–72; É. Nodet, *Essai sur les Origines du Judaïsme: De Josué aux Pharisiens*
(Paris, 1992), esp. pp. 226–36; M. Hengel, *The 'Hellenization' of Judaea in the First
Century after Christ* (London, 1989), *passim*; E. E. Urbach, *The Sages: Their Concepts
and Beliefs* (Jerusalem, 1975), pp. 576–93, 948–57; *idem, The Halakhah: Its Sources
and Development* (Jerusalem, 1986), pp. 265–68. m.Ber 3:1 itself is well discussed in
an article by I. Knohl, "A Parasha concerned with Accepting the Kingdom of Heaven,"
Tarbiz 53 (1983/4) 11–31 (Heb; Eng. summary, i–ii).

The legal lemma could be used most simply to exemplify the stereotypical view that Shammai inclined to severity whereas Hillel inclined to mildness in interpreting the law. But alternatively, one could view the disagreement in this case as stemming from whether to emphasize the communitarian value of having a common rule and practice for the praying community (so the Shammaites) or the infinite variety of individual needs and situations (so the Hillelites). This latter view would amount to a sort of rabbinic personalism or individualism. If it were not anachronistic, one would be tempted to see the Hillelite position as anticipating the cultural and historical qualifications on moral thought and obligation to which the reflections of Vico, Herder, and Hegel led. And beyond the factors of culture and history, there are the moral factors of subjectivity and personal experience which can and should be taken into account in decision-making and legislation. From this point of view, the Hillelite position could be evaluated as not merely more lenient, but also as more wise—even if it is the despair of liturgists.[8]

The story of Rabbi Tarfon's experience in trying to follow the Shammaite practice (B) was probably added because the Hillelite view was liable to be judged as libertarian, even cavalier and anarchic. Among religiously serious people, such a ruling is not usually popular or easily defensible since it is open to the charge of laxity. So the Hillelite ruling in this case needed experiential, if not supernatural, reinforcement.

Since he was a leader of the liberal wing within the Pharisaic party, many of Hillel's rulings reflect a markedly Hellenistic stamp. According to Martin Hengel, these rulings draw not only on the Hebrew Bible but also on the Socratic humanitarian tradition, and thus represent a synthesis of Judaism and Hellenism.[9] Such a view would shed another light on our mishnah.

When it comes to a comparison with Jesus, we may note the following. On the level of legal leniency, it would suffice to run through Mark's Gospel to see that, like Hillel and the Hillelites, Jesus usually—

---

[8] See, for example, J. Mahoney, *The Making of Moral Theology* (Oxford, 1987), esp. chaps. 5, 'Subjectivity,' and 6, 'The Language of Law,' pp. 175-258; J. Rohls, *Geschichte der Ethik* (Tübingen, 1991), esp. Part IV.

[9] Hengel, *Hellenization*, pp. 36–38, 42, 52.

but not always—inclines to leniency. The Marcan Jesus is lenient about the matters of tradition (7:1-23), about healing on the sabbath (1:16-34; 3:1-6), eating meals with sinners (2:13-17), fasting (2:18-22), working on the sabbath (2:23-28), dealing with the strange exorcist (9:38-41), paying taxes (12:13-17; cf. Matt 17:24-27), and the great commandment (12:28-34). The Marcan Jesus is stricter than the general run of Jewish teachers of his day regarding divorce (10:35-45). The case of adultery can be argued differently by different traditions: lenient (John 7:53-8:11) or strict (Matt 5:27-30).

The Gospel text closest to the mishnah text we have been examining is probably to be found in Matthew 6:5-6, which begins a section of instruction on prayer.

> When you pray, do not be like the hypocrites, who love to stand and pray in the synagogues and on street corners so that others may see them. Amen, I say to you, they have received their reward. But when you pray, go to your inner room, close the door, and pray to your Father in secret. And your Father who sees in secret will repay you.

One can easily find similarities, both explicit and implicit. Explicit similarities exist both in the context of instruction on prayer and in the disagreement with those who say one should stand to pray. A deeper, though implicit, similarity can be perceived in the common emphasis on a certain freedom in the posture of prayer. The Hillelites teach this directly: "They may recite it every one in his own way." The Matthean emphasis on privacy probably had the same idea in mind: that prayer is an intensely personal matter where sincerity is of the highest importance. Utter privacy would help to make posturing unnecessary.

The Matthean formulation of this basic idea has misled many readers into thinking that Jesus was thereby opposed to all common or liturgical prayer. Jesus' own practice of praying regularly in synagogues and in the Temple (as well as alone or with only a few disciples on mountain tops or gardens) rules out any such conclusion.[10] The formula, "go to your inner room, close the door, and pray" derives from the Septuagint of Isaiah 26:20 and 2 Kings 4:33.

---

[10] J. Dupont, "Jesus et la Prière Liturgique," *Maison Dieu* 95 (1968) 16–49, repr. in his *Études sur les Évangiles Synoptiques* (BETL 70; Leuven, 1985), pp. 146–79.

A search for differences between Mishnah Berakot and Matthew
6:5-6 can also be successful. The Gospel passage has a polemical tone
against unnamed fellow Jewish opponents (the mention of them praying
in synagogues makes that much plain) and the use of a term of
opprobrium (theatrical in origin) "hypocrites." There is an implicit
polemic in the Mishnah passage—particularly in the Tarfon story—but
the tone is less harsh, at times even jocular. This should not be taken to
imply that the Hillelites were not serious, too, in their way. The Gospel
passage also differs in its concern for reward, for secrecy, and in its use
of the term *Father* to refer to God. On the secrecy motif we have
already commented.

Although reward is not a theme of this mishnah, it is not foreign
to rabbinic thinking, nor indeed to sayings attributed to Hillel and Tarfon. From a number of references direct and indirect to reward in tractate 'Abot,[11] we may point out two. Hillel said, "If a man has gained a
good name he has gained somewhat for himself; if he has gained for
himself words of the Law, he has gained for himself life in the world to
come" (2:7). Rabbi Tarfon said, "The day is short and the task is great
and the laborers are idle and the wage is abundant and the master of the
house is urgent" (2:15). *Gain* and *wage* are metaphors for (heavenly)
reward.[12] On God as Father we will comment later. Thus, in sum, there
is a remarkable liberality in this Hillelite mishnah on prayer which finds
an echo in the Gospel of Matthew.[13]

Exodus 20:24b (21b in Some Numberings) and Matthew 18:20

"Where two or three are gathered together in my name, there am
I in the midst of them" (Matt 18:20). This verse provides an important

[11] Cf. *m.Ab* 1:3,7; 2:1,2,7b,8,15; 3:12,16; 4:1,4,16,17,22.
[12] A. Marmorstein, *The Doctrine of Merits in Old Rabbinic Literature* (London,
1920, repr. 1968); S-B 4.484-500; *TDNT* 4.695-728; with valuable corrections in M.
Smith, *Tannaitic Parallels to the Gospels* (Philadelphia, 1968), pp. 49-73, 161-84.
[13] B. Gerhardsson, "Geistiger Opferdienst nach Mt 6,1-6. 16-21," in *Das Neue
Testament und Geschichte*, Festschrift, O. Cullmann (Zürich, 1972), pp. 69-77; H. D.
Betz, "Eine judenchristliche Kult-Didache in Mt 6,1-18," in *Jesus Christus in Historie
und Theologie* (Festschrift, H. Conzelmann) (Tübingen, 1975), pp. 445-57; C. Dietzfelbinger, "Die Frömmigkeitsregeln von Mt 6,1-18 als Zeugnisse frühchristlicher Geschichte," *ZNW* 75 (1984) 184-201; J. Schlosser, *Le Dieu de Jésus* (LD 129; Paris,
1987), pp. 158-61; S-B 1.402.

christological basis for Christian prayer in common, as well as for other gatherings, for meeting and judging (cf. the context in 18:15-18), as well as for the purpose of sacred study (see the rabbinic parallels below). As Gnilka says, "Das Machtmittel der Gemeinde ist das Gebet."[14] It also reflects high self-esteem on Jesus' part, to put it mildly. For this reason, the verse, which comes from Matthew's special material, is usually assigned to the risen Christ rather than to the earthly Jesus.

It is a commonplace of commentaries on this verse that it is modelled on several rabbinic sayings found in m.Ab (3:2,6; 4:11; 5:17; cf. Acts 5:38-39). The shortest is attributed to R. Hananiah b. Teradion and runs: "If two sit together and words of the law are spoken between them, the Divine Presence rests between them." When the evangelist or his tradent modelled his verse on this and related mishnayoth (the numbers vary), he identified Jesus with both the Torah and with the Shekinah, the revealed will of God and Divine Presence.[15] Again, within Jewish-Christian terms, the christological claims are very high indeed.

It is the merit of Professor David Flusser to have pointed out in two essays[16] the deep roots of both Matt 18:20 and the relevant ʾAbot sayings in Exod 20:24b (21b): "In every place where I cause my name to be remembered I will come to you and bless you" (RSV; NAB begins: "In whatever place" in order to respect the nuance in בכל המקום (i.e., the Hebrew does not read בכל מקום). To be sure, this verse is not the only basis for our texts: see Jer 3:17; Ezek 43:7; Joel 2:27; Mal 3:16; 11QTemple 46.12; cf. Acts 4:31. But there is in our three texts the same combination of place, name, and divine presence.

---

[14] J. Gnilka, *Das Matthäusevangelium* II (HTKNT I.2; Freiburg, 1988), p. 140.

[15] Gnilka denies that Matthew used the ʾAbot sayings as a model. But this has recently and strongly been reaffirmed by W. D. Davies and Dale C. Allison, *The Gospel According to Saint Matthew* (ICC; Edinburgh, 1991), 2.789–90. For discussion of the problems of dating and dependence, see B. T. Viviano, *Study as Worship* (SJLA 26; Leiden, 1978), pp. 66–71; *idem*, "The Origins of Christian Study," *Cross and Crown* 29 (1977) 216–26, and J. Sievers, "'Where Two or Three ...': The Rabbinic Concept of Shekinah and Matthew 18.20," in *Standing Before God* (Festschrift, J. Oesterreicher), eds. A. Finkel and L. Frizzell (New York, 1981), pp. 171–82.

[16] D. Flusser, "Hillel's Self-Awareness and Jesus," "'I am in the midst of Them' (Mt. 18:20)," *Judaism and the Origins of Christianity* (Jerusalem, 1988), pp. 509–14, 515–25.

It may be worthwhile to consider briefly this verse of Exodus in its early and later interpretation. The verb אזכיר, commonly translated "I cause (my name) to be remembered," has also been translated "mentioned" (NJPS), "revealed" and "proclaimed" (so B. Childs in his commentary). The Targum Neofiti reads, "In every place where *you* recall my name *in prayer*, I will reveal myself to you *by my Word* and I will bless you."

Besides the coming interpreted as revealing, we note three things. Like the Syriac Peshitta, it reads תזכן as "*you* remember." Some commentators think this is a better reading. The context of prayer is made explicit. And the revelation is mediated by the Memra or Word. While some think that this targumic technical term is merely a buffer word or metonomy, others deem it to have contributed to the Johannine Logos Christology and more broadly to the general Christian idea that God saves his people through a mediator. The Targum Pseudo-Jonathan reads, "In every place where I will cause *my Shekinah* to dwell and where you *render a cult* before me, I will send over you my blessing and I will bless you." Here the Shekinah or divine presence is made explicit and the context is cult in general, not only prayer.

The Mekilta de-Rabbi Ishmael on Exodus, tractate Bahodesh, chap. 11,[17] interprets the מקום (*maqom*) or place as the Temple. This is a harmonization designed to overcome the contradiction with Deut 12:5 where the centralization of the cult is commanded. On the other hand, older critical commentators, while granting Wellhausen's assertion of the contradiction, point out that our verse indicates that altars may not be erected just anywhere, but only where God had either made a theophany or a victory (i.e., in special places).[18] In '*Abot*, the "altar" or presence of God is associated with study of Torah, the written record of theophanies and victories. In the Gospel the "altar" or locus of divine presence and the Torah are identified with a person. The Mekilta goes on to give a lesson by Eliezer b. Jacob: If you come to my house I will come to your house but if you do not come to my house I will not come to your house." Then it gives the same teaching as '*Abot* on the presence of God where 10, 3, or 2 are gathered to study Torah.

[17] *Mek.*, ed. J. Z. Lauterbach (Philadelphia, 1933), 2.287.
[18] E.g., S. R. Driver, *The Book of Exodus* (Cambridge, 1911), pp. 207–8; P. Heinisch, *Das Buch Exodus* (Bonn, 1934), pp. 161–63.

Now the little lesson given in Mekilta by Eliezer b. Jacob is attributed elsewhere to Hillel, as Flusser is quick to point out. He isolates what he believes to be three texts which suggest that Hillel had a remarkably high sense of self-esteem or self-consciousness. The three texts are as follows: First, "To the place that my heart loves, there my feet lead me; if you will come into my house, I will come into your house. But if you will not come into my house, I will not come into your house, as it is said: 'In every place where I cause my name to be remembered I will come to you and bless you.'"[19] Second, "If I am here, all is here; if I am not here what is here?"[20] Third, "My humiliation is my exaltation, my exaltation is my humiliation—it means 'Who sits exalts himself to see' (Ps 113:5f)."[21] Flusser concludes that Hillel's self-awareness flows from his awareness of the dignity of the human person as made in the likeness of God. It is therefore paradigmatic for everyone and not an expression of arrogance, since Hillel was known to be humble, whereas Jesus' self-estimate was not transferrable.

On all this we may comment, first, that Hillel's anthropomorphic theocentrism may reflect some of that Socratic Hellenistic humanism we have already mentioned, as well as his biblical heritage. Second, we note that Paul too could express himself in remarkably bold fashion in regard to his spiritual presence while he was physically absent, though always in subordination to Christ (1 Cor 5:3-5). Third, Christians share Hillel's conviction of the dignity of the human person based on Gen 1:27. This conviction is reified in visions of the graced soul experienced by saints and mystics of Eastern and Western churches. Fourth, while it is true that Jesus' unique status as Son of God is not viewed by Christians as directly or hypostatically transferrable to others, nevertheless,

[19] t.Suk 4:3; ARN 12 (Goldin trans., p. 69).

[20] b.Suk 53a; ARN 12. Note that this and the preceding text are from a context in the feast of Tabernacles, with its atmosphere of personal and national religious exaltation. The transfiguration narrative in Mark 9:2-8 with its mention of "booths" probably takes place in the same context.

[21] LevRab 1, pp. 16–17, ed. M. Margoulies (Jerusalem, 1958). To be sure, the interpretation of these sayings cannot be certain, since a complete context is lacking. Flusser's reading of them as clues to Hillel's self-understandin is not widely shared. But to undertake an independent scrutiny of them for their own sake would take us too far afield and is not part of our present purpose. See further on Exod 20:24b (=21b) the selection of Jewish commentaries in M. M. Kasher, *Encyclopedia of Biblical Interpretation*, vol. 9 (New York, 1979), pp. 238–41, esp. #438, 440, 443, 444.

Christians do hold that this unique Sonship can be shared through grace, through incorporation into his death and resurrection in baptism (Rom 6:1-11) and through being adopted sons and daughters of God in the Son (Rom 8). Fifth, those Christian exegetes who disagree with Professor Flusser on the authenticity of Matt 18:20—the present author included—do so not on dogmatic or anti-dogmatic grounds, but on the basis of a difference in the matter of estimating the sources of the Gospels. Partisans of the common two-source hypothesis (i.e., that Mark and Q are the earliest sources of the synoptic Gospels) are disposed to see a high, authentic self-consciousness of Jesus in texts like Matt 11:27 and Mark 13:32. They deem these texts to be early, even as they judge Matt 18:20 to be inauthentic both because it is part of Matthew's special material (though this in itself does not preclude authenticity) and because of the presumed lateness of the rabbinic model which Matthew, but not Jesus, could have used.

To sum up, Exodus 20:24b, m.Ab 3:2,6, and Matthew 18:20 are all texts of great religious import. They all speak of the divine immanence at times and places of sacred activity, prayer, study, and worship. In study, one wrestles with the divine word. In worship, one performs the divinely prescribed rites. In pure prayer, one struggles with God himself. In all these activities—but especially in prayer—the spirit of God and the spirit of the human meet and commune. Both the Hillelites and the early followers of Jesus drew inspiration from the beautiful promise of Exod 20:24b.

B.Beṣ 16a

Although not explicitly connected with prayer, the following *baraita* reveals a certain spirituality worth noting.

> It was taught: They related concerning Shammai the Elder that all his life he ate in honor of the Sabbath. Thus if he found a well-favored animal he said, Let this be for the Sabbath. If afterwards he found one better favored he put aside the second for the Sabbath and ate the first. But Hillel the Elder had a different trait, for all his works were for the sake of heaven, for it is said: Blessed be the Lord, day by day (Ps 68:20). It was likewise taught: Beth Shammai say: From the first day of the week prepare for the Sabbath; but Beth Hillel say: Blessed be the Lord, day by day. (b.Beṣ 16a, Soncino ed., p. 81)

Neusner points out that an earlier form of this story is found in Mekilta de R. Simeon b. Yohai, as an exegesis on Exod 20:8 which then grew into a little story.[22] In this earlier form, Hillel does not figure; Shammai is the hero. The talmudic version has been expanded and reshaped by a Hillelite partisan.[23]

Glatzer comments:

> The difference between the two men is not in their attitude to the Sabbath, revered by both, but in their attitude towards the weekday. Shammai concentrated on the Sabbath, which commanded his attention during the whole week. Hillel realized that every day brought new commitments, new demands to be taken care of as if there were no other day to follow. In the Talmud story, it is man's duty to turn every single day into a blessing.[24]

Shammai turns the whole week into a sabbath or a preparation for the sabbath. In contrast, Hillel sees the sacredness of the secular and the ordinary. Once again we see his deeply religious outlook combined with an astonishing humanism. He lives his entire life for God, like Ignatius of Loyola's *contemplativus in actione*. In modern terms he has a creation-centered spirituality, because for him all creation is holy and comes from God.[25]

The psalm reference to "day by day" suggests that for Hillel we should take each day as it comes. This conforms to a modern therapeutic outlook. We may compare this with the Jesus tradition: "Do not

---

[22] J. Neusner, *Rabbinic Traditions*, Part I, The Masters, pp. 185–87. The earlier version is from *Mekilta de R. Simeon b. Yohai*, ed. Epstein-Melamed, p. 148, lines 29–30, to Exod 20:8; cf. also A. J. Avery-Peck and J. Neusner, "Die Suche nach dem historischen Hillel," *Judaica* 38 (1982) 194–214; in English, "The Quest for the Historical Hillel: Theory and Practice," in J. Neusner, *Formative Judaism* (BJS 37; Chico, Cal.: Scholars, 1982), pp. 45–63.

[23] The authenticity of this story is suspect because the different practices of the masters correspond to the legal positions in a dispute between the much later orientations of Beth Hillel and Beth Shammai. So A. J. Avery-Peck and J. Neusner, "Die Suche," p. 208.

[24] N. N. Glatzer, *Hillel the Elder*, pp. 34–35.

[25] M. Fox, *Original Blessing: A Primer in Creation Spirituality* (Santa Fe, 1983).

worry about tomorrow; tomorrow will take care of itself. Sufficient for the day is its own evil. " This verse comes at the end of a section on trusting in divine providence rather than being anxious (Matt 6:25-34), which may be considered a radicalization of Hillel's outlook. On the other hand, many Gospel sayings about the day have an eschatological orientation which seems foreign to Hillel. "Many will say to me on that day, 'Lord, Lord, did we not prophesy in your name? ... Then I will declare to them solemnly, 'I never knew you'" (Matt 7:22-23; cf. also Prov 27:1).

The Fifteenth Benediction (Et Ṣemah David) in Recent Discussion

This standard Jewish prayer was composed after Hillel's death, between 50 and 70 C.E., yet because of its relevance to the wider terms of this symposium, I will briefly mention the recent discussion it has aroused.

The text in the Singer translation reads:

> The offspring of David, Thy servant, speedily cause Thou to spring forth; and his horn do Thou raise up through Thy *salvation*, for for Thy *salvation* we are hoping every day. Blessed art Thou, O Lord, who causest the horn of *salvation* to flourish.[26]

---

[26] S. Singer, *The Authorized Daily Prayer Book of the United Hebrew Congregations* (London, 1935), pp. 44-54; cf. also the comparative texts (not available for no. 15) in C. W. Dugmore, *The Influence of the Synagogue upon the Divine Office* (London, 1944), pp. 114-25; for discussion, see I. Elbogen, *Der jüdische Gottesdienst in seiner geschichtlichen Entwicklung* (Hildesheim, 1967), pp. 27-60; S-B 4.2, pp. 208-49; E. Schürer and G. Vermes, *The History of the Jewish People*, 2.454-63; K. G. Kuhn, *Achtzehngebet und Vaterunser und der Reim* (WUNT 1; Tübingen, 1950); L. A. Hoffmann and K. Berger, s.v. "Gebet," III, Judentum, IV, Neues Testament, *TRE* (Berlin, 1984) 12.42-60; F. Manns, *La Prière d'Israël à l'Heure de Jésus* (SBF Analecta 22; Jerusalem, 1986), pp. 141-55; J. Heinemann, *Prayer*, pp. 218-27 and *passim*; R. LeDéaut, et al., *The Spirituality of Judaism* (St. Meinrad, Ind., 1977), pp. 36-39; A. Z. Idelsohn, *Jewish Liturgy and Its Development* (New York, 1932), pp. 92-100.
   The study of Jewish liturgical prayer has received some salutary critical shocks recently. Basing himself on Yehezkiel Kaufmann's work of 1927, Prof. Shemaryahu Talmon has argued, in "The Emergence of Institutionalized Prayer in Israel," in his *The World of Qumran From Within* (Jerusalem/Leiden, 1989), pp. 200-43, that there is no trace of an institutionalized prayer in ancient Israel as represented in the Hebrew Bible. Its religion was rather one of sacrifices, usually in a (or the) temple. The psalms accompanied the sacrifices in the second Temple. (The exception to this rule is Daniel

The word *salvation*, which occurs three times, has been emphasized here to point to a curious fact. When a Christian or someone alert
to Christian interests reads this prayer, such a reader is struck by the
Hebrew word used for salvation: יְשׁוּעָה *(yšwᶜh,* or *yeshua* in more popular transliteration). The reader spontaneously thinks of the proper name
Yeshu or Yeshua, that is, Jesus in more familiar orthography, usually
interpreted as "God saves" or "Savior." Such a Christian-minded reader
would then wonder what early Jewish Christians must have felt as they
recited these words. And then, what did their non-Christian neighbors
think as they observed the Jewish Christian reaction to the words of the
Benediction? It would make the post–70 introduction of a nineteenth
benediction, against heretics—which is commonly thought to have effectively ended Jewish Christian participation in synagogue worship—
easier to understand.[27]

6:10,13). Talmon sees the start of the Amidah at Qumran and in Sirach 51:21-35. This
thesis has been radicalized by Ezra Fleischer, "On the Beginnings of Obligatory Jewish
Prayer," *Tarbiz* 59 (1990) 397–441, Eng. summary, iii–v. For him, there was no
obligatory Jewish prayer during the entire period of the Second Temple. The early
synagogue was not a place of prayer but a forum for public gathering and for reading
and studying the Law and the Prophets. The exception was the sectarians at Qumran
and perhaps the early Christians. For rabbinic Judaism, "official," statutory prayer is a
product of the period of Jamnia (ca. 75–90 C.E.), an institutional innovation, a new
commandment. The witnesses of Daniel, Sirach, and the New Testament cause the present writer to reject such drastic redatings, but they do invite us to greater critical rigor.

In a recent article, M. Weinfeld claims to have found traces of a Hebrew Grace
after meals *(birkat ha-mason)* [in Hebrew alphabet?] at Qumran (4Q434–439; cf. also
baraki napsi), dated from well before 70 C.E. This would also be relevant to our last
section on the Christian eucharistic prayer. Unfortunately, the text is in such a fragmentary state that it is difficult to be sure about his reading. See M. Weinfeld, "Grace
after Meals in Qumran," *JBL* 111 (1992) 427–40.

[27] The contemporary discussion of this subject began with K. G. Kuhn's essay,
"Giljonim und sifre minim," in *Judentum, Urchristentum, Kirche* (FS, J. Jeremias), ed.
W. Eltester (BZNW 26; Berlin, 1960), pp. 24–61; then taken up in W. D. Davies, *The
Setting of the Sermon on the Mount* (Cambridge, 1964), pp. 256–315, esp. 275–79; P.
Schäfer, "Die sogenannte Synode von Jabne: Zur Trennung von Juden und Christen im
ersten/zweiten Jh. n. Chr." *Judaica* 31 (1975) 54–64, 116–24; reprinted in his *Studien
zur Geschichte und Theologie des rabbinischen Judentums* (AGJU 15; Leiden, 1978),
pp. 49–65; B. Albrektson, "Reflections on the Emergence of a Standard Text of the
Hebrew Bible," *Congress Volume Göttingen 1977* (VT Sup 29; Leiden, 1978), pp. 49–
65; G. Stemberger, "Die sogennante Synode von Jabne und das frühe Christentum,"
Kairos 19 (1977) 14–21; S. T. Katz, "Issues in the Separation of Judaism and
Christianity after 70 C.E.: A Reconsideration," *JBL* 103 (1984) 43–76; T. C. G.
Thornton, "Christian Understandings of the Birkath Ha-Minim," *JTS* ns 38 (1987) 419–
31; R. Kimelman, "*Birkat Ha-Minim* and the Lack of Evidence for an Anti-Christian

There the matter rested, in the realm of questions and surmises, until an Israeli scholar set forth a bold hypothesis and stirred up a controversy. In 1984 Professor Yehuda Liebes published in Hebrew an article on the Fifteenth Benediction in which he argued as follows.[28] The Fifteenth Benediction is of ancient (i.e., pre-Christian) origin. It is as old as the other intermediate blessings.[29] Its prayer for the coming of the Davidic messiah is closely connected with the immediately preceding blessing for the rebuilding of Jerusalem. It probably ended originally with the formula, "who causest the horn of *David* (i.e., not salvation) to flourish."

The roots of the prayer go back to Ps 132:17a, to Ezek 29:21, and to the Hebrew expanded form of Sir 51:12 viii[30] (see also Luke 1:68-69 where God is blessed for bringing redemption and for raising a horn of salvation within the house of David). But first-century Jewish Christians altered the wording of the last phrase to the form given above, "who causest the horn of salvation to flourish," as a way of alluding to Jesus, so that it becomes a prayer for his second coming. This alteration, possible at the time because the formulas were still somewhat fluid, was found offensive to non-Christian Jews. So the fifteenth benediction was eliminated in the Palestinian recension found in

---

Jewish Prayer in Late Antiquity," in *Jewish and Christian Self-Definition*, ed. E. P. Sanders *et al.* (London, 1981), 2.226-44; W. Horbury, "The Benediction of the *Minim* and Early Jewish Controversy," *JTS* ns 33 (1982) 19-61.

[28] Y. Liebes, "Who Makes the Horn of Jesus to Flourish," *Immanuel* 21 (1987) 55-67; *idem*, "Mazmiah Qeren Yeshu'ah," *Jerusalem Studies in Jewish Thought* (=*JSJT*) 3 (1983/84) 313-48 (Heb.), Eng. summary, v-vii; critical reviews by I. M. Ta-Shma, M. Krister, and S. Morag, with responses and an addition by Liebes, *JSJT* 4 (1984/85), Eng. summaries, xv-xx, xxxv, xxxvi.

[29] Schürer, *History*, 2.460, thinks that the framework of the *Shemoneh 'Esreh* "originated during the last three decades of the first century A.D." But we prefer the view of S-B 4.218: the greater part of the prayer was known in the first half of the first century C.E. The earliest parts (the first and last blessings) are pre-Christian. Only a few blessings (the 12th and the 14th) belong definitely to the period after the destruction of the Temple. The whole received a final redaction at the time of Gamaliel II, around 90 C.E. (though the wording of blessings and even the grouping continued to evolve).

[30] In the Hebrew fragment of Sir 51, there is, after v. 12, an expansion of 16 verses not found in the Septuagint or the Vulgate. This Hebrew addition is thought to anticipate or echo the Eighteen Benedictions. The Roman numerals here follow those used by A. di Lella in his AB commentary on Sirach. —ED

the Cairo Geniza. This recension simply included a prayer for the Davidic kingdom in the preceding blessing while avoiding any mention of salvation. But this Jewish-Christian version somehow traveled to Babylonian Jewry where it was accepted as the standard form. From Babylonia it was gradually accepted as normative throughout the Jewish world and is the form used to this day. Thus far Professor Leibes. It is important to stress that only the concluding formula, not the entire prayer, is, for Professor Liebes, of Jewish-Christian provenance.

Such a bold hypothesis was quick to provoke disagreement. Several scholars rejected this reconstruction as both historically implausible and philologically unnecessary.[31] What should we say about it? The least we can say is that, while implausible, the thesis is nevertheless useful as illustrating the problem posed by Jewish Christians who continued to frequent the synagogue for a time and who gave their own interpretations to some of the prayers which they found suggestive of their own messianic convictions. The ensuing tensions doubtless contributed to the Jewish-Christian schism, as one—but only one—element. Beyond this, Leibes's hypothesis can help to explain why the Fifteenth Benediction was dropped from the Palestinian recension.

It would be ironic if the Jewish-Christian form spread throughout the Jewish world through a Babylonian tradition which did not know what it was doing. The word in question, *yeshua*, is perfectly ordinary Hebrew, and need imply no connection with Jesus at all, except for etymology which is no historical proof. Babylonian Jewry may not have been troubled by *Jewish* Christians, as Leibes says, but neither was it wholly ignorant of Christians. There were Christians in Babylonia at the time, with many monks and monasteries and outstanding leaders like Aphrahat and Ephrem.[32] Some were orthodox Catholics while others were Marcionite and later Jacobite-Monophysite or Nestorian. Their presence would have put the Babylonian Jewish sages on their guard.

Thus we must pronounce Leibes's hypothesis implausible, ironic, difficult, but not impossible. History is full of strange ironies. The

---

[31] See the critical views listed in note 27.

[32] See for example J. M. Fiey, *Assyrie chrétienne*, 3 vols. (Beirut, 1965–1968) and other works by this author; Jacob Neusner, *A History of the Jews in Babylonia*, 5 vols. (Leiden, 1965–1970), includes information on the Christians; Arthur Vööbus, *A History of Asceticism in the Syrian Orient*, 2 vols. (CSCO 197; Louvain, 1958–1960).

whole controversy illustrates the value of studying ancient Jewish sources on prayer comparatively, even if the specific hypothesis falls short of proof.

JESUS ON PRAYER

Introduction

That Jesus was a man of prayer is not in doubt. We know considerably more about his prayer life than about that of Hillel. He prayed both publicly or liturgically in synagogues (e.g., Mark 1:21) and in the Temple (Mark 11:11,17) and privately: "Rising very early before dawn, he left and went off to a deserted place, where he prayed" (Mark 1:35; cf. also the prayer in the garden of Gethsemane, Mark 14:32-42). He also set forth formal teachings on prayer. An early example runs:

> Have faith in God ... Whoever says to this mountain, 'Be lifted up and thrown into the sea,' and does not doubt in his heart but believes that what he says will happen, it shall be done for him ... All that you ask for in prayer, believe that you will receive it and it shall be yours. When you stand to pray, forgive anyone against whom you have a grievance .... (Mark 11:22-25; cf. Matt 6:5-15 and Matt 7:1-11)

Although often said to be a loose string of sayings, this Marcan passage has a logic and coherence of its own. The basis of prayer is an unshakable faith in God which involves a trust in the ultimate beneficence of the universe and the courage to be, a courage which enables people to become martyrs. On such a basis, prayer can become a political weapon which topples regimes. But this powerful prayer must, says the last verse, be linked to—indeed, preceded by—a willingness to forgive the opponent which permits love and reconciliation and not mere power to triumph. This Marcan material finds a parallel in the Q source, where Jesus goes beyond the demand for forgiveness to the more astonishing idea that we should pray for those who mistreat us (Luke 6:28b // Matt 5:44).

From the Q source come also the Lord's Prayer and the christologically crucial cry of jubilee: "I give praise to you, Father, Lord of heaven and earth, for although you have hidden these things from the wise and the learned you have revealed them to the childlike. Yes,

Father, such has been your gracious will" (Matt 11:25-27 // Luke 10:21-22). The Gospel according to John adds a postpaschal twist to this, designed to suggest the perpetual communion and intimacy in prayer between Jesus and the Father. "Father, I thank you for hearing me. I know that you always hear me; but because of the crowd here I have said this, that they may believe that you sent me" (John 11:41b-42). On this Rudolf Bultmann has the comment:

> The character of his communion with God is clearly delineated by this: he does not need to make prayer requests like others, who have to rouse themselves out of their attitude of prayerlessness and therefore godlessness; for he continually stands before God as the asker and therefore as the receiver.[33]

An interesting and relevant literary phenomenon occurs in both Luke and the Aramaic targums of the Hebrew Bible. It is well known that Luke augments the number of times Jesus prays, in comparison with the presentations in Mark and Matthew. Jesus is said to pray before his baptism (3:21), before sending out the twelve (6:12), before Peter's confession (9:18), before the transfiguration (9:28-29), before he teaches the Lord's Prayer (11:1), and of course before his passion, on the Mount of Olives (22:40-44), although this last case is part of the common synoptic tradition. A prayer that Peter's faith may not fail is Luke's way of bestowing special authority on Peter in the postpaschal situation (22:32). As in Mark, Jesus prays in deserted places (5:16; 6:12), but in the Lucan parallel to Mark 1:35, namely Luke 4:42, Jesus oddly enough is not said to pray.

Given this Lucan propensity to multiply occasions of prayer, it is striking that the same phenomenon occurs in the targums. Michael Maher has shown in two careful articles[34] that twenty-six common Hebrew verbs or expressions have been converted into terms for prayer in the targums to the Pentateuch, though not in an absolutely consistent manner. He has also shown how the targums love to portray the

---

[33] R. Bultmann, *The Gospel of John: A Commentary* (Philadelphia, 1971), p. 408.

[34] Michael Maher, "The Meturgemanim and Prayer," *JJS* 41 (1990) 226–46; "The Meturgemanim and Prayer (2)," forthcoming in *JJS*. Dr. Maher kindly permitted me to see a copy of this second part in ms.

patriarchs in situations of prayer, including Abraham, Isaac, Jacob, Joseph, Moses, Aaron, the priests, and the people. To be sure, not every case he presents is convincing. To get a more balanced picture, the competing tendency to show the patriarchs in the act of Torah study and to multiply the interpretation of verbs in that sense would also have to be set out. For example, the verb דרש (*darash*), to seek or look for, can have both senses in the targums: to pray and to study. Nevertheless, Maher has pointed to a real tendency in the texts that parallels Luke's redactional procedure.

The Lord's Prayer

The most well-known fact about Jesus and prayer is that he taught his disciples a short prayer for the coming of the kingdom of God (Matt 6:5-15; Luke 11:1-4). In both Matthew and Luke the text of the prayer is inserted in a longer catechesis on prayer. We will consider neither these catecheses nor the more familiar and frequently studied Matthean form of the prayer.[35] The shorter Lucan form is commonly judged to be taken from the Q source and to represent the prayer in its earlier form. It runs: "Father, hallowed be your name, your kingdom come. Give us each day our daily bread and forgive us our sins for we ourselves forgive everyone in debt to us, and do not subject us to the final test."

This prayer can be resolved into five elements. The first is the address to the deity, so characteristic and revelatory of Jesus' own atti-

[35] Ernst Lohmeyer, *Our Father* (New York, 1966); K. G. Kuhn, *Achtzehngebet und Vaterunser und der Reim* (WUNT; Tübingen, 1950); R. E. Brown, "The Pater Noster as an Eschatological Prayer," in *New Testament Essays*, chap. 12 (New York, 1965), pp. 275-320; Jean Carmignac, *Recherches sur le Notre Père* (Paris, 1969); J. J. Petuchowski and Michael Brocke, *The Lord's Prayer and Jewish Liturgy* (New York, 1979); Pierre Grelot, "La quatrième demande du Pater et son arrière-plan sémitique," *NTS* 25 (1978-1979) 299-314; *idem*, "L'arrière-plan araméen du Pater," *RB* 91 (1984) 531-56; Krister Stendahl, "Your Kingdom Come," *Cross Currents* 32 (1982) 257-66; Birger Gerhardsson, "The Matthean Version of the Lord's Prayer: Some Observations," in *The New Testament Age* (Festschrift, Bo Reicke), ed. W. C. Weinrich (Macon, Ga., 1984), I, 207-20; David Flusser, "Qumran and Jewish 'Apotropaic' Prayers," *IEJ* 16 (1966) 194-205, repr. in his *Judaism and the Origins of Christianity* (Jerusalem, 1988), pp. 214-29; W. D. Davies and D. C. Allison, *The Gospel According to Saint Matthew* (ICC; Edinburgh, 1988), 1.590-99 (excursus) with literature on pp. 621-24; Eugene LaVerdiere, "The Lord's Prayer in Literary Context," in *Scripture and Prayer* (Festschrift, C. Stuhlmueller), eds. C. Osiek and Donald Senior (Wilmington, 1988), pp. 104-16.

tude toward God that it will be treated in a separate section. The second element consists of the two petitions for the sanctification of the divine name and the coming of the kingdom, petitions which may be viewed as standing in synonymous parallelism. The background for the sanctification of the name in the sense of requesting that God manifest his power by saving his chosen people is probably to be found in Leviticus 11:45; Isaiah 5:16; and especially in Ezekiel: 20:41; 36:22-28; and 38:23, which reads: "So I will show my greatness and my holiness and make myself known in the eyes of many nations. Then they will know that I am the Lord."

The prayer for the coming of the kingdom presupposes the apocalyptic vision of Daniel 7:13-14 and indeed of all of Daniel. It prays for a future coming to earth of God's rule, that is, as Matthew's gloss rightly interprets, that God's will for justice and peace be realized or triumph on earth. The descent of the heavenly Jerusalem to earth in Revelation 21 is one way of visualizing this. The two parallel petitions pray for exactly the same thing—the manifestation of divine power on earth in a visible fashion—but they do so in different ways. The first does so in the vocabulary of the exilic prophets, the second in the terminology of second century B.C.E. Seleucid-Maccabean apocalyptic. In these two sets of terms a difference may be noted: the prophets think of Israel as "against the nations"; Daniel thinks in terms of world empires. Daniel ignores the Temple theocracy as petty, a Jerusalem city state. The state and society are to be found in the world empires (Dan 2:27-45; 7:2-8:17). God's rule and kingdom are in principle worldwide, even if for the present that is obscured. In the Lord's Prayer this distinction is not visible, except that all nationalist particularism is absent. The prophetic point of view is subsumed under the Danielic.[36]

The third element, the petition for bread, contains some philological difficulties which need not concern us. Yet they point to a serious difference of interpretation. Is the bread prayed for ordinary earthly bread, as is usually thought, or should it be understood as a reference to the messianic banquet in the future kingdom?[37] Although

---

[36] For a recent survey, see B. T. Viviano, *The Kingdom of God in History* (Collegeville, Minn., 1988); *idem*, "The Kingdom of God in the New Testament," *ANRW* 26, forthcoming.

[37] See Davies-Allison, *Matthew*, pp. 607-10.

certainty is not possible, the eschatological interpretation would create a thematic unity with the preceding petitions, a unity which could be extended to the final petitions and is supported by some early witnesses.

The fourth element is the petition for proportional forgiveness. A prayer for forgiveness is found in the sixth blessing of the Amidah, but not the condition that it be in proportion to our willingness to forgive. That is found rather in Sirach 27:30–28:7. Consider especially Sirach 28:2: "Forgive your neighbor the wrong he has done, and *then* your sins will be pardoned when you pray." This parallel is particularly close to both halves of the Gospel verse and is certainly of a pre-Christian date, whereas the same cannot be said for the text from the Amidah. The forgiveness in question may be that required to be prepared to receive the king when he comes in eschatological judgment.

The final petition, "Lead us not into temptation," may be interpreted as a petition for help to remain steadfast during the final trial, the apocalyptic woes, birthpangs of the messiah, or endtime ordeal, such as that described in Revelation 20:7-10. If so, this petition rejoins the second element in its request for the sanctification of the divine name, the coming of the kingdom.

In its relation to Jewish liturgical prayer, we see several possibilities. All suffer from the difficulty of secure pre-Christian dating. The closest and most certainly relevant is the Kaddish. An early form of this runs: "Exalted and hallowed be his great name in the world which he created according to his will. May he rule his kingdom in your lifetime and in your days and in the lifetime of the whole house of Israel, speedily and soon. And to this, say: Amen."

Apart from the absence of the address, "Father," the two petitions of this prayer correspond to the first half of the Lord's Prayer, though in the third rather than the second person. Proposals for the dating of the Kaddish range from the time of the Maccabees to the sixth century C.E. The divine name is blessed in Daniel 2:20; Job 1:21; and Psalm 113:2—blessed but not hallowed. M.Yoma 3:8 concludes: "Blessed be the name of the glory of his kingdom for ever and ever."

Although certitude is not possible, a strong suspicion remains that the first two petitions of the Lord's Prayer were formulated under the influence of the Kaddish. While the influence of the Eighteen Benedictions is not so obvious on the Lucan form of Jesus' prayer, an abbreviated form of them, such as is found in b.Ber. 29a, was likely used by Matthew or his community in the expansion and reformulation of the prayer.

Abba

Three times in the New Testament the Aramaic emphatic and/or vocative form of the word for father is used in contexts which manifest a strong, bold address to God: Mark 14:36; Galatians 4:6; and Romans 8:15. From this it is concluded that it was a characteristic of Jesus' personal prayer that he addressed God in Aramaic as *abba*. Joachim Jeremias built an elaborate, if implicit, Christology of filial consciousness on the part of Jesus on this basis.[38]

To summarize his position, we begin by noting that gods are sometimes referred to as fathers in the religious literature of the ancient near east. In the Old Testament, God is referred to some fifteen times as a father, with this difference from the rest of the ancient near east: it is said in a context of election of God's people in a historical action. But God is never addressed as father in prayer. In rabbinical literature, references to God as "our heavenly father" are relatively sparse and always have a collective connotation. Jeremias concludes that "there is no evidence in the literature of ancient Palestinian Judaism that 'my father' is used as a personal address to God."[39]

By way of contrast, the four Gospels show 170 cases of "father" as a title for God in the sayings of Jesus. One hundred nine of these cases are found in John. There is a clear tendency to increase the number of such cases in the later Gospels, but they presumably build on something that the earliest strata of the Jesus tradition show to be characteristic of Jesus' religious language. (This is in evident contrast with the Old Testament where the most characteristic name for God is the Tetragrammaton, as in the Septuagint it is κύριος, lord.).

Jesus refers to God as "my Father" in four important cases: Matthew 11:27 (// Luke 10:22); Matthew 16:17; Mark 13:32; and Luke 22:29 (cf. Dan 7:14 and 2Sam 7:14 // 1Chr 17:13). They all deal with the unique revelation and authority which have been given to Jesus. Their sparseness shows that Jesus did not often speak of the ultimate

[38] Joachim Jeremias, *The Prayers of Jesus* (SBT 2.6; London, 1966), pp. 11-65.

[39] Jeremias, *Prayers*, p. 29.

mystery of his mission. They belong to the esoteric teaching of Jesus, addressed only to his disciples. From his survey, Jeremias concludes "that Jesus constantly addressed God as 'my Father' (with the exception of Mark 15:34 par. Matt 27:46), and ... in so doing he used the Aramaic form *abba*."[40] This is something new in Jewish religious language. Jewish prayer and other religious literature otherwise avoided this use of *abba* as disrespectful. This usage expresses a special relationship with God.

Since Jeremias wrote, careful reexaminations of the subject of the use of *abba* in the Aramaic literature of antiquity have been undertaken.[41] One of the points at issue is what sort of Aramaic should be admitted as evidence. Should only texts written in Imperial or Middle Aramaic, such as we find in the Bible or at Qumran, be admitted (so Fitzmyer)[42], because of their certainly pre-Christian date? Or, as Alejandro Diez-Macho and Geza Vermes hold,[43] should the targums also be admitted, since they give us indirect access to the spoken language of the Tannaitic era? S. A. Kaufman has helpfully pointed out that the literary language of the moment always reflects the spoken lan-

[40] Jeremias, *Prayers*, p. 57.

[41] Jacques Schlosser, *Le Dieu de Jésus* (LD 129; Paris, 1987), pp. 105–209 gives a careful report, esp. pp. 179–209; Jacques Dupont, "Le Dieu de Jésus," *NRT* 109 (1987) 321–44; Georg Schelbert, "Sprachgeschichtliches zu 'Abba'", in *Mélanges D. Barthélemy*, ed. Pierre Casetti *et al.* (OBO 38; Fribourg/Göttingen, 1981), pp. 395–447; Adrian Schenker, "Gott als Vater – Sohne Gottes; Ein vernachlässigter Aspekt einer biblischen Metapher," *Freiburger Zeitschrift für Philosophie und Theologie* 25 (1978) 3–55; Dieter Zeller, "God as Father in the Proclamation and in the Prayer of Jesus," in *Standing Before God* (Festschrift, J. M. Oesterreicher), ed. Asher Finkel and Laurence Frizzell (New York, 1981), pp. 117–29; J. A. Fitzmyer, "*Abba* and Jesus' Relation to God," in *À Cause de l'Évangile* (Festschrift, J. Dupont) (LD 39; Paris, 1985), pp. 15–38; James Barr, "Abba Isn't 'Daddy'", *JTS* ns 39 (1988) 28–47; Witold Marchel, *Abba, Père!* (AnBib 19A; Rome, 1971); cf. the report on the "Jesus Seminar," R. J. Miller, "The Lord's Prayer and Other Items from the Sermon on the Mount," *Forum* 5 (1989) 177–86; Alon Goshen Gottstein, *God and Israel as Father and Son in Tannaitic Literature*, Diss. Hebrew University, 1986 (Heb.; Eng. abstract pp. i–viii).

[42] J. A. Fitzmyer, *A Wandering Aramean* (Missoula, 1979), esp. p. 86; *idem*, "The Aramaic Language and the Study of the New Testament," *JBL* 99 (1980) 5–21; idem and D. J. Harrington, *A Manual of Palestinian Aramaic Texts* (BibOr 34; Rome, 1978).

[43] A. Diez Macho, "Le targum palestinien," *RevScRel* 47 (1973) 169–231; G. Vermes, *JTS* ns 31 (1980) 580–82.

guage of a previous period.[44] Thus, for him, the targums in their present form date at the earliest from the Amoraic period, yet they represent our best access to the Aramaic spoken in first century Galilee. For this reason, the targums are taken into consideration in the recent studies. Yet they only confirm the picture drawn from the earlier material in this case. *Abba* is not used in prayer to God.

The one Talmudic exception, charming as it is, does not alter the picture, since it too is not a case of direct address to God. It comes from *b.Taan* 23b:

> Hanin ha-Nehba was the son of the daughter of Honi the Circlemaker. When the world needed rain, our teachers used to send school children to him, who seized the hem of his coat and said to him, 'Father, father, give us rain (אבא אבא הב לן מטרא)!' He said to God: 'Master of the world, grant it for the sake of those who are not yet able to distinguish between an *abba* who has the power to give rain and an *abba* who has not.

Note that the direct address to God is 'master of the world.'

> After the careful study of these texts," Schlosser concludes, "... we cannot any longer call upon them to doubt the originality of the New Testament as concerns *abba*. Not only are there no Jewish texts where *abba* is used as an address to God; we lack even any witness of the designation *abba* used for God in Judaism roughly contemporary with Christian origins. The fact is there. It remains to ask what it means."[45]

It is hard to interpret a silence. Jeremias explains it as a desire on the part of the rabbis to avoid familiarity or disrespect.[46] Schlosser stresses rather the desire to avoid crude anthropomorphisms, to preserve the divine transcendence. In any case the rabbis preferred אבי (*abi*; my Father) or "Father in heaven." Jesus' usage suggests an affectionate familiarity as well as a sense of God's immediacy, nearness, direct

---

[44] S. A. Kaufman, "On Methodology in the Study of the Targums and their Chronology," *JSNT* 23 (1985) 117–24.

[45] Schlosser, *Le Dieu de Jésus*, p. 200.

[46] Jeremias, *Prayers of Jesus*, p. 62.

accessibility. There is no necessary opposition between affection and respect. The opposition is rather between affection and distance.[47] In all this a Christology lies implicit. Jesus, it is safe to conclude, had a filial consciousness, a consciousness that he had a unique closeness to God, that he was the Son of the Father in some absolute sense.[48]

The Origins of the Eucharistic Prayer

Our treatment of Jesus and prayer, though not intended to be exhaustive, should not entirely pass over in silence the eucharistic prayer, which is for many Christians the supreme prayer. Our goal here is a modest one. It is once again to report on some recent research.[49]

---

[47] Schlosser, *Le Dieu de Jésus*, p. 201-9.

[48] Since writing this section a major book, a revised doctoral dissertation, has come to my attention. It attempts to make a radical revision of the consensus, based on a thorough examination of texts which refer to God as Father in the deutero-canonical/apocryphal and pseudepigraphical literature of early Judaism. I refer to A. Strotmann, *"Mein Vater bist du!" (Sir 51:10): Zur Bedeutung der Vaterschaft Gottes in kanonischen und nichtkanonischen frühjüdischen Schriften* (Frankfurter Theologische Studien 39; Frankfurt am Main, 1991).

Although it arrived too late for me to digest in its entirety, the following observations can be made. In her critique of the research tradition from Dalman and Jeremias to Schlosser, she must first concede their main points. First, the vocable *abba* is not used in prayer in the literature she surveys. (This is partly explained by the fact that much of this literature is not preserved in Hebrew or Aramaic.) Second, God is not usually addressed as Father in the *vocative* case in this literature. She shifts the terms of the debate to show that the bipolar analysis within the research tradition, which interprets the metaphor "Father" when applied to God as either absolute authority demanding obedience or as helpful kindness, care, and mercy. This move is misguided and tendentious. For the consensus, the first pole was characteristic of the Old Testament and Jewish side, and the second, of Jesus. How central this bipolar analysis was to the earlier authors is debatable, but in any case, Strotmann has credibly argued from context that the fatherhood of God in the early Jewish texts is predominantly a way of expressing God's loving care for his creatures, especially for Israel. The consensus has been corrected, but she has not entirely avoided the danger of exaggerating the significance of very fragmentary, at times textually uncertain texts (e.g., the Apocryphon of Ezekiel II).

In two recent articles, Mary Rose D'Angelo calls into question the historical certainty of Jesus' use of *Abba* (*JBL* 111 [1992] 611-30; *HTR* 85 [1992] 149-74). Her contemporary agenda is made explicit in *Horizons* 19 (1992) 199-218.

[49] J.-P. Audet, "Literary Forms and Contents of a Normal *Eucharistia* in the First Century," *Studia Evangelica* (TU 73; Berlin, 1959) 643-63, an expanded version appeared in *RB* 65 (1958) 371-99; L. Ligier, "The Origins of the Eucharistic Prayer: From the Last Supper to the Eucharist," *Studia Liturgica* 9 (1973) 161-85; T. J. Talley, "From *Berakah* to *Eucharistia*: A Reopening Question," *Worship* 50 (1976) 115-37;

The eucharistic meal is, for Christians, a great blessing of the present era of salvation, precisely because it is a foretaste or anticipation of the kingdom of God (Mark 14:25; Matt 26:29; Luke 22:18). But the narrative of the Last Supper, the institution of the eucharist, presents scholars with a number of questions related to blessing. Why do Mark and Matthew say that Jesus *blessed* the bread (εὐλογήσας), but *gave thanks* (εὐχαριστήσας) over the cup? Why do Paul (1Cor 11:24) and Luke (22:17,19) drop the term *blessing* in their accounts of the Last Supper, using only *thanksgiving* there, yet bring the blessing back in other eucharistic contexts (Luke 24:30; 1Cor 10:16; 14:16; cf. also the the pre-eucharistic context of the feeding of the multitudes, Mark 6:61; 8:7; Matt 14:19; Luke 9:16)? Why is Jesus' thanksgiving over the cup *longer* than his blessing over the bread? How did Christians move from the Last Supper to the eucharist? That is, why do they have a eucharistic prayer (or canon) rather than just the words of institution?

The answer to these questions takes us to the period of transition from the Old Testament to the New by way of the evolution of Jewish prayer forms. The standard Old Testament formula for blessing God is the stable ברוך יהוה (*baruk YHWH*), Blessed be the Lord (third person). Only in a few late texts (1Chr 29:10; Ps 119:12; 1Macc 4:30), do we find the formula "Blessed be you, O Lord" (ברוך אתה יהוה; *baruk atta, YHWH*); second person, direct address). These late texts give us a clue to the formation of the liturgical blessings in the synagogues that was going on at the time. These blessings take the stable form: "Blessed are you, O Lord our God ...." They also indicate a shift from blessings as public statements to blessings as personal address, expressing a more direct relation to God.[50] The short formula just cited is later called a חתימה (*hatimah*, seal) because it sometimes concludes a longer prayer.

Returning to our questions about the eucharist, in Mark and Matthew, Jesus *blesses* the bread in reciting the short blessing formula or *hatimah* just cited, at the start of the meal. He *gives thanks* over the

---

Talley, "The Literary Structure of the Eucharistic Prayer," *Worship* 58 (1984) 404–20; H. Wegman, "Généalogie hypothétique de la prière eucharistique," *Questions Liturgiques* 61 (1980) 263–78; C. Giraudo, *La Struttura Letteraria della Preghiera Eucaristica* (AnBib 92; Rome, 1981).

[50] W. S. Towner, "'Blessed be YHWH' and 'Blessed art thou, YHWH': The Modulation of a Biblical Formula," *CBQ* 30 (1968) 386–99.

cup, because he recites, at the close of the meal, the lengthy ברכת המזון (*birkat ha-mazon,* grace after meals) which consists of three parts: blessing, thanksgiving, and supplication or petition. Paul and Luke drop the blessing terminology because, like the early Christian text called the Didache, they sense that God's new act in Christ requires thanksgiving first and then only secondarily blessing and petition.

Jesus' words over the cup are *longer* than those over the bread because it was customary to pray briefly at the beginning of a Jewish meal and at length at the end. The New Testament eucharistic texts are brief. They do not cite in full Jewish prayers their first readers knew by heart. The New Testament is not a manual of rubrics. But the earliest eucharistic prayers outside the New Testament (Didache, Apostolic Constitutions, Hippolytus, Addai, and Mari) give us the impression that they grew out of a rearranged ברכת המזון (*birkat ha-mazon*) with the thanksgiving placed first, and then the blessing and the prayers of supplication. Within this long prayer, Jesus' words of institution were, at some point, inserted. That is how the eucharistic prayers developed out of the Last Supper.[51]

CONCLUSION

We will conclude with an exploratory question and a brief comparison between Hillel and Jesus regarding their approach to prayer.

Did Christianity "resacerdotalize" the synagogue service? Did it effect a fusion (whether conscious or unconscious) between the worship in the Temple and that in the synagogue? Did it retain more of the Levitical tradition than did the rabbis?

The normal Christian eucharistic service is commonly and rightly said to derive from the synagogue service. This is especially true for the first of its two parts, the service of the Word, which consists of scrip-

---

[51] The evolution of scholarship went something like this: Audet (see note 49) explored the connection between the Jewish ברכה *(berakah)* and the Christian eucharist. Ligier and Talley, under the influence of Joseph Heinemann, *Prayer in the Talmud* (see note 1) among others, then refined this by adding the element of תודה (*tôdah;* thanksgiving) in the Jewish grace after meals. They note that this thanksgiving can include a brief historical recollection of past divine saving interventions. This literary fact eventually emboldened the Christians to insert the *anamnesis* or memorial of the Last Supper, including the words of institution, in their eucharistic prayer.

tural readings surrounded by blessings and psalms, then usually a sermon, and often a creed. This last could be said to correspond to the recitation of the *Shema* in the synagogue. But its second part, the eucharistic meal proper, does not derive from the synagogue order of service, but, as we have seen, from the Jewish meal blessings, particularly the long grace after meals. This is in line with the Last Supper as a meal in a Passover context if not a reinterpreted Passover meal.[52] It surrounded this eucharistic prayer with offertory prayers, a salvation-historical preface which concludes with a Thrice Holy (Trisagion or Sanctus), the Lord's Prayer and related eschatological petitions, the communion rite itself, and final prayers, blessings and dismissal.

The Lord's Prayer, as we have seen, is likely a transformed Kaddish. The Sanctus may come from the Amidah, and of course remotely from Isaiah 6:3.[53] But offertory prayers (at least in some of their forms), the words of institution over the bread and wine, and the meal itself—all of these have taken on a sacrificial sense related to Jesus' death on the cross as well as to the whole system of sacrifices, offerings, and meals in the Temple. This sacrificial development began early, with such echoes of Isaiah 53 as are found in the words of institution ("blood of the covenant, which shall be shed for many") and in such texts as Mark 10:45, which strive to give a redemptive meaning to the death of Jesus. The sacrificial development was no doubt heightened by the destruction of the Temple, which removed it as a means of atonement for sin.

It was the major contribution of the Letter to the Hebrews to retrieve the Levitical dimension for Christians by transforming it. The Jews handled the crisis entailed in the loss of the Temple by means of the Yom Kippur service in the synagogues, and by replacing the sacrifices of the Temple with deeds of lovingkindness and the study of Torah, particularly the laws in the Torah relating to sacrifice.[54] The codification of the Fifth Division of the Mishnah, *Kodashim*, on these laws relating to sacrifice, are a witness to this. The Christians carried on an unbloody sacrifice in their worship. One could carry the com-

---

[52] J. Jeremias, *The Eucharistic Words of Jesus* (London, 1966).

[53] B. D. Spinks, "The Jewish Sources for the Sanctus," *HeyJ* 21 (1980) 173; D. Flusser, "Sanktus und Gloria," in *Abraham Unser Vater* (Festschrift, Otto Michel) (Leiden, 1963), pp. 129–52.

[54] ARN 4 (Goldin trans., pp. 32, 34).

parison on to the evolution and transformation of the festal calendar, but this would take us too far afield.[55]

From the few glimpses we have of Hillel and Jesus as men of prayer, we could say that Hillel represents a more creation-centered, sapiential outlook. Jesus, while capable of both wisdom teaching and acute appreciation of nature, is nevertheless stamped by a burning concern to gather and reform the people of God, to ready them for the apocalyptic redemption to come, which he expected in the near future. Both are wrestlers with God and lovers of God, who put their hope in him alone.

[55] J. Daniélou, *The Bible and the Liturgy* (Notre Dame, 1956). On resacerdotalizing or re-Leviticizing, see A. Vanhoye, *La Situation du Christ; Hébreux 1-2* (LD 58; Paris, 1969); Vanhoye, *Old Testament Priests and the New Priest according to the New Testament* (Petersham, 1986), both on the letter to the Hebrews.

EPILOGUE

HILLEL AND JESUS:
RETROSPECTIVE AND PROSPECTIVE REFLECTIONS

MY PERSONAL REFLECTIONS on thinking back to the symposium and reading the preceding chapters center first on the importance of working and thinking together as an international team of scholars, using the same methodology and seeking similar questions. The demands made upon a scholar working on Hillel or Jesus transcend the abilities of any one expert. We need the insights and data controlled by others. Philologians need archaeologists, theologians depend on historians, rabbinic specialists learn from Qumran experts—we all learn from other disciplines, especially sociology and anthropology.

I think the international team working on Hillel and Jesus came to the following generally shared conclusions:

(1) Hillel and Jesus were historical teachers and devout Jews who lived in pre-70 Palestine.

(2) Both attracted disciples and obtained fecund and efficacious insights into the meaning of creation, God, and morality.

(3) It is extremely difficult to reconstruct with certainty the authentic teachings of Jesus; the task is even more difficult with Hillel. That is because neither wrote anything, and their followers were not only dependent on fluid oral traditions concerning their teachings, but those who passed on the traditions also significantly edited what they remembered they had taught. While Jesus traditions were certainly recorded and edited in a reliable form before the end of the first century C.E., the rabbinic traditions about Hillel in some cases date from the third and even sixth century C.E. Geiger was incorrect to conclude that "Hillel is a strictly historical personage" and, unlike Jesus, was "not hidden behind legends" (*Judenthum*, pp. 99–107).

(4) Both Hillel and Jesus set in motion perspectives, commit-

ments, and means of adhering to and inculcating traditions that founded respectively Rabbinic Judaism and Christianity.

(5) It is improper to conclude that Jesus studied under Hillel (*pace* Renan and Rieger).

(6) It is probably that Jesus did teach the Golden Rule (Mt 7:12; Lk 6:31; cf. Rom 13:10), as the tradition clearly antedates both Matthew and Luke and possibly even Q as a "nucleus sermon" (as Fitzmyer suggests). Thus the tradition that Jesus taught the Golden Rule can be traced within a decade of his time. Hillel is also accredited with a similar teaching (b.Shab 31a), but the only written text that attributes it to Hillel postdates him by at least five hundred years. Thus it is difficult to trace the tradition back into the first century C.E. (see Alexander's chapter).

(7) The similarities between Hillel and Jesus are profound but that does not mean he was a Hillelite or even a Pharisee (*pace* Geiger and Falk). In the search for the Hillel and Jesus, documents other than the New Testament and Rabbinics must be studied. Among these are texts from Early Judaism, especially the Dead Sea Scrolls and the Old Testament Apocrypha and Pseudepigrapha.

(8) The New Testament writings are in places polemical documents, especially in their portrayal of the Pharisees. The latter were not hypocrites as some passages in the Gospels imply. Many Pharisees apparently loved and admired Jesus; some obviously followed him and believed in him. It is clear that these polemical sections of the New Testament were shaped by the tensions between Jesus' followers and Hillel's followers after 70 C.E.

(9) It is often misleading to compare Hillel and Jesus as historical figures (as I, Goshen Gottstein, and Alexander try to demonstrate). It is certainly probable that at times we are really comparing traditions about Hillel and Jesus; and these traditions usually reflect different times and social concerns.

The symposium opened avenues for promising areas of research. We should seek to discern how and in what ways we might learn more about both Hillel and Jesus by comparing them with the Righteous Teacher of Qumran. We need more discussion on how Hillel and Jesus fit into their time, and how they helped the Time of Transition become the Age of Standardization. In a certain sense, our methodology is imprecise: we do not know how to sift the kerygmatic and apologetic-shaped Gospels and the later post-Jamnian–shaped Rabbinics for authentic—or at least probably reliable—historical data regarding Jesus or Hillel.

INDEX OF SCRIPTURES

Hebrew Scriptures

Genesis
6:5 63n22
8:22 63n22
13:13 164
25:24 407n23
25:28 69
29:13 408
32:11 408
33:4 408
38:24-25 355n32
41:41-42 408
43:1 408
45:26 408
46:29 408
49:8 408
49:28 378
50:22 417

Exodus
3:1 420
4:22 367
8:15 97n77
12:5 344
12:6 347, 353n29
12:8 336, 358, 360
12:15 345
16:4 73nn6-7
20:2 419
20:8 440
20:12 412
20:20 88n54
20:21 331
20:24 86, 88, 331
20:24b(21b) 435-39, 38n21, 439
21:1-24:18 417
22:25 422
23:1 311
28:4 366
31:13 306n4
31:16 306n4, 314
32:33 165

Leviticus
6:2 422
11:2 407n25
11:45 448
13 338, 344
13:11 242
13:25 242
13:37 338, 339-42, 345
13:44 342
13:45f 242
15:18 199
15:31 203
18 242
18:13 342
19:3 412
19:12 69
19:3 412
19:14 63
19:18 63, 65, 66, 285, 336, 370, 386
19:32-34 63
19:34 378
19:39 63
20 242
20:10 355
21:9 355
23:14 345
25:1 63
25:17 63
25:29-30 336
25:36 63
25:43 63
26:3 407n25

Numbers
1:51 366
9:2 348, 353n29
9:2-3 354n29
9:3 348, 353n29, 354
9:11 336, 358, 360
14:2 418
15:20 336n3
16 164

19:12 352
24:17 214
28:2 46, 347
32:14-15 164

Deuteronomy
1:1 44
4:6 395
4:7 62n17
4:30 409
5:16 412
6:4 419
6:4-5 386
6:5 64n22, 65n27
6:6 67
6:7 66, 432
12:5 436, 437
13:7 64n24
15:2-3 336
15:3 358
15:8 359
15:9 313, 359
16:2 344
16:8 345
17 344
17:8ff 343
17:9 343
17:10-11 343n16
17:11 343n16
18:15 101n86
21:8-22 410
21:15-17 410
21:18 411
21:18-22 411
22:6 412
22:21 355
23:3 242
23:11-12 200
26:13 150n50
29:18 165
34:5 419

Joshua
9:27 242
15:61-62 211

2 Samuel
7:1-14 205
7:14 450
23:1 310

2 Kings
4:33 434
15:29 214
23:25 65n27

1Chronicles
17:13 450
17:16 408n29
29:10 454
29:18 63n22

Job
1:21 449
25:3 310

Psalms
1:4-6 165
1:5-6 163
7:9 163
9:16 165
15:1-5 61, 385
15:5 422
16:8 58
18:44 67
22:4 310
34:21 163
37:12-21 163
37:32 163
37:40 163
68:19 72-73
68:20 439
92:7 165
104:35 165
106:16-18 164
110 356n34
110:1 102
112:7 74, 84, 316, 357
113:2 449
113:5b 77-78, 83, 438
113:5-6 315, 328-29
119:12 454
119:126 84
145:20 165

Proverbs
3:2 326

3:6 60
10:2 163
11:9 163
11:31 163
12:3 163
12:13 163
25:7 307, 328
27:1 441

Ecclesiastes
3:4-5 81, 82
4:1 68
5:5 69

Isaiah
1:28 166
3:9 164
5:1-7 100n83
5:16 448
6:3 456
8:14 139, 214
11:1 206, 214
13:9 166
23:18 68
26:20 434
33:15 61, 385
53:12 97n77, 98n77, 456
55:7 172
56:1 61, 385
56:7 29
61:1-2 215

Jeremiah
3:17 436
48:10 68

Lamentations
4:6 164

Ezekiel
3:18-19 166
18:21-23 172
18:27 172
20:41 448
33:8-9 166
33:11 166
36:22-28 448
38:23 448
43:7 436

Daniel
2:20 448
2:27-45 448
7:2-8:17 448
7:13-14 448

7:14 450

Joel
2:27 436

Amos
5:4 385
9:11-12 205

Micah
4:8-9 207
6:8 61, 385
7:2 203

Habakkuk
2:4 61, 385

Malachi
3:16 436
4:1 166

Ezra
10:8 163

Nehemiah
13:3 163

The Apocrypha
Tobit
4:3 412
4:15 20, 368
6:14 412
13:6 172
13:8[6] 162

Wisdom of Solomon
(=Wisdom)
5:14-15 163
11:23 407n27, 412n42
12:10 412n42
17:2

Sirach
5:6 166
7:34 81n32
9:11-12 166
11:17 203
12:4 163
12:6 166
13:4 420
13:7 163
15:1 63n21
16:13 163
17:24-25 407n27
21:10 166

24 52n47, 395
26:29 421
27:30-28:7 449
28:2 449
33:14 163
33:19-33 410
41:5 163
43:33 203
44:16 412n42
51 443
51:10 454
51:12 443
51:21-35 442

Prayer of Manasseh
8 173n42, 412n42
8-14 407n27
13 412n42

1 Maccabees
1:10 162
1:34 162
2:44 162
2:48 162
2:62 162
3:5-6 162
3:8 162
3:15 162
3:18 407n28
3:60 407n28
4:30 454
5:9ff 220
6:21 162
7:5 162
7:9 162

2 Maccabees
6:18 63n21
2:21 156
8:1 156
14:38 156

3 Maccabbees 162
1:10 162

4 Macabees
5:4 63n21

Christian Scriptures
Matthew
1:18-25 210
2:74 381
3:2 407
3:7-10 398, 415n50
3:9 5n12

3:10 95
3:12 95
4:17-22 238
5:2 282
5:3 407n28
5:3-11 394
5:9 29n106
5:17 13n46, 28n102, 285
5:17-20 66, 282
5:18 218
5:19 330n30
5:25 235
5:27-30 434
5:42 29n104
5:43-48 74n10
5:44 25
5:47 162
6:5-6 434-35
6:5-15 447
6:9 98
6:11 72
6:12 391
6:25-34 72, 73n7, 441
6:34 74
7:1 83n37
7:11 421m72
7:12 13n46, 20n67, 363, 371, 381, 386, 369
7:21 101
7:22-23 441
8:5 217, 251
8:11 5n12
8:19-22 75
8:22 408
9:1 217
9:9-11 251
9:37-38 83
10:3 204
10:5 5n12
10:5-6 399n7
10:18 5n12
10:34-36 104
10:35-45 434
11:6 394
11:11-12 95
11:13 95
11:14 101n86
11:19 160
11:21-23 253
11:24 164
11:25-27 99
11:25-30 76n17, 105
11:27 439, 450
11:28-30 76, 97
12:28-34 434

12:29 97n77
12:30 84, 85, 92, 97, 98
13:12 327n21
13:24-30 237
13:27 237
13:29 327n21
13:30 95
13:32 327n21
13:52 224
13:53-58 253
13:55 151n55, 246
14:1-2 100n86
14:19 454
15:24 399n7
16:2-3 79n28
16:13-14 100n86
16:15-19 101n86
16:17-19 101n86
16:17 450
17:24-27 218
17:24-27 434
18:4 78, 330n30
18:12-14 399
18:15-18 436
18:15-22 399
18:17 399
18:20 71n1, 92, 435-39
18:23-35 399
18:32-35 252
19:1 219
19:12 220
20:1-15 237
20:12-14 90
21:14 244
21:21-31 237
21:23-27 76
21:31 241
21:32 172
21:33-46 100
21:43 5n12
22 65, 172
22:1-14 5n12
22:3-4 171
22:9 171
22:10f 251n118
22:34-40 370
22:34-44 285, 386
22:35f 63
22:36-39 64
22:41-46 102
23 67n31, 400
23:5 68, 69
23:6 69
23:12 78, 330
23:23 69

23:34 88n56
23:37 85n45
23:38-39 5n12
24:22-26 104n95
24:36 96
24:37 96
24:45 234
24:45-47 425
24:45-51 423
24:48-49 423
25:14-15 423
25:14-28 424
25:14-30 237, 252, 405n18,
  423
25:26-30 423
25:29 424
25:30 424
26:7 251n118
26:16 221
26:18 211
26:29 454
26:52 19n65
27:46 451
27:56 253
27:57 252
27:61 253

Mark
1:2-8 415n50
1:4-5 202
1:15 127
1:16-17 238
1:16-34 434
1:19-20 238
1:19f 251
1:21 445
1:22 360 360n45
1:27 360 360n45
1:35 446
1:40 242
2:1-3:6 170n36
2:1ff 219
2:6 170
2:13-17 434
2:15-17 171
2:16 160
2:17 170-175
2:18-22 434
2:20 224
2:23-27 387
2:23-28 434
2:27 19n64
3:1-6 434
3:13-19 218
3:18 204

3:28 97n77
4 20n72
4:2 401
4:33-34 401
4:55 327n21
5:22f 251
5:44 445
6:1-6 253
6:1-6a 415n50
6:3 213, 246, 247n104
6:5-15 445
6:7-13 415n50
6:14 100n86
6:14b-15 100n86
6:17-29 399
6:21 231-32
6:26 251n118
6:61 454
7 337
7:1-11 445
7:1-23 434
8:7 454
8:27-28 100n86
9:1 6, 127
9:2-10 128n24
9:33-50 263
9:38-41 98n78, 434
10:1 219, 220
10:2-12 220
10:17-22
10:42-44 425
10:45 456
10:46 244
11:3 222
11:11 445
11:11-12 220
11:17 29n109, 421, 445
11:22-25 445
11:27-12:12 49n37
11:27-33 49n37
12:1-12 100
12:13-17 434
12:28-33 65, 234
12:29-31 28n100
12:30 63n22
12:35 64n22
12:35-37 102, 356
12:38 67
12:39 69
13 25
13:21-23 104n95
13:32 6, 96n72, 439, 450
14:1 222
14:3 242, 221, 252,
  50n115

14:12 221
14:12-16 205, 250n115
14:13-14 222
14:25 454
14:32-42 445
14:36 450
14:41 162
14:48 244n93
15:1 231
15:34 450
15:40 253
15:43 252
15:47 253
16:1 253

Luke
1:5 215
1:7 19n65
1:32-33 415
1:34 215
1:36 215
1:78 216
1:80 215
2:19 210
2:24 245n96, 246n100
2:38 203
2:46-47 94
2:51 210
3:1 142
3:1-15 142
3:7-9 398
3:9 95
3:10-14 415n50
3:17 95
3:21 446
4:3 216
4:16-29 216
4:16-30 253
4:17-21 415n50
4:25-27 415n50
4:28-30 415n50
4:31 217
4:42 446
5:1-11 415n50
5:11 238
5:12 102n89, 217
5:16 446
5:29 234
5:32 173
6:12 446
6:15 204
6:20-22 394
6:24 421
6:24-25 127
6:27-38 263

6:28b 445
6:31 20n67, 363n1, 369, 386
6:33 162
6:35 421
6:37 83n37
6:46 102
7:1-2 217
7:5 212
7:6 102n89
7:11 253
7:16 101n86
7:22 215
7:30 151n55
7:34 160
7:36 142n18, 218
7:37-39 241
7:40-44 142
7:41-43 237n58
7:49 142n20
7-50-52 142
8:2 253
8:3 252, 254
8:10 327n21
8:18 101n86
9:7 100n86
9:7b-8 100n86
9:16 454
9:18-19 101n86
9:18 100n86, 446
9:20 101n86
9:28-29 446
9:49-50 98n78
9:57-62 75
9:59 412
9:60 408
9:61 102n89
10:1-20 415n50
10:2 83
10:12 164
10:13-15 253
10:17-20 415n50
10:18 127, 128n24
10:21-22 76n17, 99, 105, 446
10:22 450
10:25 63n21
10:25-28 65
10:27 63n22
10:30 244n93
10:38-42 250
11:1 142n18, 446
11:1-4 447
11:3 72
11:20 97

11:21-22 97, 98n77
11:23 84, 85, 92, 97, 98
11:37 142n18
11:45 63n21, 142n20
11:45-52 151n55
11:47 69
11:49 88n56
12:16-21 237
12:22-31 72
12:35-38 425
12:42-48 234
12:45-48 423
12:49-53 104
12:56 79n28
12:58 235
13:31ff 218
13:32 219
13:34 85n45
14 171-72
14:1-3 330
14:1-6 251
14:3 151n55
14:7 142n20
14:7-10 330
14:7-17 171
14:11 78, 330
14:15-24 421
14:21 244
14:24 171
15:1-2 160, 170, 399, 414
15:1-3 402
15:1-32 237
15:3-7 399
15:11-32 402, 413n45, 423
15:18 409n36
15:21 409n36
15:24 408
15:32 408
16:1-8 234, 421n72
16:1-9 252
16:1-12 237n58
16:8 220
16:16 13n46
16:17 66
16:19-31 421
16:20 244
17:7 237
17:7-10 425
17:12 242
17:23 104n95
18:1-8 421n72
18:2 235
18:9-14 142n18
18:14 78, 330
18:41 102n89

19:1-10 234, 251, 415
19:7 160
19:11 424
19:11-27 403-14, 416
19:12 414, 416, 424
19:13 417, 424
19:14 414, 422
19:14-15a 424
19:14-30 414
19:15 417
19:15-19 417
19:15b-25 424
19:16-17 407
19:17 407, 419
19:20 408, 417
19:21-22 422
19:24a 414
19:24 412
19:25 413
19:26 405, 424
19:27 417, 414, 422, 424
19:28-40 415
19:29 220, 413
19:30 410, 412
19:31 413
19:39 142
20:9-19 100
20:41-44 102
20:46 67, 69
22:15 221
22:17 454
22:18 454
22:19 454
22:29 450
22:32 446
22:40-44 446
24:10 253
24:13-35 106n101
24:18 208
24:30 454

John
1:28 219, 220
1:28-42 216
1:38 218
2:1 253, 254
2:13-17 216
2:16 29n109, 421
2:23 218
2:23-24 216
3:1ff 218, 252
4:3 216
4:26 253
5:3 244
6:14 101n86

7 218
7:2-3 218
7:6-8 219
7:14 219
7:50 252
7:53-8:11 434
9:1 244
10:1 244n93
10:11 237
10:31-36 100
10:40-42 220
11 221
11:1 250n115
11:52 85n45
12:1 220, 222
12:2 252, 251n118
13:1 221
14:2 29n108
18 253
18:11 19n65
18:28 221
18:39-40 221
19:25 208, 253
19:31 221, 222
19:36 221
19:38-39 218
19:39 252
20:1 253
20:28 22n81

Acts
1:6-7 415
1:7 96n72
1:13 204, 212
2 356n34
2:17 202
2:23 162
2:29 196
2:33-34 356n34
2:36 415
2:38 203
2:40 203
2:44ff 201
2:46 223n80
3:2 244
3:18-21 415
3:22 101n86
4:5 231
4:24-28 415
4:31 436
4:43ff 201
5:4 202
5:5 146n34
5:17 154
5:34 218

5:34-39 143
5:35-38 104
5:36-37 126
6:1 202
6:2-6 202
6:7 201
7:37 101n86
8:2 203
10:36 19n65
12:1-17 204
12:12ff 202
12:17 206
14:11 227n8
15:15-18 205
15:29 386
18:3 145n31
20:22-28:30 273n51
21:5ff 203
21:22 206
21:38 103
22:3 24, 143, 286n80
22:12 203
23:6 153n59
24:5 157, 274
24:2 274
24:12 274
24:17-18 274

Romans
1:3 263, 264
2:14-15 375
6:1-11 439
8 439
8:15 450
12:8-13:7 78-80
12:11 79-80, 82
12-14 263, 264
12:15 80, 81nn31-32, 82
12:17 264
12:19-21 78n25
12:21 264
13:1-7 82
13:8-10 264, 386
13:9 370
13:10 20n69, 371, 378
13:11 264
14:17-19 19n69
15:25-28 273n53
16:7 264

1 Corinthians 277-79
1:11-12 279
1:24 27n97
1:27 438
3:22 273

4:12 145n31
4:17 261
5:3-5 438
7 262
7:1-5 296n17
7:8 278
7:10 264, 274
7:10-11 262
7:12 262
7:15 19n65
8:10 296n17
9:5 267, 273n51
9:6 145n31, 273n51
9:14 262, 274, 278
9:15 278
9:19-23 81n31
9:21 162
10:16 454
11:2-16 296n17
11:23 261, 262n26, 263, 264, 274
11:23-24 263, 264
11:24 274, 454
11:25 274
12:14-26 296n17
13:2 278
13:9-11 259n11
14:16 454
14:37 274
15:1-5 267
15:3 261, 262n26, 263
15:7 204
15:5-7 273
15:28 429
16:1-4 273n53

2 Corinthians
5:16 259n13
5:17 259n13
8:2-4 273n53
8:9 251n117
9:3-15 273n53
11:4 288n83
11:26 244n93
12:11 266n39
16:1-4 273n53

Galatians 266, 279-84
1:1 269, 282n74
1:4 264, 284
1:6 288n83
1:7 279
1:7-8 282
1:8 270
1:9 270

1:12 264, 267
1:12-13 267
1:14 145, 337
1:17 203
1:18 264, 268
1:18-19 268
1:19 204
1:22 146
2:3 269
2:4 268-69
2:5 269
2:6 269
2:6-9 268
2:6-19 279
2:7-9 272
2:9 206, 264, 268, 269, 270-72
2:11 270
2:12, 271-72
2:13 273
2:14 163
2:15 162
2:15-16 174
2:17 282
2:20 282n74
3:3 268n44, 284
3:5 268n44
3:7 283
3:10 280
3:11-12 62
3:13 280, 282n74
3:14 268n44
3:21 268n44
3:22 280
3:25 280
4:4 279, 263, 264, 280-81, 282
4:1-3 259n11
4:4-5 279
4:5 280-81
4:6 450
4:10 279, 283
5:1 280
5:11 286n82
5:14 264, 284-87, 370, 386
6:2 264, 281-86, 370
6:12 272, 279
6:14 282n74
6:15 280
6:16 283, 284
6:17 282n74
11:23-24 287
12:11-18 272n49

Ephesians

4:15 327n22

Philippians
3:5 337
3:5-6 144

Colossians
3:13 264
4:2 264
11:23-24 264

1 Thessalonians
2:9 145n31
2:15 279
4-5 263
4:15-16 264, 274
5:6 264

2 Timothy
4:6-8 273n51

James
2:8 370
2:12 266
4:10 78

Jude
7 164
14-15 127n22

Revelation
21 448
20:7-10 449

Dead Sea Scrolls
1QH (=*Hodayot*) 103
3.19-23 391
4.27-29 103
5.12-6:18 394
6.6 172
6.15 215
8.6 215
8.10 215
9.24-25 77

1QpHab (=*Habakkuk Peset*) 7, 24n87,
7.1-8 393
7.4-5 103
11.4-8 194

1QM (=*War Scroll*)
3.10-11 199

1QS (=*Rule of the Com-*

munity)
1.12 64n22
1.77ff 201
2.5-18 169
3.2 64n22
3.4ff 202
3.18-4.26 125
4.20 201n28
5.13 200
6.4-5 223
6.6-8 217
6.16-17 200
6.16ff 201
7.6ff 201
9.21-26 79
10.17-20 79
11.1-2 79
13.11 64n22

1QSa (=*Rule of the Con-gregation*) 171
2.3-9 393
2.11-22 223n80

3Q15 (=*Copper Scroll*)
1.1-4.2 199
1.6-4.5 209
1.9-12 195
2.3-4 209
2.13-15 195, 199
4.13-5.14 211
8.1-10.4 220
12.10-13 211

4Q180 (=*Wicked and Holy*) 125

4Q185 (=*A Sapiential Tes-tament*) 395

4Q285 (=*Curse of Milki-resh'*)
2-5 206

4Q434-439 (=*Barki Naf-shi/Grace After Meals*) 442

4Q521 (=*On Resurrection*)
22, 215-216

4Q525 (*Beatitudes*) 394, 395

4QEnoch[c]
(=4QEnc=4Q204)

51 127n22

4QFlorilegium
(=4QFlor=4Q174)
1.10-13 205

4QpIsaᵃ (=Isaiah
Peser=4Q161-65)
161 22-24 210

4QMMT (=More Precepts
of the Torah=4Q394=99)
21-22, 154, 194, 392

4QSᶜᶠ (Cave 4 Fragments
of The Rule of the Commu-
nity=4Q259, 4Q260) 9.15-
10.2 80n30

4QSirot (=Songs of the
Sabbath Sacrifice) 391, 392

7Q5 (Greek Fragments)
223

11QMel
(=Melchizedek=11Q13)
125, 356

11QTemple (The Temple
Scroll=11Q19-20)
45.11 199
46.12 436
46.13-16 200
46.16-17 221
53.16-54.3 215
56.4 343n16
56.20-21 210
58.18 210

CD (=Cairo Damascus
Document)
1.11 393
3.7-10 164
5.7-11 342
6.12ff 206
6.15 220
6.19 220
7.5ff 215
7.15 220
7.16 205
7.19 220
8.21 220
9.1 64n27
9.18ff 206

10.10-13 200
13.11 64n22
19.34 220
20.12 220
21.1 199

**Rabbinic Writtings:
Mishnah, Talmuds, and
Tosephta**

Mishnah
m.Pirqé 'Abot (m.Ab) 39-
40, 46n32
1 39, 306
1:2 40n18, 51n42
1:3 50n40, 407n28, 435n11
1:4-5 41n18
1:6-7 41n18
1:10 240
1:10-11 141n13
1:12 39n15, 308n12,
319n83, 378
1:12-14 37, 306n2
1:13 90n59, 321, 335
1:14 84, 28, 87n52, 92, 335
1:15 40n17, 435
2 20n66, 306
2:1 435n11
2:2 435n11
2:4 87n52
2:4-7 306n2
2:5-8 37
2:5 29, 74n10, 83n37
2:6 311n36
2:7 29, 326, 335, 435
2:8 28, 323, 435n11
2:10 376
2:12 38n11, 40n16, 60, 376
2:13 51n43
2:15 435n11
3:2 435, 439
3:6 435, 439
3:7 333n40
3:12 435n11
3:17-20 37
4:1 435n11
4:2 411
4:4 407n28
4:5 39n14
4:7 412n42
4:16 435n11
4:17 412n42, 435n11
4:22 422n11
5:17 45n30, 435n11
5:22 309, 360

6:1 315n61
8 435n11

m.Abodah Zarah (m.AZ)
2:6 238

m.Arakim (m.Arak)
9:4 336n4

m.Baba Bathra (m.BB)
4:7 234n38

m.Bekorot (m.Bek)
4:4 343

m.Berakot (m.Ber)
1:3 431-32
2:5-7 313n46
4:3-4 361n51
9:3 74n8, 317n74, 357
9:5 65n27

m.Baba Mesiah (m.BMes)
3:10 417
7:4-7:7 237

m.Baba Qamma
(m.BQam)
3:11 384n25
7:7 407

m.Bikkurim (m.Bik)
3:3 240

m.Eduyot (m.Eduy) 12n43
1:1-3 336
1:12-14 313n46

m.Erubin (m.Erub)
13b 43n27

m.Gittin (m.Gitt)
4:3 134n48, 336n4, 359n42
6:2 327n20

m.Hagigah (m.Hag) 46n32
2:2 39n13, 141n13

m.Hullin (m.Hul) 10:1
59n12

m.Kelim (m.Kel)
1:1-3 325
2:2 238

m.Kiddushim (m.Kid)
4:1 242
4:14 240, 241n79

m.Ketubbot (m.Ket)
3.9 383-84
7.10 241n79

m.Kerithot (m.Ker)
1:7 149n48

m.Makkot (m.Mak)
3:1 242

m.Megillah (m.Meg)
1:7 242n85

m.Menahot (m.Men)
13:11

m.Mo ed Katan (m.MK)
3:1 242n85

m.Nedarim (m.Ned)
6:4 238

m.Pe'ah (m.Pe'a)
5:5

m.Pesahim (m.Pes)
6:1-2 351-54

m.Rosh Hashannah
4:1 313n46

m.Sanhedrin (m.Sanh)
3:3 241n79
8:1-5 410
8:3 410
8:5 410n37
10 164

m.Shabbat (m.Shab)
2:5 244n93
6:8 244
7:1 384n25

m.Shekalim (m.Shek)
8.2 117n26

m.Sheviit (m.Shevi)
10:1 307
10:3 18n58, 307, 312n44,
336n4, 358, 359n42

m.Sotah (m.Sot)
1:5 242m85
9:9 244
14a 62

m.Sukkah (m.Suk)
2:7 329
5:4

m.Ta anit (m.Ta an) 321-22
3:8

m.Yadayim (m.Yad)
4:3 323n7

m.Yebamot (m.Yeb)
4:13 242
16:6 361n50

m.Yoma (m.Yoma)
35b 327n19
3:8 449
6:4 231
8:8 412n42

m.Zebahim (m.Zeb)
14:3 242n85
14:4 59n12

Babylonian Talmud

b.Abodah Zarah (b.AZ)
18a 418
20a 150n50

b.Baba Bathra (b.BB)
12a 52n46
121b 321

b.Berakot (b.Ber)
13a-b 407n28
28b 130n33
29a 449
33b 407
34b 54n52
46a 326
60a 74n8, 317n72, 357
63a 60
64a 316n68

b.Baba Msiah (b.BMes)
37a 407
59b 343n14, 360
74a 238
75b 410

87a 242
7:9 244n93

b.Baba Qamma (b.BQam)
46a 384n25
82b 407

b.Besah (=Yom Tob)
(b.Bes)
16a 72n4, 439-40

b.Eduyot (b.Eduy) 41

b.Erubin (b.Erub)
13b 315, 327n19, 329,
360n47, 54a 329n28

b.Hagigah (b.Hag)
3a 323n7
9b 309n26
14b 324n11

b.Hullin (b.Hullin)
92a 232n32

b.Ketubbot (b.Ket)
49b-50a 412
67b 359n43, 417

b.Kiddushin (b.Kid)
29a 240
30a 360
33a 240
34a 388
49a 325n13
61b 410
66a 337n8, 140
82a 241n79

b.Me ilah (b.Me il)
17b 54n55

b.Megillah (b.Meg)
3a 22n79

b.Makkot (b.Mak)
23b-24a 61, 384

b.Nedarim (b.Ned)
55a 316n69
39b 412n42

b.Pesahim (b.Pes)
66a-b 47n33, 349n25,
141n15

115a 337n5
6:1 47n34

b.Sanhedrin (b.Sanh)
17a 329n28, 410
25b 241n79
29a 239n68
51b 355
68a 53n50
68a-72a 410
71b 410
72a 410n37
98a-b 53n50
102a 407n26

b.Shabbat (b.Shab)
14b-15a 41n21
30b 76n20
31a 64, 83n37, 76n18,
315n58, 318n78, 335, 337n7,
364-67, 371, 374, 375, 383-
84, 386-87, 385n79,
62b 325n15
73a-b 387n26
102b 238
104a 407n26
130b 361n50
153a 234n38
154b 314n50

b.Sotah (b.Sot)
22b 67
48b 53n50, 73n6

b.Sukkah (b.Suk)
20a 337
53a 85n44, 86n50, 150n49,
311n36, 331, 335n2, 438n20

b.Ta anit (b.Ta an) 321
23b 452

b.Yebamot (b.Yeb)
78b 242
122a 361n50

b.Yoma (b.Yoma)
35b 306n5, 314n53
85b 313n48
86a 412n42

Jerusalem Talmud
y.Abodah Zarah (y.AZ)
1:9 150n50

y.Berakot (y.Ber.)
1 (72b) 327n19
14b(MS Vatican 133) 74n8,
84n43, 317n73
9:3 (14a) 356

y.Hagigah (y.Hag)
1 323n7
2 324n11
2:2 42n22, 43n26
12:1-2 324n11

y.Ketubbot (y.Ket)
4:8 20n72
7.5 377

y.Nedarim (y.Ned)
9:3 375

y.Pe'ah (y.Pe'a)
1:1 (15d) 64n24
8:8 (21a) 359n43

y.Pesahim (y.Pes) 19n64
6:1 (33a) 339-40, 349

y.Ta anit (y.Taan)
68d 130n34

y.Sanhedrin (y.Sanh)
8:7 410n37

y.Shabbat (y.Shab)
31a 20n66

y.Shevi it (y.Shevi)
10:2 313n47

y.Sotah (y.Sot)
3 323n7
9 326

y.Sukkah (y.Suk)
55b 85n46, 86n48
5:4 150n49, 310n28

y.Terumot (y.Ter)
1:2 388
8:10 407n23

y.Yebamot (y.Yeb)
15:3 20n72

y.Yoma (y.Yoma)
8:5 313n48

Tosefta
t.Baba Bathra (t.BB)
3:5 234n38

t.Berakot (t.Ber.)
2:21 81n31
2:24 335n2
3:7 52n45
4:18 325
6:24 85n44
7:24 335n2

t.Baba Mesiah (t.BMes)
7:5f 237
9:11 237
9:14 234n38

t.Eduyot (t.Eduy)
1:1 336n1

t.Kiddushin (t.Kid)
1:11 239n68, 240

t.Ketubbot (t.Ket)
7.6 377

t.Ma aseroth (t.Ma as)
2:13 237
2:15 237

t.Megillah (t.Meg)
2:41 325
4(3):16 377

t. Negaim (t.Neg)
1:16 338-339

t.Nezikin (t.Nez)
1:1 361n49

t.Pe'ah (t.Pe'a)
2:2 236
4:10 359n43
5:5 after the above

t.Pesahim (t.Pes)
4:1-2 347n22
4:13-14 347n22

t.Sanhedrin (t.Sanh)
2:6 150n50
7:11 120n43, 350n27
13:5 169n34

t.Shabbat (t.Shab)
8:4 325

15:16 306n4, 313n49

t.Sotah (t.Sot)
7:9 323n7
7:12 44n28
13:3 74-5, 361n48

t.Sukkah (t.Suk)
4:2-5 311n33
4:3 86n4:3, 311n34, 330,
335, 438n19
4:4 150n49

t.Ta anit (t.Ta an)
2:12 244n93

Other Rabbinic Writings
Abot de-Rabbi Nathan
(ARN) 306-20
1-11 317-20
4 456n54
12 51n43, 438n20
37 18n56, 350n27

A
2 307n9
11 316n69, 329n26
12 143n22, 306n3, 308n15,
310n27, 311n37, 322,
329n26, 330n31, 332, 306
14 323n8, 419
15 337n7, 367
18 307n9, 323n7
19 307n9
21 307n9
27 75n11, 306n2, 307n9,
308n16,
55 309n25

B
2 307n9
14 325n12
18 307n9
21, 23a 240
22 329n26
23 307n9
24 306n3
26 64, 76n19, 75n13, 308n14,
308n14, 315n57, 368, 376,
383-384
27 306n3, 307n24, 309, 310,
311n37, 312n40, 322,
330n31
27-29 307n9
29 323n8, 367-68, 376

30 376, 60n13
56 25

Agadot Bereshit
29:1 316n71

*Amidah (=Shemoneh
'Esreh)* 412n42, 441-45

Derekh Eretz Zuta
9 329n28

Kallah Rabbati
10:3 368n2

Ma ase Rav Kahana
6 316n69

Midrashim
Genesis Rabbah (GenRab)
1:1 52n47
24:27 375, 384
63:8 407n23
63:10 70n42
71:6 408
76.5 408n29
100:10 417

Exodus Rabbah (ExRab)
2:3 420
5:4 408
45:5 307n6, 315n61,
316n69, 328

Leviticus Rabbah
(LevRab) 69
1 327, 438n21
1:5 77n22, 307n7, 315n62
12 234n38
34 75n15
34:3 91

Numbers Rabbah (Num-
Rab) 418

Deuteronomy Rabbah
(DeutRab)
2:24 409

Ecclesiastes Rabbah
(EccRab)
1:9 68n35
7:2.5 377

Song of Songs Rabbah

(SongRab)
1:4 407n25
4:12 419
7:14 419

Lammentations Rabbah
(LamRab)
18b 322
1:7 407

*Midrash Hillel Beit
Hamidrash* 328n28

*Midrash Mishlei/Midrash
on Proverbs*
6:11 418
20:3 316n69

Midrash R. Akiba
ch. 17 316n71

Midrash Tannaim 358

Midrash Tanhuma 328

Mekhilta d'Rabbi Isma'el
(Mekh) 73n6, 306n4,
313n49, 437
Bahodesh 332n38, 412
Bo 5 348n23
Bo 15:58 323n7
Pisha 326

Mekhilta de R. Shimon Bar
Yohai 324n11

Pesiqta de Rab Kahana
4:7 388n28

Pesiqta Rabbati
22:5 68
44:9 409

Pirqé de R. Eliezer
51:1 316n71

Sifra Leviticus (SifLev)
336n4, 354n31, 350n27, 339
Behar 336n4
Kedoshim 1:1 64n23
Kedoshim 4:12 375, 384
17:6 59
19:18 64

Sifre 85

Sifre Deuteronomy
(SifDeut)
Beha'alotkha 326
13:17 64n24
32 64n22
49 52n48, 64n22
116 359n43
154 343n16
203 344n17
218 410n37, 411
220 410n37
323 378n15
345 409
352 409
357 419

Sifre Numbers (SifNum)
65 348n23
142 348n23

Sifre Zutta 84-85

Sefer Ha-Ma asaiyyot
(SefMa as)
84 368n2
31 368n2

Yalqut Shimeoni 419

Pseudepigrapha to the
Hebrew and Christian
Scriptures

Ahiqar 373
8:88 20n66

Nag Hammadi Apoc-
ryphon of John (ApocJn)
II.1.5-17 183n5

Apocryphal Syriac Psalms
(ApocSyrPss)
155 242

2 Baruch
70-73 127n22

1 Enoch (1En)
1:1 163
1-5 163
1:9 127n22
1:9 167
5:4 163
5:6-7 163
7:9 163

42:1-2 16n51
42 16
98:10-16 167
100:9 167
103:7-8 167

2 Enoch (2En)
61:2 378

4 Ezra (4Ez)
13:29-40 127n22

Gospel of the Egyptians
(GEgyp)
III.2.57.6 144n26

Gospel of Thomas
(GosThom) 278
Logion 6 378
Logion 64 421
Logion 77 87
Logion 95 421

Gospel of the Nazareans
(GNaz) 1
8 423

Jubilees (Jub)
1:12 88n56
5:17-18 407
6:35 162
23:23-24 162
36:9-10 167

Protevangelium of James
(ProtJames)
9:2 213
10:1 215n58 215
17:1-2 213
18:1 213

Psalms of Solomon (Pss-
Sol)
1:1 162
2:1-2 162
2:34 168
3:11-12 168
8:13 163
13:11 168
15:10-13 168
17-18 27n98

Pseudo-Philo/Liber
Antiquiatum Biblicarum
(LAB)

11:12 20
13:3 242
16:3-6 164

Testament of Abraham
(TAb)
11:11 168
13:12 168

Testament of Joseph
3:9 407n26

Testament of Judah (TJud)
24:1-6 127n22

Testament of Levi (TLev)
18:1-10 127n22

Testament of Naphtali
(TNaph)
4:1 164

Sibylline Oracles (SibOr)
3:49 127n22

Syriac Menander
250-51 138n5

INDEX OF
GREEK AND LATIN SOURCES

Athenaeus
Deipnosophistai (Deipn)
4.156c-159d   179

Aristotle
Politics (Pol)
1.5.10   240
4.3.11-12   240
6.2.7   240
7.8.2   240

Arrian
Discourses (Diss)
3.22   184

Cassius Dio
52.34   373n8

Cicero
De Republica (Rep)
2.22   240
De Officiis (Off)
1.42   240
Ad Brutus (Brut)
73   240

Columella
De Rustica
11.1.3-29   234
12.1.1-6   234

Dio Chrysostomos
Orations (Or)
7.110   240
7.112f   239n68

Diogenes Laertius
*Lives of Eminent Philoso-
phers* (LEP)
1.19   181
1.20   180
1.36   372
2.20   308n19

2.22   308n19
2.48   308n19
6.70-71   179n13
6.99   188
6.103-5   180
6.104   179,182
7.2   182

Herodotus
Histories
2.167   239
3.142   372,373n8
7.136   372

Horace
Satires (Sat) 1.4.10   76

Isocrates
Nicocles
24   373n8
49   373n8
61   373n8
Panegyricus
81   373n8

Josephus
The Jewish War (War)
1.5.2 (§110)   337n6
1.7.2 (§143)   115n15
1.26.2 (§522)   418
1.473   231
1.667   231
2.2.1-7 (§14-38)   417n55
2.2.1 (§14)   416
2.2.1 (§16)   416
2.2.3 (§22)   416
2.6.1 (§80-100)   417n55
2.6.3 (§93)   417
2.7.3 (§111)   417
2.8.4 (§297)   337n6
2.11   217
2.14-16   231
2.17.3-4 (§§411-17)   337n6

2.24   217n66,231
2.64   231
2.118   141,157
2.119-166   193
2.122   200
2.137-142   200
2.140   82
2.162   146n33
2.163   147n39
2.237   231
2.253   244n93
2.258-260   103
2.259-64   125n15
2.287   234
2.316   231
2.318   231
2.405   232
2.410   231
2.411   231
2.433   217
2.451   151-52
2.451-53   152
2.608   253
2.626-31   151
2.627-31   148n42
2.628   151-52
2.635   238
3.54-58   220
3.173   251
3.508   238
3.520   238
4.134   244n93
4.135   229n20
4.145   195
4.159-60   149n44
4.209-15   149n44
4.239   229
4.241   229
4.406   244n93
4.419-39   229n20
4.451   229n22
5.145   196,198
6.285-99   125n15

6.312-15 125n15
6.387   209
18.5.2 (§116-19) 399
18.5.4 (§136) 399
21.571   235
Jewish Antiquities (Ant)
1.14   147n39
7.66   251
7.340   251
11.78   251
13.10.6 (§162) 337n6
13.11.1-3 (§§372-76) 111n2
13.13.5 (§§379-83) 111n2
13.16.2 (§408) 337n6
13.171   157
13.172   147n39
13.288-98 140n10
13.289   140n9
13.292   140n9
13.296   140n9
13.318-319 214
14.4.2 (§§58-59) 115n15
14   141n12
14.159   244n93
14.160   244
14.165   244
14.168   243
14.172-76 140n12,141
15.3-4   141n12
15.3-4 370   141n12
15.4   140n12
15.268   228n11
15.390   249,251
16.3.1 (§69) 418n61
16.398   147n39
17.9.3 (§219) 416
17.9.3 (§220) 416
17.9.3 (§223) 416
17.9.4 (§227) 416
17.9.5 (§237) 417
17.9.5 (§239) 417
17.11.1 (§300) 417
17.11.1 (§302) 417
17.11.4 (§320) 417
17.13.1 (§339) 417
17.159   244n93
17.318   231
18.1.3 (§12) 337n6
18.1.4 (§§16-7) 111n2
18.3   147n39
18.4   141,193
18.10   141n16
18.13-25 193
18.23   141
18.27   248

18.85-87   104,125n15
18.106-107 220
18.117   203
18.252   231
20.9.1 (§201) 337n6
20.97-98   104
20.118-36 243
20.123   231
20.213   143n24,149n46
20.219ff 250
20.223   143n24
Contra Apion (Apion)
2.27 (§208) 422
Life
1-6   194
8-9   145n29
9   231
9-10   194
11-12   194
12   147n36,194
21   148,152n57
22   152n57
32-39   232
33   231nn25-26,232
38 (§191) 337
43-45   232
63   151
71-73   237
73   151
119   231
123-25   232
134   231
189-332 151
191-92   148
191-332 148n40
193   149n45
193-96   149n43
194   231
197   150
204   149n46
217   152
217-18   153
226-27   153
229   152,153
246   231
277   152
278   231
302   152
336   153
429   147

Julian the Apostate
Orations (Or)
1.19-20 184
6.38   184

6.69   183
6.71   183
6.103   184
6.182C   181
6.182C-D 181,183
6   184
6.187C   182,183
6.187D-188A 181
6.192A   179
6.193D   179
6.201A   183
34   186
Letter of Aristeas
207 372,378
228 64

Livy
20.2.25 240

Lucian
Dialogue with Meretricus
(Dial Meret)
6.293   239n68
Demonax 184
De morte Peregrini 184

Meleager
Greek Anthology (Anth
Graec)
7.417-19 188n44

Paulus
Digest
50.17.1 388n27

Philo
Hypothetica
7 20
Apologia pro Iudaeis
1 217n66
Legum Allegoriarum (Leg
All)
3.164 73
Questiones Genesii (Quest
Gen)
§65 413n44
De Decalogo (Decal)
23 (§111-20) 412
23 (§119)   412n39
154 385
De Specialibus Legibus
1.1 385
De Abrahamo (Abrah)
26 (274) 413n44

Plato
The Republic (Resp)
2.396-371e 240
Theaetetus
160D 375
Apology of Socrates
(Apology)
29d-30d 75-6

Polybius
Histories
12.4.5   184n17

Sophocles
Antigone
518-525 74n10

Strabo
16.2.29 188n42
16.2.45 238
Suidae Lexicon
2.177   184n25

Vitruvius
On Architecture
5.1.5 303

Xenophon
Oeconomicus (Oec)
4.1-4 240
Cyropaedia (Cyr)
8.2.5 248

Patristic Sources

Augustine
De civitate dei
19.1.2-3 180
De sacra virginitate
4 215n59
Sermo
291.5 215n59
*De Sermone Domini in
Monte secundum
Matthaeum*
2.74 381n22

Clement of Alexandria
*Adumbratio in epistula
Iudae* 213

Cyril of Alexandria
Patrologia Graeca (PG)
72.876   405n18

Didache (Did)
1.2   374
8.1   224
12.3f   239n68

Didascalia Apostolorum
5.12-18   224n83

Epiphanius
Panarion (AdvHaer)
28.7.6 213n53
29.4.3 213n53
30.1-30.33 210
51:26   224n83
78.7.7 207n37

Eusebius
Ecclessiastical History
(HE)
1.7.14   214
2.1.2   213
2.23.4-6 207
2.23.7 207
2.23.8-9 207
2.23.10-19 207
3.11   208
4.22.4   208-209
4.22.5   209
4.22.7   209
5.23   224
20.200   207
Praeparatio Evangelica
(PE)
8.6   217n66
Theophania
22   423

Gregory of Nyssa
In diem natalem Christi
215n59

Hippolytus of Rome
De Benedictiones Moysis
26:1a   213n53

Ignatius of Antioch
Letter to Polycarp
3:1-2 79
Letter to the Ephesians
18.2 215n58

Jerome
De viris illustribus
2   204n32

Justin Martyr
Dialogue with Trypho
(DialTrypho)
45.4 215n4
88.8 241

Origen
Contra Celsum (c. Cels.)
6.36   240-41
Commentary on John
(Comm Jn)
I 4   213n53
Commentary on Matthew
(Comm Matt) 405n18

Theophilactus
Patrologia Graeca (PG)
123.1029 405n18

Pseudo-Clement
Recognitiones
I.65.2   144n26

Victorinus of Pettau
De fabrica mundi
3   224n83

Papyri

Berlin Papyrus
846 409n36
8502 19.12 138n5

Oxyrhynchus Papyrus
(POxy)
5.840.10-11 138n5,153n58
2.264   239n69

Confucius
Analects
15.23 373

INDEX OF
MODERN AUTHORS

Ahad Ha-Am, 379n18
Abrahams, I. 379-80n18
Adan-Bayewitz, D. 238n65, 301
Adler, A. 184n25
Adriaen, M. 139n6
Ahlstrom, S. E. 121n2
Albeck, C. 432n7
Albeck, H. 70n42, 338n9
Alberktson, B. 442n27
Alexander, P. 20n71, 34n3, 315nn 59-60, 318n79, 461
Alföldy, G. 227, 233
Allison, D. C. 73n6, 256n2, 263, 265n36, 275, 370n4, 436n15, 447n35, 448n37
Alon, G. 112n5, 116
Alt, A. 237n59
Amir, Y. 58n9, 156n2
Applebaum, S. 225
Argyle, A. W. 360n45
Arnold, 268n44
Attridge, H. W. 147n39
Audet, J.-P. 453n49, 455n51
Aune, D. 128n25, 179n14, 192n55, 398n4
Avery-Peck, A. J. 440n22
Avigad, N. 9n28, 114-115, 117n30, 118n36
Avi-Yonah, M. 120n41, 301n26

Baarda, T. 20n70
Bacher, B. Z. 311n35, 315n60
Bacher, W. 77n22, 78n23, 88n55, 309n26, 344n17, 345n18
Badian, E. 251n118, 252n120
Bagatti, B. 212n51, 214, 293n6
Bailey, K. E. 401n12, 407n24&n26, 408n31, 412n40, 413n43
Balch, D. L. 179n14, 185n29
Baldi, D. 195n4, 197n10, 208n40, 212n50, 215n61, 224n85
Ballance, M. H. 118n35
Bamberger, B. J. 73n7
Bammel, E. 399n8
Baras, Z. 97n75

Bar Ilan, M. 54n55
Bar-Kochva, B. 118n31
Baron, S. W. 232n28
Barr, J. 68n37, 122n5, 123n8, 451n41
Bassler, J. M. 142n21
Batey, R. R. 245n96, 248, 250, 253n127, 291n1
Bauckham, R. J. 24n91, 213n54
Baumbach, G. 337n6
Baumgarten, A. I. 144n28, 337n6
Baur, F. C. 258, 260, 266
Beardslee, W. A. 276n61
Beer, G. 143n23
Behm, J. 412n42
Beker, J. C. 126n20, 133n44
Ben-David, A. 63-64n22, 225, 236, 237n61
Ben-Dov, M. 112n3, 117n26
Benseler, G. 151n55
Ben-Shalom, I. 336n4, 338n9, 347n20
Berger, K. 190, 192n55, 441n26
Betz, H. D. 267n41, 435n13
Betz, O. 201n26 & n28, 202n29, 279n69, 282n72, 283
Bickerman, E. 120n46, 134
Bientenhard, H. 244n92
Billerbeck, P. 81n31, 83n37, 84n39, 182n22, 240n75, 330n29
Black, M. 198n13, 223n82, 293n9
Blenkinsopp, J. 57-58n8
Bliss, F. J. 197
Bloch, J. 123-124n11, 131n39
Bloch, M. S. 67n32
Blomberg, C. L. 401n11, 413n45, 414n47
Boccaccini, G. 129n26
Böcher, O. 23
Bockmühl, K. 211n45
Borchardt, K. 235n47
Borg, M. J. 127n23, 157n10, 397n1, 401n10
Boring, E. 398n4
Bornkamm, G. 260, 275, 412n40
Bousset, W. 57-58n8, 65, 66n28, 130n32
Bouyer, L. 431n6

Bovon, F. 413n45
Bowman, J. W. 245n96
Box, G. H. 130n31
Braaten, C. E. 259n14
Branham, J. R. 298n20
Branscomb, H. 245n96
Braun, H. 201n27, 206n34
Brawley, R. L. 405n17
Brewer, D. I. 17n55
Brinsmead, B. H. 285n78
Brock, N. 447n35
Broer, I. 406n21
Broshi, M. 23
Brown, C. 161n22
Brown, D. 381n23
Brown, R. E. 221n78, 447n35
Brownlee, W. H. 215n62
Bruce, F. F. 265, 285n78
Brunt, P. A. 226n3, 227n9, 236n56
Buber, M. 58n9, 67nn32&33, 105n100
Buchanan, G. W. 246n99, 250n117, 252
Büchler, A. 3, 10, 75n11, 76n20, 91n63,
    116n21, 138n5, 232, 240n75
Bultmann, R. 3, 11, 35n5, 259-60, 265,
    267n40, 275, 380n20, 404n15, 406n20,
    415n49, 446n33
Burford, A. 239nn68-9, 240n74, 246n103,
    249
Burridge, R. A. 35n5

Caird, G. B. 124n12
Calvin, J. 405n18
Capes, D. B. 259n14
Capper, B. J. 201n28
Carlston, C. E. 406n20, 414n46
Carras, G. 146n32
Carroll, J. T. 142n19, 416n51
Case, S. J. 248, 299n23
Casey, M. 156n4
Casper, B. 406n21
Cassetti, P. 451n41
Cave, C. H. 231n27
Cave, F. H. 231n27
Chambers, E. 298n21
Charles, R. H. 122, 130n32
Charlesworth, J. H. 9n28, 15n48, 30n110,
    33, 110n1, 124n14, 125, 129n26, 155n65,
    157n9, 171n39, 199n20, 206n35, 225n1,
    231n25, 236, 291-2n2, 294n10, 389n1,
    397n1
Chen, D. 197n9
Chernick, M. 350n26
Cipolla, C. M. 235n47
Clark, K. W. 238n63

Cohan, A. A. 96n71
Cohen, S. J. D. 111n2, 112n6, 138n5,
    139n6&n8, 148n41, 152n56, 157n6,
    343n13, 361n52
Cohn, N. 136n54
Collins, J. J. 22n76, 119n39, 124n14,
    125nn17-19, 129n26
Contbeare, F. C. 373n9
Conzelmann, H. 81n31
Cornfield, G. 229
Cosgrove, C. H. 268n44
Coulet-Cazé, M.-O. 179n13, 180nn16-18,
    184n27
Cranfield, C. E. B. 246n102
Creed, J. M. 404n14
Crossan, D. 177, 188-9, 227n4, 291, 397n1,
    401n11, 402n13, 421n71
Cullmann, O. 202n29, 435n13

Dalman, G. 198, 370n5, 453n48
Danby, H. 312nn42-43, 315n65
D'Angelo, M. R. 453n48
Daniélou, J. 207n36, 224n84, 427n1, 457n55
Danziger, A. 3n1,
Darlow, T. H. 57-58n8
Dar, S. 236
Daube, D. 120n45, 133, 134n45
Davies, D. 73n6
Davies, M. 120n46
Davies, P. R. 68n37
Davies, W. D. 117n28, 129n29-30, 130n35,
    132, 261, 274n54, 275, 277n65, 283n76,
    370n4, 436n15, 442n27, 447n35, 448n37
Deines, R. 146n32
Deissmann, A. 409n36
de Jonge, M. 397n1, 401n10
Delcor, M. 203n30
Delitzsch, F. 8, 9, 33, 389-90
Dembitz, L. N. D. 242n80
Dernberg Y. 319n84, 320n85
Derrett, J. D. M. 413n43, 419n65
de Ste. Croix, G. E. M. 226n3, 227n6, 228,
    235
de Vaux, R. 116n23, 200n23
Dibelius, M. 189n51, 397n2, 398n5, 404n14
Dickie, A. 197
Dietzfelbinger, C. 435n13
Diez-Macho, A. 451
Dihle, A. 74n10, 363-64n1, 372nn6-7,
    379n16, 380n19
di Lella, A. 443n30
Dimant, D. 343n14
Dodd, C. H. 406n21, 414n47, 423n78
Donahue, J. R. 161n19

Doty, W. G. 276n61
Downing, F. G. 177, 178n11, 185-6, 189n49, 292
Driver, S. R. 437n18
Drury, J. 404n15
Dudley, D. R. 183n23, 188nn42-3
Dugmore, C. W. 441n26
Dunbabin, K. 296n17
Dungan, D. L. 256n2, 261-3, 275, 284n77
Dunn, J. D. G. 161n21, 261, 265, 267n41, 273-4n53
Dupont, J. 434n10, 451n41

Eddy, S. 119n39
Edersheim, A. 377n14
Edwards, D. R. 228, 235, 238n64
Egger, V. 181n19
Ehrlich, A. B. 333n39
Eisenman, R. H. 216n63
Elbogen, I. 10, 441n26
Ellicott, J. 382n24
Ellis, E. E. 275n59, 375n13, 399n6, 415n48
Eltester, W. 442n27, 442n27
Engelstad, E. 298n20
Epstein, Y. N. 314n54
Evans, C. A. 4n5, 320n86, 405n17, 406n19, 420n69

Falk, H. 8, 9, 157n10, 461
Farmer, W. R. 276n62, 397n1
Fausset, A. R. 381n23
Feldman, L. 141n13, 149n46, 337n6
Fenn, R. 12n45
Fenn, W. 123n9
Ferguson, E. 179n14, 185n29
Fiensy, D. A. 231n25
Fiey, J. M. 444n31
Finkel, A. 436n15, 451n41
Finkelstein, L. 63-64n22, 64n24, 117n28, 138n3, 229, 230n23, 343n16, 344n17, 354n31
Finley, M. I. 236n56
Fischel, H. A. 190n53, 357n37
Fitzmyer, J. A. 194n2, 369n3, 404n15, 408n31, 414n47, 420n66, 451
Fleischer, E. 51n43, 442n26
Flusser, D. 7, 41n19, 71n1-3, 78n23 & n25, 80n30, 81n31&n33, 83n36, 84n39, 89n57, 90n61, 91n63, 92n64, 95n70, 96n73, 97n75, 98n79, 99n82, 101n87, 103n93, 104n94&n96&n97, 105n98, 220, 312n39, 314n51, 327n24, 356n34, 401n12, 436n16, 438n21, 447n35, 456n53
Foerster, G. 113n8, 118n35

Forkman, G. 163n26
Fox, M. 440n25
Fraenkel, Y. 306n1, 312n312, 319n84
France, R. T. 401n11
Fränkel, Y. 36n6
Frayne, J. M. 226n3
Freedman, D. N. 346n19
Freedman, H. 408n32
Frey, J.-B. 119n38
Freyne, S. 225n2, 235, 236n52, 237n58, 399-400n1
Friedmann, M. 68n38, 345n18
Friedrich, G. 49n37
Frizzell, L. 436n15, 451n41
Fuchs, M. Z. 311n35
Fuller, R. H. 22n80, 127n23
Funk, R. W. 276n62
Furfey, P. H. 245n96, 247nn106&108
Furnish, V. P. 256n1, 258n9, 259n12, 260n18, 264n31, 275
Fusco, V. 404n15

Gafni, I. 345n18, 349n25
Gager, J. 227n3
García Martínez, F. 125n18
Garlington, D. 162n24
Garnsey, P. 226n3
Garrett, W. R. 292n6
Gärtner, B. 112n5
Gaster, M. 368n2
Gätner, B. 215n57
Geiger, A. 8, 10, 17n53, 27n96, 33, 137, 460-61
Geller, M. 120n46
Georgi, D. 259n13
Gerhardsson, B. 257n3, 261-2, 275, 435n13, 447n35
Gibson, J. 161n19
Gilat, Y. D. 351n28
Ginzberg, L. 116n23, 123n11, 131, 132n43, 350n27
Glatzer, N. N. 17n52, 22n78-n79, 23, 26n95, 71n1, 71n4, 74n9, 75n11&n13, 76n18&n20, 77n22, 80n30, 81n31, 91n63, 129, 135n52, 308n19, 317n75, 432n7, 440n24
Glotz, G. 239n68, 241n77
Gnilka, J. 436nn14-15
Godfrey, R. 363n1
Goldenberg, R. 18n58
Goldin, J. 11, 134-135, 309n21, 350n27
Golomb, B. 236n49
Goodblatt, D. 137n2
Goodman, M. 111n2, 149n47, 232n30

Goppelt, L. 158
Goshen-Gottstein, A. 451n41, 461
Goulder, M. 404n15, 408n30
Gowler, D. B. 137n2
Grant, M. 226n3
Graus, F. 96n74
Greenberg, M. 427n1, 430n5
Groh, D. E. 300n24, 301n25
Gruenwald, J. 130n35
Grün, O. 298n20
Gundry, R. H. 420nn67-68
Gutman, E. M. 113n8, 116n23, 120n42
Guttmann, A. 355n33

Haas, N. 239n71
Hachili, R. 115n18, 117n30
Haechen, E. 146
Hagner, D. A. 406n19
Hall, R. G. 15n49
Halperin, D. J. 324n11
Hammerstaedt, J. 188n43
Hanson, J. S. 225, 229n20, 243
Hanson, P. D. 121n1, 124n14
Harnack, A. 122n4
Harrington, D. 451n42
Harris, J. R. 373n9
Harrisville, R. A. 259n14
Hart, Joan 2
Hata, G. 337n6
Hay, D. M. 356n34
Heiler, F. 427-30
Heinemann, J. H. 14n47, 230n23
Heinisch, P. 437n18
Heitmüller, W. 66n28, 259
Helm, R. 188n42
Hengel, M. 5n11, 49nn36-37, 50n38,
    52n49&n51, 54n53, 99n81, 111n2,
    113n10, 187-8, 189n50, 236, 243, 244n93,
    246n98, 286nn80-82, 391n7, 433
Hennecke, E. 282n73
Henry, P. 130n36
Herford, T. 21n75, 113n7, 123n11, 130n32
Herrenbrück, F. 234
Herrmann, L. 208n38
Herr, M. D. 112n4, 344n17
Hertz, J. 236
Heschel, A. J. 37-38n10
Hiers, R. H., 6n14
Higger, M. 78n24, 81n31
Hobbes, J. 379n17
Hobsbawm, E. J. 243
Hock, R. F. 185n29, 239nn68-9, 240n74
Hodder, I. 296n16
Hoehner, H. W. 231n25, 237n59, 238nn63-4

Hoffmann, L. A. 441n26
Hoifus, O. 408n30
Höisad, R. 179n12
Hollenback, P. 245n97
Holmes, O. 123n6
Horbury, W. 163, 443n27
Horovitz, H. S. 73n6, 84n42
Horsley, R. A. 225, 229n20, 243, 245n97,
    399-400n8, 422n74
Hunger, H. 198n12
Hutchison, W. R. 121n2, 123n9, 134n49
Hyldahl, N. 209n41
Hyman, A. 4n6, 24n89

Idelsohn, I. 441n26
Isaac E. 16n50

James, W. 427n1, 430
Jamieson, R. 381n23
Jastrow, M. 86n47, 230n23, 234n38,
    242nn81-3, 418n62
Jaubert, A. 223
Jeremias, G. 393n10
Jeremias J. 17n54, 138n5, 151n55, 161n19,
    232n28, 235n44, 238, 241n79, 242n84,
    244n94, , 375n13, 401n10, 406n20,
    407n22, 412n41, 415n50, 442n27, 450-51,
    452n46, 453n48, 456n52
Jewett, R. 272n49
Johnson, L. T. 158n12, 416n51
Johnson, S. E. 201n26
Johnston, R. M. 401n12
Jones, A. H. M. 226n3, 227n8, 234n38-39
Jones, C. P. 187n37
Jónsson, J. 75n16
Jüngel, E. 265

Käuhle, M. 11
Kaminka, A. 10
Kant, I. 379n17
Kapera, Z. J. 199n18, 203n30
Käsemann, E. 32n1
Kasher, M. M. 438n21
Katz, S. T. 442n27
Kaufmann, S. A. 451
Kaufmann, Y. 59n12, 321n1, 452n44
Kautsky, J. H. 233
Kedar, Y. 236n49
Keel, O. 211n46
Kelber, W. 257n5, 275, 285n78
Khun, H. W. 76n19
Kimelman, R. 169n35, 442n27
Kindler, A. 118n31
Kippenberg, H. G. 232n29

Klausner, J. 238n67, 247n108
Klein, C. 62n17
Klijn, A. F. J. 139n6, 204n32, 207n37,
    210n43
Kloppenborg, J. S. 176nn1-2, 414n47
Knohl, I. 66n30, 432n7
Koch, K. 123n10, 165n29
Koester, H. 176n1
Kon, M. 117n30
Konovitz, I. I. 144n27
Kopp, C. 292-93n6
Kosmala, H. 201n26
Kosso, P. 298n22
Kraft, R. A. 156n1, 174n44
Krauss, S. 237n61, 240n75, 241n76
Krengel, J. 339n10
Kressig, H. 225
Krister, M. 443n28
Küchler, M. 211n46
Kuhn, K. G. 223n80, 447n35, 441n26,
    442n27

Lachmann, K. 104n97
Lagrange, M.-L. 198
Lanczkowski, G. 431n6
Landau, Y. H. 236n54
LaSor, W. S. 201n26
La Verdiere, E. 447n35
Leaney, A. R. C. 80n29
LeDéut, R. 441n26
Lee, M. Y. H., 49n37
Legg, J. 373n11
Le Moyne, J. 137n2
Lenski, E. 227, 229-31, 233nn35-36,
    241n78, 243n86
Lessing, G. E. 104n97
Levine, L. I. 113nn9-10, 117n25, 118n34,
    118n37, 120n40
Lewis, A. S. 373n9
Lieberman, S.17, 63n21, 81n31, 120n44,
    134, 331n33&n35, 332n37, 337n5,
    339n10, 340, 360n46
Liebesschütz, H. 59n12
Liebes, Y. 443
Ligier, L. 453n49
Lindars, B. 356n34
Lindblom, I. 298n20
Lipmann Heller, Y. T. 353n29
Little, B. J. 295n12
Locke, J. 379n17
Loffeda, S. 217n65
Lohmeyer, E. 447n35
Longstaff, T. R. W. 291n1, 296n15, 300n24,
    301n25

Low, S. M. 298n21
Lüdemann, G. 257, 258n8, 266, 268n43,
    270-2, 273, 273-4n53
Luz, M. 188n46

Maccoby, H. 145n30
Mack, B. L. 176-177, 187, 192n55, 199, 292
MacMullen, R. 226n3, 227n7, 229, 223, 235,
    236, 240nn74-5, 243n90, 245n95
Magnin, J. 211n45
Maher, M. 446n34
Mahoney, J. 433n8
Maier, J. 201n26
Malherbe, J. A. 179n14, 180, 184n28,
    189n49
Malina, B. J. 225, 399-400n8
Malkin, I. 336nn4
Manns, F. 17n54, 441n26
Manson, T. W. 245n95, 122, 370n5, 415n49
Ma'oz Z. U. 113n8, 297n18
Margalioth, M. 4n6,
Margalit, S. 197n9
Margoulies 69n41, 91nn62-63
Marmorstein, A. 37-38n10, 435n12
Marsden, G. 122n3, 123n7
Marshall, I. H. 104n95, 106n101
Marti, K. 143n23
Marucci, C. 49n37
Mason, S. 137n1, 140n11, 142n17, 147-48,
    404n14
Maxwell, K. B. 257n5, 275
Mayer, A. 245n97
Mayer, B. 196n5, 201n26, 202n29, 223n82
Mazar, B. 112n3
McArthur, H. K. 401n12
McCollough, T. 291n1
McCown, C. C. 247n106
McGaughy, L. C. 415n49
McKane, W. 57-58n8, 59n12
McLaren, J. S. 232n28
Meeks, W. A. 179n14, 185n29
Meier, J, P. 4n7, 9n27, 93n66, 94n68,
    246n98, 291, 397n1
Meistermann, B. 198n12
Mendes-Flohr, P. 96n73
Merkel, H. 392n8
Meshorer, Y. 117n28
Metzger, B. M. 79n26, 246n102
Meyer, B. F. 184n28, 397n1
Meyers, C. L. 248n110
Meyers, E. M. 228, 248n110
Michael, O. 79n26, 198
Michel, A. 137n2, 234n40
Millar, F. 198n13, 293n9

Miller, R. J. 541n41
Miller, S. S. 232n32, 247n108, 253-4
Mitchell, H. 238n66
Moltmann, J. 158n11
Montefiore, C. G. 123-124n11, 379n18
Moore, C. A. 373n10
Moore, G. F. 57-58n8, 59-60n12, 124,
    130n32, 131, 172n40, 230n23
Morag, S. 443n28
Mossé, C. 239nn68&70
Moule, C. F. D. 276n62, 399n8
Mowinckel, S. 429-30
Muller, J. 69n39
Muncker, F. 104n97
Mussner, F. 146n35

Narkiss, B. 117n30
Naveh, J. 239n71
Naves, R. 102n92
Neale, D. A. 161n21, 166n30-n31, 173nn42-
    43
Netzer, E. 117n25, 248n110, 300
Neusner, J. 4n6, 11, 17, 18n56, 18n58,
    24n90, 26n93, 30n110, 34-35n3, 36n7,
    44n29, 116n21, 131n40, 134, 135137, 139,
    141n13&n15, 144n27, 149n48, 150,
    157n5, 158n11, 285n79, 313n45, 317n75,
    320n85, 335, 337n5, 340n12, 346n19,
    350n27, 351n28, 354n30, 356n34,
    357n36, 358n39, 359n42&n44361n50,
    432n7, 440n22, 444n32
Newsom, C. A. 391n6
Nickelsburg, G. W. E. 126, 156n1, 174n44
Nicoll, W. R. 57-58n8
Niebuhr, K.-W. 146n32, 406-407n21
Niebuhr, R. R. 276n62
Nodet, E. 338n9, 355-6n33, 432n7
Norberg-Schulz, C. 297n19

Oakman, D. E. 225, 245n97, 250n115,
    422n76, 423n77
O'Connor, M. 346n19
Oesterly, W. O. E. 401n12
Ong, W. 257n5, 275-76
Oppenheimer, A. 112n4, 115n19, 230n23
O'Rourke, J. J. 406n20
Osiek, C. 447n35
Oster, R. 291n1, 296n17
Otto, A. 76n19, 129n30
Overman, J. A. 228n11, 235, 250n114,
    253n125, 254n127

Pape, W. 151n55
Paquet, L. 188n42

Pardo, D. 340n11
Paret, H. 260
Patrich, J. 114n12
Patte, D. 350n27
Payne, P. B. 401n11
Pearson, B. A. 277n67, 278n68
Pelikan, J. 35n5
Perlman, I. 238n65
Petuchowski, J. 27, 447n35
Philippidis, L. J. 363-64n1, 372n7
Pixner B. 197nn8-9, 199n18ff, 200n25,
    200n25, 203n30, 204n31, 208n39,
    209n42, 212n49&n52, 214n56, 215n60,
    216n64, 219n70, 220, 222n79
Ploetz, K. J. 96n74
Plummer, A. 97n77, 245n96
Plumptre, E. H. 382n24
Porton, G. G. 156n1, 313n49, 354n31
Powell, M. A. 142n19
Preuss, J. 54n54
Price, J. 152n56
Puech, E. 394n13

Qimron, E. 21-22n75, 80n29, 154n62-63,
    194n3, 393n11

Rabbinowitz, J. 409n34
Rabin, I. A. 73n6
Räisänen, H. 404n15, 414n46
Rajak, T. 232
Rankin, H. D. 183n24
Rappaport, U. 117n28, 118n32, 232n33,
    343n14
Ratner, B. 336n3
Ravidovitch, S. 52n46
Recorde, R. 363-4n1
Regnsdorf, K. H. 151n55, 152n56, 399n6,
    408n33
Reich, R. 115n19, 116n24, 117n26
Reinink, G. J. 204n32, 207n37, 210n43
Renan, E. 7
Renfrew, C. 295n11, 296nn13-14
Reventlow, H. G. 427n1
Rich, A. M. 178n10
Rieger, P. 7, 9
Riesner, R. 93n67, 194n2, 196n5, 197n9,
    198n12, 201n26, 211n45, 219n70, 397n3
Rillinger, R. 233
Rist, J. M. 182n21
Rivkin, E. 137, 153n60, 154n61, 155n64
Robbins, V. K. 192n55
Robertson, R. 292n6
Robinson, J. M. 277n66
Roetzel, C. J. 266n37, 275n57

Rohls, J. 433n8
Rohrbaugh, R. L. 399-400n8, 421n73, 422n77&n76
Rollmann, H. 431n6
Rosenfield, B. Z. 62n18
Rossé, G. 142n19
Rostovtzeff, M. 226n3, 227n9, 229, 235, 237n59
Roth, C. 117n30
Roth-Gerson, L. 113n11
Rouiller, G. 413n45
Rowland, C. 124n14, 130n36
Rowley, H. H. 122n5
Ruckstuhl, E. 223n82
Russel, L. J. 381n21

Sachs, M. 77n21
Safrai, S. 87-88n54, 93n67, 115n17, 130, 225n2, 234n37, 307n8, 314n55, 316n70, 391n5
Salardini, A. J. 137, 157n6, 360n45
Salmon, M. 405n17
Sanders, E. P. 17n53, 19n62, 29n66, 32n1, 112n5, 116, 139n8, 157n6&n10, 159-61, 169n35, 170, 171n38, 184n28, 292-93, 397n1, 401n10,
Sanders, J. T. 404n15, 405, 406n20, 443n27
Sarfatti, G. B. 53n52
Sayre, F. 183n23
Schäfer, P. 442n27
Schechter, 123-124n11, 143n22
Schekbert, G. 451n41
Schenker, A. 451n41
Schiffman, L. 116n22, 125n17, 159-60, 169nn33-34
Schlatter, A. 151, 152n56
Schlosser, J. 435n13, 451n41, 452n45, 453nn47-48
Schmithals, W. 257n4, 267n41, 272-3, 404n15
Schneemelcher, W. 72n5, 282n73
Schneider, G. 399n7
Schoeps, H. J. 211n48, 257n4
Schottroff, L. 404n15
Schubert, K. 201n26
Schultz, S. 414n47
Schürer, E. 3n4, 18n56, 57n8, 143n25, 198, 227n9, 228n11, 293n9, 432n7, 441n26, 443n29
Schürmann, H. 397n1
Schwank, B. 198n12, 221n77, 223n82, 252n120
Schwartz, D. R. 343n13
Schwartz, S. 147n39, 360n45

Schwarz, A. 336n3, 345n18, 350n27
Schweitzer, A. 3, 11, 274-75
Schweizer, E. 280, 415n49
Schwemer, A. M. 391n7
Scott, B. 401n11, 415n49, 416n54, 419n64, 420n70, 424n79
Seeligman I. L. 59n12
Segal, A. F. 146n32, 157n5, 158n1155
Seidensticker, P. 193, 199
Senior, D. 447n35
Shaw, B. D. 243n90
Sievers, J. 11, 140n10, 436n15
Silberman, H. L. 57-58n8
Simons, J. 115n15
Singer, S. 441n26
Sjöberg, E. 166n31, 169n34, 173n41, 235n47
Slater, W. J. 296n17
Smend, R. 57-58n8, 58n9
Smith, G. A. 62n17
Smith, M. 34n3, 120n46, 134, 435n12
Smith, P. 239n72
Söderblöm, N. 430-31
Sperber, D. 241n77
Spinks, B. D. 456n53
Stemberger, G. 12n42, 38n11, 138n4, 157n10, 432n7, 442n27
Stendahl, K. 5-6, 78n25, 201n26, 223n80, 261-2, 447n35
Stern, D. 401n12
Stern, E. 187n40, 225n2
Stern, M. 115n17, 118n34, 234n37
Stoike, D. A. 281n71
Stone, M. E. 124n14, 147n39
Strack, H. L. 12n42, 38n11, 240n75, 330n29, 432n7
Strange, J. F. 248n110, 292n6, 294n10, 296n15, 300n24, 301
Strecker, G. 72n5
Stroker, W. D. 72n5, 87n51
Strotmann, A. 453n48
Strugnell, J. 21-22n75, 154n62-63, 194n3, 393n11
Sylva, D. D. 405n17

Talbert, C. H. 413n45, 416n53
Talley, T. J. 453-54n49
Talmon, S. 219n68, 441n26
Tal S. 87-88n54, 333n40
Taylor, A. E. 75n12
Taylor, V. 79n27, 246n102, 414n48
Thackeray, H. St.J. 150n53, 151
Theissen, G. 187n41, 190n54, 229, 399n8
Thomas, J. 202n29

Thorton, T. C. G. 442n27
Tiede, D. L. 405n17, 415n48, 416n53, 420n66
Tigay, J. H. 68n36, 69n40
Tilich, P. J. 11n40
Tomson, P. J. 261n20
Towner, S. 18n57, 454n50
Trethowan, I. 431n6
Trocmé, A. 245n97
Tuckett, C. M. 34n3
Tyson, J. B. 405n17
Tzaferis, V. 239nn71&73
Tzahor, Z. 336n4

Urbach, E. E. 18n58, 23, 25-26n92, 41n20, 42n23-n24, 60n13, 61n14&n15, 62, 63n20, 65n26, 71n3, 165n28, 169n35, 173n41, 230n23, 235n42, 316n71, 344n17, 355-6n33, 432n7

Vanhoye, A. 457n55
van Loopik, M. 81n31
Van Segbroeck, F. 404n15
Vermes, G. 3n4, 18n56, 26n94, 36n7, 53-54n52, 143n25, 198n13, 206n33, 227n9, 228n11230n23, 246n104, 293n9, 451
Via, D. O. 412n40
Vielhauer, P. 72n5, 96n71
Visotzky, B. L. 419n63
Viviano, B. T. 327nn21-22, 394n13, 436n15, 448n36
Voltaire 102-104, 374n12
von Arnim, H. 186n36
von Pöhlmann, R. 245n97
Vööbus, A. 44n32
Vriezen, K. J. H. 187n40

Wagner-Lux, U. 187n40
Ward-Perkins, J. B. 118n35

Weaver, W. P. 294n10
Wedderburn, A. J. M. 256n2, 265
Weder, H. 406-407n21
Wegman, H. 453-454n54
Weinert, F. D. 415n48
Weinfeld, M. 442n26
Weinrich, W. C. 447n35
Weiss, A. H. 309n20
Weiss, Z. 300
Wellhausen, J. 56-63, 137
Wenham, D. 401n11
Westerholm, S. 157n10
White, K. D. 226n3, 237n60
White, L. 228, 235
White, R. T. 68n37
Wilamowitz-Moelendorf 59n12
Wilckens, U. 79n26
Wilcox, M. 375n13
Wilkinson, J. 293n8
Wilson, B. 188n47
Wilson, R, McL. 72n5
Windfuhr, W. 340n10
Winter, P. 7
Wolf, C. U. 247nn107
Wrede, W. 258, 259n11
Wuellner, W. H. 238n63

Yadin, Y. 113n8, 200n24, 221
Yoder, J. H. 245n97
Young, B. H. 100n85, 401n12

Zeitlin, S. 230n23
Zeller, D. 451n41
Zerwick, M. 414n48
Zias, J. 239n72, 242n85
Ziebarth, E. 234n38